LAW AND RIGHTS: GLOBAL PERSPECTIVES ON CONSTITUTIONALISM AND GOVERNANCE

LAW AND RIGHTS: GLOBAL PERSPECTIVES ON CONSTITUTIONALISM AND GOVERNANCE

Edited by

Penelope E. Andrews & Susan Bazilli

VANDEPLAS PUBLISHING

UNITED STATES OF AMERICA

Law and rights: global perspectives on constitutionalism and governance
Andrews, Penelope E. & Bazilli, Susan *Editors*

Published by:

Vandeplas Publishing - July 2008

801 International Parkway, 5th Floor
Lake Mary, FL. 32746
USA

www.vandeplaspublishing.com

ISBN: 978-1-60042-047-4

LAW AND RIGHTS: GLOBAL PERSPECTIVES ON CONSTITUTIONALISM AND GOVERNANCE

TABLE OF CONTENTS

Constitutionalism, Separation of Powers and the Judiciary

Constitutionalism, Citizenship and Identity

Constitutionalism and Economic Justice

The Limitations of Rights Discourse

FOREWORD

A range of legal scholars have referred to the last few decades as the age of constitutionalism, especially as reflected in legal developments in the emerging democracies of Africa. In these countries, governments have adopted founding constitutional documents that guarantee and protect a range of civil, political, economic, social, and cultural rights. South Africa is one of the recent democracies to adopt a constitutional framework with a comprehensive bill of rights of rights encompassing a range of civil, political, socio-economic and cultural rights. Other countries too have included these rights in their constitutions. By incorporating these rights in their constitutions, democratic governments, commit themselves, at least formally, to fairness and transparency in their relationship with their citizens.

Although these constitutional commitments bode well for emerging democracies, the reality is that in far too many cases many governments fall short, and these documents remain only aspirational.

The contributors to this volume engage with these issues by placing them in a comparative and global perspective. They examine the democratic possibilities generated by constitutions and bills of rights, as well as their limitations, exploring the meaning of rights and their enforcement. They also investigate questions such as the separation of powers, access to justice, the particularized meaning of rights to discrete populations, including women and racial minorities. They also explore rights in political systems without bills of rights, for example, the United Kingdom and Australia.

The contributors to this volume explore these questions, not just in the narrow legal technical sense, but also as part of a comprehensive system of rights enforcement that go beyond narrow legal questions. As legal scholars and advocates in established and emerging democracies grapple with the issue of rights enforcement, this volume will make a notable contribution to the literature.

The Hon. Pius Langa
Chief Justice of South Africa
Johannesburg
May 2008

INTRODUCTION

It has been noted that "[C]onstitutional supremacy is one of the splendid achievements of North American and European legal culture."[1] This "achievement" has of late been exported to countries in the developing world, and the past two decades have witnessed a proliferation of constitutionalism in newly-democratized countries of Africa, Eastern Europe and elsewhere. Indeed, across the legal and political spectrum, it is currently the conventional wisdom that a democratic society cannot function without a constitution, or at least an entrenched system of constitutional review. Legal and other scholars, in this new age of constitutionalism, argue that constitutionalism is a precondition for democracies to flourish.[2]

The field of comparative constitutionalism has grown exponentially in the past two decades, and particularly since the end of the Cold War. Of worthy note is the ascendancy of bills of rights, and the concomitant explosion of constitutional review. Although entrenched in the United States since the landmark case of Marbury v Madison[3] (seen as the gold standard for judicial review), and also well-established in Europe in the post-World War 2 era, especially in the formation of the European Court of Human Rights, the notion of judicial review is of recent vintage for most of the developing world. Although bills of rights have been around at least since the beginning of the decolonization period in Africa and elsewhere, for the most part they have been dormant, until a revival since 1989, generated by the collapse of communism in Eastern Europe. It has been argued that as the language of rights increasingly replaced the language of redistribution, bills of rights and the rhetoric of rights, became the "lingua franca of progressive politics",[4] and that in fact this language began to supplant "all other ethical discourses".[5]

The project of constitutionalism therefore raises key questions: How should a constitution regulate human relationships? How does a constitutional framework embody shared values whilst at the same time recognizing minority derogations from such values? How does the constitution balance competing rights claims? How are the constitutional values internalized by the broader citizenry? Regarding the field of comparative constitutionalism, further questions are generated: What relationships do national constitutions have to their foreign counterparts? What analogies and distinctions can be extracted from comparative constitutional frameworks? How are national constitutions impacted by the global legal context within which they operate? Does constitutional governance strip the elected legislature of its central role of governance?

These were some of the questions raised at the conference entitled COMPARATIVE CONSTITUTIONALISM AND RIGHTS: GLOBAL PERSPECTIVES,[6] held at the University of KwaZulu-Natal in South Africa in December 2005. As the title of the conference suggested, the purpose was to explore comparative perspectives on rights enforcement, despite a diverse array of political, economic, cultural and legal contexts. The purpose was to engage some of the theoretical debates pertaining to the project of rights enforcement in a constitutional context, but also to engage in analyses of rights enforcement at an empirical level. The contributors to this volume bring to the discussion a host of questions, both standard and unique ones, regarding the project of constitutional governance and the enforcement of rights.

They demonstrate in their respective chapters the growth of the field of comparative constitutionalism, pointing out the relationship between the theoretical discourse mostly found in academic writing, on the one hand, and the organic and exciting movements for change generated by civil society, on the other. They also analyze the contested nature of rights incorporation and enforcement, and in particular the multi-layered and contested nature and context of legal interpretation.

In the first section of the volume, Dwight Newman argues, in the opening chapter, that comparative constitutionalism, thus far grounded in substantive and moral considerations, can be enriched by attention to procedural norms. Describing "process" as the "human bridge between justice and peace", Newman sees "rich possibilities" in such an exploration, choosing as his point of illustration the use of international law in the process of domestic constitutional interpretation. This focus, he argues, will highlight the issues raised by a comparative approach to normative constitutional processes. Unproblematic in the South African context, where the Constitution there mandates consideration of international law, but highly vexed in the USA, on both legal and political grounds, he suggests a framework that allows for a principled incorporation of international law. His approach respects the normative evolution of domestic constitutional law, whilst at the same time allowing the comparative constitutional project to permit a "principled intermingling" of local and international law. Although unclear as to the final result of this incorporation, that is, an improvement in domestic constitutional interpretation, or the opposite, Newman nonetheless argues that the process may generate methodological possibilities of enormous benefit to the project of comparative constitutionalism.

In his thoughtful chapter, Michael Plaxton explores the distinctions between constitutional rules and prophylactic rules, arguing that such distinction allows lawyers and legal scholars to "make better sense" of constitutional cases and doctrines. Plaxton argues that such distinction may also "clarify the relationship" between the legislative and judicial branches, particularly in the contemporary climate of accusations and counter-accusations of "judicial activism". Plaxton believes that although caution should be applied in the use of American constitutional jurisprudence, that occasional borrowing of American legal concepts may "bring order to constitutional thinking".

Taunya Banks wades into the increasingly contentious waters that concern the incorporation and justiciability of socio-economic rights. She notes that the jurisprudence on civil and political rights in the United States has resulted in a court-sanctioned hierarchy of rights, namely fundamental versus non-fundamental rights, and that the Court's balancing of these rights do not always lead to consistency or predictability. In short, Banks argues that these neatly categorized hierarchy of rights are not absolute. She cites, for example, the seminal decision of the United States Supreme Court in Brown v Board of Education,[7] in which the court jettisoned a fundamental right like the freedom of association, in favor of one that prioritized equality under the law.

She argues for the inclusion of socio-economic rights in constitutional frameworks, even though they may test the balancing capacity of courts even more, and may raise difficult separation of powers issues. Banks argues that the normal process of creating a hierarchy of rights, and the concomitant balancing required of courts, will merely incorporate another set of rights, namely socio-economic ones. Evaluating the socio-economic rights jurisprudence of the South African Constitutional Court, she is sanguine that the vexed questions raised by the incorporation of socio-economic rights in national constitutions need not tip the balance against legislatures ultimately retaining the control over state expenditure.

Martin Chanock, utilizing the metaphor of "cutting and sewing", explores the many endeavors at constitutional democracy in post-colonial Africa, and particularly the disappointing results of such endeavors. By linking the "conceptual worlds" of political science and law, Chanock anaylyzes the wave of "constitutional revival" in post independence Africa. Chanock laments the fact that bills of rights and judicial review have superceded notions of political accountability, separation of powers and the rule of law in the project for constitutional democracy. Arguing that the latter processes are actually the "primary core" of constitutional democracy, not least of which because so few of Africa's peoples "speak or are literate in the languages of constitutions, bills of rights and constitutional discourse". In fact, Chanock argues that for Africa's citizens, the "rights language" is "literally meaningless".

Using his deft skills of historical reflection, Chanock engages in a chronological narrative of post-colonial constitution making in Africa. In this account, he pays particular attention to the current concern with "failed states", a preoccupation with contemporary rule of law and good governance projects, the "explosion" of constitutional drafting in the wake of the end of the cold war, and the emergence of the contemporary global moment of free markets and diminished state oversight. Chanock ultimately reduces his chapter to the central question of the future of constitutional democracy in Africa, namely, "where to" and "how to".

The next section examines the issue of separation of powers and the role of the judiciary in the enforcement of rights. It begins with a discussion by Brian Flanagan who raises the issues of judicial review, and whether the constitutionalization of economic rights is appropriate to protect minorities. Noting the ideological polarization that the constitutional enforcement of socio-economic rights generates, he suggests a model for addressing the justiciability of economic rights on the basis of protecting welfare interests on moral grounds, one that may be accepted outside of ideological boundaries. Kirsty McClean, in her chapter continues the discussion on socio-economic rights by examining decisions of the Canadian Supreme Court and that of the South African Constitutional Court involving the right to health care. She locates her questions within the concept of "constitutional deference" in evaluating the decisions the judges reach.

Denise Meyerson explores the "complex connections between the doctrine of separation of powers and the rule of law". She argues that the "separation of judicial from executive and legislative power" furthers the rule of law because it places "the adjudication of controversies' in the judiciary that "can be relied upon to adjudicate disputes independently and impartially". This argument leads her to question the approach taken by South African and Australian courts "to the exercise of non-judicial functions by judges", an approach that she believes is too "flexible" and does not serve to protect the rule of law, and in fact contradicts the very aim of the doctrine of separation of powers. Meyerson therefore suggests that a "blanket prohibition" on non-judicial functions should be placed on judges as a means of protecting judicial independence.

Focusing on the limitation of a constitutional right, Gregoire Webber engages in an analysis of the concept of a "dialogue" between the judiciary and the legislature, in which he frames the issue of the "dialogic exchange" between the two as one of "justification". He draws on the Canadian constitutional model to explore the evolving concept of "public law as a culture of justification". He sees the Canadian experience as relevant for other democratic societies that also incorporate limitations clauses in their constitutional arrangements.

Ruthann Robson explores the question whether judicial review is "advantageous for women's sexual freedom", and in particular, "lesbian sexual freedom", and therefore, as a practical matter, whether feminists and lesbians embarking on a project of sexual freedom should "embrace" judicial review. Noting the contemporary significance of this question today as new constitutions are being drafted, she suggests ways that advocates of sexual freedom can conceptualize, to their advantage, the question of judicial review.

Section Three focuses on constitutionalism, citizenship and identity. It also pursues questions of constitutions and gender equality, and particularly how a constitution can best further women's rights, both in the public and private sphere. International and national law historically have conceptualized all forms of domestic violence as a private matter, outside the scope of state regulation. Valerie Vojdik's chapter reviews the treatment of domestic violence under international law, and then contrasts the approaches of the United States Supreme Court and the South African Constitutional Court. These two courts have taken dramatically different approaches to domestic violence under their respective constitutions. The U.S. Supreme Court has resisted efforts to constitutionalize a right to be protected from domestic or gender-motivated violence. In contrast, the Constitutional Court has held that the Constitution imposes affirmative obligations on the state to guarantee a woman's right to be free from violence, and national domestic violence legislation fulfills the state's constitutional obligation to afford women gender equality and other fundamental rights. Such affirmative obligations are also reflected in the socio-economic rights incorporated in the South African Constitution. This reflects an understanding of gender based violence as fundamental to gender inequality.

In her chapter Qudsia Mirza provides a feminist analysis of the complex relationship between issues of race, ethnicity, gender, religion and law in contemporary Britain. This analysis is placed within the context of the revival of certain forms of religious conservatism and the discriminatory attitudes that such conservatism often entails. Mirza points out that this nexus is especially pertinent for Muslim women who suffer oppression in terms of growing Islamophobia in society, and the increased exposure of 'fundamentalist' Islam. She describes a 'hierarchy of oppression' that Muslim women face in seeking legal remedies, with the unenviable task of choosing between different forms of disadvantage. Muslim women face discrimination within their communities on the basis of entrenched, conservative interpretations of scripture. Mirza examines the encounter between English law and Shari'a law which indicates that both legal cultures are being influenced by each other. She concludes that dramatic changes are being effected to Muslim practice as a result of changes imposed by English law, particularly in the area of gendered rights. She cautions that the law can become a tool by which inequalities are perpetuated leading to discrimination against Muslim women as a 'minority within a minority'. This provides lessons to other jurisdictions where increasing conflict of laws impacts adversely on women's equality rights.

Janet Calvo emphasizes that even in an increasingly globalized world, citizenship is an important basis for the protections of rights. She observes that there has been insufficient and inadequate attention paid to the constitutional protection of the right to citizenship. However, in a globalized world, changing borders and increased migration, citizenship acquisition has become increasingly controversial. There is now substantial scholarship that analyzes citizenship beyond that which is defined by a nation state. Yet citizenship continues to matter, she argues, as the world is still predominately organized by, and into, nation states. Even with unprecedented mobility for individuals, basic rights depend on the acquisition of citizenship in a nation state. Calvo reviews the various contemporary forms of citizen acquisition, before arguing that the "right" to citizenship is often the foundational right upon which other "rights" are based. The right to citizenship is "the right to have rights." But the formal acquisition of citizenship does not always mean full access to constitutional rights, and Calvo illustrates that there are many historical and current instances of second class citizenship imposed on people because of race, ethnicity, gender, and sexual orientation.

Calvo argues that constitutions should be clear and detailed about the nature of citizenship and its attendant bundle of rights. The character of this contemporary period of globalization, and the complexities that it generates with respect to citizenship, birth, descent and consent, and the growing occurrence of multiple nationalities, raises complex and contradictory questions. Calvo concludes with a strong recommendation that nation states should pursue more consistent norms with respect to citizenship, and that there is an urgent need for international standards that seriously address the issue of statelessness.

Craig Lind's shares his decade long preoccupation with elucidating the interaction between cultural norms and legal family regulation. He uses examples of same sex family regulation and polygamous family regulation in several jurisdictions, but primarily in South Africa. How does the legal system cope with real, lived, family forms which the many, if not a majority, in a particular society would prefer not to see embraced? And what effect does this interaction of law with family norm have on the lived family lives and the individual self-identities of those living in multicultural societies? Lind's inquiry seeks to reflect critically on some alternative strategies that appear to be available to the legal system in regulating the family where cultures come into conflict on the issue of family form. He pays particular attention to the fundamental rights discourse that serves as the background to legal reflection on the issues raised.

He is very concerned about the place of law in structuring the social world, and he offers us some extremely thought provoking questions about the difficult places we have reached in relation to the regulation, especially under democratic constitutionalism, of cross cultural family norms. If it is true that one of the values ascribed to multiculturalism is its contribution to the way in which we critique our own view of the world, our ambition for family regulation and gender equality should not be that it is transformed to satisfy the prescripts of one culture, but that we should be more reflective of our norms and their comparative success at resolving the problems that arise in our societies. Culturally foreign norms shine a different light on social practices and they cause us to see our practices in the light of others. They remind us that there are other ways of seeing the world and that each way provides, not complete answers to dilemmas, but answers that are partial and, at best, suit their cultural context.

Wendy Pettifer's chapter focuses on the loss of a human rights culture in the United Kingdom. Basing her analysis on her experience as both a legal aid practitioner and a clinical educator in the area of refugee and asylum law, she reviews the position of the incoming Labour Party as they prepared for government in their last days of opposition, when passage of the Human Rights Act was the centrepiece of the party's vision of a just and fair society. Pettifer sees the Prime Minister Tony Blair's recent foreign policy misadventures as the end of that vision. She looks at the passage of the Human Rights Act, which incorporated the provisions of the European Convention on Human Rights into United Kingdom domestic legislation, examining the political background within which incorporation took place.

In exploring constitutionalism and economic justice in the next section, the speakers raise the possibility of utilizing bills of rights to pursue economic equity, focusing most of their attention on litigating in pursuit of socio-economic rights on behalf of disadvantaged communities. They also explore the range of socio-economic rights that are, in fact, suitable for incorporation in constitutional texts.

Rebecca Bratspies persuasively argues that the most pressing environmental challenges, namely, global climate change, loss of biodiversity, desertification, destruction of the ozone layer, the spread of toxics and pollutants throughout the world, are beyond the capacity of any single state to resolve. No nation can, by itself, create a healthy environment. Constitutional environmental provisions are certainly a start, but they are no more than that. Although such constitutional provisions may be a necessary part of a global response, they are not, in and of themselves, sufficient. Recognizing this, however, Bratspies argues that by setting a baseline of agreed rights for individuals, and by including environmental rights as a critical counterweight to the right of development, constitutional environmental provisions can play a crucial role in developing more propitious conditions for that cooperation. She illustrates that alongside a growing body of domestic and international law governing environmental protection, there has been an unmistakable trend towards recognizing a right to a healthy environment. Almost every Constitution drafted or revised in the past 20 years has included an express textual recognition of the right to environmental protection.

In her chapter Susan Herman notes that rights discourse can overstate the role of judicially-enforced constitutional rights in effectuating change, while critiques of rights discourse can understate the role of the judiciary in implementing constitutional commitments. As many of the authors in this volume point out, the tension between these two views are often emphasized in comparison between the Constitutions of South Africa and the United States. Several of the authors in this volume question the extent to which the South African courts can truly be effective in ensuring the fulfillment of commitments to socio-economic rights. Another issue discussed throughout this volume is what, if anything, the South African courts can glean from the experiences of other countries in answering these difficult questions. Some argue that there is nothing relevant in the experience of the United States because the United States Constitution does not guarantee socio-economic rights at all. Herman cautions that this is an overly hasty dismissal of a potentially useful comparison. She argues that the experiences of the United States after the Civil War, and of South Africa after the end of apartheid, show that even a profoundly transformative event may not result in a lasting societal commitment to follow through on promised changes. In drafting a constitution, framers may accurately express their constituents' altruistic intentions to help the victims of slavery or of apartheid to build new lives. But when the personal costs of living up to that commitment become apparent, political will can and usually does dissipate. Self-interest, partisan politics, and inertia can all erode the inclination of political actors to live up to earlier promises. It is for that reason that both countries, after transformative and wrenching events, embodied their deeply held beliefs in a constitution and assigned the responsibility for interpreting that constitution to politically insulated courts. Herman answers some of her co-authors whether judicial involvement in socio-economic matters can be justified by stating that the presumption should be reversed. If a constitution confers socio-economic rights, whether explicitly or implicitly, we should have to provide justification for excluding one branch of our government from the conversation about the meaning of those rights.

Peggy Maisel and Susan Jones review the role of South African legal education in the implementation of the social and economic promise of the Constitution. Progress towards social and economic justice is South Africa's greatest challenge, complicated by the catastrophic HIV/AIDS pandemic. As noted elsewhere in this volume, the South African Constitution recognizes socio-economic rights as a necessary foundation for the enjoyment of civil and political rights. The challenge is translating these rights into opportunities for social and economic advancement by the vast majority of South Africans living in poverty – how do we make Constitutional rights "lived rights"?

Arguably, Maisel and Jones note, lawyers are among the most highly educated professionals in every society, needed to support and lead the transformation away from poverty and inequality by helping to actualize these constitutional provisions. Law students must learn about how law can be used as a tool to promote, rather than inhibit, social and economic development and they must gain the skills, values, and knowledge to assist. Under apartheid, law schools educated lawyers to maintain a system of subordination. Maisel and Jones identify ways in which legal education must continue to change in order to educate lawyers who are able to assist with South Africa's development. They analyze the contributions of clinical legal education since apartheid and some of the obstacles to its growth. It is also ironic that fewer and fewer law students are choosing to enter any form of public interest law, as the remuneration cannot compete with either government or the private sector. This very issue, the decline in human rights legal education in South Africa, was a topic very much on the agenda of the conference itself that gave rise to this volume.

In the concluding section of the volume, Patrick Kelly focuses on the emerging debate between democratic constitutionalists and populist constitutionalists about the appropriate institutions to engage in constitutional interpretation. In the United States., South Africa and other democracies with constitutions that require judicial interpretation, courts have assumed the role of final constitutional authority under the doctrine of judicial supremacy. Populist constitutionalists argue that the elected branches of government, more reflective of popular will, should dominate constitutional interpretation. Kelly is concerned that the constitutionalization of rights has expanded the role of the judiciary, thereby transferring issues of rights articulation and distributive justice from a democratic process to the courts. In this debate between adherents of constitutional democracy, on the one hand, and populist constitutionalism, on the other, there is an overlooked dynamic affecting the articulation of rights and the allocation of resources. Kelly poses the question as to what extent and by what processes international legal norms should be incorporated into domestic constitutions. He raises several concerns about the democratic legitimacy of many international legal norms and about the wisdom of the importation of international legal norms into domestic law.

Steve Ellmann enquires into the nature of war powers under the South African Constitution. He admits that this might at first glance appear a rather strange enquiry, since South Africa, certainly the post-apartheid South Africa, does not locate itself as a "war power". However, Ellmann argues that comparatively speaking, particularly in relation to other African nations, South Africa is a "well-armed state", and that in any event, South Africa is deeply immersed in peacekeeping activities in troubled regions of Africa including the Congo, Burundi and Darfur. He therefore explores what the Constitution provides for with respect to the issue of war. He concludes that the brevity of the constitution's provisions is testament to the belief of the nation's founding fathers and mothers, in the notion of peace in the wake of the brutality and violence of apartheid. In his chapter he analyzes the specific provisions that pertain to war and emergency powers, and posits hypothetical situations to outline what the South African government is enabled within its constitutional mandate of human rights and democracy.

In his chapter Christopher Gale analyzes the recent anti-terrorism legislation in the United Kingdom within a broad human rights framework. He reminds us that, again and again, when legislation is enacted hastily in response to a new and urgent situation, there is little questioning of the principles underpinning the issue the legislation is supposed to address. Governments around the world have used the 9/11 attacks as an opportunity to review anti-terrorism laws and security procedures. Indeed, as part of its own immediate response, the United States Congress hastily passed the Patriot Act. The United Kingdom followed suit by promulgating various anti-terrorism statutes. Gale argues that the legislation will contribute to far reaching infringements of civil liberties that may impede, rather than further, attempts to curb international terrorism.

Gale poses the question of why the fundamental matter of charging terrorists with specific offences has not been addressed expeditiously? He notes that because of their secretive and covert nature, allegations of involvement in terrorism are difficult to investigate. However, to subject individuals to such indeterminate restraints of liberty flagrantly violates due process rights. Gale is concerned that the current state of emergency in the United Kingdom appears unlikely to end in the near future, and that the "additional powers" provided to the government will continue to violate the due process rights of those arrested. Gale sees this as an indictment of Britain's status as a "liberal democracy".

Paul Brietzke begins his chapter, the final one in the volume, with the metaphor of the common law of tort that "every dog gets its first bite," since dogs are not deemed inherently vicious. But once that dog has bitten, its owner becomes strictly liable to prevent future bites; the dog is then said to have a known vicious propensity. Brietzke evocatively postulates that even giving the hierarchy of the United States military and intelligence network that involves private contractors and a civilian hierarchy, the benefit of the doubt, by treating it as not inherently vicious, this hierarchy has now bitten so hard, so often, and in so many contexts since September 11, 2001 that the owner is clearly obliged to take the strictest of precautions. In a democracy, the ultimate owner of this beast is the American people, but they can only exert control through the president, his bureaucratic hierarchy, Congress, the courts, the ballot box, and/or an activist media and civil society networks. Continued savagery under the rubric of torture shows the failure of such accountability devices that otherwise guarantee civilized behavior in mature democracies. Brietzke therefore argues that alternatives must be pursued to call these known vicious propensities to account.

As noted in this chapter by Brietzke, as well as in this volume by Pettifer and Gale, for both Prime Minister Blair and President Bush, the second Iraqi War is a passionately-held belief, desperately in search of a saleable moral justification. Brietzke concludes with Burke's clarion warning call: "All that is necessary for the triumph of evil is that good men [and women and institutions] do nothing". Brietzke concludes that the anti-democratic foundations of a strong and military state will continue to threaten Americans.

We are grateful to the authors of these chapters for their journey to South Africa to present them. Their thoughtful perspectives on the issues raised in this book provided the inspiration for this volume. We particularly want to thank Yasmin Tabi (CUNY School of Law Class of 2007), and Shuva Paul, Shalini Deo and Heather Muwero (CUNY School of Law Class of 2008) for their assistance in checking footnotes and references, and formatting the papers for us. We especially want to thank Wendy Stoffels for her exceptional organizational skills in ensuring that the conference in Durban ran smoothly. A special thanks as well to Dean Mike Cowling, Associate Dean John Mabuganzi, and faculty members at the Howard College School of Law for their participation in, and their support for, the conference. A special thanks to Dean Brent Cotter of the University of Saskatchewan College of Law and faculty members who presented papers at the conference. We are grateful to Chief Justice Pius Langa for introducing the issues covered in this volume in the foreword. This has been a collaborative process for the two co-editors; working together has been intellectually rewarding, and always fun. We are indebted to each other in countless ways.

Penelope Andrews
New York and Valparaiso
May 2008

Susan Bazilli
Johannesburg and Victoria
May 2008

[1] Christian Starck, *The Legitimacy of Constitutional Adjudication and Democracy,* INTERNATIONAL REVIEW OF CONSTITUTIONALISM 251, 267 (2004).

[2] See, for example, RIGHTS AND DEMOCRACY: ESSAYS IN UK-CANADIAN CONSTITUTIONALISM (Gavin Anderson ed. 1999); see also, HEINZ KLUG, CONSTITUTING DEMOCRACY: LAW, GLOBALISM AND SOUTH AFRICA'S POLITICAL RECONSTRUCTION (2000) and RAN HIRSCHAL, THE ORIGIN AND CONSEQUENCES OF THE NEW CONSTITUTIONALISM (2004).

[3] 5 U.S. 137 (1803).

[4] Boaventura de Sousa Santos, *Toward a Multicultural Conception of Human Right,* 1 ZEITSCHRIFT FUR RECHTSSOZIOLOGIE 1, 1 (1997).

[5] Upendra Baxi, *Voices of Suffering and the Future of Human Rights,* 8 TRANSNATIONAL JOURNAL OF LAW AND CONTEMPORARY PROBLEMS 125, 147 (1998).

[6] The conference was held to celebrate the tenth anniversary of the establishment of South Africa's Constitutional Court. It was organized by Penelope Andrews in her position as the Ariel F. Sallows Chair of Human Rights at the College of Law at the University of Saskatchewan. Participants attended from South Africa and other parts of the African continent, Europe, the UK, the USA, Canada, Australia and New Zealand.

[7] 347 U.S. 483 (1954).

CHAPTER 1

TRANSNATIONAL CONSTITUTIONALISM, INTERNATIONALISM, AND AN AUTHORITY-BASED CONNECTION BETWEEN INTERNATIONAL AND CONSTITUTIONAL LAW

Dwight G. Newman

Introduction

As a crude generalization, comparative constitutionalism in its modern form has, to date, tended to focus more closely on comparative analyses of legal approaches to substantive constitutional and moral questions. Those judges of the United States Supreme Court who have been ready to use comparative constitutional law have explicitly seen it as indicative of "values we share with a wider civilization" that help to guide the interpretation of specific rights.[1] Other constitutional courts invoking comparative constitutional law have similarly done so in the substantive interpretation of rights.[2] Scholars seeking to develop theories of comparative constitutional law have tended to focus on a transnational constitutionalism of substantive norms.[3] In doing so, scholars have revealed important transsytemic modalities of law; these include matters of constitutional reasoning like the use of proportionality analysis in analyzing limitations on rights[4] as well as different approaches to particular substantive questions.[5] But comparative constitutionalism, as apparent from earlier academic attention to comparative federalism,[6] need not be so confined and can ground a richer discourse.

Procedural norms, as well, can be matters involving complex theoretical considerations.[7] As Carrie Menkel-Meadow has so richly described it in another context, "process is the human bridge between justice and peace."[8] Deploying comparative constitutional analysis on procedural norms, then, has rich possibilities as a field of endeavour. Within the present argument, I will seek to draw out one particular possibility found within comparative work on norms of constitutional process. In particular, I will argue that comparative tendencies on constitutional change can actually help illuminate some of the vexed questions about the role of international law in domestic constitutional interpretation—not a controversial issue in South Africa, where the interpretive clauses of the Constitution speak explicitly to the matter,[9] but a controversial matter in many places, most notably the United States.[10]

To do so, I will set out very briefly a set of comparative modalities on constitutional change and use these to suggest a certain self-preserving character found in domestic constitutional law. I will then turn to the resort to extra-constitutional change to show a certain substitution between constitutional and international law. I will use that substitution to suggest a principled intermingling of constitutional and international law that identifies an inherent place for international law in domestic constitutional interpretation. However, in the closing section, I will advert to the dual-faced potential of this constitutional reality, suggesting that it may lead either to the improvement of domestic constitutional interpretation or risk bringing upon us something worse.

Constitutional Self-Regulation of Constitutional Change

Domestic constitutional law itself seeks to regulate constitutional change, both through constitutional texts themselves and through complex arrangements that grow up around constitutions or through additional requirements developed by judicial bodies safeguarding the constitutions. Although one could, of course, explore these claims at a more nuanced level, my main claim here is simply that constitutional law typically has a significant self-preserving character.

Most typically, constitutional amendment will require some sort of supermajority requirement provided for by the constitutional text itself. Most constitutional amendments in South Africa require a supporting vote of two thirds of the members of the National Assembly; some also require support from at least six provinces in the National Council of Provinces.[11] Amendments to the German Constitution require two thirds' support in both the Bundestag and the Bundesrat.[12] Amendments to the Indian Constitution require two thirds' support in both Houses of the Indian Parliament.[13] Amendments to the Canadian Constitution require support from the House of Commons and Senate and, typically, support of at least two thirds of the provinces with at least fifty percent of the population.[14] Amendments to the American Constitution require two thirds' support in both the House of Representatives and the Senate as well as support of three quarters of the states.[15] The list could go on.

The precise formulations of these supermajority requirements obviously differ. Most noticeably, they provide different roles for sub-national levels of government, depending on the relative importance of federalist principles within the particular constitution. Moreover, some constitutions have yet more elaborate provisions; the Russian Constitution, for instance, provides for a complex combination of votes of members of a Constitutional Assembly and votes in a popular referendum when assessing the success of a particular constitutional amendment.[16] So, there are different ways of calculating the pertinent supermajority. However, as a generalization, we can note that constitutional texts typically require some form of supermajority vote for constitutional amendment.

The constitutional self-regulation of constitutional change, however, does not end there. In some states, structural interpretation by judicial actors has effectively added further requirements for constitutional amendment. In India, article 368 of the Constitution was cast as intended to provide for a clear power of constitutional change, and the courts, in their wisdom, restricted such amendment so as not to apply to the so-called "basic structure" of the Constitution.[17] There was, of course, a specific historical and political context to this decision; that aside, the decision had the effect of further regulating future constitutional change by the philosophy behind the Constitution, or at least what the judges of a particular moment in time see as such philosophy, further judicializing the relevant political discourses.

One might presume that theories of popular sovereignty would open additional space for constitutional amendment, making constitutions subject to the determinations of the populace. However, in reality, the judicially and politically recognized role of popular sovereignty is often one functioning as an additional constraint on constitutional change. This is perhaps not entirely surprising in a rights era in which one important justification of constitutionally-protected and judicially-safeguarded rights is precisely as a protection of the ability of all members of the populace to participate and be part of the popular sovereignty the constitutional guardians now claim to protect.[18] But the effect can be to add to a self-preserving constitutional system. In Canada, the evolved practice on constitutional change, arising from the push of some towards review by popular referendum of any further constitutional amendment, has now become that any future constitutional amendment will seemingly need to be approved simultaneously by a majority vote in each of the ten provinces.[19] The effect is to render constitutional change nearly impossible, all in the name of popular sovereignty.

A combination of these two phenomena—judicial use of structural interpretation to further develop constitutional amendment provisions and complex interactions with popular sovereignty—is at the fore in the Supreme Court of Canada's judgment in the *Quebec Secession Reference*.[20] In the case, the Supreme Court of Canada was asked to adjudicate upon the legality of Quebec secession under both international law and Canada's constitutional law. Within the Court's constitutional law analysis, the Court adopted a structural approach to the implications of the Canadian Constitution on the matter, in the absence of explicit text. In so doing, the Court recognized the right of a province to seek a major change to Canada's constitutional framework,[21] including the possibility of secession,[22] but simultaneously imposed upon both the province seeking change and other political actors an obligation to negotiate in good faith,[23] guided by certain structural norms of Canadian constitutionalism.[24] One of the norms at play was the rule of law, a norm which partly dictated the obligation to negotiate in good faith so as to preserve ongoing political action in accordance with a system of legality. The function of the rule of law in the case is fascinating. The rule of law has long protected the people from governmental actors;[25] in the context of the *Quebec Secession Reference*, the rule of law effectively entered into a role of protecting the Constitution, and entrenched governmental actors, from the people.[26]

These are not an exclusive set of extratextual constraints on constitutional change. As I have argued elsewhere,[27] there can, more generally, be a "constitutional penumbra" of commitments and duties around a constitution that are not specifically law-derived. Other elements of this constitutional penumbra may also restrain constitutional amendment. It is fully possible to identify and further postulate a set of mechanisms by which domestic constitutional systems typically restrain changes to the constitutional *status quo* to a relatively limited set of incremental changes. Without in any way disparaging the motives, this is hardly surprising: entrenched power will often develop mechanisms to preserve itself, and there can be little doubting that constitutions establish certain forms of entrenched power.

Extraconstitutional Change and the Constitutional-International Substitution

An alternative to constitutional evolution, evolution typically operating subject to significant restriction, will be some form of revolution. When constitutional changes burst the established banks, when extra-constitutional constitutional amendment takes place, the alternative modality of regulation is through the altered state's quest for international legitimacy. Describing that point somewhat further, I will argue here that the presence of this alternative modality implies a sort of substitution between constitutional and international law.

In the *Quebec Secession Reference*, the Supreme Court of Canada struggled to confine Quebec's options of resorting to international law for a right of secession. In what has become a leading treatment of self-determination, the Court held that a people's right to self-determination operates internally within a state except in cases of colonialism or oppression.[28] However, the Court was unable to deny the possible implications of the principle of effectivity, which "proclaims that an illegal act may eventually acquire legal status if, as a matter of empirical fact, it is recognized on the international plane."[29] The Court could not deny that "[s]ecession of a province from Canada, if successful in the streets, might well lead to the creation of a new state."[30] The Court did introduce the international legal norm that international recognition of a new state takes account of the legality of the process by which it was created.[31] Decolonization efforts by national liberation movements may well have had more success on account of the international acceptance of the normative force of their claims,[32] and moves toward secession by a cultural minority might or might not be accepted in the same way. But the possibility of constitutional change does hinge ultimately on international law principles of recognition as a possible substitute for domestic constitutional amendment processes.[33]

A case like *Republic of Fiji v. Prasad*[34] might seem to serve as a counter to this argument. In that case, a domestic court heard the purportedly new Fijian government's claims following a *coup d'état* that the courts should recognize it as the new government, and the Court declined to do so. However, the case was simply an instance in which the Court did not see evidence of effectivity of the new government. The case did not state that there could not be an extra-constitutional change accepted through international recognition. So, the same conclusion remains that international law principles of recognition can function as a possible substitute for domestic constitutional amendment processes.

There can be a variety of significant interactions between constitutional law and international law, noteworthy within different methodological frameworks. For instance, in recent writing, Philip Bobbitt has provocatively sketched a series of interactions between the constitutional and international legal orders in the context of military technologies that he argues are both shaped by and powerfully shape human history.[35] One might develop similar sorts of political science analyses of the identified substitution between constitutional and international law. However, it also has a profound significance in terms of legal and constitutional theory.

A certain stream of legal theory writing, of course, has already been attentive to the possible significance for the legal order of revolution. Hans Kelsen described a revolution or *coup d'état* as a "law-creating fact".[36] Within his conception, there is continuity of the state in the face of extra-constitutional change only because international law determines the existence of the state.[37] John Finnis also attended to the meaning and significance of revolutions,[38] and this interest on his part has inspired some who have gone on to consider the changes in legal systems that took place in the dispossession of indigenous peoples.[39] But the identified substitution between constitutional and international law has further implications in which this stream of writers has been less interested.

If international law can substitute for domestic constitutional law in the amendment context, domestic constitutional law must meet the standards of international law if it is to have ongoing legal effect (or, if not put to the test by a specific act intended to rely on a broader international law, to be the determinative legal authority). If potentially seceding entities can have resort to international law based partly on the failure of a domestic legal order to live up to the demands of an international legal order, domestic constitutional law, more broadly, remains the determinative legal authority only if it is in accord with international law.

To put the point another way, international law recognizes a domestically extra-constitutional change (in the form of a secession or revolution) in circumstances where the domestic legal order fails to comply with the international legal order.[40] This procedural interaction shows a certain normative force of the international legal order. In one sense, this normative force hinges the legitimacy of domestic law on its coherence with international law.[41] The possible substitution of international law for domestic law implicitly renders international law into an authoritative source for purposes of domestic constitutional adjudication and sustains a certain intermingling of international and constitutional law.

Principled Intermingling of Constitutional and International Law

Comparative analysis and thought on constitutional process has thus brought matters to this interesting substantive conclusion. There is an inherent, principled intermingling of constitutional and international law coextensive with an authority-based account of the place of international law in constitutional adjudication. Facing challenges and developing this account slightly further can now flesh out some theoretical implications for approaches to the use of international law in domestic constitutional adjudication.

First, there might of course be a challenge to this account's drawing of implications for the larger corpus of constitutional law from the marginalia of constitutional amendment. There is, of course, reason to be cautious about drawing overly broad implications from a rather narrower beginning. However, processes of constitutional change can logically have much to say about the broader corpus of constitutional law. If there are reasons authorizing change in some respects, those reasons can illuminate also reasons why other constitutional content maintains authority without change. The challenge is reason only for caution.

Second, there might be a challenge that all of this speaks only of principle and not of power to enforce the norms. In so speaking, the challenge might run, the account falls into the Kantian-European model of discussion about international law and misses the insights of the Hobbesian-American model.[42] It is true that this account presupposes that principle can guide power. In so doing, however, it does not make empirical claims to a model that will predict state behaviour. It offers a normative account of an interaction of constitutional and international law, and invites an act of ethical faith and affirmation in adherence to the authority of international law,[43] all the while offering a normative account supporting that adherence.[44]

Normative accounts of this sort, however, are very much needed. Roger Alford's recent article notes that:

the notion that international and foreign material should be used to interpret the U.S. Constitution...is gaining currency. Yet proponents of this practice rarely offer a firm theoretical justification for the practice.[45]

Jeremy Waldron calls for a theory that can answer a set of complicated questions about the practice of citing foreign law.[46] Waldron's own offer is an account of legal systems facing similar problems and thus appropriately turning to solutions developed by others also applying legal science to these problems.[47] Waldron's account depends on a certain account of legal science and, as Waldron puts it, a conception of law as a "matter of reason" rather than a "matter of will";[48] this latter assumption is, of course, that there can be a normative account of law and not simply an empirical description of power. This sort of theorizing is, to a degree, at odds with realism and its innumerable legitimate and illegitimate children, but, again, that is partly the point.

If international law is to intermingle in the domestic order in a principled way, an account based on authority of the law, as has arisen in the constitutional amendment context, supposes that the international legal order will sometimes, but not always, have authoritative legal content that the domestic legal order should follow and adopt. This content will sometimes be found within international law *per se*; it will other times be found within comparative foreign law. The latter, however, is also part of the international legal order in that its content may in some instances give rise to international law *per se* either by way of general principles or by way of customary international law.[49] However, in contexts where the content of international law is indeterminate, or at least less easily subject to definitive determination,[50] it may inherently offer less guidance for domestic legal orders.

A similar point obtains where the discernible content of international law is applied to circumstances or in contexts differing substantially from those of domestic law. Accounts of comparative law must endeavour to compare systems and not simply particular rules if they are to assist in tasks of interpretation.[51] International law often tests the attainment of certain ends more than the means by which they have been obtained, recognizing that there can be a range of permissible and legitimate orders structured around partially differing domestic value determinations.[52] An account based on authority of the law thus seems to propose a somewhat less widespread application of foreign law than Waldron's account, although a further investigation of when the problems faced by different legal orders are and are not genuinely similar might further restrict Waldron's account and harmonize the conclusions. At the same time, an account based on authority of the law may call for a thicker application in the sense that there may be more principled binding force in the conclusions of international law when they are discernible.

This authority-based account certainly seems to entail the existence of more instances of binding international law than in much of the recent scholarship, which as in Vicki Jackson's recent article,[53] tends to begin from an assumption that the task is to understand how foreign law can be a persuasive source of law.[54] This authority-based account offers principled reasons why international and comparative law might be more than simply persuasive, offering rather a different form of binding law that stands outside that of *stare decisis*. At the same time, many of the considerations that come into play in writings like those of Jackson will remain applicable, particularly in the adjudicative context.

Jackson's account entails that:

the legitimacy of looking to foreign experience will vary with the issue, depending on the specificity and history of our constitutional text, the degree to which the issue is genuinely unsettled, and the strength of other interpretive sources, [and that] the persuasive value of a foreign source will depend on a combination of its reasoning, the compatibility of contexts, and its institutional origin.[55]

Nothing within an authority-based approach on the connection between international and constitutional law purports to override all normal considerations of adjudication, and those reasonably lead to the sort of considerations Jackson raises. The authority-based account will render more complex certain adjudicative decisions, in some cases adding further sources of law, but it does not transform all adjudication.

There remains a need for much further theoretical discussion of the relationship between constitutional and international law. Outside the present chapter, there would be scope for further analysis of the implications of this authority-based relationship as a possible account. In the meantime, however, it is worth turning to one further complicating factor, that of the dual-faced potential of principled intermingling of constitutional and international law.

Dual-Faced Potential of Principled Intermingling

Those who question the claim that the use of international law will automatically improve domestic constitutional interpretation (improvement in these contexts often being measured against some semi-political results-oriented aspiration) are often a particular species of American exceptionalist. They claim that "rigourous use of international materials is likely to have the most force when deployed *against* existing rights...rather than as a vehicle to extend rights",[56] which is sometimes partly a claim as to the genius of the American Founders. However, the source and tone of some of that argument does not in any way make it less than a real issue. There is a dual-faced potential contained within principled intermingling of constitutional and international law.

If constitutional law in other states is now relevant to our own (wherever that may be), constitutional law has a sort of amplified effect. There will be times when it is possible to dismiss the constitutional law of some particular states as inconsistent with the broader normative strands present within the international legal order (particularly to the extent that natural law figures into the international legal order). But there will be times when it will be more difficult to dismiss the now-amplified law of other states.

Those with particular political aspirations for the content of the domestic legal order should see potential in both directions. On the account offered here, this dual-faced potential may be particularly troubling because foreign and international law actually has some sort of authority rather than being simply something from which one can play games of *"bricolage"*,[57] as power-based accounts of law might have it. The content of international law will not always be "progressive" in the political sense of those advocating some particular interpretation of rights. Some have felt haunted by the spectre of Glendon[58] on abortion rights.[59] They might add such matters as the influence of certain Islamic fundamentalist states on women's rights more generally.[60] Given the sort of amplifying effects that arise once constitutional law enters into transnational processes, human rights advocates need to be as ready to enter into dialogue with Chinese political theory and Islamic political thought as with those who might be more apt to agree with their preferred interpretations. The account here does not necessarily make matters easier for the political groups most frequently engaged in advocacy for the use of foreign law.

The account here builds from an extension of the comparative enterprise into process issues, theorizing about the kind of regulation that governs those process issues, and works on the kind of intermingling of constitutional and international law these prior conclusions imply. It argues for the appropriateness of a more thorough-going sort of comparativism than sometimes thought but argues that this might or might not achieve the political goals comparativists have sometimes sought. It is possible that the comparative enterprise may be more complex than any have envisioned it and that there is still much further work to do. In the meantime, I look forward to learning from many of the other arguments my fellow authors in this book offer in different ways and on different facets of various related issues.

¹ *Lawrence v. Texas*, 539 U.S. 558, 575 (2003). See also *Atkins v. Virginia*, 536 U.S. 304 (2002); *Roper v. Simmons*, 543 U.S. 551 (2005).

² *E.g. United States v. Burns*, [2001] 1 SCR 283, 2001 SCC 7 at paras. 82-92; *State v. Makwanyane*, (3) SA 391 (CC) (1995). The same claim would hold across a wide range of cases. See also Stéphane Beaulac, "L'interprétation de la Charte: reconsidération de l'approche téléologique et réévaluation du rôle du droit international" 27 *Supreme Court Law Review* (2d) 1 (2005).

³ Cf. Vicki C. Jackson, "Comparative Constitutional Federalism and Transnational Judicial Discourse" 2 *International Journal of Constitutional Law* 91 (2004): 91-93.

⁴ *E.g.*, David M. Beatty, *The Ultimate Rule of Law* (Oxford: Oxford University Press, 2004).

⁵ *E.g.*, Mary Ann Glendon, *Abortion and Divorce in Western Law* (Cambridge: Harvard University Press, 1987). Articles in journals like the *International Journal of Constitutional Law* will also typically fall within one or the other of these two categories.

⁶ The classic work is Carl Joachim Friedrich, *Trends of Federalism in Theory and Practice* (London: Pall Mall Press, 1968). For a recent foray into this area once again, see Jackson, "Comparative Constitutional Federalism and Transnational Judicial Discourse". Note as well other sorts of comparative endeavours, like that of Ran Hirschl, *Towards Juristocracy: The Origins and Consequences of the New Constitutionalism* (Cambridge: Harvard University Press, 2004) (examining comparative constitutional law at a more structural level concerned with the relation between the judiciary and other political institutions).

⁷ In my own work, I have become interested in such considerations in a variety of areas: *e.g.* Dwight G. Newman, "Negotiated Rights Enforcement" 68 *Saskatchewan Law Review* 119 (2005); Dwight G. Newman, "Tsilhqot in Nation v. British Columbia and Civil Justice: Analyzing the Procedural Interaction of Evidentiary Principles and Aboriginal Oral History" 43 *Alberta Law Review* 433 (2005); Dwight Newman, "Reconstituting Promises to Negotiate in Canadian Constitution-Making" 10 *National Journal of Constitutional Law* 1 (1998-99).

⁸ Carrie Menkel-Meadow, "Peace and Justice: Notes on the Evolution and Purposes of Legal Processes" 94 *Georgetown Law Journal* 554 (2006): 580.

⁹ South Africa Constitution (1996) arts. 39, 233.

¹⁰ For some of the debate, a reader could start with sets of articles in two leading journals: "Agora: The United States Constitution and International Law" 98 *American Journal of International Law* 42 (2004); "The Debate Over Foreign Law in *Roper v. Simmons*" 119 *Harvard Law Review* 103 (2005). For other noteworthy pieces, see *e.g.* Roger P. Alford, "In Search of a Theory for Constitutional Comparativism" 52 *UCLA Law Review* 639 (2005); Sarah H. Cleveland, "Our International Constitution" 31 *Yale Journal of International Law* 1 (2005); David S. Law, "Generic Constitutional Law" 89 *Minnesota Law Review* 652 (2005); Sanford E. Levinson, "Looking Abroad When Interpreting the U.S. Constitution: Some Reflections" 39 *Texas International Law Journal* 353 (2004). See also "The Relevance of Foreign Legal Materials in U.S. Constitutional Cases: A Conversation Between Justice Antonin Scalia and Justice Stephen Breyer" 3 *International Journal of Constitutional Law* 519 (2005).

¹¹ South Africa Constitution (1996), art. 74.

¹² German Basic Law (1949), art. 79. Article 79(3) makes certain provisions unamendable.

¹³ India Constitution (1950), art. 368.

¹⁴ Constitution Act 1982 (Canada) s. 38(1). The federal government has imposed further conditions on its own agreement by way of legislation: Constitutional Amendments Act (Canada) S.C. 1996, c. 1.

¹⁵ United States Constitution (1787), art. V.

¹⁶ Russian Federation Constitution (1993), arts. 134-36.

¹⁷ *Keshavananda Bharati v. State of Kerala*, AIR 1973 SC 1461.

¹⁸ See generally John Hart Ely, *Democracy and Distrust* (Cambridge: Harvard University Press, 1980).

¹⁹ See generally Benoit Pelletier, "Les modalités de la modification de la constitution du Canada" 33 *Revue juridique Thémis* 1 (1999).

²⁰ *Reference re Secession of Quebec*, [1998] 2 S.C.R. 217.

²¹ *Ibid.* at para. 88.

[22] *Ibid.*

[23] *Ibid.*

[24] *Ibid.* at para. 90.

[25] *Ibid.* at para. 70.

[26] Cf. *ibid.* at paras. 67, 76.

[27] Newman, "Reconstituting Promises to Negotiate in Canadian Constitution-Making", 7-8.

[28] *Quebec Secession Reference,* at paras. 113-39.

[29] *Ibid.* at para. 146.

[30] *Ibid.* at para. 142.

[31] *Ibid.* at para. 143.

[32] See generally Neta C. Crawford, *Argument and Change in World Politics: Ethics, Decolonization, and Humanitarian Intervention* (Cambridge: Cambridge University Press, 2002).

[33] It is thus no surprise that an author with an academic interest in secession would see recognition as a central subject for his work on a moral account of international law: Allen Buchanan, *Justice, Legitimacy, and Self-Determination: Moral Foundations for International Law* (Oxford: Oxford University Press, 2004).

[34] [2001] FJCA 2, [2001] NZAR 385.

[35] Philip Bobbitt, *The Shield of Achilles: War, Peace and the Course of History* (New York: Penguin, 2002).

[36] Hans Kelsen, *General Theory of Law and State* (Cambridge: Harvard University Press, 1946), 220.

[37] *Ibid.* at 221. See also Hans Kelsen, *Principles of International Law* (New York: Rinehart & Company, 1952), 403.

[38] John Finnis, "Revolutions and Continuity of Law", in *Oxford Essays in Jurisprudence: Second Series,* ed. A.W.E. Simpson (Oxford: Oxford University Press, 1971), 44.

[39] Finnis supervised such students as Kent McNeil and Mark Walters: Kent McNeil, *Common Law Aboriginal Title* (Oxford: Oxford University Press, 1989), vii; Mark D. Walters, "The Continuity of Aboriginal Customs and Government Under British Imperial Constitutional Law As Applied in Colonial Canada, 1760-1860" (D. Phil. thesis, Oxford University, 1996). See also chapter 1 of F.M. Brookfield, *Waitangi and Indigenous Rights: Revolution, Law and Legitimation* (Auckland: Auckland University Press, 1999).

[40] The remedial account of secession is that a right to secession arises *only* in circumstances where it ends violations of international law: Buchanan, *Justice, Legitimacy, and Self-Determination,* at 205ff.

[41] According to Habermas, "Legitimacy means that there are good arguments for a political order's claim to be recognized as right and just: a legitimate order deserves recognition. *Legitimacy means a political order's worthiness to be recognized.*" (Jurgen Habermas, Thomas McCarthy, trans., *Communication and the Evolution of Society,* (Boston: Beacon Press, 1979), 178.

[42] Cf. Robert Kagan, *Of Paradise and Power: America and Europe in the New World Order* (New York: Knopf, 2003) (famously claiming that "Americans are from Mars and Europeans are from Venus.")

[43] Cf. Kelsen, *Principles of International Law,* 446-47.

[44] Cf. *ibid.,* 432, 444-46. Developing the account further, one could develop an international law parallel to Hart's account of the "minimum content of natural law" (H.L.A. Hart, *The Concept of Law,* 2nd ed. (Oxford: Clarendon Press, 1994), 193-200). Cf. also John Finnis, *Natural Law and Natural Rights* (Oxford: Clarendon Press, 1980), 238-45.

[45] Alford, "In Search of a Theory for Constitutional Comparativism", 639.

[46] Jeremy Waldron, "Foreign Law and the Modern *Ius Gentium*" (2005) 119 *Harvard Law Review* 129 (2005): 129-30.

[47] *Ibid.* at 143-44. Cf. also Law, "Generic Constitutional Law".

[48] Waldron, "Foreign Law and the Modern *Ius Gentium*", 146-47.

[49] Statute of the International Court of Justice (1945) art. 38.

[50] The precise wording here relates to the same sort of debates about positivism as in the domestic context.

[51] Cf. generally Richard Posner, *Law and Legal Theory in the UK and USA* (New York: Oxford University Press, 1997).

[52] *E.g.* CESCR General Comment 3, *The Nature of States Parties Obligations (Art. 2, Para. 1)*, 14/12/90, U.N. Doc. E/1991/23.

[53] Vicki C. Jackson, "Constitutional Comparisons: Convergence, Resistance, Engagement" 119 *Harvard Law Review* 109 (2005).

[54] *Ibid.* at 109n.

[55] *Ibid.* at 124.

[56] Michael D. Ramsey, "International Materials and Domestic Rights: Reflections on *Atkins* and *Lawrence*" 98 *American Journal of International Law* 69 (2004): 81.

[57] *E.g.* Mark V. Tushnet, "The Possibilities of Comparative Constitutional Law" 108 *Yale Law Journal* 1225 (1999): 1286.

[58] Glendon, *Abortion and Divorce in Western Law*.

[59] *E.g.* Roger P. Alford, "Misusing International Sources to Interpret the Constitution" 98 *American Journal of International Law* 57 (2004): 67-68.

[60] See generally Jennifer Riddle, "Making *CEDAW* Universal: A Critique of *CEDAW*'s Reservation Regime under Article 28 and the Effectiveness of the Reporting Process" 34 *George Washington International Law Review* 605 (2002).

CHAPTER 2

EXPORTING PROPHYLACTIC RULES

Michael Plaxton

Though jurists, judges, and lawyers from outside the United States should be careful when they use American constitutional jurisprudence, it may occasionally benefit them to borrow concepts from American legal scholarship and case law that bring order to constitutional thinking. The idea of prophylactic rules,[1] as distinguished from constitutional rules, belongs in this category of concepts that warrant further attention. This chapter sets out to show that we can make better sense of constitutional cases and doctrines when we draw a distinction between constitutional rules and prophylactic rules. We can also clarify the relationship between courts and legislatures. At a time when charges of 'judicial activism' are thrown around in constitutional democracies around the world, such clarification is urgently needed.

Part I will examine Ronald Dworkin's distinction between policy and principle, showing how the dichotomy can be deconstructed such that the legislature has legitimate jurisdiction to abrogate rules created by courts in constitutional cases. Part II will show how this idea is reflected in the distinction, drawn in American constitutional law, between constitutional rules and prophylactic rules. Parts III and IV will then demonstrate how constitutional cases and doctrines outside the United States can be better understood when we look at those doctrines in light of this distinction.

I. Principle, Policy, Protection

Ronald Dworkin famously drew a distinction between principles and policies. Whereas principles stem from the fundamental values of the community, he claimed, policies "set out ... economic, political, or social [goals] of the community".[2] Phrased in that way, we might think that only policies are concerned with consequences or states of affairs. On that view, if constitutions are concerned with goals at all, they must describe policies rather than principles. That conclusion would be decidedly odd inasmuch as we typically think that, if *any* legal instrument enunciates the fundamental values of the community, it must be the constitution. Indeed, it is far from clear how we could possibly square constitutions with democratic values if the will of elected legislatures could be 'trumped' on the basis that it conflicts with a mere goal of the community. After all, we have legislatures in the first place to decide which goals the community has, and which should be pursued.[3]

We need not, though, treat only policies as wrapped-up with ends. It will often be the case that the legislature cannot respect (still less, promote) the fundamental values of the community without creating, through legislation, certain states of affairs. Take, for example, s. 8 of the *Canadian Charter of Rights and Freedoms*, which provides that every Canadian citizen has the right to be free from unreasonable searches and seizures.[4] In a sense, s. 8 does not require the state to 'do' anything – it imposes an obligation to not interfere with individuals' privacy. But, as the Supreme Court of Canada noted in *Hunter v. Southam* – one of the earliest *Charter* cases to reach the Court – the state can only guarantee the right to be free from unreasonable invasions of privacy if it devises some mechanism for deterring police officers or other state agents from engaging in searches on less than reasonable and probable grounds.[5] The Court ultimately decided that any search conducted in the absence of prior judicial authorization presumptively violates s. 8, effectively holding that the *Charter* required the creation of some procedure by which search warrants could be issued. Whether or not the Court was correct to say that s. 8 requires a search warrant regime in particular, though, deterring unreasonable searches would plainly require some sort of legal mechanism. The strategy for deterring such searches might involve provisions creating a constitutional tort, a disciplinary procedure for police officers that have abused their search powers, or some other regime of legal rules, but certainly the ends dictated by s. 8 (at least as it is interpreted by the *Hunter* Court) do demand a strategy.

Once we see both principles and policies as concerned with goals, we find that the values underpinning legal rules cannot always be neatly classified as *either* principles *or* policies. This is in part because principle obviously exerts a pull on the kinds of policies that can be pursued. An economic policy of low taxation might be utterly foiled by a strategy for protecting rights that requires significant state resources – for instance, state-funded counsel.[6] A social policy that we should prosecute rape cases as successfully as possible might be seriously undermined if we tried to protect the presumption of innocence through the use of corroboration rules.

We can complicate the policy-principle divide also because policy can affect the viability of certain means of promoting or respecting principles. An example of this idea can be found in one of Dworkin's few forays into the realm of criminal procedure. In *A Matter of Principle*, Dworkin set out to show that a community may acknowledge the injustice or 'moral harm' of a wrongful conviction and yet refuse to commit itself to the most accurate procedural rules possible.[7] He made that claim on the basis that people do not aspire to avoid moral harm 'at any cost'.[8] They aspire only to have their status, as agents who pursue moral projects, respected enough that the risk of wrongful convictions is kept low. Rules of criminal procedure, then, do not need to be perfectly reliable; their reliability need only satisfy a minimum threshold. Critically, Dworkin does not prescribe any particular procedural rules: the legislature may adopt any rules of procedure it likes, so long as the criminal justice system prevents wrongful convictions to the extent minimally required by citizens' moral aspirations.[9]

If the minimum threshold is a matter of principle, and so non-negotiable, it seems as though considerations of policy cease to play a role; as if there is no 'balancing' of social interests against individual rights. Yet administrative efficiency plainly *does* matter, as does financial cost. Dworkin reconciles these competing claims on citizens' well-being by arguing that considerations of efficiency and cost come into play when the legislature decides which procedural strategy to use. This affects, to some extent, how much protection the legislature will offer criminal defendants. If the legislature has to choose from among ten possible strategies, all of which offer defendants the same risk of wrongful conviction, the legislature is entitled (indeed, one intuits, obligated) to adopt the least costly model. The community's economic goals (as well as any political and social goals that depend on having a certain amount of resources available) rightly affect the means by which the principle that an innocent person should not be punished can be respected.

We can find another example of the pull policy can have on principle by looking to a relatively recent Supreme Court of Canada decision, *Newfoundland v. N.A.P.E.*[10] There, the Court noted that a requirement on the province to pay an affirmative action settlement, given its dire economic circumstances at the time, would seriously impact the quality of health care and the job security of many provincial employees. On that basis, the Court held that, although the province's failure to pay the settlement amounted to a violation of women employees' equality rights under s. 15 of the *Charter*, it was justified under s. 1. There was no question that the province had an obligation to treat its employees equally. The province's economic and social goals, however, were recognized as valid reasons for not adopting a particular strategy (that is, the payment of a settlement) for achieving equality.

The distinction between policy and principle, then, is not hard-and-fast. The decision to promote or respect a given principle in a particular way may be itself a matter of policy. This is, no doubt, one reason why Dworkin suggested that the values underpinning legal rules cannot be exhaustively classified as either principles or policies. Often, a constitution will demand the implementation of some regime of legal rules – that is, it will require the courts or legislature to devise some strategy for achieving the goals dictated as a matter of principle – without requiring the implementation of one specific strategy. Where the ends required by the fundamental values of the community – those expressed in the constitution – can be achieved through the deployment of only one strategy, that strategy is *per se* required as a matter of principle. The means by which the specified end is achieved is as much a 'constitutional rule' as the rule that that end must be achieved in the first place. Where, on the other hand, a principled goal can be reached through one of several possible strategies, none are *per se* required by the constitution. The lawmaker must choose to implement one of those strategies, since adopting such a course would mean failing to achieve the results demanded by principle; she has, however, a measure of discretion when deciding which measure to implement. We will refer to the means ultimately selected as a 'protective rule', since it protects constitutional values without *per se* being required by the constitution.

The distinction is of much more than theoretical significance. If we accept Dworkin's claim that matters of principle are the responsibility of the courts, and matters of policy that of the legislature, we might think that rules devised by courts in constitutional cases cannot be legitimately subjected to legislative interference. But once we see that the decision to protect constitutional values in a particular way can (and often will) represents a policy decision, we likewise see that the legislature can legitimately abrogate a judicially-crafted rule – even one made in a constitutional case.

Recognizing the distinction between protective rules and constitutional rules sweeps the legs out from under many claims that the courts, when devising rules in constitutional cases, have become 'activists' or have acted undemocratically. If a high court 'discovers' a constitutional rule, that rule is effectively immutable unless and until the court overrules itself. The state must conform to the rule. (In many constitutional democracies, the legislature may choose not to conform, but only if it is prepared to say explicitly that it intends to act unconstitutionally. Such a move is politically perilous and so, for all intents and purposes, a finding that a constitutional rule exists ties the hands of the legislature.) No doubt, there will be some occasions where the courts must, if they take their interpretive responsibilities seriously, find that a constitutional rule exists. In such cases, they tie the hands of the legislature. That is a legitimate exercise of power in a constitutional democracy. Courts invite the charge of activism when they suggest (either implicitly or explicitly) that every rule they craft in constitutional cases is constitutionally mandated. That sort of claim neither rings true, nor seems compatible with a respect for democratic institutions. Acknowledgment that the rules created in some, perhaps many, constitutional cases are provisional rather than final – that they may be reviewed, abrogated, and replaced by the legislature – muffles the criticism that the courts are engaging in a power-grab.

II. American Law and Prophylactic Rules

American constitutional criminal procedure has long distinguished constitutional rules from 'prophylactic rules'. The latter are rules created specifically by the *courts* to protect constitutional values, but which are not themselves required by the Constitution. There is an obvious similarity between protective rules and prophylactic rules – both are, in a sense, disposable. We might hesitate, however, to equate the two, given that prophylactic rules have been traditionally regarded as subject to abrogation by statute even if no replacement strategy is put forward. As we will see, however, we arrive at a better view of prophylactic rules, as they have been deployed by the courts, when we treat them as protective rules. There are two reasons to think so.

First, we should note that there is nothing inherent in the idea of a prophylactic rule requiring us to treat it as unconditionally subject to abrogation. Prophylactic rules are distinct from constitutional rules by virtue of their disposability. They are distinct from other non-constitutional rules by virtue of the fact that they protect constitutional values. Nothing in those two premises prevents us from taking the view that prophylactic rules may reflect a constitutionally-mandated level of protection, the satisfaction of which requires some sort of procedural infrastructure. The rule itself is disposable, but the standard is not. For reasons already discussed, moreover, there is good reason to think that constitutional provisions often require just such an infrastructure. With this in mind, it is simply inadequate to draw a rigid line between rules that can be abrogated by statute and those which cannot. American constitutional jurisprudence might simply recognize a third class of rules – that is, protective rules. But there seems little reason to do that, when the idea of prophylactic rules is already part of the law, and substantially overlaps with protective rules anyway.

A second reason is this: when we treat prophylactic rules as unconditionally subject to abrogation, we find much of the law surrounding the most prominent of these rules difficult to fathom. Take, for example, the rule enunciated in *Miranda v. Arizona*.[11] In that case, a majority held that the Fifth Amendment requires officers to inform a suspect held for custodial interrogation that "he has the right to remain silent",[12] "that anything said can and will be used against the individual in court",[13] "that he has the right to consult with a lawyer and to have the lawyer with him during interrogation",[14] and "that if he is indigent a lawyer will be appointed to represent him".[15] In *Dickerson v. United States*,[16] a majority of the Court relied on the idea that *Miranda* laid down a "constitutional rule",[17] in finding that an attempt by Congress to abrogate the *Miranda* rule could not succeed.

It is difficult to understand, though, how *Miranda* could have created a constitutional rule. In the years following *Miranda* and before *Dickerson*, the Court crafted a number of exceptions to the *Miranda* doctrine. As Scalia J. correctly noted in *Dickerson*, these exceptions plainly show "that it is possible – indeed not uncommon – for the police to violate *Miranda* without also violating the Constitution."[18] If the Constitution does not require the *Miranda* rule, there seems no reason to think that Congress lacks the power to remove it. For this reason, the *Miranda* rule was generally believed to be prophylactic before the Court's decision in *Dickerson*.

We find ourselves in something of a quagmire when we try to reconcile the *Dickerson* holding with the *Miranda* jurisprudence. We escape it when we recognize that prophylactic rules can be only conditionally disposable. Suppose that the *Miranda* majority, first and foremost, declared that the Fifth Amendment mandated a particular level of protection owed to suspects – a level of protection not provided by law prior to *Miranda*. The warning-and-waiver regime was not, on this view, a rule *per se* required by the Fifth Amendment; instead, it was one of a number of possible strategies available for providing the constitutionally-mandated level of protection. As one of several possible strategies, the *Miranda* rule is not (contrary to the suggestion of the *Dickerson* majority) a 'constitutional rule', insofar as the legislature or the Court itself could strip away the rule without failing to satisfy the demands of the Constitution. The legislature could only take that step, though, if it replaced the rule with one also capable of protecting constitutional values to the extent necessary. Because Congress attempted to abrogate the *Miranda* rule without providing an alternative strategy, the attempt failed and the *Miranda* rule survived. By understanding the *Miranda* rule as a prophylactic rule in a modified sense, we clear up some of the difficulties we have in reconciling the *Miranda* case law with the majority's holding in *Dickerson*.

We can see a further example of a prophylactic rule in the exclusionary rule for Fourth-Amendment violations. The bulk of Fourth-Amendment case law, since *Boyd*,[19] has grounded the exclusionary rule in the claim that it is an expedient means of ensuring compliance with the Fourth Amendment, not a rule required by the Constitution itself.[20] No matter how efficient it is, however, the exclusionary rule – at least in its application to the individual states via the Fourteenth Amendment – has proven highly controversial. This is partly because such application should only be possible if it is a constitutional rule. Suppose, though, that the Fourth Amendment, like s. 8 of the *Charter*, requires some rule or regime of rules whereby unreasonable searches are effectively deterred. In that case, the Fourteenth Amendment may be understood as imposing an obligation on the states to have some means of deterring unreasonable searches to the extent required by the Fourth Amendment. The exclusionary rule devised by the U.S. Supreme Court, as merely one possible means, can be regarded as susceptible to abrogation by the individual states when and if they decide to use some other strategy capable of achieving the constitutionally-mandated ends.

Thus, we can unravel some of the more intractable difficulties in categorizing rules as either constitutional or prophylactic, when we more closely equate prophylactic rules with protective rules. Furthermore, once we take that step, we find that the American concept of prophylactic rules is able to help us resolve constitutional difficulties outside the United States. In the following two sections, we will see how the distinction between protective or prophylactic rules and constitutional rules can help us to make sense of constitutional cases and doctrines in Scotland and Canada. In each section, we will see the courts devising rules that are ostensibly grounded in a constitutional (or quasi-constitutional) document, but which are difficult to understand when we look at them as constitutional rules. We will find that the introduction of the concept of prophylactic rules will help us understand better the relationship of the courts and the relevant legislatures, and perhaps also the substantive doctrines themselves.

III.   The Privy Council and Disclosure

In Scotland, a legislative or executive act, to be valid, must conform to the European Convention on Human Rights.[21] The Convention (or ECHR), then, has the status of a quasi-constitutional document. Just as the distinction between constitutional and prophylactic rules can help us understand constitutional doctrines in the United States, so it can assist us when we try to make sense of ECHR cases and doctrines. To make this point, we can examine *Holland* and *Sinclair*, two recent decisions in which the Privy Council found that article 6(1) of the ECHR confers an obligation upon the Crown to "disclose to the defence all material evidence for or against the accused".[22]

In *Sinclair*, the Crown accused the defendant of striking the complainant in the face with a hammer and a pair of scissors. The Crown had corroborated evidence that the complainant was assaulted in this manner. P.R., a Crown witness, provided the necessary corroboration[23] that it was the defendant who delivered the blows. Much, then, could turn on whether the jury accepted P.R.'s version of events.

In police statements, P.R. said that she had seen the defendant stab the complainant in the face with the scissors. She made no mention of a hammer, except to say that *the complainant had told her* that the defendant had used a hammer during the alleged assault. The Crown did not disclose the contents of this statement to defense counsel. Nothing suggests that this failure to disclose was motivated by malice or 'gamesmanship' – it appears, since even trial counsel for the Crown did not have a copy of P.R.'s statement on hand during her examination, that no one believed that anything would turn on her testimony. (Defence counsel, who could have applied for disclosure of the police statement, did not.)

At trial, everyone was taken by surprise when P.R. testified that she in fact *saw* the defendant strike the complainant with a hammer. Though neither Crown nor defense counsel had a copy of P.R.'s statement, and may have had no first-hand knowledge of its contents, it seems that the testimony of other witnesses led them to spot the inconsistency. Crown counsel, during the examination and re-examination, pressured P.R. to concede that she did not mention having seen the defendant use a hammer during her police interview. Defence counsel, on cross-examination, attempted to do the same thing. P.R. stated, by turn, that she could not remember what she told the police; that she told the police that she saw the defendant use the hammer; that she 'must' have told the police that; and that, if the police asked her, she would have told them that she saw the defendant use the hammer. Neither Crown nor defense counsel could shake P.R. from her story, since neither could confront her with the statement itself. The defendant was convicted.

The defendant argued that the Crown, by failing to disclose P.R.'s police statement, breached his article-6(1) right to a fair trial. The Judicial Committee of the Privy Council agreed. Following *Edwards v. United Kingdom*,[24] the Committee found that article 6(1) of the ECHR confers an obligation upon the Crown to "disclose to the defence all material evidence for or against the accused".[25] Since the police statements of any witness to be called at trial "must contain material evidence against or, in some cases, in favour of the accused", the Crown has a duty to disclose those statements in every case.[26] Likewise, in *Holland* (released the same day), the Privy Council observed that the Crown has an obligation to disclose the prior convictions of and outstanding charges against witnesses.[27]

The decisions, though, are incoherent if we attempt to ground them directly in the terms of the European Convention. The Privy Council refused to say that the failure to disclose material evidence is *per se* a violation of article 6(1). There are two reasons for this hesitation. First, the failure to disclose is only problematic if the undisclosed evidence is relevant to a *material* issue. An issue may not turn out to be material until the trial is well under way. Nothing may turn on it at all. In *Sinclair*, for example, P.R.'s police statement was relevant to a material issue only when P.R.'s trial testimony deviated from the prior statement. Until that moment, no one was arguing over what she said to the police. Only when P.R. maintained that her police statement and trial testimony were consistent, did their (in)consistency become a material issue.

The first point leads to the second: since the Crown has a measure of control over which issues become material and which do not, the Crown can choose not to disclose evidence, without falling afoul of article 6(1), so long as it (or someone else) takes steps to mitigate the prejudice resulting to the accused. Thus, Lord Rodger pointedly observed that, had trial counsel for the Crown obtained and disclosed P.R.'s police statement the moment it became clear that something would turn on its contents, the Crown would have preserved the fairness of the trial and there would have been no violation of article 6(1).[28] We can also suppose that, had the accused in *Sinclair* successfully applied for disclosure of P.R.'s police statement (as he was entitled to do), he would have been in a position to effectively cross-examine P.R. on her prior statement, and the trial would have been fair. This is not to suggest that we should penalize Sinclair for failing to make such an application by declaring that any unfairness was his own fault and that there was, on that basis, no unfairness (properly speaking) at all.[29] It is to make the substantially milder claim that Sinclair could have helped the Crown meet its obligation to try him fairly and, by choosing not to do so, made the Crown's failure to disclose relevant for article-6(1) purposes. Had he chose to assist the Crown by making the application, though, the failure to disclose would have ceased to matter. There were several possible ways by which Sinclair's trial could have complied with article 6(1). Though the Privy Council clearly approved a new Crown Practice Statement requiring near-automatic[30] disclosure of all witness statements, there is no indication that such a rule is *per se* demanded by the accused's right to a fair trial.

It is not obvious, moreover, that the right to a fair trial in and of itself requires the Crown to automatically disclose prior convictions and any outstanding charges against witnesses. In *Holland*, Lord Rodger noted that the Crown would *voluntarily* disclose previous convictions if the accused could show their relevance to a proposed defence.[31] He found this discretionary approach to disclosure unseemly given, first, the Crown's adversarial position in the trial; and, second, the fact that defence counsel's knowledge of a witness' prior convictions will often 'materially assist' the accused.[32] Importantly, though, there is nothing in that procedure that *automatically* leads to a violation of the accused's right to a fair trial – the Crown, taking its role as 'minister of justice' seriously, might exercise its discretion in a generous fashion. Indeed, the Privy Council remarked that disclosure had long been a non-issue precisely because the Crown traditionally adopted an attitude of open-ness with regard to documents in its possession.[33]

It is precisely because there may be more than one path to a fair trial that, as Lord Rodger observed in *Holland*, the European Convention does not generally prescribe specific rules of evidence. He stated:

> It is trite that the Convention does not concern itself with the law of evidence as such. In particular, it does not lay down that certain forms of evidence should be regarded as inadmissible. Such questions are left to the national legal systems. What article 6 does is guarantee a fair trial and so, when the introduction of some form of evidence is said to have infringed the accused's article 6 rights, the question always is whether admitting the evidence has resulted in the accused not having a fair trial in the circumstances of the particular case.[34]

The Privy Council made the similar point in *Brown v. Stott*[35] that, although the right to a fair trial is 'absolute' (in the sense that the state cannot justify subjecting an accused to an unfair trial), the rules (or bundles of rules) that *make* a trial fair – for instance, the privilege against self-incrimination or the duty of disclosure – may be justifiably limited. The issue in *Brown* was whether the legislature had justifiably limited one such 'derivative right', whereas *Sinclair* and *Holland* required the Privy Council to determine the nature of the 'derivative rights' in existence absent legislative involvement. Nonetheless, all assume that there is a certain amount of 'wiggle-room' when delivering a fair trial.

But if the right to a fair trial contained in the European Convention does not prescribe particular rules of evidence or criminal procedure – if, as we have seen, an accused may have a fair trial in the absence of specific rules mandating Crown disclosure of certain kinds of evidence – it becomes unclear how we are to understand the rules laid down in *Sinclair* and *Holland*. *Sinclair* and *Holland* were, in one respect, easy cases, since both defendants suffered actual breaches of their fair-trial rights. What about cases where the Crown fails to act according to the rules enunciated in *Holland* and *Sinclair*, but does not, in fact, compromise the accused's right to a fair trial? As we have seen, it is not just possible but probable that this will happen in at least some circumstances. In those cases, can we say that the Crown has violated the accused's rights under article 6(1), even though the violation is notional, not actual? That seems an odd result, not least because article 6(1) does not say that the state is precluded from implementing rules and practices that *might* lead to an unfair trial. Furthermore, if we are to say that the accused's right to a fair trial has been violated merely because the absence of disclosure *might* undermine trial fairness, it seems difficult to explain how the Privy Council (or the European Court of Human Rights in *Dowsett*)[36] could countenance an exception to the duty of disclosure – if disclosure is to be regarded as *per se* necessary for a fair trial, there seems no reason to think it any less necessary when the materials to be disclosed concern the identity of informants, or police investigative tactics. We might think other rights or state interests at stake in the privileging of that kind of information, but it is difficult to believe that the Privy Council would want to say that, for the sake of those other rights and policies, the fair-trial rights of criminal defendants can be *limited* or *violated*, given that it has remarked elsewhere that the right to a fair trial is absolute.

We can make sense of *Sinclair* and *Holland* by bringing the American language of prophylaxis into the discussion. The issue in those cases was, first and foremost, whether the particular defendants had been given a fair trial in accordance with article 6(1). (As we have seen, they had not.) There was, however, an additional issue: what sort of common law rule should the court impose on the Crown to minimize the possibility of future deprivations of the right to a fair trial? The ECHR may preclude a certain amount of 'risk-taking' with regard to the fair-trial rights of citizens (though, as we have seen, it is far from clear that this is so); in that case, the ECHR requires the court or domestic legislature to create some sort of procedural rules to keep the Crown's gambling to a 'constitutionally' acceptable minimum. The precise content of that rule, however, would not be determined by the ECHR – so long as the rule secures fair-trial rights to the minimum extent the ECHR requires, it satisfies the Convention. Alternatively, we might think that the ECHR precludes no Crown risk-taking with fair-trial rights (so long as the accused can contest the fairness of her trial after-the-fact through a right of appeal).[37] If true, the Privy Council *could* have chosen not to devise *any* common law rule. That sort of antinomian strategy, though, would not necessarily do the Crown any favours: by not imposing a rule on the Crown, the Privy Council would allow it to take its chances with ECHR-compliance, leading to the prospect of more unfair trials in the future. Moreover, the Privy Council had reliable indications that the Crown did not *want* to take that kind of chance with ECHR-compliance – the Lord Advocate had already changed Crown practice with respect to the disclosure of witness statements and criminal records, presumably to avoid the unfairness attending non-disclosure in at least some cases. The Privy Council may, on this basis, have simply taken it upon itself to create a common law duty of disclosure possibly going far beyond anything required by article 6(1) *per se*. (To be sure, the common law rules created by the court went beyond the procedures fashioned by the Lord Advocate, but they nonetheless reflect the same concerns.)

In either case, the duty of disclosure is not a rule of the ECHR, but a prophylactic rule designed to protect values contained in the ECHR. On this view, the duty created in *Sinclair* and *Holland* is not *per se* required by the ECHR, and could be replaced by other procedural rules that satisfy its minimum standards. The duty is grounded not so much in the authority of the ECHR but in the law-making authority of the Privy Council. Thinking of the matter in these terms helps us resolve (or, at least, re-frame) the questions that earlier confronted us. Because the precise dimensions of the duty are not required by the terms of the Convention, exceptions can be carved into that duty where other Convention rights or pressing state objectives demand them – thus, the Privy Council could envision limits on Crown disclosure where, for example, the identity of informants was at issue, without imagining that the accused's article 6(1) rights could be violated or limited. Furthermore, the courts *may* later decide that a breach of the Crown's duty of disclosure need not automatically trigger a finding that the Crown acted contrary to the ECHR; on the other hand, the courts may fashion a remedy of their own to deal with cases where the Crown is *only* guilty of having failed to disclose in accordance with *Sinclair* and *Holland*. By importing the language of prophylaxis, we improve our understanding of 'constitutional' law in Scotland.

IV.   The Supreme Court of Canada and 'Dialogue'

In the Canadian context, the language of prophylaxis can help us make sense of problems associated with 'dialogue theory' – that is, the view that courts and legislatures share responsibility for interpreting the Constitution.[38] Dialogue theory is meant to explain how we can square democratic values with the striking-down of legislation by courts; that is, with so-called 'judicial activism'. If a judicial pronouncement represents the beginning of a 'dialogue' in which the courts and legislature together decide what the *Charter* demands, it is more difficult to criticize constitutional case law as illegitimate over-reaching. In that case, the judiciary begins to look less like a usurper than a conscientious advisor of the Crown.[39] The trouble with the dialogue metaphor is that, ultimately, somebody must have the last word when it comes to interpreting the Constitution. If the courts and the legislatures disagree about what the *Charter* requires, they cannot both be right. As a matter of convention, the courts have the last word.[40] But, if the courts have the last word, we fall back into the problem that dialogue theory was supposed to resolve. Furthermore, we wind up with problems we would not have with naked judicial activism, inasmuch as legislatures will be more inclined to challenge judicial interpretations of the Constitution, in the process wasting time and scarce resources, as well as calling into question the constitutional role of the courts and creating more room for uncertainty in constitutional law.

Consider, for example, the situation that arose after the Supreme Court of Canada's split decision in *O'Connor*.[41]   Section 7 of the *Charter* gives every criminal defendant the right to full answer and defense. *O'Connor* concerned the extent to which criminal defendants are entitled, by virtue of s.7, to records held by third parties. Increased disclosure would give accused persons greater opportunity to prepare their respective cases, but would also subject victims to greater intrusions on their privacy – intrusions which, particularly in sexual assault cases, could be considerable enough to engage women's equality and privacy rights. The Court had to decide what procedure for obtaining third-party records would achieve what the Constitution required. The majority declared that a particular procedure (A), whereby accused persons could obtain third-party records, would make it too difficult for defendants to acquire them. It devised an alternative procedure (B), with obstacles far easier for defendants to hurdle. The remaining members of the Court took the view that procedure A was preferable; that procedure B made it too easy for defendants to invade the privacy of victims.

After *O'Connor*, the Canadian Parliament considered how much access criminal defendants should have to the personal records of sexual assault complainants. It enacted legislation that effectively swept away the procedure devised by the

O'Connor majority, replacing it with that proposed by the *O'Connor* dissent. The constitutionality of that legislation was at issue in *Mills*.[42] Plainly, if the majority judgment in *O'Connor* accurately described the minimum requirements of s. 7, Parliament's new legislation could not survive. The Court, however, upheld the legislation, invoking the dialogue metaphor.

As we have already observed, though, the dialogue metaphor is problematic. By enacting the legislation at issue in *Mills*, did Parliament truly carry on a 'dialogue' with the courts concerning what the *Charter* demands, or did it attempt to bulldoze unconstitutional legislation past the courts in the hope that judges would be too timid to strike it down? When the Court upheld the legislation, did the Court accept an alternative interpretation of s. 7, or did it simply acquiesce to an insistent legislature, abdicating its constitutional responsibilities? In deciding *Mills*, the Court never indicated that it was adopting a different interpretation of the *Charter*, and never referred to any fresh arguments to justify a changed interpretation. Given that *Mills* was decided only four years after *O'Connor*, it is difficult to imagine that the Constitution itself changed in the interim. Nor does it obviously matter that Parliament followed the lead of the *O'Connor* dissent. We seem forced to conclude that the Court buckled under pressure from the legislature.

Acknowledging the place of protective rules in constitutional law would allow us to cast *Mills* in a more favourable light. Suppose that the procedure adopted by the *O'Connor* majority was not the only procedure capable of respecting all of the constitutional interests at stake. It may be that the *Charter* only required that accused persons have *some* measure of access to third-party records, short of absolute access (in recognition of the privacy interests of sexual assault complainants). If true, there was no constitutional reason why either procedure A or B could not be adopted. Nonetheless, some procedure needed to be implemented; otherwise, the requirements of the *Charter* would not be satisfied. A decision needed to be made. It simply happens that, in *O'Connor*, a majority of the Court found that procedure B was preferable to procedure A. In that case, the procedural regime created in *O'Connor* was not a constitutional rule but a protective or prophylactic one. As such, it could be replaced with another rule or regime of rules in the event that the legislature decided that some other rule would better promote the economic, social, or political goals of the community. So long as Parliament provided the constitutionally mandated level of access to third-party records, it could ignore both or either of the contending rules devised by the two factions on the Court.[43]

If we understand *O'Connor* as laying down a prophylactic rule, rather than a constitutional rule, Parliament's legislation becomes a legitimate attempt to advance social policies without sacrificing constitutional values. Moreover, the *Mills* Court's refusal to strike down the legislation no longer looks like abdication of their constitutional responsibilities, and begins to look like humble recognition that the legislature is better placed to decide how the community's social goals can best be advanced. Yet *O'Connor* and *Mills* remain unsatisfying for the Court's failure in those cases to say expressly what it was doing. Had the *O'Connor* majority said that the procedural regime it created was not required *per se* by s. 7 of the *Charter*, the legislature could be expected to know – not just guess – that it would be appropriate to re-evaluate that approach to protecting the accused's right to full answer and defense. As matters stand, we may suspect that Parliament simply rolled the dice and hoped that the Court would not thwart its attempt to re-write the procedure for obtaining third-party records. That is not an efficient way to craft legislation in a constitutional democracy.

Nor is it a proper means of engaging in a 'dialogue'. Had the *O'Connor* majority envisioned the rule it created as a constitutional rule, Parliament's only conceivable role in a dialogue would have involved persuading the Court that a new interpretation of s. 7 was both available and preferable. Given that Parliament could bring nothing new to the Court in support of a new interpretation, it would have been quite appropriate for Parliament to yield to the interpretation devised in *O'Connor*. Effectively, the 'dialogue' would have ended. The courts and Parliament had something to talk about only if the rule crafted by the *O'Connor* majority is envisioned as a prophylactic device. Only then could a fruitful dialogue truly develop. Without saying whether the rule was constitutional or prophylactic, the courts put Parliament in the position of having to guess whether, by crafting new legislation, it was acting consistently with the constitution. Under those circumstances, Parliament might have been deterred from participating in any dialogue at all. That ought to concern us, since Parliament has far more resources than the courts when it comes to deciding how policies and principles can best be promoted.[44]

It is not enough, in short, to know that prophylactic rules are 'out there'. If the courts are to act in a way that is respectful to the legislature, they must change the way they create rules in constitutional cases. They must do two things. First, they must indicate whether the rules created are constitutional or prophylactic. This will give legislatures a heads-up that a given rule is open to re-consideration; that abrogation of the rule may be consistent with respect for constitutional values. Second, the courts must indicate what sort of standard any replacement rule would need to satisfy to pass constitutional muster. This allows the legislature to use its resources efficiently and in such a way that there is little risk that any replacement will run afoul of the Constitution.

Taking these steps will do much to improve the relationship between courts and legislatures not just in Canada, but in constitutional democracies everywhere. In today's political climate, that sort of peacemaking is urgently needed. That we can use the concept of prophylactic rules to achieve that result, in turn, serves as a reminder that, whatever the limits of comparativism, there is much to be gained in looking beyond our respective borders.

[1] See Brian K. Landsberg, "Safeguarding Constitutional Rights: The Uses and Limits of Prophylactic Rules" 66 *Tenn. L. Rev.* 925(1999): 926 (defining prophylactic rules as "risk—avoidance rules that are not directly sanctioned or required by the Constitution, but that are adopted to ensure that the government follows constitutionally sanctioned or required rules"); Joseph D. Grano, "Prophylactic Rules in Criminal Procedure: A Question of Article III Legitimacy" 80 *Nw. U. L. Rev.* 100 (1985): 105 (defining them as "rules that function as a preventive safeguard to insure that constitutional violations will not occur").

[2] Ronald Dworkin, *Taking Rights Seriously* (Harvard, 1978), 22.

[3] For the view that legislative authority is justified chiefly on the need for coordination, see Joseph Raz, *Ethics in the Public Domain* (Oxford: Clarendon Press, 1994), 198 (discussing the normal justification thesis); John Finnis, *Natural Law and Natural Rights* (Oxford, 1979), ch. 9. See also Leslie Green, "Three Themes From Raz" (2005) 25 *O.J.L.S.* 503 (2005): 509—16.

[4] *Canadian Charter of Rights and Freedoms*, being Schedule B to the *Canada Act 1982* (U.K.) 1982, c. 11, s. 8 [*Charter*].

[5] See *Hunter v. Southam*, [1984] 2 S.C.R. 145 at 160.

[6] See *R. v. Prosper*, [1994] 3 S.C.R. 236 (refusing to find that the *Charter* requires the provinces to fund duty—counsel).

[7] Ronald Dworkin, "Principle, Policy, Procedure" in *A Matter of Principle* (Harvard, 1985).

[8] *Ibid.* at 86.

[9] *Ibid.* at 90—2.

[10] *Newfoundland v. N.A.P.E.*, 2004 SCC 66.

[11] *Miranda v. Arizona*, 384 U.S. 436 (1966).

[12] *Ibid.* at 468.

[13] *Ibid.* at 469.

[14] *Ibid.* at 471.

[15] *Ibid.* at 473.

[16] *Dickerson v. United States*, 530 U.S. 428, 120 S. Ct. 2326, 147 L. Ed. 2d 405, (2000) [case cited to S. Ct.]. For a summary of the decision, see Note, "The Supreme Court — Leading Cases" 114 *Harv. L. Rev.* 179 (2000): 199—209.

[17] *Dickerson, ibid.* at 2333.

[18] *Ibid.* at 2340.

[19] *Boyd v. United States*, 116 U.S. 616 (1885). The Fifth Amendment explicitly requires courts to exclude certain kinds of evidence, but the Fourth does not. The Fourth Amendment merely states that the government shall not conduct unreasonable searches and seizures; it does not say that the proceeds of such searches should or must be excluded at trial. The Supreme Court in *Boyd* held that a Fourth—Amendment violation is necessarily a violation of the Fifth, that an unreasonable search invariably amounts to a constructive infringement of the searchee's right not to incriminate herself under the Fifth Amendment. To give effect to the intention of the Framers of the Fifth Amendment, an exclusionary rule must, the *Boyd* Court claimed, be read into the Fourth. *Boyd* is discussed and criticized in Jacob W. Landynski, *Search and Seizure and the Supreme Court* (John Hopkins Press, 1966), 57—61; Polyvios G. Polyviou, *Search and Seizure* (Duckworth, 1982), ch. 1.

[20] Hence, in *Wolf v. Colorado*, 338 U.S. 25 (1949), a majority found that the exclusionary rule applied only in federal criminal cases. The Court, it found, could not exclude evidence obtained through unreasonable seizures under the Fourteenth Amendment, since the exclusionary rule was merely one possible means of enforcing the requirements of the Fourth. The Court later narrowly overruled *Wolf* in *Mapp v. Ohio*, 367 U.S. 643 (1961) again on the basis of expedience. The decision has been criticized as unprincipled. See Polyviou, *ibid.* at 345—8. For a general overview of the debate over the exclusionary rule's constitutional status in Fourth—Amendment jurisprudence, see Wayne R. LaFave, *Search and Seizure: A Treatise on the Fourth Amendment* (West, 1987), Vol. 1, § 1.1.

[21] Scotland Act 1998, s. 29, s. 57. This does not apply to legislation from Westminster.

[22] *Sinclair v. H.M. Advocate* 2005 S.L.T. 563; *Holland v. H.M. Advocate* 2005 S.L.T. 553. For commentary on the cases, see Peter Duff, "Sinclair and Holland: A revolution in 'disclosure'" 2005

S.L.T. (News) 105; Fiona E. Raitt and Pamela R. Ferguson, "Re—Confirming Scots Criminal Procedure – Seismic Shifts" 10 *Edinburgh L. Rev.* 102 (2006).

[23] In Scotland, evidence establishing every 'crucial fact' must be corroborated. See Margaret Ross, ed., *Walker and Walker's The Law of Evidence in Scotland*, 2d. Ed. (Edinburgh: T & T Clark, 2000), chap. 5.

[24] *Edwards v. United Kingdom* (1992) 15 EHRR 417.

[25] *Ibid.* at para. 36, as cited in *Sinclair, above* note 24 at para. 48 (per Lord Rodger of Earlsferry).

[26] *Sinclair, ibid.* at paras. 33, 48—9.

[27] *Holland, above* note 24 at paras. 72—3.

[28] *Sinclair, above* note 24 at paras. 43, 48.

[29] A point made by Lord Hope: *Sinclair, ibid.* at para. 21.

[30] The Privy Council made it clear that certain kinds of privileged information need not be disclosed.

[31] *Holland, above* note 24 at para. 67.

[32] *Ibid.* at para. 72.

[33] *Ibid.* at para. 66.

[34] *Ibid.* at para. 39. See also James Chalmers, "Hearsay, Discretion, and the ECHR" 2003 S.L.T. (News) 181: 183—5.

[35] See *Brown v. Stott* 2001 SLT 59; 2001 SC (PC) 43; 2001 SCCR 62.

[36] *Dowsett v. United Kingdom* (2003) 38 EHRR 845.

[37] The Privy Council, in *Sinclair* and *Holland*, frequently notes the importance of a right of appeal: see, *e.g., Holland, above* note 24 at para. 41. We might, of course, wonder if a right of appeal could be effective if the accused does not know what information was withheld at trial.

[38] For some of the essential scholarly commentary on dialogue theory in Canada, see Peter Hogg and Allison Bushell, "Constitutional Dialogue Between Courts and Legislatures" 35 *Osgoode Hall L. J.* 75 (1997); Peter W. Hogg and Allison A. Thornton, "Reply to 'Six Degrees of Dialogue'" 37 *Osgoode Hall L. J.* 529 (1999); Carissima Mathen, "Constitutional Dialogue in Canada and the United States" 14 *N.J.C.L.* 403 (2003); Kent Roach, *The Supreme Court on Trial: Judicial Activism or Democratic Dialogue* (Toronto: Irwin, 2001). For a skeptical treatment of dialogue, see Christopher P. Manfredi and James B. Kelly, "Six Degrees of Dialogue: A Response to Hogg and Bushell" 37 *Osgoode Hall L. J.* 513 (1999).

[39] See *In re References by the Governor—General in Council* (1910), 43 S.C.R. 536 at 547, aff'd [1912] A.C. 571 (P.C.).

[40] A point made, in the American context, by Larry Alexander and Frederick Schauer, "On Extrajudicial Constitutional Interpretation" 110 *Harv. L. Rev.* 1359 (1997). In Canada, the notwithstanding clause empowers Parliament to act contrary to *Charter* rights; that is, contrary to a constitutional rule. Parliament, however, does not change the Constitution – or reformulate the constitutional rule – when it employs the notiwthstanding clause. The clause merely gives Parliament temporary authority to act *as if* the constitutional rule did not exist. But the constitutional rule does exist and the Supreme Court has the last word with respect to defining its scope and contours. The notwithstanding clause does not allow Parliament to assert control over *Charter* interpretation; it only allows Parliament to act in certain respects 'notwithstanding' the constitutional rule as interpreted by the Supreme Court. In other words, the notwithstanding clause is a vehicle by which Parliament can choose to temporarily make constitutional interpretation a non—issue.

[41] *R. v. O'Connor*, [1995] 4 S.C.R. 411.

[42] See *R. v. Mills*, [1999] 3 S.C.R. 668.

[43] See Jamie Cameron, "Dialogue and Hierarchy in Charter Interpretation: A Comment on R. v. Mills" 38 *Alta. L. Rev.* 1051 (2001): 1058.

[44] See *Doucet—Boudreau v. Canada*, 2003 SCC 62 at para. 34.

CHAPTER 3

BALANCING COMPETING INDIVIDUAL CONSTITUTIONAL RIGHTS: RAISING SOME QUESTIONS

Taunya Lovell Banks

"[L]aw is a compromise of contending forces and interests in society."[1]

Introduction: The Debate about Constitutionalizing Socio-economic Rights

In 1996 United States Supreme Court Justice Ruth Bader Ginsburg noted that many of the more than 200 new constitutions adopted since 1970 contain guarantees of socio-economic rights like housing, health care and education. But, she opined, Americans would quickly reject amending their Constitution to include these rights.[2] The Justice reminded her audience that in 1944 President Franklin D. Roosevelt urged the enactment of a "second bill of rights" that would take care of human needs because "necessitous men are not free men."[3] And for a brief period, as American constitutional scholar Cass Sunstein points out, the Warren Court quietly, but unsuccessfully, attempted to move the country in that direction.[4] Instead of constitutionalizing socio-economic rights the United States chose a federal-state arrangement of entitlements, many of which have been, or currently are being, dismantled by a hostile executive and congress. Without constitutional protection socio-economic benefits once conferred easily can be withdrawn.

Despite increasing support for global human rights, as exemplified by the International Covenant on Civil and Political Rights[5] and the International Covenant on Economic and Cultural Rights,[6] some scholars and constitutional democracies, like the United States, continue to resist constitutionalizing socio-economic rights. Socio-economic rights, unlike political and civil constitutional rights that usually prohibit government actions, are thought to impose positive obligations on government. As a result, constitutionalizing socio-economic rights raises questions about separation of powers and the competence of courts to decide traditionally legislative and executive matters.[7]

Sunstein, writing about the late twentieth century constitutions in Eastern Europe, also argued that constitutionalizing socio-economic rights compels governments to interfere with free markets.[8] He even argued, somewhat patronizingly, that constitutionalizing socio-economic rights "may promote attitudes of welfare-dependency and become a counterincentive to self-reliance and individual initiative."[9] Others argue that the inherent difficulty in judicial enforcement of socio-economic rights weakens public faith that constitutional rights will be enforced.[10]

Concerns about the enforceability of rights even plague those countries whose constitutions protect only political and civil rights. Most courts find it difficult to insure equality when faced with competing constitutional rights claims. In Germany, for example, the Constitutional Court in reconciling conflicting constitutional rights refers to the structural unity of its constitution applying "the principle of 'practical concordance' (*praktische Konkordanz*)" by which conflicting constitutional rights are "harmonized" and balanced so that each is "preserved in creative tension with one another."[11]

Thus there are no absolute rights.[12] The German Constitutional Court in harmonizing and balancing conflicting constitutional rights has created a de facto hierarchy of rights. As a result, the jurisprudence of that court is inconsistent and unpredictable. Sometimes the court's jurisprudence rests on rigorous analysis, and other times on bewildering ex cathedra pronouncements.[13]

Another approach to the balancing problem adopted by the United States Supreme Court, among others, is to create a formal hierarchy of constitutional rights privileging some individual rights over others. First Amendment rights, including freedom of association, are considered fundamental rights, whereas the right to equal protection of law is not. Yet this formal hierarchy is not absolute. There are a few exceptional cases where the Supreme Court prefers a non-fundamental right over a so-called fundamental right.

Perhaps the most well-known example is the U.S. Supreme Court's seminal 1954 decision, Brown v. Board of Education.[14] In Brown the right of black Americans to equality under law in access to public education was protected at the expense of the associational rights of white Americans hostile to being educated with blacks. Some constitutional scholars, while applauding the demise of the separate but equal doctrine, complained about the court's departure from its articulated hierarchy of rights.

Legal scholar Herbert Wechsler in a 1959 essay about the Brown decision wrote:

> [A]ssuming equal facilities, the question posed by state-enforced segregation is not one of discrimination at all. Its human and its constitutional dimensions lie entirely elsewhere, in the denial by the state of freedom to associate, a denial that impinges in the same way on any groups or races that may be involved . . . .
>
> But if the freedom of association is denied by segregation, integration forces an association upon those for whom it is unpleasant or repugnant. Is this not the heart of the issue involved, a conflict in human claims of high dimension, not unlike many others that involve the highest freedoms . . . .[15]

Constitutional scholars raised similar questions about the U.S. Supreme Court's departure from its stated hierarchy of constitutional rights in the restrictive covenants cases, Shelly v. Kramer[16] and Jones v. Mayer.[17] Neil Gotanda writes: "Legal scholars who believed in a constitutionally required freedom of contract and private sector right to discriminate (subject to certain restrictions), found [the Supreme Court's refusal to enforce racially] restrictive covenant[s] ...hard to justify."[18] The questions raised by Herbert Wechsler and other American constitutional scholars about these exceptional departures from the accepted formal hierarchy of rights, continue to generate discussion today within academic circles.

As Justice Ginsburg suggests, the American constitution once a model of modern constitutions, looks antiquated next to late twentieth century models like the South African Constitution. That country's constitutionalizing of socio-economic rights, while the United States gradually dismantled much of the New Deal and 1960s socio-economic programs, caused Cass Sunstein to reconsider his position on constitutionalizing those rights.[19] The transformative nature of the South African

Constitution is evident in the document's repeated references to the protection of human rights.[20]

But when transitional democracies, like South Africa, choose to constitutionalize socio-economic rights, courts inevitably must grapple with their role in the realization of those rights. Where courts have both declaratory and enforcement obligations under the constitution, a commitment to human rights, while laudable, may be difficult to attain. Two questions immediately come to mind: (1) whether it is possible to treat conflicting constitutional rights equally, or whether a hierarchy of rights, either formal or informal, is an inevitable result; and (2) whether in a true participatory democracy courts should be placed in the position of determining this hierarchy of constitutional rights, or whether the ordering of rights is an inherently political task.[21]

A related question is whether when vast socio-economic inequities exists among the citizenry a judicial approach is more appropriate until that society has reduced those inequities. Citizens who lack adequate food, shelter and basic education are disadvantaged politically even in the most liberal democracy. A nation-state's approach to these questions is reflected in the mechanisms adopted to enforce socio-economic rights.

Modern state constitutions that incorporate socio-economic rights usually adopt one of three approaches to enforceability of these rights. Some constitutions treat socio-economic rights as judicially enforceable, the same as other individual rights.[22] Other constitutions distinguish socio-economic rights from political and civil rights by making the former non-justiciable aspirational targets for the legislature and executive branches.[23] Still other constitutions adopt a middle position designating some socio-economic rights as justiciable and others not.[24]

The South African Constitutional Court was mindful of the controversy surrounding constitutionalizing socio-economic rights.[25] Former Constitutional Court Justice Richard Goldstone writes that the court "has successfully enforced the constitution's provisions for social and economic rights while balancing the state's interest in managing its political affairs."[26] He rejects as a false dichotomy the distinction many legal scholars and jurists draw between socio-economic and civil or political rights arguing that enforcement of both sets of rights often involves expenditures of public funds, citing as an example the costs of school bussing to enforce the U.S. Supreme Court's integration mandate in Brown v. Board of Education.[27] But, as mentioned previously, even American scholars concede that Brown was an exceptional case. Thus the South African Constitutional Court's treatment of socio-economic constitutional rights during its first decade of existence merits closer scrutiny.

When modern democracies like South Africa constitutionalize socio-economic rights and declare these rights justiciable, judicial enforcement is an issue.[28] This chapter argues that some hierarchy of rights that privileges one set of rights over another is inevitable, especially where neither the state constitution nor the court clearly creates a formal hierarchy of rights. It uses the right to housing cases decided during the Constitutional Court's first decade to explore this question.

Enforcing Constitutional Socio-Economic Rights in South Africa

The South Africa Constitution provides that everyone, citizen and non-citizen[29], is entitled to reasonable access to health care, food, water, social security, housing and education.[30] The Constitution also prohibits government from carrying out arbitrary evictions or refusing emergency medical treatment.[31] Although phrased in the negative, these last two provisions compliment or reinforce the positive socio-economic rights to housing and health care. Also reinforcing these socio-economic rights are the constitutional rights to equality, human dignity and life[32] which impose restraints as well as affirmative obligations on government. But the Constitution also qualifies some socio-economic rights like access to housing and health care by explicitly providing that those rights are to be progressively realized "within available resources" of government.[33]

In early decisions interpreting socio-economic rights, the Constitutional Court addressed many questions raised by opponents of constitutionalizing socio-economic rights. It sought to assuage separation of powers concerns by normalizing the enforcement of socio-economic rights saying that courts traditionally make decisions that have budgetary implications. Thus the enforcement of socio-economic rights is not substantially different from judicial tasks normally conferred on courts by a bill of rights.[34] Therefore, under the South African Constitution all socio-economic rights are, with certain limitations, justiciable.[35]

Conceding justiciability raises two important questions: what standard of review is appropriate in reviewing constitutional socio-economic rights claims, and how do courts enforce these rights when violated by government. These are difficult questions that the Constitutional Court says "must be carefully explored on a case-by-case basis."[36] Addressing the appropriate standard of review the court initially adopted, and then discarded, a rationality test. In Soobramoney v. Minister of Health, Justice Chaskalson wrote that "[a] court will be slow to interfere with rational decisions taken in good faith by ...authorities whose responsibility it is to deal with such matters."[37]

In Soobramoney the court ruled that access to dialysis treatment could be restricted because of limited government resources and not violate the right to health care. The court said that limiting dialysis treatment to individuals eligible for a kidney transplant was a rationale policy decision. But application of a rationale basis standard results in an extremely deferential attitude toward those governmental entities responsible for health care decisions. This minimal review standard also seems inconsistent with the transformative view of the new South African Constitution and Constitutional Court.

Four years later in Republic of South Africa v. Grootboom, a seminal socio-economic rights case, the court replaced the rationality test with a reasonableness test,[38] a more demanding standard. Thus the issue when socio-economic rights are asserted is whether "the measures taken by the state to realize the right ... are reasonable."[39] The exact meaning of reasonable, however, is to be worked out case-by-case. The reasonableness test as announced seems an ad hoc and somewhat unpredictable approach to constitutional decision-making. Undoubtedly the court adopted this cautious approach mindful of separation of powers concerns. Arguably, a reasonableness standard preserves executive and legislative prerogatives in determining how limited financial resources should be allocated.

Scholars characterize the court's reasonableness test as an "administrative law" approach to the adjudication of socio-economic rights.[40] The unit of government whose policy is challenged, and to whom the Constitution assigns the responsibility, must explain the rationale for its policy— why it prioritized the allocation of its limited resources the way it did. The court's role is one of oversight only, namely to guard against "unreasonable" resource allocation.

Separation of powers concerns also may explain the court's resistance to arguments for a minimum core of socio-economic rights.[41] The United Nations Committee General Comment 3 states: "a minimum core obligation to ensure the satisfaction of, at the very least, minimum essential levels of each of the rights is incumbent upon every State party."[42] Although amicus briefs in Grootboom argued for a minimum core obligation, the Constitutional Court, for the moment at least, rejects this argument.[43] Justice Yacoob writes that the court does not have enough information "to determine the minimum threshold for the progressive realisation of the right of access to adequate housing without first identifying the needs and opportunities for the enjoyment of such a right."[44]

At the same time the court concedes that there might be circumstances where this type of inquiry would be appropriate.[45] Since, as the court acknowledges, lack of shelter can result in the denial of "human dignity, freedom and equality,"[46] it is instructive to look at whether, when balancing the rights of private property owners against the access to housing rights of landless people, the Constitutional Court tends to favor the former or latter. In other words, the inquiry is whether the court, in fact rather than by formal policy, treats access to housing for homeless society members as a minimum core obligation.

Access to Housing: Grootboom as Setting the Stage

In a series of cases the South Africa Constitutional Court explored one aspect of the access to housing right – the protection against arbitrary evictions. During the apartheid era arbitrary evictions by government and third parties were commonplace, and disproportionately affected non-whites.[47] Mindful of this unfortunate past, section 26(3) of the Bill of Rights provides: "No one may be evicted from their home, or have their home demolished, without an order of court made after considering all of the relevant circumstances. No legislation may permit arbitrary evictions." The Constitutional Court acknowledges that section 26 (3) is designed to prevent apartheid-type evictions and property-related injustices from recurring in the new South Africa.[48]

Debates about whether to preserve common law property rights persisted throughout drafting of the new South Africa Constitution. Ultimately, nationalization of land was rejected. Instead, the Bill of Rights protects both "existing entrenched rights and privileges … [while] extending 'the enjoyment of rights to all.'"[49]

The protection of property rights is contained in section 25 of the Bill of Rights. Section 25 (1) provides: "No one may be deprived of property except in terms of law of general application, and no law may permit arbitrary deprivation of property." Under section 25 (2) "[p]roperty may be expropriated only in terms of law of general application - for a public purpose or in the public interest" and only where the landowner has been compensated. Unanswered by sections 25 and 26 is how to balance the rights of homeless society members with those of private property owners, some of whom acquired land during the apartheid era.[50] Specifically, the question is whether the dignity and access to housing rights of South Africans include the right not to be left homeless and if so, whether the enforcement of these rights often will occur at the expense of private landowners.

The South African Constitutional Court in Grootboom said in passing that the right of access to housing contained in section 26(1) implicitly imposes, "at the very least, a negative obligation ... upon the state and *all other entities and persons* to desist from preventing or impairing the right of access to housing."[51] (emphasis added) Whether this negative constitutional obligation to take no action that would leave individuals homeless applies horizontally to non-governmental entities is left unresolved.[52] Other language in Grootboom can be read either way. The Constitutional Court said, for example, that in addition to the State "other agents within our society, including individuals themselves, must be enabled by legislative and other measures to provide housing."[53] Since the court's role in these cases is oversight, not policymaking, the court's language seems purposefully vague deferring to those branches of the State assigned the responsibility by the Constitution of determining the means of fulfilling the government's housing obligation.

When the State fails to provide access to adequate housing for those members of society most in need, individuals are forced to resort to self-help measures, like land invasions. In turn land owners whose property is invaded, to protect their rights, must initiate ejectment proceedings against the unlawful occupants. But under Section 8 (1) of the South African Constitution, courts are considered state actors, so they are bound by provisions of the Bill of Rights, including section 26, when issuing ejectment orders. As a result, according to Geoff Budlender, a "court may... stay the eviction to a stipulated date... to enable the evictees to find another place ... [to] live... [or] order an eviction conditional upon the state's first finding another place where the evictees may settle."[54] Thus the right of a property owner to eject squatters is qualified. Grootboom illustrates some of resulting problems faced by property owners in this situation.

In Grootboom hundreds of adults and children living in an informal community under intolerable conditions moved on to vacant privately owned property designated for government subsidized low-cost housing and built makeshift homes rather than wait indefinitely for better housing.[55] The landowner obtained an eviction order from the magistrate court but Mrs. Grootboom and the others resisted saying that they would be homeless if evicted.[56] Nevertheless, they were forcibly evicted during harsh weather and under conditions reminiscent of "apartheid-style evictions."[57] They sued alleging, among other things, that they were being denied access to housing as guaranteed by section 26 of the South African Constitution.[58]

In Grootboom Justice Yacoob notes that the post-apartheid government, consistent with section 26 (2), was making progress in addressing the housing problem.[59] Had the court applied the rationality test announced in Soobramoney the court might have concluded that the government's decision to focus on permanent rather than temporary housing could be justified as rational. But applying a reasonableness standard the Constitutional Court found that the government housing plan was unreasonable and fell short of its constitutional obligation[60] because it did not provide temporary housing for society members living in "intolerable conditions" or crisis situations.[61] To make matters worse, the Cape Metro Council, the government entity responsible for housing, took no action after it became aware of the squatters, and its inaction allowed the settlement to grow substantially.[62] So the problem in Grootboom was the result of a two-fold failure by government of its constitutional obligation.

The court, in passing, also noted that the state may have failed to have executed the evictions of the plaintiffs in a humane manner. Section 26 (3) prohibits unreasonable evictions. In determining whether to grant an ejection order the court must consider all the "relevant circumstances." An important factor in determining the reasonableness of an eviction is whether the evictees will be left homeless.[63] But since this issue was not raised by the plaintiffs in <u>Grootboom</u> the court did not rule on the reasonableness of the evictions.[64] Thus the <u>Grootboom</u> case did not squarely pit the right of private property owners against the right to housing for the poorest of the poor. Mrs. Grootboom and the other plaintiffs already had been ejected. But the Constitutional Court's decision in that case suggested that private landowners might have difficulty ejecting some unlawful occupants.

Balancing the Rights of Landless and Landowners

The <u>Grootboom</u> decision triggered a vigorous debate within South Africa about its impact on common law landowner rights.[65] Legal scholars wondered whether the Constitutional Court was saying that the new constitution modified common law property rules by limiting the power of courts to order an otherwise lawful eviction because of the impact on those ejected.[66] Six months after <u>Grootboom</u> another case, <u>Minister of Public Works v. Kyalami Ridge,</u> raised a similar issue and provided some insights on the question. But once more the court was not squarely faced with a case that directly pitted the rights of private landowners against landless individuals.

<u>Kyalami Ridge</u> involved 300 people in Alexandra Township outside of Johannesburg who lost their housing due to flooding. Initially the flood victims were given temporary shelter "in overcrowded and unhealthy circumstances without sufficient water and sanitation."[67] Subsequently the government, responding to the court's mandate in <u>Grootboom</u>, allocated money to provide temporary housing on state-owned land located near an affluent white neighborhood. The neighboring property owners, who had not been consulted about the relocation beforehand, objected, raising environmental concerns and questioning the authority of government to act without a public meeting. When the landowners obtained an order from the High Court to stop the construction, the government, joined by a flood victim, appealed, and the Constitutional Court reversed the order.[68]

The property owners conceded that government has an obligation to act reasonably to provide adequate access to housing for the flood victims, but argued that the proposed relocation would adversely affect their property values.[69] The Constitutional Court rejected their argument saying that the interests of neighboring landowners were insufficient to constitute a constitutional violation.[70] Instead the court treated the matter like a common law nuisance claim. Thus the court reasoned that the neighboring property owners had no right to object to another landowner's reasonable use of its property, even when it adversely affected neighboring property owners.[71] The State, like any private landowner, could make reasonable use of its property and that was what it was doing.[72]

Theoretically, however, the State in this instance really was not acting like a common law landowner because it has an affirmative obligation under the Constitution to assist homeless or intolerably housed residents find adequate housing.[73] This constitutional obligation trumped the conflicting, but tangential, rights of the neighboring landowners. Despite the absence of any direct impact on private property rights, the court volunteers that in reconciling conflicting constitutional rights, "proportionality which is inherent in the Bill of Rights is relevant to determining what fairness requires."[74]

If proportionality is the measure of how to strike the balance between competing constitutional rights, then the rights of private property owners will almost always have to give way to the rights of poor homeless persons or poor people living in intolerable conditions. This approach seems consistent with the overall goal of the South African Constitution to ensure that the government brings about the progressive realization of socio-economic rights. As the Court in Grootboom says, "Those whose needs are the most urgent and whose ability to enjoy all rights ... is most in peril, must not be ignored by the measures aimed at achieving realisation of the right."[75]

Mass land invasions by homeless members of South African society have become more commonplace as dissatisfaction with the slow pace of the government's housing program increases. Anticipating South Africans' increasing frustration about government's slow response to the housing problem the Constitutional Court in Grootboom warned the State that if "people in desperate need are left without any form of assistance with no end of sight.... [t]he consequent pressure on existing settlements inevitably results in land invasions by the desperate."[76] This is exactly what happened after Grootboom.

Three years after that decision the housing situation in the area had deteriorated because the government still had not prioritized emergency or temporary housing for the poorest of the poor in allocating its limited financial resources.[77] When the City of Cape Town, the successor to the government entity in Grootboom, applied to evict land invaders from a public park, a High Court judge, while condemning land invasions, refused the city's application.[78] The High Court judge noted when Grootboom was decided the house backlog was 206,000 houses and this number was being reduced by 2000 housing units per year.[79] But by November 2001 the backlog had grown to 250,000 houses, and the backlog was increasing at a rate of 15,000 annually. Further "[t]he yearly demand was growing by 25,000 units as against a supply of 10,000 per year."[80] The housing crisis had become even more severe. But like Kyalami Ridge, the land invasion in this lower court case involved public, not private land so no private property rights were at issue. Nevertheless, the import of this court's reading of the Grootboom mandate was clear. When government fails to fulfill its obligation under section 26 to provide adequate temporary housing for people most in need of shelter, they cannot be evicted from land they occupy unlawfully if they will be left homeless.

Four years after Grootboom the Constitutional Court in Port Elizabeth Municipality v. Various Occupiers squarely faced the problem of balancing the interests of property owners and homeless unlawful occupants who invade private lands.[81] Here 68 people, including 23 children, had been living in an informal community on private property located within the Municipality of Port Elizabeth for two to eight years. The property owners and their neighbors, a total of 1600 people, appealed to the city to evict the squatters.

The unlawful occupants agree to leave if "given reasonable notice and provided with suitable alternate land."[82] But the parties could not agree upon a suitable existing housing site, and the municipality resisted building housing for the squatters. The government argued that the squatters would be "queue-jumping", benefiting from their unlawful conduct at the expense of law abiding individuals equally in need of housing.[83] The Supreme Court of Appeals set aside the High Court's ejectment order because the unlawful occupants would be homeless if evicted, and the municipality appealed to the Constitutional Court. Thus the issue of conflicting constitutional rights was squarely framed.

The Constitutional Court recognized that the protection of property rights in section 25, and the housing and eviction rights in section 26 of the Bill of Rights "are closely intertwined,"[84] but noted that under the new Constitution private property rights are qualified and "subject to societal considerations."[85] A consideration that courts must take into account when interpreting section 25 rights is the need to redress "the grossly unequal distribution of land" which is a legacy of the apartheid era.[86] But exactly how the new constitution reconfigures conventional views of private property rights remains unclear.[87] The only guidance is that the end goal in striking this balancing of rights, according to the court, is the affirmation of "the values of human dignity, equality and freedom."[88] Invoking these values as components of section 26 (3) restrictions on evictions automatically establishes a basis for some informal ranking or hierarchy of rights. This qualification also sounds a lot like the balancing language used by the German Constitutional Court.

According to Justice Sachs the role of the court in cases where these two rights are in conflict is "to balance out and reconcile the opposed claims in as just a manner as possible taking account of all the interests involved and the specific factors relevant in each particular case."[89] The end result in these cases seems clear, if the unlawful occupants will be left homeless, eviction is unlikely. As Geoff Budlender predicted, unlawful occupants will remain on the private property until the government finds suitable alternate housing.

The unlawful occupants in Port Elizabeth Municipality lived in a relatively settled community, thus Justice Sachs reasoned, courts should be "reluctant" to issue ejectment orders unless reasonable alternative housing or land is available.[90] Reflecting the court's growing frustration with government's housing program, and the complex balancing required in the ejectment cases he opined: "[t]he judiciary cannot of itself correct all the systemic unfairness to be found in our society.... [but] it ...[can] soften and minimise the degree of injustice and inequity which the eviction of the weaker parties in conditions of inequality of necessity entails."[91]

But in these cases the private landowner is caught in the middle, unable to eject unlawful occupants until the government provides suitable housing. The adverse effect on individual property rights is not mitigated by the court's characterizing the eviction provisions of section 26(3) as "defensive rather than affirmative," a negative rather than a positive right.[92] Under the Constitutional Court's rationale the property rights of private landowners will be restricted or subject to limitations until the housing situation in the country is more equal.

In the abstract this outcome seems like a reasonable compromise given the alternative, nationalization of private property and more equitable redistribution by the government. But the reality of having an informal settlement of strangers in your backyard for years must be disquieting for landowners. For the moment, at least, private property rights must gave way whenever the choice is between leaving groups of people homeless and protecting a property owner's right to use his or her property. Homeless individuals will prevail and thus an informal hierarchy is created that privileges the right of temporary housing for homeless individuals over the right of private property owners to eject unlawful occupants.

The Constitutional Court in a more recent decision illustrates how application of the court's balancing approach tries to minimize the adverse affects on private landowners. In President of the Republic of South Africa v. Modderklip, approximately 40,000 individuals were living on approximately 50 hectares (approximately 123 acres) of the Modderklip Company's land.[93] In the 1990s the squatters had moved from an overcrowded township to a neighboring informal settlement from which they subsequently were evicted by the municipality. They moved onto the Modderklip property in May 2000, believing it to be public land. The municipality notified the company saying that the law required the company to institute ejectment proceedings.[94]

Given the number of unlawful occupants Modderklip believed that the ejectment proceeding was a government responsibility, and initially declined to sue for an order.[95] The company also tried, without success, to sell the occupied land to the municipality. Finally, Modderklip sought and obtained an ejectment order within the legally established time limits. But the cost of executing the order and lack of an alternate settlement for the squatters caused the order not to be effectuated. Frustrated the company sought relief in the court on constitutional grounds.

Modderklip claimed that its property rights under section 25 (1), as reinforced by section 7(2) of the Constitution, had been infringed Section 7(2) provides that "the state must respect, protect, promote and fulfill the rights in the Bill of Rights." The company also alleged that the rights of the unlawful occupants to adequate housing under section 26 had been violated. In other words, the government's failure to comply with its housing obligations under section 26 also resulted in a violation of the landowner's property rights as protected by section 25.[96] The government countered that the case presented no constitutionally enforceable infringement of property rights because the controversy was between private parties.[97] But a unanimous Constitutional Court disagreed.[98]

The court acknowledged that under the Constitution private property owners are primarily responsible for protecting their property.[99] Thus Modderklip could not sit idly by and leave a mass invasion of its land unchallenged. While once more condemning land invasions, the court reaffirmed government's affirmative duty under section 26 to "progressively ... ensure access to housing or land for the homeless."[100] Acting Chief Justice Langa writes sympathetically: "I am mindful of the fact that those charged with the provision of housing face immense problems.... [Nevertheless] the progressive realization of access to adequate housing... requires careful planning and fair procedures made known in advance to those most affected."[101]

At the same time government is obligated to provide more than the legal mechanisms and institutions to enforce Modderklip's property rights.[102] In this case the court concluded that an award of compensatory damages was appropriate.[103] Arguably, there had been a de facto expropriation of the company's land caused by the government failure to provide temporary housing in accordance with the Grootboom mandate and thus compensation was warranted. Rather than construing this result as evidence that socio-economic rights might be horizontally enforceable, the court characterizes the situation in Modderklip as "extraordinary."[104]

Unfortunately, the land invasion at issue in Modderklip is far from extraordinary. A quick glance through any South African newspaper indicates that mass land invasions by homeless individuals are increasing and wide-spread. For the moment at least, the Constitutional Court continues to side-step the question of whether property rights under section 25 are horizontal, and if so, under what circumstances.[105] It also avoids answering whether the state can order expropriation of privately held land in these circumstances.[106] Thus, the rights and obligations of private property owners' in relation to homeless society members remain unclear.

Conclusion

There was no judicial review provision or Bill of Rights in the old South African Constitution. Instead, during the apartheid era, the parliamentary-based legal system "was essentially one of 'repressive law' [leaving black South Africans] deep[ly] alienation from the formal legal structures."[107] The Bill of Rights in the new South African Constitution was designed to restore faith in the rule of law by serving as a check on potential political government abuses. In Jaftha v. Schoeman and others (2005) Justice Mokgoro wrote that section 26 of the Bill of Rights represents a "decisive break from the past,"[108] and a recognition that "access to adequate housing is linked to dignity and self-worth."[109] Yet the Constitutional Court's approach to the enforcement of socio-economic rights is cautious and largely declarative rather than transformative.

Years after the Constitutional Court's decision in Grootboom the people of that community continued to live in intolerable conditions.[110] In a country that has some of the world's widest disparities in wealth, and where approximately 60 percent of its children and more than 40 percent of the total population live in poverty,[111] the realization of adequate access to housing is an enormous task. "[T]he South African Human Rights Commission's annual reports on Economic and Social Rights consistently indicate[]… a significant gap between the promise of housing, medical care, basic infrastructure and the delivery thereof."[112] Thus the court's access to housing cases illustrate that judicial declarations of socio-economic rights do not necessarily translate into realization of those rights.

One disillusioned South African scholar writes that for socio-economic relief to be meaningful it must be "capable of immediate implementation," especially where government grants relief to the most desperate segment of society.[113] While the Constitutional Court is unwilling to concede the immediacy point, in Fose v. Minister of Safety and Security (1997) it noted that: "without effective remedies for breach, the values underlying and the right entrenched in the Constitution cannot properly be upheld or enhanced…. [and t]he courts have a particular responsibility … and are obliged to 'forge new tools' and shape innovative remedies, if needs be, to achieve this goal."[114] But the court has not been forthcoming in fashioning new tools and innovative remedies in this area.

The Constitutional Court, by ordering payment of compensatory damages to the landowner in Mudderklip directly affected by land invasions, has taken only a small step in this direction. The ongoing debate within South Africa is whether the Constitutional Court can and should fashion more effective remedies to realize its orders involving socio-economic rights.[115] This debate over the proper role of the court in enforcing socio-economic rights goes to the very heart of the criticism about constitutionalizing socio-economic rights.

In Minister of Health and Others v. Treatment Action Campaign and Others (TAC)[116] the High Court's order included a structural interdict requiring the government to revise its policy about not providing the anti-viral drug Nevirapine to reduce mother-to-child transmission of HIV and submit it to the court for review.[117] The Constitutional Court upheld the ruling but substituted its own order declaring the government's refusal to provide appropriate treatment in public clinics within its available resources unreasonable, and a violation of the right of access to health care. Rather than squarely address the lawfulness of the interdict order, the court avoided the issue saying that the order was unnecessary because "[t]he government has always respected and executed orders of this Court [and t]here is no reason to believe that it will not do so in the present case."[118] Articulating separation of powers concerns the Constitutional Court added: "Courts are ill-suited to adjudicate upon issues where court orders could have multiple social and economic consequences for the community."[119]

The government in response to the court's ruling almost immediately developed a program for pregnant HIV-positive women which included, when appropriate, access to Nevirpine. To many the court's ruling in the TAC case was a bold move with financial implications, and a far cry from its more deferential stance on access to health care in Soobramoney. But without the internal and world-wide political pressure on the government generated by South African AIDS activists, one wonders whether the government would have responded so quickly.

Scholars remain divided when assessing the Constitutional Court's record on socio-economic rights during its first decade. Few question whether the court can issue declaratory orders or, in extreme cases, exercise supervisory jurisdiction over the implementation of its orders.[120] Some scholars applaud the court while others express disappointment, especially about the court's record on enforcement of rights. The court's critics divide along two lines. One group argues for bold remedies like constitutional damages.[121] Even bolder remedial suggestions include preventive damages[122] or reparation in kind, where the court might order the state "to provide appropriate remedial services for the benefit of a whole community that has suffered a long-term violation of its socio-economic rights."[123]

A second group criticizes the court's approach to deciding socio-economic rights cases. High Court judge and law professor Dennis Davis, for example, argues that there is no suggestion in the court's jurisprudence of "a new legal method which could assist in the implementation of the promise held in … the constitutional text."[124] Instead the Constitutional Court prefers to rely on administrative law and the occasional, perfunctory application of international law.[125] Further, Davis argues, the court seems reluctant "to impose additional policy burdens upon government" or hold the government accountable for the socio-economic rights it declares, especially in cases involving the right to housing, health care and rights of children.[126] He concludes that for the moment, at least, South Africans seeking enforcement of their socio-economic rights may find quicker relief following the political rather than the judicial route.[127]

There is some merit to Davis' argument. Many observers believe that the court never would have ruled in favor of the litigants in TAC but for the political pressure generated world-wide by AIDS activists. Unlike TAC there are no major politicized housing organizations nationally or internationally, only small housing rights movements throughout South Africa. Currently, these organizations do not have the visibility and political clout of South Africa's AIDS activists.

Land invasions and questionable evictions continue throughout the country. Housing in some urban areas, like Cape Town, has become unaffordable or unavailable for all but the very affluent. On one hand, wealthy Europeans, Americans and South Africans push up the prices of homes; on the other, poor people from rural areas and other African countries continue to crowd into already overcrowded informal communities or invade land to create new communities. Local residents continue to be displaced or threatened by floods and unhealthy living conditions. Perhaps in the end, the political branches of government will be forced by both landowners and landless people to make access to adequate housing for the poorest of the poor more readily available.

Finally, there is an alternate less damning interpretation of the Constitutional Court's first decade. Arguably, the South African Constitutional Court, mindful of the arguments against constitutionalizing socio-economic rights, is proceeding cautiously hopeful that the State will fulfill its constitutional obligations as declared by the court. Perhaps the court is giving the State time to stabilize its economy and more completely actualize its plans for progressive realization of socio-economic rights like access to housing. If so, then the court may be unwilling to act more forcefully until there is a longer record of inaction by the political branches of government.

More importantly, it may be too early to judge the direction of the South African Constitutional Court. Perhaps another decade must pass and more founding court members be replaced before any meaningful predictions of direction can be made. In twenty years the court will have a longer record and more expertise and may be more willing to take bold steps, especially if the plight of residents like Mrs. Grootboom and her neighbors has not improved or worsened.

But there also is a real danger in the court's delaying bolder action. South Africans may lose faith in the ability of the courts to enforce socio-economic rights and rights in general. Memories of the apartheid era abuses are still fresh in their minds. Judicial pronouncements of rights that are not actualized weaken the public's respect for the rule of law. Perhaps the Constitutional Court judges will be motivated by the bolder actions of some high court judges. The High Court judge in Grootboom, for example, in directing the government to provide the evictees with adequate basic temporary shelter pursuant to their right of access to adequate housing spelled out these requirements rather than leave it to the State to determine.[128]

Human rights advocates worldwide will be watching and hoping that South Africa succeeds in its transformative mission. South Africa and its Constitutional Court in particular, have an opportunity to serve as a model for other nations seeking to transform their societies into more egalitarian communities that respect human rights. Time will tell whether it is possible to realize this goal while humanely balancing competing constitutional rights.

[1] Jack M. Balkin, "Plessy, Brown, and Grutter: a play in three acts," *Cardozo Law Review* 26 (2005):1689, 1691. Balkin continues: "when law participates in social change, law is complicit in the new forms of social stratification that replace older, discredited forms. As law recognizes and outlaws some forms of inequality, it fails to recognize or it legitimates others." Id.

[2] Peter Shinkle, "Justice Ginsburg: Constitution "Skimpy"," *The Advocate*, October 25, 1996, News section, B1, free abstract *available at* http://www.2theadvocate.com/. Specifically, Shinkle reported that Justice Ginsburg said "Any bid to add the types of rights found in other constitutions to this country's Constitution would be dealt a defeat "far more stunning" than the Equal Rights Amendment for women, which failed in the 1980s." Most "post-World War II European constitution-makers . . . supplemented traditional negative liberties with certain affirmative social and economic rights or obligations." Mary Ann Glendon, "Rights in Twentieth-Century Constitutions," *University of Chicago Law Review* 59 (1992): 519, 520-21.

[3] Shinkle, "Justice Ginsburg."

[4] *See generally,* Cass Sunstein, *The Second Bill of Rights: FDR'S Unfinished Revolution and Why We Need It More than Ever* (New York: Basic Books, 2004).

[5] G.A. Res. 2200A, U.N. GAOP, 21st Sess., Supp. No. 16, U.N. Doc. A/6316 (1966), 999 U.N.T.S. 171, entered into force January 3, 1976.

[6] G.A. Res. 2200A, U.N. GAOR, 21st Sess., Supp. No. 16, U.N. Doc. A/6316 (1966), 993 U.N.T.S. 3 entered into force January 3, 1976.

[7] "One commentator, invoking the separation of powers doctrine, has suggested that constitutional courts should not make decisions that have significant effects on social and economic policy." Amanda Littell, "Can a Constitutional Right to Health Guarantee Universal Health Care Coverage or Improved Health Outcomes?: A Survey of Selected States," *Connecticut Law Review* 35 (2002): 289, 307 (citing David Beatty, "The Last Generation: When Rights Lose Their Meaning," in *Human Rights and Judicial Review: A Comparative Perspective*, ed. David Beatty (Boston: Springer, 1994), 321, 350-51). "Critics of positive rights argue that such provisions are inherently nonenforceable, at least by courts, which are said to be poorly positioned to compel compliance with open-ended social and economic concerns." Helen Hershkoff, "Positive Rights and the Evolution of State Constitutions," *Rutgers Law Journal* 33 (2002): 799, 827 (discussing positive rights in the context of American state constitutional law).

[8] Cass Sunstein, "Against Positive Rights," *East European Constitutional Review* 2 (1993): 35, 36.

[9] Id. at 37. But c.f., Sadurski Wojciech, "Post Communist Chapters of Rights in Europe and the U.S. Bill of Rights," *Law and Contemporary Problems* 65 (2002): 223, 230.

[10] Frank B. Cross, "The Error of Positive Rights," *UCLA Law Review* 48 (2001): 857, 901(arguing that "positive rights offer a poor bargain for the disadvantaged"). Further, Sunstein and others argue that enforceable socio-economic rights could adversely affect negative constitutional rights. Sunstein, "Against Positive Rights," 254 (citing John Elster, "Human Rights and the Constitution-Making Process," in *Papers of the International Conference: Human Rights and Freedoms in New Constitutions in Central and Eastern Europe*, ed. Andrzej Rzeplinski (Warsaw: Helsinki Foundation for Human Rights, 1992), 25.

[11] Donald P. Kommers, "Comparative constitutionalism: German Constitutionalism: a Prolegomenon," *Emory Law Journal* 40 (1991): 837, 851. Thus even a constitutional amendment could be unconstitutional if it does not conform to the notion of the structural unity. Id. at 852. While the German Constitutional Court claims the authority to find constitutional amendments unconstitutional, unlike the Indian Supreme Court, it has never actually exercised this authority. Although the German Constitutional Court's claim may stem in part from more general considerations, most scholars would say that this authority flows primarily from Article 79 (3) of the Basic Law, which prohibits amendments that "affect" the principles of human dignity (including, in part, the principles set forth in the Basic Rights of Part I of the Basic Law), or certain structural principles of the Basic Law set forth in Article 20.

[12] Id. at 857. Although some rights "are cast in unqualified language, others in conditional language [i]n actuality ... no right under the Constitution is absolute. . . . [T]he task of the Court [when rights conflict] is to apply a balancing test consistent with the interpretive principle of concordance. The broad principle of human dignity, ... which under the explicit terms of Article 1 (1) binds all state authority, may also serve to limit the exercise of a so-called unconditional right." Id.

[13] *See, e.g.,* the discussion of the court's jurisprudence in the area of freedom of expression in David P. Currie, *The Constitution of the Federal Republic of Germany* (Chicago: University of Chicago Press, 1994), 33 et seq.

[14] 349 U.S. 294 (1955).

[15] Herbert Wechsler, "Toward Neutral Principles of Constitutional Law," *Harvard Law Review* 73 (1959): 1, 34. Neil Gotanda writes:

> "The constitutional guarantee of freedom of association—the right to choose whether to associate with another person—has also served to protect racially discriminatory conduct in the private sector. .... Wechsler's article anticipated modern analyses of private sector discrimination. Constitutional protection of an individual's right to limit personal associations requires constitutional protection of that individual's decision to discriminate on the basis of race.... The effect of focusing exclusively on associational issues is a promotion of white people's freedom to exercise economic and social domination."

Neil Gotanda, "A Critique of "Our Constitution is Color-Blind,"" *Stanford Law Review* 44 (1991): 1, 9-10.

[16] 334 U.S. 1 (1948).

[17] 392 U.S. 409 (1968).

[18]Gotanda, "A Critique," 9, n. 32 (citing Wechsler, "Toward Nuetral Principles of Constitutional Law," 29). Wechsler writes: "Assuming that the Constitution speaks to state discrimination on the ground of race but not to such discrimination by an individual even in the use or distribution of his property, although his freedom may no doubt be limited by common law or statute, why is the enforcement of the private covenant a state discrimination rather than a legal recognition of the freedom of the individual? . . . What is not obvious, and is the crucial step, is that the state may properly be charged with the discrimination when it does no more than give effect to an agreement that the individual involved is, by hypothesis, entirely free to make." Id.

[19] Cass R. Sunstein, *Designing Democracy: What Constitutions Do* (Incorporated: Oxford University Press 2001), 221-38.

[20] *See, e.g.,* the Preamble which declares among its objectives strong regard for human rights where two of the four objectives stated in the Constitution are: "To heal the divisions of the past and to establish a society based on democratic values, social justice and fundamental rights. . . . [and] "To improve the quality of life of all citizens and to free the potential of each person." Further, the first provision in the Constitution's Bill of Rights reaffirms this commitment to "human dignity, equality and freedom," cornerstones of human rights. Section 7 (1). *See also* sections 1 (a) (stating the values upon which the Constitution is based are "human rights, dignity, the achievement of equality and the advancement of human rights and freedoms."), 36 (1) (limitations of rights is "reasonable and justifiable" only after taking "human dignity, equality and freedom" into account) and 39(1) (a) (interpretation of Bill of Rights "must promote... human dignity, equality and freedom.").

[21] One American scholar suggests using popular referendums to determine fundamental rights. *See* Benjamin N. Smith, "Using Popular Referendums to Declare Fundamental Rights," *Boston University Public Interest Law Journal* 11 (2001): 123. Given that the tyranny of popular democracies is widely acknowledged, perhaps Smith is overly optimistic in suggesting that the majority will not act "inappropriately" and trample the rights of various minority or political less powerful groups, at least with respect to gay rights. Id. at 138-39.

[22] Wojciech, "Post Communist Chapters," 234. The author cites as an example the post communist constitutions in Belarus, Bulgaria, Croatia, Estonia, Georgia, Hungary, Latvia, Lithuania, Macedonia, Romania, Russia, Ukraine, Yugoslavia, Montenegro, and Serbia. Id.

[23]Littell, "Can a Constitutional Right," 293. The author calls these programmatic socio-economic rights found in the constitutions of Nordic countries, France, Greece, Italy, and Spain. Id.

[24] Wojciech, "Post Communist Chapters," 235. The author cites as an example the post communist constitutions in Albania, Moldova, Poland, and Slovenia. Id. at 235, n. 73.

[25] *R.S.A. v. Grootboom*, 2001 (1) S.A. 46 (CC), ¶ 20, n. 20. (citing numerous articles debating this point in South African political and legal journals).

[26]Richard J. Goldstone, "A South African Perspective on Social and Economic Rights," *Human Rights Brief* 13 (2006): 4.

[27] Id.

[28] According to the Constitutional Court of South Africa, the socio-economic rights contained in the 1996 Constitution are justiciable, but as the Court acknowledges, the problem is "how to enforce them in a given case." *Grootboom*, 20.

[29]Goldstone, "A South African Perspective," 5, n. 4. The author notes that in *Khosa v. Minister of Social Development; Mahlaule v. Minister of Social Development*, 2004 (6) SA 505 (CC), the Constitutional Court held that the use of the term "everyone" in the Constitution included non-citizens as well as citizens. Id. at 4.

[30] Constitution of the Republic of South Africa, ch. 2 §§ 26 (1), 27 (1), 29 (1)(a) (Oct. 11, 1996), *available at* http://www.polity.org.za/html/govdocs/constitution/saconst.html?rebookmark=1. In addition, § 28 (1)(c) provides for children's socio-economic rights and § 35 (2)(e) grants socio-economic rights to incarcerated individuals whether convicted or awaiting trial.

---

[31] Id. at §§ 26 (3), 27(3).

[32] Id. at §§ 9, 10, 11.

[33] § 26 (2) guaranteeing a right to housing provides: "The state must take reasonable legislative and other measures, within its available resources, to achieve the progressive realisation of this right." The same qualification is found in § 27 (2) guaranteeing health care, food, water and social security along with similar language in § 29 (1) (b) guaranteeing a right to education.

[34] *In re Certification of the Constitution of the Republic of South Africa*, 1996 (4) SA 744 (CC), ¶ 77.

[35] Ex Parte Chairperson of the Constitutional Assembly: *In Re Certification of the Constitution of the Republic of South Africa*, 1996 (4) SA 774 (CC), ¶ 78. "[T]hese rights are, at least to some extent, justiciable…. At the very minimum, socio-economic rights can be negatively protected from improper invasion." Id. ¶ 8.

[36] *Grootboom*, ¶ 20.

[37] *Soobramoney v. Minister of Health* [KwaZulu-Natal], 1997 (12) BCLR 1696 (CC), ¶ 30.

[38] *Grootboom*.

[39] Id. ¶ 33.

[40] *See, e.g.*, Sunstein, *Designing Democracy*, 224-37. But c.f., Murray Wesson, "*Grootboom* and Beyond: Reassessing the Socio-Economic Jurisprudence of the South African Constitutional Court," *South African Journal on Human Rights* 20 (2004): 284, 289-95.

[41] The Constitutional Court in *Minister of Health v. Treatment Action Campaign (TAC)*, 2002 (10) BCLR 1033 (CC), reaffirmed its limited role in this area saying: "The Constitution contemplates … a restrained and focused role for the Courts…. In this way the judicial, legislative and executive functions achieve appropriate constitutional balance." Id. ¶ 67-70. For a discussion of the debate about a minimum core obligation, compare Sandra Liebenberg, "The Right of Social Assistance: the Implications of *Grootboom* for Policy Reform in South Africa," *South African Journal on Human Rights* 17 (2001): 232; Pierre De Vos, "*Grootboom*, the Right of Access to Housing and Substantive Equality as Contextual Fairness," *South African Journal on Human Rights* 17 (2001): 258 with David Bilchitz, "Giving Socio-Economic Rights Teeth: The Minimum Core and its Importance," *South Africa Law Journal* 119 (2002): 484; Wesson, "*Grootboom* and Beyond," 297-305.

[42] General Comment 3, *The Nature of State Parties' Obligations* E/1991/23 paragraph 10.

[43] *See, e.g.*, *Grootboom*, ¶ 31-33.

[44] Id. at ¶ 32. He continues: "These will vary according to factors such as income, unemployment, availability of land and poverty. The differences between city and rural communities will also determine the needs and opportunities for the enjoyment of this right. Variations ultimately depend on the economic and social history and circumstances of a country." Id.

[45] Id. at ¶ 33. "The determination of a minimum core in the context of 'the right to have access to adequate housing' presents difficult questions. … There may be cases where it may be possible and appropriate to have regard to the content of a minimum core obligation to determine whether the measures taken by the state are reasonable. However, even if it were appropriate to do so, it could not be done unless sufficient information is placed before a court to enable it to determine the minimum core in any given context." Id. The Court concluded that *Grootboom* was not such a case. Id.

[46] Id. at ¶ 23.

[47] For an overview of apartheid era evictions see, Kate O'Regan, "No More Forced Removals? An Historical Analysis of The Prevention of Illegal Squatting Act," *South Africa Journal Human Rights* 5 (1989): 361.

[48] *Port Elizabeth Municipality v. Various Occupiers*, 2004 (12) BCLR 1268; 2004 SACLR LEXIS 25, ¶¶ 8-10. Justice Sachs wrote: "In the pre-democratic era the response of the law to a situation like the present [eviction proceeding] would have been simple and drastic….Once it was determined that the occupiers had no permission to be on the land, they not only faced summary eviction, [but] were liable for criminal prosecution…. PISA (Prevention of Illegal Squatting Act) was an integral part of a cluster of statues that gave a legal/administrative imprimatur to the usurpation and forced removal of black people from land and compelled them to live in racially designated locations…. Residential segregation was the cornerstone of the apartheid policy….Differential on the basis of race was … not only a source of grave assaults on the dignity of black people. It resulted in the creation of large, well-established and affluent white urban areas co-existing side by side with crammed pockets of impoverished and insecure black ones." Id.

[49] Marie Huchzermeyer, "Housing Rights in South Africa: Invasions, Evictions, the Media and the Courts in the Cases of *Grootboom*, *Alexandra* and *Bredell*," *Urban Forum* 14(1) (2003), *available at* http://www.ihrn.gov.za/Seminars/March%202004/23%20Huchzermeyer.pdf   (citing   de   Vos, "*Grootboom*, the Right of Access to Housing," 261).

[50] For a discussion of this point *see* Heinz Klug, *Constituting Democracy: Law, Globalism and South Africa's Political Reconstruction* (Cambridge: Cambridge University Press, 2000), 124-38. According

to Klug: "The final property clause.... Not only guarantees the restitution of land taken after 1913 and a right to legally secure tenure for those whose tenure is insecure as a result of racially discriminatory laws or practices, but also includes an obligation on the state to enable citizens to gain access to land on an equitable basis." Id. at 135.

[51] *Grootboom*, ¶ 34. The court in *Jaftha v. Schoeman*, 2005 (1) BCLR 78 (CC), 2004 SACLR LEXIS 23, more directly addresses the right to access to adequate housing contained in § 26(1) of the Bill of Rights.

[52] South African litigator Geoff Budlender raises, but does not explore, the extent to which application of a negative constitutional obligation contained in the South African Bill of Rights applies to non-governmental parties. Geoff Budlender, "Justiciability of the Right to Housing – The South African Experience," (Paper delivered at ICJ conference in New Delhi, India, 2001) *available at* http://www.humanrightsinitiative.org/jc/papers/jc_2003/judges_papers/budlender_housing_ms.pdf.

[53] Id. at 8 (citing *Grootboom*, ¶ 35). The court continues: "The State must create the conditions for access to housing for people at all levels of our society." Id.

[54] Id. at 4.

[55] Prior to moving onto the private land the litigants in this case, 510 children and 390 adults, lived in an informal settlement which was prone to flooding and had no water, sewage, trash collection and little electricity. Some of the litigants had been on the waiting list for municipal provided subsidized low-cost housing for seven years with no idea of when they would get housing. *Grootboom*, ¶ 7.

[56] Id. at ¶ 9.

[57] Id. Following their eviction Mrs. Grootboom and the others sought shelter on a sports field constructing temporary structure with plastic sheeting which proved ineffective when the winter rains began. Id. at ¶ 11.

[58] The plaintiffs alleged that the government's action violated their constitutional right to access to housing under section 26 and the right of children to shelter contained in section 28 (1) (c) . Id. at ¶ 15.

[59] Id. at ¶ 53.

[60] Id. at ¶ 95.

[61] Id. at ¶ 52.

[62] *Grootboom*, ¶ 87.

[63] Id. at ¶ 88.

[64] Id. at ¶ 6.

[65] Budlender, "Justiciability of the Right to Housing," 6.

[66] Id. at 7. Budlender writes that in 2002 the Supreme Court of Appeal, the highest court in South Africa, except the Constitutional Court for constitutional matters, rejected the idea in *Brisley v. Drotsky*, 2002 (4) SA 1 (SAC), ¶ 42. Id.

[67] *Minister of Public Works v. Kyalami Ridge Environmental Association*, 2001 (7) BCLR 652 (CC), 2001 SACLR LEXIS 154, ¶ 2.

[68] Id. at ¶ 17.

[69] The neighboring property owners also argued that they have a constitutional right to procedurally fair administrative actions. See § 33 (b) of the Constitution.

[70] Kyalami Ridge, ¶ 99.

[71] Id. at ¶ 95. The State property at issue was formerly a prison farm and according to the Court well suited as a temporary housing site. Id. at ¶ 98. Lawyers for Mr. Mukwevho, the flood victim, argued that he and the others were destitute, and that the housing guarantee in sections 26 (1) and (2) of the Constitution obligates the State "to take reasonable measures" to help the flood victims achieve this right. Id. at ¶ 19. The State agreed saying that as owner of the property sections 85 (2) (b) and (e) of the Constitution vests it with the executive authority to carry out its constitutional functions, in this case to fulfill its obligation under sections 26 (1) and (2). Id. at ¶ 40. These sections give the President along with the Cabinet the power to "develop[] and implement [] national policy" and perform[] any other executive function provided for in the Constitution or national laws." §§ 85 (2) (b) and (e).

[72] Id. at ¶ 105.

[73] The Court notes that the government even as a private property owner must act lawfully in carrying out its constitutional obligations. Id. at ¶ 114.

[74] Id. at ¶¶ 101-03.

[75] *Grootboom*, ¶ 44.

[76] *City of Cape Town v. Rudolph*, 2003 (11) BCLR 1236 (C),2003 SACLR LEXIS 43, ¶ 65.

[77] Id. at ¶¶ 107-12. Cape Metro Council, the applicant in *Grootboom*, was the predecessor of the City of Cape Town, the applicant in this case. Id. at ¶ 112. The High Court noted that in 2000 the house backlog was 206,000 houses and this number was being reduced by 2000 housing units per year (citing *Grootboom*, ¶¶ 57-58. By November 2001 the backlog had grown to 250,000 houses and "the backlog was no longer being reduced, but was increasing at the rate of 15,000 houses per year. The yearly demand was growing by 25,000 units as against a supply of 10,000 per year. Id. at ¶ 111.

[78] *City of Cape Town v. Rudolph*, 2003 (11) BCLR 1236 (C),2003 SACLR LEXIS 43.

[79] Id. at ¶ 112 (citing *Grootboom*, ¶¶ 57-58).

[80] Id. at ¶ 111.

[81] *Port Elizabeth Municipality*.

[82] Id. at ¶ 2.

[83] Id. at ¶ 3.

[84] Id. at ¶ 19. In balancing the competing constitutional rights the court discussed the apartheid government's approach to illegal squatting as exemplified by the Prevention of Illegal Squatting Act 52 of 1951 and contrasting it to approach adopted in the Prevention of Illegal Eviction from and Unlawful Occupation of Las Act 19 of 1998. Id. at ¶¶ 8-13.

[85] Id. at ¶ 16.

[86] Id. (citing Justice Ackermann's words in *First National Bank of SA Limited t/a Westbank v. Commissioner for the South African Revenue Services*; *First National Bank of SA Limited t/a Westbank v. Minister of Finance*, 2002 (4) SA 768 (CC); 2002 (7) BCLR 702 (CC)).

[87] Id. Later in the opinion the court writes: "In sum, the Constitution imposes new obligations on the courts concerning rights relating to property not previously recognised by the common law....The expectations that ordinarily go with title could clash head-on with the genuine despair of people in dire need of accommodation." Id. at ¶ 23.

[88] Id. at ¶ 15.

[89] Id. at ¶ 23.

[90] Id. at ¶ 28.

[91] Id. at ¶ 38.

[92] Id. at ¶ 20.

[93] *President of the Republic of South Africa v. Modderklip*, 2005 (8) BCLR 743 (CC).

[94] Both the High Court and the Supreme Court of Appeals ruled that the government's inaction violated Modderklip's property rights under section 25(1) and the occupiers' right to adequate housing under sections 26(1) and (2). Id. at ¶ 4. The court cited section 6(4) of the Prevention of Illegal Eviction from and Unlawful Occupation of Act 19 of 1998 which requires the landowner "to institute eviction proceedings against the unlawful occupiers." Id.

[95] Id. at ¶¶ 4-5. The company chose instead to bring criminal trespass charges against the squatters.

[96] The High Court ruled that the government's inaction constituted an unlawful expropriation of Modderklip's property, also infringing on the company's equality rights under sections 9(1) and (2) of the Constitution by requiring the to bear what should be a state burden of providing accommodation to the occupiers. Id. at ¶ 15. The court also imposed a structural interdict whereby the state had to develop and present a comprehensive plan to implement the court's order and present it to the court and other parties in the matter. Id. at ¶ 16. The Supreme Court of Appeals agreed with the High Court's basic rationale for its ruling but went a step further ordering the state to pay Modderklip "constitutional damages." Id. at ¶¶ 18-21. The Supreme Court of Appeals ordered the State to pay the company compensatory damages to compensate it for the loss of the use of its property, since the private property owner was performing essentially a state obligation – providing temporary housing for homeless individuals. Id. at ¶ 20 (citing *Modderfontein Squatters v. Modderklip Boerdery (Pty) Ltd.*, 2004 (6) SA 40 (SCA), ¶ 43).

[97] The state also argued that Modderklip was not entitled to prevail because it had failed to comply with state law requiring it apply for a timely eviction order. Id. at ¶ 22.

[98] Id. at ¶ 66.

[99] Id. at ¶ 29.

[100] Id. at ¶ 49.

[101] Id.

[102] Id. at ¶¶ 43-46.

[103] Id. at ¶ 66.

[104] Id. at ¶ 47.

[105] Id. at ¶ 26.

[106] Id. at ¶¶ 63-64.

[107] For a discussion of this point *see* Alfred Cockrell, "The South African Bill of Rights and the "Duck/Rabbit,"" (1979), 60 *The Modern Law Review* 60 (1979): 513, 516.

[108] *Jaftha*, ¶ 29. The court imposed limitations based on the constitutional right to housing on the circumstances under which debtors who failed to satisfy judgments against them could be forced to sell their homes to satisfy their debts.

[109] Id. at ¶ 27.

[110] See, Mia Swart, "Left Out in the Cold, Crafting Constitutional Remedies for the Poorest of the Poor," *South African Journal on Human Rights* 21 (2005): 215-16.

[111] Id. at 216, n. 8 (citing two 2002 reports).

[112] Dennis Davis, "Adjudicating the Socio-Economic Rights in the South African Constitution: Towards "Deference Lite?,"" *South African Journal on Human Rights* 22 (2006): 301, 314 (the five Commission annual reports can be found at http://www.sahrc.org.za).

[113] Swart, "Left Out in the Cold," 217.

[114] *Fose v. Minister of Safety and Security*, 1997 (3) SA 786 (CC); 1997 BCLR 851 (CC), ¶ 69.

[115] *See, e.g.*, Davis, "Adjudicating" 301 (arguing that the South African Constitutional Court's record on enforcement of socio-economic rights as been less than transformative).

[116] *Minister of Health v. TAC*.

[117] Id. at ¶ 28. The High Court in Modderklip also ordered a structured interdict. *Modderklip*.

[118] Id. at ¶ 129.

[119] *Minister of Health v. TAC*, ¶ 38.

[120] The Court in at least one case, *August v. Electoral Commission*, issued mandatory interdicts directing the Electoral Commission "to make all reasonable arrangements necessary to enable prisoners to register as voters ... and to vote in [an] upcoming election." Swart, "Left Out in the Cold," 227. (citing *August v. Electoral Commission*, 1999 (3) SA 1 (CC)). *See also* Sandra Liebenberg, "South Africa, Evolving Jurisprudence on Socio-economic Rights: An effective tool in challenging poverty," (2002), *available at* http://www.communitylawcentre.org.za.

[121] Swart, "Left out in the Cold," 225-26.

[122] Wim Trengove, "Judicial Remedies for Violations of Socio-Economic Rights," *ESR Rev.* 1(4) (1999), *available at* http://www.communitylawcentre.org.za/ser/esr1999/1999march_trengove.php.

[123] Swart, "Left out in the Cold," 238. In *Port Elizabeth Municipality* Justice Sachs wrote that "courts may need to find expression in innovative ways." *Port Elizabeth Municipality*, ¶ 39. He was referring in this case to voluntary or compulsory face-to-face mediation. Justice Sachs calls on poor and landless people not to view themselves as "helpless victims" but mediation is hardly an effective tool in eviction cases when there is considerable socio-economic imbalance of power between the two sides.

[124] Davis, "Adjudicating," 304.

[125] Id.

[126] Id. at 304. Davis cites *Soobramoney v. Minister of Health* (Kwa-Zulu), 1998 (1) SA 765 (CC) and *Minister of Health v. TAC* as examples of the Court limiting the right to health care contained in sec 27. Id. at 305-306. He also cites *Grootboom*, Id. at 306-307.

[127] Davis, "Adjudicating," 326.

[128] *Grootboom*, ¶ 4 (citing *Grootboom v. Oostenberg Municipality*, 2000 (3) BCLR 277 (C). According to the High Court "tents, portable latrines and a regular supply of water...would constitute the bare minimum." Id.

CHAPTER 4

CUTTING AND SEWING: GOALS AND MEANS IN THE CONSTITUTIONALIST PROJECT IN AFRICA[1]

Martin Chanock

Lord Acton contrasted the urge towards revolution, democracy and the proclamation of rights with the careful processes of creating the institutions to maintain these goals. This chapter will discuss the continuing tensions between cutting and sewing and suggest that rights scholarship has overlooked the importance, for the achievement of rights, of the design and maintenance of democratic constitutionalist institutions, as well as the conventional concerns of constitutional scholarship with limiting and balancing the exercise of power. The West has long espoused the export of democracy. The decolonisation of Africa was one such exercise. The "second wave" of democratisation in the 1980's and 1990's has not led, South Africa so far aside, to the establishing of successful constitutional democracies. Throughout the post colonial period many African analysts have viewed the forms of constitutional democracy that were adopted, and then failed, in Africa as alien to African political culture, and have argued that Africa must search for indigenous forms of government. But the struggle for freedom in Africa is part of a universal struggle and the failures raise the question of why African states still stand outside of the global spread of democratic institutions.

This essay seeks to consider the limited success of the attempt to revive constitutionalism in post independence Africa. It seeks to marry two conceptual worlds, those of political science and law, which are still surprisingly separated in considerations of the project of constitutionalist democracy for Africa. And it seeks also to supplement the vision of public law that sees Bills of Rights and judicial review as the core of the constitutionalist project. It will suggest that an older version of constitutionalism, which emphasised political accountability, the separation of powers and the rule of law, are the primary core of the project. It may be pertinent to start with the observation that in all African countries only a very small proportion of the people speak or are literate in the languages of constitutions, bills of rights and constitutional discourse. For most these are "literally meaningless."[2] Neither constitutionalist concepts nor the language of rights have, therefore, been grounded in popular discourse.

The enquiry has a number of present day questions in mind. One concerns the current concern with weak and failing states[3] and the search for a model of what legitimately a strong state might look like in the era of reducing state capacities.[4] The very high price that has been paid when states collapse makes the issue of state capacity to govern perhaps the primary human rights issue on the continent. Another concerns the so called "rule of law" revival[5] and its connection to the processes of democratic state building which has been a feature of the post cold war world.[6] A third, related to this, is the proliferation of new constitutions world-wide in the last two decades, an explosion of constitutionalism and concern for human rights that has affected Latin America; Eastern Europe; Africa and elsewhere. A fourth is the growth of the interest in good governance and the consequent focus on corruption, which has exerted pressure on aid-dependent states. Fifth and underlying many of these is the dominance of free market policies and property rights and the dismantling of the vast apparatus of state-led development across Africa.[7] The role of the state in development and the model of state directed development which dominated the activities of the independent African states in the first decades of their existence is crucial to the story of the collapse of the rule of law broadly conceived. The urgency and needs of "Development" were the justifications for the abandonment of democracy, formal legalism, and political freedoms. Ultimately the paradigm behind the new constitutionalist endeavour is that of the connection made by the World Bank and others between democracy, liberalism, property rights and market. However, as we shall see, the much of the failure of the democratization project of the 1990's is due to its links with marketisation. Which raises the questions not just *where to now;* but *how* to now?

In the light of these concerns it may be useful to look at an earlier period of constitution making, and democracy and rule of law promotion, a period that in Africa at least was singularly unsuccessful (if these were serious goals). In analysing the decades of political failure in Africa from independence to the present neither historians nor political scientists have paid much attention to matters of formal legal structures, or the nature of legality generally. It might be said that political scientists came to treat constitutional issues even less seriously than African politicians as an essential component of analyses of the decline of democracy and the possibility of its revival. There is good reason for this: the ease with which constitutions were swept away seemed to prove that they were irrelevant to the real world of politics. There was also remarkably little international support during the cold war years for democratic and constitutionalist practices by the new states. The emphasis was rather on supporting stability of governments and effective anti-communism. I would stress the importance of the absence of international support for African democracy and constitutionalism. And also to be noted is the virtual absence of support from the 'progressive' side of politics, and from intellectuals, both in Africa and outside. However in the present international environment democracy and constitutionalism are internationally supported with sanctions for departures from democratic norms (for example in the Commonwealth and by donor institutions and countries) and by the international subsidisation of powerful "democratic" NGO's to assist in the creation of democratic societies. In contrast to the earlier period of state-making when the creators of the new states had little faith in democracy, constitutionalism and adherence to the rule of law, these are now embodied in new constitutions which are expected to succeed. These expectations provide another reason for looking back at the role of constitutional legality in the earlier period. De Smith's judgment then was that "In developing countries constitutional factors will seldom play a dominant role in the shaping of political history."[8] In the light of the processes of democratisation that have swept Africa since 1989, (and what has been called the "constitutional fetishism" of the new South Africa), should this judgment be revised, or have many countries engaged again with an illusion?

The overwhelming message of the political science analyses about the new African states in the decades between independence and the end of the 1980's, was that constitutionalism and democracy were not of importance in understanding African politics. Zolberg in his classic analysis in 1968[9] warned against "reification" of categories of analysis like constitution, civil service and army, positing essentially that the constitution did not exist. He observed constitutional arrangements, which in the absence of supporting norms and institutions had little reality beyond their physical existence as a set of written symbols deposited in a government archive; ...the civil service, in which the usual bureaucratic norms are so rare that it is perhaps better to speak of 'government employees'...even of the 'the Army' which far from being a model of hierarchical organization, tends to be an assemblage of armed men who may or may not obey their officers....[10]

As Richard Sklar wrote in an important article in 1987 political science was the "dismal science" for the third world.[11] "Steeped in 'realism' political science tells a future of dictatorial rule for most of those who face the prospect of increasing physical misery." Political scientists had described the new generation of third world Leviathans, capturing the "spirit of the beast" in the concept of "developmental dictatorship." "From all sectors of the spectrum - left, centre, right – analysts have asserted or conceded the historical necessity of developmental dictatorships to cope with the causes and consequences of economic underdevelopment."[12] Democratic forms of development were proclaimed to be irrelevant to the third world. Samuel Huntington thought in 1968 that "the limits of democratic development in the world may well have been reached."[13] Third world scholars on the whole shared the view that western concepts of democracy were part of a "tyranny of borrowed paradigms."[14] As Sklar says it was a widely accepted tenet of "realism" that the idea that democracy itself "may be the mainspring of development appears to put the proverbial cart before the horse." Democratic institutions which meant greater popular participation could even be damaging in that they might lead to demands for egalitarian welfare policies that would consume capital resources and impede growth. Political science "explains dictatorship as an unavoidable, if not indeed necessary, condition of social order..."[15] It is not surprising then that wondering about what had happened to constitutionalism was not a mainstream concern of political science in these years.[16]

It is still the case that analyses of the continuing rise and flourishing of democracy and its promotion, focussed around Eastern Europe and Latin America (with little to say about Africa) has produced a literature which, given its size and scope, has relatively little to say about legal institutions and processes. There is recognition of Africa's new semi-authoritarians, and their reliance on patronage; as well as the concept of "illiberal democracy" – democracies resulting from the 1990's transitions without habits of law based liberalism.[17]

Legal Transplants

The processes of democratisation and marketisation have been accompanied by the large scale transfer of law and legal institutions across the world as parts of deliberate efforts to re-structure both the public institutions and private law of recipient countries. The changes associated with globalization; the collapse of communist states; and the new pressures on developing states, have simultaneously contributed to this global movement of law. The fundamental tensions between approaches which insist on the distinctiveness of legal cultures and the huge problems involved with the idea of transplanted law, and those who see transplantation as simple and functional, remain. The extent it which law does or does not "fit" cultures has been the issue.[18] But whether or not inter-cultural understanding, or a "real" acceptance of a legal institution, idea or rule from one culture into another is even possible, the facts are that on the ground the purported transfer of law is taking place all around us without a great deal of agonizing about what this might mean in the short or long term. Indeed as legal elites increasingly are much like each other, trained in the same way in the same institutions across the world, their assumptions and the facility with which they communicate and comprehend each other, tends to push the questions of the cultural "fit" of law into different societies into the background. The real "receivers" of transplanted law are not societies at large, but only the legal (as distinct even from the political) elites who work with the new law.

The transplanting of law is particularly significant in the public law area where the world's repertoire of models upon which states draw is limited. Even where there are different variations of prime ministerial and presidential constitutions the universalisation of human rights jurisprudence has created a key area of transplantation of a global scale.[19] While the transplanting of other areas of law often takes place over long time spans, in constitutional law it is more typically part of major political transitions: in the African case the end of colonialism; the later collapse of the dictatorial regimes; and the end of apartheid. The process of constitutional transplanting is not gradual, the time span is short. This process, as we have noted, failed the first time in Africa, and may have failed in most countries again. The legal transplant issue in Africa is central to the understanding of the failure of states to develop "a rule of law" culture. Transplanting took place in a context in which the incapacities of states meant that the absence of law reports, and even more basic the unavailability of statutes, meant that law was simply unavailable. When it was it was in language hardly anyone was competent in. The failure to integrate the received and customary laws into national legal systems, though it had been at the outset a priority for many interested in African legal matters, lay at the base of the failure of the rule of law. Because of this, state courts were rarely seen as either the first places to go, or the first line of defence, by ordinary African litigants.

A major theme in African constitutionalist scholarship has been the foreign origins of the constitutional order and on the need to find an indigenous version of the African state. Hutchful links this with the failure to deal with ethnicity because it meant that "little effort was made in post-independence constitutionalism to indigenize the state and constitution in order to reflect the diversity and pluralistic basis of African society."[20] Another key theme has been to contrast Western individualism and African collectivism. Shivji writes:

> The point of reference for democratic organization in Africa has always been the Western parliamentary form…The gravamen of this form relates to the way the state is organized *inter se* and the relation of the state to the *autonomous* citizen…. The western liberal democratic form has been tried again and again in Africa and totally failed.[21]

Hutchful argued also that the inherited constitutional formula had "limited relevance to African social formations," assuming nationhood when it was problematic and sanctioning "parliamentarism," which was "a democratic practice for which there was no experiential basis in colonial or pre-colonial society…"[22] This drove a wedge between the formal and the more extensive informal political sphere including the entire realm of traditional authority relations. "Parliamentarism established a privileged political discourse with normative prescriptions accessible only to a small minority of the population" and drove large areas of the political underground. The liberal constitutional model also defended individual but not collective rights. "[I]ndividual property rights received constitutional recognition, while the collective property rights fundamental to traditional social organization were ignored" as were "gerontocratic institutions."[23]

Bills of Rights

The transplanting of Bills of Rights and the cultural aspects of this has generated over time a substantial literature.[24] Oddly perhaps, there is a far greater acceptance of the universality of rights discourse than of other areas of public law. Indeed extra-territorial borrowing of human rights law has been a key to the working of high courts' implementation of bills of rights. I do not want to review this question again here, but to consider this aspect of public law transplanting within the context of the collapse of constitutional government in post-colonial Africa, and the rise of the international human rights movement. It is easy to see how the second should have been invoked as the remedy for the first. However the reasons for the failure of constitutionalism in Africa may not, on examination, bear much relation to the constitutional provision of rights, or their absence. This will come as no surprise to realists. As I have said, one of the most marked features of the accounts of Africa produced by political scientists, historians, and scholars of development, is an absence of consideration of constitutionalism, of the "hows" of, and the values of government. But there is a third history that must be added, and that is the history of the idea of constitutionalism. While "rights" scholars understand constitutional government in terms of Bills of Rights and judicial review, rights, the older constitutionalist paradigm has been one which stresses government limited by law, the primacy of the rule of law in general, the structures of relations between legislatures and executives; the degree of centralisation; the electoral system; the separation of powers and the independence of the judiciary; and other issues of constitutional design and balance. One of the problems with a constitutional scholarship that focuses on rights, rights interpretations and visions, and judicial review, is that it pushes into the background the matters that should still be of primary concern. To be something more than a piece of paper a Bill of Rights must be set within a governmental process which habitually respects the rule of law, and constitutional processes. These habits are not arrived at overnight. Nor will they be arrived at outside of the context of accountable and democratic government. This makes the stories of democracy and constitutionalism in Africa the key parts of our narrative.

Democracy and Constitutionalism in Africa

The struggle for democracy and human rights in Africa has been part of a powerful universalist search for ways to organise state power. But it has also been an African struggle against African governments. Those who were the victims of the despotic governments which abandoned their independence constitutions were Africans. Their history has been submerged in the many accounts of the colonial legacy, and the search for African Democracy. We may begin with the "legacy issue." The colonial period from which the new independent states derived both the machinery of government handed over, and the style of government in the period immediately preceding independence, gave little in the way of an example for democratic and constitutional rule.[25] Apart from elections in the final phases of transition it was based on a racist denial of the capacity of Africans to be self-governing. Its style of decision making was autocratic; its laws embodied very wide discretions; and authority rested on the ready use of coercive force. Accordingly there was no space for a constitutionalist mode to develop. Many scholars have placed an emphasis on the nature of the colonial heritage. Emphasis was correctly placed on the essence of colonial rule being "coercion and command."[26] Democratic institutions and the idea of a state limited by law were introduced only at the point of the transfer of power. As Shivji observed the colonial state's legal order "was exactly the opposite of that prescribed in the notions of constitutionalism." This essential feature was passed on to the successor states where the organising principle became the concentration of power, not its separation.[27]

Our narrative really begins with decolonisation, which was accompanied by a self conscious attempt by the colonial power to hand down constitutional democracy. The time span for preparation for independence was far shorter than had been envisaged. In 1945 the talk in Whitehall in relation to Africa was still of "generations."[28] In the early 1950's it was of "decades," but less than a decade later, it was all but done.[29] The old model of developing democratic institutions in local government as part of a long haul towards independence was cast aside. Thinking about how the new devolved institutions, (which were premised on understandings and conventions in British political practice) would work in the African context was minimal, as political pressures led to the production of one "Westminster model" constitution after another. Nationalist leadership had remarkably little time to adjust to its new role. And while devolving constitutional democracy was felt to be a "good thing," there was little belief among policy makers that it would succeed as they contemplated the fierce regional and ethnic conflicts which emerged in the final years of the artificial colonial states, and the anticipated collapse in administrative capacity as colonial administrators withdrew.[30] Crucially, there was little support for it once independence had been granted, either among the leaders of the new countries or from the former colonial power. The critical contextual factors in the rapid decolonisation were the crisis of colonial government in Africa and the Cold War. British and American interests supported "stable" governments which were not communist. The American Secretary of State John Foster Dulles, pointed out to the British Prime Minister Harold Macmillan in 1958, the "unwisdom of promoting the virtues of popular election" and thought that we should get a "few people to consider at a high level how we could stop ourselves from being carried away down the stream of uncontrolled democracy which might submerge the existing order of things" and leave the communists able to set up their own dictatorships.[31] British interests also more narrowly supported those still within an informal sphere of British influence.[32] There was little interest post-independence in supporting democratic institutions, and no condemnatory reaction to the move towards one party states (apart from right wing delight at the proven incapacity of Africans for self rule).

The international context of these developments was crucial. Two matters are central to understanding. The rushed nature of African independence could not in the context of colonial rule be opposed, because to do so was to suggest that the premise of colonialism, that Africans were unfit to govern themselves, was correct.

This held true for the restraint of most criticism of post- independence developments. Secondly, these developments took place within the context of the Cold War at a time in which there was overt competition for influence over African states. As we have seen when the process of devolution in British Africa got underway, John Foster Dulles, the American Secretary of State, expressed his hesitation about the suitability of democracy for backward states. Strong, if necessary authoritarian, rule was preferable to weaker democracies. This preference for stability over democracy created a specific space for authoritarian developments in Africa which began to close closed when the cold war ended.

Many of the devolved constitutions had Bills of Rights. (Ghana was not offered one, Tanzania declined). But extensive emergency powers, inherited from the final years of colonial rule, remained in place. In the earlier process of Asian constitution making lawyers in Whitehall had been scornful of such provision. The Joint Select Committee on the Bill which became the Government of India Act of 1935 thought that the recent history of Europe "suggested that the most effective way of subverting human rights was to embody them in a Constitution, where they must prove either of no practical value, or impediments to effective legislation...."[33] The Ceylon independence constitution, crafted in London, had no bill of rights. By contrast inn India, where the constitution was made by the Indians themselves, there was both a bill of rights and a statement regarding the directing principles of state policies. In Malaysia also local political pressures favoured a Bill of Rights. Compelling local input of this kind was absent in the African transition. Prior to independence Britain had already brought the African colonies under the European Convention as a piece of image making, though this was in practice meaningless.[34] The Bills of Rights devolved on African countries were modeled on this convention. (Some made reference to the Universal Declaration of Human Rights). The purpose of these rights declarations was less the protection of civil liberties and more a strategy (the other being forms of federal or regional devolution) to deal with "tribalism," and the anxieties of ethnic minorities about their position once independence had been achieved.[35] As the immediate post-colonial constitutional order collapsed across Africa, these Bills of Rights played a small but insignificant role in the ways in which states were governed. Only in Nigeria, alone in having had a large legal profession, were real – but unsuccessful – efforts made to hold government to account using the constitutional bill of rights. The African judiciary in these years, largely British, or drawn from elsewhere in the Commonwealth, and all educated in common law constitutionalism, had little knowledge or appreciation of rights jurisprudence. Nwabueze blamed the English lawyers' literalism and analytical positivism for their narrowness of outlook. As Prempeh was later to write, a liberal constitution does not guarantee a liberal judiciary.[36]

The Commonwealth African states quickly shrugged off the constraints on executive power that their independence constitutions had imposed. Of greater significance than the failures of the Bills of rights was that all countries swiftly moved to nullify, either in law or in fact, the influence of their legislatures. All moved towards de facto or de jure one party government (in Nigeria in the States rather than at the centre). The imperatives of national unity, national integration and development were cited as requiring and justifying this course. There was frequently voiced disagreement with the idea of a constitutionalised Opposition (an alternative government in waiting) which was an essential feature of the Westminster model. African indigenous states, it was said, new of no such constitutionalising of divisions. Amidst the extreme cynicism among leaders about legal forms, high levels of corruption made an early appearance.

The details of the story are on course different for each country and it is of the greatest importance to be aware that in most there was strong opposition to this process. (I shall here focus on three cases: Ghana, Nigeria and Tanzania). In the "emblematic" case of Ghana[37] the then Prime Minister Nkrumah rapidly moved towards the creation of a one party state; introduced a new constitution with himself as Life President with presidential power to legislate by decree; and made frequent use of preventive detention to deal with opposition. Not only was there strong civilian opposition but he was overthrown in 1964 by a military coup, after which there was a quick return to civilian rule. The model for the second return of democracy was extraordinarily conventional. Produced by English trained lawyers, it tried to re-establish Westminster democracy based on the rule of law.[38] This failed a second time. A second period of military rule, a second failed attempt to re-introduce civilian democracy with a constitution tailored slightly more to Ghanaian conditions, followed by a third military coup, were the next steps. Attempts to maintain judicial independence (fatal in the case of three judges) continued.

In Nigeria, the collapse of the astonishingly badly designed first federation which ended in the assassination[39] or imprisonment of its leaders was followed by a prolonged period of firmly authoritarian military rule (during which there was a bitter secessionist civil war). After the first military coup the Federal Supreme Court had attempted to hold the military government to the rule of law and was swiftly crushed by legislative reversal and a denial of competency to question the proclamations of the military government. But the 1970's were a time of prolonged constitutional ferment and constitutional design, which bear witness to the strength of the local struggles for democracy. These culminated in the adoption of a complex new federal constitution in 1979 in which the designers had taken on board (they thought) all of the causes of Nigeria's political failures, and which established a democratic state with constitutionalised rights protections. Like the later Ghanaian constitutions, and most of the other Commonwealth African constitutions, the Westminster model was abandoned in favour of an executive presidency and a formal separation of powers.[40] This state collapsed after four years amid widespread corruption of the electoral processes. The crucial point, in relation to our concerns here, is that while the courts begun to proceed fairly boldly in their use of the bill of rights, this proved irrelevant in the face of failure of the politicians to operate the processes of democracy. Another prolonged period of military rule, another failed attempt to return to constitutional democracy in the election winner was imprisoned and died, and a further prolongation of military rule was to follow. Because of the far greater size and sophistication of the legal profession in Nigeria, a constitutionalist tradition was far stronger and its goals were never repudiated, despite the violence and corruption of politics. And it is of importance that while the Westminster model of constitutionalism and the overhang of common law precedent had been a strongly inhibiting factor on judiciaries in Africa, that under the new constitutional model in Nigeria after 1979 the Nigerian Supreme Court had begun to carve out of new role for itself, with a mode of interpretation of Bill of Rights that departed from the common law method of treating constitutional instruments as ordinary statutes.

In Tanzania, however, the western democratic goals were very quickly repudiated. Resisting the incorporation of a bill of rights at independence, Tanzania moved quickly to amend its independence constitution, creating a one party state with an avowedly socialist policy, with powers concentrated in the President and the Party.[41] The de jure one party state embodying forms of "socialism," as the state led development model was described, became popular across both Commonwealth and formerly French Africa. The notions of the separation of powers and the rule of law were abandoned. The Tanzanian judiciary co-operated with and did not resist this process. As the Trinidadian Chief Justice of Tanzania was to say "Socialism was sung as a song. And we had to sing it."[42] At the time, Georges did not disagree with the Nyerere's rejection of the idea of judicial neutrality. It was necessary, he thought, for judges and magistrates to interpret the laws with "a strong regard for public policy." Their independence was

> not being safeguarded to set them apart from the people. Its purpose was really to enable them to better serve the people of whom they were a part. Judicial independence would hardly survive where it appeared to encourage the growth of judicial arrogance.[43]

Georges encouraged judges to join the ruling party. "The concept of the judge as a neutral, belonging to no party in a multi-party democracy," he wrote, "can have no meaning here."[44]

It is of significance that the specific rejection of multiparty democracy and the rule of law in Tanzania were developments that were treated favourably by progressive opinion in Africa and outside.[45] "Tanzaphilia" was not upset by the crushing of opposition and trade unions, nor by the extra-legal and coercive villlagisation of the peasantry. It was not until the mid 1980's, as part of the structural adjustment reforms imposed on African states by the World Bank, that under pressure Tanzania began to make its way towards a multi-party system and a constitutionalised bill of rights. As in Nigeria, the Tanzanian judiciary, moved towards giving it meaning, indicating that the extreme judicial scepticism about rights which had been part of the early post-colonial phase was over.[46] External pressures had created the opportunity.

In Uganda another poorly designed federation quickly fell apart and parliamentarians legislated a new constitution which they had not been given time to read. A military coup was to follow; the brutal dictatorship of General Idi Amin toppled by invasion from Tanzania; and further significant periods of violence followed by an attempt to introduce a "no party" democracy.[47] The process in Kenya was slightly different. The constitution created a plural state and the first parliament had strong opposition to the government. But the opposition politicians (as they were to do in other African countries), calculating that they had no chance of ever winning and unwilling to be excluded from power and its spoils simply crossed the floor to join the government. Thus a "consensual" one party state was formed and this allowed the government, and its bureaucracy, to govern essentially without law.[48]

Development

The most important contextual factor was the accepted model of economic development, and the dominant ideas about the role which the state should play in it.[49] It is important, given the strengths of contemporary critiques of the imposition of the market economy on "disciplined democracies,"[50] that contemporary constitutionalist scholars do not lose sight of the difficulties of combining other models of economy with a constitutional state and the rule of law. Political scientists and development economists alike, in the early decades of independent African states, celebrated far more than they condemned the course taken by African states (and other developing states) in this period. It was argued that the deliberately fractionalized map of power created by the independence constitutions was a serious liability in the drive for rapid economic development.[51] In the prevailing paradigm it was the state which inevitably (and legitimately) took the lead in the development process and which had therefore to have the necessary powers. Control over all aspects of economic life, and the required discretions that government needed to attempt this, was seen as a necessity if new states were to escape neo-colonial control. The dominant ideology of developmentalism superseded both law and politics. Statute law was enabling, empowering the executive organs to the state in wide and unrestrictive terms. The concept of contract, the key to liberal legal systems, played a minor role in this legal system organized around domination.[52] Overall there was what Hutchful has called "an effacement of the boundaries" between state and economy and civil society.[53] This is something which liberal constitutionalism, with its careful delineations of the spheres of the political, of the rights of citizens and the powers and functions of government, was not designed to cope with. While the legacy of legality bequeathed by colonialism was meagre, it was further attenuated by this model of development.

By the end of the 1970's and the early 1980's the paradigm of state led development came under severe pressure from international institutions like the World Bank. The identification of the bloated state sectors as being incapacitating "rent-seekers" rather than the creators of wealth, and the subsequent demands for structural adjustment, was an assault on the state-dependent ruling class all over Africa.[54] And it was this context that began some of the democratic and constitutionalist revivals referred to above. This process intensified after the end of the Cold War, and the global acceleration of democratisation. The new model for the so called "disciplined democracies" imposed real limits upon the role of the state. In place of the state's role in leading development, it was the market, operating within a liberal-legal framework guaranteed by the state that was to be the path towards development. In this model, limited government and the rule of law, and also the protection of individual civil and property rights, were not only not irrelevant, they were considered to be the key to successful economic development and therefore to the success of the new states.[55]

The 1980's and 1990's in which this paradigm of the state dominated, were, accordingly, a period of so called democratic renaissance in Africa. Continent wide, regimes reinvented themselves as democracies, especially after the end of the cold war. While based on a different set of premises, they were, by and large, no more successful than their predecessors and reversions, coups, civil wars and other forms of state collapse and weakness were prevalent.. Changing the state form had not changed the states' problems. Exercising effective control in the often worsening economic conditions which accompanied structural adjustment, and within new democratic constitutional frameworks which both intensified competition for power and raised the expectations of newly empowered electorates, was very difficult. States, stripped of many of their functions, and sources of revenue, were simply too weak to cope with the role they had been allocated. Political and social conditions in states in varying degrees of failure were not conducive either to constitutionalism or to the realisation of rights. Also, electorates did not embrace the neo-liberal order, and the new political competition forced politicians to make promises incompatible with it. Thus while the democratic, market and rights oriented model was triumphant discursively, in practice it its triumphs were limited. The international diagnosis of this failure was that it was not the market that had failed the institutions, but the institutions which had failed the market. To the extent that institutions were undermined by ever more rampant corruption there was some validity in this. The remedy was to stress the need for a stronger state, with more transparent, more accountable institutions.[56]

Learning the Lessons? Democracy, Constitutionalism and Rights

One of the most canvassed reasons for failure has been the fractionalised ethnic composition of the successor states. Reliance on ethnic centres of power had been a part of colonial rule. The rulers of the new "nations" demanded national unity both as part of the state-building project where each state feared disintegration, and as an imperative for development. This demand, where the "nation" was made up of diverse ethnic groups, created impossible pressures on weak democracies which had neither institutionalised political cultures or constitutional habits. As An-Na'im notes, "one of the most problematic aspects of constitutionalism throughout the world is the status and rights of minorities" whether defined in ethnic religious or linguistic terms. The core questions were how to achieve resolution of the competing claims to self determination within a unified state, or how to protect the status and rights of minorities within a constitutional order.[57] The British answer to this, on withdrawing from Africa, was varying forms of federalism and decentralisation which did not survive the subsequent pressures for centralisation. The legacy bills of rights did not conceive of nor protect national, collective or cultural rights. Even in Nigeria, with its scarring experience of ethnic conflict, the attempt to re-build a democratic state in 1979 was based on a constitution which in its "Fundamental Objectives and State Principles" and political mechanics which "implicitly banned ethnic and regional parties" was deliberately assimilationist.[58] Shivji wrote that the issue of the "right to self-determination" have been central to struggles in Africa. Both liberal and statist perspectives have rejected this right: the liberal because it was unable to deal with the concept of collective rights; while the statist opposed the further splintering of African states. The area of ethnicity remains a key challenge for both constitutional design and rights jurisprudence.

While effective and functioning democracy has by no means been established in Commonwealth Africa, nowhere is the one-party dictatorship a legitimate goal. While a rule of law constitutionalism is weak, it is no longer dismissed as irrelevant to Africa's problems. But neither of these is necessarily secure. I have told this story in order to emphasise that bills of rights are a secondary part of constitutional design for the establishment of democratic rule-governed polities, and to think about the future of rights we need to think first about the framework that is necessary to sustain them. And we must pay attention to the political contexts in which rights may be "enforced" as well as the institutional context. I have stressed that constitutional rights instruments made their way back into Africa as a part of a governance package which enjoined market led economic policies for development. These policies have everywhere led to widening gaps between richer and poorer, with concomitant political tensions.[59] The gap between the rhetoric of both democracy and rights and the realities of economic life both weakens democracy and makes the judicial enforcement of second and third generation rights seem fanciful.[60] The future of rights must therefore be imagined within the context of these tensions.

Rights discourses, and the institutions which enforce the constitutionalised bills of rights, now operate in a context of democracy without choice. This is sometimes simply because though elections take place there is no alternative government (as in South Africa, though it is Africa's most successful democracy), but because the international context prevents the pursuit of different political agenda. This, combined with the new attack on civil liberties occasioned by the war on terror, produces new tendencies towards authoritarianism. It is exceptionally tempting in this situation to see the enforcement of rights by courts as an alternative to the choices which might "normally" be taken by democratic legislatures. The story I have told above indicates that weak democracy and the failure of constitutional institutions is the greatest threat to the achievement of rights. Where they fail the courts cannot take their place. Executives and legislatures must be strong, effective, and democratically accountable before courts can have a really effective role. Without this there is no reason why governments should take any notice of courts at all. Early in this paper I noted the obvious, that in the authoritarian one party states in Africa, the rule of law and rights were both ignored. But sometimes democracy itself can create conditions of the absence of political accountability where the governing party has no prospect of defeat.

I shall end by posing two questions. The first concerns cultural indigeneity. The constitutions and constitutional practices which failed in Africa were all imported. I have noted the persistent search for an African version which has romantic vision but as yet few answers. What role might there be for African cultural traditions or legal concepts to be a part of a developing African constitutional tradition? Is constitutionalism something other a technology of rule? Invoking of African tradition was a common part of constitutional discourse in Commonwealth Africa. The major component was the notion of African consensual politics, and the foreign nature of an official 'Opposition' to governing authority. This cultural discourse was a core part of rejection of liberal democratic and constitutionalist politics. But could it amount to anything else? This is ultimately a more important question than the much traversed discussion of whether rights are universal or cultural.

The second relates to the virtual unanimity of the political science literature which limits the ability to sustain democracy to countries which have a certain level of GNP and a "middle class" with an effective interest in defending property and other rights.[61] If this is the case what is the fate of the countries of Africa which do not meet these criteria and which will not meet them in the foreseeable future? We need to imagine how poor countries are to be governed. They appear to have rejected developmental authoritarianism. But what future awaits them?[62]

In conclusion, let us not put to great a burden on the courts and their powers of creativity in interpretation. It is the politicians who must deliver the promises of the constitution and it is in the political (and public) cultures that respect for rights must be founded. Courts can certainly contribute to this, their contribution is vital but theirs is unlikely to be the largest contribution. And while traditional public law scholarship has put its emphasis on the need to control executive power, in the African context it is the lack of executive capacity that is a greater problem. Without this capacity no basic rights can be fulfilled even by governments willing to abide by courts' decisions.

In his seminal article Rustow[63] distinguished between the transition to democracy, and its "habituation." The problem of habituation remains the key to maintaining constitutional democracy in Africa. Bills of Rights may contain the ultimate promises of transition but it may be that their role in the establishing of rights discourses in the political society at large, rather than the success of High Courts in "imposing" duties on governments that they are unable to fulfil, will be the core of the contribution of "rights." Sensitivity to the problems of habituation, such as maintaining the integrity of electoral processes; and routine embedding of a rule of law orientation in the both the political leadership and the bureaucracy; and the acceptance of a separation of powers culture, appear to me to be the primary matters, which Rights may follow, but not precede.

[1] The title of this paper is adapted from Lord Acton's remark that the French in 1789 had borrowed from the Americans 'their theory of revolution not their theory of government – their cutting but not their sewing'. Quoted in Fareed Zakaria, *The Future of Freedom: Illiberal Democracy at Home and Abroad*, (New York: W.W. Norton, 2003), 44.

[2] E Hutchful, 'Reconstructing Political Space: Militarism and Constitutionlism', in Issa G. Shivji, *State and Constitutionalism: An African Debate on Democracy* (Harare: Sapes Books, 1991), 192.

[3] *See* Robert I. Rotberg, ed. *When States Fail: Causes and Consequences* (Princeton: Princeton University Press, 2003) and Martin Chanock, "Customary Law, Sustainable Development and the Failing State," in *The Role of Customary Law in Sustainable Development*, edited by Peter Orebech, et al. (Cambridge: Cambridge University Press, 2005), 338-83.

[4] *See, e.g.*, Sheldon Garon, Patricia L. Maclachlan, and Francis Fukuyama, ed. *State Building: Governance and World Order in the 21st Century* (Ithaca: Cornell University Press, 2004).

[5] *See* Thomas Carothers, "The Rule of Law Revival," *Foreign Affairs* 77, n. 2 (1998).

[6] Very large sums of aid money have been spent on rule of law and democracy projects. *See* Heinz Klug, *Constituting Democracy* (Cambridge: Cambridge University Press, 2000).

[7] *Sub-Saharan Africa: From Crisis to Sustainable Growth: a Long Term Perspective Study* (Washington D C: World Bank 1989) and *Adjustment in Africa: Reforms, Results, and the Way Ahead)* Washington D.C: World Bank, 1994). *See also* Hernando De Soto, *The Mystery of Capital: Why Capitalism Triumphs in the West and Fails Everywhere Else* (London: Black Swan, 2000).

[8] *Quoted in* B. O. Nwabueze, *Constitutionalism in the Emerging States* (London: C. Hurst, 1973), 55. De Smith's lack of faith is of note in that he was the leading English legal authority on the constitutional design of the new states.

[9] Aristide R. Zolberg, "The Structure of Political Conflict in the New States of Tropical Africa," *American Political Science Review* 62 (1968).

[10] Id. at 72.

[11] Richard Sklar, "Developmental Democracy," *Comparative Studies in Society and History* 29 (1987): 686.

[12] Id.

[13] Samuel Huntington, *quoted in* Sklar, "Developmental Democracy." 687.

[14] Ib. at 687.

[15] Sklar, "Developmental Democracy," 690, 709.

[16] There are notable exceptions. In particular, *see* books by B. O. Nwabueze; *Constitutionalism in the Emerging States*; *Judicialism in Commonwealth Africa* (London: C. Hurst, 1977); *Presidentialism in Commonwealth Africa* (London: C. Hurst 1974); *Nigeria's Presidential Constitution 1979-1983 The Second Experiment in Constitutional Democracy* (London: Longman, 1985). *See also*, the laudable classic, Yash P.Ghai, *Public law and Political Change in Kenya: A Study of the Legal Framework of Government from Colonial Times to the Present* (London: Oxford University Press, 1970).

[17] In an echo of the earlier 'development now, democracy later' paradigm of the 1960s we have the emergence of a 'marketisation now, democracy later' view. *See* Fareed Zakaria, *The Future of Freedom*.

[18] *See* David Nelken, "Comparatists and Transferability," in *Comparative Legal Studies: Traditions and Transitions*, ed. Pierre Legrand and Roderick Mundy (Cambridge: Cambridge University Press, 2003), 437 et seq. The literature of the legal donors is instrumental, and has little intimation of failure. There is not much sense in it of the political struggles within receiving countries; or more generally of the problems which might emerge from the modernisation paradigm.

[19] *See* Rachel Murray, *Human Rights in Africa: From the OAU to the African Union* (Cambridge: Cambridge University Press, 2004), 99 et seq. for an account of how the African Union has now adopted the whole democratic and human rights 'package.' The Constitutive Act of the African Union, adopted in 2000, commits states to democracy, while the African Charter on Human and Peoples rights contains both a bill of rights and, in chapter two, a distinctive statement of duties. *See* 'Appendices.'

[20] Shivji, *State and Constitutionalism*, 187.

[21] Shivji, *State and Constitutionalism*, 42.

[22] E Hutchful, 'Reconstructing', in Shivji, *State and Constitutionalism*, 186.

[23] Id. Looking towards the future some identified as a reason for failure the absence of any wider popular involvement in the processes of constitution making. The post-colonial constitutions were negotiated without popular involvement, as were many of the later wave. The processes adopted to

foster wide involvement in the production of South Africa's final constitution, and those in Kenya were departures from this mode, though the Kenyan attempt may not have succeeded.

[24] For my own comments, see "A Post-Calvinist Catechism or a Post-Communist Manifesto? Intersecting Narratives in the South African Bill of Rights Debate" in *Promoting Human Rights Through Bills of Rights*, ed. Philip Alston (Oxford: Oxford University Press, 1999) and "Human Rights and Cultural Branding: Who Speaks and How" in *Cultural Transformation and Human Rights in Africa*, ed. Abdullahi A. An-Na'im (London: Zed Books, 2002). *See also* the other essays in this volume and Yash Ghai, *Human Rights and Governance: the Asia Debate* (Asia Foundation, Occasional Paper, 1994).

[25] *See* Crawford Young, *The African State in Comparative Perspective* (New Haven: Yale University Press, 1994).

[26] *See, e.g.,* E.Hutchful, Reconstructing', in Shivji, *State and Constitutionalism*, 185 et seq.; Achille Mbembe, *On the Postcolony* (Berkeley: University of California Press, 2001); Jean-Francois Bayart, *The State in Africa: the Politics of the Belly* (London: Longman, 1993).

[27] Shivji, *State and Constitutionalism*, 27 et seq.

[28] Of course the devolution of democratic constitutions in countries formerly part of the British Empire was nothing new. It had been done in the case of the white dominions (including South Africa) and was underway in Asia. India, Pakistan, Sri Lanka, Burma, and Malaysia had all become independent before the process began in Africa. The constitutions given to African countries were developed in these earlier processes.

[29] *See, e.g.,* J.M. Lee, *Colonial Development and Good Government* (Oxford: Clarendon Press, 1967); A. B. Cohen, *British Policy in Changing Africa* (London: Routledge and Kegan Paul, 1959).

[30] *See* the volumes in the series *British Documents on the End of Empire* London: Institute of Commonwealth Studies.

[31] In the account given by the Foreign Office. See UK National Archives, FO 371/152113 'Democracy in Backward Countries' Steering Committee Report. This was a year after Ghana's independence. Dulles, explained the British embassy in Washington, had been essentially worried about Latin America where dictatorial regimes were outmoded but were leaving no foundations for popular institutions.

[32] *See* A. Stockwell, 'Ending the British Empire: What Did They Think They Were Doing?' (Egham: Royal Holloway University, 1999).

[33] *Quoted in* J. N. D. Anderson, ed. *Changing Law in Developing Countries* (London: Allen and Unwin, 1963), 85. This was before the notorious U.S.S.R. Constitution of 1936 with its extensive and meaningless Bill of Rights.

[34] *See* A. W. Brian Simpson, *Human Rights and the End of Empire: Britain and the Genesis of the European Convention* (London: Oxford University Press, 1991). Fundamental scepticism remained in Britain. Lord Chandos had diverted early Nigerian suggestions of a bill of rights by saying about the constitution 'Why not put in God is Love?' Id. at 863.

[35] The key discussion is in run up to Nigerian independence when the Willink Commission came up with the strategy of offering a Bill of Rights in lieu of creating more states Cmnd 505, 1958. (London; Her Majesty's Stationery Office)

[36] *See* B. O. Nwabueze, *Judicialism in Commonwealth Africa*; A. N. E. Amissah, *The Contribution of the Courts to Government: A West African View* (Oxford: Clarendon Press, 1981); Kwasi Prempeh, 'A New Jurisprudence for Africa,' *Journal of Democracy* 10 (1999). The deployment of English precedents, such as the notorious majority judgement in *Liversidge v. Anderson*, 1942 A C 206, dampened efforts to hold Ministers accountable for decisions.

[37] Because it was the first so-called black African state to receive independence. The Sudan was the first African state to do so, (not counting white South Africa's independence). After decolonisation in 1956 its democracy quickly deteriorated, culminating in a military coup.

[38] There was and is a fundamental difficulty in framing African constitutions (in both explicit terms and ideological underpinnings) that are 'African.' *See* E.Hutchful, 'Reconstructing', in Shivji, *State and Constitutionalism*, noting the 1968 constitutional proposals in Ghana "claimed to have extracted its recommendations from values "animating our traditional social institutions" but is in fact replete with quotations from Locke, Mill and Plato." Id. at 199.

[39] An example which was followed by Ghana's state sanctioned executions of former Heads of State. After the overthrow of civilian President Hill Liman in 1982, the Rawlings regime 'tried' and executed Generals Afrifa, Acheampong, and Akuffo.

[40] *See* B. O. Nwabueze, *Presidentialism*. The idea was to make executives secure by reducing their dependence on legislative support and giving them the necessary strength, by constitutional means, to

carry out heir developmental tasks. This change, it was thought, would do away with the temptation for executives to sweep their constitutions aside.

[41] For President Julius Kambarage Nyerere's views on constitutionalism, law and democracy see *Freedom and Unity* (Dar es Salaam: Oxford University Press, 1967); and *Freedom and Socialism* (Dar es Salaam: Oxford University Press, 1968).

[42] *Quoted in* Jennifer A. Widner, *Building the Rule of Law: Francis Nyali and the Road to Judicial Independent in Africa* (New York: W. W. Norton, 2001), 28. For Georges' speeches in full *see* R. W. James and F. M. Kassam, *Law and its Administration in a One Party State. Selected Speeches of Telford Georges.* (Nairobi: East African Literature Bureau, 1993).

[43] Widner, *Building the Rule of Law*, 107-08.

[44] Id.

[45] *See* Robert Martin, *Personal Freedom and the Law in Tanzania: A Study of Socialist State Administration* (Nairobi: Oxford University Press, 1974) (an example of a 'progressive' discounting of the value of liberal human rights in Tanzania).

[46] *See* C.M. Peter, *Human Rights in Tanzania Selected Cases and Materials* (Koln: Rudige Koppe Verlag, , 1997) and Luitfried Mbunda, "Securing Human Rights Through the Rule of Law in Tanzania" in *Human Rights, the Rule of Law, and Development in Africa*, ed. Paul Tiyambe Zelesa and Philip J. McConnaughay (Philadelphia: University of Pennsylvania Press, 2004), 144 et seq.

[47] This was probably the most significant attempt to create a state built on African concepts of government. *See* Holger Bernt Hansen and Michael Twaddle, *From Chaos to Order: the Politics of Constitution-Making in Uganda* (London: James Currey, 1995); *Changing Uganda: the Dilemmas of Structural Adjustment and Revolutionary Change* (London: James Currey, 1991).

[48] *See* Ghai and McAuslan, *Public Law.*

[49] *See* Colin Leys, *The Rise and Fall of Development Theory* (Oxford: James Currey, 1996). On the shift from modernization theory to the development of underdevelopment, *see* Walter Rodney, *How Europe Underdeveloped Africa* (Dar es Salaam: London and Tanzanian Publishing House, 1972) and Andre Gunder Frank, *On Capitalist Underdevelopment* (New York: Oxford University Press, 1975). *See also*, Robert B. Seidman, *State, Law and Development* (London: Croom Helm, 1978).

[50] *See* Rita Abrahamsen, *Disciplining Democracy: Development Discourse and Good Government in Africa* (London: Zed Books, 2000).

[51] H Okoth Ogendo 'Constitutions Without Constitutionalism', in Shivji, *State and Constitutionalism*, 11.

[52] Shivji, *State and Constitutionalism*, 30-31.

[53] E. Hutchful, Reconsturction' in Shivji *State and Constitutionalism*, 189.

[54] *Sub-Saharan Africa: From Crisis to Sustainable Growth: a Long Term Perspective Study* (Washington D C: World Bank, 1989) and *Adjustment in Africa: Reforms, Results, and the Way Ahead* (Washington D.C.: World Bank, 1994).

[55] As Widner notes, in the era of state led development the government was necessarily a party to many legal disputes – as a major employer, investor, contractor and supplier. Widner, *Building the Rule of Law*, 26. Its courts could not readily treat it as just another litigant. Widner writes, liberalization "lowered the stake executive branch officials had in controlling the courts, and created a private sector constituency for an independent judiciary," Id.

[56] On the state, *see* Fukuyama, *State Building*. Significant pressure on the corruption issue is being exerted by donor states and institutions.

[57] Abdullahi A. An-Na'im, 'The National Question, Secession and Constitutionalism: The Mediation of Conflicting Claims to Self-Determination', in Shivji, *State and Constitutionalism*, 101-15. On importance of national unity, *see* Dankwart A. Rustow, "Transitions to Democracy: Toward a Dynamic Model" reprinted in *Transitions to Democracy*, ed. Lisa Anderson (New York City: Columbia University Press, 1999), 14 et seq.

[58] Shivji, *State and Constitutionalism*, 35; E. Hutchful, 'Reconsturction', in ibid, 198.

[59] In addition to greater inequalities the market can inflame ethnic tensions. *See* Amy Chua, *World on Fire* (London: Heinemann, 2003).

[60] For declining political engagement in South Africa *see* Robert S Mattes, "South Africa: Democracy Without the People?," *Journal of Democracy* 13 (2002).

[61] *See, e.g.,* Seymour Lipset's seminal article, "Some Social Requisites of Democracy: Economic Development and Political Legitimacy," *American Political Science Review* 53 (1959); Dankwart A.

Rustow, "Transitions;" Samuel P. Huntington's well known monographs *Political Order in Changing Societies* (New Haven: Yale University Press, 1968) and *The Third Wave: Democratisation in the late 20th century* (Norman: University of Oklahoma Press, 1991); and the recent study by Adam Przeworski et al., *Democracy and Development: Political Institutions and Well-Being in the World, 1950-1990* (Cambridge: Cambridge University Press, 2000).

[62] In 1987 the historian Michael Crowder wrote, in a widely read paper, that the ambition to establish liberal democracy in Africa was not an African one, but a 'Eurocentric dream'. Michael Crowder, "Whose dream was it anyway? Twenty Five Years of African Independence," *African Affairs* 86 (1987).

[63] Rustow, "Transitions."

CHAPTER 5

JUDICIAL REVIEW: CAN MINORITY PROTECTION JUSTIFY A CONSTITUTIONALISATION OF THE ECONOMY?

Brian Flanagan**

The conventional focus of the socio-economic rights debate is whether judges should be granted the same scope in the protection of welfare interests that they possess in relation to other interests. The latter are typically described as 'first generational' and include, for instance, the interest in voting, in speaking one's mind and in associating with one's friends and allies. In the common law world, such interests are generally justiciable as matters of constitutional law. Legal discussion thus leads to an argument over the constitutional justiciability of socio-economic interests – whether one should have a legally enforceable right to a particular quantity or quality of consumption not clearly specified by an enacted text.

Disputing scholars tend to shy away from substantive moral theory when formulating a position on justiciability; instead they concentrate on neutral concepts such as polycentricity,[1] positivity,[2] universality,[3] and imperfect obligation.[4] This is not the place for a detailed discussion of the merits of these ideas, but it is submitted that there is a limit to what they can achieve in the context of what is primarily a normative debate. One reason why theorists and commentators prefer to base their arguments on justiciability on neutral rather than normative grounds is that the alternative is to leave their conclusions open to peremptory rejection by ideological counterparts. This paper attempts to address this problem. Though it outlines a model for addressing the justiciability of welfare interests that proceeds on overtly moral footings, they are footings which, in principle, many partisans would accept. In summary, they are (a) the notion that societies ought to make basic provision for their indigent members and (b) that a society's political decisions ought to correspond to the political inclinations of its members. These ideas are placed in the context of the modest distinctions that seem to exist in the structure of socio-economic and civil-political rights. I conclude that socio-economic interests should not be made constitutionally justiciable. This is far from the only or demonstrably best conclusion that can be drawn from the interplay of these moral propositions and the structural characteristics of first and second generational rights. However, it is an effort to tackle the issue in a way that is apposite to the moral substance of the task while avoiding an ideological posture which would leave it summarily irrelevant to one half of the debate. The terms of argument will be presented, followed by the case itself.

1. 'RIGHTS'

In any debate involving 'rights,' clarity as to the meaning of the term is essential. This is particularly the case in the socio-economic debate since the question of justiciability tends to invite circular reasoning as to the relationship between law and morality. In a society, an individual or group right is a means to an end; he who has a right to X can, in principle, receive the social means by which he can satisfy the morally legitimate interest society has deemed him to have in the realisation of X. For present purposes, we may assume that an element of the social means denoted by any given 'right' will be justiciability – be that a cause of (legal) action on the basis of a detailed statutory provision *or* on the basis of an imprecise constitutional text. The 'right' to X is simply a function of society's normative judgment that X is a legitimate interest for the individual or group to realise.[5] Thus a right is not itself a moral phenomenon but a tool with which moral phenomena are realised. Consequently, if the marshalling of social means in relation to moral phenomena could be divided into conceptually distinct categories, we could not draw any normative conclusion from this fact alone, since an instrument is not a normative proposition. In order to assess the relative moral merits of the use of different means we need a moral theory. As such, the classification of rights as, say, positive or negative cannot conclude an argument about the legitimacy of a normative proposition, such as whether to recognise socio-economic rights in a given case.[6] Likewise, though we might argue that socio-economic rights entail more financial means than civil rights, we could not draw any conclusion as to whether and how one or the other should be recognised from such arguments alone.

It follows that for a satisfactory understanding of rights, we need to take a careful look at the nature of social means. The means at a society's disposal to achieve normative ends in the individual's interest are enormous compared with the means available to the individual herself – consider how difficult it would be for the individual to enjoy any civil-political or economic interest if she lived under anarchy or in a Hobbesian 'state of nature.' Two broad types of social means present themselves – the tangible and the intangible. Intangible means are those which are the product of will. In most cases, it is a matter of social will whether an individual will be in a position to enjoy a moral interest. At its simplest, there is strength in numbers and if a society resolves to arrest or confine a man, thereby breaching his liberty interest, that is what will happen. This reality is often concealed by the apparent necessity of the prevailing set of power relations within a given society. But an element of 'resolution,' 'choice' or 'will' in the political configuration of a society is invariably present. Without a degree of social support or acquiescence, no would-be leadership can expect (or probably even want) to enforce its ideas on others. This point has nothing to do with majorities or voting; it is simply that the kind of power needed to ensure normative outcomes is nearly always a social rather than individual phenomenon. Its social character means that at a certain level the end to which the power is being directed must be in some way persuasive to the human agents of that power. As such, whatever normative outcomes prevail in a given society are products of their persuasiveness to the agents of its power. Consequently, we can say that if a man is not under arrest or in prison, it will ordinarily be the result of a social choice not to interfere with his freedom of action. As a means of moral action, 'will' is intangible in that it does not in itself possess material qualities; it is quite literally a figment of individual or collective imagination. It is thus unquantifiable and infinitely renewable.[7] By contrast, tangible means possess (or represent) material qualities. They are finite, concrete and measurable. Such means are capable of being given a price by a market and for most purposes they may be captured by the term 'financial resources.' Tangible means need to be physically produced, maintained and reproduced – they cannot simply be imagined.

2. IS PROPERTY A SOCIO-ECONOMIC INTEREST?

The second definitional move is to describe the proper subject matter of the debate. Within Western political culture, the right to private property is historically a 'first generational' right. Conceptually, however, an individual's interest in private property is indistinguishable from her interest in the social provision of a consumption minimum. Evidence of this point is apparent from a brief analysis of an antithesis – Robert Nozick's celebrated libertarian manifesto, *Anarchy, State, and Utopia*.[8] In short, Nozick's theory holds that the only just transaction is a voluntary one. Hence, justice requires only a minimal state in which taxation may be levied to assure public order and the protection of just transactions but which excludes the redistribution of wealth for other reasons. Nozick premised this position on a rejection of John Rawls' idea that inequalities in natural talents (and in the character it takes to exploit them) should be offset on the ground that, being the product of genetic inheritance, environment and upbringing, they are undeserved.[9] On the contrary, if these dimensions of human beings were subtracted, even for the sake of argument, no coherent conception of a 'person' would remain.[10] The tension here is evident; in advocating the retention of the social means required to preserve the institutions of private property and bodily integrity, Nozick sought to neutralise certain human inequalities such as physical strength which might deny weaker or outnumbered wealth generators the enjoyment of their asserted material. In other words, the logical outcome of Nozick's protection of 'just transactions' (ie private property etc.) is a plea for society to offset imbalances in certain personal characteristics, thereby contradicting the basis of his objection to taxation aimed at relieving poverty. The tension reveals the conceptual commonality between welfare and property rights; both involve the assertion of exclusionary interests in material resources and a corresponding demand for the social means to permit the enjoyment of those interests. As Nozick recognised, a state of anarchy provides cold comfort for the prospective property owner. The latter needs the protection of a (ideally minimal) state, but the consequence is that property, like welfare, becomes a social good, such that categorical distinctions between the nature of property and welfare as moral claims become redundant.[11] In light of this conceptual unity, it is not surprising that commentators sympathetic to the notion of justiciable welfare rights find private property a particularly unsustainable element of theories privileging the justiciability of first generational rights.[12] However, in their focus on the proper organisation of material resources, theories of property and welfare are conceptually distinct from theories of civil-political interests, such as the interests in voting, speech, assembly, association and strike which focus on the proper organisation of social decision-making. In section 4, we shall see the relevance of this distinction for questions of constitutional justiciability.

It would be remiss to finalise the proper scope of the socio-economic justiciability debate without considering the contribution of Ernst-Ulrich

Petersmann.[13] In the context of international trade law, Petersmann has characterised the freedom of contract (and certain other economic 'freedoms') as an indivisible member of the family of 'liberty' interests that includes conventional civil-political interests. If this were the case, an implicit conceptual dichotomy would be established between an individual's moral interest in the material for which he has freely contracted with another and his interest in any non-contracted material that he claims for his welfare. In other words, if freedom of contract were recognised as an individual liberty interest, it would be difficult to object to a construction of the right to specifically transacted material resources as a conceptually different moral claim on our attention than welfare rights. Via its association with civil-political interests, the former could be characterised as concerning the allocation of social decision-making rather than the allocation of material resources. Such a conceptual difference would pave the way for a possible distinction in justiciability between welfare and property without the need for a theorist to pronounce private property as morally more important than the availability of a consumption minimum.

The theoretical foundation of Petersmann's vision is that the freedom of contract derives from our inherent human dignity. One problem with this is that the freedom of contract for labour or resources is a liberty interest which can only be enjoyed by those who are productive or who are favoured by the productive. Since productive humans are only a subset of mankind, we are left with people whose inherent dignity is not represented or expressed by an interest in the freedom of contract. As such, it is difficult to appreciate the deontological necessity for it to be protected as a 'human' interest. Conversely, it could be argued that the fact that the interest in individual self-determination cannot be meaningfully exercised by children or the mentally disabled is not seen as affecting its status as a *human* interest in most moral theories. Likewise, a solution to the human dignity problem could be sought in the introduction of a redistributive economic system which would permit all to enjoy some of the material fruits of the 'Invisible Hand.' On closer scrutiny, however, neither argument is adequate for the task. The status of childhood or the possession of a mental disability indicates that full mental human maturity has not been reached. The extent of the right of children and the mentally disabled to self-determination grows in a manner proportionate to their mental development. Yet we do not consider unemployed persons generally to lack any form of human maturity.[14] As a group, what such people lack is a job, not the capacity to make moral claims on society at a level *formally* equal to that of other members of society. Of course, a number of other factors may well impact on moral demands that the unemployed might assert, say, to a second home or a weekend at the Ritz. But these demands will not be morally evaluated according to whether unemployed claimants deserve free access to such resources; rather they will be evaluated according to whether claimants *generally* deserve free access to such resources. In other words, the unemployed would be recognised by society as fully formed moral agents. Moreover, children and the mentally disabled have partial rights to exercise self-determination in the sense that a society rarely permits their compulsion unless it is hypothetically in their best interest, whereas the unemployed may not exercise any right to trade despite it being generally accepted as in their best interest to do so. Evidently, this analysis proceeds on foot of certain moral assumptions; but accepting these, it is clear that while the affirmation of human dignity may involve self-determination for every mature individual, it does not entail the freedom of contract.[15]

The second defence of the moral importance of contractual freedom is to say that market rights create wealth – wealth which can be redistributed to ensure that every individual enjoys at least a consumption minimum.[16] But this approach is merely an instrumental method of grounding the freedom of contract; it does not provide it with a moral basis in its own right. Moreover, a deontological defence of the freedom of contract premised on the notion of compulsory redistribution involves the use of an antithetical condition – thus calling the freedom's coherence into question. Undoubtedly, both generations of rights require the redistribution of resources; the right to vote necessitates the provision of polling booths and staff, the right to protest involves the provision of policing. Yet the redistribution required to facilitate such rights is not antithetical to their raison d'être. Certainly the right to free expression sometimes requires regulation so as to allow everyone to exercise it. But while the regulation of speaking slots might be regarded as antithetical to a restricted individual's right to speak, given sufficient time, there would be no need for such regulation. In this context, time and other resources can be characterised as external factors, which would, if available, remove the necessity to curtail the individual interest protected by the right to free expression so that this interest might be properly protected within a community of similar interests. However, even if people had an abundance of time in which to trade or acquire skills, the unlucky and unqualified would remain unable to protect their interest in a minimum level of consumption via the right to trade. With the freedom of contract, there is a direct and ineluctable conflict between an individual's interest in 'his' material and the material redistribution necessary to assure the material interests of humans generally. Within a market morality, there are no 'external' factors which might alleviate the need to curtail an individual's interest so as to protect each individual's interest, since there can be no concept of a market without scarcity. In short, the 'right to contract' is not a credible question of morality as it cannot be coherently reconciled with even a formal theory of moral equality. It should not therefore muddy discussion as to the appropriate legal response to moral claims on the material resources under a society's ultimate control. Thus, the second definitional move focuses our attention on the central issue in the justiciability debate; whether there is any reason for a society to treat an individual's economic interests – to both property and welfare – as less justiciable than his civil-political interests.

3. DEMOCRACY AND MORALITY: SOME PRELIMINARIES

Space does not permit a defence of the notion that a society's politics ought to be sensitive to the views of its inhabitants or the view that those politics should be sensitive to the basic needs of its indigent members. But a little clarification of what is meant by political sensitivity is in order. The question of whether a political arrangement is democratic is irrelevant to the question of whether that arrangement is as democratic as we would like. The former is a matter of observation – are political decisions made by processes governed by political equality? The latter is a question of critical morality – what does the theorist think? If a political arrangement has been produced by a democratic mechanism, it is democratic regardless of the views of any theorist on the democratic credentials of that arrangement (as opposed to those of the mechanism which produced it). But a theorist may locate herself in the realm of theorising about justice rather than theorising about law. If so, her views on the democracy of political arrangements that have been democratically enacted could be compelling. It is from this critical moralist perspective that my argument proceeds.[17]

The first point to note is that there can be no equation of the democratic credentials of a directly, regularly elected legislature with those of an appointed, securely tenured court. Other things being equal, when set in opposition, the views of the latter cannot claim to represent the will of the electorate since they operate only to replace a more immediate and direct imprint of that will with an older, more remote one.[18] In this regard, Marius Pieterse has argued that:

> [t]he process of rights-based judicial review may further be said to require awareness of and sensitivity to societal convictions to an extent far greater than that of legislating and as such it may be said that, compared to the legislative process, 'judicial review facilitates a better reflection and implementation of the will of the people'. This is arguably illustrated by the reality that the public make use of the judiciary to secure basic rights where they are unable to do so through more direct democratic means.[19]

Evidently, it is likely that citizens will tend to use all convenient means at their disposal to move the politics of their society in a favourable direction. The fact that all individuals have the opportunity to overturn assembly decisions by way of judicial review does not make the practice democratic. When an individual participates on an equal basis with the other members of a society in the election of its legislators, the ensuing legislation cannot be revised without reference to that participation while remaining optimally democratic. The discretionary revisions of a body of judges do not refer to that participation since they do not invoke its terms – the taking into equal account the views of all members of the society on the matter. In referring instead to the participation of a tiny number of lawyers, judicial review undercuts the norm of political equality. Likewise, testing the political responsiveness of an elected assembly cannot be done from the perspective of a securely tenured bench – an election was only held because it was thought to be the best way of determining the legislative intentions of the people. If judges were in a position to differentiate between representative and 'unrepresentative' electoral consequences, there would be little point in holding elections at all given that a more reliable assessment of the views of the people could be furnished by the courts.

But political equality is not the only facet of justice. A theory of the good society that seeks to establish majority rule but which would delimit its operation by reference to certain moral extremities is eminently conceivable. The classic *Carolene Products*[20] scenario of a discrete and insular minority being victimised by a selfish majority is a distinct possibility to which judicial review offers a plausible, if fallible antidote. The prospect of 'stirred up majorities'[21] and populist demagoguery prejudicing vulnerable groups cannot be discounted. Of course, even here, there is no doubt that judicial review comes at a cost in terms of the value of political equality. My argument simply supposes that in some circumstances the balance of justice may fall in favour of establishing such review. Assuming also that the balance favours review for civil-political interests, the question which arises is whether measures that seem injurious to the indigent, qua indigent, are as readily conceivable as incidents of injustice given that a major factor in those decisions will be an assessment of how best to *renew* the *tangible* means at a society's disposal. The case for establishing a securely tenured elite as a remedy for prejudice is that they may be in a better position to treat it than a popularly elected assembly. It seems more doubtful, however, that life tenure and political insulation make one better able to oversee an economy.[22] Equally, all popularly elected majorities, no matter how critically unjust their intentions, would appear to have an interest in the successful stewardship of the national economy.

4. CONSTITUTIONAL JUSTICIABILITY?

The key difficulty with constitutionalising economic rights is that the existence and extent of such rights bear heavily on how well the state can produce material resources. Put simply, economic rights cost more to maintain than civil-political ones.[23] As such, their nature and extent are more consequential for macro-economic policy than civil-political rights. Moreover, economic rights often directly affect how specific economic policy levers may be deployed. Consider the potential implications for national prosperity (positive and negative) of the use of compulsory purchase orders or the regulation of the labour market. The ability to compulsorily purchase land is often of critical importance in the construction of state's basic economic infrastructure. Evidently, the institution of private property is an obstacle to such orders. Where that institution is regulated by a judiciary on the basis of a vague text, the power of elected politicians to direct the economy is undercut. In relation to labour regulation, the setting of a minimum wage may have considerable effects on national productivity, business confidence and incentives to enter the workforce. Where a minimum wage comes under judicial oversight, elected politicians find themselves sharing control of one of the economy's central levers. The point is that rather than simply coming under judicial pressure to manipulate the economy in such a way as to provide sufficient funds for a discrete measure, say, the provision of polling booths, economic rights often require the government to use a particular economic lever in particular fashion. An important part of a government's thinking on which economic interests to recognise as morally compelling is likely to be a perspective on how such recognition will affect the range of economic tools at its disposal. There is no question that the recognition of economic rights has a major impact on the moral interests of directly affected individuals. Crucially, however, it can also have a significant effect on the ability of the state to secure the economic conditions and future revenue required to satisfy all moral claims.[24]

Furthermore, unlike say, dissident political speech or the bodily integrity of criminal suspects, the achievement and maintenance of national prosperity is presumably in the self-interest of all members of the society. For instance, it is likely that a political majority would have a self-interest in arranging for the state-wide provision of education in order for the economy as a whole to maximise its gains from globalised capital. Likewise, it would probably have a self-interest in providing for a utilitarian compulsory purchase regime which (by virtue of its utilitarianism) would occasionally injure the interests of its some of its own members to the general good. Consequently, it seems that welfare and property rights do not deal *solely* in the kind of currency we have taken to represent the strongest case for judicial review, namely the protection of individuals and minorities from majority abuse. In other words, those whose interests lose out in an economic decision appear structurally less likely to have been prejudiced or victimised by that loss because those in the majority have a self-interest in pursuing what they see as rational macroeconomic policies. Economics is of course a deeply politicised science. But it is viewed by virtually all political actors (and evidently by economists) as a rational and scientifically oriented discipline, which, when applied appropriately, generates favourable material outcomes. It seems improbable that any partisan would attach such a utilitarian proviso to a purely moral platform. Thus, when we consider the financial implications of economic rights, the immediacy of their impact on policy formulation and the inevitably forward looking element of economic policymaking, the case for full-bodied economic review by the courts becomes less compelling.

The notion of justiciability encounters a further incidental problem in the interplay between the macroeconomic and fairness aspects of economic decisionmaking. This is brought out in the South African caselaw. An interesting feature of the South African Constitution is that its text appears to establish certain absolute socio-economic rights. In its *Grootboom* decision,[25] the Constitutional Court took a brief and pragmatic look at article 28's seemingly unconditional guarantee of shelter for children.[26] The Court read the article as nominating parents rather than the state as the primary providers of the right to shelter, so as to avoid undercutting article 26's 'within the available resources' saver on the state's duty to provide housing to everyone. While this approach seems economically sensible, it bore a somewhat unconvincing relation to the text, and taken with the robust approach to remedies set out in the *TAC*[27] and *Sibiya*[28] cases, implies that children might have enforceable constitutional rights against their parents should they be unable to supply shelter. Counsel for the state picked up on this point in the *TAC* case,[29] pleading that according to article 28, parents were obliged to provide life-saving AIDS drugs for their children rather than the state. The Court adopted a different approach here however, finding that since parents were unable to provide the medicine, article 28 obliged the state to do so. However in *Grootboom*, the fact that the parents were similarly unable to provide the material in question did not engage the state with an article 28 obligation. The inconsistency seems suggestive of the difficulties which courts face in weighing constitutionalised economic preferences when the economic consequences can vary so greatly.[30]

Assuming a court of last resort has not changed its mind as to the fairness of a precedent, it may still be reluctant to follow it where equivalent individual merits might beget a substantially different economic impact. The court might thus find itself sacrificing fairness for the sake of financial prudence. There is nothing intrinsically wrong with this, nor are such trade-offs entirely absent from civil-political decisions. Nonetheless, as traditionally conceived, courts are primarily concerned with the work of righting wrongs. We may not want to place institutions of this nature in a position where they will be faced with making anti-fairness tradeoffs. Given our institutional expectations, ensuring fairness in individual cases while concurrently maintaining sound macroeconomic policy may be too great a burden for a court of law to bear. The weight of this burden is more apparent when contrasted with that of a legislature, which we tend to imagine as having the luxury of declining to carry its fairness logic through to the ultimate conclusion.

On the other hand, a number of commentators dispute the notion that judiciaries lack advantages over assemblies in relation to economic decisionmaking. Pieterse, for instance, argues that:

> Courts are . . . ideally suited to lend content to social rights and the standards of compliance that they impose. The legal process is rational and deliberative and is tailored towards producing fair and well-reasoned results . . . their knowledge or expertise in specialist policy-making areas may in fact exceed that of members of the legislature or bureaucracy. Further, 'courts handle real cases and thus can test more

effectively the particular implications of abstract principles and discover problems the legislature could not forecast.'[31]

The problem with this kind of argument is that, assuming the truth of its claims, it quickly transforms into a case for giving judges complete control over economic policy. An advocate would have difficulty in limiting judicial control out of respect for political accountability because the argument leaves no metric for determining the importance of that value. We know accountability is not of controlling significance; otherwise it could not be balanced away to permit justiciability. But accountability is not something that can come into play only when we agree with the results reached by politically accountable representatives since that would give no true weight at all to the value of listening to what the electorate thinks. As Pieterse's language suggests – 'expertise,' 'rational,' 'fair and well-reasoned results' – it is difficult to construct a policymaking advantage for courts without an underlying judgment that they tend to make better policy. It is, in turn, difficult to separate that judgment from a judgment as to whether, in a given case, an assembly has made as sound a decision as a court would likely make. An argument for deferring to a legislature which was critically 'wrong' simply because it was directly elected seems doubtful to gain much traction in this equation and political accountability is thus unlikely to bear any real weight. It is worth noting that a theory which assumes that an assembly's decisions have a macroeconomic merit equal to or greater than those of a court can provide a relatively accessible metric for weighing the importance of accountability. Through denying judicial review for moral questions involving substantial amoral factors, such a theory might demonstrate that there would be no case at all for review but for a judicial advantage in getting the moral factors right. As such, it could give real weight to political accountability.

Conversely, by apparently separating the elements of economic decisionmaking that relate to fairness,[32] Justice Albie Sachs of South Africa misconstrues the nature of the potential judicial advantage in this sphere:

An implication of placing social and economic rights in a constitution is to say that decisions which, however well-intended, might have the consequence of producing intolerable hardship, cannot be left solely in the hands of overburdened administrators and legislators. Efficiency is one of the great principles of government. The utilitarian principle of producing the greatest good for the greatest number might well be the starting-off point for the use of public resources. But the qualitative element, based on the respect for the dignity of each one of us, should never be left out. This is where the judiciary, tunnelled in the unshakeable direction of securing respect for human dignity, comes into its own.[33]

In characterising the tension produced by constitutional justiciability as a conflict between the notions of dignity and efficiency, Sachs downplays the nature of the institutional clash. 'Efficiency' is not a property which can be evaluated by reference to one's preferred qualitative or critical morality. It is merely a measure of a legal instrument's effectiveness in achieving a moral end. As such, the desirability of efficiency is solely a function of a normative evaluation of the measure's moral end. A government could never be 'too efficient' and thereby insufficiently attentive to the underlying moral end. On the contrary, if a government offends qualitative morality it can only be the result of its being insufficiently efficient or having a faulty set of moral priorities. In relation to welfare interests, moral priority is largely determined by how much financial resources are due to be distributed for their fulfilment – it always being more efficient vis-à-vis the satisfaction of a particular interest to have more resources with which to treat it. Where a court, believing its economic decisionmaking advantage to lie in correcting 'excesses' of efficiency, sidesteps a confrontation with an assembly's moral priorities for the economy, strange results can emerge. A good example of this is *Grootboom* itself (where Sachs was a member of a unanimous Court). There the Court found fault with the government's denial of short-term shelter to indigent citizens despite an acknowledgment that the concentration of resources on the construction of durable housing would be more efficient in the long run.[34] Thus under the Sachs approach the government was efficient – most durable housing for most people – but insufficiently attentive to its moral goal – it neglected individuals who would be bereft of short-term shelter due to its focus on efficiency.

Logically however, sacrificing durable for short-term shelter inevitably increases the amount of money required to fulfil the efficiency position of the most housing for the most people since the short-term variety must be continually renewed whereas the other is permanent. Increasing the overall shelter budget means changing the state's moral priorities. In other words, Sachs would have to disagree with the government's morality rather than with its zeal for efficiency in order to coherently criticise its neglect of short-term housing. In avoiding that characterisation, Sachs, and the Court itself, settled *Grootboom* by leaving less accommodation of any kind for the indigent in the long-term, that is, an inefficient outcome. Thus it seems that judicial modesty as to the court's strengths in economic decisionmaking may lead to the worst of both worlds – the popular will of the community as to its moral priorities is ignored while the countermanding elite fails to provide a sure path to meet its own moral priorities.

None of this is to say that constitutional justiciability for economic interests is unsupportable, simply that the bar should be higher than it is for civil-political ones. Scenarios where justiciability might be justified due to grievous relational unfairness can certainly be imagined; perhaps the government has decided to provide one race with twice the unemployment assistance provided to another or has denied women the right to hold and alienate property in their own name.[35] Evidently, the question of what constitutes 'grievous relational unfairness' is critical and contentious. Leaving its resolution to one side means leaving any theory of justiciability perilously incomplete. Nevertheless, reliance on such a placeholder does keep the trigger for judicial review in the realm of morality – something which permits a coherent defence of why we should allow judges to second guess elected legislators in the first place.[36] At best, this paper provides only a partial analysis of the constitutional justiciability of economic interests. But insofar as it goes, one plausible idea to emerge is that the greater the financial implications of a decision, the stronger the case for an unelected decision-maker to defer to an elected one. There is moral value in the self-determination expressed by a majoritarian distribution of social means; a value undercut by constitutional justiciability. This difficulty is not overcome by classical judicial strengths since tangible social means would have to play a substantial part in any economically just distribution. As judges lack a natural advantage over elected policymakers in the successful husbandry of such means,[37] my own conclusion is that economic interests should not, as rule, be justiciable.

5. CONCLUSION

Given its implications for a society's manner of government, a positive or negative position on the constitutional justiciability of welfare interests is best served by a moral theory of what society should look like. Two moral values have a compelling case for inclusion in the construction of such a theory – individual self-determination and the basic material well-being of our fellow men and women. Likewise, given the similarity of their demands, theories that call for the justiciability of property interests should either treat welfare interests in like fashion or indicate, in overtly moral terms, why not (and vice versa). The outcome proposed by this paper is the result of only one of a range of possible moral weightings that might be attributed to the interests in play. In particular, the role performed by individual self-determination might be conceived in a more complex manner, with moral value arising both in relation to the proper disposal of material incidentally in the individual's possession, 'micro value,' and as regards the proper distribution of political input into a society's government, 'macro value.' That is, one might imagine a moral case for providing the individual with the social means to control the destiny of resources that have come into her possession via no social institution. As implied above, a potential micro role for self-determination in justifying the individual's control over material resources could not rely on 'the freedom of contract' since the products of contracts are *social* goods which are themselves in need of moral justification. In the absence of more sophisticated moralities, perhaps the simple notion of 'finders' keepers' has a role to play. In any case, it is time for justiciability theorists to join the moral debate.

[1] *See, e.g.*, Lon Fuller, "The Forms and Limits of Adjudication," *Harvard Law Review* 92 (1978): 353.

[2] *See, e.g.*, Richard Posner's judgment in *Jackson v. City of Joliet*, 715 F.2d 1200, 1203 (7th Cir. 1983).

[3] Onora O'Neill, "The Dark Side of Human Rights," *International Affairs* 81 (2005): 427-28.

[4] Amartya Sen, "Elements of a Theory of Human Rights," (2005) 32 *Philosophy & Public Affairs* 32 (2005): 315, 337.

[5] Note that a right does not have to protect the interests of the individual – it can just easily be a tool for the realisation of a moral end deemed (by society) to be legitimately desirable despite its apparently negative implications for individuals.

[6] For example, *Gosselin v. Quebec (Attorney General)*, (2002) 4 SCR 429 (stating, "I leave open the possibility that a *positive* obligation to sustain life, liberty, or security of the person may be made out in *special circumstances*. However, this is not such a case. . . The frail platform provided by the facts of this case cannot support the weight of a positive state obligation of citizen support." (emph. added)). Id. ¶ 83.

[7] It is submitted that the notion of intangibility is the key to unlocking the problem of infinite regress (identified by Tom Palmer in his review of Sunstein and Holmes' *The Cost of Rights: Why Liberty Depends on Taxes*, *Cato Journal* 19 (2) (1999): 332-33) in the conception of rights as a social construction.

[8] Robert Nozick, *Anarchy, State, and Utopia* (New York: Basic Books, 1974).

[9] John Rawls, *A Theory of Justice* (Cambridge: Harvard University Press, 1971).

[10] Hence, his rejection of a state which attempts to alleviate poverty by taxing those who are wealthy.

[11] The point is not that moral ideas such as 'earning' and 'need' do not conflict in interesting and consequential ways in attempts to theorise the correct approach to property and welfare. Rather, it is that both property and welfare concern the proper *social* organisation of material resources.

[12] *See* Ciarán Lawlor, "The Conscience of the Nation: Socio-Economic Rights and the Irish Constitution," *University of Calif. Davis L. Rev.* 5 (2005): 56-57.

[13] Ernst-Ulrich Petersmann has developed the ideas discussed below in several publications; for convenience I will concentrate on their exposition in "Time for a United Nations 'Global Compact' for Integrating Human Rights into the Law of Worldwide Organisations: Lesson from European Integration," *European Journal of International Law* 13 (2002): 621-50.

[14] If we did, we would have to imagine large swathes of the population of many countries as critically immature at one time or another during their adult lives.

[15] In effect, both Petersmann and I are using the term 'dignity' as a placeholder for 'that which is morally required.' Id.

[16] *See* Petersmann, "Taking Human Dignity, Poverty and Empowerment of Individuals More Seriously: Rejoinder to Alston," (paper presented to the Jean Monnet Working Paper No.12/02, Symposium: Trade and Human Rights: An Exchange, New York City, U.S., 2002) *available at* http://www.jeanmonnetprogram.org/papers/02/021201-03.rtf. "The basic EC and WTO guarantees of liberty [of contract] and non-discrimination [amongst economic actors] should also be recognized . . . as human rights protecting personal liberty and human dignity. . . [J]ust as EU protection of human rights has usefully complemented protection under the ECHR, so too consideration of the human rights obligations of WTO Members in interpreting WTO rules could . . . help create the resources needed for the enjoyment of human rights." Id. at 3-4.

[17] By contrast, in characterising the institution of judicial review as undemocratic, the recent liberal challenge to it invokes questions of *legal* theory. *See, e.g.*, Jeremy Waldron's "The Core of the Case Against Judicial Review," *Yale Law Journal* 115 (2006): 1346 and *Law and Disagreement* (New York: OUP, 1999). For a critique, *see* Brian Flanagan, "Judicial Rights Talk: Defects in the Liberal Challenge to Judicial Review," *South African Journal on Human Rights* 22 (2006): 173.

[18] Evidently, this relative elderliness and remove also applies to the constitutional text whose enactment typically pre-dates by some time the enactment of the legislation that is the subject of judicial review.

[19] Marius Pieterse, "Coming to Terms with Judicial Enforcement of Socio-Economic Rights," *South African Journal on Human Rights* 20 (2004): 391.

[20] *United States v. Carolene Products Co.*, 304 U.S. 144 (1938). In this otherwise unremarkable case, Justice Harlan Stone planted the seeds for a new approach to judicial review. In footnote four, Stone cautiously asserted that certain types of legislation might not merit presumptive judicial deference as to their constitutional validity. His most noted proviso was the suggestion that prejudice directed against discrete and insular minorities may call for a 'more searching judicial inquiry.'

[21] U.S. Supreme Court Justice Ruth Ginsburg, "Looking Beyond our Borders: The Value of a Comparative Perspective in Constitutional Adjudication," *Yale Law & Policy Review* 22 (2004): 329.

[22] I am conscious of the substantial economic power granted by elected politicians to central bankers. However, the analogy is imperfect in that states which have delegated monetary policy to unelected bodies invariably reserve fiscal and budgetary policy powers for politicians. Likewise, politicians tend to exercise greater control over central bankers than they do over judges – with the exception of the European Central Bank, I am not aware of any central bank whose institutional command over interest rates is constitutionally prescribed. Nor I am familiar with any state (including the Eurozone) whose central bankers enjoy constitutionally guaranteed security of tenure (the ECB's chief decision-making body is largely comprised of serving national central bank governors). For a brief discussion of 'oversight' see n. 25.

[23] In the UK, for instance, the state's public expenditure is highly biased towards funding economic interests. See the departmental breakdown for 2002/03, http://www.hm-treasury.gov.uk/media/1BD/28/1BD2833C-BCDC-D4B3-166DB51D1D949FA3.xls. Excluding subventions to Northern Ireland, Scotland, Whales and local government, the cumulative capital and resource spend for the 'socio-economic' departments of Education, Health, Transport, Industry, Environment, International Development, Work and Pensions and the Chancellor amounts to over two thirds of total public expenditure. In truth, this underestimates the proportion of resources spent on economic interests since it takes no account of the property protecting functions of law enforcement, justice and defence expenditure, not to mention the 'socio-economic' nature of most local government spending (see http://www.lga.gov.uk/Documents/Publication/localgovtmatters05.pdf at 8). Likewise, a departmental breakdown of Ireland's Current Expenditure Projections for 2007 and 2008 reveals public spending to be directed mainly towards socio-economic rather than civil-political interests; see http://www.budget.gov.ie/2006/downloads/BudgetTables.xls (Table 4a). The budgetary tilt of the British and Irish exchequers tallies with what one would expect to find in a modern welfare state. Given that Ireland and Britain have each maintained a fairly constant (and high) level of individual civil-political freedom since the 1920's, we can be relatively confident that civil-political rights may be successfully maintained independently of the establishment of 'social democracy.' Moreover, the tilt suggests that the packages of socio-economic rights Western societies regard as morally compelling are significantly more demanding on their tangible resources than the equivalently treasured packages of civil-political rights. Indeed, Cass Sunstein and Stephen Holmes essentially concede as much in their book, *The Cost of Rights: Why Liberty Depends on Taxes* (New York: WW Norton, 1999). 'From the perspective of public finance, the three generations of rights occupy a continuum, rather than being radically distinct kinds of claims.' Id. at 127.

[24] It is useful to be clear on what exactly judicial 'oversight' implies. It is not necessarily a question of judges being involved in the creation or administration of policy. Rather it is the existence of an institution that may potentially countermand the decisions of the policymakers and administrators. To the extent that they operate in this capacity, judges bear a measure of responsibility for government policy insofar as its maintenance is dependent on their (often tacit) assent. Likewise, government policymakers seem likely to formulate their policies in line with what they expect are the 'red lines' of an overseeing judiciary.

[25] *Government of the RSA v. Grootboom*, (11) BCLR 1169 (CC).

[26] Art. 28(1) Every child has the right . . . (c.) to basic nutrition, shelter, basic health care services and social services. Constitution of the Republic of South Africa Art. 28(1).

[27] *Minister of Health v. Treatment Action Campaign (TAC)*, 2002 (10) BCLR 1033 (CC).

[28] *Sibiya v. Dir. of Public Prosecutions (Johannessburg High Court)*, 2005 (1) SA 105.

[29] Id. at ¶ 76.

[30] In *TAC*, the state could have provided the disputed medicine at little or no cost. *Minister of Health v. TAC*.

[31] See *Carolene Products*, 394.

[32] As opposed to macroeconomic policy. In effect, macroeconomic policy is a forward looking species of 'efficiency' that is focussed on the husbandry of resources for future use This may be contrasted with the notion of efficiency in the use of resources. Put differently, macroeconomic policy concerns keeping the goose which lays the golden eggs, Sachs' efficiency concerns the methods of distributing those eggs.

[33] Justice Albie Sachs, "The Judicial Enforcement of Socio-Economic Rights," (Inaugural Human Rights Lecture, Law Society of Ireland, June 23, 2005), 10.

[34] Holding that "[t]he nationwide housing programme falls short of obligations imposed upon national government to the extent that it fails to recognise that the state must provide for relief for those in desperate need. They are not to be ignored in the interests of an overall programme focussed on medium and long-term objectives." *Grootboom*, ¶ 66.

[35] Assuming a resource scarce scenario, the only way an analysis of economic justice can logically proceed is through an examination of relational fairness, that is, equality analysis. Thus, it is not possible to draw a coherent distinction between a constitutional equality guarantee which is used to review socio-economic justice and a constitutionalised socio-economic right.

[36] *See* notes 21 and 32.
[37] Note that this is not based on the idea that judiciaries are inherently worse at creating macroeconomic policy, simply that they seem to have no particular advantage in the area.

** I would like to thank Christopher McCrudden, Jeff King, Penelope Andrews, Ciarán Lawlor, Richard Waghorne and David Whelan for their valuable comments on earlier drafts of this article. The usual disclaimer applies.

CHAPTER 6

JUDICIAL INDEPENDENCE IN AUSTRALIA AND SOUTH AFRICA: COMPARATIVE LESSONS

Denise Meyerson

There are complex connections between the doctrine of separation of powers and the rule of law. In this article I focus specifically on the connection between the rule of law and the separation of judicial power, showing how the separation of judicial from executive and legislative power serves the rule of law by placing the adjudication of controversies in the hands of a branch of government which can be relied upon to adjudicate disputes independently and impartially. Relying on this analysis, I criticise the approach of the South African and Australian courts to the exercise of non-judicial functions by judges. These courts take the view that conferral of non-judicial functions on judges is permissible provided that the functions are not "incompatible" with judicial office. I suggest that the flexible concept of incompatibility is ill-suited to protect the rule of law interests served by the separation of judicial power.[1] I argue that if we pay attention to the fact that there may be good reasons for rigidly following rules, we will be led to a blanket prohibition on the conferral of non-judicial functions on judges as a more effective way to protect the constitutional role of the courts as independent and impartial arbiters of disputes.

I. THE INCOMPATIBLITY TEST

Montesquieu saw that the concentration of power in any one branch of government is a threat to liberty and that dividing or separating power is therefore central to its control.[2] In fact, as MJC Vile points out, the dispersion of power among the different arms of government is at the heart of Western constitutionalism and is the antithesis of totalitarianism. As Vile remarks, "in the totalitarian State every aspect of the State machine is seen merely as an extension of the party apparatus, and subordinate to it ... The 'ideal' of the totalitarian state is that of a single all-embracing agency of government."[3]

The separation of judicial power, which is the specific focus of this article, prevents the political branches of government from undertaking judicial tasks and the judiciary from undertaking legislative and executive tasks. Although it must be conceded that there is no bright line distinction dividing the concept of a "judicial" task from a "non-judicial" task,[4] the concepts are clear enough in general terms for these joint preclusions to assist in controlling the exercise of power in the following ways.

First, by confining the exercise of judicial functions to a branch of government that has tenure and remuneration protections, the separation of judicial power ensures that the adjudication of disputes will be immune from political interference or manipulation. This is of particular importance in disputes between citizens and the political branches of government, providing an important protection for individual rights and a guarantee against the abuse of power. As Ralf Dahrendorf notes, "[s]uch independence of the 'judicial department' may indeed be regarded as the very definition of the 'rule of law': it is certainly an important part of it .... [T]he partisan administration of law is in fact the perversion of law, and the denial of the rule of law".[5]

Secondly, since judges are neither elected nor accountable in the ordinary way, the legitimacy of judicial decisions depends on their being controlled by pre-existing law. If judges were to make decisions free of the constraints of law, this would be the rule of men, not laws. As Montesquieu wrote:

> there is no liberty, if the judiciary power be not separated from the legislative and the executive. Were it joined with the legislative, the life and liberty of the subject would be exposed to arbitrary control; for the judge would be then the legislator. Were it joined to the executive power, the judge might behave with violence and oppression.[6]

The separation of judicial power prevents the arbitrary exercise of power by courts by confining them to the exercise of judicial functions.

The essence of the rule of law, as Chief Justice Murray Gleeson of the High Court of Australia observes, is the idea that "all authority is subject to, and constrained by, law".[7] The separation of judicial power plays a central role in securing such subjection and constraint. By protecting judicial decisions from outside interference and ensuring that they are made according to pre-existing legal norms, it guarantees an independent judiciary, faithful only to the law, on which the public can rely to apply the law without "fear, favour or prejudice".

Yet in both South Africa and Australia, countries in which the separation of judicial power is constitutionally entrenched (albeit only at federal level in Australia),[8] the courts are willing to allow judges to exercise non-judicial functions, such as conducting governmental enquiries, serving as tribunal members and issuing warrants authorising telephone taps. The Australian courts have traditionally upheld arrangements of this kind on the basis of a distinction between the exercise of non-judicial power by courts on the one hand and by individual judges on the other. They have taken the view that it is permissible for federal judges to perform non-judicial functions in their personal capacity—as so-called "personae designatae" — rather than in their capacity as a judge, even if being a federal judge is a condition for conferral of the power.[9]

More recently, however, the High Court of Australia has sought to cut down on the persona designata doctrine, and for good reason, because it has obvious difficulties. One problem is its artificiality. Members of the public are especially likely to find it difficult to distinguish judges in their personal capacity from judges "as such".[10] A second problem is the fact that there are clearly circumstances in which service by a judge in a non-judicial role, even in a personal capacity, can threaten the rule of law values served by the separation of judicial power. For instance, when judges play roles which cause them to be caught up in contentious political and social conflicts, this is likely to damage the reputation of the judiciary for independence and impartiality and diminish public confidence in the capacity of judges to perform their judicial functions with integrity.[11]

George Winterton discusses several cases of this kind. One is the case of Justice Roberts of the Supreme Court of the United States who chaired a Presidential Commission inquiring into the Japanese attack on Pearl Harbour. The Commission exonerated the President and attached blame to some commanding officers in Hawaii. These findings caused great controversy and led to a congressional investigation of the Commission's work. Justice Roberts later spoke of his regrets at accepting the invitation to chair the Commission, admitting: "I do not think it was good for my position as a justice nor do I think it was a good thing for the Court".[12]

Recognising that the persona designata doctrine has the potential to threaten the interests served by the separation of judicial power, the Australian High Court has recently introduced the incompatibility test. This test restricts the circumstances in which the persona designata doctrine is applicable. Thus in the case of *Grollo v. Palmer*,[13] although the power in question was held to be validly conferred, the High Court held that certain non-judicial functions may not be conferred on federal judges even in their personal capacity. In their joint majority judgment, Brennan CJ, Deane, Dawson and Toohey JJ stated two limitations on the persona designata doctrine. First, a non-judicial function cannot be conferred without the judge's consent, and secondly, the performance of non-judicial functions by a persona designata must not be incompatible with the performance of his or her judicial functions or with the "proper discharge by the judiciary of its responsibilities as an institution exercising judicial power".[14] Performance of the function must not, for instance, impair a judge's ability to carry out his or her judicial functions with integrity, or diminish public confidence in the integrity of the judiciary as an institution.[15]

In the subsequent case of *Wilson v. Minister for Torres Strait Islander and Aboriginal Affairs*,[16] the joint majority judges (Brennan CJ, Dawson, Toohey, McHugh and Gummow JJ) mentioned the following considerations as relevant to deciding whether a non-judicial function is likely to diminish public confidence in the integrity of the judiciary or in the capacity of individual judges to perform their judicial functions. First, if the function is not closely connected with the functions of the political branches of government it will not be incompatible with judicial office. A second issue relates to whether the function is "required to be performed independently" of "any non-judicial instruction, advice or wish". If the function is not required to be performed independently, it will be incompatible with judicial office. Third, if the judge is required to exercise discretion on political grounds, the function will be incompatible with judicial office.[17]

The Constitutional Court of South Africa adopted the incompatibility approach in the case of *South African Association of Personal Injury Lawyers v. Heath.*[18] A unanimous Court found that the separation of judicial power does not absolutely forbid judges from serving in non-judicial roles, and stated that it all depends on whether the non-judicial functions are incompatible with judicial office. The Court took the view that a case-by-case approach is essential, stating that "[t]he question in each case must turn upon considerations ... which come to the fore because of the nature of the particular function under consideration".[19] Applying the incompatibility test (though seemingly unaware of the reasons why it was introduced in Australia), the Court did not uphold the challenged function, which involved the appointment of a judge as head of a Special Investigating Unit, vested with wide powers to investigate allegations of corruption and maladministration and to litigate on behalf of the state. The Court took the view that these functions were essentially partisan. Furthermore, the head of the Unit had been appointed on an indefinite basis. He had not been able to perform his judicial duties for more than three years and might, in fact, never return to them. These considerations led the Court to conclude that the particular arrangement under scrutiny threatened the independence of the judiciary and was therefore in breach of the separation of powers.[20]

II. THE BENEFITS OF RIGIDITY

The key feature of the incompatibility test is its flexibility. Eschewing rigid adherence to a rule precluding the exercise of non-judicial functions by judges, it prefers to ask whether the particular role under scrutiny is likely to undermine the interest in judicial independence and impartiality which is served by the separation of judicial power. On the face of it, such a contextual, case-by-case approach is attractive and sensible. If, as I have argued, the purpose of the separation of judicial power is to secure the independence and impartiality of the judiciary, what possible reason can there be for invalidating conferral of a particular non-judicial function on a judge when the function is not a threat to these values? Would this not involve what Peter Strauss calls "technical positivism"[21] —elevating form above substance, or making a fetish of a rule for the sake of doctrinal purity?

The answer to this is that there can be good reasons to enforce a blanket ban on judges exercising non-judicial functions which have nothing to do with a doctrinaire desire for doctrinal purity. It is useful in this connection to consider Frederick Schauer's work on the nature of rules and the reasons to follow them.[22] Schauer's starting-point is the fact that we use rules in an instrumental way to serve an underlying purpose. Consider, for instance, the rule that freedom of speech should be respected. One of the reasons why we recognise this rule is because we believe that freedom of speech advances the goal of self-realisation. Schauer calls this a background justification for respecting freedom of speech. Yet respect for freedom of speech is only statistically, or as a matter of probability, related to this background justification or underlying purpose: though freedom of speech usually assists in self-realisation, it is not guaranteed to do so. After all, suppression of a particular view might not undermine the goal of self-realisation. Furthermore, suppression of a particular non-communicative or non-speech activity might undermine the goal of self-realisation.[23] Another way of putting this is to say that our rule about respecting freedom of speech is over-inclusive and under-inclusive relative to the purpose it is intended to serve.[24] It is therefore a "crude implement": it protects acts "that its background justifications would not protect, and [fails] to protect acts that its background justifications would protect".[25] The consequence is that decision-making which protects freedom of speech as a rule is necessarily "sub-optimal": there will inevitably be cases in which the results indicated by the rule are inferior to the results indicated by direct application of its underlying justifications to particular cases.[26]

But does this mean that instead of respecting freedom of speech as a rule it would be better to consider whether following the rule will serve its underlying purpose in each and every case which confronts us? Should we, in other words, adopt what Schauer calls a "particularistic" approach—an approach which aims to reach the optimal decision in every case,[27] and which thus seeks to avoid the errors caused by the "inevitable grossness" of rules?[28]

Lon Fuller would appear to be in favour of such an approach. He argues that it is irrational to follow rules when to do so will defeat the purpose why they were enacted. In his view, we should have regard to the spirit of the law—to what those who drafted it thought it "ought to be" —rather than to its literal meaning. Indeed, Fuller believes that we really only know what a rule means when we understand its purpose.[29] Fuller's purposive approach to interpretation has the effect of treating rules as merely provisional or rough guides to decision-making. Though rules are usually useful, they should be ignored when the circumstances are unsuitable for their application because decision-makers should attend to all the moral and political considerations that may be relevant to achieving a justifiable result in each individual case. Fuller writes: "the judicial process is something more than a cataloguing procedure. The judge does not discharge his responsibility when he pins an apt diagnostic label on the case. He has to do something about it, to treat it, if you will." [30]

But a rule-guided approach, non-ideal as it must be conceded to be, may nevertheless have certain advantages over a results-oriented or instrumental approach such as Fuller's. Schauer points out that there are two kinds of error. There are the inevitable errors that result, as we have seen, from the under-inclusiveness and over-inclusiveness of rules. But errors can also be made when decision-makers attempt to make the best decision, taking into account all relevant factors. Though the contextual approach is *in theory* the optimal approach—whereas rules are necessarily sub-optimal—the truth is that, in the real world, case-sensitive decision-makers may produce worse results on average or in the long run than rule-guided decision-makers. After all, real-world decision-makers are imperfectly rational, not usually in possession of all the relevant information and may suffer from bias and self-deception. These and other human imperfections may lead them to make mistakes. This is especially likely to be the case when the relevant considerations are complex and difficult to assess.[31]

Consider freedom of speech again and its connection with self-realisation. Case-sensitive decision-makers, who regard it as their responsibility to ascertain whether a particular restriction on the right to freedom of speech will undermine the goal of self-realisation, may arrive at the wrong answer *more* often than decision-makers who protect freedom of speech as a rule. *Disabling* decision-makers from inquiring whether respect for the right will, in a particular case, promote the goal which underlies it may therefore be the better way to *promote* that goal in the long term.

As Schauer says:

> If we believe that judges would, for various reasons, err with some frequency in applying the background justifications directly to particular cases, then we might prefer the rule-based approach, one whose under-inclusiveness and over-inclusiveness prevents judges from reaching the optimal result in every case, but whose probabilistic simplification may also be optimal over the aggregate of cases by preventing the even larger number of errors that might be the product of a particularistic approach.[32]

Joseph Raz's analysis of the nature and benefits of authority supports this point.[33] Raz points out that we can have valid reasons for *not* acting on our own assessment of the reasons that apply to us. Raz's argument is as follows. When I am deciding whether to do something—visit my friend, say—all sorts of reasons will be relevant to my decision, some of these in favour of visiting my friend, some against. We can call these my first-order reasons. It is natural to suppose that in deciding whether I should visit my friend, I should rely on my own assessment of what it would be best for me to do, on the basis of all the first-order reasons that apply to me. But Raz points out that this is not necessarily the case. I might have a second-order reason to disregard or *not* to act on my own, independent assessment of what would be the best thing to do. Raz calls a second-order reason of this kind an exclusionary reason.[34]

Exclusionary reasons apply to us when other people have justified authority over us. When we accede to an authority's order we do what we have been told to do, regardless of our own view of the merits of the instruction. Such blind adherence to authority is justified if we are more likely to reach the right result indirectly (that is, by following the authority's views), than directly (by trying to evaluate and weigh up the consequences of various actions ourselves). I might, for instance, be more likely to make the best decision if I rely on the opinion of an expert rather than my own opinion as to what the balance of reasons requires. Thus I am more likely to get well if I take the medicine a doctor prescribes for me rather than rely on my own views as to what will make me feel better. Again, in cases where I am short of time, or need to coordinate my actions with large numbers of other people, an authoritative directive may assist me to achieve my goals. Raz calls this a "service conception" of authority because the authority performs a service for us. We hand over to the authority the task of weighing up the pros and cons of different courses of action, in the belief that the authority is better placed to do this than we are.[35]

Schauer's and Raz's arguments show that we can be justified in rigidly following rules, or treating them as authorities, without considering the merits of doing so and without having regard to whether following the rule will serve its underlying rationale in the particular case. This will be so if the more reliable way to achieve the rule's purpose over a whole series of cases is to ignore the question whether applying it will achieve its purpose in the instant case. "Acontextual"[36] decision-making of this kind is therefore justified not out of irrational "rule-worship",[37] or a misplaced desire for doctrinal purity, but rather by reference to the very considerations which seemed at first sight to argue *against* an acontextual approach, namely, the need to serve a rule's purpose. Though a more fine-grained, individualised and contextual approach holds out the *hope* of achieving the rule's purpose more consistently, in the real world of imperfect decision-makers and complex calculations a rigid, rule-following approach may be the better strategy.

III. INCOMPATIBILITY AND THE INSTITUTIONAL INTEGRITY OF THE COURTS

This analysis can now be applied to the separation of judicial power and the issue of judges exercising non-judicial functions. The purpose served by the separation of judicial power is, as we have seen, that it assures the independence and impartiality of the judiciary, thereby serving as a guarantee of the rule of law. Let us now reflect on the best strategy for maintaining the institutional integrity of the courts. Should courts use a contextual approach, trying to ascertain on a case-by-case basis whether a particular non-judicial function is incompatible with judicial office and therefore likely to erode the institutional integrity of the judiciary? Or should they rather apply a strict rule which prohibits judges from exercising non-judicial functions?

In my view, this is exactly the sort of context in which strict rules are likely to be the lesser of two evils. It is quite possible that a mechanical prohibition on judges exercising non-judicial functions will sometimes yield the wrong results, because it is quite likely that there are certain non-judicial functions which judges can perform without threatening the independence and impartiality of the judiciary. But the dangers of a flexible approach are likely to be even greater, because the difficulties in applying it are likely to present a real risk to the rule of law values served by the separation of judicial power. This is in virtue of the kinds of questions that judges applying the flexible approach are required to answer. It will be remembered that the High Court of Australia in the case of *Wilson v. Minister for Torres Strait Islander and Aboriginal Affairs* [38] called attention to such matters as whether a particular non-judicial function is to be performed independently, or is closely connected with the functions of the political branches of government, or threatens the ability or apparent ability of the judiciary to act as an independent check on those branches.

Answers to questions like these are very uncertain and subjective. In fact, in the two persona designata cases in which the High Court of Australia has used the incompatibility test there was considerable disagreement on these very issues. In the case of *Grollo v. Palmer*,[39] the majority found that the use of judges to issue warrants authorising telephone taps for the purpose of criminal investigations would not compromise judicial integrity or public confidence in the courts. But the minority judge, McHugh J, disagreed, arguing that if judges were allowed to authorise telephone taps this would weaken the public perception that the federal courts are independent of the federal government. He made the following powerful points.

First, he said, judges were being asked to authorise what would otherwise be an unlawful invasion of privacy and to approve police activity. Secondly, the issuing of a warrant did not depend on compliance with objective conditions which had been precisely formulated. As McHugh J pointed out, "the legislation [put] the persona designata in the uniform of the constable",[40] requiring the judge to consider whether the information would be likely to assist in connection with the investigation. This might lead members of the public to conclude that the judge had preferred the interests of government to those of ordinary citizens. Thirdly, the judge participated in secret procedures, forming part of the criminal investigation process. Finally, there was the possibility of direct conflict with a judge's judicial functions should proceedings involving the subject of a warrant subsequently come before him or her. This was in virtue of a duty of secrecy under the relevant Act to keep the circumstances surrounding the issue of a warrant confidential. Given this duty, the only option for such a judge would be to disqualify himself or herself without being able to state the reasons, and this would erode public confidence in the judiciary. McHugh J was furthermore disinclined to believe that judges are more likely to take an impartial approach to requests for warrants, noting that of the 2639 applications made between 1988 and 1994, only 13 had been refused or withdrawn.[41]

Comparable disagreement surfaced in the case of *Wilson*.[42] In terms of the *Aboriginal and Torres Strait Islander Heritage Protection Act 1984* (Cth), the Minister had the power to make declarations preserving Aboriginal sites and objects, but before doing so he had to have considered a report from a "person" nominated by him. He nominated a judge of the Federal Court to fulfill the reporting function. The majority found that her appointment was invalid because her role was equivalent to that of a ministerial adviser. She was not required by the Act to act independently of the Minister and the decisions she was required to make were political in nature. But Kirby J dissented, on the basis that the judge's appointment as a reporter *did* satisfy the compatibility test. He thought that the reporter's duties were much closer to those of the holder of a judicial office than the duties which had been upheld in *Grollo*. And he dismissed the fear that performance of the reporting function would diminish public confidence in the judiciary. On the contrary, Kirby J thought that "the Australian community ... would feel more comfortable that the task of reporting was being performed by a judge".[43]

The indeterminacy of the incompatibility test is confirmed by its subsequent history in Australia. In *Kable v. Director of Public Prosecutions (NSW)*,[44] the incompatibility doctrine was applied in very different circumstances – not to test the permissibility of the appointment of a federal judge as a persona designata, but rather to invalidate State legislation which vested non-judicial power in a State Supreme Court. Although the State Constitutions do not entrench the separation of judicial power, State courts can be vested with federal jurisdiction in terms of s 71 of the Commonwealth Constitution and are therefore capable of exercising federal judicial power. The majority of the High Court held in *Kable* that the separation of judicial power contained in the Commonwealth Constitution imposes certain limits on the kinds of non-judicial powers that State parliaments can confer on State courts as bodies capable of exercising federal judicial power. In particular, they cannot confer powers on such courts which are incompatible with their exercise of federal judicial power.

The legislation challenged in *Kable* – the *Community Protection Act 1994* (NSW) – authorised the Supreme Court of New South Wales to order the preventive detention of "a specified person" if satisfied on reasonable grounds that he was likely to commit an act of serious violence and that his detention was "appropriate" for the protection of a particular person, or persons, or the community generally. The express object of the Act was stated in s 3(1) to be "to protect the community by providing for the preventive detention ... of Gregory Wynne Kable". Kable was a prisoner who had written threatening letters while in prison and whose sentence was about to expire. The majority judges (Toohey, Gaudron, McHugh and Gummow JJ) held in related formulations that the function conferred on the Supreme Court – to imprison Kable without the benefit of the ordinary processes of the law – would undermine public confidence in the Court's independence from the political branches of government and in its processes, compromising its integrity and thereby the integrity of the integrated Australian court system. The power vested in the Supreme Court was therefore, to use Gaudron J's phrase, "repugnant to or incompatible with [its] exercise of the judicial power of the Commonwealth".[45]

The High Court has continued to affirm the *Kable* doctrine and has even extended it to Territory courts.[46] At the same time, in two post-*Kable* cases – *Fardon v. Attorney-General (Qld)*[47] and *Baker v. The Queen*[48] – there were significant differences of opinion on whether the challenged legislation conferred powers on State Supreme Courts which damaged their institutional integrity and were therefore incompatible with their status as repositories of federal judicial power.

Fardon concerned the validity of the *Dangerous Prisoners (Sexual Offenders) Act 2003* (Qld), which authorised the Supreme Court to detain in prison prisoners who had served their sentences on the basis that they posed an unacceptable risk of serious sexual offence. *Baker* concerned the *Sentencing Act 1989* (NSW), in terms of which prisoners who had been given life sentences could apply to the Supreme Court for the fixing of a minimum sentence, after which they were able to apply for release on parole. Special conditions, however, applied to a certain class of life prisoners, a class which was constituted by a small number of identifiable individuals. They could not apply for a minimum term unless they could satisfy the Supreme Court that "special reasons" existed. It was argued that their difficulty in satisfying this requirement created the impression that the Supreme Court had been enlisted in a legislative plan to ensure they would never be released.

In both cases, the majority of the High Court found that the legislation did not compromise the institutional integrity of the State courts and was therefore not incompatible with their status as recipients of federal jurisdiction. However, Kirby J vigorously dissented, pointing to the similarities, as he saw it, between the legislation invalidated in *Kable* and that upheld in *Baker* and *Fardon* – an analysis with which some commentators agree.[49] If the *Community Protection Act* gave rise to an apprehension that the Supreme Court was being used as an instrument of government policy to secure a person's imprisonment in a way anathema to the judicial process, it is difficult to see why the same is not true of the *Dangerous Prisoners (Sexual Offenders) Act* and the *Sentencing Act*. As Oscar Roos points out, the High Court in *Baker* and *Fardon* authorised radical new forms of detention, in the form of indeterminate life sentences with no prospect of release and indefinite detention after the serving of a sentence – practices which until that point were largely foreign to the Australian legal system.[50] These seemingly intractable differences in opinion as to whether legislation infringes the incompatibility condition confirm the suspicion that incompatibility is an unsatisfactorily vague concept, the application of which is very difficult to predict.[51]

If so, this may perhaps help to explain why the majority of the High Court reasoned in a way which made it unnecessary to pay detailed attention to the notion in the most recent challenge based on the *Kable* line of reasoning, the case of *Gypsy Jokers Motorcycle Club Incorporated v. Commissioner of Police*.[52] The issue here was whether s 76(2) of the *Corruption and Crime Commission Act 2003* (WA) was invalid for damaging the institutional integrity of the Supreme Court of Western Australia. The section provided that the Police Commissioner might identify information as confidential in review proceedings if its disclosure might prejudice police operations, in which case such information would be for the Court's use only. The court below had interpreted the provision as meaning that the Supreme Court could not exercise its own judgment about the matter of confidentiality. Relying on this interpretation, the appellant argued that the Supreme Court was dictated to by an executive official in the independent performance of its review function, a state of affairs which was incompatible with the Court's institutional integrity. However, the majority of the High Court read s 76(2) as not rendering the Commissioner's claim for confidentiality unexaminable by the Supreme Court. The effect of construing the section in this somewhat unexpected way was to take the wind out of the applicant's sails. Once read in this way, as Gleeson CJ observed, "the principal foundation for the appellant's argument on validity disappears".[53]

I have argued thus far that the incompatibility test is plagued by uncertainties which make its application unforeseeable. A second problem with it is that it can be argued that it has an inbuilt skewing tendency which makes it more likely than not to yield the wrong results. This is precisely *because* it demands a case-by-case approach. Judged on a case-by-case basis, the benefits of conferring non-judicial functions on judges will be concrete and immediate, whereas the impact on the institutional integrity of the courts will necessarily be remote, speculative and difficult to quantify. Even social scientists would find it difficult to determine the long-term effects of persona designata appointments on the independence and appearance of independence of the courts. How much more difficult, then, are courts likely to find such a task, ill-equipped as they are to make such complex, empirical judgments and lacking most, if not all, of the relevant information? The long-term costs of conferring non-judicial functions on judges are as a result likely to be underestimated and in any particular case the temptation for courts will be to uphold the conferral of the challenged functions. It can therefore be argued that the incompatibility test is likely to lead to "incremental erosion" of the institutional integrity of the judiciary – an effect which will not become apparent until it is too late.[54]

Given the indeterminacy and unreliability which are built into the incompatibility test, I therefore conclude that the best way to achieve the purposes which underlie the separation of judicial power is indirectly rather than directly. Courts should not attempt to determine whether a particular non-judicial function is incompatible with the purposes of the separation of judicial power. Instead they should follow a strict rule that judges should be confined to judicial functions, because the best strategy for promoting judicial independence and impartiality in this context is the indirect one of rigid rule-following.

[1] See also Denise Meyerson, "Extra-Judicial Service on the Part of Judges: Constitutional Impediments in Australia and South Africa," (3) *Oxford University Commonwealth Law Journal* 181 (2003), in which some of the points made here are argued for in more detail.

[2] Charles de Montesquieu, *The Spirit of the Laws*, trans. Thomas Nugent (New York: Hafner, 1949), Book XI, ch 6. Montesquieu's theories are illuminatingly discussed in Laurence Claus, "Montesquieu's Mistakes and the True Meaning of Separation," 25 *Oxford Journal of Legal Studies* 419 (2005).

[3] M.J.C. Vile, *Constitutionalism and the Separation of Powers* (Oxford: Clarendon Press, 1967), 15-16. See also Philip Pettit, *Republicanism: A Theory of Freedom and Government* (Oxford: Clarendon Press, 1997), 177-178.

[4] On this issue see Geoffrey Marshall, *Constitutional Theory* (Oxford: Clarendon Press, 1971), 119; Eric Barendt, "Separation of Powers and Constitutional Government," *Public Law* 599 (1995): 603-606

[5] Ralf Dahrendorf, "A Confusion of Powers: Politics and the Rule of Law," 40 *Modern Law Review* 1 (1977): 9. See also Joseph Raz, "The Rule of Law and its Virtue," 93 *Law Quarterly Review* 195 (1977): 201.

[6] Montesquieu, *The Spirit of the Laws*, Book X1, ch 6.

[7] Murray Gleeson, "Courts and the Rule of Law" in Cheryl Saunders and Katherine Le Roy (eds), *The Rule of Law* (Sydney: The Federation Press, 2003), 179.

[8] In both countries the doctrine is inferred from the structure and provisions of their respective Constitutions. In Australia the separation of judicial power applies only to the so-called "Chapter III Courts", these being courts in which federal judicial power is vested in terms of s 71 of the Commonwealth Constitution - the High Court, other federal courts created by Parliament and other courts it invests with federal jurisdiction. There is no constitutional doctrine of separation of powers at State level in Australia.

[9] See *Drake v Minister for Immigration and Ethnic Affairs* (1979) 46 F.L.R. 409; *Hilton v. Wells* (1985) 157 C.L.R. 57.

[10] In *Hilton's* case (note 9), the minority justices, Mason and Deane JJ, noted that it would surprise an observer unversed in "distinctions without differences" to "learn that a judge, who is appointed to carry out a function by reference to his judicial office and who carries it out in his court with the assistance of its staff, services and facilities, is not acting as a judge at all, but as a private individual". Such an observer could with some justification think that the persona designata doctrine is an "elaborate charade" (at 84).

[11] George Winterton, "Judges as Royal Commissioners," 10 *University of New South Wales Law Journal* 108 (1987): 118; A.J. Brown, "The Wig or the Sword? Separation of Powers and the Plight of the Australian Judge," 21 *Federal Law Review* 48 (1992): 81; T. Sherman, "Should Judges Conduct Royal Commissions?," 8 *Public Law Review* 5 (1997): 8; The Hon Justice R S French, "Courts under the Constitution," 8 *Journal of Judicial Administration* 7 (1998): 18-19.

[12] Winterton, "Judges as Royal Commissioners," 118.

[13] *Grollo v. Palmer* (1995) 184 C.L.R. 348.

[14] *Ibid.*, 365.

[15] *Ibid.*, 365.

[16] *Wilson v. Minister for Aboriginal and Torres Strait Islander Affairs* (1996) 138 A.L.R. 220.

[17] *Ibid.*, 230-1.

[18] *South African Association of Personal Injury Lawyers v. Heath* 2001 (1) SA 883 (CC).

[19] *Ibid.*, para 31.

[20] *Ibid*, paras 45-6.

[21] Peter L. Strauss, "*Bowsher v. Synar*: Formal and Functional Approaches to Separation-of-Powers Questions – A Foolish Inconsistency?," 72 *Cornell Law Review* 488 (1987): 512.

[22] I use Schauer's analysis of rule-following to critique the Constitutional Court of South Africa's approach to the right to privacy in the case of *S v. Jordan* (2002 (6) SA 642 (CC)). See "Does the Constitutional Court of South Africa Take Rights Seriously?: The Case of *S v. Jordan*," *Acta Juridica* 138 (2004).

[23] Frederick Schauer "The Second-Best First Amendment," 31 *William and Mary Law Review* 1 (1989): 5-7.

[24] *Ibid.*, 7; Frederick Schauer, *Playing by the Rules: A Philosophical Examination of Rule-Based Decision-Making in Law and in Life* (Oxford: Clarendon Press, 1991), 28-34.

[25] Schauer, "Second Best," 13.

[26] Schauer, *Playing by the Rules*, 100.

[27] *Ibid.*, 77-8.

[28] *Ibid.*, 149.

[29] Lon L. Fuller, "Positivism and Fidelity to Law – A Reply to Professor Hart," 71 *Harvard Law Review* 630 (1958): 669.

[30] *Ibid.*, 666.

[31] Schauer, *Playing by the Rules,* 149-155.

[32] Schauer, "Second best," 19.

[33] I provide a fuller account of Raz's theory in *Understanding Jurisprudence* (Oxford and New York: Routledge-Cavendish, 2007), 55-9.

[34] Joseph Raz, *The Authority of Law: Essays on Law and Morality* (Oxford: Clarendon Press, 1979), 17.

[35] Joseph Raz, *Ethics in the Public Domain: Essays in the Morality of Law and Politics* (Oxford: Clarendon Press, 1994), 214.

[36] This is Schauer's word in *Playing By the Rules*, 135.

[37] This is J.J.C. Smart's phrase in J.J.C. Smart and Bernard Williams, *Utilitarianism: For and Against* (Cambridge: Cambridge University Press, 1973), 10.

[38] See note 16.

[39] See note 13.

[40] *Grollo* (note 13), 379.

[41] *Ibid.*, 382.

[42] See note 16.

[43] *Wilson* (note 16), 256.

[44] *Kable v. Director of Public Prosecutions (NSW)* (1996) 189 C.L.R. 51.

[45] *Ibid.*, 103.

[46] See *North Australian Aboriginal Legal Aid Service Inc v. Bradley* (2004) 218 C.L.R. 146.

[47] *Fardon v. Attorney-General (Qld)* (2004) 223 C.L.R 575.

[48] *Baker v. The Queen* (2004) 223 C.L.R. 513.

[49] See, for instance, Dan Meagher, "The Status of the Kable Principle in Australian Constitutional Law," 16 *Public Law Review* 173 (2005): 185.

[50] Oscar Roos, "*Baker v The Queen* and *Fardon v Attorney General for the State of Queensland*," 13 *Deakin Law Review* 271 (2005): 279.

[51] This point is also made by Meagher, "The Status of the Kable Principle," 184. See also Fiona Wheeler, "The *Kable* Doctrine and State Legislative Power over State Courts," 20(2) *Australasian Parliamentary Review* 15 (2005): 22, 30.

[52] *Gypsy Jokers Motorcycle Club Incorporated v. Commissioner of Police* (2008) 242 A.L.R. 191.

[53] *Ibid.*, [7].

[54] This phrase is used by Brennan and Marshall JJ in *Commodity Futures Trading Commission v. Schor* 478 U.S. 833, 861 (1986). See also Strauss, "Formal and Functional Approaches," 522; Colin Campbell, "An Examination of the Doctrine of Persona Designata in Australian Law," 7 *Australian Journal of Administrative Law* 109 (2000): 114-5, 117-8; K. Walker "Persona Designata, Incompatibility and the Separation of Powers," 8 *Public Law Review* 153 (1997): 163.

CHAPTER 7

THE COURT AS A FORUM FOR JUSTIFICATION

*Grégoire C. N. Webber***

Introduction

The relationship between democracy and constitutional supremacy in a democratic constitutional State is a central question of constitutional theory. Simply stated, how should one negotiate democratic claims ("what the people will should be law") with constitutional constraints ("there are limits to what the people should will")? With respect to constitutional rights in particular—the focus of this essay— the negotiation is no less difficult. And the difficulty in answering this question manifests itself in another central question of constitutional theory: the relationship between the judicial and legislative branches.

In many democratic constitutional States, the role of the judiciary in reviewing legislation for compliance with constitutional rights is described with references that include "guardian of the Constitution" and "protector of rights". In so much as language structures one's understanding of the world, it also has the potential to deceive and to restrict that understanding. The vocabulary of "guardian" and "protector" has bred the assumption that the Constitution and, more specifically, constitutional rights are in need of a guardian or in need of protection from the encroachments of the legislature. In turn, this has led to the somewhat familiar refrain that the legislature[1] is interested in "policy" without (sufficient) regard to matters of "principle", the latter being reserved to the (exclusive) domain of the court. As a result, the court is identified (and, critically, has self-identified) as *the forum of principle*, the forum for the protection of rights.[2] The role of the legislature as regards constitutional rights is said to be to listen to the teachings of the court. The legislature, it would seem, cannot be trusted to engage in reasoned debate as to the meaning and application of constitutional rights: legislators are irresponsible, in the sense of being unaware of or indifferent to constitutional rights when formulating legislation, and the legislature allows for the tyranny of the majority and therefore is liable to violate the rights of minorities.

Resting on the strength of these widespread assumptions, this understanding of the relationship between the legislature and the court is often put forward—albeit with more subtlety than this cursory exposition—to justify judicial review. It is also often resisted on the ground that not only are the assumptions false (the legislature does take rights seriously, the court is not exclusively a forum of principle, etc.), but also on the ground that disagreements about constitutional rights between court and legislature are rarely about obvious cases: they occur in non-obvious cases where reasonable disagreement is expected and endemic. In such cases, why should the words of a few (the judges) take precedence over the words of the many (the legislators)? Yet, this latter view is too often neglected or even unacknowledged. In this way, we do well to remind ourselves that "[m]etaphors in law are to be narrowly watched, for starting as devices to liberate thought, they end often by enslaving it".[3]

Given these considerations, how should the court undertake the task of judicial review when a claimant contends that a right has been violated by a legislative act? Constitutional scholarship tends to assume that it is for the court to articulate the meaning of a constitutional right and to evaluate the legislation's compliance with that specification.[4] In this essay, I will argue for an alternative role for the court in judicially reviewing legislation for compliance with constitutional rights. Proposing a conception of the court as *a forum for justification*, I will argue that legislation should be understood as attempting to give meaning by specifying constitutional rights and that the role of the court should be to evaluate the legislature's justification for its rights-specifications. This account will focus on the legislature's *reasons* supporting the specification of a constitutional right and whether, taken together, those reasons can justify the specification of the right. This account aims to participate in the growing and promising idea of public law as a culture of justification.[5]

A. Some Preliminaries

Five assumptions govern what follows.

First, constitutional rights are in need of *specification* or synonymously: *delimitation* or *concretization*. Charters and bills of rights often proceed with commanding declarations, announcing indeterminate rights with contours not wholly worked out. Often if not always, strict adherence to constitutional text and recourse to dictionary definitions will not satisfy the search for constitutional meaning. As a result, the process of applying a constitutional right must proceed through the instantiation of that right. For example, though the guarantee of expressive freedom orients the inquiry into restrictions on hate speech, it does not without more determine whether hate speech is constitutionally protected. A specification of the constitutional guarantee of free expression must be performed in order to determine its application in the case of hate speech. Should it be concluded that hate speech is not within the properly specified scope of free expression, then no violation of the constitutional right would result from a legislative prohibition on hate speech. In this way, the specification or delimitation of a right should not be confused for its infringement, violation, or impairment, all of which assume that a right has already been specified or delimited.

Second, in an engaged society committed to rights, there is reasonable disagreement as to the specification of rights.[6] The open-ended, indeterminate formulations of constitutional rights command wide-spread agreement, which is indicative of a genuine commitment to a culture of respect for constitutional rights.[7] However, wide-spread agreement tends to decrease as the specificity of the contours and content of rights increases. This disagreement is a function of the challenge of delimiting a constitutional right, which could be described as,

> the challenge of deciding how best to achieve, how best to "instantiate," in a particular context that implicates the norm, the political-moral value (or values) at the heart of the norm; it is the challenge of discerning what way of achieving that value, what way of embodying it, best reconciles all the various and sometimes competing interests at stake in the context at hand.[8]

Two persons committed to the same open-ended, indeterminate constitutional right can disagree, reasonably and in good faith, about how to resolve the challenge of specifying that right. This disagreement between reasonable persons is merely demonstrative of the more fundamental point that each one of us, in participating in the difficult and complex exercise of specification, will appreciate the availability (in most cases) of different reasonable specifications of any given right. Reason will often eliminate countless unreasonable specifications, but will in turn often be exhausted before identifying a single specification as the only reasonable one. In this way, reasonable disagreement results in the reasoned availability of different rationally available specifications of any given right.

Third, the legislature (as the author of law)[9] and the court (as the institution traditionally associated with constitutional review) are the candidates for "who" is to do the specification of constitutional rights. The executive has neither the power of authorship of law (except by way of regulation) nor of review (except incidentally through the administration of law). Though this assumption focuses on institutions, this should not be taken to deny the importance of "popular constitutionalism", which includes the citizen as an interpreter of the Constitution.[10]

Fourth, the legislature is a democratic legislature and participates in the ideal of equal political participation. The legislature may at times and in certain respects fail to satisfy this ideal, but it strives to realize it by correcting unequal political participation where identified. Moreover, consistent with the second assumption, the legislature does not "take the attitude that it will do anything it can get away with and let the Supreme Court worry about the Constitution".[11] Rather, the legislature is a forum for debating reasonable disagreement about rights and for deciding, for the community, which specification of a right will be favoured, until a different specification commands the legislative assembly. As will be reviewed below, the legislature undertakes this task as a forum of justification.

Fifth, the court is independent of the legislature. With the exception of the process for appointing judges by political actors (or their delegates), the court does not participate in the ideal of equal political *participation*, although it may claim that its role is necessary in order to maintain the conditions necessary for such equal participation. Its decision-making process tends to constrain the modes of argumentation, and privileges legal-technical reasoning over more open-ended political-moral reasoning.

With these assumptions stated, I turn to review how the legislature and in turn the court can be understood as fora of and for justification.

B. The Forum of and the Fora for Justification

In a democracy, the legislature should aspire to be a *forum of justification*. Legislators should appeal to the idea of public reason and seek to convince each other that the specification of a right they favour ought to be shared by other legislators. Purported justifications for the specification of a right should be evaluated in the legislature, questioned by fellow legislators on the floor of the chamber and in committee rooms. Through the exchange of reasons, legislators should seek to justify to each other (and to the citizens they represent) why the proposition for legislative action they favour should be adopted by the assembly. As a forum for the resolution of the questions of political society, the legislature should encourage its members to share a commitment to reason and justification.

In this way, the authority of the legislature is derived not only from its democratic pedigree, but also from its decision-making process. The legislature's openness and deliberative ethos imbues it with an authority derived from the participation (however indirect) of all citizens in the decision-making process. In this sense, one should conceive of the legislature's law as 'a set of publicly adopted reasons for adopting or rejecting proposals for action'.[12] However, because the legislature is self-consciously fallible—that is, because the legislature makes its decisions in the course of disagreement among legislators who may come to recognize that legislative action has proceeded in error—a legislative destination should not be conceived of as permanent. Legislative action is always accompanied by the possibility of a different destination. The possibility of a change in the legislative course commits the legislature 'to considering [the inevitable] dissenting voices, and [to] seeking to acknowledge and address those voices in the laws by which all in the community must live'.[13]

The exchange of reasons *within* the legislative assembly is central to an account of the legislature as a forum of justification, but it does not exhaust it. The legislature should also speak of justification to all citizens. The legislature's justificatory stance should be both *inward* looking (legislators should seek to justify legislative initiatives to *themselves*) and *outward* looking (the legislature should seek to justify legislative initiatives to *citizens*). In this respect, the outward looking justificatory stance provides the citizen who did not participate directly in the deliberations in the legislative chamber with a criterion for evaluating legislative initiatives. The citizen may ask: Has the legislative specification of a right been justified with good and sufficient reasons?

The legislature's role as a forum of justification does not come to an end the moment that a right-specification and its justification are adopted. By construing the law-making project '*self-reflexively*, in a manner similar to the self-reflexive construction of the administration of justice', one 'furnish[es] the legislature with the authority to review its own activity'.[14] The legislature is the first body responsible for evaluating whether the purported justification for a right's specification is valid. It is also the first body responsible for evaluating whether this justification continues to be valid with the passage of time, as the community's relationship with reason evolves. (Consider the decrease in appeals to religion to justify legislative action.)

Just as the evaluation, criticism, applause, and rejection of a legislative specification of a right do not end the moment it is adopted by the legislature, nor do these activities remain confined to the legislative chamber. News media, public opinion, and non-governmental organizations question the specification of a right and the proposed legislative justification and, at times, encourage the legislature to re-consider. In this way, they are countless *fora for justification*; that is, fora for the legislature to defend its justification for a right's specification. The force of public opinion in a democracy compels the legislature to position itself within a culture of justification, especially as pertains to matters of fundamental political-moral importance like constitutional rights. Evaluated this way, the court is an *additional* forum for justification. When seized by a claimant criticizing and calling for the rejection of a legislative specification of a right, a court compels the legislature to justify its right-specification. However, unlike the other more informal fora for justification, the court is a *unique* forum: it has the power to declare legislative specifications of rights unconstitutional.

As a forum for justification, the relevant question for the court is not whether the right-specification is one that the court would have adopted. Rather, the question for the court is whether the legislature has adopted a valid justification for the specification of a constitutional right. The role of the court should not be to specify constitutional rights and to restrict legislative action in consequence. It should rather be for the legislature to articulate the specification of rights and the court should appreciate this. On this account, the court upholds the Constitution by scrutinizing the reasons adopted by the legislature in justification of its specification of constitutional rights. Indeed, constitutional scholars often neglect the possibility that '[a] court can just as well uphold the Constitution, thus performing its duty under the Supremacy Clause, by taking the meaning of the Constitution to have been settled by another authority'.[15]

Accepting that the legislature should be a forum *of* justification and the court a forum *for* justification, how should they interact? What, in short, should be the performance of justification?

C. The Performance of Justification

Understanding the court as a forum for justification and the legislature as a forum of justification focuses constitutional review neither on the constitutional right nor on the legislation in isolation, but rather on the interaction *between* legislation *and* constitutional rights. It nuances the relationship between legislation and constitutional rights by allowing for the understanding that legislation participates in instantiating rights. This view distances itself from an understanding of legislation as either infringing or complying with rights, but never as a source for concretizing rights. This shift in emphasis has the following potential consequences. First, there is a distinction between "limiting" (understood in the sense of *specifying* and *concretizing*) and "violating" a constitutional right such that "a law which limits a right set out in the [Constitution] will only violate the Constitution if it is not justified."[16] In this way, the legislature should be understood to be a responsible actor, seeking to comply with its best understanding of the Constitution. By articulating the reasons supporting its constitutional reading of a right, the legislature illustrates that it has sought to comply, and not to violate, the Constitution. If its reasons amount to a valid justification, then its right-specification should be accepted as a reasonable reading of the Constitution, irrespective of the possibility that a court favours an alternative reasonable reading.

Second, the assumption that the court is the only institution responsible for specifying constitutional rights is resisted. The legislature is responsible both for the provision of legislation and for the articulation of the specification of rights *in legislation*. The legislature undertakes an active (rather than passive or incidental) responsibility to debate and to articulate the specification of constitutional rights in the context of a legislative scheme. By legislating the specification of rights, the legislature both exercises its democratic mandate and recognizes the existence of proper constraints on its mandate. If the legislature cannot adduce good and sufficient reasons, it has failed to justify its specification on a constitutional right and therefore has failed to act in a manner required by the Constitution.

As a forum for justification, the court ought to evaluate the reasons put forward by the legislature in justification of its specification of a constitutional right. The relevant question for the court is not whether the right-specification proposed by the legislature is one that the court would have adopted, but rather and only whether the legislature has justified the specification. To ask whether a specification is *justified* is to limit the inquiry to the reasons put forward by the legislature; by contrast, to ask whether a specification is *justifiable* requires the court to evaluate whether there are good and sufficient reasons available, including but not limited to those offered by the legislature. Why limit the role of the court in this way? Why limit the court to *reviewing* the justification proposed by the legislature? The answer lies in a community's collective, democratic responsibility for engaging in the plethora of political-moral considerations relevant to specifying constitutional rights. By positing the responsibility for evaluating constitutional meaning with the legislature itself rather than exclusively with the court, the legislature must grapple with the difficult questions raised by indeterminate constitutional rights and is required to provide a justification for its choices which goes beyond "because a majority of us—the legislators—voted for it". This approach buttresses majoritarian decision-making with a criterion of correctness, which is satisfied when a justification is demonstrated for the democratic choices made in specifying a constitutional right.

In order for justification to be performed, the legislature, in approaching and framing its legislative choices, ought to be devoted to providing justification for why its specification of a constitutional right is reasonable. It may be argued that "legislative reasons" are not possible to identify: one legislator may vote for reasons that are not the same as the reasons supporting another legislator's vote. Moreover, defending the constitutionality of legislation before the court is usually undertaken by the executive (for example, by the Attorney General) rather than by the legislature directly. This creates the real possibility that the reasons supporting the specification of a constitutional right could be *discovered* after the fact by legal counsel rather than being those reasons that motivated the enactment of the legislation. Not enough will be said about these important challenges in this essay, except for the following: with all its imperfections, the role of the Attorney General in defending the specification of a right in legislation is likely to be guided—even if it is not determined—by the reasons that were exchanged by legislators prior to the enactment of a bill and by the logic animating the structure, provisions, and omissions of the enactment. This suggests that a commitment to identifying and using legislative reasons is possible, though more needs to be done to confirm and perfect this practice. For example, the legislature may aim to render explicit its understanding of the reasonableness of the specification of rights it seeks to justify. One tool which is increasingly used in Canada is the legislative preamble, wherein the legislature may outline the justification for the specification of a right.[17] In addition, legislation may contain a statement of principle,[18] or a section outlining the purpose of the legislative scheme.[19] These methods seek to identify, in the legislative act itself, the justification for a right's specification and thereby participate in preventing the subsequent discovery of justificatory reasons.

But why, one may ask, should the legislature be called upon to demonstrate again its justification for a legislative specification—the legislature has, after all, already justified the specification in the process of law-making? Two different, yet related answers are available. First, the legislature may have good reason to demonstrate its justification in a different forum. Doing so may appease resistance from those who wish to challenge the right-specification, including those who do so before the court. In this respect, it is frequently observed that the court, "through its history, has acted as a legitimator of government".[20] Second, committed to the proper specification of constitutional rights, the legislature should remain open to the possibility that the court (and, of course, the other more informal fora for justification) will convince it that its justification is not (or is no longer) valid. The court may highlight weaknesses in the reasons put forward by the legislature. As importantly, knowing that legislative choices about the specification of constitutional rights may be subject to justificatory review encourages legislators to consider the putative justification throughout their deliberations.

Now, it cannot be denied that a court unrestrained by intellectual and institutional modesty could well find fault with almost any legislative justification. The mere setting of a standard of judicial review cannot, in and of itself, constrain the court. The argument of this essay proceeds on the assumption that the court can, should, and perhaps will exercise intellectual and institutional modesty. A court recognizing that the responsibility for delimiting constitutional rights should rest with the legislature, that the specification of rights proceeds not exclusively by rational deduction but also with political judgment and choice, and that innumerable incommensurables confront the legislature in articulating the specification of a right will hesitate before concluding that a legislative justification is not made out. A court thus directed will be guided, perhaps, by what Thayer articulated in 1893 as the rule of the clear mistake: that is, that the question for the court "is not one of the mere and simple preponderance of reasons for or against, but of what is very plain and clear, clear beyond a reasonable doubt".[21]   This orients the institutional humility that ought to guide the court in reviewing the legislative specification of constitutional rights.

Now, the court—a forum *for* justification—will at times assume the function of forum *of* justification. That is, the court will, at times, itself be engaged in a process of justification. If the court concludes that a legislative justification is invalid, it should provide reasons to justify this disagreement. The activity of justification in the court will be somewhat different from the activity of justification in the legislature: it will be focused on providing reasons for disagreement with the legislature's justification. It will not be oriented to providing reasons for adopting the specification of a right. Now, in the same way that the court should reject the legislative specification of a constitutional right if it is not supported by a valid justification, the legislature would be entitled to maintain that its justification is valid if the court's finding to the contrary is affirmed without reasons in justification. The performance of justification requires a commitment from and disposition of both institutional actors, without which it can but fail.

Conclusion

Framing the court as a forum for justification promotes the legislature's role in rights-discourse, which has the far from inconsequential benefit of infusing politics with an understanding of the priorities identified by constitutional rights. To posit the court as the protector of the Constitution—as does much constitutional scholarship—has the potential effect of confirming the court as the sole "forum of principle". Citizens may "become careless as to whom they send to the legislature" and may be satisfied that "these few wiser gentlemen on the bench are so ready to protect them against their more immediate representatives."[22] It is said to be a consequence of judicial supremacy that it

> leads easily to judicial exclusivity and institutional disrespect for the constitutional opinions of the elected branches of government. It can also result in the over-

legalisation of constitutional discourse and the consequent snuffing out of forms of popular constitutionalism.[23]

By contrast, understanding the court as a forum for justification promotes an epistemological interchange of legislative reasons purporting to justify specifications of constitutional rights and of judicial reasons rejecting (or accepting) the justification. The force of reason—rather than the assertion of institutional respect—is a most important component. Without an articulated basis for justifying a specification of a constitutional right, the constitutionality of legislation is questionable and, accordingly, should be held unconstitutional. Without an articulated basis for rejecting a legislature's justification, the authority of judicial review is questionable. Understanding the court as a forum for justification, in this sense, rests not only on a theory of judicial review; it also rests on a theory of legislative action. It provides that legislation must comply with the Constitution in order to be valid, and this is demonstrated by the provision of good and sufficient reasons justifying the right-specification set out in legislation. This dual foundational component to the court as a forum for justification highlights the reciprocity—explicit or not—inherent in all theories court-legislature relationships.

[1] Unless context suggests otherwise, I refer to 'legislature' and 'court' in the singular for the purposes of alleviating the text.

[2] The phrase "forum of principle" is generally attributed to Ronald Dworkin, "The Forum of Principle" 56 *New York University Law Review* 469 (1981). See also Ronald Dworkin, *Taking Rights Seriously* (London: Duckworth, 2000).

[3] *Berkley v Third Ave Railway*, 244 N.Y. 84, 94; 155 N.E. 58, 61 (1926) (New York Court of Appeals) (Cardozo J.).

[4] See e.g. Andrei Marmor, "Are Constitutions Legitimate?" 20 *Canadian Journal of Law and Jurisprudence* 69 (2007).

[5] See e.g. David Dyzenhaus, "Law as Justification: Etienne Mureinik's Conception of Legal Culture" 14 *South African Journal on Human Rights* 11 (1998).

[6] See John Finnis, *Natural Law and Natural Rights* (New York: Clarendon Press, 1980), ch. VIII and John Finnis, "Some Professional Fallacies About Rights" 4 *Adelaide Law Review* 377 (1971-1972): 385-86, for the difficult, contingent, and complex exercise involved in specifying rights.

[7] Jeremy Waldron, "Some Models of Dialogue Between Judges and Legislators," 23 *Supreme Court Law Review* (2d) 7 (2004): 12.

[8] Michael J. Perry, "Protecting Human Rights in a Democracy: What Role of the Courts?" 38 *Wake Forest Law Review* 635 (2003): 651 (footnote omitted).

[9] In making this assumption, I bracket the lessons of legal pluralism which identify the normativity of society in its implicit and inferential norms, not in its explicit and formulaic representations. I thank Roderick Macdonald for this clarification.

[10] One important matter that is overlooked (in part) in this third assumption is that it is far from evident that constitutional rights are primordially a matter for those with legal training. We could easily imagine a council of philosopher-kings, or social workers, or economists as possible alternatives.

[11] Neal Devins and Louis Fisher, *The Democratic Constitution* (New York: Oxford University Press, 2004), 74 (quoting Justice Scalia).

[12] John Finnis, "Commensuration and Public Reason" in Ruth Chang (ed.), *Incommensurability, Incompatibility, and Practical Reason* (Cambridge, Massachusetts: Harvard University Press, 1997), 215.

[13] *Reference re Secession of Quebec*, [1998] 2 SCR 217, (1998) 161 DLR (4th) 385 [68] (SCC).

[14] Jürgen Habermas, *Between Facts and Norms: Contributions to a Discourse Theory of Law and Democracy* (Cambridge: Polity Press, 2004), 242 (emphasis in original).

[15] Alexander M. Bickel, *The Least Dangerous Branch: The Supreme Court at the Bar of Politics* (2nd edn.) (New Haven: Yale University Press, 1986), 10.

[16] *R v Swain*, [1991] 1 SCR 933, 997 (SCC).

[17] Kent Roach, "The Uses and Audiences of Preambles in Legislation" 47 *McGill Law Journal* 129 (2001).

[18] See e.g. Criminal Code, R.S.C. 1985, c. C-46 (Canada), § 25.1(2).

[19] See e.g. Tobacco Act, 1997, c. 13 (Canada), s. 4.

[20] Charles L. Black Jr., *The People and the Courts* (New York: The MacMillan Company, 1960), 52. See also Robert A. Dahl, "Decision-Making in a Democracy: The Supreme Court as a National Policy-Maker" 6 *Journal of Public Law* 279 (1957): 294.

[21] James Bradley Thayer, "The Origin and Scope of the American Doctrine of Constitutional Law" 7 *Harvard Law Review* 129 (1893): 151.

[22] James Bradley Thayer, *John Marshall* (Boston: Houghton Mifflin, 1901), 103-104.

[23] Stephen Gardbaum, "The New Commonwealth Model of Constitutionalism" 49 *American Journal of Comparative Law* 707 (2001): 747 (footnote omitted).

** I wish to thank Penelope Andrews, Graham Gee, Kate Hofmeyr, Roderick Macdonald, Owen Rees, and Stéphanie Vig for their instructive comments; I also thank John Finnis for enlightening discussions with regard to a previous draft on which this essay is based.

CHAPTER 8

ACHIEVING SEXUAL FREEDOM THROUGH CONSTITUTIONAL STRUCTURES: THE PROBLEM OF JUDICIAL REVIEW

Professor Ruthann Robson

I. Introduction

Judicial review—the power of an often unelected judiciary to declare acts of a usually elected legislative body void as unconstitutional—remains a divisive subject despite its reputation as a cornerstone of democratic constitutionalism. Stated in very basic terms, one perspective is that judicial review is necessary to curb the excesses of democracy which can lead to "mob" rule and the oppression of minorities or even statistical majorities who are less powerful. Phrased equally reductively, the opposing view is that judicial review is an elitist and aristocratic notion which thwarts democracy, imposing the unchecked views of an appointed oligarchy on the people.

Sexual rights such as equality for women, reproductive rights, the decriminalization of sexual practices, and family rights for sexual minorities serve as the contemporary flashpoints for controversies about judicial review. The mainstream jurisprudential arguments regarding the "counter-majoritarian difficulty"[1] often proceed in abstract or historical terms, as if judicial review is unrelated to particular contemporary politics and devoid of women or sexual minorities. The classic neo-liberal defense of judicial review, articulated and refined most persuasively by John Hart Ely, is the "representation-reinforcing" theory of judicial review, arguing that Acourts should protect those who cannot protect themselves politically.[2] In the current political climate, it is predominantly (although not always) conservatives who voice arguments against judicial review of legislation, especially legislation seeking to limit reproductive or sexual rights or to limit family rights to traditional heterosexual families.

The ultimate question this chapter posits is whether judicial review is advantageous for women's sexual freedom, and most specifically lesbian sexual freedom. At a practical level, the question is whether feminists and lesbians working toward sexual freedom in democracies should embrace judicial review. This would mean advocating that judicial review be included in new constitutions that are being promulgated and be defended in nations, including the United States and Canada, in which judicial review is being assaulted.

This chapter will first outline the theoretical debates regarding judicial review centered largely on the United States experience. Thereafter, the chapter will explore specific instances of sexual freedom and particular processes of legislative action or judicial review, focusing on California, the Netherlands, and South Africa. Lastly, the chapter offers some preliminary suggestions for advocates of sexual freedom confronted with controversies regarding judicial review.

II.   The Problem of Judicial Review: "American-Style"[3]

Judicial review has been called one of the United States' "chief contributions to world thought"[4], and "one of the U.S.A's "best-selling (and least remunerative) exports."[5] New constitutions in new democracies, often drafted under United States influence, generally contain provisions for judicial review which give the judiciary the power to declare democratically promulgated laws void as unconstitutional. For example, under Chapter 7, Art. 6 of Afghanistan's constitution, the "Supreme Court, upon request of the Government or the Courts can review compliance with the Constitution of laws, legislative decrees, international treaties, and international conventions, and interpret them, in accordance with the law." Similarly, the new constitution of Iraq, announces that the constitution is the "Supreme Law of the land," that any legal provision that conflicts with it is "null and void," and grants the Federal Supreme Court original and exclusive jurisdiction to review claims that a law, regulation or directive issued by the federal or regional governments is inconsistent with the constitution. Likewise, nations from the former Soviet Union and on the continent of Africa all include provisions for judicial review.

Meanwhile, in the United States itself this very power of the judiciary is incessantly and continuously contested. Best selling books such as *Men in Black: How the Supreme Court is Destroying America*, stridently advance the thesis concisely articulated in the title, despite the failure to recognize the two women then-members of the United States Supreme Court.[6] The more historical and less conservative approaches of legal scholars such as Larry Kramer and Mark Tushnet similarly argue that "judicial supremacy" should yield to a "popular constitutionalism" in which "the Supreme Court is our servant and not our master."[7] Legal scholar Jeremy Waldron, a native of New Zealand and now a professor in the United States, takes a similar view, articulating his "opposition to American-style judicial review."[8] Certainly such concerns are not new. James Thayer's famous 1893 article sought to provide a guide to restrain courts from declaring acts unconstitutional.[9] Recently, the two hundredth anniversary of the United States Supreme Court's 1803 opinion in *Marbury v. Madison,* which reputedly established judicial review, occasioned several symposia issues of law reviews devoted to the problems of judicial review.[10]

Abroad, Americans may not be promulgating judicial review as enthusiastically as it might appear. For example, regarding the drafting of the Iraqi constitution, at least one advisor from the Bush administration argued that Iraq's constitution limit the power of judicial review, lest Iraq be faced with a situation of unacceptable judicial decisions comparable to those in United States[11], such as those granting the right of abortion. Furthermore, the distrust of judicial review is not solely a preoccupation in the United States. In *The Most Dangerous Branch: How the Supreme Court of Canada has Undermined Our Law and Our Democracy,* law professor Robert Martin argues that "feminists and feminist ideology have come to dominate" the legal system and the Canadian Supreme Court to the extent that there is a "matriarchy in charge."[12]

Thus, contemporary critiques of judicial review are inflected with anti-feminist and anti-sexual freedom overtones. As the Iraqi anecdote previously mentioned illustrates, there is a continued preoccupation with abortion and other types of sexual freedom in the criticisms of judicial review. Indeed, the United States Supreme Court's 1973 decision in *Roe v. Wade*[13] has become a symbol of judicial activism, joining the previous paradigmatic example of judicial activism attributed to *Brown v. Board of Education*[14], in which the Court in 1954 declared racial segregation and separatism—however "equal"—

unconstitutional, issuing in an era of attempted racial integration. Interestingly, the scholarship and rhetoric castigating the Court are startlingly similar. Consider these two statements:

> The Supreme Court of the United States, with no legal basis for such action, undertook to exercise their naked judicial power and substituted their personal political and social ideas for the established law of the land; the Supreme Court created a new right that is not inferable from the Constitution, in any values derived from provisions in it or in the intent of its Framers . . . never had their reasoning been so spurious, so lacking in careful scholarship, or so overtly based on a philosophy of relativism.

The first statement is from the Southern Manifesto, a statement by members of Congress rejecting the Court's decision in *Brown v. Board of Education*[15], while the second is a statement by a United States Senator introducing a bill to amend the United States Constitution to provide that "a right to abortion is not secured by this Constitution."[16]

The coupling of accusations of "judicial activism" with "intent of the Framers" is a hallmark of conservative rhetoric; the reference to original intent is meant to serve as the proper leash on the judiciary. In the United States, this means that the equality and liberty interests articulated in the Fourteenth Amendment are "time-dated" at the year 1868, when the Amendment was passed.[17] Or perhaps earlier. In a 2005 speech before the conservative Federalist Society, presidential advisor Karl Rove extolled the Founders who gathered in the 1770s as "the greatest assemblage of political philosophers since ancient Athens."[18] This display of what Justice Kirby of Australia's High Court would surely label "ancestor worship"[19], is joined to a lambast of four recent court cases, half of which concern sexual matters.[20] Perhaps more surprisingly, even a defender of judicial review can resort to original intent when he disagrees with a conclusion of reproductive freedom. John Hart Ely found *Roe v. Wade* "frightening" because he did not believe a right to abortion was "inferable from the language of the Constitution" or "the framers' thinking respecting the specific problem in issue."[21] His theory that the judicial role is to correct the malfunctionings of representative democracy by protecting those in the minority[22] did not extend to abortion as a constitutional right; he theorized that fetuses are even more entitled to minority status than women.[23] Further, he reasoned that "Compared with men, very few women sit in our legislatures....But *no* fetuses sit in our legislatures."[24]   Accusations of judicial activism, accompanied by references to the Constitution's silence and the intent of the framers, are voiced from within the judiciary itself. In the abortion cases, several Justices have argued that "abortion" is not in the text of the Constitution, that it has been criminalized and therefore was not recognized by the framers as a protected right, and that the issue should be left to the democratic process. In *Lawrence v. Texas*, the 2003 Supreme Court decision declaring a state statute criminalizing homosexual sodomy unconstitutional, Justice Scalia, dissenting, stated that "it is the premise of our system" that judgments regarding sexual and other types of morality are to be made through "normal democratic means" and not "imposed by a governing caste."[25] He argued that the state's choice to criminalize homosexual sodomy "is well within the range of traditional democratic action, and its hand should not be stayed through the invention of a brand-new 'constitutional right' by a Court that is impatient of democratic change." Scalia seems to attribute the Court's impatience to the fact that the "Court has taken sides in the culture war, departing from its role of assuring, as neutral observer, that the democratic rules of engagement are observed." He views the Court as a "product of a law-profession culture" that has largely signed on to the so-called homosexual agenda."[26]

Several years earlier, Justice Scalia's dissenting opinion in *Romer v. Evans*, in which the Court declared unconstitutional Colorado's Amendment Two which barred anti-discrimination laws which protected "homosexuals, lesbians, and bisexuals," was equally rancorous.[27] Justice Scalia again stressed the democratic quality of the state law, which in the case of Amendment Two might be viewed as democracy in its purest form because it resulted from a voter referendum rather than from a representative legislative process. In the dissenting opinion, Justice Scalia declared that since the Constitution of the United States is silent on the issue, "it is left to be resolved by normal democratic means" and the "Court has no business imposing upon all Americans the resolution favored by the elite class from which the Members of this institution are selected."[28] That Amendment Two had resulted from the success of "homosexuals" on the local level using the democratic process to enact anti-discrimination laws was characterized by Scalia as attributable to "the geographic concentration and the disproportionate political power of homosexuals."[29] Lest he be accused of criticizing democratic processes, he added, "I do not mean to be critical of these legislative successes; homosexuals are as entitled to use the legal system for reinforcement of their moral sentiments as is the rest of society. But they are subject to being countered by lawful, democratic countermeasures as well."[30] Importantly, these criticisms seek to raise themselves above mere disagreements about the outcome, but impugn the power of the courts to decide the issue at all.

In the United States, the exercise of judicial review by the federal courts of democratically promulgated legislation by states also implicates the problem of federalism and so-called "states rights." In both *Lawrence v. Texas* and *Romer v. Evans*, the United States Supreme Court was reviewing democratic enactments by states. Yet the problem of federalism in the United States is not neatly mapped onto the judicial review landscape. For example, the Massachusetts' Supreme Court's decision in *Goodridge v. Department of Public Health*, holding that the Commonwealth of Massachusetts may not "deny the protections, benefits, and obligations conferred by civil marriage to two individuals of the same sex who wish to marry," is the product of a state highest court reviewing its own state laws.[31] Despite previously articulated preferences for states' rights and local control, this decision was condemned by President Bush in his State of the Union Address in 2004 as a product of "activist judges" who have "begun redefining marriage by court order, without regard for the will of the people and their elected representatives," and who "insist on forcing their arbitrary will upon the people."[32] The support for a constitutional amendment which would define marriage as limited to one man and one woman is justified, by President Bush and others, as responsive to "activist judges." In his 2005 State of the Union Address on February 3, Bush reiterated his position: "Because marriage is a sacred institution and the foundation of society, it should not be redefined by activist judges. For the good of families, children and society, I support a constitutional amendment to protect the institution of marriage."[33] And again in 2006, George W. Bush included his view that "many Americans, especially parents," are "discouraged by activist courts that try to redefine marriage."[34] The judicial review in this scenario is accomplished by state court judges interpreting their own state constitution, yet the invocation of "judicial activism" trumps any fealty to states rights.

Divorcing the constitutional structure that permits judicial review from the particularities of a case of judicial review can be exceedingly difficult. Even those who argue against judicial review most stridently and most expressly, including Justice Scalia, are more accurately quarreling with the results in particular cases rather than judicial review generally. In the instance of Justice Scalia, such a conclusion is buoyed by his resort to judicial review to declare other democratically promulgated legislation unconstitutional. During the 1994-2000 terms, Justice Scalia voted to declare unconstitutional federal, state or local acts 25 times, a statistic that bears comparison to Justices Souter, Ginsburg, and Breyer, with 17, 14, and 14 votes to declare legislation unconstitutional.[35]

Indeed, it is a mistake to view judicial review as co-extensive with a progressive political agenda. One of the most prolonged and vigorous exercises of judicial review by the United States Supreme Court was directed at declaring unconstitutional federal and state statutes granting economic rights to workers. During the so-called Lochner era, derived from the case of *Lochner v. New York* in 1905 in which the Court declared unconstitutional a New York statute limiting the working hours of bakers to sixty hours per week[36], the Court invalidated numerous laws that were part of the progressive effort to curb the excesses of capitalism. This era, now widely discredited, ended with FDR's "New Deal" and his threat to confront the power of the United States Supreme Court itself, through what has become known as his "court-packing plan" among other strategies.

Moreover, the more recent Rehnquist Court, 1986-2005, is unarguably an activist Court, especially in relation to Congress, declaring almost twice as many Congressional statutes unconstitutional than the Warren Court, 1954-1969, and more than Burger Court, 1969-1986.[37] The federal statutes voided by the Court included a federal law providing a civil remedy for violence against women[38], two regulating the possession of guns[39] and two prohibiting employment discrimination.[40]

Regarding the enforcement of state laws and judgments, the Rehnquist Court, from 1986-2003, invalidated 128 state or local laws.[41] Such invalidations included two state anti-discrimination laws with protections for sexual minorities. In *Hurley v. Irish-American Gay Group*[42] and *Boy Scouts v. Dale*[43], the Court concluded that state anti-discrimination laws were overridden by the First Amendment rights of private organizations that professed homophobia as a part of their claim. Certainly, an accurate or nuanced portrait of the practice of judicial review cannot be reduced to statistics; perhaps the most activist decision of the Rehnquist Court—*Bush v. Gore* in which the Court effectively determined the outcome of the 2001 presidential election—did not result in any laws being declared unconstitutional.[44] Further, the generally available statistics capture only an activist stance which prevailed; one could calculate the times a Justice voted to declare a government act unconstitutional but was part of the minority dissent. Nevertheless, it is impossible to refute the fact that the Rehnquist Court has declared many federal and state statutes unconstitutional, which satisfies the basic definition of an activist court.

Despite such realities, it remains true that "activism" is generally an accusation hurled at judges rendering liberal decisions and that liberals and neo-liberals tend to support judicial review in a strategy of defensiveness. "Ideological drift"[45] and similar conceptions attempt to explain the tendency of most progressives to continue to support judicial review. Judicial review on the whole once benefited progressive causes such as racial equality and reproductive rights, symbolized by the cases of *Brown v. Board of Education* and *Roe v. Wade*, and the Warren Court. That era has long since ended, despite some—perhaps just enough—successes to convince one that the trend persists. One might intellectually realize that theories of constitutional interpretation including judicial review "do not have a fixed normative or political valence"[46] but vary over time, yet might be "stuck in the past" remaining comfortable with "old positions"[47], or convinced that the "underlying structure" is sound despite a superficial "tilt on the surface."[48] Lastly, it is argued that the preference for judicial review arises from a "sensibility"[49] of paternalism, elitism, and a mistrust of the masses who are "emotional, ignorant, fuzzy-headed, and simple-minded," even if one would prefer these traits be described with "kinder, gentler adjectives."[50]

III.   Global Perspectives

In light of the rhetoric discussed above, it might seem as if in the United States sexual freedom has only ever been advanced through judicial decisions. Yet in the United States as throughout the world, sexual freedom for lesbians, other sexual minorities, and women has been broadened both through judicial review and through legislative and other democratic processes. Assuming that rights to same-sex marriage can be a component of sexual freedom, a proposition which is certainly debatable[51] it is noteworthy that despite the attention paid by conservatives to the Massachusetts Supreme Court's opinion in *Goodridge* as an example of judicial activism, other states have also enacted quasi-marital protections through the legislative process as in Connecticut[52], or through a combined judicial and legislative process as in Vermont.[53]

The California situation confounds much of the conservative rhetoric blaming "activist judges" for subverting the legislative democratic process in the area of same-sex marriage. On September 7, 2005, the California legislature passed a bill that provided that Amarriage is a personal relation arising out of a civil contract between two persons," thus allowing same-sex marriage. Governor Schwarzenegger of California vetoed the state legislature's bill, saying that the "matter should not be determined by legislative action," but by "court decision" or a direct vote of the people. Certainly the governor's action is complicated by the fact that there had been a successful ballot initiative restricting marriage to opposite sex couples in 2000, that the initiative had been declared unconstitutional by lower California courts, and was (and still is) making its way through the California judicial courts. Yet it demonstrates the contradictory positions regarding judicial review amongst those who do not advocate same-sex marriage.[54] As one conservative opined, the California law sought to impose same-sex marriage by Alegislative snub," comparable to the Massachusetts court's "judicial fiat," as well as to the Aexecutive decree" of mayors performing same-sex marriages in San Francisco and New York.[55]

Outside of the United States, the relationship between the availability of judicial review in constitutional democracies to sexual freedom, especially for lesbians, is equally unclear. The examples of the Netherlands and South Africa are illustrative. Both nations would certainly be identified in any list of constitutional democracies whose legal systems are most protective of the rights and freedoms of sexual minorities. Yet their constitutional structures and provisions are quite distinct.

The Netherlands Constitution specifically prohibits judicial review: Article 120 provides in full that "The constitutionality of laws and treaties shall not be reviewed by the courts." The Constitution, however, does specify rights, including positive rights and rights as against private parties. Article 1 states that "All persons in the Netherlands shall be treated equally in equal circumstances. Discrimination on the grounds of religion, belief, political opinion, race, or sex or on any other grounds whatsoever shall not be permitted." Subsequent articles provide for rights of association, privacy, "inviolability of the person," health, education, work, and aid from the government for subsistence. Thus, although certain rights are enumerated and entrenched in the Netherlands Constitution, they are judicially unenforceable. Given this structure, it is predictable that any advancements for sexual minorities have been accomplished through acts of Parliament, although it is not necessarily predictable that the Netherlands would be in the vanguard of providing protections for sexual minorities. In late 2000, Netherlands became the first nation to provide for same-sex marriage, when Queen Beatrix signed what is usually translated as the "Act on the Opening Up of Marriage" which amended the marriage laws to provide that "A marriage can be contracted by two persons of different sex or of the same sex."[56] Companion acts amended language in other laws to make it gender-neutral, amended adoption laws, and amended laws respecting presumed parenthood. These acts of parliament followed a previous pattern in which the Netherlands had enacted a registered partnership scheme which had gradually become more similar to marriage. In the nonmarital realm, the Dutch Parliament had enacted the General Equal Treatment Act in 1994, which included both sexual orientation and marital status as protected grounds. Sodomy had been decriminalized since 1811. Additionally, other activities had been decriminalized such as prostitution (although pimping continues to be criminalized), some drug use, and euthanasia.

While the legislative process has been paramount, there has been some invocation of judicial power. The Dutch Supreme Court, the Hoge Raad, had been presented with a case regarding same-sex marriage in 1990, as did a lower court in Amsterdam. The petitioners argued to the court that it could interpret the law to include same-sex partners, or in the alternative, that if the law was limited to opposite-sex couples it violated the Dutch Constitution, the European Convention on Human Rights, and the International Covenant on Civil and Political Rights. The courts rejected the claim that the law could be interpreted to include same-sex couples. The courts side-stepped the constitutional and international claims, stating that such issues were reserved to the Parliament, although the Netherlands Supreme Court did engage in some analysis of the issues. Interestingly, the Netherlands Supreme Court did not make a pronouncement that Parliament should address any inequalities as it had several years earlier in cases involving the unequal treatment of married and unmarried parents.[57]

Unlike the Dutch Constitution, the South Africa Constitution, adopted in its final form in 1997 1996, provides for a robust judicial review. Supremacy of the constitution is proclaimed as a value of the democratic state of South Africa in the first section of the Constitution (in addition to "human dignity, the achievement of equality and the advancement of human rights and freedoms," "non-racialism and non-sexism," and universal adult suffrage).[58] The following section explicitly provides for the supremacy of the constitution and further states that Alaw or conduct" inconsistent with the Constitution is invalid.[59] Section 167 of the Constitution establishes the Constitutional Court, which "makes the final decision whether an Act of Parliament, a provincial Act or conduct of the President is constitutional," and even Adecide on the constitutionality of any amendment to the Constitution" and "decide that Parliament or the President has failed to fulfill a constitutional obligation."[60]

The constitutional provisions that the Constitutional Court must enforce include a vigorous Bill of Rights, including both negative and positive rights, similar to the Dutch Constitution but much more expansive. The South Africa Constitution, however, is the first—and remains the only—constitution to specifically guarantee equality to sexual minorities. Section 9, entitled "Equality," provides in subsection 3 that "The state may not unfairly discriminate directly or indirectly against anyone on one or more grounds, including race, gender, sex, pregnancy, marital status, ethnic or social origin, colour, sexual orientation, age, disability, religion, conscience, belief, culture, language and birth."[61] The next subsection extends these protections to private conduct and further imposes a duty on the national government to enact legislation to Aprevent or prohibit unfair discrimination." Moreover, such legislation may be in the form of positive promotion of equality, or as it is generally known in the United States "affirmative action," under subsection 2.

Several cases have come before the Constitutional Court of South Africa relating to sexual freedom.[62] In the first, predictably involving the constitutionality of the criminalization of sodomy, the Court ruled the crime of sodomy (which applied only to males), the common law crime of unnatural sexual acts, and an array of accompanying criminal laws unconstitutional as inconsistent with the Constitution's equality sections.[63] The Constitutional Court has also applied the equality provisions protecting sexual orientation to require that same-sex partners be accorded equal treatment in the consideration of residence permits[64] in the award of benefits provided to married partners under the Judges Remuneration Act[65], allowing same-sex couples to adopt as joint parents[66] and allowing same-sex couples to both be named as parents in cases of Aartificial insemination"[67]

Undoubtedly, judicial review in South Africa, coupled with the inclusion of "sexual orientation" in the Constitution's Bill of Rights, has furthered the legal protection of sexual freedom in the nation. Yet the Constitutional Court has not been a solitary force. Indeed, in most of the cases mentioned above, the Constitutional Court has been affirming judgments of other courts, and importantly, these judgments have been largely unopposed by the executive branch members named as opposing parties. Moreover, legislative action has occurred to include protections for sexual minorities in areas such as employment, medical benefits, rental housing, and domestic violence. The Parliament promulgated The Choice on Termination of Pregnancy Act of 1996 which provides a trimester scheme in which a woman may terminate a pregnancy in the first 12 weeks, may terminate only with the advise of a doctor from weeks 13 until 20, and afterwards only if there is risk to the woman or the fetus.

In such a context, and considering the opposition of government entities in the litigation, perhaps it was not surprising that the Constitutional Court of South Africa invoked the legislative branch when it rendered its decision regarding same-sex marriage in December 2005.[68] After finding that the limitation of marriage to opposite sex couples violated South Africa's Constitution, Justice Albie Sachs, writing for the Court, noted that "Ordinarily a successful litigant should receive at least some practical relief," but that this Ais not an absolute rule."[69] In supporting the Court's conclusion to allow Parliament "to cure the defect within twelve months"[70], the Court interestingly relied upon the need for security for a "section of society that has known protracted and bitter oppression."[71] Justice Sachs reasoned that Parliament might later choose a remedy other than a simply "reading-in of the words 'or spouse'" in legislation which was sex-specific, as the Court would do[72], and the Court's "temporary remedial measure would be far less likely to achieve the enjoyment of equality as promised by the Constitution than would lasting legislative action compliant with the Constitution."[73] This somewhat co-operative model is similar to the process that occurred in the United States jurisdiction of Vermont, which resulted in the legislature passing a civil union statute available only for same-sex couples[74]; a regime which has been criticized as imposing a "separate and unequal" system of marriage.[75] Interestingly, however, the South Africa Constitutional Court maintains judicial supremacy—should the South Africa Parliament fail to remedy the situation within twelve months, the Court's remedy will be instated.[76]

Comparing the legal schemes governing sexual freedoms in South Africa and the Netherlands, even in a cursory manner, warrants several conclusions. Legal protection of sexual freedom does not require it be achieved solely by either judicial review or representative democratic processes. Further, even in legal systems with definite positions on judicial review, there is an interplay with the supposedly non-dominant branches of government. Moreover, the achievements of legal guarantees for sexual freedom are exceedingly contextual, and provisions for judicial review are only one of the conditions. For example, the status of the Netherlands in the vanguard of sexual freedoms is often linked to its secularism and the lack of organized religious fundamentalism. On the other hand, the status of South Africa as a vanguard in rights generally and the inclusion of sexual minority rights specifically, is often explained by historical contingencies and coalition work, accomplished despite organized religious and cultural fundamentalism largely attributable to the abiding influence amongst the now minority Afrikaners of the Dutch Reformed Church, as well as the popular portrayal of homosexuality as un-African.[77]

Further, even if from the perspective of the United States the legal protections appear relatively positive, there remain gaps and lacunae. Lastly, and more implicitly perhaps, an examination of the legal structures provides a partial and superficial, portrait of sexual freedom and the lived realities of sexual minorities and women in the respective societies.

IV. Preliminary Conclusions

It is tempting to succumb to an unbounded contextualism admitting of no general principles, especially if the goal is the achievement of sexual freedom. Legal structures, civil societies, and cultural conditions might be simply too diverse to support any sort of general theorizing. In the United States, neither the history of judicial review in the United States nor contemporary practices provide clear conclusions. Comparing two nations that have been in the forefront of the protection of sexual freedom reveals two constitutional democracies with very distinct approaches toward judicial review. The Netherlands Constitution prohibiting judicial review and the South Africa Constitution creating a constitutional court can seem incomparable, and the fact that each nation has advanced the rights of sexual minorities can seem mere coincidence. Rather than consider judicial review, perhaps advocates of sexual minority rights should devote themselves exclusively to cultural change.

Yet without developing theories about judicial review, advocates of sexual freedom are sidelined in the vociferous debates around sexual freedom, including the rights of sexual minorities, the rights regarding reproductive choices, and even the criminalization of sexual practices. Further, advocates will be marginalized in other controversies regarding equality, including racial and economic equalities, in which advocates of sexual freedom must participate. For example, advocates of sexual freedom must participate in the litigation surrounding economic rights, which too often is based upon family policies which privilege and reify particular notions of family, which may not be conducive to sexual freedom.

At the very least, it is necessary to debunk the neutral stance assumed by conservatives arguing against sexual freedom, whether such principles are advanced as "judicial activism" or "legislative snub." The argument regarding judicial review in constitutional democracies is not abstractable from the specific controversies at stake.

Moreover, it is vital to assert that framing judicial review in contrast to democracy presents a false dichotomy. It remains true that the judiciary is informed by popular will and sentiment and by actions of legislatures. It is also true that popular sentiment is informed by judicial pronouncements, as is the legislative process. This does not occur only as a "backlash," but can be a positive acceptance of declarations of rights. The Canadian discourse on a constitutional "dialogue" between the judiciary and the legislature is pertinent here, as it recognizes that a conversation between the various branches of government enhances accountability and therefore a democratic process that is protective of rights.[78][79] Importantly, however, the Canadian Supreme Court has recognized that "the concept of democracy is broader than the notion of fundamental rule, as fundamental as that may be."[80]

Finally, neither judicial review nor unbridled democracy alone is sufficient to procure sexual freedom. Both have severe shortcomings, especially given the entrenchment of biases against sexual minorities and women, and the ability of such biases to be manipulated by powerful interests which can be wielded with regard to a small and select judiciary, an identifiable legislature, and a diffuse electorate. At one time, feminist and lesbian theorists dreamed that we might "invent" a world of sexual freedom.[81] Working within the frameworks of constitutional democracies should not hobble such desires.

[1] Alexander Bickel, The Least Dangerous Branch: The Supreme Court at the Bar of Politics (New Haven: Yale University Press, 2d ed. 1986 [1ˢᵗ ed. 1962]).

[2] John Hart Ely, Democracy and Distrust: A Theory of Judicial Review, (Cambridge: Harvard University Press, 1980), p. 181, 152.

[3] Jeremy Waldron, Law and Disagreement. (Oxford: Claredon Press, 1999), p. 15.

[4] Steven G. Calabresi, 'Why Professor Ackerman is wrong to prefer the German to the U.S. Constitution' (2001) 18 Constitutional Commentary 51-104 at 53.

[5] Steven G. Calabresi, 'Thayer's Clear Mistake' (1993) 88 Northwestern University Law Review 269-277 at 269.

[6] Mark R. Levin, Men in Black: How the Supreme Court is Destroying America (Washington, D.C.: Regnery Publishing, Inc. 2005).

[7] Larry D. Kramer, The People Themselves: Popular Constitutionalism and Judicial Review (Oxford: Oxford University Press, 2004), p. 227-248; Mark Tushnet, Taking the Constitution Away from the Courts (Princeton: Princeton University Press, 1999).

[8] Waldron, Law and Disagreement, p. 15.

[9] James B. Thayer, 'The Origin and Scope of the American Doctrine of Constitutional Law' (1893). 7 Harvard Law Review 129-156.

[10] See e.g., Symposium: Marbury at 200: A Bicentennial Celebration of Marbury v. Madison, 20 CONST. COMM. 205-436 (2003); Symposium: Marbury and Its Legacy: A Symposium to Mark the 200th Anniversary of Marbury v. Madison, 36 GEO. WASH. INT'L L. REV. 505-693 (2003); Symposium, Marbury v. Madison and Judicial Review: Legitimacy, Tyranny, and Democracy, 37 JOHN MARSHALL LAW REV. 317-627 (2004); Symposium, Marbury v. Madison: 200 Years of Judicial Review in America, 71 TENN. L. REV. 241-313 (2004); Symposium, Marbury v. Madison: A Bicentennial Symposium, 89 VA. L. REV. 1105-1573 (2003); Symposium, Judicial Review: Blessing or Curse? Or Both? A Symposium in Commemoration of the Bicentennial of Marbury v. Madison, 28 WAKE FOREST L. REV. 313-838 (2003).

[11] Larry Diamond, Squandered Victory (New York: Henry Holt and Company, 2005), p. 158.

[12] Robert Martin, The Most Dangerous Branch: How the Supreme Court of Canada has Undermined Our Law and Our Democracy (Montreal & Kingston: McGill-Queen's University Press 2003), p. 124.

[13] Roe v. Wade, 410 U.S. 113 (1973).

[14] Brown v. Board of Education, 347 U.S. 483 (1954).

[15] 102 Cong. Rec. 4515-16 (1956) (Signed March 1956 by 19 Senators and 81 Representatives).

[16] Statement of Senator Hatfield, in support of Constitutional Amendment on Abortion, S.J. Res. 3, Congressional Record, June 27, 1983, at 17311, 17326.

[17] Antonin Scalia, A Matter of Interpretation: Federal Courts and the Law (Princeton: Princeton University Press, 1997) p. 149.

[18] Karl Rove, Against judicial imperialism. Text of Federalist Society Speech. On November 11, 2005, available at http://www.opinionjournal.com/extra/?id'110007537 (accessed November 25, 2005).

[19] Honorable Justice Michael Kirby, 'Constitutional Interpretation and Original Intent: a Form of Ancestor Worship (2000) 24 Melbourne University Law Review 1-14.

[20] The two cases regarding sexuality are Goodridge, the same-sex marriage case decided by the Massachusetts Supreme Court, Goodridge v. Department of Public Health, 798 N.E. 2d 941 (Ma. 2003), and discussed infra, and an unnamed federal district court case in which a judge decided that Afederal obscenity laws violated the pornographers' right to privacy," which undoubtedly refers to United States v. Extreme Associates, Inc. 352 F.Supp. 2d 578 (W.D. Pa. 2005). The other two cases, both unnamed, are a Ninth Circuit Court of Appeal case which Adeclared the phrase 'under God' in the Pledge of Allegiance to be unconstitutional," and a United States Supreme Court case in which Afive Justices on the Supreme Court decided that a 'national consensus' prohibited the use of the death penalty for murders committed under the age of 18." The first is a reference to the 2002 case of Newdow v. U.S. Congress, 292 F.3d 597 (9th Cir.2002), which was reversed on other grounds by the United States Supreme Court in Elk Grove Unified Sch. Dist. v. Newdow, 542 U.S. 1 (2004). The second reference is to Roper v. Simmons, 125 S. Ct. 1183 (2005).

[21] John Hart Ely, 'The wages of crying wolf: a comment on Roe v. Wade' (1973), 82 Yale Law Journal 920-949 at 935-36.

[22] John Hart Ely, Democracy and Distrust: A Theory of Judicial Review, p. 136. [cited in note 2].

[23] Ely, Wages of Crying Wolf, p. 934-5.

[24] Ely, Wages of Crying Wolf, p. 933. [use Ibid? not in Cambridge manual?]

[25] Lawrence v. Texas, 539 U.S. 558 (2003).

[26] Lawrence, 539 U.S. at 603-604.

[27] Romer v. Evans, 517 U.S. 620 (1996).
[28] Romer, 517 U.S. at 636.
[29] Romer, 517 U.S. at 647.
[30] Romer, 517 U.S. at 646.
[31] Goodridge v. Department of Public Health, 798 N.E. 2d 941 (Ma. 2003).
[32] George W. Bush, Text of State of Union Address, "We Have Not Come All This Way . . . to Falter," Wash. Post, Jan. 21, 2004, at A18.
[33] George W. Bush, Text of State of Union Address, "Let Us . . . Build a Better World," Wash. Post, Feb 3, 2005 at A14.
[34] George W. Bush, Text of State of Union Address, "America is Addicted to Oil," Wash. Post, February 1, 2006, at A14.
[35] Thomas M. Keck, The Most Activist Supreme Court in History: The Road to Modern Judicial Conservatism (Chicago: University of Chicago Press, 2004) p. 251. This statistic is not an anomaly, and a comparison of Justice Scalia's decisions from his appointment to the Court in 1986, with other Justices, shows a similar pattern. Epstein, L., J. A. Segal, H. J. Spaeth, and T.G. Walker. The Supreme Court Compendium: Data, Decisions & Developments. (Washington, D.C.: Congressional Quarterly Press., 3rd ed. 2003) p. 588-590 [Table 6-8]. A manual review of the cases decided in subsequent terms reveals a consistent result.
[36] Lochner v. New York, 198 US 45 (1908).
[37] Keck, The Most Activist Supreme Court in History, p. 40.
[38] United States v. Morrison, 529 U.S. 598 (2000).
[39] United States v. Lopez, 514 U.S. 549 (1995); Printz v. United States, 521 U.S. 898 (1997).
[40] Kimel v. Florida Board of Regents, 528 U.S. 62 (2000); Board of Trustees of University of Alabama v. Garrett, 531 U.S. 356 (2001).
[41] Keck, The Most Activist Supreme Court in History, p. 41. Again, data is readily available only until the 2003 Term, but the trend has not significantly altered. For comparison, this is less than the "activist" Warren Court, 1954-1969, in which 186 state and local laws were invalidated, and significantly less than the "moderate" Burger Court, 1969-1986, in which 309 state and local laws were invalidated. Ibid.
[42] Hurley v. Irish-American Gay Group, 515 U.S. 557 (1995).
[43] Boy Scouts of America v. Dale, 530 U.S. 640 (2000).
[44] Bush v. Gore, 531 U.S. 483 (2000).
[45] J.M. Balkin, 'Ideological drift and the struggle over meaning' (1993) 25 Connecticut Law Review 869-891.
[46] Balkin, 'Ideological drift,' p. 870.
[47] Tushnet, Taking the Constitution Away from the Courts , p. 131 [cited note 7].
[48] Tushnet, Taking the Constitution Away from the Courts , p. 132. [ibid?]
[49] Richard Parker, "Here, the People Rule": A Constitutional Populist Manifesto (Cambridge: Harvard University Press, 1994).
[50] Kramer, The People Themselves: Popular Constitutionalism and Judicial Review, p. 242- 3 [cited note 7].
[51] Ruthann Robson, 'Assimilation, marriage, and lesbian liberation' (2002) 75 Temple Law Review 709-819.
[52] Connecticut General Statutes, ' '46B-38aa to 46B-38oo (effective October 1, 2005). [typographical note: last two characters of 38oo are the letter Ao"].
[53] In Baker v. State, 744 A.2d 864 (Vt. 1999), the Vermont Supreme Court decided that the exclusion of same-sex couples from the benefits of marriage violated the state constitution and directed the legislature to remedy the situation. The legislature passed the Vermont Civil Union law, Vt. Stat. Ann. tit. 15, §§1201-1206 (2002). For a more detailed discussion, see Robson, Assimilation, p. 740-746.
[54] Press Release, Statement by Gubernatorial Press Secretary Margita Thompson on AB 849, September 7, 2005. The Press Release, however, began: "In Governor Schwarzenegger's personal life and work in public service, he has considered no undertaking more noble than the cause of civil rights. He believes that gay couples are entitled to full protection under the law and should not be discriminated against based upon their relationship."
[55] Jeff Jacoby, The People's voice on gay marriage. Boston Globe, October 5, 2005.
[56] Wet van 21 december 2000, Stb. 2001, 9. For an English translation of the text of the law, see the summary translation by Kees Waaldijk, <http://ruljis.leidenuniv.nl/user/cwaaldij/www/NHR/transl-marr.html>.
[57] For a fuller discussion of these developments, see Nancy Maxwell, 'Opening civil marriage to same-gender couples: a Netherlands - United States comparison.' (2001) 18 Arizona Journal International and Comparative Law 141-208.
[58] Constitution of the Republic of South Africa, ' 1.
[59] Constitution of the Republic of South Africa, ' 2.
[60] Constitution of the Republic of South Africa, ' 167.
[61] Constitution of the Republic of South Africa, ' 9.
[62] For two excellent discussions of the South Africa jurisprudence on sexual minorities, see Pierre DeVos, 'Same-sex sexual desire and the reimagining of the South African family' (2004) 20(2) South African Journal on Human Rights 179-206; Kerry Williams, (2004) "I do" or "we won't": legalising same-sex marriage in South Africa' (2004) 20(1) South African Journal on Human Rights 32-63.

[63] National Coalition for Gay and Lesbian Equality v. Minister of Justice, 1999.

[64] National Coalition for Gay and Lesbian Equality v. Minister of Home Affairs, 1999.

[65] Satchwell v. The President of South Africa and the Minister of Justice, 2002.

[66] Du Toit and De Vos v. Minister for Welfare and Population Development, 2002.

[67] J and B v. Director General of the Department of Home Affairs, 2003.

[68] Lesbian and Gay Equality Project and Eighteen Others v. The Minister of Home Affairs, 2005.

[69] Ibid, paragraph 133.

[70] Ibid, paragraph 161.

[71] Ibid, paragraph 136.

[72] Ibid, paragraph 135.

[73] Ibid, paragraph 136.

[74] See note * supra.

[75] Barbara Cox, 'But Why Not Marriage: An Essay on Vermont's Civil Unions Law, Same-Sex Marriage, and Separate but (Un)Equal' (2000) 25 Vermont Law Review 113, 132-33.

[76] *Lesbian and Gay Equality Project and Eighteen Others v. The Minister of Home Affairs*, 2005, THE ORDER, paragraph 2(e).

[77] Carl F. Stychin, A Nation by Right: National Cultures, Sexual Identity Politics, and the Discourse of Rights (Philadelphia: Temple University Press, 1998), p. 52-88.

[78] In Vriend v. Alberta, [1998], 1 S.C.R. 493, the Supreme Court of Canada relied on notions of a constitutional "dialogue" between the branches, inherent in the Canadian constitutional Charter of Rights, to hold that sexual orientation must be a protected category for purposes of discrimination.

[79] Id. at 140

[80] Id. at 140.

[81] For example, as Nicole Brossard has written, "a lesbian who does not reinvent the world is a lesbian in the process of disappearing." Brossard, Nicole. 1985. The Aerial Letter 136 (tr. Malene Wildeman) Toronto: The Women's Press. Similarly, Monique Wittig's famous instruction in Les Guérillerčs is "Make an effort to remember. Or, failing that, invent." (tr. David LeVay 1969). New York: Avon Books. 89.

CHAPTER 9

DECONSTRUCTING DEFERENCE: A COMPARATIVE ANALYSIS OF JUDICIAL APPROACHES TO HEALTH CARE IN SOUTH AFRICA AND CANADA

Kirsty McLean**

The testing right is a principle of the Devil.[1]

Introduction

In democratic countries, courts are generally reluctant to make decisions on how scarce medical resources should be allocated.[2] This reticence on the side of courts is, in part, attributable to a notion of deference to the other branches of government in policy decision-making. This chapter explores and contrasts two judgments in Canada and South Africa involving health care. It begins with a general discussion of the concept of 'constitutional deference' and then uses this notion to analyse the two judgments. The chapter concludes with some general observations on the two judgments and the value of using constitutional deference in evaluating judicial reasoning.

Deference in Judicial Review

Judicial review is the evaluation undertaken, by courts, of the exercise of public power—whether by a public or a private body—for consistency with a set of pre-defined or constructed legal norms.[3] The power under review may be exercised by any of the branches of government—the executive, including the public administration, the legislature and even the judiciary itself. The exercise of public power is similarly wide-ranging, including executive and judicial decision-making, policy formulation (by the legislature or executive), legislation (primary or delegated) or the implementation of legislation or policy. Courts undertake judicial review when they consider whether such legislation, policy or action is consistent with these norms. The precise content of those norms will depend on the constitution; the values of the dominant culture; the type of democracy which a country espouses as well as the court's understanding of its role and of judicial review.

The justification for judicial review is broadly so that the courts can act as a check on the use of public power, ensuring that it is exercised in a manner consistent with the constitution (in the wide sense) of a particular country.[4] This justification is grounded in the rule of law, as well as the separation of powers doctrine and the system of checks and balances that derives from the doctrine. In addition to this justification, in countries with a written Constitution which provides for judicial review, the courts are mandated to uphold the Constitution, through, amongst other means, the process of judicial review. Such courts have, therefore, direct constitutional legitimacy for the exercise of their power.

In applying these norms, courts have a degree of discretion regarding the strictness with which they are applied. In other words, they can apply the norms strictly, applying a high level of judicial scrutiny, or they can apply them more leniently, preferring to accept the word of the legislature or executive (or judiciary) that it has in fact met the standard required by the norm in question. It is this degree of discretion that is encompassed in the notion of deference. Deference, as a principle of judicial decision-making, therefore, includes the approach of the courts to the level of scrutiny applied in the process of judicial review and consequently— as the reverse side of the coin—to the amount of weight which a court gives to the decisions of the institution or person under review. Deference also operates in other respects, such as the choice of remedy or the way in which the remedy is crafted, or in the manner in which the court defines the content of the right itself. Deference is therefore not an all-or-nothing approach, but rather a range of approaches to the institution whose action is under review as well as the action itself. Deference reflects the court's understanding of its role and the role of the other branches of government in judicial adjudication.

This understanding of deference differs from others which seek to describe a theory of when it would be appropriate for courts to defer and when it would not.[5] Instead, the analysis of deference developed in this chapter arises out of the separation of powers doctrine and must be understood as a general principle of constitutional adjudication. For this reason, the term 'constitutional deference' is used to indicate that deference, in the sense used in this chapter, is a principle of judicial adjudication. Thus the reasons which underpin a court's deferential approach (in the sense of a great degree of deference) in choosing a lower standard of review, for example, are the same as those which inform a court's 'ordinary' standard of review. This approach has been chosen for two reasons. First, it is more conceptually coherent to discuss a court's use of a high level of deference within the broader framework of its overall approach to judicial review and adjudication. Second, delimiting the theoretical underpinnings of judicial approaches to adjudication through the lens of deference enables greater scrutiny of 'ordinary review' and helps focus discussion on how courts adjudicate particular areas of the law.

Despite the non-determinant nature of the concept, it is possible to draw out a number of principled, underlying considerations which influence the ways in which the courts have used the notion of deference. These considerations may be grouped into three categories, and courts' understanding of constitutional deference is dependent on the interplay of these three factors, namely, the appropriate role of the court *vis-à-vis* the institution under review, the capacity of the court *vis-à-vis* the institution under review, and the content of the matter before the court.[6] These three factors together make up a court's specific approach to constitutional deference. These considerations are analogous to Cartesian coordinates, with each factor operating as an axis.[7] In principle, these axes operate independently, that is, there is no necessary relationship between the approaches taken for one to determine the approach taken on another. In practice, however, these three issues may be used instrumentally so that the approach taken in all three may be similar, and there may be substantial overlap between the axes. An example may be useful here: a court, in considering the legality of an alleged extra-legal rendition of a foreign national, suspected of terrorist activities, to a country with which the home country has friendly relations, may decide that, for reasons of comity and international relations, it would ordinarily afford the executive a high degree of constitutional deference in deciding where and when to deport non-nationals suspected of terrorism. At the same time, however, it may decide that the rights of the individual to liberty and due process, as well as the principle of rule of law, would demand a low level of constitutional deference in these circumstances. Here the two axes, that of democratic competence and the nature of the interests at stake, point in different directions. The third axis, that of institutional competence, may or may not be raised to defend a high or low degree of deference. Alternatively, the court could decide that it wishes to adopt a low degree of constitutional deference, and then use all three arguments of democratic competence, institutional competence, and the importance of the right in question to justify its finding.

Constitutional deference operates on two levels. First, a court (whether that be an individual judge, a particular court such as a constitutional court, or the judiciary of an entire country) can have a general approach to deference, that is, it can be characterised as a 'deferent' court or a non-deferent court. Such an approach may parallel the characterisation of a court as non-activist or activist respectively (or executive-minded or non-executive-minded). The second level on which constitutional deference operates is on a case-by-case basis. Here, a judge (or judges) will assess the specific matter before her and decide (albeit often intuitively) what the appropriate level of deference is, depending on the three factors outlined above. The approach adopted in a particular case may relate to the general, overarching approach of the court, but is not necessarily determined by it. In the remainder of this chapter, it is the second approach to deference which will be used.

In short, constitutional deference is the principle that a certain amount of weight, or *respect*,[8] should be accorded to the decisions of the executive or legislature in assessing the legality of those decisions in an exercise of constitutional review. The principle of constitutional deference can never be reduced to a bright-line test. It is a complex notion relating to doctrines of separation of powers, justiciability and comity. How and when courts choose to defer is determined by their approach to three considerations, that is, the court's understanding of its institutional role, the court's understanding of its institutional competence, and the nature of the matter before the court. These three factors are discussed, in more detail, separately below.

(a) Principles of Democracy

The first aspect making up a court's approach to constitutional deference relates to its understanding of the institutional independence or interdependence of the three branches of government, in particular, the role of the courts in a democracy when engaged in the process of judicial review. This issue has also been described by Jeffrey Jowell as one of 'constitutional competence', involving 'a normative assessment of the proper role of institutions in a democracy.'[9]

The democratic legitimacy of judicial review has been the subject of intense academic debate.[10] It is important to note at the outset that this discussion of the debate focuses on whether the institutional practice of judicial review is, in itself, democratic, and not on the efficacy of rights protection through a system of judicial review. That is a separate question.[11] Neither does this discussion consider the political objections to a rights-based discourse which argues that rights-discourse impoverishes our conception of society and leads to a preoccupation of the individual with his or her rights, rather than a more group-based approach to rights.[12] The argument that judicial review is a preferable or even a necessary means to ensure adequate protection of constitutional rights does not equate with the question of the democratic legitimacy of judicial review. Rather, the 'democracy versus juristocracy debate' is one that hinges on the countermajoritarian nature of judicial review, since unelected (and therefore democratically unaccountable) judges, in engaging in judicial review, overturn the decisions of the democratically-elected majority representatives. This is the 'paradox' of judicial review in constitutional democracies: on the one hand, separation of powers requires that courts hold government accountable to the standards set out in the constitution; yet the power given to the courts may be used to thwart the very right to political participation by withdrawing debate from the public arena to the domain of the courts.[13]

Advocates of judicial review have essentially three arguments open to them in the face of this objection to judicial review. First, they can limit the scope of judicial review to procedural matters in order to remove the democratic objections to substantive judicial review. This is the approach promoted by John Ely.[14] The second avenue open to judicial review proponents is to question the assumption that democracy is the sole determinant of legitimacy. Such theorists would accept the undemocratic nature of constitutional review, but argue that it is nonetheless valuable as it affords greater protection for rights. The final option is to challenge a notion of democracy that excludes judicial review, that is, properly understood, democracy is in fact enhanced by judicial review—an argument advanced by theorists such as Ronald Dworkin.[15]

It is clear that there is a range of reasonable and defensible views which a court could adopt. Whatever jurisprudential position a court adopts on this 'spectrum' of understandings, this position will be crucial in determining that courts' approach to constitutional deference.

(b) Institutional Capacity

The second consideration underpinning a court's approach to deference relates to perceived institutional limitations in the various branches of government and is based on a 'practical evaluation of the capacity of decision making bodies to make certain decisions'.[16] This justification is given further weight in the modern bureaucratic State with its reliance on specialist expertise in almost all areas of the government machine. Thus, it is seen as inappropriate for courts to engage in review of complex government policy, or 'polycentric decision-making', as judges lack the experience, knowledge or resources to make these types of decisions, in particular, to assess what the consequences of their decisions may be and to respond flexibly to unanticipated results of those decisions. For the same reasons, as a general rule, courts will be far more willing to defer to other agencies where the matter is one of fact or policy rather than of law or constitutional interpretation. For Lord Steyn, the 'relative institutional capacity' of the courts is the critical factor in deciding whether courts should defer to the other branches of government.[17]

Lon Fuller's famous posthumous article on polycentricity is often cited as authority for the view that courts are not appropriate forums to decide sufficiently polycentric matters, that is, that courts should not decide matters which involve a large, complex, interrelated web of relationships, such that a change to one factor, will produce incalculable changes to other factors.[18] Fuller argues that almost all judicial decisions contain elements of polycentricity and that the distinction between polycentric and non-polycentric decisions is really one of degree.[19] It is only when a polycentric decision has reached a sufficiently high degree of polycentricity that it falls outside of the limits of adjudication.[20] Fuller does not argue that such decisions are incapable of resolution, only that their resolution should not be undertaken through the judicial system. Moreover, the question of whether a court should adjudicate a polycentric decision or not, is dependent on the way in which precedent operates in a particular legal system. The more rigorously courts apply the doctrine of stare decisis, the less inclined courts should be to decide polycentric issues since successive courts will be bound to a rigid decision. If, on the other hand, 'judicial precedents are liberally interpreted and are subject to reformulation and clarification as problems not originally foreseen arise, the judicial process as a whole is enabled to absorb these covert polycentric elements.'[21] Fuller's understanding of the problems relating to polycentric adjudication is therefore dynamic and involves an understanding of the specific consequences of polycentric adjudication on the legal system in question. He does not draw a bright line between polycentric decisions as non-justiciable and non-polycentric decisions as justiciable. Instead, his work can be used to support a more subtle approach, where the degree of polycentricity is one of the factors that influences a court's approach to justiciability or deference.

Since decisions involving social policy or socio-economic rights are normally thought to involve polycentric issues and complex issues of policy, courts are often reluctant to adjudicate on such matters and will usually accord the State a high level of constitutional deference in such adjudication.[22] In particular, where there are competing socio-economic theories, or a decision would have far-reaching resource-allocation implications, courts will be more reluctant to make policy choices. One would expect, however, that where a domestic constitution expressly includes socio-economic rights, such as in South Africa, courts would adopt a lower level of constitutional deference as socio-economic matters move from being those of pure 'policy' into the realm of justiciable rights.[23] Another issue affecting the institutional competence of courts to adjudicate certain matters is the nature of the evidence placed before the court. Where evidence relates to complex social science matters, courts will be more deferent to the decision-making of the other branches of government.[24] There is also, of course, a limit to the quantity of evidence that can be placed before the court and which judges can be expected to assimilate.[25]

(c) The Political Nature of Rights

The third consideration relates to the nature of the subject matter under review. There are a number of ways in which this can affect the level of deference applied by a court. First, where the action is one characterised by greater political discretion (such as the appointment of officials), courts will tend to be more deferential to the institution under review. This is clearly demonstrated in the British decision of *A* where Lord Bingham expressly stated that one of the reasons for affording deference to the executive in its conclusion that the United Kingdom is facing a 'threat to the life of the nation' is because this is a 'pre-eminently political judgment':

The more purely political (in a broad or narrow sense) a question is, the more appropriate it will be for political resolution and the less likely it is to be an appropriate matter for judicial decision. The smaller, therefore, will be the potential role of the court. It is the function of political and not judicial bodies to resolve political questions. Conversely, the greater the legal content of any issue, the greater the potential role of the court, because under our constitution and subject to the sovereign power of Parliament it is the function of the courts and not of political bodies to resolve legal questions.[26]

This simple distinction between 'legal' and 'political' questions, however, threatens to unravel, particularly where two competing rights or interests are at play. The example above, for instance, begs the question: why is the interpretation of what constitutes a 'threat to the life of the nation' purely a political question where it also constitutes a statutory pre-condition for legitimate derogations from the Human Rights Act 1988? Surely this could equally be characterised as a legal question?

A second instance where courts are more likely to be deferential to the decisions of the executive or legislature is where the constitution or right in question permits a wide range of legitimate responses, or where the right has to be balanced against another right.[27] And third, when fundamental rights, highly prized in a particular society, are in issue, a court is less likely to defer to choices made by the agency in question. This approach often results in courts drawing lines between what they will protect as 'fundamental human rights' and those which are non-justiciable or which require a greater degree of deference. This approach of differing levels of review is famously expounded by Justice Stone in the United States Supreme Court in *United States v Carolene Products Co* in the fourth footnote. In that note, Justice Stone explained that the new deferential method expounded by the Court in that case did not mean that the same level of deference was necessarily to be applied in all constitutional litigation and that legislation aimed at 'particular religious, or national, or racial minorities', for example, may call for a 'more searching judicial enquiry'.[28]

Socio-economic rights are a good example of a category of rights where many judges would accept that a highly deferent approach should be adopted—that is, if they are to be considered justiciable at all. Decisions with resource-allocation implications are another category of cases where courts will generally show a great degree of deference to the decision-making of the executive or legislature.[29] As Sandra Fredman points out, however, just as a strict distinction between 'legal' and 'political' decisions is dubious, the category of 'social or economic' decisions or those with resource implications is difficult to sustain.[30]

In addition to these three contextual factors, others can be postulated. For instance, it is arguable that the subject matter should affect the level of review imposed where the agency has an interest in the outcome and may be perceived as biased in the decision-making process. In such cases it is important for the court to be seen as an independent arbiter. A good example is where political rights are involved, such as the right to vote. Where a dispute arises in Parliament or amongst the executive, around voting regulations or practices, a court should be quick to adjudicate the matter and apply a high level of scrutiny in constitutional review. This justification arises out of a more pragmatic conception of separation of powers.

Comparative Approaches to Health Care

The second part of this chapter discusses two recent judgments dealing with public health care in Canada and South Africa in order to illustrate how the principle of constitutional deference contributes to an understanding of judgments involving complex social and economic matters.

(a) *Chaoulli*

The *Chaoulli v Quebec*[31] judgment was handed down in June 2005 and has generated extensive discussion both within Quebec and throughout Canada more generally, on the role of the State in regulating access to health care, as well as on the role of the courts in reviewing that regulation.[32] The judgment concerned the validity of section 15 of the Health Insurance Act and section 11 of the Hospital Insurance Act, under the Quebec Charter and the Canadian Charter.[33] These two provisions prohibit Quebeckers from taking out private medical insurance for services in the private sector that are available under the provincial health system. The rationale of these provisions is the ethical claim that health care services should be provided on the basis of need, and not on the basis of wealth. The appellants claimed that the waiting times in the public health system, coupled with the prohibition on private medical insurance, created an obstacle to medical treatment, resulting in unnecessary suffering. As a result, the appellants argued, section 7 of the Charter, which protects the right to life, liberty and security of the person is infringed.[34] The approach of the majority and minority differ markedly in their approach to evidence and in their reasoning, and a discussion of the two approaches is informative of differing approaches to constitutional deference.

The majority, per Deschamps J, found that there was an infringement of section 7 of the Charter, since waiting times within the public health care system meant that it was 'inevitable that some patients will die if they have to wait for an operation'.[35] Moreover, this infringement was not justified under the Charter since there was no proportionality between the measure adopted and the objective of the provisions, namely, 'to preserve the integrity of the public health-care system'.[36] While Deschamps J found that there was a rational connection, she held that the Attorney General had not demonstrated that this measure met the minimal impairment test.[37] In coming to this conclusion, Deschamps J relied extensively on comparative evidence from other Canadian provinces and OECD countries showing that the integrity of the public health care system could be maintained, even with private medical insurance allowed.[38]

In her reasoning, Deschamps J made a number of comments on the level of deference required in this judgment. Her starting point, in this discussion, is that government must be able to justify any measures it takes which infringe Charter rights. In assessing whether such a limitation is justifiable, courts can consider any evidence they wish and, provided that courts are satisfied that they have all the evidence necessary to make an assessment, they must do so. It is only where the State explains why evidence is too complex to be understood by the court, that a measure of deference is required.[39] Moreover, none of the other reasons justifying deference, such as 'the prospective nature of the decision, the impact on public finances, the multiplicity of competing interests, the difficulty of presenting scientific evidence and the limited time available to the state' were, according to

Deschamps J, applicable in this case.[40] Rather, '[t]he instant case is a good example of a case in which the courts have all the necessary tools to evaluate government's measure'. Thus, Deschamps J emphasises the second principle underpinning the notion of constitutional deference discussed earlier, namely the institutional competence of the courts to decide complex social matters. In addition, she adopts a narrow understanding of competence, arguing that the level of deference to be applied will depend on the factual assessment of whether the court has sufficient evidence before it to decide the matter, rather than a deeper appreciation of the inherent limitations on the courts for adjudication of complex, polycentric matters. Thus, for Deschamps J, deference is something to be applied (or not) depending on the circumstances and evidence before the court. This is a very thin conception of deference, and one which fails to appreciate how the notions that underpin deference have already contributed to her reasoning. Notably, her discussion of deference is 'tagged on' to the end of her judgment, after she had already made her finding that 'the prohibition of private insurance contracts is not justified by the evidence'[41] and therefore does not meet the minimal impairment test. This approach is inconsistent with earlier Canadian jurisprudence which generally considers the level of deference appropriate at the beginning of the limitations analysis.[42]

The concurring judgment of Chief Justice McLachlin and Major J (with Bastarache J) similarly found that the purpose of the legislation was to protect the public health system and that there was an infringement of section 7 of the Canadian Charter as the provisions in question restricted access to private health care, while 'failing to provide public health care of a reasonable standard within a reasonable time'.[43] Such an infringement, they concluded, failed to meet the rational connection requirement, and went further to characterise the provisions as 'arbitrary'.[44] Moreover, the provisions failed to meet the minimal impairment test as 'the prohibition goes further than necessary to protect the public system'.[45]

The majority and concurring judgments therefore characterise the question before the Court as whether the prohibition on private medical insurance is justifiable given the waiting times within the public health system, and the legislative objective of protecting the public health system. The dissenting approach, per Binnie and LeBel JJ (with Fish J), by contrast, defines the question before the Court as a question of constitutional competence.[46] Similarly, the minority defines the objective of the legislative provisions differently to the majority and concurring judgments, which define the legislative objective vaguely as protecting the public health care system:

> Quebec's legislative objective is to provide high quality health care, at a reasonable cost, for as many people as possible in a manner that is consistent with principles of efficiency, equity and fiscal responsibility. Quebec (along with the other provinces and territories) subscribes to the policy objectives of the *Canada Health Act*, which include (i) the equal provision of medical services to all residents, regardless of status, wealth or personal insurability, and (ii) fiscal responsibility. ... The legislative task is to strike a balance among competing interests.[47]

In dealing with this issue, the minority adopted a far more deferential approach than the majority. The minority held that the debate on this issue could not be resolved by the courts, and that it is impossible for courts to assess when health care services are 'reasonable' as the concurring judgment of MacLachlin CJ and Major J held. While this criticism, given the jurisprudence of the South African courts, is perhaps overstated,[48] it is warranted insofar as the concurring judgment failed to discuss how and why it reached this conclusion. In considering the evidence before the Court, Binnie and LeBel JJ emphasised the importance of appropriate deference to the institutional competence of government in making policy decisions.[49]

> In our view, the appellants' case does not rest on constitutional law but on their disagreement with the Quebec government on aspects of social policy. The proper forum to determine the social policy of Quebec in this matter is the National Assembly.[50]

Similarly, the minority emphasise the constitutional competence of the State to decide certain matters:

> Still less can we say that the boundaries of the Quebec health plan are dictated by the Constitution. Drawing the line around social programs properly falls within the legitimate exercise of the democratic mandates of people elected for such purposes, preferably after a public debate.[51]

Thus, in contrast to the majority, the minority are more keenly aware of the role of the courts in adjudicating social and economic policy, and adopt a more deferential approach to the adjudication of these issues. The majority approach has been criticised for its unprincipled approach to deference, for its inadequate handing of complex evidence, and for failing to take into consideration the rights of vulnerable groups.[52] It has also been received negatively by the executive and the public, and may, for this reason, be a good example of where the relevant legislation should be re-enacted with the 'notwithstanding clause'.[53]

(b) New Clicks

The second judgment to be considered is the South African decision of *Minister of Health v New Clicks*.[54] Discussion of the South African courts' approach to deference is more difficult than for jurisdictions such as Canada, since South African courts have generally not yet engaged directly in a discussion of deference. Deference appears to still be equated with apartheid 'executive-mindedness' and a more sophisticated understanding of constitutional deference has yet to emerge.[55] The *New Clicks* judgment is no exception to this. Nevertheless, the doctrine and the principles underlying it, do inform the judicial reasoning of the various judgments and it is informative to examine the judgment from this perspective.

New Clicks concerned the constitutionality of certain regulations promulgated by the Minister of Health in order to regulate the pricing of medicines in South Africa in giving effect to section 27 of the Constitution—the right to have access to adequate health care services.[56] Various regulations were challenged by the pharmaceutical industry on standard administrative law grounds of review, most notably that the 'dispensing fee', which was determined by the Pricing Committee, was not appropriate and that the decision-making process in determining that fee was flawed on a number of grounds. A narrow majority of the Court (6:5) held that the dispensing fee was not appropriate and referred the decision back to the Pricing Committee for reconsideration.[57] The judgment makes a number of important statements on administrative law—but unfortunately, none of these remarks are concurred in by a majority of judges. The judgment is therefore hugely

disappointing for administrative lawyers and represents an opportunity missed by
the Court to clarify several important issues. This chapter will not consider further
any of the substantive provisions of the judgment, and will, instead, consider how
the concept of constitutional deference can be used to throw light on the approaches
adopted by the judges. There are five separate judgments dealing with the merits,
and three concurring judgments. The judgment as a whole begins with a judgment
by 'The Court' in which the facts are set out as well as the order, and a useful
summary of the findings in the various judgments.

The first substantive judgment is provided by Chaskalson CJ. Chaskalson CJ
begins by emphasising that the judgment concerns a legal issue, not a political one,
and that the judgment concerns the legality of government policy, not its wisdom.
He goes on to point out that this is not unusual and is part of the day-to-day role of
the courts in a democracy.[58] Further into his judgment, in response to an assertion by
the State that 'Courts are ill-equipped to deal with economic matters and ought not
to sit in judgment on what are essentially political decisions taken by the Executive
in making regulations', Chaskalson CJ is careful to reaffirm that the exercise of all
public power is subject to constitutional control and that 'it is the duty of Courts if
called upon to do so to determine whether or not power has been exercised
consistently with the requirements of the Constitution and the law.'[59] Thus
Chaskalson CJ again emphasises the democratic and constitutionally mandated role
of courts in upholding the Constitution and ensuring that government action is
consistent with the Constitution. There is also a hint of deference to the
constitutional and institutional competence of the executive in deciding what factors
are relevant to decision-making:

> Courts must be sensitive to the special role of the executive in making regulations.
> This, and the special expertise of the Pricing Committee, are factors to which due
> regard must be paid in the present case. What is or is not relevant, and what is
> appropriate, were in the first instance matters for the Pricing Committee and the
> Minister to decide.[60]

Chaskalson CJ then goes on to say that, despite this, courts should not 'rubber
stamp' decisions of the executive and must scrutinise them for consistency with the
Constitution.

The remainder of Chaskalson CJ's judgment is remarkable only for its measured
objectivity, balanced assessment of the evidence, and emphasis on the 'legal' nature
of the reasoning and the importance of preserving neutrality. Chaskalson CJ appears
to be acutely aware of the political context in which this judgment is given, and goes
to extraordinary lengths (literally—his printed judgment is well over 100 pages) to
maintain balanced, careful and objective judicial review. Only one thing strikes the
reader as remarkable in his judgment, and that is the extent to which he goes to cure
the defects in the various regulations which otherwise, would be struck down: of the
eight instances in which the regulations are founds to be defective, six are corrected
through either the severance of words or through reading down, or both, and only
two remaining regulations are referred back to the Pricing Committee and Minister
for reconsideration.[61]

The second substantive judgment is provided by Ngcobo J. The tone of the
judgment is much the same as that of Chaskalson CJ, and Ngcobo J is similarly
careful to place his reasoning squarely within traditional administrative law
justifications. A passage from his judgment demonstrates this well:

It follows that the Pricing Committee and the Minister exercise some discretion in the determination of the appropriate dispensing fee. But they must remain within the range of what is appropriate and observe the limits for the exercise of discretion. What must constantly be borne in mind is that Courts have a limited role in reviewing the exercise of an administrative discretion. They should guard against substituting their views on what is appropriate for that of the Pricing Committee and the Minister. Their role is to ensure that administrative action is lawful, reasonable and procedurally fair.[62]

Ngcobo J goes on, however, to point out that courts should recognise the expertise of the Pricing Committee in determining an appropriate fee, and 'should interfere with a fee fixed by the Pricing Committee only if the fee is one that is beyond the range of what is appropriate'.[63] In his discussion of the facts and application of administrative law, Ngcobo J's judgment is similar to that of Chaskalson, although he does find a number of additional flaws in other regulations. He is therefore more extensive in scope of matters considered, but not in his level of scrutiny of the regulations.

The Ngcobo J judgment is followed by the Sachs J judgment, which takes a different approach to the question of whether section 33 of the Constitution, which provides a right to just administrative action, covers regulatory rule making. Sachs J found that it does not, and that the notion of legality should be used to cover the 'lacunae' left by this absence.[64] In his discussion of what this standard of legality would require, Sachs J quotes the *TAC* judgment,[65] noting that courts are 'ill-suited to adjudicate upon issues where Court orders could have multiple social and economic consequences for the community',[66] thereby emphasising the institutional limitations of courts to decide complex, polycentric matters. Rather, all that is required of the courts, by the Constitution, is to evaluate the reasonableness of State action.[67] For Sachs J, if courts are to 'arrogate to themselves the right to declare that Parliament has not acted reasonably in adopting a certain piece of legislation' this would constitute 'a political judgment that would be both institutionally and constitutionally inappropriate'.[68] Thus, for Sachs J, the source of the courts' authority must lie in the Constitution.

The minority judgment, concurred in by four other judges, adopts a different position on the main question before the Court, namely, whether the dispensing fee is 'appropriate' within the meaning of the Medicines Act. The judgment, written by Moseneke J, turns largely on its assessment of the evidence, and whether the dispensing fee could be considered 'reasonable'. For Moseneke J, the evidence on whether the dispensing fee would undermine the financial viability of pharmacies was inconclusive, and therefore there were no substantive grounds for considering the dispensing fee inappropriate. In coming to this conclusion, Moseneke J concluded that because it could not be shown by the pharmacies that the dispensing fee was unreasonable it could not be demonstrated that there was any procedural unfairness.[69] This reasoning stands in contrast with the majority who found that the Pricing Committee and the Minister had not demonstrated procedural fairness by failing to demonstrate that they had taken into consideration all relevant circumstances. Moseneke J did, however, find that, in the case of rural and courier pharmacies the dispensing fee was inappropriate as the Pricing Committee and the Minister had failed to apply their minds to the special circumstances of these two categories of pharmacies.[70] Again, procedural unfairness was found on the basis on substantive unreasonableness.

The second minority judgment by Yacoob J, and concurred in by the same judges who concurred in the Moseneke J judgment, found a number of the regulations which the majority had found void for vagueness, to be acceptable. In his discussion, Yacoob J goes to great lengths to read the provisions in question in a manner that makes them intelligible. In doing so he strains the ordinary linguistic meaning of the text in a manner often inconsistent with norms of statutory interpretation, to create a 'subtle and creative' regulatory system.[71] The two minority judgments, therefore, demonstrate a high level of constitutional deference, one in which the courts will go to all possible lengths to uphold government rule-making.

Conclusion

It is perhaps unfair to compare these two judgments, since the *Chaoulli* decision involved substantive review of a legislative measure under the Canadian Charter, while the *New Clicks* decision was an administrative law decision, which did not, on the face of it, deal with the substantive merits of the regulatory measures. Moreover, the majority approach in the *Chaoulli* decision is (arguably) extraordinary it its analysis and approach to deference. Nevertheless, both judgments deal with matters which have complex social and economic consequences—and both are good examples of the adjudication of polycentric issues. For this reason it is instructive to compare the approaches adopted by the various judges as illustrative of the possible routes that could have been travelled.

The approach of the majority of the Supreme Court of Canada in *Chaoulli* demonstrated astonishingly little deference, and was far less deferential than the minority judgment, and all the judgments of the South African Constitutional Court in *New Clicks*. The majority of the Court struck down legislative provisions which prohibited Quebeckers from taking out private medical insurance for services in the private sector that are available under the provincial health system—a decision with far-reaching consequences for public health care in Quebec, and in Canada more generally. For the majority in *Chaoulli*, the question of deference is a question of whether the court is in a position to assess the evidence before it properly, focussing almost exclusively on the institutional competence of the courts to adjudicate such matters. By contrast, the judges in the South African Constitutional Court, in particular, the judgment of Chaskalson CJ, are acutely aware of the political context in which the decision was handed down. The underlying thread informing the judges' various approaches is the importance of constitutional competence, locating the judgment squarely within the traditional confines for judicial review of administrative action.

There is an important difference in the Constitutions of these two jurisdictions which should be noted: South Africa has a set of justiciable socio-economic rights, including a right to have access to health care services, while Canada does not. While neither *Chaoulli* nor *New Clicks* were decided on the basis of a right to health care, one would expect the existence of the right in the South African Constitution to have some impact on the constitutional landscape in which the adjudication of *New Clicks* took place. Indeed, it appears as if the existence of a right to have access to health care while, far from yielding a less deferential approach on the part of the Constitutional Court to the review of health policy, instead was used to justify a more deferential approach. It was, in part, the fact that the State sought to give effect to the right to access to health care in promulgating the regulations in question, and the Court's sympathy for this project, which underpinned its accommodating interpretation of the regulations and the remedies given. The minority, in fact, would have applied an exceptionally low standard of review—surprising given the patent errors in many of the regulations. Comparing the two judgments also illustrates the contextual nature of constitutional deference and its dependence on the political culture in which it operates. South African courts are still wary of 'overstepping the mark', particularly in relation to executive action, and are careful to situate their role within the broader constitutional project.

Finally, it would be useful to summarise the value which an understanding of constitutional deference can bring to the analysis of case law: first, the concept creates a framework within which to understand and critique the rhetoric of deference employed by the courts; second, it provides a perspective to understand what the courts are doing even when they don't use the language of deference; third, it allows for analysis of judicial reasoning across different types of cases and provides a framework for such an analysis; and fourth, and perhaps most importantly, it provides a framework within which judges themselves should understand their approach to a particular case. In this sense, a doctrine of constitutional deference is a call for greater transparency and self-reflection in judicial reasoning. There is no single or 'correct' approach to deference, or a correct deferential standard which the court should apply, just as there can never be a 'correct' understanding of democracy. Rather, this approach to constitutional deference brings about a greater consideration of the underpinning principles of constitutional deference and greater transparency and engagement on the part of the courts and commentators with these principles.

---

[1] President Paul Kruger (Transvaal Republic) on Judicial Review (1897) cit in J Dugard, 'The Judicial Process, Positivism and Civil Liberty' (1971) 88 *South African Law Journal* 181, 184.

[2] *See, e.g., R v. Cambridge Health Authority, ex parte B*, 1995 (2) ER 129 (CA) (United Kingdom), 137; *Cruzan v. Dir. Missouri Department of Health*, 497 U.S. 261, 303 (1990) (United States); and *Soobramoney v. Minister of Health, KwaZulu-Natal*, 1998 (1) SA 765 (CC), 30 (South Africa). For a contrasting approach, see *Paschim Banga Khet Mazdoor Samity v. State of West Bengal*, (1996) AIR SC 2426 (India).

[3] This general discussion is limited to a characterisation of countries with a democratic system of government and an independent judiciary.

[4] There are a number of competing theories on the justification for judicial review which will not be covered in this chapter. *See* Christopher Forsyth, ed. *Judicial Review and the Constitution* (Oxford: Hart Publishing, 2000) for a good overview of the debate in the United Kingdom, in the context of administrative law.

[5] *See, e.g.,* Lord Steyn, "Deference: A Tangled Story," *Public Law* [2005]: 346, 350; and M. Hunt, "Sovereignty's Blight: Why Contemporary Public Law Needs the Concept of "Due Deference,"" in *Public Law in a Multi-Layered Constitution*, ed. Nicholas Bamforth and Peter Leyland (Oxford: Hart Publishing, 2003), 337, 345.

[6] There may, of course, be unprincipled reasons for a court adopting a particular position in relation to deference. These will not be considered here.

[7] In mathematics, Cartesian coordinates are used to describe the position of a point in relation to set of intersecting axes.

[8] *See* David Dyzenhaus, "The Politics of Deference: Judicial Review and Democracy," *The Province of Administrative Law*, ed. Michael Taggart (Oxford: Hart Publishing, 1997), 279 for a discussion of deference as respect.

[9] Jeffrey Jowell, "Of Vires and Vacuums: The Constitutional Context of Judicial Review," *Judicial Review and the Constitution*, ed. Christopher Forsyth (Oxford: Hart Publishing, 2000) 327 at 330. Jowell's argument is set out in relation to administrative judicial review, but is nevertheless applicable to constitutional review.

[10] For a good overview of this debate in the United States, *see* Barry Friedman, "The Birth of an Academic Obsession: The History of the Countermajoritarian Difficulty," *Yale Law Journal* 112 (2002): 153.

[11] *See* Wojciech Sadurski, "Judicial Review and the Protection of Constitutional Rights," *Oxford Journal of Legal Studies* 22 (2002): 275, 276.

[12] *See, e.g.,* Chantal Mouffe, "Hegemony and New Political Subjects: Toward a New Concept of Democracy," in *Marxism and the Interpretation of Culture*, ed. Cary Nelson and Lawrence Grossberg (Urbana: University of Illinois Press, 1988) 89, 100; and Jeremy Waldron, "Nonsense Upon Stilts?—a Reply," in *Nonsense Upon Stilts: Bentham, Burke and Marx on the Rights of Man*, ed. Jeremy Waldron (London: Methuen, 1987), 151, 183–190.

[13] Ran Hirschl, "Looking Sideways, Looking Backwards, Looking Forwards: Judicial Review vs. Democracy in Comparative Perspective," *University of Richmond Law Review* 34 (2000): 415, 421.

[14] John Ely, *Democracy and Distrust: A Theory of Judicial Review* (Cambridge: Harvard University Press, 1980).

[15] Patrick Lenta, "Democracy, Rights Disagreements and Judicial Review," *South African Journal on Human Rights* 20 (1) (2004): 8–13.

[16] Jowell, "Vires and Vacuums," 330.

[17] Lord Steyn, "Tangled Story," 352. *See also*, Jeffrey Jowell, "Judicial Deference and Human Rights: A Question of Competence," in *Law and Administration in Europe: Essays in Honour of Carol Harlow*, ed. Paul Craig and Richard Rawlings (Oxford: Oxford University Press, 2003), 67, 80; and Jeffrey Jowell, "Judicial Deference: Servility, Civility or Institutional Capacity?," *Public Law* (2003): 592, 598.

[18] Lon L. Fuller, "The Forms and Limits of Adjudication," *Harvard Law Review* 92 (1978): 353.

[19] Id. at 397.

[20] Id. at 398.

[21] Id. at 398.

[22] See, e.g., *RJR-MacDonald Inc v. Canada (AG)*, 1995 (3) SCR 199, 68-70; *R v. DPP ex parte Kebilene*, 2000 (2) AC 326, 381; and *International Transport Roth GmbH v. Secretary of State for the Home Department*, 2002 EWCA Civ 158, 139.

[23] Here, such an argument would constitute and overlap between issues of institutional competence, and the third axis, which considers the nature of the right or subject matter under review.

[24] See, e.g., *MacDonald*, 67–68.

[25] Lord Walker, "Second-Guessing Government: Judicial Deference and Human Rights," (unpublished paper delivered at Oriel College, Oxford, February 17, 2005), 19.

[26] *A v. Secretary of State for the Home Department; X v. Secretary of State for the Home Department*, 2004 UKHL 56, 29.

[27] See, e.g., *R v. Edwards Books & Art Ltd.*, 1986 (2) SCR, 147; *Irwin Toy Ltd v. Quebec (AG)*, 1989 (1) SCR 927, 74, 81–88; and *Kebilene*, 380.

[28] 304 U.S. 144 (1938) at 152 (n 4). See the discussion of this case in Daniel Solove, "The Darkest Domain: Deference, Judicial Review, and the Bill of Rights," *Iowa Law Review* 84 (1998–1999): 941, 989–995.

[29] Lord Hoffmann, "The Combar Lecture 2001: Separation of Powers," *Judicial Review* 137 (2002): 19, 26. Contrast Martin Chamberlain, "Democracy and Deference in Resource Allocation Cases: A Riposte to Lord Hoffmann," *Judicial Review* 12 (2003): 5–10; Lord Steyn, "Tangled Story," 357.

[30] Sandra Fredman, "From Deference to Democracy: The Role of Equality Under the Human Rights Act 1998," *Law Quarterly Review* 122 (2006): 53, 58–59.

[31] *Chaoulli v. Quebec (Attorney General)*, 2005 SCC 35.

[32] *See, e.g.*, the page on the University of Toronto website dedicated to the debate around *Chaoulli* at http://www.law.utoronto.ca/healthlaw/ (last accessed November 21, 2005); and Colleen M. Flood, Kent Roach, and Lorne Sossin, eds. *Access to Care Access to Justice: The Legal Debate Over Private Health Insurance in Canada* (Toronto: University of Toronto Press, 2005).

[33] For the purposes of this discussion, the provisions of these charters relevant to this judgment are substantially the same, and reference will be made to the Canadian Charter in the subsequent discussion for ease of comparative reference. It should be noted, however, that the judgment was ultimately decided on the basis of the Quebec Charter, and the finding of the court was inconclusive with regard to the Canadian Charter since Deschamps J reserved judgment in this regard, with the result that three judges found a violation of the Canadian Charter, while three did not.

[34] *Chaoulli*, 37.

[35] Id. at 40.

[36] Id. at 56.

[37] Id. at 84.

[38] Id. at 70–84.

[39] Id. at 85–92.

[40] Id. at 95.

[41] Id. at 84.

[42] See, e.g., *Irwin Toy*, 74; *Thomson Newspapers Co. v. Canada (AG)*, 1988 (1) SCR 877, 113–117; and *Delisle v. Canada (Deputy AG)*, 1999 (2) SCR 989, 126–132.

[43] *Chaoulli*, 105.

[44] Id. at 155.

[45] Id. at 156.

[46] Id. at 161.

[47] Id. at 236.

[48] The South African courts have adopted a 'reasonableness test' is assessing the constitutionality of State socio-economic policy. In the realm of health care, this test has been applied by the Constitutional Court in *Soobramoney* and *Minister of Health v. TAC*, 2002 (5) SA 721 (CC).

[49] See, e.g., *Chaoulli*, 164.

[50] Id. at 167.

[51] Id. at 170.

[52] Jeff A. King, "Constitutional Rights and Social Welfare: A Comment on the Canadian *Chaoulli* Health Care Decision," *Modern Law Review* 69 (2006): 631, 636–639.

[53] Section 33 of the Canadian Charter is known as the 'notwithstanding clause' and permits Parliament to enact or re-enact legislation 'notwithstanding' the fact that it is or may be inconsistent with the Charter, thereby immunising the legislation from constitutional review.

[54] *Minister of Health v. New Clicks South Africa (Pty) Ltd.*, 2006 (2) SA 311 (CC).

[55] Some academic writing has called for such a development. *See, e.g.*, C. Hoexter, "The Future of Judicial Review in South African Administrative Law," *South African Law Journal* 117 (2000): 484; and C. Hoexter, *The New Constitutional and Administrative Law*, 2 vols. (Lansdowne: Juta, 2002), vol II, *Administrative Law* at 82–83.

---

[56] *New Clicks,* 1. Section 27 of the South African Constitution provides: '(1) Everyone has the right to have access to—(a) health care services … . (2) The state must take reasonable legislative and other measures, within its available resources, to achieve the progressive realisation of each of these rights.'

[57] Id. at 17.

[58] Id. at 30–33.

[59] Id. at 313. This assertion by the State is remarkable given its repeated reappearance in socio-economic matters and its rejection by the Constitutional Court.

[60] Id. at 390.

[61] Id. at 22.

[62] Id. at 521.

[63] Id. at 522.

[64] Id. at 581-83.

[65] *Minister of Health v. Treatment Action Campaign,* 2002 (5) SA 721 (CC).

[66] *New* Clicks, 634.

[67] Id.

[68] Id. at 635.

[69] Id. at 674.

[70] Id. at 772, 781 and 783.

[71] Id. at 833. *See, e.g.,* ¶ 803, where Yacoob J states the following after quoting the definition of a 'single exit price': 'Some point was made about the fact that the word "price" is used twice in the definition and that the definition can make sense only if the word "price" means something different in each of its uses. I do not see how it matters if the word "price" does have a different meaning in each of its uses in the definition provided that the different meaning is clear and provided further that the fact that the word has a different meaning in each of its uses does not confuse.'

** The author wishes to thank Cathryn Costello, Jeff King, Jonathan Klaaren, John O'Dowd, her doctoral supervisor, Paul Craig, as well as participants at the Comparative Constitutionalism and Rights Conference (December 2005), for helpful comments on earlier drafts of the paper.

CHAPTER 10

DOMESTIC VIOLENCE AND GENDER EQUALITY UNDER THE U.S. AND SOUTH AFRICAN CONSTITUTIONS

Valorie K. Vojdik

Introduction

Domestic violence against women is a global pandemic. The World Health Organization (WHO) in 2006 concluded that domestic violence against women is widespread.[1] In 15 nations studied by WHO, 15% to 71% of women in intimate relationships reported having been physically assaulted by an intimate male partner.[2] Both international and national law historically have conceptualized domestic violence as a private matter between individuals within the family, outside the scope of state regulation.[3] Over the past decade, however, the international community has recognized that violence against women reflects and reinforces women's subordination, denying them the right to equality and enjoyment of fundamental freedoms, including life, liberty, and security of the person. The Declaration for the Elimination of Violence Against Women, adopted by the United Nations General Assembly in 1994, condemns violence against women and imposes affirmative duties upon states to prevent and eliminate it.[4]

In this paper, I discuss the treatment of domestic violence under international law and then compare the approaches of the United States Supreme Court and the South African Constitutional Court. The highest courts of the United States and the South Africa have taken dramatically different approaches to domestic violence under their respective constitutions. The U.S. Supreme Court has resisted efforts to constitutionalize a right to be protected from domestic or gender-motivated violence. In recent decisions, the Supreme Court has held that the United States Constitution does not impose affirmative obligations on the federal government to prevent violence between private persons, that Congress lacked the power to create a federal civil rights remedy intended to redress gender-motivated violence, and that there is no constitutionally protected property interest in the enforcement of a mandatory arrest statute under the Due Process Clause. In contrast, the South African Constitutional Court has held that the South African Constitution imposes affirmative obligations on the state to protect women from private violence and that national domestic violence legislation fulfills the state's constitutional obligation to afford women gender equality and other fundamental rights.

The difference in approach does not reflect merely differences in the content of the constitutions, but also differences in the courts' conceptualization of the nature and effect of domestic violence upon women. The United States Supreme Court has conceptualized domestic violence as a violent crime subject to state regulation rather than an issue of gender subordination or discrimination that warrants federal constitutional protection. In contrast, the South African Constitutional Court has repeatedly recognized that domestic violence, and violence against women, subordinates women and denies them access to the rights of equality, dignity and other fundamental constitutional rights. The courts' understanding of domestic violence as an issue of gender equality, therefore, has critical implications for the decision to recognize that the prevention and punishment of domestic violence is entitled to constitutional protection.

a. International law regarding intimate violence

The Declaration for the Elimination of Violence Against Women, adopted by the United Nations General Assembly in 1994, defines violence against women broadly to mean "any act of gender-based violence that results in, or is likely to result in, physical, sexual or psychological harm or suffering to women" – whether occurring in private or public life. [5] The Declaration recognizes that violence against women "is a manifestation of the historically unequal power relations between women and men" and a means of subordination of women that is an obstacle to equality. [6] It states that violence against women

> constitutes a violation of the rights and fundamental freedoms of women and impairs or nullifies their enjoyment of those rights and freedoms... [7]

The Declaration imposes positive duties upon states to eliminate and prevent violence against women. [8] Such action includes legal measures to protect women against violence not only by the state, but by private persons. [9] The Declaration provides that states should pursue a policy of eliminating violence against women that includes

> exerci[sing] due diligence to prevent, investigate and in accordance with national legislation, punish acts of violence against women, whether they are perpetrated by the State or by private persons[]... [10]

Specifically, states should develop

> preventative approaches and all those measures of a legal, political, administrative and cultural nature that promote the protection of women against any form of violence. [11]

The Convention for the Elimination of Discrimination Against Women (CEDAW) outlaws discrimination against women but does not specifically address domestic violence. The Committee on the Elimination of Discrimination Against Women, however, has interpreted its nondiscrimination mandate to prohibit violence against women. [12] General Recommendation 19 of CEDAW specifically addresses violence against women. [13] It recognizes that gender-based violence is not merely a crime between individuals, but also a form of discrimination that inhibits women's ability to enjoy rights and freedoms on an equal basis with men. [14] General Recommendation 19 requires states to take positive measures to eliminate violence against women. [15] Moreover, it states that

> under general international law and specific human rights covenants, States may also be responsible for private acts [of violence] if they fail to act with due diligence to prevent violations of rights, or to investigate and punish acts of violence, and for providing compensation. [16]

The Organization of American States in 1994 adopted the Inter-American Convention on the Prevention, Punishment and Eradication of Violence Against Women. The preamble states that violence against women "is a manifestation of the historically unequal power relations between women and men." [17] Violence against women is defined broadly to include "physical, sexual and psychological violence." [18] Article 3 specifically provides that women's rights are "to be free from violence in both the public and private sphere." [19] States must "pursue, by all appropriate means and without delay, policies to prevent, punish and eradicate such violence." [20]

The international community thus recognizes that violence against women is not merely a private family matter but a fundamental human rights issue that requires affirmative state action. [21] Historically, state governments have engaged in a widespread pattern of non-enforcement of criminal sanctions against perpetrators of domestic violence. Because domestic violence occurs within private familial or intimate relationships, states have rationalized nonintervention by invoking the public/private dichotomy in which domestic violence is categorized as a private matter rather than a public harm. The United Nations' Special Rapporteur on Violence Against Women explicitly rejected this dichotomy, explaining that states actively construct the status, rights, and remedies of women within the family through a host of laws that have reinforced women's subordination. [22] These include laws regulating sexuality, violence, privacy, divorce, adultery, property, succession, employment, and child custody. [23]

United States: Resistance to Constitutionalizing the Right to Protection from Domestic Violence

In contrast to the international treaties and documents locating domestic violence as a means of gender subordination, the United States Supreme Court has not treated domestic violence as an issue of gender discrimination or equality that justifies constitutional protection. Its approach rests upon an artificial distinction between the public and private, in which domestic violence has been conceptualized as a private harm to individuals that occurs within the privacy of the family rather than as an issue of gender discrimination or subordination that impedes women's enjoyment of equality, life, liberty, or property.

While the United States Constitution does not explicitly guarantee the right to gender equality, the Fifth and the Fourteenth Amendments guarantee individuals the right to equal treatment under the law as well as protection from the arbitrary deprivation of life, liberty, and property by the state. [24] The Due Process Clause of the Fifth Amendment applies to the federal government and provides inter alia that no person .... shall "be deprived of life, liberty, or property without due process of law." [25] The Fourteenth Amendment provides inter alia that "no State shall deprive" any person of "life, liberty or property" without "due process of law" nor deny any person "equal protection of the laws." [26] The Supreme Court has interpreted the Fifth and Fourteenth Amendments to guarantee the right to equal protection on the basis of gender.

The Supreme Court has interpreted the right to equal treatment and due process quite narrowly. First, the Supreme Court has interpreted the Constitution to guarantee negative rather than positive rights. The Constitution guarantees individuals freedom from state action that interferes with the exercise of the constitutional rights; it does not positively obligate the state to take affirmative action to ensure access or fulfillment of such rights. [27] Second, the Supreme Court has interpreted the Fifth and Fourteenth Amendments to prohibit intentional discrimination by state actors, not private persons. Third, facially neutral policies with discriminatory effects alone do not violate the right to equal protection; proof of specific discriminatory intent is required. Fourth, as feminist scholars have long recognized, the right to gender equality has generally been considered to embrace formal equality, not substantive equality. Formal equality rests on the notion that "likes should be treated alike" and requires that men and women be treated the same to the extent that they are similarly situated. [28] The issue for courts is whether the state has treated men and women differently without sufficient justification. [29] In contrast, substantive equality considers the effects of state action upon women, recognizing that women are often differently situated from men for a number of reasons, including past discrimination or disadvantage, and that such differences may justify differential treatment.

Constitutionalizing a right to protection from domestic violence under U.S. equality jurisprudence, therefore, is extremely difficult. The Supreme Court in *DeShaney v. Winnebago County Dept. of Social Services* held that the Fourteenth Amendment does not impose an affirmative duty upon the state to protect the life, liberty, and property of its citizens against invasion from other citizens. [30] The petitioners, Joshua DeShaney and his mother, sued to recover damages sustained by Joshua, who at four years of age suffered severe brain damage at the hands of his father, whom a state social service agency had investigated for suspected child abuse but had taken no action. [31] Petitioner sought to recover damages from the state, alleging the state had deprived him of his liberty without due process of law by its failure to protect him, in violation of his rights under the Due Process Clause of the Fourteenth Amendment. [32]

The Supreme Court in *DeShaney* held that the state's failure to provide the petitioner with adequate protection against his father's violence did not violate the substantive component of the right to Due Process. [33] The Court held that the Due Process Clause forbids the state itself from depriving individuals of life, liberty, and property without due process of law; it does not, however, affirmatively require the state to protect its citizens from harm by other citizens. [34] Thus, the Due Process Clause operates as a "limitation on the State's power to act, not as a guarantee of certain minimal levels of safety and security." [35] Under *DeShaney*, the state has no affirmative duty as a matter of substantive due process to protect women from private violence. [36]

Constitutional challenges to state policies of non-enforcement of domestic violence statutes are also difficult. Under the Fourteenth Amendment, it is possible to challenge discriminatory state statutes or policies that permit the non-enforcement of domestic violence statutes as violations of the right to equal protection. As a practical matter, however, such statutes or policies are usually phrased in gender-neutral terms (referring, for example, to "spousal violence"). [37] To prove unlawful gender discrimination, it must be established that the state acted because of an intent to discriminate on the basis of gender; evidence that non-enforcement disparately affects women (since women are disproportionately the victims of domestic violence) is insufficient to establish a violation. [38] Consequently, numerous federal courts have held that facially neutral spousal assault policies do not discriminate on the basis of gender. [39]

To redress the lack of enforcement of domestic violence statutes, federal and state legislators have enacted various reforms to remedy a systematic bias against prosecution of domestic violence. These have included adoption of the federal Violence Against Women Act, which created a federal civil rights remedy for victims of domestic violence, and adoption by numerous states of mandatory arrest statutes, designed to eliminate police discretion in refusing to enforce domestic violence criminal laws. [40] Unfortunately, the Supreme Court has been hostile to attempts to create federal civil rights and constitutional remedies for victims of domestic violence. [41]

In *United States v. Morrison*, the Court struck down Section 13981 of the federal Violence Against Women Act (VAWA) that created a federal civil remedy for victims of gender-motivated violence. [42] The United States Congress adopted VAWA to prevent and redress violence against women. [43] Section 13981 of VAWA radically redefined violence against women as a civil rights issue. [44] Section 13981 provided that "persons within the United States shall have the right to be free from crimes of violence motivated by gender." [45] To enforce that right, VAWA provided a civil right of action against persons who commit "a crime of violence motivated by gender" for compensatory and punitive damages, injunctive and declaratory relief. [46] The statute defined a crime motivated by gender as "a crime of violence committed because of gender or on the basis of gender, and due, at least in part, to an animus based on the victim's gender." [47]

In adopting VAWA, Congress relied on a substantial record of factual findings that gender-motivated violence affected interstate commerce, limiting and interfering with women's employment opportunities, impoverishing women, and causing significant state expenditures for health care and other costs that affect the United States economy. For example, Congress found that three out of four American women will be victims of violent crimes sometime during their life; [48] "as many as 50% of homeless women and children are fleeing domestic violence;" [49] between 2,000 and 4,000 women die yearly from domestic abuse; [50] and that, according to partial estimates, violent crime against women costs the United States at least $3 billion per year. [51] Congress also found that states had discriminated against women in their treatment of gender-based crime, perpetuating discriminatory stereotypes that often result in insufficient investigation, prosecution, and punishment of gender-motivated crime. [52] Attorney generals from 38 states supported the adoption of the federal civil rights remedy, conceding that "the problem of violence against women is a national one, requiring federal attention, federal leadership and federal funds." [53]

Despite the voluminous fact-findings of the impact of domestic violence, the Supreme Court held that federal civil rights remedy for gender-based violence in VAWA was an unconstitutional exercise of Congressional power. [54] The Court rejected the argument that Congress had the authority to create the federal cause of action under the Commerce Clause, which permits Congress inter alia, to regulate activities "having a substantial relation" to, or that "substantially affect," interstate commerce. [55] Gender-motivated crimes of violence, the Court held, are not "economic in nature."[56] The Court held that Congress relied on an improper "method of reasoning" that purported to regulate noneconomic, violent crime because of its nationwide, aggregated impact upon the national economy. [57] The Commerce Clause, the Court held, requires a distinction between "what is truly national and what is truly local." [58] Violence against women, the court held, is non-economic, violent crime, traditionally a "local" concern regulated by states.

The Court also rejected the argument that VAWA's civil remedy was a proper exercise of Congress' remedial power under Section 5 of the Fourteenth Amendment, which authorizes Congress to enforce through legislation the equal protection and due process guarantees of the Fourteenth Amendment. [59] Although Congress found pervasive bias in the state justice systems against victims of gender-motivated violence, VAWA created a civil remedy created against private actors, not the state actors who had discriminated on the basis of gender. [60] The Court held that Congress' Section 5 powers do not extend to the conduct of private actors. [61]

In holding that VAWA did not regulate interstate commerce, the Court ignored Congressional findings documenting the devastating impact of domestic violence upon the lives of women and the national economy. As the dissent points out, the Court also ignored that gender-motivated violence operates in a similar manner to racial discrimination in the 1960's. In *Heart of Atlanta Motel, Inc. v. United States* and *Katzenbach v. McClung*, the Supreme Court relied upon evidence of the consequences of racial discrimination by motels and restaurants on interstate commerce to uphold Title II of the Civil Rights Act of 1964, which banned racial discrimination in hotels and restaurants, against challenges under the Commerce Clause. [62] In contrast, the Court rejected similar evidence in *Morrison* – evidence which was much more voluminous and well-documented.

Rather than engage in a contextual analysis of the statute that took into account Congressional findings regarding the impact on women's civil rights, [63] the Court substituted a formalistic analysis that framed the legal issue as whether the legislation regulated the "truly local" v. the "truly national" and economic v. noneconomic activity. Ignoring the discriminatory impact of gender-motivated violence on women, the Court re-characterized "gender-motivated violence against women" as "violent crime," which it then categorized as a "local" concern unworthy of constitutional protection. Seen through the lens of categorical formalism, VAWA becomes a statute about crime, not a statute creating a civil rights remedy to punish and deter the discriminatory effects of gender violence.[64]

While *Morrison* can be read as a part of the Rehnquist Court's efforts to limit the power of the federal government to legislate matters concerning the states, it also rests on the public/private distinction that historically has underpinned the state's refusal to enforce criminal laws against perpetrators of violence within the family. [65] In categorizing domestic violence as a local concern, the majority ignores the myriad of federal laws that regulate the family, including federal tax law, pension law, property, divorce, and child custody law. [66] By ignoring the crucial role that federal law plays in constructing women's status and rights within the family, *Morrison* reinvokes the pubic/private distinction that the Declaration for the Elimination of Violence and CEDAW have condemned.

In *Castle Rock*, the Supreme Court in 2005 rejected another attempt to constitutionalize the right to protection from domestic violence. The Court held that a Colorado mandatory arrest statute did not give a woman a constitutionally protected property interest in the enforcement of a restraining order against her physically abusive husband. [67] The petitioner had obtained a restraining order against her estranged husband, who violated the order and took the couple's three children from the family home around 5:00 p.m. [68] Petitioner repeatedly called the police, begging them to enforce the restraining order and arrest her husband, but the police refused. [69] At around 1:30 a.m., the husband arrived at the police station with a shotgun and killed himself; the police found the murdered bodies of the couple's children in his vehicle outside. [70] Petitioner sued the police for damages, claiming that Colorado's mandatory arrest statute created a property interest which the state could not arbitrarily deny under the Due Process Clause.[71]

The statute at issue was adopted by the Colorado state legislature for the purpose of eliminating police discretion in enforcement of restraining orders. [72] It stated that "A peace officer shall use every reasonable mean to enforce a restraining order." [73] It directed that

> a peace officer shall arrest or if an arrest would be impractical under the circumstances, seek a warrant for the arrest of a restrained person when the peace officer has information amounting to probable cause [that s/he has violated the order]. [74]

The issue of whether the Colorado statute gave the plaintiff an entitlement to enforcement of the restraining order which enjoyed procedural due process protection, the Court held, was left open in *DeShaney*. [75] The Court held it did not. [76] As a matter of procedural due process, a benefit is not a protected entitlement if government officials may grant or deny it in their discretion. [77] The majority held that the Colorado statute did not create a truly mandatory duty to enforce the restraining order. [78] The majority held that it did not override a "well-established tradition of police discretion" in enforcing criminal statutes, even those that seemed mandatory. [79] Given this tradition of police discretion, the Colorado legislature had not adequately indicated that it intended its statute to be a true mandate of police action, despite having used the word "shall" in the statute. [80] Moreover, the statute mandated either arrest or seeking an arrest warrant and, therefore, did not mandate a particular course of action. [81] Even assuming that the duty was mandatory, the majority held that would not necessarily mean that the law conferred a personal entitlement to enforcement of the statute. [82]

Further, the majority held that "it is by no means clear that an individual entitlement to enforcement of a restraining order could constitute a property interest for purposes of the Due Process Clause." [83] Under *Board of Regents of St. Colleges v. Roth*, the property interests subject to protection under the due process clause "extend well beyond actual ownership of real estate, chattels or money" and include state-conferred benefits and services, including welfare benefits, public education, and drivers' licenses. [84] The right to enforcement of a restraining order, however, does not have "some ascertainable monetary value," which the majority held is implicitly required by *Roth*.[85] Further, the alleged property interest arises incidentally from a function that government actors have always performed, i.e. arresting people whom police have probable cause to believe have committed a crime.[86]

Given its analysis in *DeShaney*, the majority in *Castle Rock* concluded that "the benefit that a third party may receive from having someone arrested for a crime" does not trigger protection under either substantive or procedural due process.[87] These decisions, the Court explained, reflect its reluctance to treat the Fourteenth Amendment as a "font of tort law' that would impose liability upon state and municipal actors. [88]

The Court's analysis of the mandatory arrest statute in *Castle Rock* is entirely acontextual, ignoring the long history of police inaction that has resulted in the adoption of mandatory arrest statutes in numerous states specifically to eliminate police discretion in this area. In a dissent joined by Justice Ruth Bader Ginsburg, Justice Stevens wrote that the Court gives "short shrift" to the unique case of mandatory arrest statutes in the domestic violence context adopted by states with the "unmistakable goal of eliminating police discretion in this area." [89] The dissent locates the Colorado statute within the context of a nationwide movement of states that sought to redress "the crisis of police underenforcement in the domestic violence sphere" by adopting mandatory arrest statutes to eliminate police discretion. [90] Other state courts have interpreted these mandatory arrest statutes to eliminate the police's traditional discretion to refuse enforcement. [91]

In concluding that Gonzales had a legitimate claim of entitlement to enforcement created by state law, the dissent concluded that Colorado intended to eliminate police discretion and, the dissent concluded, the text "perfectly captures" this purpose by using the word "shall." [92] While the precise means of enforcement may have been to arrest or to seek an arrest warrant, the dissent noted that the police lacked the discretion to simply do nothing. [93] Moreover, the statute conferred a direct benefit of enforcement on a specific group of persons, i.e. recipients of domestic restraining orders, defined as "protected person[s]" in Section 18-6-803.5(1.5)(a). [94] As the dissent observed, *Roth* recognized that a purpose of the institution of property is to protect the interests of persons on claims upon which they rely in their daily lives. [95] Police enforcement of protective orders, the dissent stated, provides a valuable benefit similar to that provided by a private security company that should constitute a protected property interest. [96] Police enforcement of a restraining order is a government service "no less concrete and no less valuable" than other government services, such as education. [97]

As the dissent's analysis illustrates, the majority in *Castle Rock* replaced a contextualized analysis of the failure of police to enforce restraining orders with a formalistic analysis that ignored the gendered nature of domestic violence. The Court entirely ignored the value of mandatory enforcement of restraining orders to millions of women in the United States, for whom protection from domestic violence is often a matter of life-and-death. In characterizing Ms. Gonzalez' claim as that of a "third party" seeking an arrest of another, the majority further ignored the fact that states adopted mandatory arrest statutes to protect women from the state's historical refusal to protect women from violence in the family. By ignoring the gendered nature and impact of domestic violence, as well as the critical role of the state in protecting women from violence, the Supreme Court has interpreted the Constitution to grant women an enforceable property interest in the right to obtain a driver's license but not in a court order to protect their lives and their enjoyment of fundamental civil liberties.

In *Morrison* and *Castle Rock*, the Supreme Court thwarted the use of the federal constitution to redress systematic gender-based discrimination against women by the state. In both cases, the Court rejected a contextualized understanding of the enormous effects of domestic violence upon millions of women's lives in favor of a formalistic analysis that reinvokes the public/private dichotomy and ignores the role of the state in perpetuating and condoning domestic violence. Rather than conceptualize domestic violence as impairing women's equality or fundamental civil rights, the Supreme Court in *Morrison* categorized domestic violence in gender-neutral terms, i.e. as a "violent crime" that implicates "local" concerns that do not justify federal constitutional protection. In *Castle Rock*, the Court narrowly defined "property" to obscure the reality that mandatory arrest statutes protect women's right to life itself. The Supreme Court's reasoning implicitly rests upon the public/private dichotomy explicitly rejected in the Declaration for the Elimination of Violence Against Women, CEDAW, and the Inter-American Convention on the Prevention, Punishment and Eradication of Violence Against Women.

South Africa: State is Constitutionally Required to Prevent and Eliminate Domestic Violence

The South African Constitutional Court, in contrast to the United States Supreme Court, recognizes that domestic violence is a means of gender subordination which the state has an affirmative obligation to eradicate. The difference in approach reflects substantive differences in the nature and scope of the two constitutions, as well as in the willingness of the Constitutional Court to understand domestic violence as gender subordination with concrete effects on women's civil liberties.

The South African Constitution differs substantially from that of the United States, explicitly guaranteeing the right to gender equality as a foundational constitutional norm, recognizing that equality has not yet been achieved, and authorizing measures to protect and advance persons disadvantaged by unfair discrimination. [98] In contrast to the United States, whose constitution was drafted by men, women activists in South Africa played a fundamental role in insuring a constitutional and political commitment to gender equality in post-apartheid South Africa. [99] Because the struggle for women's equality occurred within the context of the struggle for national liberation, South African women activists effectively mobilized the political and organizational skills acquired during the struggle for racial equality to compel the inclusion of women's issues in the new Constitution. [100]

While the struggle against racial apartheid took precedence over issues of gender equality, women in the African National Congress (ANC) began to press for the inclusion of gender equality as part of the national liberation struggle and the transition to post-apartheid South Africa. [101] In 1992, the ANC Women's League organized a meeting of about 40 women's organizations with the goal of developing a Charter of Women's Rights to identify the needs of women and include their concerns in the constitution. The league subsequently formed the Women's National Coalition (WNC), a broad coalition of over 115 national and regional women's organizations, to coordinate a national political campaign to mobilize and educate women and entrench equality for women in the new Constitution. [102]

During the transition to democracy, the WNC and women activists succeeded in developing a consensus concerning women's subordination in South African society and in securing a political commitment to the role of the state in eliminating gender inequality. [103] As Catherine Albertyn explains, the WNC "sought to construct an understanding of equality that took account of the social, economic and cultural reality of women's lives." [104] The women's movement in South Africa was supported by international feminist groups, activists, and scholars engaged in similar struggles. [105] During the negotiations over the new constitution between the major South African political parties, the WNC lobbied the participants to include the right to gender equality in the new Constitution. [106] They also successfully persuaded the ANC to name female candidates to one-third of its electoral lists of parliamentary candidates in the 1994 election, insuring substantial representation by women in parliament. [107]

As a result of their efforts, they succeeded in securing both a constitutional and political commitment to gender equality and non-sexism. Section 9 of the South African Constitution expressly guarantees the right to equality on the basis of gender. [108] The Constitution also specifically guarantees the right to dignity, [109] right to bodily and psychological integrity, [110] and the right not to be treated or punished in a cruel, inhuman, or degrading way. [111] Unlike the U.S. Constitution, which guarantees merely negative liberties, Section 7 of the Constitution obliges the state to respect, promote, and fulfill the Bill of Rights. [112] Thus, the South African Constitution affirmatively obligates the state to take steps to realize the rights guaranteed by the Constitution.

The right to equality under the South African Constitution is much broader in scope than the right to equal protection in the U.S. Constitution. Section 9(3) provides that the state "may not unfairly discriminate directly or indirectly" on several enumerated grounds, including sex and gender. [113] While the U.S. Supreme Court has interpreted the right of equal protection to prohibit only intentional discrimination, the Constitutional Court has held that "conduct which may appear to be neutral and non-discriminatory may nonetheless result in discrimination." [114] Consequently, lack of specific evidence of intent is not dispositive. [115] While the Supreme Court has interpreted the right to equal protection to apply only to state action, Section 9(d) expressly prohibits any "person" from unfairly discriminating on one or more of the enumerated grounds. [116] Unlike the right to equal protection under the U.S. Constitution, the right to equality under the South African Constitution embraces substantive rather than formal equality. As Saras Jagwanth explains, in interpreting Section 9, the Constitutional Court "has rejected a rigid, formal approach in favour of a substantive, contextual and asymmetrical analysis" that interprets the right to equality in light of past and continuing discrimination. [117]

Applying these constitutional provisions, the Constitutional Court has held repeatedly that the Constitution provides women with the right to be free of domestic violence and that the state has an affirmative obligation to prevent and eliminate such violence. The Court has explicitly adopted a nuanced and contextual analysis of domestic violence that recognizes that it is a form of gender subordination that impedes women's equality, liberty, and other fundamental liberties.

In *Carmichele v. Minister of Safety & Security & Another*, [118] the Constitutional Court expressly held that the South African Constitution imposed positive duties upon the state to take preventive measures to protect individuals whose lives are at risk from the criminal acts of others. In *Carmichele*, the female appellant had been violently attacked by Francois Coetzee, who was free on bail pending trial on charges of raping a woman. [119] The police and prosecutor had recommended that Coetzee be released without bail and failed to inform the court regarding a prior conviction. [120] The applicant sued the Minister for Safety and Security and the Minister of Justice and Constitutional Development for damages, claiming that the police and prosecutors had negligently failed to prevent Coetzee from harming her. [121] The applicant claimed that the police and prosecutors owed her a duty to ensure her constitutional rights to life, dignity, freedom and security, privacy and freedom of movement. [122] Further, she argued that the Constitution imposed a particular duty on the state to protect women against violence crime and sexual abuse. [123]

Rejecting the U.S. approach in *DeShaney*, the Constitutional Court held that the state's obligation to protect the right to life was not limited to adopting criminal laws to deter the commission of crime.[124] The Court held that the South African Constitution entrenches the right to life, dignity, and freedom and security of the person.[125] The Constitution does not merely prohibit the state from interfering with these rights but imposes certain positive duties upon the state and all of its organs to promote and protect these rights.[126] In particular situations, the state has a positive obligation to take preventive measures to protect an individual whose life is at risk from the criminal acts of another.[127]

Although the common law did not recognize such a duty on the part of the state, the Court held that the Bill of Rights applies to the common law and that Section 173 of the Constitution gives all higher courts the power to develop the common law taking into account the interest of justice.[128] Section 39(2) provides that, when developing the common law, every court must promote the spirit, purport and objects of the Bill of Rights. The Constitutional Court's analysis, therefore, was informed by its understanding that the South African Constitution is transformational in nature.[129] Whether the police had a legal duty to act must be decided "in the context of a constitutional state founded on dignity, equality and freedom and in which government has positive duties to promote and uphold such values."[130]

In contrast to the categorical formalism employed by the Supreme Court in *Morrison* and *Castle Rock*, the Constitutional Court's analysis in *Carmichele* focused on the gendered nature of sexual violence and its impact upon women's freedom and equality. The Court held that "few things can be more important to women than freedom from the threat of sexual violence."[131] Sexual violence "goes to the core of women's subordination in society" and is "the single greatest threat to the self-determination of South African women."[132] As a state agency, the police are responsible to protect the public in general and women and children in particular from violent crime.[133] The Court also held that South Africa had a duty under international law to prohibit gender-based discrimination that impairs women's enjoyment of fundamental rights and freedoms and to take steps to prevent the violation of those rights.[134] Applying these principles, the Supreme Court of Appeals affirmed the judgment of the High Court on remand that the police and prosecutors owed the applicant a legal duty to protect her against the risk of sexual violence by Coetzee.[135]

Further, in *State v. Baloyi*, the Constitutional Court upheld the Prevention of Family Violence Act 133 of 1993 ("the 1993 Act").[136] The appellant, Godfrey Baloyi, challenged the Act after his wife obtained an interdict pursuant to the Act enjoining Baloyi from assaulting his wife and their child, as well as a warrant for his arrest, which was suspended pursuant to the terms of the Act.[137] Subsequently, the appellant allegedly assaulted the complainant and threatened to kill her; he was convicted by a magistrate for violation of the interdict.[138] Baloyi argued that the Act unconstitutionally infringed on his right to be presumed innocent and have his guilt proved beyond reasonable doubt.[139] The Constitutional Court held that the 1993 Act, properly construed, does not impose a reverse onus on the accused to prove his innocence.[140]

As in *Carmichele*, the Court in *Baloyi* held that the state has a constitutional obligation to deal effectively with domestic violence.[141] While recognizing that all crime harms society, the Constitutional Court distinguished domestic violence, focusing on "its hidden, repetitive character and its immeasurable ripple effects on our society and, in particular, on family life." [142] Domestic violence "cuts across class, race, culture and geography, and is all the more pernicious because it is so often concealed and so frequently goes unpunished." [143] The Court noted the devastating social and economic costs of domestic violence to the victims and the nation's communities. [144]

The Court held that the Constitution obligated the state to take affirmative action to prevent and eliminate domestic violence. Section 12(1) provides that

> Everyone has the right to freedom and security of the person, which includes the right
> . . . (c) to be free from all forms of violence from either public or private sources. [145]

Section 7(2) of the Constitution provides that "the state must respect, protect, promote and fulfill the rights in the Bill of Rights." [146] The Court held that, read together, these sections obligate the state to protect the right of everyone to be free from private or domestic violence. [147] In addition, the Constitution obligates the state to protect the right to bodily and psychological integrity, the right to dignity, the right to not be subjected to torture in any way, and the right to not be treated or punished in a cruel, inhuman or degrading way. [148] The Court also held that international law (including the Universal Declaration of Human Rights, the Declaration on the Elimination of Violence Against Women, CEDAW, and the African Charter on Human and People's Rights) obligated the government to seek to remedy the injustice of domestic violence. [149]

While the U.S. Supreme Court has ignored the gendered dimension of domestic violence, the Constitutional Court in *Baloyi* held that domestic violence implicates the constitutional right to gender equality. [150] Justice Sachs explained that domestic violence is "systemic, pervasive and overwhelmingly gender-specific." [151] As such, "it reflects and reinforces patriarchal domination and does so in a particularly brutal form." [152] The Court recognized that notions of patriarchy, autonomy, and privacy have been used to justify non-interference by the state into what is perceived as a private or intimate matter. [153] The Court specifically recognized that the ineffectiveness of the criminal justice system in addressing family violence

> intensifies the subordination and helplessness of the victims. This also sends an unmistakable message to the whole of society that the daily trauma of vast numbers of women counts for little. The terrorization of the individual victims is thus compounded by a sense that domestic violence is inevitable. Patterns of systemic sexist behavior are normalized rather than combated. [154]

Nonenforcement violates the foundational commitment to non-sexism and the right to gender equality under the South African Constitution. [155]

The Constitutional Court reiterated these principles in a 2005 decision upholding the Domestic Violence Act of 1998 (the "Domestic Violence Act"), the successor to the domestic violence act analyzed at issue in *Carmichele*. In *Omar v. The Government of the Republic of South Africa*, the Constitutional Court upheld the constitutionality of Section 8 of the Domestic Violence Act, which provides for a court to authorize a warrant of arrest when it issues a protective order. [156] The Court held that Section 8 does not violate the rights to freedom and security of the person, a fair trial and access to the Courts guaranteed by the South African Constitution. [157]

In its analysis, the Court considered the social context and purpose of the Domestic Violence Act. In its preamble, the Act recognizes that domestic violence is a serious social evil and that the South African Constitution assures the right to equality and freedom of security of the person. [158] The stated purpose of the Act is to "afford the victims of domestic violence the maximum protection from domestic abuse that the law can provide" and to ensure that the state gives full effect to the protections of the Act and to convey that the state is committed to the elimination of domestic violence. [159]

Declaring the high incidence of domestic violence as "utterly unacceptable," the Court recognized that domestic violence causes severe psychological and social harm. [160] Significantly, the Court stated that "the gendered nature and effects of violence and abuse as it mostly occurs in the family, and the unequal power relations implicitly therein, are obvious." [161] Citing *Baloyi*, the Court in *Omar* reiterated that domestic violence reflects and reinforces patriarchal domination and that the ineffectiveness of the criminal justice system in addressing such violence exacerbates the subordination of the victim and normalizes sexist behavior. [162]

The Court concluded that domestic violence "brutally offends the values and rights enshrined in the Constitution," including non-sexism, human dignity, equality and the advancement of human rights and freedoms. [163] In addition, domestic violence offends various rights guaranteed in the Constitution: the right to freedom and security of the person, which includes the right to be free from all violence whether public or private; the right to dignity; life; equality; and privacy. [164] Again citing *Baloyi*, the Court held that the South African Constitution obligates the state "to deal effectively with domestic violence." [165] Moreover, international law obligates South Africa to prohibit gender-based discrimination and to take reasonable measures to prevent the violation of women's fundamental rights and freedoms. [166] The Court recognized that the Act addresses "the historical ambivalence of the role of law enforcement" by requiring the police to take specific steps in addressing complaints of domestic violence. [167]

Conclusion

More than ten years after the adoption of the Declaration for the Elimination of Violence Against Women, the U.S. Supreme Court has refused to recognize a constitutional right to protection from domestic violence. In contrast, the South African Constitutional Court has recognized that the state has affirmative obligations to prevent and eliminate domestic violence. The difference does not merely result from doctrinal differences; it also reflects different jurisprudential conceptions of domestic violence and its relationship to gender equality and civil liberties. By understanding domestic violence as a means of gender subordination, the Constitutional Court has been able to acknowledge the role of the state both in perpetuating violence and in eliminating domestic violence to assure women gender equality and the full enjoyment of the rights and liberties guaranteed under the South African Constitution. The United States Supreme Court, on the other hand, has ignored the role of the state and law in perpetuating domestic violence and has characterized domestic violence as a gender-neutral crime that occurs between private individuals. Rejecting the contextualized analysis of violence and equality offered by both international and South African law, U.S. constitutional jurisprudence continues to deny that freedom from intimate violence is a fundamental prerequisite to gender equality, liberty, and other fundamental civil liberties.

[1] World Health Organization, *The WHO Multi-country Study on Women's Health and Domestic Violence Against Women* (2006), available at http://www.who.int/gender/violence/who_multicountry_study/summary_report/chapter2/en/index.html

[2] *Ibid.*

[3] UNICEF, "Domestic Violence Against Women and Girls," 6 *Innocenti Digest* 8 (June 2000), available at http://www.unicef-icdc.org/publications/pdf/digest6e.pdf.

[4] Declaration on the Elimination of Violence Against Women, G.A. Res. 48/104, U.N. GAOR, 48th Sess., 85th plen. mtg., Supp. No. 49, U.N. Doc. A/48/49 (Dec. 20, 1993).

[5] *Ibid.*, art. 1.

[6] See, *ibid.*

[7] See *ibid.*

[8] See *ibid.*

[9] See *ibid.*

[10] *Ibid.*, art. 4(c).

[11] *Ibid.*, art. 4(f).

[12] See General Recommendation No. 12: Violence Against Women, in Report of the Committee on the Elimination of Discrimination Against Women, 8th session, U.N. Doc. A/44/38 (1989).

[13] See General Recommendation No. 19: Violence Against Women, in Report of the Committee on the Elimination of Discrimination Against Women, 11th session, U.N. Doc. No. A/47/38 (1992).

[14] *Ibid.*, ¶ 1.

[15] *Ibid.*, ¶ 4.

[16] *Ibid.*, ¶ 9.

[17] Inter-American Convention on the Prevention, Punishment, and Eradication of Violence Against Women, June 9, 1994, 27 U.S.T. 3301, General Assembly of the O.A.S., Doc. OEA/Ser.PAG/doc.3116/94 rev. 2., reprinted in 33 *ILM* 1534.

[18] *Ibid.*, art. 2.

[19] *Ibid.*, art. 3.

[20] *Ibid.*, art. 7.

[21] See Declaration on the Elimination of Violence Against Women.

[22] Preliminary Report by the Special Rapporteur on Violence Against Women, Its Causes and Consequences, Commission on Human Rights, E/CN.4/1999/68/Add.4 (1999).

[23] *Ibid.*, art. 2(7).

[24] U.S. CONST. amends. V, XIV.

[25] *Ibid.*, amend. V.

[26] *Ibid.*, amend. XIV.

[27] Robin West, "The Constitution and the Obligations of Government to Secure the Material Preconditions for a Good Society: Rights, Capabilities, and the Good Society", 69 *Fordham L. Rev.*, 1901, (2001): 1906-7.

[28] Katharine T. Bartlett, "Gender Law", 1 *Duke J. Gender L. & Policy* 1, (1994): 2-5.

[29] *Ibid.*

[30] *DeShaney v. Winnebago County Dept. of Soc. Servs.*, 489 U.S. 189, 195 (1989).

[31] *Ibid.*, 193.

[32] *Ibid.*

[33] *Ibid.*, 203.

[34] *Ibid.*, 196.

[35] *Ibid.*, 195.

[36] See *ibid.*, 196.

[37] See Reva B. Siegal, "The Rule of Love: Wife Beating as Prerogative", *105 Yale L. J.* 2117, (1996): 2189-90.

[38] See, e.g., *Personal Adminstr. of Mass. v. Feeney*, 442 U.S. 256 (1979).

[39] Siegal, "The Rule of Love," 2191 (noting that a number of federal courts have not subjected facially neutral spousal assault policies to heightened scrutiny); See *Thurman v. City of Torrington*, 595 F. Supp. 1521 (D. Conn. 1984).

[40] Violence Against Women Act of 1994, 42 U.S.C. § 13981 (2006).

[41] See *Town of Castle Rock, Colo. v. Gonzales*, 125 S.Ct. 2796 (2005).

[42] See *United States v. Morrison*, 529 U.S. 598 (2000).

[43] See 42 U.S.C. § 13981(a).

[44] *Ibid.*

[45] *Ibid.*, § 13981(b).

[46] *Ibid.*, § 13981(c).

[47] *Ibid.*, 1§ 3981(d)(1).

[48] See H. R. Rep. No. 103-395, p. 25 (1993).

[49] S. Rep. No. 101-545, p. 37 (1990).

[50] *Ibid.*, 36.

[51] *Ibid.*, 33.

[52] See *Morrison*, 529 U.S. at 620.

[53] 1993 Crimes of Violence Motivated by Gender: Hearing Before the Subcomm. On Civil and Constitutional Rights of the House Comm. on the Judiciary, 103rd Con. (1993), 34-36.

[54] See *Morrison*, 529 U.S. at 625.

[55] *Ibid.*, 609.

[56] *Ibid.*, 617.

[57] *Ibid.*

[58] *Ibid.*, 617-18.

[59] *Ibid.*, 627.

[60] *Morrison*, 529 U.S. at 626.

[61] *Ibid.*

[62] See *Heart of Atlanta Motel, Inc. v. U.S.*, 379 U.S. 241 (1964); *Katzenbach v. McClung*, 370 U.S. 377 (1964).

[63] See Siegal, "The Rule of Love", 2189-90.

[64] See Julie Goldscheid, "United States v. Morrison and the Civil Rights Remedy of the Violence Against Women Act: A Civil Rights Law Struck Down in the Name of Federalism", 86 *Cornell L. Rev.* 109 (2000).

[65] See *ibid.*, 2201.

[66] Judith Resnik,,'"Naturally" Without Gender: Women, Jurisdiction, and the Federal Courts', 66 *N.Y.U. L. Rev.* 1682, (1991): 1721-1722.

[67] 125 S.Ct. at 2810.

[68] *Ibid.*, 2800-01.

[69] *Ibid.*, 2801, 2802.

[70] *Ibid.*

[71] *Ibid.*, 2802.

[72] See *ibid.*, 2805.

[73] Colo. Rev. Stat. § 18-6-803.5(3)(a) (West 2006).

[74] *Ibid.*, § 18-6-803.5(3)(b).

[75] See *Castle Rock*, 125 S.Ct. at 2803.

[76] *Ibid.*, 2809.

[77] See *ibid.*, 2807-08.

[78] *Ibid.*, 2805.

[79] *Ibid.*, 2806.

[80] *Ibid.*

[81] See *Castle Rock*, 125 S.Ct. at 2807-08.

[82] *Ibid.*, 2808.

[83] *Ibid.*

[84] *Ibid.* (citing *Bd. of Regents of St. Colleges v. Roth*, 408 U.S. 564, 572 (1972)).

[85] *Ibid.*

[86] *Ibid.*

[87] *Castle Rock*, 125 S.Ct. at 2810.

[88] *Ibid.*, 2810.

[89] *Ibid.*, 2816 (Stevens, Ginsburg, JJ, dissenting).

[90] *Ibid.*, 2817.

[91] *Ibid.*, 2818.

[92] *Ibid.*, 2822.

[93] *Castle Rock,* 125 S.Ct. at 2819-20.

[94] *Ibid.,* 2823.

[95] *Ibid.*

[96] See *ibid.,* 2823-85.

[97] *Ibid.,* 2822.

[98] See Justice Zak Yacoob, "Some perspectives on the movement towards and the struggle for equality in out context", in *Equality Law: Reflections from South Africa and Elsewhere,* eds. Saras Jagwanth & Evance Kalula, (Landsdowne, South Africa: Juta & Co., 1994), 1-2.

[99] Penelope Andrews, "Violence Against Women in South Africa: The Role of Culture and the Limitations of the Law", 8 *Temp. Pol. & Civ. Rts. L. Rev.* 425, (1999): 441; Catherine Albertyn, "Women and the transition to democracy in South Africa", in *Gender and the New South African Legal Order,* ed. Christina Murray (1994), 47-63.

[100] Andrews, "Violence Against Women in South Africa", 441-443; Felicity Kaganas and Christina Murray, "Law and Women's Rights in South Africa: An Overview", in *Gender and the New South African Legal Order,* ed. Christina Murray (1994), 1.

[101] Albertyn, "Women and the transition to democracy in South Africa", 48.

[102] 51

[103] Gay W. Seidman, "Gendered Citizenship, South Africa's Democratic Transition and the Construction of a Gendered State", 13 *Gender & Society* No.3, 287 (1999): 302.

[104] Albertyn, "Women and the transition to democracy in South Africa", 52.

[105] Andrews, "Violence Against Women in South Africa", 427-428.

[106] See Albertyn, 57-61.

[107] Andrews, 440-441.

[108] S. AFR. CONST. 1996, sec. 9.

[109] *Ibid.,* sec. 10.

[110] *Ibid.,* sec. 12(2).

[111] *Ibid.*

[112] *Ibid.,* sec. 7.

[113] *Ibid.,* sec. 9.

[114] *City Council of Pretoria v. Walker,* 1998 (3) BCLR 257, para. 31 (CC).

[115] *Ibid.* The Court noted, however, that absence of an intent to discriminate may be relevant in determining the unfairness of discrimination.

[116] See S. AFR. CONS. 1996, sec. 9(4); Saras Jagwanth, "Affirmative Action in a Transformative Context: The South African Experience", 36 *Conn. L. Rev.* 725 (2004): 726-27.

[117] Jagwanth, *"Affirmative Action in a Transformative Context",* 727.

[118] *Carmichele v Minister of Safety & Sec. & Another* 2001 (10) BCLR 995 (CC).

[119] *Ibid.,* paras 13 and 23.

[120] *Ibid.,* para 13.

[121] *Ibid.,* para 25.

[122] *Ibid.,* para 27.

[123] *Ibid.,* para 29.

[124] *Carmichele,* 2001 (10) BCLR 995, at para 39.

[125] *Ibid.,* para 43.

[126] *Ibid.,* para 44.

[127] *Ibid.,* para 45.

[128] S. AFR. CONST. 1996, sec. 173.

[129] See Christopher Roederer, "The Constitutionally Inspired Approaches to Police Accountability for Violence Against Women in the U.S. and South Africa: Conservation Versus Transformation", 13 *Tulsa J. Comp. & Int'l L.* 91 (2005); Karl E. Klare, "Legal Culture and Transformative Constitutionalism", 14 *S. Afr. J. Hum. Rts.* 146 (1998).

[130] *Carmichele,* (10) BCLR 995 at para. 43.

[131] *Ibid.,* para 62.

[132] *Ibid.*

[133] *Ibid.*

[134] *Ibid.*

[135] *Carmichele v Minister of Safety & Sec. & Another,* 2004 (2) BCLR 133, at para 73.

[136] *S v Baloyi (Minister of Justice & Another Intervening),* 2000 (2) SA 425 (CC) (At the time of the decision, the Act was about to be replaced by the Domestic Violence Act 116 of 1998).

[137] *Ibid.*

[138] *Ibid.*

[139] *Ibid.,* para 8.

[140] *Ibid.,* para 25.

[141] *Baloyi,* 2000 (2) SA 425 at para 29.

[142] *Ibid.*

[143] *Ibid.*

[144] *Ibid.,* para 13.

[145] *Ibid.,* para 10.

[146] S. AFR. CONST. 1996, sec. 7(2).

[147] *Baloyi,* 2000 (2) SA 425 at para 11.

[148] *Ibid.*

[149] *Ibid.,* para 13.

[150] *Ibid.,* para 12.

[151] *Ibid.*

[152] *Ibid.*

[153] *Ibid.,* para. 12.

[154] *Ibid.*

[155] *Ibid.,* para. 12.

[156] *Omar v Government, RSA & Others* 2006 (2) BCLR 253 (CC).

[157] *Ibid.,* para 60.

[158] *Ibid.,* para 11.

[159] *Ibid.*

[160] *Ibid.,* para 13.

[161] *Ibid.*

[162] *Omar,* 2006 (2) BCLR 253 at para 16.

[163] *Ibid.,* para 17.

[164] *Ibid.*

[165] *Ibid.*

[166] *Ibid.*

[167] *Ibid.,* para 21.

CHAPTER 11

BRITISH MUSLIMS, MINORITY RIGHTS, AND GENDER

Qudsia Mirza[*]

Introduction

In the early years of South Asian immigration to the UK, it was assumed by policy makers that the newly arrived migrants would abandon their religious affiliations, leaving them behind in the countries of their origin. These 'original' immigrants consisted mostly of single young men for whom religious expression was not of primary importance. It was only when such men were reunited with their families, who began to join them a few years later, that the role of religion assumed a greater and more central importance. However, the new focus on religion was seen as a largely transitional phase, subsisting only while such immigrant communities adapted and assimilated to their new, more overtly secular, environment. Focussing particularly on Muslim migrants, Nielsen asserts that it was assumed that 'Muslims would become, if not secularized, at least like most north European Christians in confining their religious life to a small private niche.'[1]

In the last forty years since the first significant phases of immigration, Muslims have attempted to negotiate their way through state secular provisions and requirements which conflict with their Islamic values and ideals. This process has involved identifying those aspects of life which are culturally relative – and open to jettisoning or modification—from core Islamic values, which are seen as inviolable and must remain absolute. The objective is integration, and this is defined as the participation of Muslims, both as individuals and at group level, in the social structures of the host society, whilst allowing them to retain the distinctive features of their culture and identity. As a result, we can see the emergence of a distinct European Islamic culture, one that is predicated upon established norms and precepts imported from the countries of origin of Muslim migrants. However, what is also clear is that through encounters with European social structures, Islamic cultures are undergoing a process of change and transformation and being configured into new forms,[2] generically termed 'European Islam.' This is an inadequate term as the Muslim presence, a substantial religious minority in Europe, is a considerably varied group in terms of religious practice, national origin, linguistic diversity, ethnicity and race[3] and can therefore be differentiated along discrete ethnic, social and cultural lines.[4]

The global community of Muslims is defined as the *umma* and there is a distinct paradox that lies at the heart of any definition of the Muslim diaspora.[5] At the most basic level, a body of fundamental principles characterises Islamic doctrine and practice. However, this universalist core and the notion of a unified Islamic identity which is attendant upon it, is refracted through the prisms of cultural differentiation, of 'ethnicisation', of political differentiation and through generational distinctions to produce a countervailing specificity. The notion of the *umma* clearly embodies this contradiction as it acknowledges the diversity of Muslim peoples in respect of cultural, social and other vectors of differentiation, whilst simultaneously incorporating the affirmation of an eternal, unifying and universal Muslim identity which transcends the differentiations outlined above. One of the most interesting and, indeed, challenging questions for the Muslim diaspora in Europe—which constitutes a significant contingent in the global *umma*—is to what extent we will see the reconfiguration and 'secularisation' of religious traditions and practices as Islam is subjected to complex processes of acculturation. Indeed, there is a growing body of evidence that points to the development of new, hybrid forms in Islamic social and cultural practices, customs and laws, arising as a result of this process, particularly in the area of gendered legal rights.[6]

Although the idea is often contested and challenged by conservative factions in Muslim communities, it is generally accepted that some degree of the secularisation of Islam through state institutions is necessary for the integration of minority Muslim communities into the polity, and for the formation of a Britain that is culturally and socially diverse. From the state perspective, the problem of how secularism can accommodate religious normative frameworks is often an acute one and it is becoming increasingly recognised that differences between the majority society and minority Muslim communities have to be located within an overall political, social and legal consensus. As a society, Britain has endeavoured to find this consensus in institutional frameworks, in identifying a nucleus of common social values, and in a form of national identity which is both unifying and able to accommodate cultural difference. This has been achieved with varying degrees of success both in Britain and in the broader European context.[7] Most recently, legal, social and political developments in respect of Muslim communities and their place in many European countries have been characterised as conflictual and antagonistic.[8] It is clear that much progress has been made in terms of integration and equality; on the other hand, signs of a counter-movement of acute segregation, marginalisation and inequality are also observable in most countries.[9] For this reason, any reference to the 'Muslim' population is misleading as it denies the complex heterogeneity of different Muslim communities and societies, both in Europe overall and within specific member states. For the same reason, the absence of a unified, homogenous Muslim population within the context of national boundaries, makes it more difficult for the state to respond to Muslim concerns and demands.

Focussing on the British context, the earliest policy initiatives in response to the arrival of Muslim migrants[10] were oblivious to the huge diversity within such migrant populations and were centred almost solely on the subsuming of Muslim minority groups so that they assimilated as completely as possible within mainstream society. Public discourse at the time was dominated by the rhetoric of assimilation with little recognition of the need to accommodate cultural and religious difference. A precedent already existed within Britain in that the position of Jewish communities, at least until the end of 18th century, was very similar to the position of modern Muslim communities: newly arrived Jewish communities had demonstrated a substantial separation from mainstream society. This separation dissolved considerably by the 20th century with the assimilation of the Jewish community in British society. To many of those who were involved in formulating policies for the recent Muslim arrivals, this past example was deemed to be a useful template for these new communities to follow.[11]

After the first policies of assimilation, a number of different approaches have been adopted over the years in response to Muslim migration to Britain.[12] From 'absorption' and 'assimilation' at one end of the spectrum to 'pluralism,' 'multiculturalism' and 'cultural diversity'[13] at the other, there has been an assortment of state initiatives introduced to address the issue of religious pluralism and Muslim participation. As mentioned above, over the years, Britain has moved away from assimilationist policies proposed during the initial stages of Muslim immigration, in which the complete absorption of Muslim communities into British society was the primary aim of state policies.[14] Broadly speaking, this was based upon the denial of cultural difference. However, as the Muslim population increased, it became clear that this policy approach was untenable and, under a policy of liberal cultural pluralism, the formal recognition and facilitation of Muslim difference became an accepted and much needed objective. The contemporary position in Britain is that state initiatives combine elements of both the assimilationist and the multicultural or pluralist approach. However, the accommodation of Muslim difference is not unlimited and is tempered by the fact that when the pluralist approach conflicts with any aspect of society's 'core shared values', the latter always take precedence. Where this occurs, Muslims are expected to abandon their religiously sanctioned practices[15] and conform or assimilate to the 'shared' standards of society. The central issue, of course, is what constitutes these 'shared values' in British society. Furthermore, if priority is to be given to these standards, to what extent will the state allow exceptions to Muslims when (so-called) Islamic values conflict with any core societal values.[16]

Policies of multiculturalism and social inclusion are, thus, based upon a recognition or accommodation of Muslim values, which can sometimes be at variance with certain aspects of established state policies. One of the areas where the inconsistency between the two is most acute is in the area of gender equality and the state's objective of eliminating gender-based power differentials in society. This is the point at which it has been suggested that Muslim communities need to re-assess certain Islamic interpretations of gender equality, in order to reconcile these with state policies which aim to guarantee women and men legal and social equality. Within Muslim communities, there is some recognition that the normative basis of *Shari'a* is located in a variety of unjustifiable social and cultural practices which do not have a theological or doctrinal basis. Such practices not only contradict state laws and policies, but also deny the fundamental ideals of equality, freedom, and justice upon which *Shari'a* itself is based. Thus, British Muslims need to embark urgently upon a project of recognising how significant normative aspects of *Shari'a* have been based incorrectly upon discriminatory social practices. This reappraisal of the foundational roots of Islamic norms has the potential to lead to the reconfiguring of legal and social standards within Islam on questions of gender equality. Discussing this possibility within the broader European context, Malik is optimistic as she contends that the development of Islamic laws 'within a framework of European constitutional values which take freedom, tolerance and equality as their starting point may not be as problematic as some may imagine. It may prove a catalyst for re-discovering the ideals which underpin legal norms within the Islamic tradition.'[17]

In any reappraisal of Islamic norms, the relationship between English law, as the officially sanctioned system of law and *Shari'a,* as an unofficial counterpart, plays a pivotal role. The nexus between the two legal cultures is characterised by an informal legal pluralism in which *Shari'a* operates in parallel to English law but is not officially recognised as a legal system and is thus constrained by, and within, the boundaries of English law. This encounter has produced considerable changes in the area of Islamic gendered rights as a legal dimension has been created whereby certain *Shari'a* norms on women's rights have been suspended or marginalised in favour of a state-imposed gender equality. The now well-established incorporation of liberal feminist ideals within the framework of English law has resulted in the suppression of key 'Islamic' values[18], particularly in the context of marriage and divorce, rights of inheritance and succession as well as in the rules of evidence. English law has thus imposed strict controls on 'Islamic' rights granted to men and denied women in a number of key areas as these are considered antithetical to the principle of non-discrimination against women. These include finding the male right to polygamy unlawful under English law; there is a prohibition of a husband's right to unilateral divorce; English law restricts men's greater rights of custody over children (often in favour of women); Islamic law prohibits Muslim women the right to marry non-Muslim men, whilst in English law, no such restrictions apply. In addition, *Shari'a* directives on women's lesser rights of inheritance, and the unequal rules of evidence which pertain to women, are also prohibited in English law. Thus, where there is conflict between conservative interpretations of Islamic norms on the rights of women, and the principle of gender equality, viewed as a key societal 'shared value,' the latter unequivocally takes precedence over the former.

Assimilation, Accommodation, and *Angrezi Shari'at*

British Muslims can be defined as living in a state in which religion and law are viewed as existing in separate domains and 'secularism is de facto the majority creed.'[19] Muslims—both at community and at individual level—are negotiating pragmatic ways in how to practice their religion and live with the non-Muslim majority.[20] With the need to reconfigure or modify Islamic precepts in the context of secularisation, law is viewed as one of the primary (although by no means the only, or even the most effective) ways by which such a religious reconstruction takes place. Liberal law effects this reconstruction largely by re-classifying Islam into concepts that are rationalised in the modern world. Thus, Islam is categorised as religion, morality and law, a typology which contains an artificial and forced classificatory separation in order to accommodate Islam within the modern legal system.

By projecting Islamic law as a 'legal system' which functions side by side with other legal systems similarly conceived, Islamic law is endowed with a meaning which corresponds to a Western conception of legality.[21] Two consequences flow from this construction. First, particular issues of Muslim etiquette, personal behaviour, and other purely 'religious' precepts–primarily concerns of individual conscience–become reconfigured as 'rules' existing within the boundaries of Islamic law. Such issues become open to state intervention and enforcement. Second, the legal ordering of religion becomes problematic if religion is not rendered into a form recognisable and amenable to the language of law. Consequently, law 'translates' religion from a matrix of practices, rituals and obligations into a set of particular rights which formally recognise and guarantee these matters of religious observance. Thus, religions 'jostle for position' in that each is evaluated on the basis of what claims it makes and the state decides whether such claims are to be recognised in relation to other religious demands.

The popular understanding of *Shari'a* merely as Islamic law is both simplistic and reductive as it does not necessarily delineate clear boundaries between the three categories of religion, morality and law, mentioned above. The basic meaning of *Shari'a* as 'path or way' represents the normative order that delineates the totality of an Islamic way of life. Modern Muslim jurists define *Shari'a* as revealed or divine law in order to distinguish it from two other conceptions of law: first, *fiqh*, the jurist's law, which represents the jurists' interpretation of *Shari'a* and second, *qanun*, defined as state law. This is a significant distinction in the typology as it places primary importance on the divine nature and origin of *Shari'a*, thus establishing that *Shari'a* norms possess normative and binding effect precisely because of their divine origin.[22] The idea of *Shari'a* as a homogenous, distinct category of law is also untenable in view of the significant differences between *Shi'a* and *Sunni* conceptions of law and between the main schools of jurisprudence, which often evince irreconcilable differences in their interpretations of specific legal issues. Furthermore, the foundational texts of *Shari'a* are fundamentally different in nature from secular laws. The primary source is the *Qur'an*, considered to be the eternal and absolute divine word, revealed over a number of years to the Prophet Muhammad. The secondary source of *Shari'a* is the collection of *hadith* literature, which outlines the words and traditions of the Prophet Muhammad and his companions. These narratives elaborate a more detailed understanding of the broad principles and norms of the *Qur'an*. These sources are all supplemented by a copious anthology of exegetical texts, the *tafsir* literature, including the corpus of writing on *usul ul-fiqh*, Islamic jurisprudence. Substantive and methodological tools in *Shari'a* such as *ikrah* (compromise), *darura* (necessity), *maslaha* (public welfare) and *takhayyur* (selection)are also utilised as aids to interpretation; other methodological tools such as local custom, and public interest, are also used increasingly in diasporic Muslim communities to supplement the main foundations of Islamic law.[23]

The demands and claims made by Muslims are assessed primarily against the standards of largely secular obligations and values: the state determines which Muslim differences are to be accommodated within the legal domain and in this way brought within the scope of the liberal state. This is effected by utilising the idea of what is deemed to be an 'acceptable difference.' As mentioned above, the idea of a society's set of 'shared values' is deployed to differentiate those aspects of religious practice that are viewed as worthy of legal protection and exclude those considered not part of such a societal consensus. What is of central importance to Muslims is determining which elements of their religious practice will be recognised and facilitated by the state and which will be rejected.

During the last few decades of migration to Britain, English law has recognised certain aspects of personal law systems[24] based on different religious and cultural traditions. In the context of the Muslim diaspora, although some significant concessions have been made to accommodate Muslim difference, there has been considerable reluctance on the part of the state to grant full recognition to *Shari'a* as an integral or official part of the British legal system. Some Muslims have insisted on the primacy of *Shari'a*, calling for the greater legal autonomy of Muslim communities in the legal system. In contrast, English law operates upon the basis of complete adherence to, and supremacy, of its own rule of law models. In respect of the calls for the institution of *Shari'a*, Zubaida, writing in a more general context, argues that such demands are driven by a complex array of ideological and political motives, including a certain social conservatism which aims for 'the restoration of patriarchal authority, of order and hierarchy and the moralization of public space and cultural activity.'[25] Although this sweeping statement can be applied in a more nuanced way in the British context, it is nonetheless clear that many demands for the official recognition of Islamic law are predicated upon an understanding of *Shari'a* norms in which the notion of gender equality is compromised and falls short of a variety of English legal provisions which guarantee women equal rights with men.

The common understanding of English law is that it is rooted in a uniform secularism and that it takes a broadly neutral and equal approach to all religious groups. The deeply religious basis of many contemporary laws in Britain belies the simplicity of this account. There are also notable exceptions to the idea that English law treats all religious groups in an equal manner in that, historically, beneficial legal provisions have been established for Jews, Quakers, and Sikhs.[26] In addition, a number of religious groups have been recognised by the courts as a 'racial group' and thus gained protection within the ambit of anti-race discrimination legislation enacted in the mid-1970s. Conspicuously, Muslims have repeatedly been denied such recognition and protection. The explicit non-recognition of Muslims as a 'racial group'[27] under the provisions of the Race Relations Act 1976 is the most striking instance of the exclusion of Muslims from official legal recognition.[28] As a result, *Shari'a* occupies an unclear position in relation to English law. As Pearl and Menski assert, 'Muslim law, in such a scenario, is pushed into the realm of the unofficial, the extra-legal, the sphere of 'cultural practice' or perhaps 'ethnic minority custom'...rather than being treated as officially recognised law'.[29] In this framework, English law represents the site of official, established law whilst *Shari'a* is designated as one of its unofficial 'counterparts.'

Thus, the relationship between the two legal cultures is characterised by the fact that, first, there is no official recognition of Islamic law as a legal system running parallel with, and having equal status, with English law. Second, a number of concessions have been made to accommodate Muslim requirements. As a result, it can be said that the English legal system is moderately flexible in accommodating Muslim needs and that there is widespread legislative and judicial recognition of the needs and requirements of Muslim communities. As far as the courts are concerned, decisions in areas such as criminal law, the law of slander and tort law all illustrate a certain judicial flexibility in responding to Muslim claims.[30] This multicultural approach can also be found in areas such as family law and employment law, and in the form of specific exemptions allowed Muslims such as the relaxation of regulations over the slaughtering of animals.[31] The passing of the Finance Act 2003 is the most recent major legal provision designed to accommodate Muslim difference. In *Shari'a,* the levying of interest (*riba*) is deemed to be unlawful and in order to avoid this, Muslims have been forced to put in place complex mortgage arrangements whereby the tax payable on the purchase of property – Stamp Duty – is paid twice by Muslims who wish to avoid the paying of interest. This punitive measure has been abolished by the 2003 Act, thereby facilitating the taking out of mortgages which both comply with *Shari'a* precepts and do not place an excessive financial burden on observant Muslims.

Returning to the problematic issue of which Muslim claims are to be accommodated, the mechanism used to filter out those demands perceived to be unworthy of protection, is the notion of 'shared values' mentioned above. According to Poulter, this includes democracy, the rule of law, natural justice, freedom of expression, religious toleration and the English language.[32] The key question, of course, is who determines what these shared values are to be; Pearl and Menski conclude that there are certain beliefs and practices that Muslims would be forced to renounce as these run counter to one or more of these shared core values.[33] In a sustained critique of what they view as the contemporary Orientalism of state attitudes to Islamic law, Pearl and Menski argue first, that Islamic law is reduced to being defined as 'customs' and 'exotic practices.' Second, Islamic law is perceived as inferior as it fails to provide effective human rights protection, particularly in areas such as gender equality.[34] Third, and perhaps most controversially, Pearl and Menski contend that colonial history continues to play a part in the marginalisation of Islamic law in Britain. They argue that contemporary debates about Islamic law in Europe are still underpinned by the colonial encounter and the 'persistent view that overseas concepts and values are inferior.'[35] Thus, whilst it was legitimate to respect and uphold Islamic law for subjects under colonial rule, limitations on the application of such laws in contemporary British society is justified by invoking a false notion of the unity and uniformity of English law.[36] These key concerns enunciated by Pearl and Menski have particular resonance when considering the possibility of instituting *Shari'a* rights for women within the fabric of English law.[37]

The framework above delineates the relationship between English and Islamic law in a broad sense as either assimilation or accommodation: under a policy of assimilation, English law does not recognise certain *Shari'a* ideals and Muslims are expected to jettison their attachment to such ideals[38]; under a policy of accommodation, those aspects of *Shari'a* which are viewed as compliant with society's notion of 'shared values' are formally recognised and protected by English law. A closer investigation can provide us with a more nuanced reading of the relationship between the two. The use of hybridity is instructive in this regard as this concept incorporates the creation of new identities beyond binary opposites. If English law and *Shari'a* form the polarised, binary points of an encounter, what new legal hybrid identities does this encounter produce? Although the development of hybridity can be located at certain points, one area of law where it is very difficult to locate any hybridity is in the encounter between the English law of blasphemy and *Shari'a* concepts of blasphemy. Far from creating an 'in-between' space[39] for the forging of new hybrid identities, English law insists on its capacity to construct the Other. The trajectory of the cases brought against the publication of *The Satanic Verses* can be viewed as an example of the resistance of English law to any new relationship with the Other, especially Islam. When Muslim groups sought to use the English law of blasphemy against Rushdie's book, the legal discourse developed representations of Islamic law and Muslims in terms that essentialised Muslims as 'backward' and *Shari'a* as lacking basic norms of human rights protection.[40] This attempt by Muslims was characterised as a conflict with one of society's most inviolable 'shared' values, freedom of expression. The courts' rejection of Muslim demands indicates that, at least in this area, there is no legal recognition or acceptance of Muslim difference. Thus, Muslims were expected to assimilate unquestioningly to the notion of freedom of expression, and in challenging *The Satanic Verses*, have been characterised as antagonistic to this core 'shared value'.

In this way, English law establishes a hierarchy, with it as the official form of law, and in a position to determine when and to what extent legal recognition is to be given to Muslim demands. Although this represents the formal situation, it is apparent that Muslims have developed means by which official laws can be legitimately avoided.[41] Using the concept of hybridity once again, the state tolerance of certain elements of *Shari'a* has created a space for the development of a fused scheme or structure of rules which is based upon a basic adherence to *Shari'a* but one that has been modified to avoid conflict with English law. Muslims are following those aspects of English law they consider appropriate or not in direct conflict with Islamic precepts, thus incorporating elements of both legal cultures – Islamic obligations as well as aspects of English law – and developing a hybrid form of *Shari'a*. This hybridised '*Angrezi Shari'at*' remains unrecognised by English law as a coherent legal system, but is a potent and dominant force in many British Muslim communities.[42] An example of this emerging form of hybridity can be seen in the area of marriage. In order to comply with *Shari'a* requirements, a couple has to undergo the Islamic *nik'ah* ceremony. However, this is not recognised in English law; furthermore, requirements in English law need to be met in order to formally register a marriage. Therefore, in addition to completing the *nik'ah* (which is not prohibited in English law but also not formally recognised), Muslims also undergo a civil marriage ceremony and the two are grafted onto each other to form a new, hybridised marriage process. Consequently, Muslims are being selective in which parts of *Shari'a* they consider absolute and inviolable and those elements of English law that must be complied with which do not conflict with *Shari'a* principles. Thus, Yilmaz argues, Muslims can be viewed as 'skilful legal navigators who apply different laws in relevant contextual situations in order to meet the demands of different overlapping normative orderings.'[43]

The Gender Perspective

With the revival of certain forms of religious conservatism and the discriminatory attitudes that such conservatism often entails, the nexus between gender, religion and law is one that is increasingly salient for a growing number of women.[44] This is especially pertinent for Muslim women who suffer oppression on the basis of gender, religion, and often also race. Discriminatory attitudes towards such women in terms of their adherence to Islam exists both 'externally' and 'internally': the former in terms of increasing Islamophobia in society; the latter in the form of the increasingly conservative nature of 'fundamentalist' or 'political' Islam.[45] In the British context, the forms of discrimination Muslim women face are often complex and challenging and the question of religion must be viewed not simply as an additional form of disadvantage to 'throw into the multiple discrimination pot' with other forms of discrimination such as race and gender. In particular, the relationship between race and religion is especially convoluted and, as Fredman argues cogently, 'ethnicity is intimately bound up with religion.'[46] She highlights the difficulties the British courts have faced in severing ethnicity from religion in cases such as the seminal decision in *Mandla v Dowell Lee*[47] in which the House of Lords set down a list of criteria by which to determine whether an individual belonged to a 'racial group' and thus was afforded protection from racial discrimination. The list of criteria has been applied in subsequent decisions in such a way that Muslims have been excluded from the definition of 'racial group' in contrast to other racial/religious groups such as Sikhs and Jews.[48] The situation has been eased somewhat by the passing of the Employment Equality (Religion or Belief) Regulations 2003 which protect all religious communities against discrimination. Muslim women face an additional burden in the form having to prove gender discrimination. A 'hierarchy of oppression' is put into place whereby women are faced with the unenviable task of choosing between different forms of disadvantage if legal remedies are sought – a problem difficult enough when trying to distinguish between sex and race discrimination, rendered even more problematic if the question of religion is added.

A key problem with legislating against religious discrimination is the natural tension that exists between certain beliefs and values of a religion, on the one hand, and fundamental principles that have been enshrined in law by a secular society, on the other. From a feminist perspective, problems arise when the state accommodates 'religious' practices when they are, in fact, merely social or cultural traditions which are defined incorrectly as theologically legitimate. The porous nature of the divide between theological/religious doctrine and social and cultural traditions and norms in Islam has made this a particularly problematic issue for Muslim communities. This tension became apparent during the time of the publication of Salman Rushdie's *The Satanic Verses* and the calls for the implementation of the *fatwa* against him as well as calls for the extension of blasphemy laws in Britain. Feminist Muslims[49] argued that Islamic sensibilities were being characterised in an over-simplistic manner in that self-appointed unrepresentative elites were speaking on behalf of the great diversity of opinion within British Muslim communities. Feminists felt that the specific concerns that Muslim women had over the publication of the book were either marginalised or misrepresented by their male counterparts, who falsely projected themselves as representing the entirety of the British Muslim population. The courts have also been persuaded by arguments that depicted Islam in a stereotypical way, particularly in the characterisation of women's role and rights in the family. Fixed ideas of Muslim women as passive victims in cases involving forced marriage is an example of how the courts have deployed such stereotypical representations to determine cases. Specifically, the courts have accepted particularly orthodox versions of the gender roles within Islam in the operation of nullity in cases of marriage.[50] These cases illustrate the courts' almost unquestioning acceptance of the assertion that Islamic doctrine is detrimental to women as it legitimates gender roles in which women are viewed as inferior to men.

Posing the policies of assimilation, accommodation, and *Angrezi Shari'at* (as a nebulous form of hybridity) as three distinct models, it is possible to map the relationship between English laws and *Shari'a*[51] in relation to Muslim women's rights under one of these three frameworks. To take the most straightforward first, accommodation consists of cases where the recognition and facilitation of Muslim women's difference is incorporated into the fabric of official law either by formal legislative change or by judicial intervention. A current example is the acknowledgment that a woman can be discriminated against in the workplace on the basis of wearing the *hijab* and that she must be afforded legal protection against such discrimination. Britain has complied with recent developments in European law such as the Equal Treatment at Work Directive,[52] promulgated under Article 13 of the EC Treaty, which outlaws discrimination in the workplace on a number of grounds, including religion. This has now been implemented by Britain in the Employment Equality (Religion or Belief) Regulations 2003 and has outlawed religious discrimination in the workplace generally. Muslim women who adhere to the practice of wearing the *hijab* are among the main beneficiaries of these Regulations as it is possible to assert the right to wear the *hijab* and instigate a claim of religious discrimination if an employer restricts or prohibits the exercise of this right.

The second approach, of hybridity, comes into play when Muslims develop strategies for legitimately avoiding compliance with official laws. As mentioned above, the area of marriage laws may be seen as an example of this approach whereby the *nik'ah* ceremony in *Shari'a*, although not formally recognized by English law, functions as an integral part of the marriage ceremony and is incorporated or fused within British civil procedures. A Muslim woman is able to benefit from the rights which accrue from the civil marriage and the state registration of that marriage and also comply with the religious/*Shari'a* requirements of the *nik'ah* ceremony. Finally, the assimilation model, which operates where there is a conflict between English laws and *Shari'a* injunctions. Here, liberal ideals come into play and there is a clear rejection of Muslim religious difference on the basis that Muslim demands do not comply with so-called secular ideals such as gender equality. What is most interesting about the assimilationist model is that this is creating an environment leading to the development of legal measures for Muslim women that are radically less discriminatory than conservative interpretations of such rights under *Shari'a*. The assimilationist rationale underpins the complete rejection by the state of conservative interpretations of *Shari'a* under which we see the ordering of rights such as polygyny, men's unilateral right of divorce, mothers' lesser rights of child custody, women's reduced rights of inheritance, the diminished weight accorded a woman's evidence against a man, and the prohibition inter-marriage between Muslim women and non-Muslim men.

Taking the first of the examples above, polygamy, the British ban on this practice has resulted in women not having to doctrinally challenge versions of *Shar'ia* which allow their husbands' 'right' to take on additional wives. The practice is banned under the English laws of bigamy and is implicitly incorporated when a Muslim woman marries a Muslim man in Britain by complying with official legal requirements under English law. Of course, the possibility always remains that the husband may take on additional wives in *Shari'a* but these will not be recognised under English law and the rights of the 'first' wife under English law will not be affected. What is important to note is that British Muslim men are not asserting their 'Islamic' right to take on additional wives. It may be too dramatic to characterise this as a re-configuration of *Shari'a*, but in practical terms, this appears to be the development that is taking place. In the same way, the philosophy of assimilation underpinning the rejection of the other matters outlined above (divorce, custody, inheritance, etc) has led to the entrenchment of greater legal rights for women. Other rights for women also flow from the state registration of marriage such as greater custody rights of children upon divorce.

Many Muslim women are unaware of their rights, under either *Shari'a* or English law.[53] Even when women are aware of their rights, their ability to access these legal rights may be limited. Predetermined and fixed cultural norms, and the social and cultural stigma attached to such issues as divorce, have resulted in women failing to properly access their legal rights, both in English courts and Islamic community institutions. As far as the latter is concerned, such organisations are often associated with weak enforcement mechanisms which are considered less effective than the stronger, more coercive enforcement measures of the English legal system. Enforcing rights under English law requires litigants to possess substantial financial and other resources, something that poorer Muslim women will not have ready access to. Migrant Muslim women may also encounter substantial language problems in pursuing legal claims in British courts. Accessing their rights in community institutions may be equally problematic as reliance on forms of alternative dispute resolution in local community courts and tribunals may result in decisions which are based on traditional interpretations of *Shari'a* and which discriminate against women in the key areas outlined above. A continued problem is that many interpreters and enforcers of *Shari'a* are imams of local mosques and male community elders, 'experts' who interpret women's legal rights in a conservative manner, reinforcing entrenched patriarchal interpretations of scripture. These individuals are also called to appear in the British legal system to provide expert evidence, and courts are dependant upon such interpreters to give definitive interpretations of Islamic law.

In conclusion, the ideals of *Shari'a* are clearly based upon freedom, equality, and justice. However, social mores and stratifications in Muslim societies have restricted or denied these ideals to the extent that they have not been realised. This is particularly so in the realisation of gendered rights – a reality that has just as much application in Western states where there are substantial Muslim diasporic communities, as well as in the wider Muslim world. As Masud contends, 'at the social level, women and non-Muslims suffered most from the inner contradictions between *shari'a* ideals and social norms in Muslim cultures.'[54] This is largely due to the fact that a number of discriminatory social norms, denying gender equality, have been assimilated into the fabric of *Shari'a* and are now considered to be normative and immutable rules governing men and women's respective legal rights. At the heart of the problem is a great divergence between legal norms which have now become instituted and entrenched in Muslim communities, and Islamic ethical values which guarantee gender equality.

Muslim women face discrimination on the basis of race, gender and religion in mainstream British society. They also face discriminatory attitudes within their communities on the basis of entrenched, conservative interpretations of scripture. The encounter between English law and *Shari'a* indicates that both legal cultures are being influenced by each other to varying degrees. To what extent each is being transformed by the other, is a complex question. What is undeniable, however, is that dramatic changes are being effected to Muslim practice as a result of changes imposed by English law, and this is particularly so in the area of gendered rights. However, the official non-recognition of *Shari'a* or the non-recognition of certain aspects of *Shari'a* militates against Muslim women who wish to live their lives according to Islamic precepts. Therefore, it is worth considering an approach that recognises the centrality of Islam in women's lives and the need to reconcile this with more 'secular' notions of equality. Writing more broadly in the Indian context, Mullaly argues that what is needed is 'a dialectic between constitutional essentials and the actual politics of multicultural societies.'[55]

Muslim feminists are re-interpreting scripture and traditions and arguing that Islamic precepts can be adapted and modified. This is based on an understanding of Islam and *Shari'a* as shifting and being contested rather than as fixed and static – a too common representation of both within British society. By perpetuating the notion that Islamic norms are fixed in patriarchal tradition, *Shari'a* standards have been characterised as immutable and dangerous for Muslim women.[56] Liberal feminism's recent assault on multicultural politics as 'bad for women'[57] is bound up with such depictions of religious systems and this is a position that needs urgent re-evaluation. Muslim communities also need to acknowledge that women have a right to challenge, question and dissent from established norms and that feminist interpretations of religious tradition should form an important part of the internal discussions that need to take place urgently within such communities. Returning to the question of law, there is a risk that, in granting legal rights to Muslims on the basis of their collective religious identity—without incorporating these feminist, egalitarian interpretations of gendered rights—an accommodation of Muslim demands may be made which infringes or limits women's rights in such communities. It is essential, therefore, to ensure that any laws which guarantee the exercise of religious practices do not unwittingly entrench conservative and discriminatory interpretations of Islam.[58] If this were to happen, law could be used not only as a tool which guarantees freedom from discrimination for religious groups, but also as an instrument by which inequalities against groups within a religious community are maintained. The discrimination against Muslim women as a 'minority within a minority' then continues and is perpetuated by the force of law.

[*] This is a version of a chapter entitled "Legal Pluralities: Shari'a, English Law and Gender" published earlier in "Jurisprudence, Religion and Political Identity" (Adam Gearey and Marinos Diamantides eds. 2008).

[1] Jorgen Nielsen, *Muslims in Western Europe* (Edinburgh: Edinburgh University Press, 1995),157. *See* also W.A.R. Shahid and P.S. van Koningsveld, ed., *Religious Freedom and the Neutrality of the State: The Position of Islam in the European Union* (Leuven, Sterling: Peeters, 2002).

[ii] In historical terms, this is by no means a new phenomenon. Through the centuries, Islam has transplanted itself in new locations and grafted on the social and cultural trappings of that particular environment. It should also be noted that Islam in the 'West' does not have a monopoly on being open to adaptation and syncretism. The practice of Islam in Muslim countries is also dynamic and open to modification and change.

[3] For detailed country by country population analyses, see www.islamicpopulation.com. There are slightly conflicting statistics on the Muslim population in Britain. One estimate is approximately 2 million – the largest minority faith group in the UK: Humayan Ansari, "The Legal Status of Muslims in the UK," in *The Legal Treatment of Islamic Minorities in Europe*, ed. Roberta Allufi and Giovanna Zincone, (Leuven: Peeters, 2004), 255. According to the 2001 Census, there are 1.6 million Muslims in Britain: see Tariq Modood, *Multicultural Politics, Racism, Ethnicity and Muslims in Britain* (Minneapolis: University of Minnesota Press, 2005), 151. For general analyses, *see* Joel S. Fetzer and Christopher Soper, *Muslims and the State in Britain, France, and Germany* (Cambridge, New York: Cambridge University Press, 2005); Jytte Klausen, *The Islamic Challenge: Politics and Religion in Western Europe* (Oxford, New York: Oxford University Press, 2005); Iftikhar Malik, *Islam and Modernity: Muslims in Europe and the United States* (London, Sterling: Pluto Press, 2004); Jocelyne Cesari, *When Islam and Democracy Meet: Muslims in Europe and in the United States* (New York: Palgrave Macmillan, 2004).

[4] *See* Prakash A. Shah and Werner Menski, ed., *Migration, Diasporas and Legal Systems in Europe* (London: Cavendish, 2006); Silvio Ferrari and Anthony Bradney,ed., *Islam and European Legal Systems,* (Aldershot: Ashgate, 2000); Steven Vertovec and Ceri Peach, ed., *Islam in Europe: The Politics of Religion and Community* (London: Macmillan, 1997); W.A.R. Shahid and P. S. van Koningsveld, ed., *Intercultural Relations and Religious Authorities: Muslims in the European Union* (Leuven, Dudley: Peeters, 2002); Brigitte Marechal, ed., *Muslims in the Enlarged Europe*, (Leiden, Boston: Brill, 2003); Tariq Modood et al., ed., *Multiculturalism, Muslims and Citizenship: A European Approach* (London, NY: Routledge, 2006); Shireen Hunter, ed., *Islam, Europe's Second Religion: The New Social, Cultural and Political Landscape* (Westport: Praeger, 2002).

[5] For a comparative analysis of the Muslim diaspora, *see* Everett Jenkins, ed., *The Muslim Diaspora: A Comprehensive Reference to the Spread of Islam in Asia, Africa, Europe and the Americas*, (Jefferson: McFarland, 1999).

[6] *See* Werner Menski and David Pearl, *Muslim Family Law* (London: Sweet and Maxwell, 1998); Ihsan Yilmaz, *Muslim Laws, Politics and Society in Modern Nation States* (Aldershot: Ashgate, 2005). For a discussion of a nebulous form of legal and cultural hybridity emerging in the context of the laws of marriage in Britain, see Qudsia Mirza, "Islam, Hybridity, and the Laws of Marriage," *Australian Feminist Law Journal* 1, (2000), 14. For the counter-argument in the context of the law of blasphemy see Qudsia Mirza, "Sacred and Secular Blasphemies,"*Griffith Law Review*, 12, 2, (2003), 336.

[7] Jocelyne Cesari and Sean McLoughlin, ed., *European Muslims and the Secular State* (Aldershot; Ashgate, 2005).

[8] For one of the earliest surveys of the position of Muslims in a particular European context, *see* W. A. Shahid, "The Integration of Muslim Minorities in the Netherlands," *Int. Migration Rev.*, 25,2 (1991), 355, although some of his conclusions have not been borne out.

[9] W.A.R. Shadid and P.S. van Koningsveld, ed., *Religious Freedom and the Neutrality of the State: The Position of Islam in the EU* (Leuven: Peeters, 2002), 5.

[10] In the context of this essay, 'British Muslims' refers mainly to Sunni Muslims of South Asian descent. These first arrived in significant numbers in the early 1960s.

[11] Silvio Ferrari, "Islam in Europe: An Introduction to Legal Problems and Perspectives," *The Legal Treatment of Islamic Minorities in Europe*, ed. Roberta Allufi and Giovanna Zincone, (Leuven: Peeters, 2004), 2; *See* also Anwar, M and Bakhsh, Q, *British Muslims and State Policies* (Warwick: University of Warwick, 2003) for a recent survey of state responses to the Muslim presence.

[12] See Sebastian Poulter, *Ethnicity Law and Human Rights*, (Oxford: Clarendon Press, 1998); Tariq Modood et al., *Ethnic Minorities in Britain: Diversity and Disadvantage*, (London: Policy Studies Institute 1997); Tariq Modood et al., *Changing Ethnic Identities*, (London: Policy Studies Institute, 1994); Tariq Modood, *Racial Equality: Colour, Culture and Justice*, (London: Institute for Public Policy Research,1994); Colin Brown, *Black and White Britain: The Third PSI Study*, (London: Policy Studies Institute, 1984).

[13] For a stimulating study of cultural and legal pluralism and the relationship between the two, see Prakash Shah, *Legal Pluralism in Conflict: Coping with Cultural Diversity in Law* (London: Glass House, 2005).

[14] Mohammad Siddique, ed., *British Muslims: Loyalty and Belonging*, (Islamic Foundatin, 2003; Roger Ballard, *Desh Pradesh: The South Asian Experience in Britain*, (Hurst, 1994); Colin Clarke et al., *South Asians Overseas Migration and Ethnicity*, (Cambridge University Press, 1990); Milton Israel and Narendra Wagle, ed., *Ethnicity, Identity, Migration: The South Asian Context*, (University of Toronto Press, 1993); Pearl and Menski, *Muslim Family Law*, (Sweet & Maxwell, 1998).

[15] Whether a practice is religiously sanctioned or prescribed is a contested issue and one that depends largely upon a variety of different interpretations.

[16] For further analyses see Sebastian Poulter, "The Limits of Legal, Cultural and Religious Pluralism," Jonathan Montgomery, "Legislating for a Multi-Faith Society: Some Problems of Special Treatment," Tariq Modood, "Cultural Diversity and Racial Discrimination in Employment," in *Discrimination: The Limits of Law*, ed. Bob Heppele and Erika Szyszczak, (Mansell, 1992).

[17] Maleiha Malik, "Accommodating Muslims in Europe Opportunities for Minority Fiqh," *ISIM Newsletter*,13 December 2003, 11.

[18] Or the manner in which *social/cultural* norms in Muslim cultures (which should be open to challenge and contestation) have been crystallised as Islamic *legal* norms (which are often defined wrongly as 'Islamic' and are not open to any form of challenge).

[19] Tariq Modood, ed., *Church, State and Religious Minorities* (London: Policy Studies Institute, 1997), 12.

[20] *See*, generally, Richard Jones and Gnanapak Welhengama, *Ethnic Minorities in English Law* (Trentham: 2000); Samia Bano, "Muslim and South Asian Women: Customary Law and Citizenship in Britain," in *Women, Citizenship and Difference*, ed. Nira Yuval-Davis and Pnina Werbner, (London, New York: Zed Books, 1999), 165 on the relationship between the liberal underpinnings of English law and minority Muslim laws.

[21] Michael King, ed., *God's Law Versus State Law* (London: Grey Seal, 1995), 108.

[22] Muhammad Khalid Masud, *Muslim Jurists' Quest for the Normative Basis of Shari'a* http://www.isim.nl/files/inaugural_masud.pdf.

[23] Humayan Ansari, "The Legal Status of Muslims in the UK," in *The Legal Treatment of Islamic Minorities in Europe*, ed. Roberta Allufi and Giovanna Zincone, (Leuven: Peeters, 2004), 262.

[24] *See*, in particular, Sebastian Poulter, "The Claim to a Separate Islamic System of Personal Law for British Muslims," in , *Islamic Family Law*, ed. Chibli Mallat and Jane Connors, (London, Boston: Graham & Trotham,1990).

[25] Sami Zubaida, *Law and Power in the Islamic World* (London, New York: IB Taurus, 2003), 222.

[26] For a discussion of such exceptions in the law of marriage see Qudsia Mirza, *Islam, Hybridity and the Laws of Marriage*. Poulter also discusses a selection of recent cases in which there is judicial recognition of different cultural and religious backgrounds, including "Islam: Multiculturalism and Human Rights for Muslim Families in English Law," in *God's Law Versus State Law*, ed. Michael King, (Grey Seal Books, 1995), 83.

[27] Or 'ethnic group' under the terms of the *Rae Relations Act*, 1976.

[28] The exclusion of Muslims is in contrast to Sikhs and Jews who have been afforded protection under the Race Relations Act 1976 as members of a 'racial group': *Mandla v Dowell Lee* [1983] IRLR 209, HL; *Siede v Gillette* [1980] IRLR 427. *Ahmad v ILEA* [1978] 1 All ER 574, is a case in which a Muslim teacher was denied the protection of the RRA 1976. The case progressed to the European Court of Human Rights, which affirmed the decision of the British courts: *Ahmed v UK* [1982] 4 EHRR 126.

[29] Pearl and Menski, *Muslim Family Law*, (Sweet & Maxwell, 1998), 51.

[30] Sebastian Poulter, "Multiculturalism and Human Rights for Muslim Families in English Law," in *God's Law Versus State Law*, ed. Michael King, (London: Grey Seal, 1995), 2.

[31] Sebastian Poulter, "Muslim Headscarves in School: Contrasting Legal Approaches in England and France," *OJLS* 43 (1997) 49.

[32] Sebastian Poulter, *Ethnicity, Law and Human Rights* (Oxford: Clarendon Press,1998) 22 – 26.

[33] Pearl and Menski, *Muslim Family Law*, (Sweet & Maxwell, 1998), 68.

[34] Many critics have countered this crude depiction of Islamic law and have pointed out the similarities between the ideals of secularism and the core ideals of Islamic law. One of the most vocal is Engineer, who asserts categorically, that 'Islam upholds pluralism, freedom of conscience and human and democratic rights and thus does not clash with the concept of secularism': Asghar Ali Engineer, "Islam and Secularism" in *Islam in Transition Muslim Perspectives*, ed. John Donohue and John Esposito, (New York, Oxford: Oxford University Press, 2007).

[35] Pearl and Menski, *Muslim Family Law*, (Sweet & Maxwell, 1998), 66.

[36] *Ibid.*

[37] In the context of Muslim migrant communities in Canada, Razack has delineated the caricatures of the 'imperilled Muslim woman' and the 'dangerous Muslim man' and how the former has to be 'saved' from the latter and his use of patriarchal Islamic norms to justify discriminatory practices: Sherene Razack, "Imperilled Muslim Women, Dangerous Muslim Men and Civilized Europeans: Legal and Social responses to Forced Marriages," *Feminist Legal Studies*, 12 (2004) 129. It can be argued that the continued deployment of such negative representations of Islamic norms is predicated upon the Orientalist attitudes outlined by Pearl and Menski.

[38] In contrast to these examples where Muslim difference has been accommodated, the prohibition of polygyny, and unilateral divorce, are some of the areas affecting Muslims where the legal response rejects the accommodation of such demands and demonstrates an assimilationist approach. Additionally, it is important to note that there are other assimilationist laws, particularly in the areas of immigration law and marriage and divorce procedures, that affect minority communities generally, and therefore include Muslim communities.

[39] See Homi Bhabha, *The Location of Culture* (London: Routledge, 1996) for the notion of hybridity in the cultural sense.

[40] See Qudsia Mirza, for a critique in "Sacred and Secular Blasphemies." The case was also brought before the European Court of Human Rights which affirmed the decisions of the British courts.

[41] In some cases, Muslims have developed regulatory obligations systems which are mechanisms internal to the community itself. The development of *Shari'a* courts applying Muslim law is the main means by which Muslims have managed to avoid official legal processes. Official organisations such as the Muslim Council of Britain and its related Shari'a Council exercise a number of regulatory powers.

[42] This is a term coined by Pearl and Menski and translated, means 'British Shari'a' (see Pearl and Menski, *Muslim Family Law*).

[43] Ihsan Yilmaz, *Muslim Laws, Politics and Society in Modern Nation States*, (Aldershot: Ashgate, 2005), 3.

[44] See Oonagh Reitman, "Feminism and Multiculturalism: Compatibility, Incompatibiity or Synonymity," *Ethnicities*, 5 (2005) 2.

[45] 'Fundamentalist' and 'political' Islam are, of course, contested terms.

[46] Sandra Fredman, "Equality: A New Generation," *ILJ* 30, 2, (2001) 158.

[47] [1983] IRLR 209 HL. There was no gender dimension to this case.

[48] The courts in *Nyazi v Rymans Ltd*, EAT 86 (10 May1988, unreported) specifically excluded Muslims. See also *J H Walker Ltd v Hussain* [1996] IRLR 11. In *CRE v Precision* (1991), the courts also clarified that direct racial discrimination was not unlawful against Muslims; as the group of Muslims was predominantly of Pakistani origin, racial discrimination could be found against them on the basis of this ethnic origin.

[49] Gita Sahgal and Nira Yuval-Davis, ed., *Refusing Holy Orders: Women and Fundamentalism in Britain*, (London: Virago, 1992).

[50] See Hilary Lim, "Messages From A Rarely Visited Island: Duress and Consent in Marriage," *Feminist Legal Studies* 4 (1996) 195, for this critique.

[51] See Jochen Blaschke, ed., *Multi-Level Discrimination of Muslim Women in Europe* (Berlin: Ed. Parabolis Books, 2000).

[52] 2000/78/EC.

[53] It is important to note the burgeoning feminist literature exploring women's legal rights in Islam and the manner in which this work is challenging restrictive notions of gendered rights. For an overview, see Qudsia Mirza, *Islamic Feminism:Possibilities and Limitations* in *Law After Ground Zero*, ed. John Strawson, (London: Cavendish, 2002).

[54] Masud, *Muslim Jurists' Quest for the Normative Basis of Shariah*, p7.

[55] Siobhan Mullaly, "Feminism and Multicultural ilemmas in India: Revisiting the Shah Bano Case," OJLS 24 (4) (2004) 690.
[56] Natasha Bakht, "Were Muslim Barbarians really Knocking on the Gates of Ontario?: The Religious Arbitration Controversy – Another Perspective," http://www.lawsite.ca/OLR_Barbarians-Arb_Article.pdf, 13.
[57] Susan Moller Okin, "Is Multiculturalism Bad For Women?" in *Is Multiculturalism Bad For Women?: Susan Moller Okin with Respondents*, ed. J. Cohen, J. Howard and M. Nussbaum, (Princeton: Princeton University Press, 1999).
[58] For a discussion of minority group rights generally in this context, see Ayelet Shachar, "The Puzzle of Interlocking Power Hierarchies: Sharing the Pieces of Jurisdictional Authority," Harv. C.R.-C.L. Rev 385 (2000) 25. See also Ayelet Shachar, *Multicultural Jurisdictions: Cultural Differences and Women's Rights*, (Cambridge: Cambridge University Press, 2001).

CHAPTER 12

THE CONSTITUTIONAL RIGHT TO ACQUIRE CITIZENSHIP: COMPARATIVE PROVISIONS AND ISSUES

Janet M. Calvo

Citizenship is an important basis for the protections of rights even in an increasingly globalized world. There is an insufficient and inadequate focus on constitutional protection of the right to citizenship. There has been recent focus on constitutional provisions that promote a universal concept of rights that recognizes the dignity of every person. In some more recent constitutions there has been an explicit attempt to address the human rights of all.[1] There has also been a substantial amount of scholarship that appropriately looks at citizenship beyond that defined by a nation state.[2] Yet citizenship continues to matter.

The world is still predominately organized by and into nation states. Even in the context of international organizations or cross-national unions, the ultimate power and resources to enforce rights still lie in the component nations.[3] Citizenship provides the basic right to indefinitely live in a country and not be forcibly removed. The right to citizenship determines who will be the continuing inhabitants protected by a nation state's constitutional provisions. Thus even in an increasingly mobile and international world, basic rights depend on the acquisition of citizenship in a nation state.

Moreover, most constitutions, even those with a human rights focus inevitably limit some important rights to citizens.[4] This is most particularly true with regard to political rights. The implementation of rights in nation states is predominately left to the political process and political participation most often depends on citizenship.[5] There is particular significance in comparing the basic provisions of constitutions regarding citizenship in democracies. The definition of citizenship in a democracy defines who has the right to determine how the society is run and gain the benefits the society has to offer, as well as who takes responsibility for the society as a whole and for others in that society.

Frequently socio-economic rights, if protected at all in constitutions, are protected for only citizens.[6] Further protection of a person when in other countries is limited by citizenship; nations protect their citizens from other nations through diplomatic effort and force.[7] Therefore the "right" to citizenship is often the foundational right upon which other "rights" are based. The right to citizenship is "the right to have rights."[8]

There is a caveat. The formal acquisition of citizenship does not always mean full access to the rights and responsibilities of a member of a society. There is unfortunately a myriad of historical and current instances of second class citizenship imposed on people who clearly meet a constitutional norm, but who face discrimination because of race, ethnicity, gender, and sexual orientation.[9] Further, constitutional provisions have been distorted from their plain meaning to promote a discriminatory objective in practice. For example, in the Dominican Republic, the provision in the Constitution that provides citizenship to children born in the country, except those born to persons in transit, has been interpreted to mean that parents of Haitian heritage are perpetually in transit.[10] Constitutional protection of citizenship means little if the means to prove citizenship is not available. In many countries there is not an accepted means of registering births, so birth on the soil of the country is impossible to prove. This has provided an excuse for countries to deny rights to and responsibility for those who claim citizenship.[11]

A full assessment of the right to citizenship that includes how constitutional provisions are interpreted and empirical evidence about what factually happens is beyond the purpose of this chapter. This chapter focuses on understanding what choices have been made at a basic and fundamental level because the formal right to citizenship protected in a Constitution is the necessary base upon which other important rights rest. There is a need to understand what guarantees have been made about citizenship as membership and participation since these choices impact the issues underlying human rights and democratic function.

This chapter will analyze various constitutional protections[12] of the right to acquire citizenship and nationality for the purpose of describing different approaches and understanding the consequences of these choices. First it reviews in general the various approaches to the acquisition of citizenship. Next it surveys approaches to citizenship in a number of constitutions to ascertain how a variety of nations have or have not addressed the basic notions of citizenship. Third it sets forth four issues raised by citizenship acquisition provisions in an increasingly globalized world; statelessness, permanent under classes, multiple nationalities and socio political cohesiveness. The chapter concludes that there is insufficient protection of the right to citizenship in a number of constitutions. As a consequence, the notion of democratic participation is undermined. Further the pressing issues that emerge from choices about citizenship acquisition are not sufficiently addressed. This results in uncertainty regarding the protection of other basic rights and presents opportunities to undermine the well being of non citizen populations through statelessness and exclusion from membership in the nation of their residence.

Various Approaches to Citizenship Acquisition

There are a few basic approaches to citizenship acquisition, but a number of variations. Here the term citizenship is presumed to include the term nationality. The terms are often used interchangeably.[13] In many Latin countries, the term citizenship is reserved for adults while nationality refers to all members of the population.[14]

One view sees citizenship as being the province of those who constitute a people with common ethnicity and culture and familial connection. This is called citizenship by blood or *jus sanguinis*. Acquisition of citizenship through family has a historical gender bias that still remains in some constitutions. Another view is based on a notion of a society as a geographical community. Under this approach, citizenship derives from birth on the soil of the country, called *jus soli*. Also the concept of citizenship based on presence in territory is found in constitutions that reflect changing borders or systems, e.g. all persons who are present in the geographical territory at the time of the establishment of the constitution are viewed as citizens of the "new" nation. A third approach is citizenship by choice and qualification through naturalization. Naturalization requires an individual with one citizenship to choose to acquire another and to meet the criteria for eligibility.

None of these approaches is exclusive. It is common for constitutions to combine variations of all three. However there is often a strong preference expressed for *jus soli* or *jus sanguinis*. In an age of increased migration these approaches frequently result in the acquisition of multiple nationalities. Constitutions vary in how they deal with this consequence.

1. Citizenship based in territory

Citizenship through birth on the soil of the country is sometimes afforded to a child regardless of the citizenship status of the parents. The constitution of Ecuador simply provides nationality to a child born in Ecuador.[15] In other constitutions limitations are imposed. The most common limitation excludes children born on the soil to persons who are in the service of a foreign government or organization.[16] However, in some constitutions there are restrictions that require choice by the parent or child. The Costa Rican Constitution recognizes the citizenship of a child born to foreign parents on Costa Rican soil, but requires that the parent register a minor child or that the child self registers by age twenty-five.[17] The Constitution of East Timor recognizes the citizenship of a child born to a foreign father or mother, if the child declares the desire to be a national of East Timor when the child is over seventeen.[18]

The qualification for citizenship may also be based in the parent's status. East Timor also recognizes the citizenship of a child who is born on the soil of East Timor if the child's parents are stateless, incognito or of unknown nationality.[19] The United States Constitution provides citizenship to all children born in the United States and "subject to the jurisdiction thereof."[20] Some propose, against current interpretation, that this means that the child's parent must be a legal resident of the country for a child to be a citizen at birth.[21] As explained below, in a number of countries birth on the soil alone is not recognized, but is combined with birth through heritage requiring both birth in the territory and a citizen parent.

A concept of citizenship based on presence in the territory is also reflected in constitutions of nations that have emerged from changed systems or changed borders. For example the Indian constitution recognizes those in the territory attributed to India to be citizens, but excludes those in the territory designated as belonging to Pakistan from citizenship.[22] These constitutions vary in whom, both inside and outside the physical territory, were considered citizens of the "new" state. Gambia recognized those who were citizens in the territory before the new Constitution.[23] Nigeria recognized those who belonged to a community indigenous to Nigeria who had a parent or grandparent who was born in Nigeria.[24] India recognized those with one Indian parent or five continuous years of residence in India.[25] A variation in citizenship based on territory is also reflected in constitutional treatment of indigenous populations that straddle borders. For example, the constitution of Ecuador allows indigenous people in border areas to choose Ecuadorian citizenship.[26]

2. Citizenship based in heritage, ethnicity, race and or culture

Citizenship through heritage is a predominant form of citizenship protected in constitutions and has been formulated in a number of ways. In some circumstances citizenship both inside and outside the country is dependent on parental citizenship. The Polish constitution protects Polish citizenship by birth to parents who are Polish citizens.[27] The Gambian Constitution requires that one parent be a citizen of Gambia for a child to be a citizen whether the child is born inside or outside of Gambia.[28] Citizenship is sometimes afforded to children who are born outside of the country's territory if the child is the descendant of a person who has citizenship or in some cases if the child shares an ethnic and cultural heritage. A common constitutional approach is acquisition of citizenship by a child at birth if one parent is a citizen of the nation.[29] Others constitutions have provisions that require both parents to have the relevant citizenship.[30]

Some constitutions have a gender bias in citizenship acquisition. They allow citizenship acquisition through a father, but not a mother. For example, the current Kenyan constitution states that a person born outside of Kenya is a citizen "at the date of his birth if at that date his father is a citizen of Kenya."[31]

A few constitutions go further in recognizing "blood" as a basis for citizenship. Some provide citizenship to persons who are descendants of grandparents who had citizenship.[32] "[A] person born in or outside of Ghana...shall become a citizen of Ghana...if either of his parents or grandparents is or was a citizen of Ghana."[33] Some limit citizenship to a certain ethnic group. The constitution of Liberia provides:

> In order to preserve, foster and maintain the positive Liberian culture, values and character, only persons who are Negroes or of Negro descent shall qualify by birth or by naturalization to be citizens of Liberia.[34]

Some constitutions express general ethnic solidarity:

> [The] Irish nation cherishes its special affinity with people of Irish ancestry living abroad who share its cultural identity and heritage.[35]

Some direct that persons with cultural heritage be given easier access to citizenship. "Individuals of Armenian origin shall acquire citizenship of the Republic of Armenia through a simplified procedure."[36]

3. Citizenship through marriage

The concept of citizenship through marriage was initially based in notions about the subjugation of women to their husbands. A married woman lost her citizenship when she married and acquired the citizenship of her husband because husband and wife were one and the one was the male.[37] Some constitutions provide for acquisition of citizenship through marriage for only a woman. The Dominican constitution states that a foreign woman who marries a Dominican shall have her husband's status unless she declines it and chooses to retain her nationality.[38] The Nigerian Constitution allows any woman who is or has been married to a Nigerian citizen to register as a citizen of Nigeria.[39]

Most constitutions that recognize citizenship through marriage generally do so without regard to gender. These provisions often provide an opportunity for a spouse to choose the citizenship of the other spouse or maintain original citizenship. For example, Bolivia provides that foreigners married to Bolivians acquire Bolivian nationality provided they manifest their consent and reside in the country.[40]

Removal of the gender based notion that a woman acquired the citizenship has ironically harmed some women. The mere removal of a wife's acquisition of her husband's citizenship without providing for citizenship through marriage in general has left some non- citizen married women without independent access to legal status or citizenship in the country in which they reside.[41] Others have to meet naturalization criteria.

4. Citizenship based on choice through naturalization

Citizen through choice via naturalization is promoted by some Constitutions and discouraged by others. Some constitutions do not mention naturalization at all.[42] Some direct that the law shall provide for naturalization[43] and some merely allow naturalization to be established.[44] Those constitutions that designate criteria for naturalization do so with varying degrees of difficulty. Some provisions allow for naturalization with very limited criteria. For example Argentina requires only two years of continuous residence.[45] Many require some amount of time in residence before naturalization. The time can be moderate, for example, two years in Bolivia[46], five years in Haiti[47] to more onerous such as Nigeria and Gambia's requirement of fifteen years.[48] Some require less time of residency of persons with ethnic connections or who are married to a citizen. Venezuela requires ten years of residence, but only five years for those with Spanish, Portuguese, Italian or Latin American heritage or those who are married to a Venezuelan.[49] Brazil requires fifteen years, but only one year of residence for persons whose country of origin is Portuguese speaking.[50]

Some provisions also have additional criteria that relate to character or language capacity[51] or assimilation. For example, the constitution of Kenya requires good character and knowledge of Swahili in addition to a period of residence.[52] Panama requires five years residence, and that applicants

> declare their intention to become naturalized, expressly renounce their citizenship of origin or any other citizenship, and establish that they have a command of the Spanish language and an elementary knowledge of Panamanian geography, history and political organization.[53]

Panama allows refusal of naturalization for reasons of morality, security, health and physical or mental impairment.[54] The Nigerian constitution contains an example of more onerous criteria, requiring in addition to fifteen years of residence, full age and capacity, good character, clear intention to be domiciled in Nigeria, and that the applicant be acceptable to the local community in which he is to live permanently, has been assimilated into the way of life of Nigerians in that part of the Federation, is capable of making useful contribution to Nigeria and has taken an oath of Allegiance.[55] A significant limitation related to the acquisition of multiple nationalities is whether the naturalization criteria require renunciation of original citizenship. The constitution of Mozambique allows foreigners to naturalize only if "they renounce their previous nationality."[56]

5. *Acquisition of multiple citizenships*

The continuing controversy regarding multiple nationality is reflected in the number of ways constitutions address or do not address the concept.[57] Individuals can obtain multiple nationalities in two basic ways. A person can acquire more than one citizenship at birth, for example, if a child is born in the geographical territory of a country that recognizes citizenship at birth on the soil to parents with citizenship of a country that recognizes citizenship through heritage. A person can also acquire multiple nationalities through naturalization. Some constitutions like that of the United States are silent on the issue. A number of constitutions reject multiple nationalities.[58] Some constitutions explicitly state that dual or multiple nationalities is not allowed. The Cuban constitution states "Dual citizenship shall not be allowed."[59] Some state that acquisition of another citizenship results in the automatic loss of the original citizenship.[60]

A number of nations allow multiple nationalities on various bases. Some explicitly allow multiple nationalities in general. "An Iraqi may have multiple nationalities."[61] Some limit multiple nationalities to nationals by birth. "Salvadorans by birth have the right to enjoy double or multiple nationalities."[62] The Mexican constitution accepts multiple nationalities for born, not naturalized citizens, but also requires that the law establish the rights of dual nationals and regulate them to prevent conflict.[63]

Some allow the acquisition of a foreign nationality for their citizens. "The right of a Dominican to acquire a foreign nationality is recognized."[64] Some additionally recognize the multiple nationalities of those who acquire their citizenship:

> The Bolivian nationality is not lost by acquisition of a foreign nationality. Those who acquire the Bolivian nationality shall not be compelled to renounce their nationality of origin.[65]

Some accept dual nationality for children, but require choice of one citizenship by the person at majority.[66] Others like Ecuador allow dual nationality only through a treaty.[67]

Still others recognize multiple nationalities in a regional area; for example, Guatemala recognizes the multiple nationalities of nationals of other countries in the Central American Federation if they have a domicile in Guatemala and declare a desire to be a Guatemalan citizen.[68] Other constitutions recognize multiple nationality only if necessary for the well being of their citizens. The Brazilian constitution states that a Brazilian will lose Brazilian nationality if he acquires another nationality except in cases of a foreign law imposing naturalization upon a Brazilian residing in a foreign country as a condition for remaining in its territory or for exercise of civil rights.[69]

Overall approaches to citizenship acquisition in individual constitutions

Surprisingly there is little in a number of Constitutions that protects the acquisition of citizenship. A few constitutions articulate nothing about citizenship acquisition.[70] Often acquisition of citizenship is delegated to the law in general[71] or the legislature[72] with no direction or limitation. For example, the Japanese Constitution states, "The conditions necessary for holding Japanese citizenship are determined by law".[73] The Italian Constitution states, "The State has exclusive legislative power with respect to...citizenship..."[74] In the Ukraine, "The President of the Ukraine...adopts decisions in the acceptance of citizenship."[75]

Some constitutions leave citizenship acquisition to the legislative branch but impose general limits on the legislation. This approach attempts to allow legislative discretion for change over time but with some general control over outcome. A prime example is the South African Constitution which states that "national legislation must provide for the acquisition...of citizenship." However, it further states that this right is one that

> may be limited only in terms of general application to the extent that the limitation is reasonable and justifiable in an open and democratic society based on human dignity, equality, and freedom....[76]

It further states that all children have a right to a nationality.[77] Another more general example is the Constitution of Malawi that states:

> Parliament may make provision for the acquisition [of citizenship] but citizenship shall not be arbitrarily denied or deprived. [78]

Some constitutions designate some categories of people as citizens and then leave additional designation to the legislative branch. An example is found in the Untied States Constitution, which establishes birthright citizenship, gives Congress the power to set a uniform system of naturalization but is silent on the issue of citizenship through heritage.[79] Some constitutions try to comprehensively address acquisition of citizenship by providing for nationality through birth on the soil and through heritage, naturalization and addressing the issue of multiple nationality.[80]

Issues raised by current constitutional choices regarding citizenship acquisition

There has been a long term tension between citizenship based on a concept of heritage and culture and citizenship based on a notion of a geographical participant community. However in a world of globalization, changing borders and increased migration, citizenship acquisition has become increasingly controversial. In developing countries attempting to enforce rights and equalize access to resources, tensions abound about who is entitled to the nation's protections and resources.[81] Newly formed or reformed nations attempt to respond to historical violence and conflict. Developed countries face increasingly diverse migration. Responses have included limitations placed on long term residents in the acquisition of citizenship, arguments about birthright citizenship and attempted restrictions on multiple nationalities. The focus on citizenship also has become important as nation states try to avoid socio-economic obligations to persons migrating across their borders.[82] Significant issues raised by choices regarding constitutional protections of citizenship include statelessness, permanent under classes, multiple nationalities and socio political cohesiveness.

1. Statelessness

There are an estimated eleven million stateless human beings in the world; they have no effective nationality or citizenship.[83] There are stateless people in every region of the world.[84] The condition of statelessness highlights the continuing import of citizenship since stateless people cannot participate in their own governance and have no guaranteed legal protections. They are frequently the targets of discrimination and violence and have difficulty finding a means of support and accessing basic services.[85] Statelessness has a particularly adverse impact on women and children and ethnically mixed people.[86]

Statelessness results from a number of causes that are reflected in the citizenship acquisition provisions of various constitutions. Statelessness can be caused when a person is caught in the differing citizenship acquisition criteria. A child can be stateless if born in a country that does not recognize citizenship from birth on the country's soil or only recognizes it if the parents have a particular status. The parents may be from a country that does not recognize citizenship through heritage in those particular circumstances. This is a particular problem for the children of guest or undocumented workers. Children a birth can also be stateless when their country of birth recognizes citizenship through the paternal, but not the maternal line. This has been particularly troublesome when children are born to a female national and a solider or peacekeeping troop member of another nationality.[87] Statelessness can also be caused when members of a resident population in a country cannot naturalize but have lost the citizenship of their country or origin.

Stateless can be also be caused by emergence of new nations, border disputes and ethnic, racial and religious conflict. There are unfortunately numerous examples and only a few follow. The partition of India and Pakistan and the conflict between these two nations still has the consequence of a number of stateless people in their territories. The creation of Bangladesh resulted in a number of stateless people and is an example of the difficulties of citizenship denial based in ethnic conflict; the Bihari excluded from citizenship in what is now Bangladesh sided with what was then Western Pakistan in the Bangladesh struggle for independence. Rohingya Muslims were expelled from Burma.[88] Resented Russian minorities in countries emerging from the USSR became stateless.[89] Palestinians living in Europe and countries of the Middle East are stateless sometimes because of a political decision to refuse them citizenship in their countries of residence to preserve their national identity in the conflict with Israel.[90]

The People's Republic of China declared that every Chinese person in the world is a Chinese citizen.[91] The Chinese constitution states "All persons holding the nationality of the People's Republic of China are citizens of the People's Republic of China."[92] Yet this is not in reality effective citizenship and ethnic Chinese are essentially stateless in various countries, e.g. Indonesia, Korea.[93] The Roma are a significant stateless and denigrated population in countries across Europe.[94] Mauritania declared people with dark skin not Mauritanians and expelled them and they live stateless predominantly in Senegal and Mali.[95]

Very few constitutions address this significant world wide problem directly. Fiji has a general provision for the prevention of statelessness.[96] Mozambique and East Timor both allow birthright citizenship to children of stateless people.[97] Some of the underlying causes of statelessness could be addressed by explicit provisions in constitutions. Every person should be guaranteed a right to a nationality. Birthright citizenship should guarantee the citizenship of each child born in a nation or at least specify that articulated birthright citizenship standards will be modified when needed to prevent the statelessness of a child born in the country. Removal of gender distinctions, allowing citizenship through a mother as well as a father, would also help. Further, reasonable naturalization standards for those living in a territory would help eliminate some statelessness. This would be particularly true with regard to those who are currently permanent under classes including guest workers or those without status who have informally been encouraged to work in a country.

The statelessness resulting from changing borders and deep seated ethnic and political conflict could be addressed by individual nations seriously reviewing the realities of each country's population and coming to terms with a citizenship that includes diversity. Some constitutions specifically articulate the difficulties of the past and attempt to provide for a means to counter them in the future. The Rwandan constitution states that the "people of Rwanda" are "resolved to fight the ideology of genocide," asserts that they have a common culture, shared history and vision of destiny and promises adherence to the principles of human rights.[98] It then explicitly provides that every person has the right to a nationality and no person shall be arbitrarily deprived of nationality. It further specifies that no person may be deprived of Rwandan nationality of origin, that all persons originating form Rwanda and their descendants have the right to acquire Rwandan nationality.[99]

Some constitutions have tried to address prior ethnic and racial conflict, violence and abuse by articulating a broad concept of who constitute a people. The South African constitution protects the right of every child to a nationality, asserts a common South African citizenship, recognizes a myriad of languages and cultures as South African and incorporates the protections of international human rights documents.[100] The Ethiopian constitution attempts to deal with a history of violent ethnic conflict by recognizing the right of "Nationalities and Peoples" to establish at any time their own state[101] thus promoting a policy of ethnic federalism, giving ethnic self determination a freer reign.[102] However, resolution of who are citizens and thereby mutually dependant and respected members of a society is a difficult endeavor when the conflicts have a deep history and are based in previous violence and mutual discrimination among the groups. Elimination of statelessness based in ethnic, racial and religious conflict will require more attention to international standards, international mediation and serious multi nation diplomatic effort.[103]

2. Permanent under classes

The existence of groups of people living within nation states that have no realistic vehicle to becoming citizen's results in permanent under classes and this undermines democratic structure and human rights goals. Those who cannot achieve citizenship in the country of their residence become a persistent vulnerable population. This causes difficulties with adequate police protection, public health controls, and effective implementation of labor laws as well as resentment that can lead to public unrest.[104]

Permanent under classes often result from provisions in constitutions and laws that limit citizenship by birth on the soil and impose restrictive naturalization requirements. In wealthier immigrant receiving countries, underclasses are often comprised of guest workers or undocumented populations induced to enter a country to perform cheap labor or refugees seeking asylum and their children.[105] Wealthier immigrant receiving countries have demonstrated some recent resistance to birthright citizenship for children of migrant under classes thus extending the under classes into the next generation. The Irish Constitution provides:

> It is the entitlement and birthright of every person born in the island of Ireland...to be part of the Irish nation.[106]

However a recent change in the Irish Nationality and Citizenship Act restricts Irish citizenship for the children with non national parents to those whose parent was a resident of Ireland for three years.[107] The U.S. constitution provides citizenship to all persons born in the U.S and subject to the jurisdiction thereof, which has for almost two hundred years been interpreted to mean that all children born in the U.S. are U.S. citizens except for the children of diplomats.[108] Yet arguments have recently been made that subject to the jurisdiction thereof includes only children born to citizens or permanent residents.[109]

Constitutional provisions and laws that impose onerous naturalization criteria perpetuate permanent under classes. Long years of residence are a clear barrier as are rigorous levels of required language proficiency. Requiring approval of local communities or subjective familiarity with customs and habits can lead to discriminatory denial. Requiring renunciation of original nationality blocks citizenship since people often hold to their origins for emotional and practical reasons.[110]

3. Multiple nationalities

Until relatively recently multiple nationality was disfavored from an international perspective and in the constitutional provisions of many countries.[111] As described above the constitutions of some countries explicitly reject multiple nationality but a recent trend as indicated in the constitutions of other countries is to provide constitutional protection for multiple nationality. The international law concerns with problems of allegiance and diplomatic protection caused by multiple nationalities has diminished with recognition of the concept that primacy should be given to the nation with which the person has primary contacts.[112]

The practical realties in an age of increased migration also undermined opposition to multiple nationalities. Sending countries want to keep the connections with the migrating citizen. Sometimes this comes from a dependence on remittances which comprise large portions of some countries GNP.[113] Receiving countries find that integration of migrants through citizenship acquisition is beneficial even if the person keeps citizenship connections with the country of origin.[114]

Multiple nationalities are however not without controversy.[115] It has been opposed particularly opposed in economically developed nations in response to increased migration from less wealthy areas whose populations may also have different ethnic and religious heritage. Some opponents in the United States have condemned dual nationality as civic bigamy.[116] If analogy to family structure is appropriate, a more apt analogy could be found in the parent child relationship. A child can have more than one parent and a parent can have more than one child with equal or varying degrees of commitment to and concern and affection for each.

4. Societal cohesiveness

Attempts to respond to the movement of people in a globalizing world by integrating migrants is reflected in constitutional provisions that ease access to naturalization, recognize birth citizenship and accept multiple nationalities. This trend however has been undermined by concerns about societal cohesiveness especially in the recent context of concerns about terrorism. However, a greater threat to societal cohesiveness may be the consequence of constitutions that do not adequately protect the right to citizenship.

As detailed above a number of constitutions do not address who is or can become a citizen at all or leave the issue to the law or legislature. This leaves the basis for such a fundamental notion as citizenship subject to political change over time. Having no designation of who has a right to be a citizen is especially troublesome in democracies since the power and authority for governance are supposed to flow from the citizenry.

A possible rationale for legislative control is that it allows change in response to circumstance and majoritarian will. However this is also where problems lie. Constitutions set rights that form the base of the society and protect these rights from the passion of a particular time or incident and the subjugation of a minority from an abusive majority. Without a designation and protection of the right to citizenship in a constitution, legislation regarding citizenship acquisition can go beyond notions of descent into notions of narrow ethnicity and bar participation to those who are in reality full members of a society. This can cause statelessness and uprooting of those with a nation's boundaries who do not fit the ethnic profile and failure to recognize full membership to people living working and raising families in the society. Constitutions best provide the means for socio political cohesiveness if they provide detailed provisions that guarantees citizenship by including children born in the country, children born to citizens outside the country, reasonable criteria for naturalization and multiple nationalities.

Conclusion

There is great variety in the degree to which constitutions protect the acquisition of citizenship. In those constitutions that are more explicit and thorough with regard to citizenship, the provisions vary considerably. In other constitutions the acquisition of citizenship by birth in the nation, by heritage or naturalization is left to developing law and thus leaves the basis upon which rights exist constantly subject to political change. Nation states should pay closer attention to citizenship and recognize that it is the right to have rights. Constitutions should be clear and detailed about citizenship. A more globalized world requires a more complex approach that combines notions based on birth, descent and consent and effectively deals with the reality of multiple nationalities. If citizenship is left to a legislative or political body, a constitution should at least limit legislative discretion to prevent discrimination or violence. Nation states should engage in establishing some more consistent norms about citizenship. International standards that seriously address the issue of statelessness are especially needed.

[1] Jonathan Klaaren, *Contested Citizenship in South Africa* in The Post-Apartheid Constitutions; Perspectives on South Africa's Basic Law, 304 (Penelope Andrews and Stephen Ellman, eds., Witwaterstrand University Press and Ohio University Press, 2001).

[2] See e.g. Heinz Klug, *Contextual Citizenship*, 7 Ind. J. Global Legal Stud. 567 (2000); Linda Bosniak, *Citizenship Denationalized*, 7 Ind. J. Global Legal Stud. 447 (1999-2000)

[3] Rainer Baubock, Global Commission on International Migration, *Citizenship Policies: international, state, migrant and democratic perspective* (Jan. 2005) at 3, http://www.gcim.org/attachements/GMP%20No%2019.pdf

[4] Klaaren, *supra* note 1 at 307-310, 316-317

[5] T. Alexander Aleinikoff and Douglas Klusmeyer, Citizenship Practices for an Age of Migration, 42 (The Brookings Institution Press, 2002).

[6] Rett R. Ludwikowski, *Constitutionalization of Human Rights in Post-Soviet States and Latin American: A Comparative Analysis*, 33 Ga. J. Int'l & Comp.L.J. 47, 48 (2004)

[7] Ruth Donner, The Regulation of Nationality in International Law, ___ (Transnational Publisher, Inc. 2004, 2nd Edition).

[8] *Perez v. Brownell*, 356 U.S. 44, 64-65 (1958)

[9] Stephen Castles and Alastair Davidson, Citizenship and Migration: Globalization and the Politics of Belonging, 11 (Routledge, 2000); Penelope Andrews, *The Stepchild of National Liberation: Women and Rights in the New South Africa, supra* note 1 at 326; Ruthann Robson, *Sexual Minorities and "the State": Some Struggles and U.S. Perspective*, 2 Flinders J.L.Reform 67, 68 (1997)

[10] M. Lynch, Ph.D., Refugees International, *Lives on Hold: The Human Cost of Statelessness* (Feb. 2005), at 30., http://www.refugeesinternational.org/files/5051_file_statelessness_paper.pdf

[11] Lynch, *supra* note 10 at 5, 29, 30, 31

[12] Unless otherwise noted, all Constitutional citations were translated and/or reprinted from I-XX Constitutions of the Countries of the World (Oceana Publications) or see http://www.oceanalaw.com, last visited April 1, 2008 (Dr. Rainier Grote, Dr. Dr. h.c. Rudiger Wolfrum and Gisbert H. Flanz, eds., 2006)

[13] Greta Gilbertson, Migration Policy Institute, *Citizens in a Globalized World*, http://www.migrationinformation.org/Feature/print.cfm?ID=369 (Jan. 1, 2006)

[14] Const. of Mexico, Ch. 4, art. 34(I); Const. of Chile, Ch. 2, art. 13

[15] Const. of Ecuador, Ch. 1, art. 7.1, also e.g. Const. of Venezuela, Ch. 2, art. 32.1

[16] E.g. Const. of Cuba, Ch. 2, art. 29(a); Const. of Guatemala, Ch. 2, art. 144

[17] Const. of Costa Rica, Tit. 2, art. 13(3)

[18] Const. of East Timor, Part I, art. 3.2(c)

[19] Const. of East Timor, Part I, art. 3.2(b) and 3.2(c)

[20] U.S. CONST., amend. XIV, § 1

[21] H.R. 698, 109th Cong. (2005)

[22] Const. of India, Part II, art. 6

[23] Const. of Gambia, Ch. 3, art. 8

[24] Const. of Nigeria, Ch. 3, art. 25(1)(a)

[25] Const. of India, Part II, art. 5(b), (c)

[26] Const. of Ecuador, Title 2, ch. 1, art. 8(5)

[27] Const. of Poland, Ch. 2, art. 34.1

[28] Const. of Gambia, Ch. 3, art. 9.1, 10

[29] Const. of East Timor, Part 1, art. 3(3); Const. of India, Part II, art. 8

[30] Const. of Panama, Tit. II, art. 9.2 (if establish domicile in the nation); Const. of Venezuela, Tit. II, Ch. 2, art. 32(2)

[31] Const. of Kenya, Ch. 6, art. 90. The proposed but rejected Kenyan constitution would have allowed citizenship through a mother or a father. *The Proposed New Constitution of Kenya*, Kenya Gazette Supp. No. 63, Aug. 22, 2005, at 16.

[32] Const. of Ghana, Ch. 3, art. 6(2); Const. of Nigeria, Ch. 3, art. 25(1)(b)

[33] Const. of Ghana, Ch. 3, art. 6(2)

[34] Const. of Liberia, Ch. 4, art. 27(b)

[35] Const. of Ireland, Art. 2

[36] Const. of Armenia, Ch. 1, art. 11.3

[37] See Janet Calvo, *Spouse-Based Immigration Laws: The Legacies of Coverture*, 28 San Diego L.Rev 593 (1991)

[38] Const. of the Dominican Republic, Tit. 3, Sec. 1, art. 11.4, para III

[39] Const. of Nigeria, Ch. 3, art. 26(2)(a)

[40] Const. of Bolivia, Tit. 3, Ch. 1, art. 38

[41] See Janet Calvo, *A Decade of Spouse-Based Immigration Laws: Coverture's Diminishment, But Not Its Demise,* 24 No. ILL L.R. 153 (2004)

[42] See e.g. the Constitutions of Finland, Iran and Armenia.

[43] Const. of Uganda, Ch. 3, art. 13; Const. of the Dominican Republic, Tit. 3, sec. 1, art. 11(4); U.S. CONST., art. I, §8

[44] Const. of Guatemala, Ch. 2, art. 146; Const. of Cuba, Ch. 2, art 30(a); Const. of Mexico, Ch. 2, art. 30(B)(I)

[45] Const. of Argentina, Part 1, ch. 1, art. 20

[46] Const. of Bolivia, Part 1, Tit. 3, ch. 1, art. 37(2)

[47] Const. of Haiti, Tit. 2, art. 12-1

[48] Const. of Nigeria, Ch. 3, art. 27(2)(g)(i); Const. of Gambia, Ch. 3, art. 12(1)

[49] Const. of Venezuela, Ch. 2, art. 33(1) and (2)

[50] Const. of Brazil, Ch. 3, art. 12(II)(a) and (b)

[51] Const. of Panama, Tit. 2, art. 10(1); Const. of Ghana, Ch. 3, art. 9(2)

[52] Const. of Kenya, Ch. 6, art. 93(b), (d) and (e)

[53] Const. of Panama, Tit. 2, art. 10(1)

[54] Const. of Panama, Tit. 2, art. 12

[55] Const. of Nigeria, Ch. 3, art. 27(2), (a)-(g)

[56] Const. of Mozambique, Ch. 2, sec. 2, arts. 21(a) and 22(a)

[57] Ludwikowski, *supra* note 6 at 47

[58] Const. of Iran, Ch. 3, art. 41; Const. of Haiti, Tit. 2, art. 13(a); Const. of Uganda, Ch. 3, art. 15(1); Ludwikowski, *supra* note 6, at footnote 204

[59] Const. of Cuba, Ch. 2, art. 32

[60] Const. of Fiji, Ch. 3, art. 14(1); Const. of Mozambique, Ch. 2, sec. 3, art. 24

[61] Const. of Iraq, Sec. 2, ch. 1, art. 18(4)

[62] Const. of El Salvador, Tit. 4, art. 91

[63] Const. of Mexico, Ch. 2, art. 32 and Ch. 4, art. 37 (A) and (B)(1)

[64] Const. of Dominican Republic, Sec. 1, art. 11(4), para. I

[65] Const. of Bolivia, Tit. 3, Ch. 1, art. 39

[66] Const. of Fiji, Ch. 3, art. 14(2); Const. of Kenya, Ch. 6, art. 97(3) (b); Const. of Mozambique, Part I, Ch. 2, sec. 3, art. 24(d)

[67] Const. of Ecuador, Tit. II, Ch. 1, art. 10

[68] Const. of Guatemala, Tit. III, Ch. 2, art. 145

[69] Const. of Brazil, Tit. II, Ch. 3, art. 12, § 4(II)

[70] e.g. Const. of Pakistan; The Constitution of China states only that Chinese nationals are Chinese citizens, Ch. 2, art. 33.

[71] e.g., Const. of Algeria, Ch. 4, art. 30; Const. of Bahrain, Ch. 3, art. 17; Const. of Belarus, Sec. 1, art. 10; Const. of Cent. African Repub., Tit. IV, ch.3, art. 58; Const. of Dem. Repub. Of Congo, Title 2, ch. 2, art. 10; Const. of Repub of Eq. Guinea, Part 1, art. 12; Const. of Egypt, Pt. 1, art. 6; Const. of France, title 5, art. 34; Const. of Georgia, Ch. 2, art. 12; Const. of Greece, Pt 2, art. 4; Const. of Kazakhstan, Sec. 2, art. 10; Const. of Kuwait, Pt. 3, art. 27; Const. of Macedonia, art. 4; Const. of Netherlands, Ch, 1, art. 2; Const. of Qatar, Ch.3, art. 41; Const. of Russia, Ch.1, art. 6; Const. of Yemen, Pt. 2, art. 43

[72] e.g., Const. of Cameroon, Part 4, art. 26(2)(b.1); Const. of Cote d' Ivoire, Title 5, art. 71; Const. of Senegal, Title 5, art. 67.

[73] Const. of Japan, Ch. 3, art. 10.

[74] Const. of Italy, Part 2, Tit. 5, art. 117(i)

[75] Const. of Ukraine, Ch. 5, art. 106(26)

[76] Const. of South Africa, Ch. 2, art. 3(3), and Ch. 2, art. 36(1)

[77] Const. of South Africa, Ch. 2, art. 28(1)(a); Const. of Ethiopia, Art. 36(1)(b)

[78] Const. of Malawi, Ch. 5, art. 47(2).

[79] U.S. CONST., amend. XIV and Art. 1, §8

[80] e.g., Const of Brazil, Title 2, ch. 3, art. 12; Const. of Fiji, Ch. 3, arts. 8-20; Const. of Nigeria, Ch. 3, arts. 25-31

[81] Klaaren, *supra* note 1 at 314-315

[82] Aleinkoff and Klusmeyer, *supra* note 5 at 1-3

[83] Refugees International, *New Report by Refugees International Documents Plight of "Stateless" People,* http://www.refugees international.org/content/publication/detail/5051 (last visited on June 23, 2006)

[84] Maureen Lynch, *The People Who Have No Country...,* International Herald Tribune, Feb. 18, 2005, available at http://www.iht.com/articles/2005/02/17/opinion/edlynch.php.

[85] Refugees International, *supra* note 83.

[86] Lynch, *supra* note 10 at 1.

[87] Lynch, *supra* note 10 at 5.

[88] Kavita Shukla, Refugees International, *Ending the Waiting Game: Strategies for Responding to Internally Displaced People in Burma* (June 2006) at 9, http://www.refugeesinternational.org/files/8705_file_EndingtheWaitingGame/pdf.

[89] Lynch, *supra* note 10 at 40.

[90] Lynch, *supra* note 10 at 28, 29 and 40.

[91] Lynch, *supra* note 10 at 34.

[92] Const. of China, Ch. 2, art. 33

[93] Donald K. Emmerson, *Indonesia in 1990: A Foreshadow Play*, Asian Survey, Vol. 31, No. 2, A Survey of Asia in 1990: Part II (Feb. 1991), 179-187, 180 and Lynch, *supra* note 10 at 34 and 36.

[94] Adam M. Warnke, *Vagabonds, Tinkers, and Travelers: Statelessness Among the East European Roma*, 7 Ind. J. Global Legal Stud. 335, 335-336 (Fall 1999).

[95] *Citizenship and Equality in Practice: Guaranteeing Non-Discriminatory Access to Nationality, Protecting the Right to be Free from Arbitrary Deprivation of Nationality, And Combating Statelessness*, submission to U.N. Office of High Commissioner for Human Rights (Open Society Justice Initiative, Washington D.C), Nov. 2005 at 10-11, available at http://www.justiceinitive.org/db/resource2/fs/?file_id=16592.

[96] Const. of Fiji, Ch. 3, art. 20; Const. of Bosnia and Herzegovina, Art. I, part 7(b)

[97] Const. of Mozambique, Ch. 2, sec. 1, art. 11(1)(b); Const. of East Timor, Part 1, art. 3(2)(b)

[98] Const. of Rwanda, Preamble 2, 7 and 9

[99] Const. of Rwanda, Title 1, ch. 1, art. 7

[100] Const. of South Africa, Ch. 2, art. 28(1) (a); Ch. 1, art. 3(1); Ch. 2, art. 30 and 31(1); and Ch. 2, art. 39

[101] Const. of Ethiopia, Ch. 4, art. 47(2)

[102] Isaak I. Dore, *Constitutionalism and the Post-Colonial State in Africa: a Rawlsian Approach*, 41 St. Louis U. L.J. 1301, 1315-1316 (1997).

[103] Lynch, *supra* note 10 at 25-26; Dore, *supra* note 102 at 1317.

[104] Joseph H. Carens, *On Belonging: What We Owe People Who Stay*, Boston Review (summer 2005), available at http://www.bostonreview.net/BR30.3/contents.html

[105] Carens, *supra* note 103

[106] Const. of Ireland, Art. 2

[107] Irish Nationality and Citizenship Act, Sec. 2, art. 4 at 6(A) (2004)

[108] U.S. Const., amend. XIV; *U.S. v. Wong Kim Ark*, 169 U.S. 649, 18 S.Ct. 456 (1898)

[109] *supra*, note 20

[110] Castles and Davidson, *supra* note 9 at 86-88

[111] Baubock, *supra* note 3 at 6

[112] Aleinkoff and Klusmeyer, *supra* note 5 at 40

[113] Baubock, *supra* note 3 at 9

[114] Aleinkoff and Klusmeyer, *supra* note 5 at 37

[115] Aleinkoff and Klusmeyer, *supra* note 5 at 27-37

[116] John Fonte, Ph.D., *Dual Allegiance: A Challenge to Immigration Reform and Patriotic Assimilation* (Ctr. For Immigration Studies, Washington, D.C.) November 2005, at 8.

CHAPTER 13

UNANSWERABLE DILEMMAS? LEGAL REGULATION FOR CROSS CULTURAL FAMILY NORMS

Craig Lind

Abstract

In this chapter I wish to examine the interaction between cultural norms and legal family regulation. I am interested in the way in which varying family norms found within individual legal jurisdictions are reflected in their legal regulatory regimes. How does the legal system cope with real, lived, family forms which the many, if not a majority, in a particular society would prefer not to see embraced? And what effect does this interaction of law with family norm have on the lived family lives and the individual self identities of those living in multicultural societies?

While the paper is unlikely to resolve the problems that will be posed, it will seek to reflect critically on some alternative strategies that appear to be available to the legal system in regulating the family where cultures come into conflict on the issue of family form. It will pay particular attention to the fundamental rights discourse that serves as the background to legal reflection on the issues raised. The paper will use as its paradigm examples same-sex family regulation and polygamous family recognition. It will consider these family forms in the light of the legal and social positions operating, principally, in South Africa where most of the research for this paper has been conducted (although other jurisdictions will also feature in the work).

1. Introduction

In this chapter I wish to explore an issue that has preoccupied me for almost ten years. I will offer some thoughts on the difficult place we have reached in relation to the regulation—especially under democratic constitutionalism—of cross cultural family norms (especially in South Africa, although the problem can be extrapolated beyond that jurisdiction).

I will outline some of the research fragments that have brought me to a point at which I find only complicated answers to the problems that I perceive to arise when family norms diverge dramatically between different cultures in a single jurisdiction. In the process of outlining these research fragments it will become evident that I have become more and more concerned about the place of law in structuring the social world, and the profound dilemma that lies at the heart of legal admiration of social diversity.

My conclusions will, therefore, appear incomplete. They will set out the impossibility of any resolution which would have an (even approximately) ideal consequence.

2. Breaching Borders: Travelling Families

My overarching interest is in the way in which states attempt to regulate family relationships when cultural family norms travel relatively easily from one geographic space to another. In other words, family norms in any legal jurisdiction are often quite contradictory because of the ease with which people travel and settle away from the place in which their family norms are commonly observed. These people take their attitude to "family" with them and, more often than not, they adhere in their new homes, to the tenets of their received beliefs on family structure (at least in part).

I am, in short, interested in the salient features of cross cultural family regulation. Two particular family norms have formed the focus of my research; I am interested in the way in which same sex relationships have come to be recognised in South African law. That interest took a cultural turn when South Africa proposed a constitution which undertook to prevent discrimination on the grounds of sexual orientation.[1] At that time I began to wonder about both the cultural process by which such a legal alteration could take place, and the cultural consequences that recognition of same sex families would have. I will explain these interests in more detail below.

Once I was some way into my consideration of the cultural conundrums that same sex families and their regulation created, I began to be interested in what I conceptualised as a reverse cultural phenomenon. I became interested in the way in which the legal regulation of polygamous families might have cross cultural influences. Towards the end of this chapter I will try to give reasons for the appeal that these two family forms began to have for me. I will also try to offer some thoughts on what I think regulation of each tells us about the way in which cross cultural family law can be framed.

I will, therefore, deal with each in turn and then turn to a consideration of the ideas that an interest in both has spawned.

3. Same Sex Families[2]

a. Equality jurisprudence and same sex families

Same sex families have become a significant feature in the analysis of family law in many, if not all, western jurisdictions.[3] They have also grown in significance in the analysis of the contours of South African family law.[4]

In the analysis that follows I wish to discuss some cultural observations I have begun to make in the aftermath of the inclusion of sexual orientation in the equality clause of the South African constitution.

My interest began with the constitutional transformation in South Africa. When the constitution determined that sexual orientation was no longer to be a permissible ground for discrimination in 1993 I argued[5] that the consequence of the equality clause for family regulation would have to be the full legal recognition and regulation of same sex marriage (like different sex marriage). The argument was a rather bland equality argument that asserted that the only significant difference between same sex and different sex relationships was the thing which the constitution determined could not be used as the basis for discriminatory treatment.

Although I think that that argument remains powerful, I am no longer persuaded that the conclusions I reached then are necessary or inevitable[6] (despite recent court decisions).[7] Although I do still think that, in the current jurisprudential climate in South Africa, those conclusions remain the more powerful.

b. The politics of the legal transformation of same sex families

But what made the subject more interesting was not whether or not South Africa achieved same sex marriage, but the way in which it progressed to that goal, especially in the immediate aftermath of the interim constitutional settlement.

In the four years after the passing of the interim constitution it is noteworthy that no formal legal progress was made to achieve same sex family recognition.[8] Clearly there were politics at work which required that, despite the guarantee of constitutional protection, that protection should not be enforced in the courts—at least, not immediately. By 1997 I had begun to be interested in why, after so much time, so little progress had been made towards achieving same sex family recognition. The period between the interim and final constitutions seemed to be a period of remarkably little activity that would achieve real equality.

It soon became apparent that the reticence to take full advantage of the constitutional change was probably rooted in concern that too much progress made too quickly would damage the long term political strategy towards full equality. Progress on particular issues in the interim period might prejudice the shape of the equality clause in the final constitution.[9]

During the four years in which the interim constitution held sway in South Africa the lesbian and gay political movement operated remarkably coherently. This was unlike the parallel movements elsewhere in the western world which were often significantly fragmented,[10] and also much bigger and much more politically active (in the visible public arena).[11]

The explanation for this altered pattern of development seemed relatively simple to me. Sexuality politics in South Africa had developed completely differently from the parallel development in most of the western world.[12] Fairly profound legal protection had arrived in South Africa whereas most western jurisdictions had had to satisfy themselves with much more limited success.[13] All that was achieved arrived despite the limited visibility (at the time) of a grass roots lesbian and gay political movement, and a morally conservative voting population.

In essence, my view was that a tolerant political elite had seen to the entrenchment of protection for lesbians and gay men in South Africa whereas grass roots movements were still actively engaged in convincing politicians and voting populations of the merits of such an approach in places like the USA, Canada, Australia and Europe.[14] The elite political group[15] negotiating the interim constitutional settlement had clearly come to view discrimination on the grounds of "sexual orientation" as sufficiently similar to the other more public forms of invidious discrimination which had polluted South African history. On that basis it, like all other forms of invidious discrimination, had to be outlawed.

But in other (western) jurisdictions legal change had been much slower and necessarily the result of a ground swell of lesbian and gay political activity which worked to persuade politicians, judges and, in the final analysis, majorities of their voting populations of the merits of tolerance.[16] I was—and remain—convinced that western societies are more likely to be tolerant of homosexuality than is South

African society.[17] The significant difference, though, is that whereas western politicians were simply keeping up with (often bare) majorities of their voting populations, South African politicians had managed to move ahead of their electors (largely insulated from any negative reaction to that move because of the more important issues at the forefront of transformation politics, namely, the serious disadvantage caused by racial segregation, issues of gender inequality, and overwhelming poverty).

c. The origins of homosexuality

This conclusion led me to reflect again on the nature of the sexuality that was being protected in the South African constitution. The history of sexuality, written in Europe and America, rooted the binary division of identity creating sexuality (in which heterosexual and homosexual serve as opposite personal identities) firmly in the social history of western countries and of western philosophical thought.[18] While a similar history could be written in South Africa[19] that history would be, it seemed to me, written with an entrenched western historical knowledge, philosophy and identity outcome in mind. It would be, in short, a history which mimicked <u>western</u> historical writing on <u>western</u> sexuality. It would seek out and find same sex sexual conduct in patterns similar to those discovered in the Europe and America and would, in the way western history had done, discover homosexual identity in its practitioners.

Gevisser's history of the lesbian and gay movement in South Africa[20] appears to me to be that kind of history. It seems to be patterned on Weeks's history of homosexuality in England (or any of a number of similar histories of western sexuality in western jurisdictions).[21] It knows what homosexuality is, and traces its origins in South African society. But Weeks and Trumbach were writing to demonstrate the creation of the 20th century "homosexual" in Europe, and to trace its development to the politics of the present day. Like so many consequences of colonialism, this was just another. Where western historians and philosophers had been demonstrating that homosexual practices did not simply lead to an unproblematic homosexual identity[22], Gevisser was tracing the history of those who had already assumed that identity. And, in writing a history of lesbian and gay politics in South Africa in the aftermath of the constitutional settlement, it sought out to find western style homosexuals in black same sex sexual and social practices.[23]

What is missing in Gevisser's account of South African sexuality is a rigorous exploration of what same sex sexual practices existed in cultures beyond those most profoundly influenced by western social norms. If those had been discovered, and the significance that was attached to them by their own cultures were uncovered, we would begin to discover a culturally specific sexuality indigenous to South African cultures. And those sexualities might have been more or less inclined to require constitutional protection of the sought granted in the Bill of Rights.

It is possible that the variety of South African sexualities might have had much in common with western sexuality. But, however similar they were, it is almost inevitable that some measure of difference in identity would, on closer examination, have been found.[24] And those differences might have caused subtle differences in the sexuality politics that has played itself out in South Africa to have occurred.[25]

In the light of social theory which pointed to social conditions as the necessary precursor's to the creation of sexualised identities it was inevitable that I would begin to wonder what an African "sexual orientation" might have been like, without western influence. If we were able to examine (in an idealised anthropological way) the same sex sexual practices of people in the African past what might we have discovered of the cross cultural need for the kind of protection granted to lesbians and gay men in the constitution? Would the homosexual/heterosexual binary of the contemporary west have been replicated in African society? Some, admittedly contested, anthropology[26] has clearly suggested that African attitudes towards sexual practices were remarkably different from western attitudes (much of the politics around HIV and AIDS in South Africa seem to confirm the view that indigenous cultures are suspicious of western attempts to (continue to) direct African sexual practices). Caldwell, et al, suggest that African cultures were more concerned with matters of social position, family role and family responsibility than with individual sexual behaviour.[27]

If we were able to isolate this historical trajectory and anticipate a future for it, I did wonder whether or not the potential absence of controversy surrounding same-sex sexual conduct would have meant that no sexualised identities might have existed in (some, at least) African societies. Western history of sexuality suggests the emergence of homosexual identity from the growing problematisation of same sex sexual conduct in the Victorian era.[28] It is that problematisation that requires a policy response, either to subvert the behaviour—in the way the Victorians tried to do[29]—or to protect its practitioners—as western democracies seem now more likely to wish to do. If a similar problematisation is not apparent from African histories, then a similar response would not be necessary.

But of course, that historical trajectory cannot be isolated. The west has had a profound influence on the way in which life is lived in Africa. And that influence extends to sexual behaviour and to sexualised identities.[30] In these circumstances the advent of legal (indeed, constitutional) protection for minority sexualities is clearly necessary. But it may not be universally necessary across cultures. And, if that is so, the protection granted may have an effect on those cultures which was not considered when protection was granted. Legal protection is culturally loaded and has cultural consequences beyond the culture for which it is appropriate.

d. Sexuality and the family

My concern with the origins of, and the transformations that might occur in relation to, sexuality are, of course, rooted in the legal regulation of the family. The family is a particularly personal space in which most, if not all, individuals, across cultures, have strong emotional attachments both to other people (family members) and to the family norms that sustain them and, consequently, to their society.[31]

One of the consequences of the rising prominence of homosexuality in western societies has been the creation—in fact, if not in law—of same sex family relationships. These have in many ways mimicked the norms of heterosexual family life. And that has given rise to the growing claims of same sex couples to legal recognition of their families, a recognition that it is claimed should match the recognition afforded to different sex families.[32] The public face of western style sexuality has been enhanced by the public political battles for same sex family recognition and ultimately by the legal acceptance of those relationships.[33]

e. Constitutional protection and the creation of sexuality

Constitutional protection and the pursuit of legally protected family life in South Africa was, therefore, bound to raise the public profile of western style homosexuality in South Africa, not least because the battle for legal recognition of same sex families took on a progressively more public face.[34] This, I became convinced, would have a consequence on understandings of same sex sexual practices beyond the culture at which constitutional protection had been aimed.

This became the central dilemma I was to face and which was to take me to my second paradigm problem (the regulation of polygamy). As a lawyer my object seemed always to be fairly straight forward. I would be recommending some variation in the way in which legal regulation was conducted. That meant that I had to decide whether I approved of the constitutional provision that offered protection to individuals free from discrimination on the basis of sexual orientation. Or did I wish to see it changed? And if I believe that cultural concerns do compel us to consider change, what change would I wish to see fostered? And to what end?

My concern had become one about the potential constitutive effect of legal regulation and its resulting politics on African sexualities. In particular I began to wonder what effect the legal recognition of same sex relationships would have on perceptions of same sex sexual practices in cultures whose "homosexualities" were not western? How would alternative (unexplored) African sexualities be transformed by the legislation, case law and concomitant politics of western style homosexuality? In contemplating this dilemma I began to wonder whether or not law would be instrumental in creating a binary idea of sexuality that would replicated the one which served as the foundation of western sexuality; And would that binary division give rise to prejudice and approbrium on the basis of sexuality in cultures in which those notions had not been prevalent before.

It seemed to me to be clear that an African version of western sexuality was already being created in South Africa, at least in part, by the constitutional provision (and its politics) which ought to have protected people engaging in same sex sexual conduct.[35] The South African Gay and Lesbian Archive (housed in the University of the Witwatersrand's William Cullen Library) is full of examples of the way in which perceptions of same sex sexual conduct in South Africa have been, and are being, westernised (although not always in a uniform unidirectional way).[36]

f. Culture, sexuality and family regulation

I have attempted to argue that the constitutional stipulation for the protection of people from discrimination on the grounds of sexual orientation has created (or at least entrenched) a vision of sexual orientation into cultures in which that vision was foreign. The social transformation that I have argued has taken place has occurred because western cultural norms around sexuality and the family have, through constitutional politics (amongst other things)[37], been absorbed into other cultures. The absorption is not even. But the transformation has occurred as a result, in part at least, of the powerful social discourses around sexuality and the family.

The consequence of this transformation is not that we should revisit the legal inscription of these cultural norms. In a way it is too late for that. The changes have already occurred. However, the imposition of western social norms on African society did make me wonder about whether or not—and, if so, to what extent— African social norms might be absorbed into western culture through the legalisation of "other" (culturally divergent) family norms.

Same sex sexuality and the family regulation that flowed from its protection were western imports which began to take root in (some fragments, at least) of African culture. And so I began to wonder whether the reverse process might be possible. Could African family norms and their regularisation in the legal system— most importantly, perhaps, through the rights based (western democratic) constitution[38]—have an influence beyond the culture in which the norms found their home. I was also intrigued by the promise of the South African constitution to protect cultural norms which, it seemed to me, were likely to be threatened by the advent of western constitutionalism. Polygamy is, in my view, one of the clearest examples of a cultural norm which offends western sensibilities, but which the western style constitution of South Africa sets out to protect.[39]

We turn, therefore, to polygamy under African customary law.

4. Polygamy in customary law[40]

a. The potential for reverse cultural influence

Polygamy seemed to me to be an ideal reverse paradigm. It is still a prevalent practice in South Africa which, superficially at least, defies western liberal notions of gender equality.[41] And the west has a strong tradition of antagonism towards it.[42] That tradition was exported to Africa in the colonial era and maintained in the era of apartheid.[43] But the post-apartheid era opened up the space for a renegotiation of the place of African cultural norms in the new legal and political dispensation.[44] The Constitution had brought about an altered legal, moral and political climate in which the legal rules governing cultural variation in marriage might be settled.[45]

b. The constitutional conundrum

Unfortunately, the constitutional framework did not suggest a clear way forward.[46] There was a profound tension operating at the heart of the new constitutional dispensation. Two of its fundamental principles[47] clashed when applied to adult family relationships. The problem was simply stated; the constitutional promise of respect for cultural diversity[48] and the promise of equality between the sexes[49] could not be easily reconciled when polygamous family relationships were under consideration.

There is a superficial appeal to the logic of this clash of principle; because South African customary polygamy is uniformly polygynous,[50] men and women are treated unequally. However, there were, amongst the great variety of views expressed on the issue, those who sought to justify the recognition of customary marriage in South African law on both cultural and equality grounds.[51] Two sorts of defences can be discerned: Firstly, there were those who sought a feminist analysis that would deal pragmatically with the gendered harm suffered by individuals (women) in customary relationships.[52] And secondly, there were those who defended the practices on more overtly cultural grounds.[53] Although I think that the former strand of argument was more successful in the South African debate, I wish to consider both types of argument here because of what I have to say about the importance, in cross cultural societies, of diverse (sometimes offensive) family norms. I will start, therefore, with the argument about cultural diversity, and return to the argument on gender equality.

i. The value of cultural diversity

In offering fundamental rights based protection to different cultures the South African constitution indicated that it valued cultural traditions that had been subverted by apartheid. That ascription of value rests on the ideological assumption that a cultural practice which is familiar to those whose practice it is and serves social functions for them retains its value and can be justly protected in law even if it is foreign and even offensive to those whose practice it is not.[54] The constitution saw the dawning of an era in which life ways could be equally valid when remarkably very different from one another. Social problems could, legitimately, attract different, equally valid, responses in different cultures, without the state ascribing a hierarchy of value to them.

Polygamous marriage is a social practice of this sort. Traditional societies in South Africa[55] celebrate these unions.[56] But, although culturally rooted—and, at least in some respects, popular[57]—they have been deemed offensive to those for whom they are foreign and, in legal terms, denigrated,[58] and subordinated[59] under both colonial and apartheid legal systems.[60] The source of this negative attitude—manifested in the laws of western colonialists and then apartheid rulers—is not difficult to fathom; Although there have been western versions of polygamous practice[61] they are unusual. And the last two millennia have been dominated by a strong western tradition of legally recognised and socially structured monogamous marriage.[62]

In South Africa, therefore, the advent of a constitutional dispensation that wished to celebrate cultural diversity ushered in an era in which the western tradition of monogamy might have to coexist with an African tradition of polygamy.[63] For some the legal recognition of alternative cultural norms—like customary marriages—would have a deeper, more profound significance, than simply honouring tradition. They attributed to it some inherent value of its own which, in an era of celebrated cultural diversity, would make a positive contribution to the peaceful coexistence of different cultures. This was, after all, at the heart of South Africa's renewed constitutionalism. In relation to the customary family rules and practices, Nhlapo says, for example, that

> the overriding value in the African family is reflected in the *non-individual nature of marriage*, sometimes called the collective or communal aspect of the marriage relationship. This notion embodies the idea of marriage as an alliance between two kinship groups for purposes of realizing goals beyond the immediate interests of the particular husband and wife. This does not mean that the two parties are unimportant—they are—but only as the point at which the two families, lineages or clans are joined for purposes which have community-wide significance.[64]

Its value to the greater (national) society lies in its divergence from another cultural tradition. Any alteration in that tradition, or the termination of it, would deprive the composite culture of its alternate worldview. If this defence of an offensive cultural practice is accepted the state's response must be to offer the cultural institution protection. But that protection must extend further than to the parties to the relationships in question. It must protect the institution itself.

However, the problem for polygamy was that the value at the heart of the offence it causes others is itself a value protected in the constitution. Although the practice has a claim to recognition (by virtue of its status as a traditional, socially inscribed, living, cultural practice)[65] it remains ideologically problematic because it is always polygynous. It defies western ideas about gender based equality.

ii. Gender, equality and feminist argument in favour of polygyny

The South African Constitution clearly espoused the principle of equality between the sexes.[66] Given polygamy's cultural roots a debate was, therefore, inevitable about whether or not the constitution would permit legal recognition of polygamous marriages under customary law.

Although there were many strong feminist arguments waged against recognition of polygamous customary unions, there was one that did not disparage the institution so completely. And that argument was remarkably pragmatic.[67] If polygynous practices were to continue whatever the state of the law[68], it was necessary for law to offer protection to vulnerable participants, especially if their vulnerability was exacerbated by their historically subordinated status. In effect, it was argued, women in South Africa were prejudiced (and denied their equal citizenship) by the profound operation of social patriarchy. This was so in traditional (customary law) settings as much, if not more, than in settings beyond the gaze of traditional cultural norms. And law that refused recognition to polygynous relationships would not undermine that subsisting patriarchy. Marriages would still be celebrated within the customary norms of a traditional society. The only consequence would be that vulnerable parties would be at the additional disadvantage of being beyond the scope of legal protection. To avoid that double disadvantage polygyny had to be recognised in law, and safeguards provided for those who were most likely to be rendered vulnerable as a result of it. The Law Commissioners and legislators recognised the need to do just that.

But the premise of this recognition is that particular forms of patriarchy are resilient in the face of legislative measure to undermine them. Commentators who took this view still wished to see patriarchy undermined. And if the greater gender equality project were to succeed, if traditional patriarchal conventions were undermined, it would become unnecessary (and ideologically untenable) to continue to recognise polygyny. If those conditions were finally achieved in South Africa polygyny would have died a natural death (and some might applaud the customary law style of its demise).[69] The legislation could then be repealed. Until that time, though, polygamy had to be regulated in law.

c. *The legislative settlement*

I will not rehearse the many other arguments and recommendations made to the South African Law Commission when it investigated the future of customary marriages in South African law.[70] Nor do I wish to summarise the Law Commission's findings or its recommendations. It is enough to observe that the final outcome of the Commission's work was legislation recognising customary marriages—the Recognition of Customary Marriages Act.[71] In that Act the more obviously unacceptable features of customary marriages were altered[72] but polygyny was not one of them.[73]

But it is also clear that the Law Commission had in mind the regulation of polygyny until it did, eventually, disappear from customary practice. It recommended regulation of customary marriages so as to protect participants, but not so as to preserve its fundamental character. Indeed, it forecast the end of polygyny, and did not seem to be unduly perturbed that that should occur.[74]

Another interesting feature of the recognition of customary marriages in law is the form that it takes. The Act[75] recognises customary unions, but only if imposed threshold conditions (formal and other requirements) are met. It also alters most of the significant consequences of customary marriages.[76] It has been argued that the Act barely recognises customary marriages at all. Instead it is a codification of a new form of civil marriage, based broadly on customary practices but relying heavily on the common law traditions of family law and law reform to remedy perceived defects of customary practices. It is, in effect, only the ghosts of customary marriages that are recognised and then only to impose on them a completely new set of rules, all of which are derived from common law authority.[77]

Codification of customary unions becomes, therefore, the creation of a new genus of statutorily regulated marriage. The "customary" status of customary marriages was denuded of most of its content. And it is likely that, over time, further amendments—like the termination of recognition for polygynous unions—will take place. By gradual accretion the statute will completely redefine the parameters of "customary" marriage.

d. *Cross cultural impacts?*

Of course, I am, in this chapter less interested in the legal outcome than in the consequences, for other cultures, of the process that brought us to this legal solution. The debate on the legal recognition of polygyny, like the debate on the recognition of same sex marriage, took place on a very public stage. It involved the Law Commission in a programme of wide spread public consultation.[78] This gave rise to a considerable public debate in the press.[79] This public debate clearly incorporated, for many, a public reconsideration of the nature of marriage and of the legal regulation of marital relationships. And although focussing on the marriages of one culture, it took place across the spectrum of cultures and the relationships they recognised.

It is, therefore, appropriate that we should ask how the debate and subsequent legislation did affect, or might affect, other cultures. Did the reflections on the "offensive", gender privileging polygynous characteristics of customary marriage cause us to reflect on the state of common law marriage? Did one set of family norms, freshly inscribed with legal vitality, influence the family norms of other cultures.[80] And if so, how? In this respect I am less certain of the effects than I was when considering same sex relationship recognition and the effect that its politics had on identity formation in South Africa. I will, therefore, limit myself to a few observations—mostly in the form of questions—before concluding.

i. Is there a polygamous element to western marriage?

It was never likely that African polygamy would "create" polygamy in non-African South African cultures (in the way that a particular sexual identity might have been created in one culture by the debate on another culture's understanding of it). Aside from religious and cultural polygamy, South African marriage was always likely to remain, in the strongest western tradition, monogamous. Indeed, monogamy was more likely to be "spreading" its cultural grasp.[81] However, I do wonder if debate on the legalisation of polygamy, and on the way it operates in other South African cultures might not have caused us to reflect on western marriage (with its endemic divorce and all that that entails).[82] Is it, in some ways, a modern version of polygamy (not just polygyny, and so gender neutral)? Most potentially polygamous marriages are, in fact, monogamous. And many monogamous marriages end in divorce and become, in effect polygamous;[83] although marriage is formally over a substituted family relationship continues. In this relationship slightly altered marital support usually obligations continue and child care obligations are created and performed in new ways.

ii. Is marriage's gender problem better resolved in the common law?

The married family of western family law (that is, monogamous) has long been the subject of a detailed critique which set out the problematic problematic gendering of the family. That critique explains the privileging of men in the public world of work while women are relegated to the private unpaid work of the home.[84] But, interestingly, this gendered division of labour, and the financial advantage that it gives men continues almost unabated. In the era of substantial divorce the transformed family burdens and obligations of the post-divorce family are disproportionately borne by women.[85] Consequently, family law has come to regard its remit to include the neutralisation of gender in family disputes.[86] But this has not been performed with unremitting success. It is, therefore, not clear that a proper social valuing of the gendered division of family labour, or a polygamous, gendered redivision of family labour, might not provide a better real solution to the gender problems of family life and family law.[87]

iii. Should legalised polygyny be limited to cultures in which it is traditionally practiced?

The answer to this question is frequently given as obvious. And the passion and rationality that fuels opposition to polygyny from a western perspective does explain the strength of the view espoused. However, limiting polygyny to certain cultures in which they have a traditional footing does create some obvious problems for a constitutional settlement which espouses fundamental individual and cultural rights.

What happens, for example, when people in a cross cultural relationship wish to adopt the polygynous model of marriage? And if the husband is the outsider to the culture, and is allowed to take further wives, how is he legitimately distinguished from a man who is married in a western style monogamous marriage? But even in the "easy" case—of a couple completely outside the traditions of a polygynous culture wishing to adopt polygynous marriage norms—a problem presents itself. Why should the couple be prevented from adopting new cultural norms? And who should be the arbiter of the decision as to whether or not they should? What becomes of individual autonomy, and the advantage of cultural diversity in this case?

iv. Is it self evident that the solution to the gendered problems of polygyny is to work to undermine it universally rather than to espouse polygamy universally?

Once again commentators seem to take it as self evident that the solution to the gendered problems of polygyny is monogamy and not polygamy[88] (or "polyamory".[89] And yet, it seems an explanation is required. If the state of western marriage and post-marital consequences are properly considered it is clear that a problem exists for which we have not found a proper solution. Why would a universal system of potential polygamy not answer the problems of gender based inequality?

5. Conclusion

I wish to draw this chapter to a close by making two observations by way of conclusion. The one is a pragmatic suggestion for a solution to the problem of recognising polygyny in law. The second is to reflect, once again, on the metaphysical influences that cultures bring to bear on one another where their "offensive" norms are admitted to the fold of legal regulation in the name of cultural diversity.

a. The practical solution

When we are contemplating the problems of the legal regulation of relationships that offend some fragment of our multi-cultural societies—which applies to both same sex family regulation and to polygynous families—we seem often to become confused because of the attempt we make to draw unacceptable family norms into the fold of acceptable norms. We wish to recognise some, and leave others outside the scope of recognition.

And yet, society keeps producing new and varied ways of conducting family life, particularly as we become aware of the ways in which other cultures conduct their family lives. There is no single family norm, even within a single culture. Trying to regulate patterns of family life as if there could be one framework type, therefore, seems to be a project doomed to failure. Why should we be discussing whether or not law will recognise the marriages of same sex couples or of polygynous groups when we know that, whether or not we "recognise" the marriages in question a time will come when we will have to decide whether or not to enforce a just outcome for the parties when a dispute arises. In short, whether or not we recognise same sex marriage or polygynous marriage, there will be those living in relationships we do not recognise. And they will (from time to time) justly call upon the law for an equitable resolution to their family disputes.[90]

Instead of trying to allow same sex couples to marry, or to give legal recognition to polygamous marriages, perhaps the more appropriate response is a much more pragmatic, and much less categorical one. If we were to ask what roles we believe family members should perform, and then set out to discover who, in fact, fulfills those roles, we would begin to ascribe legal solutions to circumstances in which law matters. Where law is immaterial it would be unnecessary to ascribe any consequence. But where it matters, to refuse a solution on the basis of a judgement on inscribed family status seems, in the multi-cultural era of autonomous rights holding individuals, to be inappropriate. It would be to allow a dominant culture to determine whether or not a subsidiary culture can be admitted to the privileged status of the dominant culture. And that judgement is too easily influenced by ideological views of what deserves "status" and what should be excluded from it. It does not reflect the justice of particular situations. Nor does it give vent to the underlying reason for promoting multicultural diversity.

Relying on a functional analysis of what family members should do for one another, and what particular people have been doing, would seem to approximate, more closely, a just response.[91] This pragmatic approach to family regulation would require family lawyers to devise appropriate touchstones of family function, and to go on to create tests for each function so that people would have a sense of their family obligations and rights. They would know what the consequences would be when their real, pragmatic family lives fail in some remediable way.

If this approach were to be adopted same sex family recognition and polygamy would both disappear as political problems requiring refined legislative solutions. Instead, the nature of lived family life would be at the root of solutions to problems that arise in the family.

b. The metaphysical dimension

My interest in this subject began because of a concern about the way in which identity in one culture might become constructed in another because of the law and politics that surrounded a particular issue of some significance to the one culture. I started out with an ambition to try to protect a cultural understanding from the pollution of another culture so that it might be properly used (at least properly understood before its demise). But I am no longer convinced—if I ever really was —that such a project is possible. Cross cultural influence is simply unavoidable and uncontrolled by law. And cultures do change.

And yet, I do think that, to the extent that we are able to exercise power so as to manipulate cultural change, we should do so to foster mutual cultural exchange (rather than one sided cultural transfers). Cultures should influence each other. We should resist the trend for dominant cultures simply, by virtue of their dominance, to dictate the direction of cultural change.

If it is true that one of the values ascribed to multiculturalism is its contribution to the way in which we critique our own view of the world, our ambition for family regulation and gender equality should not be that it is transformed to satisfy the prescripts of one culture, but that we should be more reflective of our norms and their comparative success at resolving the problems that arise in our societies. Culturally foreign norms shine a different light on social practices. They cause us to see our practices in the light of others. And they remind us that there are other ways of seeing the world and that each way provides, not complete answers to dilemmas, but answers that are partial and, at best, suit their cultural context.

[1] Initially in s 8 of the interim constitution (Constitution of the Republic of South Africa Act, No. 200 of 1993) and then in s 9 of the final constitution (Constitution of the Republic of South Africa, Act No. 108 of 1996).

[2] For a more detailed analysis of some ideas outlined in this section see Craig Lind 'Importing Law, Politics and Sexuality' in Mikki van Zyl and Melissa Steyn *Performing Queer: Shaping Sexualities 1994 – 2004, vol.1* (Kwela Books, Roggebaai, 2005).

[3] See Robert Wintemute and Mads Andenaes (eds) *Legal Recognition of Same-Sex Partnerships: A study of National, European and International Law* (Hart, Oxford, 2001). See too Craig Lind 'Time for Lesbian and Gay Marriage?' (1995) 145 *New Law Journal* 1553.

[4] See, in particular, *Fourie v. Minister of Home Affairs* 2005 (3) BCLR 241 (SCA), 2005 (3) SA 429 (SCA) where the right of same sex couples to marry was upheld by the Supreme Court of Appeals. The South African Constitutional Court upheld that decision in *Minister of Home Affairs v Fourie* (CCT 10/05, decided 1 December 2005) but it delayed implementation of the decision, allowing the government to legislate to repair the deficiency of the law in failing to admit same sex couples to legal marriage, or an appropriate alternative. Some of the many articles written on the subject of same sex family regulation include: Pierre De Vos 'Same-sex sexual desire and the re-imagining of the South African family. (2004) 20 *South African Journal on Human Rights* 179, Craig Lind 'Politics, Partnership Rights and the Constitution in South Africa ... (and the Problem of Sexual Identity)' in Wintemute and Andenaes note 3 above, Elsa Steyn 'From Closet to Constitution: The South African Gay Family Rights Odyssey' in John Eekelaar and Thandabantu Nhlapo *The Changing Family: Family Forms and Family Law* (Hart, Oxford 1998), Lorraine Volhuter 'Equality and the Concept of Difference: Same-Sex Marriages in the Light of the Final Constitution' (1997) 114 *South African Law Journal* 389, the special edition of the South African Journal on Human Rights: 'Focus on Same-sex Marriage' (1996) 12 *SAJHR* 533, Craig Lind 'Sexual Orientation, Family Law and the Transitional Constitution' [1995] 112 *South African Law Journal* 481, and Pierre De Vos 'The Right of a Lesbian Mother to have Access to her Children: Some Constitutional Issues' (1994) 111 *South African Law Journal* 687.

[5] See Lind 'Sexual Orientation', note 4 above.

[6] For a pragmatic sceptical argument, see Kenneth McK Norrie 'Marriage is for heterosexuals—may the rest of us be saved from it' 2000, 12 *Child and Family Law Quarterly* 363. For philosophical arguments expressing some scepticism about same sex marriage see Davina Cooper 'Like Counting Stars? Re-Structuring Equality and the Socio-Legal Space of Same-Sex Marriage' in Wintemute & Adenaes, note 4 above, p. 75 and Paula Ettelbrick 'Since when is marriage a path to liberation' in William B. Rubenstein (ed) *Lesbians, Gay Men, and the Law* (The New Press, New York, 1993) 401 (But Cf William N. Eskridge 'The Ideological Structure of the Same-Sex Marriage Debate (and some Postmodern Arguments for Same-Sex Marriage) in Wintemute & Adenaes, note 4 above, p.113 and Janet Halley 'Recognition, Rights, Regulation, Normalisation: Rhetorics of Justification in the Same-Sex Marriage Debate.' in Wintemute & Adenaes note 4 above, p.97.

[7] Note 4 above.

[8] See Lind 'Politics', note 4 above.

[9] During the tenure of the interim constitution negotiations were taking place to settle the final constitution.

[10] In the United Kingdom, for example, there were two principle lesbian and gay lobbying groups— Stonewall and Outrage—which operated very differently. Stonewall lobbied diplomatically by talking to and impressing important politicians and policy makers, while Stonewall engaged in direct action protest politics (like invading television studios during the news, or staging 'kiss ins' in Piccadilly Circus).

[11] Gay Pride marches have been held annually in most western capital cities and in other large urban centres starting with the first pride march in New York City a year after the Stonewall riots: see Jeffrey Weeks *Coming Out: Homosexual Politics in Britain, from the Nineteenth Century to the Present* (Quartet, London 1977) p. 189. South Africa's first gay pride march took place 20 years later, in 1990: see Mark Gevisser 'A Different Fight for Freedom: A History of South African lesbian and gay organisation from the 1950s to the 1990s' in Mark Gevisser and Edwin Cameron *Defiant Desire: Gay and Lesbian Lives in South Africa* (Routledge; New York, 1995) p.14 at p. 77.

[12] This is not to say that traces of a similar trajectory cannot be found in South Africa: see Gevisser, note 11 above. But it is to question the cultural pervasiveness of the parallel movement at grass roots level.

[13] Even now—in 2006—South Africa has the most overt, comprehensive protection available to lesbians and gay men. Those other countries which have made progressive moves towards the protection of their lesbian and gay communities (including the Scandanavian countries, most of the rest

of Europe, and some US states) have done so in a piecemeal fashion. Canada is, perhaps, the noteworthy exception. But even in Canada, the constitutional protection granted to lesbians and gay men was granted by judicial interpretation of the constitution rather than by an explicit provision in it: see *Egan v Canada* [1995] 2 *SCR* 513. See Wintemute and Adenaes note 3 above.

[14] For some writing on the poitics of equality struggles see, for example, Urvashi Vaid, *Virtual Equality: The Mainstreaming of Gay and Lesbian Liberation* (Anchor Books, New York, 1995), Weeks, note 11 above, and Dennis Altman *Homosexual: Oppression and Liberation* (Allen Lane, London, 1974).

[15] See Simon Nkoli 'Wardrobes: Coming out as a black gay activist in South Africa' (p. 249) and Ivan Toms 'Ivan Toms is a Fairy?: The South African Defence Force, the End Conscription Campaign, and me' both in Gevisser and Cameron, note 11 above, p. 258 for some personal stories of prominent anti-apartheid activists who were also out gay men.

[16] See, for example, the transformation of law and politics in the UK because of the change from Conservative to Labour governments in 1997. The Conservative government had been responsible for legislation like the notorious section 28 of the Local Government Act 1988 which prohibited the promotion of same sex families as 'pretended families'. Labour, in its turn, has been responsible for passing the Human Rights Act 1998 (which allowed the Courts to treat unmarried same sex couples like unmarried different sex couples in *Ghaidan v Godin-Mendoza* [2004] UKHL 30), the Civil Partnerships Act 2004 (which set up a same sex equivalent of marriage) and the Adoption and Children Act 2002 (which explicitly recognised that same sex couples should be allowed to adopt children; see ss. 68(3) and 144(4)).

[17] See Annie Leatt and Graeme Hendricks ' Beyond identity politics: homosexuality and gayness in South Africa' in van Zyl and Steyn note 2 above. It has never surprised me that some of the most outspoken and vitriolic criticisms of lesbians and gay men have been uttered by the leaders of other Southern African Societies: see Stephen O Murray 'Sexual Politics in Contemporary Southern Africa' in Stephen O Murray and Will Roscoe (eds) *Boy-Wives and Female Husbands: Studies in African Homosexualities* (Palgrave; New York, 1998) esp. p. 247ff (on homophobic comments made by leaders in Zimbabwe, Namibia, and Botswana in the mid 1990s). This is not, however, to assert that African societies are more 'homophobic' – in a western sense – than are western societies. It is simply to acknowledge that cultural constructions of sexuality are different.

[18] See, in particular, Michel Foucault *The History of Sexuality, Volume 1: An Introduction* (London, Penguin, 1978) (translated by Robert Hurley).

[19] See Gevisser note 11 above.

[20] Above, note 11.

[21] See Weeks, note 11 above, Jeffrey Weeks *Sex, Society and Society: The regulation of sexuality since 1800* (2ed) (London, Longman, 1989), and Randolph Trumbach 'The Birth of the Queen: Sodomy and the Emergence of Gender Equality in Modern Culture, 1660-1750.' in Martin B. Duberman, Martha Vicinus and Jeffrey Chauncey, Jr (eds) *Hidden From History: Reclaiming the Gay and Lesbian Past* (London, Penguin, 1991) p. 129. See too Dennis Altman *Global Sex* (Allen and Unwin, Crows Nest, 2001) ch 6.

[22] These authors all do what Foucault, note 18 above, had suggested they do in order to trace the origins of sexuality. They had looked to the discourse of the era to trace the construction of individual sexuality.

[23] I don't want to suggest that there is anything wrong with Gevisser's history of homosexual politics in the late 20th century. However, I do wish to argue that that history is one of several that could be written and that others might have a very different understanding of sexual identity and identity formation. See, for example, Rudi C. Bleys *The Geography of Desire: Male-to-male Sexual Behaviour outside the West and the Ethnographic Imagination 1750 – 1918* (Cassell; London 1996) and Stephen O Murray and Will Roscoe (eds) *Boy-Wives and Female Husbands: Studies in African Homosexualities* (Palgrave, New York, 2001).

[24] See Altman, note 21 above.

[25] I have argued elsewhere (Lind note 2 above) that African homo-sexualities might have been dramatically different requiring no constitutional need for protection because no real disadvantage might have attached to it: see especially J.C.Caldwell , P. Caldwell, and P. Quiggin 'The Social Context of AIDS in sub-Saharan Africa.' 15 (1989) *Population and Development Review* 185. But see too B.M. Ahlberg 'Is there a distinct African sexuality? A critical response to Caldwell.' 64 (1994) *Africa* 220. The consequence of such a view would, I have suggested, be to have created categories to which prejudice attaches where none might have arisen if an indigenous sexuality had been more rigorously sought.

[26] See Caldwell, et al, and Ahlberg note 25 above.

[27] Caldwell et al, note 25 above.

[28] See Foucault, note 18 above. See too Weeks (1989) note 21 above and Trumbach, note 21 above.

[29] See Weeks (1989) note 21 above.

[30] See Altman note 21 above.

[31] See Alison Diduck, *Law's Families* (LexisNexix, London 2005).

[32] See Andrew Sullivan *Virtually Normal* (Random House, New York, 1995). In the South African context, see Lind 'Sexual Orientation' note 4 above.

[33] In the USA cases like *Baehr v Lewin* 852 P2d 44 (1993 *Baker v Vermont* 170 Vt. 194; 744 A.2d 864 and *Goodridge v Department of Public Health* (SJC, Mass) 440 Mass. 309; 798 N.E.2d 941 have ignited political turmoil and resulted in numerous pieces of legislation which range from statutes to recognise same sex couples to those which outlaw same sex marriage (most influencially, the Federal Defence of Marriage Act 1996 – 1 US Code s. 7 and 28 USC s. 1738C); see Evan Wolfson 'The Hawaii Marriage Case Launches the US Freedom-to-Marry Movement for Equality' in Wintemute and Andenaes, note 3 above.

[34] See Lind 'Politics' note 4 above.

[35] This is self evident in the rise of the vibrant, multicultural, political face of sexuality in South Africa since the constitutional transformation: see Gevisser and Cameron, note 11 above, and van Zyl and Steyn, note 2 above.

[36] See Altman, note 21 above

[37] It is as well to note, at this stage, that law and the politics that surrounds its uses, are not the only influences that are brought to bear upon cultures. The media (in both news and fiction), as well as a myriad other circumstances contribute to the way in which individuals within cultures reflect on their cultures. And some attempts to harness particular kinds of power to control culture or identity can have very different impacts than the impact they desire. The cultural impact of resistence to the use of law (and other socially powerfull devices) to control gay men has attracted much noteworthy analysis: see Foucault, note 18 above, Weeks (1989) note 21 above, amongst many others.

[38] See R. Panikkar 'Is the Notion of Human Rights a Western Concept?' in Peter Sack (ed.) *Law and Anthropology* (1992) 7 on scepticism about rights (as western exports to cultures in which they are not absolutely comfortable).

[39] Section 15 (3) of the final Constitution, note 1 above.

[40] In this chapter I will deal only with polygamy in African customary law: See South African Law Commission *Project 90: The Harmonisation of the Common Law and the Indigenous Law—Report on Customary Marriages* (Aug 1998), Thandabantu Nhlapo 'African Family Law under an Undecided Constitution: the Challenge for Law Reform in South Africa' in John Eekelaar and Thandabantu Nhlapo *The Changing Family: Family Forms and Family Law* (Hart, Oxford 1998) p. 617; T.W. Bennett *Human Rights and African Customary Law under the South African Constitution* (1995). Felicity Kaganas and Christina Murray 'Law, Women and the Family: the Question of Polygyny in a new South Africa' 1991 *Acta Juridica* 116, and June Sinclair (with Jackie Heaton) *The Law of Marriage: Vol 1* (Juta, Cape Town, 1996), p.164. I will not deal with Religious polygamy practiced, for example, in Muslim communities in South Africa.

[41] For some discussion of the clash of cultures in relation to gender see Kaganas and Murray Note 40 above. See too Sinclair, note 40 above.

[42] See Frances Raday 'Culture, Religion and Gender' (2003) 1 *International Journal of Constitutional Law* 663, Prakash A. Shah 'Attitudes To Polygamy In English Law' (2003) 52 *International and Comparative Law Quarterly* 369, And see Cheshire Calhoun 'The Meaning of Marriage: Who's Afraid of Polygamous Marriage? Lessons for Same-Sex Marriage Advocacy from the History of Polygamy' (2005) 42 *San Diego Law Review* 1023 on the end of Mormon polygamy in the USA.

[43] See SA Law Commission, note 40 above, paras 2.1.4 and 2.1.5

[44] See Vera Sacks 'Multiculturalism, Constitutionalism and the South African Constitution' 1997 *Public Law* 672. And see Martin Chanock 'Law, State and Culture: Thinking About 'Customary Law' After Apartheid' 1991 *Acta Juridica* 52 at 65 for an appealing way forward that does not require us to worry about whether or not traditions of marriage subsist.

[45] See Judith Sloth-Nielsen and Belinda Van Heerden 'The Constitutional Family: Developments In South African Family Law Jurisprudence Under The 1996 Constitution' (2003) 12 *International Journal of Law, Policy and the Family* 121. See too South African Law Commission, note 40 above, para 2.3.

[46] This is unlike the constitutional framework which governs same sex sexuality, where the way forward seemed relatively clear: see Lind 'Sexual Orientation', note 4 above. There may be a parallel, however, if religious authorities wish to assert the right to undermine the rights of individuals with a protected sexuality on the grounds of religious conviction.

[47] Fundamental principles which were to ground the final constitution were agreed to and laid out in Schedule 4 of the interim constitution (note1 above). These included: the principle against discrimination on race and gender grounds (principle III), the principle of equality before the law (principle V), the princple to promote multicultural diversity (principle XI), and the principle

protecting indigenous laws and customs which do not offend the fundamental rights established in the constitution (principle XIII).

[48] Set out most explicitly in s 30 and s 31 (and in s 15(3) in relation specifically to customary marriage) of the Constitution (note 1 above).

[49] Section 9(1) of the Constitution (note 1 above). But s 15(3) of the Constitution which allows for legislative recognition of customary marriages also contains the proviso that the protections offered by the bill of rights in the constitution should not be undermined.

[50] One man may marry more than one woman (but a woman may only have one husband). See SA Law Commission, note 40 above, para 2.2 and para. 6.1

[51] These include Kaganas and Murray, note 40 above, Nhlapo, note 40 above, and C.R.M. Dlamini 'The Role of Customary Law in meeting Social Needs' 1991 *Acta Juridica* 71.

[52] Kaganas and Murray, note 40 above are, perhaps, the chief proponents of this defence.

[53] Dlamini, note 51 above, is one of the chief proponents of this defence.

[54] In the context of this chapter, it is necessary to remind ourselves that same sex families are also based on practices that are offensive to large portions (probably majorities) of the greater national community.

[55] And most of sub-Saharan Africa, at least: see Bennett note 40 above at p. 301.

[56] See T.W. Bennett *A Sourcebook of African Customary Law* (1991).

[57] Elsje Bronthuys 'Accommodating Gender, Race, Culture and Religion: Outside Legal Subjectivity' 18 (2002) *South African Law Journal* 41, at 49. But see the claim of the Law Commission in its 1998 report that polygamous practices are dying out (or likely to die out): SA Law Commission, note 40 above, para. 6.1.14 and 6.1.25.

[58] This sentiment was universalised in *Seedat's Executors v The Master (Natal)* 1917 AD 302 at 307 where the court said that polygyny was 'reprobated by the majority of civilized peoples, on the ground of morality and religion', and again in *Ismail v Ismail* 1983 (1) SA 1006 (A) at 1026 where the court said that it was 'contrary to the accepted customs and usages which are regarded as morally binding upon all members of our society.' See too *Prior v Battle* 1998 (8) BCLR 1013 (Tk), *Mthembu v Letsela* 1997 (2) SA 936 (T), 1998 (2) SA 675 (T), 2000 (3) SA 867 (SCA) and *Metiso v Padongeluksfonds* 2001 (3) SA 1142 (T).

[59] Principally under the Black Administration Act 38 of 1927.

[60] See Chuma Himonga 'The advancement of African women's rights in the first decade of democracy in South Africa: The reform of the customary law of marriage and succession' 2005 *Acta Juridica* 82 at 101. See too Law Commission, note 40 above, para. 6.1.16

[61] See, for example, Alyssa Rower 'The Legality of Polygamy: Using the Due Process Clause of the Fourteenth Amendment' (2004) 38 *Family Law Quarterly* 711 and Stephanie Forbes '*Why Have Just One?: An Evaluation of the Anti-Polygamy Laws Under the Establishment Clause*' (2003) 39 *Houston Law Review* 1517 (on the history of polygamy in the USA). Mormon polygamy was brought to a formal (legal) end in the USA by the Morrill Anti-Bigamy Act ch. 126, 12 Stat. 501 (1862), upheld in *Reynolds v. United States* 98 U.S. 145 (1878).

[62] The source of much of common law authority on the prerequisites of a valid marriage is the statement of Lord Penzance in *Hyde v Hyde* (1866) LR 1 P & D 130 : 'I conceive that marriage, as understood in Christendom, may be defined as the voluntary union for life of one man and one woman to the exclusion of all others'. In Roman Law marriage was also strictly monogamous: see J.A.C. Thomas *Textbook of Roman Law* (North-Holland, Amsterdam, 1976), at p.424.

[63] See, especially, section 15(3) of the final Constitution, note 1, above.

[64] T.R.Nhlapo 'The African Family and Women's Rights: Friends of Foes?' 1991 *Acta Juridica* 135 at 137 (footnotes omitted). See too Dlamini, note 51 above.

[65] On the difficulties of outlawing a practice that is ideologically suspect, but actively practiced in communities across the country, see T.W.Bennett 'The Compatibility of African Customary Law and Human Rights' 1991 *Acta Juridica* 18 and the SA Law Commission note 40 above, paras.2.1.18—2.1.22, and 6.1.19.

[66] See s 9(3) of the Constitution (note 1 above). For a discussion of the transformation of family law after the constitution, particularly in the light of gender problems endemic to family law, see Sinclair note 40 above ch 1.

[67] See Kaganas and Murray note 40 above. See too Sinclair, note 40 above, p 164 and Bennett note 65 above.

[68] See Bennett, note 65 above, at 32: 'The most powerful argument in favour of sustaining customary law, and hence allowing free pursuit of cultural rights, is that this law ... endorses current social practice, and therefore, rests on a foundation of popular acceptance... There is telling evidence to suggest that reforms affecting such domestically sensitive matters as patriarchy are either ignored or actively combated.' (footnotes omitted).

[69] See Law Commission, note 40 above, para. 6.1.14.

[70] See, for example, Kaganas and Murray, note 40 above. For a summary of some of the debate, see Sinclair, *Law of Marriage* note 40 above, p. 164.

[71] 120 of 1998. For a discussion of the Act see Chuma Himonga 'The advancement of African women's rights in the first decade of democracy in South Africa: The reform of the customary law of marriage and succession' 2005 *Acta Juridica* 82 and June Sinclair, 'Embracing New Family Forms, Entrenching Outmoded Stereotypes: Building the Rainbow Nation' in Peter Lødrup and Evan Modvar (eds) *Family Life and Human Rights* (Gyldendal, Trondheim, 2004) p. 801. See too Bronthuys note 57 above. See too Chanock note 45 above.

[72] Notably in relation to the 'minority' status of women (s. 6), the proprietary consequences of marriage (s. 7), and divorce (s. 8): see Himonga, note 71 above.

[73] SA Law Commission, note 40 above, para 6.2.

[74] SA Law Commission, note 40 above, para. 6.1.25.

[75] note 71 above.

[76] For a critique of the Act a disingenuous attempt to honour customary law (by imposing the common law on customary relationships through statute) see Himonga, note 71 above.

[77] Himonga note 71 above.

[78] See the public consultation methods adopted by the Law Commission described and discussed in ch. 1 of their report, note 40 above. These included public workshops, meetings, and debates (some targeted to particular audiences, and others open to anyone who wished to participate). There were also numerous opportunities to submit written opinions to the Law Commission on the subject.

[79] Sinclair, note 40 above, (at fn 426, p. 162).

[80] For an interesting analysis of the influence that the legalisation and regulation of polygamy might bring to family regulation, see Maura I. Strassberg 'The Challenge of Post-Modern Polygamy: Considering Polyamory' (2003) 31 *Capital University Law Review* 439

[81] note 74 above.

[82] Notably, post divorce financial support and property allocation, and post divorce child care arrangements.

[83] Calhoun talks of monogamous marriage in which divorce is easy as 'serial polygamy'. See Calhoun, note 42 above.

[84] See, for example, Katherine O'Donovan *Sexual Divisions in Law* (1985) and Albie Sachs and Wilson *Sexism and the Law: A Study of Male Beliefs and Legal Bias in Britain and the United States* (1978). See too Sinclair, note 40 above, ch 1.

[85] See June Carbone 'Feminism, Gender and the Consequences of Divorce' in Michael Freeman (ed) *Divorce: Where Next?* (Ashgate, London, 1996) 181.

[86] For an excellent English example of one attempt to do this, see the House of Lords decision in *White v White* [2001] 1 All ER 1, [2001] 1 AC 596, in which the court set out to value the domestic work of women in a non discriminatory way by refusing to value the paid work of men at a higher rate.

[87] See Kaganas and Murray, note 40 above.

[88] See Sinclair, note 40 above and the Law Commission's view that polygyny was – and should be – a dying tradition: Law Commission, note 40 above, para. 6.1.25.

[89] For a discussion of 'polyamory' as a solution see Strassberg, note 80 above.

[90] Noteworthy in this context is the call that has been made by many to offer legal solutions to the problems of unmarried cohabitants: see, for example Craig Lind 'Domestic partnerships and marital status discrimination' 2005 *Acta Juridica* 108

[91] See Sinclair (2004) note 40 above and Chanock note 44 above.

CHAPTER 14

UK; THE INCORPORATION OF HUMAN RIGHTS AND NEW LABOUR SUCCESS OR FAILURE?

Wendy Pettifer

Introduction

The Universal Declaration of Human Rights in 1948 provided a template for the collective dream that every individual has the right to live their life with dignity, and that the world would never be revisited with the horrors of World War II. Its sentiments strongly contrast with European hostility towards refugees in the 1930s as reflected in the content of the Evian Conference in the United States in 1938 called to discuss the plight of Jews in Germany and Austria. "No country in any part of the world wanted to add to its population destitute and demoralized outcasts. For such many of the refugees had become."

The Declaration's principles are embodied in the international treaty of the European Convention on Human Rights[1] ("the Convention") and its numerous protocols adopted in 1950, ratified by the UK in 1951 and entered into force in 1953. The Convention aims to protect the right of every individual to life, **protection from torture and inhuman or degrading treatment**, protection from slavery or compulsory labour, the right to liberty and security of person, **to a fair trial**, protection from retrospective criminal offence, of private and family life, freedom of thought conscience and religion, of expression, of association and assembly, the right to marry and found a family, freedom from discrimination, the right to property, education, free and fair elections and the abolition of the death penalty in peacetime. (Articles 2, 1 12 and 14, Articles 1-3 of the First Protocol, Article 1 of the sixth Protocol.)

The UK's historic isolationist position with regard to Europe was reflected in its marked reluctance to incorporate the principles of the Convention into domestic legislation.

For centuries the idea prevailed that UK political and legal institutions were perfectly suited to protecting human rights and required no fundamental change.[2]

As New Labour prepared itself for Government in its last days as the opposition there was a genuine belief that the passing of the Human Rights Act was the centrepiece of the party's vision of a just and fair society.

"This bill will bring human rights home….Our courts will develop human rights throughout society. A culture of an awareness of human rights will develop."[3]

During its election campaign of 1997, the Labour Party therefore promised incorporation as part of its election Manifesto: "the HRA will allow citizens…statutory rights to enforce their Human rights in the UK courts."[4]

In this paper I look at the incorporation of the Human Rights Act 1998 which gave effect to the provisions of the Convention in UK domestic legislation from the point of view of a legal aid practitioner with particular reference to Articles 3 and 6 of the Human Rights Act within the context of the availability of Legal Aid. I look at the political background within which incorporation took place, two examples of relevant case law relating to the support of asylum seekers and the detention of non-EU suspected terrorists within the context of the changing perception of Human Rights before the terrorists attacks of 9 November 2001 (US) (9/11) and after 7 July 2005 (UK) (7/7).

Incorporation

The incorporation of the Human Rights Act 1998 into UK domestic legislation in 1999 represented a commitment to Convention principles, in the absence of a written constitution. Its objective was to promote a culture of mainstream rights. Since that time, and particularly since 9/11 and 7/7[5] such incorporation has failed to protect the human rights of the minority against the perceived need to protect the majority from "terror". The defeated proposal in the House of Commons in November 2005 of New Labour's ninety-day detention proposals in the Terrorism Bill reflects the alarming (albeit defeated) intention of a democratic Western Government to incorporate into UK law provisions which equate with those of internment in South Africa prior to the abolition of apartheid. It is ironic that in the 1970s the UK was a persuasive force in the UN's authorisation of reports on South Africa during apartheid which undermined the self-confidence of that Government and sustained internal opposition organisations and encouraged international support for regime change.

In Western Europe and North America the formalisation of right-wing racist ideas into government policies imbues such ideas with legitimacy:

> They undertake a double displacement of responsibility, identifying Others as the source of economic, social or cultural tensions, and deflecting onto the mass of the population, the state's own interest in stimulating prejudice.[6]

Incorporation of Human Rights must be seen within the dominant populist Christian, xenophobic perspective: Bush and Blair are both ardent Christians. Combine this dominant social culture with the current unregulated economic interests of globalised industry, finance and services and non-Christians, especially Muslims immediately become a major threat to order: the enforcement of Human Rights is therefore based on membership of the right social community not common humanity. The sub-text of the racist agenda of Bush and Blair 'others' non-Christians, particularly Muslims. This gives rise to a conflict between the positive obligation of the state to protect its population against the threat of terror and the need to protect the human rights of alleged terrorists—particularly with regard to Article 3.[7]

Incorporation could only ever have worked if set within the political will to change from the Executive. Now both senior members of the judiciary and junior members of the executive have experienced confrontation with the Cabinet over enforcement of human rights. The first illustration below on section 55 cases[8] shows how the incorporation of human rights assisted radical lawyers and community groups in minimising the harsh effects of a specific piece of legislation in 2002/03. Unfortunately the second illustration of the Belmarsh cases and the Prevention of

Terrorism Act 2005 shows how the response of the Government to a fair and progressive decision by the judiciary has been to shift the goal posts by introducing new legislation within the space of eighteen months, and particularly since 7/7.

Case A: Section 55 (Nationality Immigration and Asylum Act 2002)

The aim of section 55 was to make it harder for illegal entrants to use asylum as a means of entering and staying in the UK with a hidden agenda of obtaining work. It prohibited the grant of housing and financial support from the National Asylum Support Service (NASS) to asylum seekers who failed to seek asylum *'as soon as reasonably practicable'* (interpreted to mean within seventy-two hours of entry into the UK) leading to destitution and homelessness pending an initial determination of asylum claims. Section 55(5) allows a discretionary deviation from the above where an Article 3 breach of the Human Rights Act would be engaged should destitution ensue from a negative decision.   By late 2003 an estimated 500 people were sleeping rough in London because of the rule.

In 2003 I joined a lobbying group which included about thirty lawyers and many other organisations working with asylum seekers (Housing and Immigration Group—(HIG)) to oppose these restrictions. The broad base of our campaign enabled us to bring alive the 'human interest' of our clients stories and together we brought over 700 challenges to decisions to refuse NASS support based on s 55 in the High Court. A key element of the legal challenge was the engagement of Article 3 in accordance with Article 5(5) as we argued that the circumstances in which asylum seekers found themselves amounted to inhuman and degrading treatment. Regular meetings of HIG were held throughout the campaign and a lengthy dossier compiled which included expert evidence from numerous NGOs e.g. Refugee Arrival Project, Liberty. A succession of High Court decisions with *Limbuela*[9] as the leading case found that if the destitution amounted to inhuman and degrading treatment[10] Article 3 was engaged.

The Home Department appealed the matter which was finally decided in the House of Lords unanimously in favour of asylum seekers on appeal from the Home Secretary on 3rd November 2005 with NGOs Justice, Liberty and Shelter intervening.[11] Lord Bingham of the Law Lords commented:

> I have no doubt that the threshold (of suffering) may be crossed if a late applicant with no means and no alternative sources of support himself is, by deliberate action of the state, denied shelter, food or the most basic necessities of life.

Adam Sampson, Shelter's director commented that: The government should now remove this inhumane and degrading piece of legislation from the statute book.[12]

As a result of this sustained campaign on 7 August 2006 the Home Department issued an Interim Policy Bulletin 75 providing guidance on section 55.[13] The Bulletin promotes a flexible approach to the *'as soon as reasonably practicable test'* extending it beyond seventy-two hours. It allows 'in-country' applications in certain circumstances (e.g. a military coup in country of origin)[14] and gives six different examples where NASS caseworkers may or may not grant support in accordance with s 55.

Strategic litigation around *Limbuela* publicised the injustice of destitution faced by newly-arrived asylum seekers, mobilised support and resulted in a de facto change to the statutory guidance. As a result of the collective working between refugee agencies on the ground who were providing food and sometimes shelter for the destitute asylum seekers, the asylum seekers themselves, experienced caseworkers and qualified and experienced solicitors and barristers, those working on cases within the campaign were able to:

- Identify the strongest case to lead the challenge on a point of law from a pool of cases
- Involve Justice, Liberty and Shelter as effective interveners able to shed light on the 'bigger picture'.
- Maximise the impact of the *Limbuela* judgement through the broader campaign.

The collective evidence of examples of bad decisions by NASS and the resultant destitution swayed the opinion of the High Court Judges who in the majority of cases granted *ex parte* injunctions ordering NASS to grant support and accommodation pending the outcome of—eventually—*Limbuela*. It was indeed a positive experience to obtain such an injunction from an empathetic Judge who immediately understood the background of the case by phone at 8:00 pm. The whole process from implementation of the statute in January 2003 to the change in policy after the final decision in *Limbuela* in August 2006 took about two years.

The final positive outcome demonstrated the difference between the stated intention of Government policy (to dissuade "bogus" asylum claims) from the reality (destitute asylum seekers sleeping outside NASS' offices). Sadly, the limited judicial remedies available and the lack of power to dis-apply primary legislation in order to enforce human rights means that in spite of achievements like the "success" of the s 55 Campaign, such rights have not been incorporated into UK mainstream culture. The modest positive legal reform resulting from the s55 Campaign may be due to the fact that those adversely affected fell within a relatively structured and clearly defined group.

A long-term benefit from the campaign is the forging of strong links between community groups and lawyers. HIG is currently working with Eritrean NGOs on a different facet of unjust law which denies support to Eritreans unable to obtain travel documents and therefore re-admission to their country of origin after failed asylum claims. HIG has also raised money to fund an advocacy representation service for asylum seekers who appeal original negative NASS decisions to an Adjudicator.

> Strategic litigation can publicise injustices, mobilise support and sometimes even change the law. But this is only one way to make a difference and as history has shown, is rarely enough on its own.[15]

Two salaried caseworkers provide representation at the Asylum Support Adjudication Service, co-ordinate a rota of pro bono volunteers with a minimum of five years experience as either solicitors or barristers, train NGOs in appropriate representations to support appeals. Access to language line is also funded.

Proportionality

The doctrine of proportionality means that human rights are only ever taken into account in proportion to the effect that their implementation will have on the majority, particularly with regard to cost and issues of national security. The UK Courts have established five factors to be considered in respect of the test of proportionality:

1. whether 'relevant and sufficient' reasons have been advanced in support of it
2. whether there is a less restrictive alternative
3. whether there has been some measure of procedural fairness in the decision-making process
4. whether safeguards against abuse exist
5. whether the restriction in question destroys the 'very essence' of the Convention right in issue.

The judiciary cannot "trump" Parliamentary legislation and strike it down: it can only declare legislation incompatible with the Human Rights Act. The political climate within which proportionality is considered by the judiciary has been altered by 7/7 and the question of the exercise of individual human rights is increasingly balanced against the need to maintain national security.

To what extent should the courts defer ... to the judgements of the executive and of parliament in striking a balance between the interests of national security and the need to protect fundamental rights?[16]

A see-saw situation has evolved in the UK whereby each time the judiciary make a decision which favours the human rights of the individual within the context of "terrorism" or immigration, Parliament reacts to the judgement by introducing legislation which erodes that right. This is clearly illustrated in the Belmarsh judgement and the Prevention of Terrorism Act 2005 (which also responds to 7/7).

Case B – the Belmarsh Judgement[17]

In fact in only seven cases in the UK have the Courts made declarations that public authorities' decisions are incompatible with human rights legislation. Seen within the context of an onslaught of change within criminal justice policy and legislation, decisions such as that in **Belmarsh** have inevitably resulted in a subsequent legislative backlash, as illustrated below.

In May 2003 sixteen **non-UK nationals** were detained under the Anti-Terrorism, Crime and Security Act 2002. In October 2003 eleven eminent psychiatrists had found all the detainees to be suffering from mental health problems due to their lengthy detention and uncertain future. They remained in detention until their appeal was heard in the House of Lords over eighteen months later in December 2004. The UK was subjected to a serious terrorist attack in London on 7 July 2005.

The House of Lords held by a majority of eight votes to one that the conditions of indefinite detention of nine of the detainees without trial were unlawful as they invoked Article 3 Human Rights Act as amounting to inhuman and degrading treatment. Eight of the nine Law Lords in the judgment accepted the government's claim that the threat to the UK posed by Al Qaeda-related terrorism posed a 'public emergency threatening the life of the nation' within the meaning of Article 15 of the Convention. In the leading *Belmarsh* judgement Lord Bingham, who also gave the lead judgement in *Limbuela* clearly articulates the importance of the impartiality of the judiciary:

> It is of course true that the judges in this country are not elected and are not answerable to parliament. It is also of course true...That parliament, the executive and the courts have different functions. But the function of independent judges charged to interpret and apply the law universally recognised as a cardinal feature of the modern democratic state is a cornerstone of the rule of law itself. The Attorney-General is fully entitled to insist on the proper limits of judicial authority, but he is wrong to stigmatise judicial decision-making as in some way undemocratic. *(para 42)*

He goes on to confirm at paragraph 42 that the Human Rights Act 1998 gives the court "a very specific, wholly democratic mandate".

Having been charged by parliament with the task of reviewing the compatibility of government actions and legislation with fundamental rights, the court must ask hard questions of the balance that ministers and parliament strike in respect of counter-terrorism measures.

However, the Lords still held that such treatment constituted discrimination against non EU citizens in accordance with Article 14 Human Rights Act[18] and their decision illustrates the importance of the courts in holding fast to their independent constitutional role and acting as a check on legislative action. Lord Bingham also commented:

> The real threat to the nation is not terrorism but a Government which invokes 'acts of terrorism to restrict liberty'...the function of independent judges charged to interpret and apply the law is universally recognised as a cardinal feature of the modern democratic state, a cornerstone of the rule of law itself.

Lord Carlisle one of the five judges compared to the position of the British Government to that of the South African Government prior to the release of Nelson Mandela.

Tony Blair subsequently expressed doubt as to whether the above dictum would be issued after the bombings of 7 July 2005.

The Government's Reaction

Tony Blair abandoned any serious commitment to Human Rights after the terrorist attacks of 7 July 2005. The numerous proposals to combat "terrorism" including those contained within the Prevention of Terrorism Act 2005 made law in the UK on 30 March 2006 are based on the premise that further serious terrorist attacks will take place. "Let no one be in any doubt...the rules of the game are changing," Tony Blair.[19] These include:

1. the ability to remove non-nationals suspected of terrorist offences with exceptional/humanitarian/indefinite leave to remain in the UK, thereby breaching Article 3 of the Human Rights Act by accepting that such removal was likely to lead to death or torture.

2. the extension of the maximum limit of detention for those detained under suspicion of terrorism offences to twenty-eight days.[20]
3. the creation of the criminal offence to "glorify, exalt or celebrate terrorism" over the past twenty years carrying a maximum sentence of five years imprisonment.
4. The extension of control orders beyond foreign nationals to include UK citizens

The Act gives British police the toughest powers in Europe to detain suspects without charge. For example in France and Spain the maximum periods of detention are four and thirteen days respectively.

On 5 August 2005 the Prime Minister warned: "We will legislate further including, if necessary, amending the Human Rights Act in respect of the interpretation of the European Convention on Human Rights."

Legal Aid

Legal Aid in the UK is administered by the Legal Services Commission (LSC) which is part of the Department of Constitutional Affairs. Effective incorporation of Human Rights depends on adequate funding for legal representation. In effect the LSC acts as gatekeepers of justice and the Government has very effectively used the tool of reducing funding to deny access to justice. Neither the s 55 nor the Belmarsh decisions could have happened without the grant of Legal Aid to the individuals concerned.

Within the context of the both the overall reduction in the availability of Legal Aid and restrictions in immigration and asylum appeal rights including specifically in 2003 curtailment of the high court judicial review mechanism to scrutinise decisions, the cuts in funding for immigration work have been extreme.

In April 2004 the Government announced proposals to:

- withdraw devolved powers to grant Legal Aid from all but the largest suppliers
- introduce cost and/or time 'thresholds' limiting the amount of permissible contract work on a case without prior LSC authorisation
- withdraw funding for legal representation at Home Office interviews[21]
- require all immigration practitioners undertaking LSC funded work to achieve "accreditation" by passing two exams and a skills assessment.

After the effective introduction of these proposals in April 2005 further restrictions were introduced so that Legal Aid could only be granted retrospectively on a successful application for reconsideration by a High Court judge of a decision of the Asylum and Immigration Tribunal on an error of law AND reconsideration which supports the appellant.

The UK implementation of the EU Directive laying down minimum standards for the reception of asylum seekers from February 2005 is likely to fail to meet minimum provision in the area of the availability of legal assistance.[22]

Such reforms combine to exacerbate the difficulties for asylum seekers in accessing justice and for legal aid practitioners in running a cost-effective practice.

Although an alliance of lawyers and organisations worked together to retain limited high court scrutiny of decisions of the Asylum and Immigration Tribunal, the reductions in Legal Aid are now effective. This has led to: "many individuals being denied a vital human right, namely a fair hearing before an independent judiciary assisted by effective legal representation."[23]

The availability of Legal Aid for the s 55 cases enabled lawyers to launch such cases in the High Court whilst carrying out some pro bono research outside the scope of individual Public Funding Certificates even though in the majority of cases costs were finally met *inter partes* by the Home Department thereby keeping "public purse" expenditure to a minimum.

There are now 'advice deserts' in the UK (e.g. South Yorkshire and Humberside)[24] where practitioners are no longer willing or able to provide advice and assistance for little or no profit in refugee and asylum work. NGOs valiantly try to take up the challenge and the role of the pro bono advisor becomes ever more crucial in an ironic mirror of legal services provided by much poorer countries.

There is a persuasive argument that to deny non-English speaking appellants legal representation in Tribunals whose negative decisions will lead to their destitution is serious enough to engage Article 6 (1) Human Rights Act 1998.[25]

Conclusion

Many of the rights contained in the Human Rights Act are embodiments of the English common law tradition stretching back for centuries: the right not to be detained without lawful justification: to live with dignity and not be exposed to inhuman and degrading treatment: to have a fair trial.

A culture of Human Rights has **not** developed in the UK from the implementation of the Human Rights Act. Alvaro Gil-Robles, the Council of Europe's Commissioner for Human Rights prefaced his report on the UK by noting:

> That the UK government had introduced a series of measures on the very limit of what respect for human rights allows …..human rights are not a pick and mix assortment of luxury entitlements, but the very foundation of democratic societies.[26]

My own experience as both a practitioner and a clinical educator is that legislation can only ever reflect cultural mores. Sadly Aristotle's definition of law as "reason unaffected by desire" finds little common parlance today.

Whilst the intention of the Labour Party in opposition was genuinely to promote and improve the position of the oppressed individual within society, once in power and faced with the *"terror phenomena"* the agenda shifted. The success of the "s 55 campaign" rested on the positive decisions of the High Court in 2003/04 prior to 7.7. Since that date it has become far more likely that the judiciary may decline to interfere with a government decision or express doubts about the compatibility of legislation on the ground that the court is ill-placed to second-guess the 'institutional competence' of the executive or parliament on matters of national security. The event of 7/7 has accelerated the increasingly revisionist agenda of New Labour and as Tony Blair opined over the Belmarsh judgement, it is unlikely that either the s 55 cases or the decision in Belmarsh would be the same today.

Today the incorporation of human rights into domestic legislation in the UK fails to protect those most vulnerable sectors of the community—particularly asylum-seekers and now, notably, non-Christians against a political mainstream of increasingly xenophobic and reactive thought.

Helena Kennedy, a well-known QC and human rights activist in the UK states:

> Human Rights activists abroad are devastated to see the UK loosen the constraints we have placed upon the state because they lose one of their strongest arguments for change within their own systems. That is one reason why it matters so much when the Government is cavalier with the principles of justice and due process: many presidents or prime ministers around the world see parallels which would justify their abandonment of principle and process too.[27]

If rich Western countries fail to protect economic and social rights there is little hope for "developing " countries who cannot afford to do so without either large scale economic aid or rapid economic growth.

UK politicians and state officials justify their renegation from incorporation of Human Rights into domestic legislation as a response to mass opinion: the State is merely reflecting the concerns of its citizens over national security. To incorporate for effect alone has not assisted the vulnerable members of society but has brought about conflict between the legislature and the judiciary, confusion over the interpretation of judgements and a backlash leading to ever more restrictive legislation. The incorporation of human rights into the UK constitution has not guaranteed human dignity and the sentiments echoed in the Evian Conference nearly seventy years ago remain the same. The test for the UK judiciary today post 7/7 is to hold fast to its constitutional role in safeguarding those values enshrined in the Human Rights Act 1998.

[1] European Convention for the Protection of Human Rights and Fundamental Freedoms ('the Convention') Cmnd 8969 (1950).

[2] Keir Starmer, *European Human Rights Law* (London: Legal Action Group, 1999), 1.

[3] Lord Irvine, *Human Rights Bill* (1995, HL 2nd reading 3, November 1997)

[4] Labour Party Election Manifesto (1997).

[5] 7/7 - 7th July 2005 when 53 London commuters died and several hundred were injured as a result of 3 suicide bombings on public transport.

[6] Philip Marfleet, *Refugees in a Global Era* (London: Palgrave Macmillan, 2006), 280.

[7] Human Rights Act 1998 – Sched. 1, Art. 3: "Prohibition of torture" – no one shall be subjected to torture or to inhuman or degrading treatment or punishment.

[8] Nationality Immigration and Asylum Act 2002, section 55, enforceable from 8 (January 2003).

[9] *R(Limbuela) v Secretary of State for Home Dept* [2004] EWHC 219 (Admin).

[10] *Pretty v UK* [2002] 35 EHRR 1. Defines the threshold which must be crossed to establish "Article 3 destitution" as "ill-treatment that attains a minimum level of severity and involves actual bodily injury or intense physical or mental suffering".

[11] *R v Secretary of State for Home Dept ex p Adam, ex p Limbuela ex p Tesema* [2005] UKHL66.

[12] A. Sampson "Withdrawal of Support breaches asylum-seekers' human rights say Lords" Legal Action Group Bulletin (2005), 4.

[13] NASS Policy Bulletin 75: Section 55 (Late Claims) 2002 Act Guidance – Home Department, (August 7, 2006).

[14] Ibid., p. 3

[15] Katie Ghose, *Beyond the Courtroom: a lawyer's guide to campaigning*, (London: Legal Action Group, 2005), 29.

[16] E. Metcalfe, *Judges and terrorism after the 7.7 attacks*, Legal Action Group Bulletin (September 2005).

[17] *Ajouaou and A B C and D v Secretary of State for Home Dept* [2003] UKSIAC 1/2002 [2004]UKHL 56

[18] Human Rights Act (1998) Sched. 1, art. 14 – the prohibition of discrimination – 'the enjoyment of the rights and freedoms set forth in this Convention shall be secured without discrimination on any ground such as sex, race, colour, language, religion, political or other opinion, national or social origin, association with a national minority, property, birth or other status

[19] Press Conference 5 (August 2005), available at: *www.number-10.gov.uk*

[20] The period of 90 days was decided by a majority of 323 to 290 in the House of Commons on 9 November 2005, thereby defeating a previous Government proposal that detention be extended to 90 days.

21 This making it unlawful to support or fight in a revolution outside the UK even if it has aims generally supported within the UK.

[21] *R(Dirshe) v Sec State Home Dept* [2005]EWCA Civ241 CA - held that the presence of a representative …provided a safeguard against poor interpreting or inaccurate record-keeping. Without that safeguard there was a risk of procedural unfairness if tape-recording was not permitted.

[22] Council Directive 21/EEC of September, 2003 on the standard of accommodation for asylum seekers introduces a common policy for the reception of asylum seekers 'to ensure them a dignified standard of living and comparable living conditions in all member states'

[23] Bail for Immigration Detainees (BID) and Asylum Aid, *Justice Denied :asylum and immigration legal aid – a system in crisis: Evidence from the front-line* (June 2005).

[24] Report to the Department of Constitutional Affairs by Legal Services Commission (North West Area), November 2005.

[25] Sched. 1, Art. 6(1) Human Rights Act (1998) – Right to a fair trial 'in the determination of his civil rights and obligations….everyone is entitled to a fair and public hearing within a reasonable time by an independent and impartial tribunal established by law…'

[26] Report by Mr.Alvaro Gil-Robles, Commissioner for Human Rights visit to the UK, 4, (November 12), for the attention of the Committee of Ministers and the Parliamentary Assembly.

[27] Helena Kennedy, *Just Law* (London: Vintage, 2003), 56.

CHAPTER 15

ON CONSTITUTIONALIZING ENVIRONMENTAL RIGHTS

Rebecca M. Bratspies

Everyone has the right to enjoy and live in a healthy environment. This should be regarded as a fundamental human right, which is a prerequisite and basis for the exercise of other human, economic and political rights.[1]

Since the dawn of civilization, and more specifically since the industrial revolution, the environment had been treated as the "away" in the phrase "throw it away" —a residual dumping ground for all the poisons and hazardous byproducts of an industrial society. *Silent Spring*, Rachel Carson's 1962 indictment of DDT and other chlorinated pesticides[2] shattered social complacency with this status quo, sending tremors through American society, and indeed the world. Together with the first Earth Day in 1970,[3] Silent Spring marked the beginning of a period of intense awareness about the social consequences of pollution's toxic legacy. Along with the growing recognition of the adverse environmental consequences of economic activity came the conclusion that governments must act to protect their citizens from environmental harms.

Thus, nascent environmental regulation emerged from this period, generally as legislative responses to specific environmental catastrophes. Between 1970 and 1980, the United States enacted ten major environmental regulatory regimes that were often breathtakingly ambitious in scope. The Santa Barbara Oil Spill and the Cuyahoga River[4] fire led to the Clean Water Act's declared goal of eliminating all discharge of pollutants into navigable waters by 1985.[5] Love Canal[6] led to enactment of the Comprehensive Environmental Response, Compensation and Liability Act's (CERCLA or Superfund) to clean up closed and abandoned hazardous waste disposal sites;[7] and the Bhopal tragedy[8] to the Emergency Planning and Community Right to Know Act's institution of the Toxic Release Inventory.[9] A similar phenomenon occurred throughout the rest of the world as infamous incidents like the Minamata mercury poisonings[10] underlined a deep and growing anxiety about the results of pollution and environmental degradation. Despite these ambitious legislative initiatives, however, actual progress towards ensuring a cleaner and more wholesome environment was slow.

A 1985 British Antarctic Survey publication documenting a hole in the ozone layer[11] provided a much needed jolt to international complacency and ensured the successful negotiation that same year of the Vienna Convention for the Protection of the Ozone Layer.[12] Within two years, the details of this international agreement had been hammered out in the Montreal Protocol on Substances that Deplete the Ozone Layer,[13] which became effective in 1989. In contrast to the typically glacial pace of global treaty formation, this negotiating process was astonishingly rapid, and real-world behavioral changes were equally speedy. Indeed, the Montreal Protocol stood atop a transformative moment—it was no longer possible to deny that anthropogenic forces were changing the earth itself, and making it less conducive to human existence. (Today, global climate change is perhaps the most visible such concern.)[14]

With renewed urgency, states turned to environmental questions and negotiated a series of environmental agreements intended to halt and reverse environmental degradation.[15] Along with the UN charter, the Universal Declaration and the various tribunals that decide international law questions, this process has sometimes been termed the "constitutionalization" of international law.[16] Nevertheless, despite this proliferation of agreements, and dispute resolution mechanisms, there is an ongoing debate about the effectiveness of these multilateral environmental agreements.[17] Because these international agreements treaties tend to be long on glittering generalities but short on enforceable commitments to action, measuring effectiveness can be a challenge. Many treaty regimes have weak enforcement mechanisms and compliance is often spotty.[18] Moreover, diplomatic wording in many treaties papered over disagreements, producing agreements without actual consensus as to their meaning.

As a result, until recently, state determination to protect the environment often gave way to a willingness to degrade nature whenever material reward beckoned or whenever environmental features had no apparent monetary value. Decisions were based largely on material and economic calculations. The lack of moderation and balance embedded in this approach has grown more evident with each passing year. For this reason, alongside a growing body of domestic and international law governing environmental protection, there has been an unmistakable trend towards recognizing a right to a healthy environment. This trend finds reflection in the fact that almost every state constitution drafted or revised in the past 20 years has included an express textual recognition of the right to environmental protection.[19] Indeed, of the 191 member states of the United Nations, 131 have some kind of explicit environmental provision in their national constitution.[20] These provisions fall into three general categories, either: 1) protecting environmental rights as fundamental rights of individuals;[21] 2) instructing legislatures to provide environmental amenities, or to protect the environment for the benefit of current and future generations;[22] 3) guaranteeing citizens a right of access to environmental information and/or a right of participation in environmental decision-making.[23] A few constitutions do not provide for enforceable rights, but do include non-binding, aspirational statements of national policy.

Given this near universal incorporation of some form of environmental rights in national constitutions, it becomes important to explore the consequences that flow from constitutionalizing environmental rights. The decision to recognize environmental rights has far reaching ramifications. Echoing the Universal Declaration of Human Rights,[24] most national constitutions promise a "right to property"[25] and many also guarantee "a right to development."[26] Without a concomitant constitutional commitment to a safe and wholesome environment, society's basic compact is skewed towards short-term development demands at the expense of the environment.[27] This continues to be true even though in the medium and longer term, a safe and wholesome environment is the single most important condition for ensuring the long-term sustainability of that development. Including an environmental provision in a constitution can right this skewed analysis by placing environmental rights on equal footing with these other fundamental rights. Environmental rights thus serve as an expression of societal values in guiding interpretation of legislative and administrative mandates, much the same way that property rights do. The move to include environmental rights among the basic guarantees ensured by a constitution may therefore mark a profound normative shift in how humans view their relationship to the natural environment.

Each nation's constitution reflects that society's notion of ordered liberty, and together the striking convergence that these documents exhibit about environmental rights can be read as something of an international consensus.[28] While the ultimate normative significance of environmental constitutional provisions hinges on both the specific content of the provisions themselves, and on the constitutional environment in which these provisions are interpreted,[29] there are some general conclusions that can be drawn. This chapter will detail the rationales for including environmental rights in constitutions as well as the primary arguments opposing such rights. These arguments primarily flow from the notion that positive rights, including environmental rights, are either undemocratic or are too indeterminate to be judicially enforceable. The rest of this chapter will explore and reject the validity of these objections to environmental rights, before concluding with some of the significant advantages that come from constitutionalizing environmental rights.

Background: Constitutions as Constitutive Documents

A constitution is the "fundamental and paramount law of the nation,"[30] an expression of the will of the people that articulates the consensual basis for sovereignty.[31] It expresses the state's priorities of rights, obligations, and responsibilities, and in many ways marks a society's standard of legitimacy. As such, a constitution occupies a unique place in the national consciousness, delineating the institutions of government and the relationship between a state and its citizens. In many ways, the constitution embodies a society's idealized vision of a just state.[32] Not surprisingly, given this defining role, the scope and kinds of rights that should be included in a constitution has been a matter of vigorous debate.

Many scholars draw a line between negative constitutional rights (sometimes referred to as first-generation rights) and positive constitutional rights (also called second-generation or social rights).[33] Other theorists argue that the distinction is of questionable value in shaping the constitutional restraints on government power.[34] These latter scholars emphasize that a modern government's greatest power is often its ability to allocate or prohibit access to scarce resources. Under this reasoning, too great a focus on a positive/negative rights distinction misunderstands the myriad ways in which government can confer advantage or cause harm in the modern state.[35] To some extent, this positive/negative dichotomy is more dependent on how a particular right is characterized than on the inherent aspects of the right itself. Nonetheless, for purposes of this discussion, I am assuming that positive and negative rights can be sorted on the following basis: negative rights are those rights that involve limitations on state power while positive rights are those that involve invocation of state power. Thus an individual asserts a negative right to prevent governmental invasion of certain liberty or property interests and asserts a positive right to obtain access to certain governmentally-created or bestowed benefits. Negative rights can thus be characterized as a shield that can be used to protect a sphere of private autonomy from the power of the state.[36] Positive rights, by contrast, act more like a sword and can be invoked as an affirmative claim to substantive goods or services from the government. Environmental rights are typically characterized as positive rights—the right to demand that the state do, as opposed to refrain from doing, something.[37]

The United States Experience: Objections to Positive Rights

With the exception of the right to a jury trial (a right to which there have been increasing procedural hurdles obstructing easy access),[38] the United States constitution itself is typically considered to contain little in the way of positive individual guarantees.[39] Instead, the United States Constitution is viewed primarily as a charter of negative liberties—composed of various individually-held rights to demand that the government refrain particular actions.[40] Indeed, in various contexts the Supreme Court has announced that "the due process clause grants no affirmative rights"[41] and that "governmental inaction is not actionable."[42]

Perhaps not surprisingly given this predisposition, a string of federal decisions uniformly rejected suggestions that the United States Constitution might currently guarantee environmental rights.[43] More than once, amendments intended to expressly incorporate environmental protection into the federal constitution have foundered in congress.[44] That leaves the United States in a small class of nations with no environmental provisions in their national constitutions, and perhaps as a corollary, extremely hostile to the notion that the national constitution, or for that matter, the "law of nations,"[45] includes any environmental rights.

This unambiguous rejection of environmental rights as a foundational right in society stands in sharp contrast to much of the rest of the world and stems from a highly idiosyncratic vision of the propriety of positive rights in a constitution. The notion that constitutions are intended to enshrine only negative rights has assumed talismanic qualities in the United States. Negative rights, the theory goes, carve out spheres of activity that are to remain free from government intrusion, thereby creating the necessary pre-conditions for democratic governance.[46] Rights beyond this necessary minimum, however, are viewed as inconsistent with a democratic, market-oriented society. Thus, positive rights are characterized as a threat to democracy for many of the same reasons that negative rights are viewed as democratic safeguards. In addition to this objection to positive rights as anti-democratic, a second objection argues that these rights are indeterminate, and thus compromise the careful balance of power between the various branches of government. The next sections explore each of these contentions in turn.

Are Environmental Rights Anti-Democratic?

If democracy is understood to be the unadulterated will of the majority, then all constitutional rights, positive and negative, are equally vulnerable to attack as anti-democratic. If the actions of the legislature and the executive are viewed wholly as the will of the people, any interference with the expression of that will by definition thwarts majority rule. Taken to its extreme, a pure "majority rule" vision of democracy entirely discounts the democratic legitimacy of the judiciary because it would reject any system of checks and balances that places constitutional constraints on the legislature and the executive. Of course, few argue for such an interpretation.

Constitutional protection of civil and political rights is the foundation of democratic governance precisely because most agree that majorities (and markets) cannot be trusted to fully value them.[47] These foundational constitutional rights counterbalance this tendency to undervalue rights by incorporating them into the social contract that defines the powers of the legislature and the executive in the first instance. After all, it cannot be an effective criticism to point out that constitutional rights prevent the legislature and executive from exercising powers that have been constitutionally withheld from their purview. Thus, properly recognized constitutional rights do not undermine democracy even though such rights limit the contours of the constitutional powers that can be exercised by the legislature and the executive.

The more likely democracy-based argument against positive rights grows from the proposition that while some basic rights are necessary preconditions to make democracy possible, rights beyond those institutionally-necessary minima, particularly when the rights require the government to do something rather than refrain from doing something, amount to undemocratic constraints.[48] This is the realm in which much of the relevant discourse about environmental rights occurs.

The argument against including environmental rights in a constitution begins from the clear, though typically unarticulated, assumption that the existing array of rights is a result of, and therefore reflects, the majority's political will. Public choice scholars[49] and critical legal theorists[50] have, for different reasons, cast substantial doubt on this initial premise. Instead, both lines of reasoning suggest that the existing array of rights has at least as much to do with private power seeking its own advantage as with majoritarian values.[51] From Madison onward, thinkers have grappled with this dilemma and have concluded that while self-interested factions are inevitable, the key to preserving democratic governance is to craft a governmental structure that minimizes their influence.[52]

If a primary justification for enshrining civil and political rights (the conventionally sanctioned array of negative rights) in a constitution is a mistrust of the ability of the political process to otherwise secure these rights, that same reasoning suggests that environmental constitutional provisions are equally necessary. Where the justification for civil and political rights stems from the belief that majorities cannot be trusted to fully value such rights, it is a mistrust of the political process's abilities to consider and appropriately weigh environmental interests against economic claims that leads many to propose including environmental rights in a constitution.

Thus, by focusing attention on the structural barriers to achieving majority will on topics of environmental protection, the rationale justifying civil and political rights also offers a powerful argument for including environmental protection in constitutions. Overwhelming majorities of citizens routinely express the desire for clean air and water, safe disposal of toxics and biohazards and foods that are fit for human consumption.[53] Yet most governments have a poor track record of delivering these environmental goods. Expedience, and the power of small, well-funded interest groups, too often persuades legislatures to adopt environmentally unsound tradeoffs.

To answer that concern with a stricture that the best means to solve this problem is through the political process ignores the reason for the concern in the first place—that without constitutional environmental rights as a backdrop, the democratic process is incapable of protecting and preserving a healthy environment. To the extent that the observable failures of environmental protection stem from a structural flaw in how the democratic processes themselves function, a structural solution makes sense. The major contribution that environmental rights make is to elevate the environmental beyond "just another factor" in legislative and administrative horse-trading, thereby limiting the influence that lobbying groups and corporate special interests can wield *vis-à-vis* environmental protection. Such a course is profoundly democratic.

Are Environmental Rights Indeterminate

Another major criticism of the move to enshrine environmental rights in constitutions focuses on the alleged indeterminacy of such rights and the suggestion that enforcement of positive rights is beyond the institutional competence of courts.[54] This line of thinking is a logical corollary of the claim that environmental rights are undemocratic. It raises the possibility that full enforcement of constitutional environmental rights would put courts in the position of either demanding that legislatures enact legislation, or of creating environmental policies themselves in the absence of such legislation. Both options are posited to intrude on the legislative function, thereby disrupting the carefully constructed balance of power at the heart of constitutional governance.[55] United States courts have frequently expressed this concern, most fully articulated in *Tanner v. Armco Steel*:

> the judicial process, through constitutional litigation, is peculiarly ill-suited to solving problems of environmental control. Because such problems frequently call for the delicate balancing of competing social interests, as well as the application of specialized expertise, it would appear that their resolution is best consigned initially to the legislative and administrative processes. Furthermore, the inevitable trade-off between economic and ecological values presents a subject matter which is inherently political, and which is far too serious to relegate to the ad hoc process of 'government by lawsuit' in the midst of a statutory vacuum.[56]

It is true that many rights enshrined in constitutions are relatively absolute—for example, the right to be free from discrimination, or cruel and unusual punishment (or at least it seemed so before the so-called war on terror). In interpreting these rights, a court engages in no balancing of interests, or assessing costs and benefits. Instead, a court measures the challenged activities against the constitutional standard. Actions either violate the standards or not, and are accordingly either prohibited or not.

Environmental rights are different. Most supporters of environmental rights acknowledge that there is no absolute right to a healthy environment, but is instead a matter of degree.[57] We are largely unwilling to live in an unmodified environment as that would entail foregoing essentially all economic activity.[58] That fact alone, however, does not damn the attempt to draw fundamental boundaries around a right to a healthy environment. The right that emerges from this inquiry is in many ways akin to the right to property, which similarly exists within a social context that shapes the contours of the right. In both a right to property and a right to a healthy environment, there are often competing fundamental interests at stake. Thus, environmental rights, like property rights, typically involve balancing and proportionality—a right to be free from *unacceptable* harm.[59]

The specter of courts second-guessing every economic and scientific decisions is just that, a specter—an insubstantial shade that disappears under the bright light of examination. Courts interpreting environmental rights will do what they always do—examine records to make sure that government actors perform their constitutional duty, in this case protecting the environment to the fullest extent possible consistent with other countervailing constitutional duties. This inquiry will be no different than any other constitutional analysis. It is thus not up to a court to determine precisely the content of the term "a healthy environment" but to rigorously ensure that for any challenged administrative or legislative action, the state can make the necessary showings that it has not only fully considered the environmental effects but has also taken all reasonable and prudent steps to minimize those effects. Courts are as capable of that analysis as they are of scrutinizing any other state action that implicates a constitutional right. As Joseph Sax notes: "If environmental claims are to be taken as more than rhetorical flourishes or broad aspirational statements and are to be set in the context of rights, it is necessary to ask how they fit into the values underlying other basic rights."[60]

Moreover, even if there is some validity to this line of reasoning when a court is being asked to find an implicit environmental right in a constitutional text that does not provide for an explicit right, to argue that express environmental constitutional provisions are inappropriate on the ground that the necessarily delicate balancing of competing social interests is best left to the legislature misses the point. It was, after all, precisely an unwillingness to leave environmental rights to the legislature that prompted these constitutional provisions in the first place. By including such rights in a constitution, the people as ultimate sovereign, have instructed all branches of government that in making necessary trade-offs between economic and ecological values (or between private property rights and environmental rights) they are to accord full weight to both sets of concerns.

Of course, merely showing that the primary objections to incorporating environmental rights in a constitution can be overcome is not the same as offering a positive reason for choosing to incorporate such rights. The next section offers a positive agenda for environmental rights, arguing that such rights are necessary for a just society.

So, Why Have Environmental Provisions in a Constitution?

Environmental provisions can serve many vital roles in national constitutions.[61] After all, the institutional structures specified in a constitution inevitably shape the policies that a government produces. A constitution can entrench current social and political practices, either explicitly or by implication, to ratify a nation's existing identity. However, constitutions can also be a vehicle to transform social and political practices, thereby remaking a nation's identity.[62] As such, constitutions are far more than a mere recitation of rights and government structures, they are a site of the ongoing political contest to create or circumscribe social meaning.

Environmental rights tend to fall into this latter category. These constitutional provisions define a zone of environmental interests that cannot be compromised by governments looking to solve short-term problems. By doing so, these provisions impose a constitutional limit on the interpretation of other legal rights, thereby reshaping the terms of social debate over resource preservation or exploitation, and, in particular, recalibrating the proper balance between environmental and property rights.

A Social Justice Imperative for Constitutionalizing Environmental Rights

The United States' experience teaches us the difficulties of establishing claims for environmental justice in the absence of express constitutional rights guaranteeing a healthy environment or citizen participation in environmental decision-making. While these rights can be guaranteed by statute, and indeed are in the United States, there are reasons to be dissatisfied with such an approach. The more we learn about ecosystem functioning, the clearer it becomes that individual choices about consumption and land use influence the communal welfare in direct and dramatic ways. As a result, the traditional vision of property as absolute dominion increasingly runs into a web of regulation based on the reality that individual property choices, particularly those about exploiting or developing resources and consumption directly affect the property and liberty interests of others.[63] It is this recognition that often animates the drive to constitutionalize environmental rights.

Environmental challenges pose a classic "circumstance of justice" to use the Rawlsian term. There is a moderate and growing scarcity of resources (in this case environmental amenities such as clean air, clean water, safe foods, healthy ecosystems) a shared geographic territory, and a capacity for non-altruistic persons with conflicting claims to either help or harm each other.[64] However, attempts to exercise statutory environmental rights often conflict head on with constitutional property rights, at least as they have traditionally been interpreted. In the tug of war between property rights grounded in constitutional protection, and legislative environmental rights, the environment, and environmental rights holders often lose categorically. This imbalance can have serious and undesirable consequences because the unfettered exercise of property rights has often had serious environmental repercussions that are borne by society at large.

Moreover, the environmental burdens generated by private activity are not allocated equally across society. Instead it is the poorest and most vulnerable among us who face the most dangerous environmental situations and are least likely to have access to help or remedies. It is invariably the poor who live in the least wholesome environments. They are overwhelmingly more likely to be exposed as children to lead,[65] and throughout their lives to dangerous levels of heavy metals, toxics and other pollutants that have a disastrous immediate and long-term effect on health and welfare.[66] Without an environmental right to balance the scales, this inequity can be, and too often is, dismissed as a natural by-product of market forces.[67]

This problem of differential exposure to environmental harms exists within nation states[68] and between them.[69] The Basel Convention[70] and the POPS Treaty[71] are just two of the many recent attempts to stem the flow of dangerous and toxic chemical wastes from the global north to the global south.[72] While neither treaty expressly recognizes itself as vindicating the right to a healthy environment enshrined in the national constitutions of so many states, these treaties are in the vanguard of an emerging global norm embodied in these constitutional guarantees of a right to a healthy environment.

This emerging norm represents the basic conviction that poverty ought not be the criterion for distributing exposure to the sorts of human-generated toxic and hazardous wastes that create an unwholesome environment. It is for this reason that essentially every modern constitution addresses environmental rights in some fashion. A constitutional right to a healthy environment can be a powerful tool to challenge the existing distribution of environmental harms, and the power relationships that distribution embodies.

Removing Environmental Rights from the Realm of Politics as Usual

This brings me to the second justification for constitutionalizing environmental rights—such rights remove environmental protection from sole and complete dependence on the vicissitudes of power politics. This justification is in many ways the flip side of the objection explored above that environmental rights are undemocratic.

As already mentioned, the United States has an extensive set of environmental laws. Many of these laws have become models that are widely copied throughout the world. However, the rights provided by those statutes are continually under siege, both in the legislature and the courts, as incompatible with express constitutional guarantees, most particularly the right to property. This constant battle diverts energy away from the struggle over the content of environmental rights and has contributed to the failure of statutory environmental law to achieve its fundamental goal—the protection of human and ecological communities.

Obviously, including environmental guarantees in a constitution eliminates this entire strain of litigation and agitation, thus preserving resources and energy for the real fight—the appropriate content of these environmental rights, and the proper balance between competing constitutional imperatives when these environmental rights conflict with other constitutional rights.[73] Providing environmental rights at the constitutional level entrenches recognition of the importance of environmental protection and offers the possibility of unifying principles for legislation and regulation.

Such provisions respond to the structural limitations of existing constitutional rights that otherwise permit business interests to trump environmental issues, especially with regard to future generations, and act as a counterweight to development pressures that systematically and structurally devalue a healthy environment in favor of more easily quantifiable interests. With environmental rights included, the constitutional enterprise becomes an attempt to balance or harmonize competing constitutionally important interests. Thus, at root, a constitutional right to a wholesome environment can be a counterweight to the rights to property and development—a means for channeling these rights into sustainable paths. At the same time, certain types of environmental constitutional provisions enhance the possibility of democratic participation in decision-making.[74] Such provisions can empower legislatures by providing solid footing from which to pass laws aimed at furthering environmental protection. Thus, constitutional environmental provisions can expand the range of possible legislative responses to environmental challenges.

Adopting this perspective, the Philippine Constitutional Court interpreted Article 2 §16 of the Philippine constitution, which directs the state to "protect and advance the right of the people to a balanced and healthful ecology in accord with the rhythm and harmony of nature" broadly. In *Oposa v. Factoran*, a case challenging timber concessions as inappropriately granted, the court affirmed that environmental rights are enforceable, and noted that such rights were incorporated into the constitution:

> because of the well-founded fear of its framers that unless the rights to a balanced and healthful ecology and to health are mandated as state policies by the Constitution itself, thereby highlighting their continuing importance and imposing upon the state a solemn obligation to preserve the first and protect and advance the second, the day would not be too far when all else would be lost not only for the present generation, but also for those to come —generations which stand to inherit nothing but parched earth incapable of sustaining life. [75]

In short, the Philippine Supreme Court acknowledged that, in the absence of an enforceable constitutional provision to the contrary, it is all too easy for short-term economic considerations and powerful interest groups to trump environmental concerns.

Finally, environmental constitutional provisions affect the public's behavior by creating or altering social norms. Constitutional constraints influence how citizens conceive of themselves as social actors, and often guide the conduct of legal and political reform activities. After all, most people, most of the time, do not resort to courts to claim and enjoy their constitutional rights. By shaping the construction of social meanings, an environmental constitutional provision can influence the behavior of social actors in a fashion that makes resort to the police powers of the state to achieve environmental goals less necessary. *Oposa* is an example of this phenomenon. Though this ruling has hardly "solved" the problem of over-exploitation of natural resources in the Philippines, it has been influential in shaping environmental rhetoric and advocacy both in the Philippines and around the world.

Some Caveats about Environmental Constitutionalism and a Suggestion

It is easy to get carried away with the possibilities represented by environmental constitutionalism. Many nations have such a constitutional provision and yet still do not enjoy vital environmental amenities like clean air or clean water. It is not enough to merely declare as a matter of constitutional fiat that individuals or "the people" have a right to a healthy environment. Nor does judicial recognition of these rights alone guarantee anything—for example, the *Oposa* case did not transform timber practices in the Philippines where deforestation remains a pressing concern, nor did it even result in the cancellation of the challenged timber licenses. A clear-eyed and sober analysis of the possibilities of environmental constitutionalism must confront the futility of rights without power, and the cynicism that can be engendered by constitutional language that creates environmental expectations that either cannot be or are not fulfilled by governments.

While the critique applies to all levels of environmental protection, after all, many nations possess extensive environmental laws and regulations but still fall far short on providing their citizens with a wholesome environment, it has a special resonance in the context of constitutional rights simply because constitutions are so often perceived as foundational. There are unfortunately numerous examples from various countries of the right to a wholesome environment being honored wholly in the breach, or interpreted out of existence.[76] The reasons for this failure range from a lack of effective enforcement mechanisms, to corruption, to the pressures introduced by a need (perceived or actual) for development. Such situations raise the specter that an unenforceable right will diminish the constitutional project in its entirety by eroding trust in state institutions.

This same argument applies with equal force to other fundamental rights protected in constitutions —the discrepancy between the ideal and the real can undermine public confidence in law and engender public cynicism that is destructive to constitutional democracy. There is nothing about environmental rights that uniquely poses this challenge, and the risk, though real, is no more of an issue for environmental rights than for any other right, whether positive or negative, guaranteed by a constitution.

Obviously constitutional rights are not a panacea.[77] They are only as good as those charged with enforcing and respecting them. To a large extent, the drive to constitutionalize environmental rights has been built on the assumption that content will flow into the form once it is established. History has not always borne out this assumption. More attention must be devoted to how these constitutional environmental rights can be made meaningful, including developing strategies for legislative and administrative implementation, as well as ensuring for rigorous jurisprudential interpretation and oversight. States with plain and unambiguous constitutional language, and direct procedural access to courts are likely to lead the way.[78] It is in these states that environmental rights will fare the best and reach their highest potential. In this era of globalized communication and converging visions of law, the experience of these vanguard states may open a path that other states, with more ambiguous constitutional language, can follow in interpreting the scope of a constitutional right to a healthy environmental.

One way to implement the constitutional right to a healthy environment might be by using a substantive version of the relatively common environmental impact assessment (EIS) as a tool for assessing whether an environmental right has been violated or upheld. EISs are a common procedural device employed by governments worldwide as a means to manage and cope with environmental change.[79]

As a procedural device, EISs have their roots in the United States' enactment of the National Environmental Policy Act of 1969.[80] NEPA requires that every federal agency:

> include in every recommendation or report on proposals for legislation and other major Federal actions significantly affecting the quality of the human environment, a detailed statement by the responsible official on — (i) the environmental impact of the proposed action; (ii) any adverse environmental effects which cannot be avoided should the proposal be implemented; (iii) alternatives to the proposed action; (iv) the relationship between local short-term uses of man's environment and the maintenance and enhancement of long-term productivity; and (v) any irreversible and irretrievable commitments of resources which would be involved in the proposed action should it be implemented.[81]

From this domestic law beginning, the EIS process spread around the world.[82] By the time the United Nations convened its Conference on Environment and Development—the 'Earth Summit'—in 1992, the EIS process had gained international support. Indeed, Principle 17 of the Rio Declaration recognized the important role that EISs play in international law.[83]

At present, EIS's are most often performed to satisfy procedural rather than substantive requirements.[84] However, the EIS process need not be a mere "paper tiger."[85] There is nothing inherent in the EIS process that would prevent its adaptation to satisfy substantive requirements. Thus an expansive, or slightly creative, use of the EIS process may be the best means of achieving the goals embodied in environmental constitutional provisions.

For example, imagine if the EIS process was required as part of a substantive interpretation of constitutional provisions guaranteeing a right to a healthy environment. It is easy to see how this substantive EIS process would work. The government would have the obligation not only to assess environmental impacts by to fully minimize adverse environmental effects and consider whether alternative projects or sites, or additional mitigating measures would offer more protection for the environment as proposed without unduly curtailing non-environmental benefits.

Whenever a proposed governmental activity compromised an environmental right,[86] a more probing inquiry would necessary (much like other fundamental rights). The burden would be on the government to show that the actual balance of costs and benefits is necessary to a compelling government purpose and does not, on its face, insufficiently weigh environmental protection.

Thus, full recognition of a constitutional right to a healthy environment will at the very least, counteract notions that there is a right to unfettered exploitation of environmental goods. Many states already have begun down this path and are interpreting their constitutions in a manner vastly different than United States' stringent rejection of environmental rights.[87] For example, in 2004, the Costa Rican Supreme Court used the Constitution's Article 50 guarantee of a "healthy and ecologically balanced environment" to hold customs officials responsible for not cracking down on fishing vessels using local ports to ship shark fins.[88]

Conclusion

The most pressing environmental challenges—global climate change, loss of biodiversity, desertification, destruction of the ozone layer, the spread of toxics and pollutants throughout the world—are beyond the capacity of any single state to resolve. No nation can, by itself, create a healthy environment. Constitutional environmental provisions are certainly a start, but they are no more than that. Although such constitutional provisions may be a necessary part of a global response, they are not, in and of themselves, sufficient. International and global cooperation will be necessary. By setting a baseline of agreed rights for individuals, and especially by including environmental rights as a critical counterweight to the right of development, constitutional environmental provisions can play an important role in developing more propitious conditions for that cooperation.

[1] Fundepublico v. SOCOPAV, Ltda. Case No. T-101, Judgment No. T-415 (Republic of Columbia Constitutional Court, June 17, 1992)

[2] Rachel Carson, *Silent Spring* (1972)

[3] For general information about earth day, *see* Senator Gaylord Nelson, *How Earth Day Came About*, available at: http://earthday.envirolink.org/history.html.

[4] For more information about the Cuyahoga River incident, *see* EPA, Cuyahoga River Area of Concern, available at: http://www.epa.gov/glnpo/aoc/cuyahoga.html.

[5] 33 U.S.C.§ 1251(a)(1).

[6] A comprehensive collection of materials documenting the Love Canal saga is available at http://ublib.buffalo.edu/libraries/projects/lovecanal.

[7] 42 U.S.C §9601 et seq.

[8] Bhopal is considered one of the worst industrial accidents in modern times. At a Union Carbide pesticide plant (now owned by Dow Chemical) 45 tons of methyl isocyanate gas were released sometime during the night of December 2, 1984. The toxic cloud killed at least 3,500 persons immediately (estimates run to 20,000) and injured at least another three hundred thousand people. *See* James Kenneth Mitchell, *The Long Road to Recovery: Community Responses to Industrial Disaster* (United Nations University Press, 1996). The Indian government brought suit in the Southern District of New York on behalf of the victims, but the case was rejected on forum non conveniens grounds. *In re Union Carbide Corp. Gas Plant Disaster in Bhopal, India*, 809 F.2d 195 (2d Cir. 1987), cert. denied, 484 U.S. 871 (1987). In 1989, Union Carbide Corporation paid the Indian government $470 million in damages, but many lawsuits and criminal charges remain unresolved.

[9] 42 U.S.C.§11,001 et seq.

[10] Timothy S. George, *Minamata: Pollution and the Struggle for Democracy in Postwar Japan* (Boston: Harvard University Press, 2001).

[11] J. C. Farman, B. G. Gardiner, J.D. Shanklin, "Large losses of total ozone in Antarctica reveal seasonal ClO_x/NO_x interaction", 315 *Nature* 207 (May 16, 1985) (summarizing data collected by the British Antartic Survey showing that ozone levels had dropped to 10% below normal January levels for Antarctica). For more information, see www.theozonehole.com.

[12] Vienna Convention for the Protection of the Ozone Layer, Mar 22, 1985, T.I.A.S. No. 11,097, 1513 U.N.T.S. 293, 26 I.L.M. 1529 (1987).

[13] Montreal Protocol on Substances that Deplete the Ozone Layer, Sept. 16, 1987, S. Treaty Doc. No. 100-10, 1522 U.N.T.S. 3, 26 I.L.M. 1541, 1550 (1987).

[14] In 1992, the United Nations negotiated the Framework Convention on Climate Change (UNFCCC). United Nations Framework Convention on Climate Change, opened for signature May 9, 1992, S. Treaty Doc. No. 102-38, 1771 U.N.T.S. 164, 166. To implement the UNFCCC, the World Meteorological Organization and the United Nations Environmental Program established the Intergovernmental Panel on Climate Change as the international clearinghouse charged with collecting information to implement the Framework Convention on Climate Change. For more information, *see* http://www.ipcc.ch/. The Kyoto Protocol was negotiated to implement the UNFCCC. Kyoto Protocol to the United Nations Framework Convention on Climate Change, Dec. 10, 1997, 37 I.L.M. 22, *available at* http://unfccc.int/resource/docs/convkp/kpeng.html. In 2001, the Bush Administration famously withdrew from the Kyoto Protocol, throwing international efforts to combat climate change into chaos.

[15] According to at least one expert, there are over 700 multilateral environmental agreements that express some kind of binding commitment between states. Ronald B. Mitchell, "International Environmental Agreements: A Survey of their Features, Formation, and Effects", 28 *Annual Rev. Env. Resour.* 429 (2003). Significantly more than half of these agreements have been negotiated since 1972. Robert O. Keohane, Peter M. Haas, & Mark A. Levy, *The Effectiveness of International Environmental Institutions* (1993).

[16] Jürgen Habermas, *America and the World , A Conversation with Jürgen Habermas (with Eduardo Mendieta),* LOGOS 3.3 (Summer 2004), *available at* http://www.logosjournal.com/habermas_america.pdf

[17] *See, e.g.*, Carsten Helm & Detlef Sprinz, "Measuring the Effectiveness of International Environmental Regimes", 44 *J. Conflict Resolution* 630 (2000); Thomas Bernauer, "The Effects of International Environmental Institutions: How Might We Learn More", 40 *International Organization* 351 (1995). *See also* Report of the United Nations Conference on Environment and Development, Agenda 21, U.N. GAOR, 47th Sess., U.N. Doc. A/CONF.151/26 (1992), available at http://www.un.org/esa/sustdev/documents/agenda21/english/Agenda21.pdf [hereinafter Agenda 21].

[18] The effectiveness of multilateral environmental regimes depends on state (and regional) implementation of the legal principles and/or resource management practices adopted in the treaty. For a stark assessment of the failures on this front, *see* Report of the Secretary-General's High-level Panel on Threats, Challenges and Change, A More Secure World: Our Shared Responsibility, UN GAOR, 59th Sess., Supp. No. 565, UN Doc. A/59 (2004), para 52-58, available at: http://www.un.org/secureworld/report.pdf.

[19] For example, in 2005, France amended the preamble to its constitution to read "The French people solemnly proclaim their attachment to the Rights of Man and the principles of national sovereignty as defined by the Declaration of 1789, confirmed and complemented by the Preamble to the Constitution of 1946, and to the rights and duties as defined in the Charter for the Environment of 2004." 1958 Fr. Const. pmbl,, available at: http://www.assemblee-nationale.fr/english/8ab.asp. The French Conseil Constitutionnel has declared that rights enumerated in the Preamble have the full force of constitutional provisions. *See* Cons. const., July 16, 1971, J.O. July 18, 1971, 7114. Article 1 of the Charter for the Environment, which is now part of the French Constituion, guarantees "Each one has the right to live in a balanced and respectful environment of health." *Id.*

[20] A detailed breakdown of environmental provisions in national constitutions is on file with author.

[21] Fifty-four national constitutions contain the explicit and individual right to a healthy environment. For example, the constitutions of Angola, Peru, Ivory Coast, Costa Rica, Norway, Slovakia, South Africa and Portugal, *inter alia* guarantee every person a right to a healthy environment. Most of these constitutions contain an unfettered individual right. Some, like the South African constitution qualify the right with the phrase "through reasonable legislative and other measures." South Africa Const. Art. 4(b)

[22] More than 70 national constitutions impose a state duty to protect or preserve the environment ranging from Afghanistan to Zambia.

[23] For example, Art. 45 of the Slovakia Constitution provides: "Everyone has the right to timely and complete information about the state of the environment and the causes and consequences of its condition." Article 110b of Norway's Constitution provides: "In order to safeguard their right in accordance with the foregoing paragraph, citizens are entitled to be informed of the state of the natural environment and of the effects of any encroachments on nature that are planned or commenced."

[24] Universal Declaration of Human Rights, available at: http://www.un.org/Overview/rights.html.

[25] *Ibid.*, art. 17. Article 75(22) of Argentina's constitution incorporates the Universal Declaration and 9 other international human rights agreements into the state constitution. For the range of state constitutional provisions protecting the right to property, see e.g., United States Const., Amend. V ("No person . . . .shall be deprived of ...property without due process of law; nor shall private property be taken for public use without just compensation); Taiwan Const. Art. 15 ("The right to live, the right to work, and the right to own property shall be guaranteed to the people"); Japan Const. Art. 29 ("The right to own or to hold property is inviolable. 2) Property rights shall be defined by law, in conformity with the public welfare. 3) Private property may be taken for public use upon just compensation therefore"); Macedonia Const. Art. 8.1 ("The fundamental values of the constitutional order of the Republic of Macedonia are: . . .the legal protection of property.) Interestingly, another clause in that same constitutional provision also identifies "proper urban and rural planning to promote a congenial human environment, as well as ecological protection and development" as a fundamental constitutional value.

[26] The right to development is guaranteed by many modern constitutions including *inter alia* those of Oman, India, and Ethiopia.

[27] It was at the Stockholm Conference on the Human Environment that the linkage between human rights and the environment was first clearly articulated in the international legal arena. Stockholm Declaration of the United Nations Conference on the Human Environment, U.N. ESCOR, 21th Sess., pmbl. art. 1, at 1, U.N. Doc. A/CONF.48/14/rev. 1 (1973) ("Both aspects of a man's environment, the natural and the man-made, are essential to his well-being and to the enjoyment of basic human rights and the right to life itself.") The general assembly has not specifically proclaimed the existence of a right to a clean environment, although it ratified the Stockholm Declaration generally. The General Assembly has, however, on more than one occasion explicitly recognized a right to development. *See e.g.,* Declaration on the Right to Development, G.A. Res. 41/128, Annex, U.N., GAOR 41st Sess., No. 53, U.N. Doc. A/4/53 (Dec. 4, 1986); Alternative approaches and ways and means within the United Nations system for improvising the effective enjoyment of human rights and fundamental freedoms, G.A. Res. 34/46, U.N. GAOR, 34th Sess., Supp. No. 46 at 170: ¶ 8, U.N. Doc. A./Res./34/46 (1979). However, the Vienna Declaration and Programme of Action, U.N. Doc. A/CONF.157/23 (July 12, 1993), adopted at the 1993 World Conference on Human Rights cautioned that "[t]he right to development should be fulfilled so as to meet equitably the developmental and environmental needs of present and future generations."

[28] For an overview of the comparative law discourse, *see* Mathias Reimann, "The Progress and Failure of Comparative Law in the Second Half of the Twentieth Century," 50 *Am. J. Comp. L.* 671 (2002).

[29] For example, Martin Jänicke argues that the material, institutional and socio-cultural capacity of a country are more relevant predictors of environmental policies than is the presence or absence of a constitutional provision. Martin Jänicke, "Conditions for environmental policy success: An international comparison", 12 *The Environmentalist* 47 (1992).

[30] *Marbury v. Madison*, 5 U.S. (1 Cranch) 137, 177 (1803)

[31] For varied theoretical explorations of the role and form that popular consent takes in constitutional government, *see generally*, Alan Brudner, *Constitutional Goods* (Oxford University Press: 2004); Ronald Dworkin, *Sovereign Virtue* (Harvard University Press: 2000); Jurgen Habermas, *Between Facts and Norms*, trans. William Rehg (Polity Press, 1998); John Rawls, *Political Liberalism* (New York, NY: Columbia University Press, 1993); Robert Nozick, *Anarchy State and Utopia* (Basic Press, 1974); John Locke, "Second Treatise on Government" in *Two Treatises of Government*, ed. Peter Laslett (Cambridge Univ. Press, 1988),1690.

[32] *See*, Larry Siedentop, *Democracy in Europe* (New York, NY: Columbia Univ. Press, 2001), 96-97 ("there are some respects in which liberal constitutions have a fundamental impact on citizens' lives and mark out borders on the maps of their personal identity. Constitutions have this potential of creating provinces in the mind.") Jürgen Habermas, "Why Europe Needs a Constitution", 11 *New Left Review* 5, (Sept./Oct. 2001):14 and 17.

[33] *See* Craig Scott & Patrick Macklem, "Constitutional Ropes of Sand or Justiciable Guarantees: Social Rights in a New South African Constitution", 141 *U. Pa. L. Rev.* 1, (1992), 4 ("Social rights refer, at a minimum, to rights to adequate nutrition, housing, health, and education.") Susan Bandes, "The Negative Constitution: A Critique", 88 *Mich. L. Rev.* 2271 (1990): 2272. Some, like Philip Alston, plead for caution in creating new rights without becoming mired in this positive/negative dichotomy. Philip Alston, "Conjuring Up New Human Rights: A Proposal For Quality Control", 78 *Am. J. Int'l L.* 607 (1984).

[34] *See* Alan Gewirth, *The Community of Rights* 41 (1996); Mary Ann Glendon, "Interdisciplinary Approach: Rights in Twentieth-Century Constitutions", 59 *U. Chi. L. Rev.* 519, (1992): 537; *see also* Amartya Sen, *Resources, Values and Development* 313 (1984). ("(C)onsequential reasoning can justify--indeed require--many positive actions in pursuit of negative freedom . . . .") Seth F. Kreimer, "Allocational Sanctions: The Problem of Negative Rights in a Positive State," 132 *U. Pa. L. Rev.* 1293 (1984).

[35] Kreimer, *Allocational Sanctions, supra* note 34; Thomas H. Marshall, *Citizenship and Social Class* (Pluto Press, 1950). The ill-starred European Convention was built on T.H. Marshall's three-fold manifestation of citizenship as legal, political, and social/economic.

[36] Richard A. Epstein, "The Uncertain Quest for Welfare Rights", 1985 *B.Y.U. L. Rev.* 210 (1985); *see also* Nozick, *supra* note 31.

[37] If civil and political rights are first-generation rights, and social and economic rights are second-generation rights, there is also a so-called "third generation" of rights which is where environmental rights are typically categorized. For purposes of this chapter, however, the relatively arcane distinctions between second- and third-generation rights are irrelevant and I will use the term second-generation rights broadly to include environmental rights.

[38] United States Constitution, Amendment VI provides:

> In all criminal prosecutions, the accused shall enjoy the right to a speedy and public trial by an impartial jury of the State and district wherein the crime shall have been committed; which district shall have been previously ascertained by law; and to be informed of the nature and cause of the accusation; to be confronted with the witnesses against him; to have compulsory process for obtaining witnesses in his favor, and to have the assistance of counsel for his defense.

This amendment thus secures individuals a number of affirmative rights against the state.

[39] *See DeShaney*, 489 U.S. at 196 (holding that the Federal Constitution's due process clauses do not confer a positive right to government aid, "even where such aid may be necessary to secure life, liberty, or property interests of which the government itself may not deprive the individual"); *see also* Jackson 715 F.2d at 1203.

[40] See, e.g., *DeShaney v. Winnebago County Dept. of Social Servs.*, 812 F.2d 298, 301 (7th Cir. 1987) *affd.*, 489 U.S. 189 (1989); *Rogers v. City of Port Huron*, 833 F. Supp. 1212, 1216 (E.D. Mich. 1993) (noting that "the Constitution is a charter of negative rather than positive liberties" (citing *Harris v. McRae*, 448 U.S. 297, 318 (1980)); *Jackson v. City of Joliet*, 715 F.2d 1200, 1203 (7th Cir. 1983), *cert. denied*, 465 U.S. 1049 (1984) (same.) At least one of the United States has taken a different path in

interpreting its state constitution. *See, e.g., Goodridge v. Dep't of Pub. Health*, 798 N.E.2d 941, 959 (Mass. 2003) ("The individual liberty and equality safeguards of the Massachusetts Constitution protect both 'freedom from' unwarranted government intrusion into protected spheres of life and 'freedom to' partake in benefits created by the State for the common good.")

[41] *DeShaney*, 489 U.S. at 196.

[42] *City of Canton v. Harris*, 489 U.S. 378, 395 (1989) (O'Connor, J., concurring in part and dissenting in part).

[43] Indeed, US federal courts have repeatedly declined to interpret existing constitutional language to include any fundamental environmental rights. *Stop H-3 Ass'n v. Dole*, 870 F.2d 1419, 1429 (9th Cir.1989) (declining to find a fundamental constitutional right to a wholesome environment within the equal protection clause of the 14th amendment); *Izaak Walton League of America v. Marsh*, 655 F.2d 346 (D.C.Cir.,. 1981) (declaring that generalized environmental concerns do not constitute a liberty or property interest); *Ely v. Velde*, 451 F.2d 1130, 1139 (4th Cir., 1971) (same). In the early 1970's, a string of district court cases fleshed out this position, most notably *Gasper v. Louisiana Stadium and Exposition District*, 418 F.Supp. 716 (E.D.La.,1976) (stating that the courts have never seriously considered the right to a clean environment to be constitutionally protected under the 5th and 14th amendments); *Haggadorn v. Union Carbide*, 363 F.Supp. 1061 (D. W. Va.,, 1973); *Tanner v. Armco Steel Corp.*, 340 F. Supp. 532, 535 (S.D.Tex., 1972) ("The Ninth Amendment, through its 'penumbra' or otherwise, embodies no legally assertable right to a healthful environment."); and *Envtl. Def. Fund, Inc. v. Corps of Eng'rs of U.S. Army*, 325 F. Supp. 728, 738-39 (D.C.Ark., 1970) (holding that there is no Constitutional right to a healthy environment under the 5th, 9th or 14th Amendments), aff'd, 470 F.2d 289 (8th Cir., 1972), cert. denied, 412 U.S. 931 (1973). For a discussion of these cases, see Carole L. Gallagher, "The Movement to Create an Environmental Bill of Rights: From Earth Day, 1970 to the Present," 9 *Fordham Environmental. L.J.* 107, 112-17 (1997). Federal courts thus rely exclusively on an interstate commerce nexus as support for federal environmental legislation. Recent Supreme Court jurisprudence suggests that this reliance may be becoming tenuous. *See Rapanos v. United States*, 547 U.S.ref?? ___, 126 S. Ct. 2208 (2006); Solid Waste Agency of Northern Cook Cty. v. Army Corps of Engineers, 531 U.S. 159 (2001).

Where the United States Supreme Court has found that the "right to life" guaranteed in the Fifth and Fourteenth Amendments does not have an environmental component, the Indian Supreme Court has interpreted comparable language in Art. 21 of the Indian constitution to contain a right to a wholesome environment as an integral part of the right to life. *See Subash Kumar v. State of Bihar*, (1991) I.S.C.R 5 (India)(granting redress for a claim that environmental pollution violated the Indian Constitution's guarantee of a right to life.)

[44] E.g., H.R.J. Res. 1321, 90th Cong. (1968); H.R.J. Res. 1205, 91st Cong. (1970); S.J. Res. 169, 91st Cong. (1970) ("Every person has the inalienable right to a decent environment. The United States and every state shall guarantee this right."). By contrast, the constitutions of many individual states within the United States include some form of positive environmental rights. The state constitutions that phrase environmental rights most explicitly in terms of individual rights are Montana and Illinois. *See* Mont. Const. art. II §3 (All persons are born free and have certain inalienable rights. They include the right to a clean and healthful environment); Ill. Const. art. XI, §§ 1-2)("Each person has the right to a healthful environment. Each person may enforce this right against any party, governmental or private, through appropriate legal proceedings subject to reasonable limitation and regulation as the General Assembly may provide by law.") Many other state constitutions contain provisions relating to the environment ranging from explicit provisions securing environmental rights to "the people," *see* HAW. CONST. art. XI, §9; MASS. CONST. art XLIX; PA. CONST. art. I, § 27; to more general directions that the state protect environmental resources. *See, inter alia,* CAL. CONST. art. X; FLA. CONST. art. II, § 7; GA. CONST. art. III, § 6; LA. CONST. art. IX, § 1; MICH. CONST. art. IV §§ 51, 52.

[45] *Beanal v. Freeport-McMoRan, Inc.*, 197 F.3d 161 (5th Cir., 1999) (stating that because environmental treaties and agreements do not enjoy universal acceptance in the international community, and state merely abstract rights and liberties that cannot be the basis for establishing customary international law); *Flores v. Southern Peru Copper Corp.*, 414 F.3d 233 (2d Cir., 2003) (concluding that plaintiffs failed to demonstrate that high levels of environmental pollution within a nation's borders violate well-established, universally recognized norms of international law); *see also* Sarah C. Rispin, "Litigating Foreign Environmental Claims in U.S. Courts: The Impact of Flores v. Southern Peru Copper Corporation", 34 *Envtl. L. Rep.* 10,097 (2004) (noting difficulty for plaintiffs to find documented international law violated by corporations in environmental cases).

[46] Nozick, *supra* note 31.

[47] For this reason, there is almost unanimous agreement that constitutions must ensure universal suffrage, the right to free speech, and due process and equal protection of the law.

[48] Nozick, *supra* note 31.

[49] *See, e.g.*, James Buchanan, "Politics Without Romance: A Sketch of Positive Public Choice Theory and Its Normative Implications," in *The Theory of Public Choice*--II, ed., J. Buchanan and R. Tollison, (1984), 11 (suggesting that public choice theory replaces "a romantic and illusory set of notions about the workings of governments" with more realistic notions.) The basic insight of public choice theory is that small cohesive groups enjoy organizational advantages in the political process over diffuse majorities, and thus even nominally majoritarian political process may not produce majoritarian results. One can take public choice theory too far. For example, Farber and Frickey detail empirical studies suggesting that legislation is not a "mere commodity" sold to interest groups, but that legislators base their votes on an array of factors including ideology, institutional ambitions, and even conceptions of the public good. Daniel A. Farber & Philip P. Frickey, *Law and Public Choice* (Chicago: University of Chicago Press, 1991).

[50] There is a wealth of literature exploring the role that power and various interests including race and gender play in how law functions. Two good introductions are: Robert W. Gordon, "Critical Legal Histories," 36 *Stan. L. Rev.* 57 (1984); James Boyle, "The Politics of Reason: Critical Legal Theory and Local Social Thought," 133 *U. PA. L. REV.* 685 (1985).

[51] *See* Mark Seidenfeld, "A Civic Republican Justification for the Bureaucratic State," 105 *Harv. L. Rev.* 1511, 1565-66 (1992) (discussing the capture of the deliberative process by those with superior organization and funding).

[52] *The Federalist* Nos. 10 and 39 (J. Madison) (C. Rossiter ed. 1961).

[53] For example, a 2005 Harris poll reported that three in four U.S. adults (74%) agree that "protecting the environment is so important that requirements and standards cannot be too high, and continuing environmental improvements must be made regardless of cost." In addition, a plurality of adults (47%) agree that "there is too little government regulation and involvement in the area of environmental protection." "Nearly Half of Americans Cite 'Too Little' Environment Regulation," *Wall St. J.,* October 13, 2005. The poll itself is available at http://www.harrisinteractive.com/harris_poll/index.asp?PID=607. *See also* Special Environment Eurobarometer "Attitudes of Europeans towards the Environment" available at http://ec.europa.eu/environment/barometer/index.htm (surveying environmental opinions in 25 European states); *Only One-Third of Russians are Satisfied with the Environment,* Poll by the Public Opinion Foundation (June 14, 1999) *available at* http://bd.english.fom.ru/report/cat/az/E/environment/eof992405. For a more comprehensive treatment of this topic, *see* Riley E. Dunlap, "International Opinion at the Century's End: Public Attitudes Towards Environmental Issues," in *Environmental Policy: Transantional Issues and National Trends,* eds., Lynton K. Caldwell & Robert V. Bartlett, (Quorum Books, 1997), 201.

[54] *See e.g., Dandridge v. Williams*, 397 U.S. 471, 485 (1970) (concluding that administration of public welfare assistance "raises "intractable economic, social, and even philosophical problems" that "are not the business" of the Court); Cass R. Sunstein, "Against Positive Rights", *E. Eur. Const. Rev.,* Winter 1993, at 36 (claiming that a constitution cannot adequately protect the environment and cautioning that constitutions incorporating such rights threaten to become "mere pieces of paper, worth nothing in the real world"); *but see* Elizabeth F. Brown, Comment, "In Defense of Environmental Rights in Eastern European Constitutions," *U. Chi. L. Sch. Roundtable* 191 (1993) (arguing that environmental provisions in a constitution encourage long-term conservation); *see generally* Stephen Loffredo, "Poverty, Democracy and Constitutional Law," 141 *U. Pa. L. Rev.* 1277, (1993): 1388-89 (criticizing the Court's approach as ignoring the structural role of money in American politics).

[55] The identical objection, from a slightly different political perspective, terms this is a strategy of "hegemonic preservation" by a confluence of political, economic, and judicial elites. *see* Ran Hirschl, *Towards Juristocracy: The Origins and Consequences of the New Constitutionalism* (Cambridge, 2003), 11.

[56] *Tanner v. Armco Steel Corp.*, 340 F.2d 532, 536 (S.D. Tex., 1972)

[57] Professor Richard Lazarus aptly points out the perils of this generalization. "[T]here are individuals on both sides of the environmental protection debate who summarily reject any characterization of environmental lawmaking as the attempt to balance competing economic interests. Each camp views their position as being supported by absolute, not relative, rights. The right to human health. The right to a healthy environment. The rights of nature itself. The right to private property. The right to individual liberty and freedom from the will of the majority .... Each side tends to view the other as

beginning from an unacceptable moral premise." Richard J. Lazarus, *The Making of Environmental Law* (Chicago, IL: University of Chicago Press, 2004), 28.

[58] *See* Victor Flatt, *"This Land is Your Land (Our Right To The Environment)"*, 107 *W.Va L. Rev.* 1 (2004) (pointing out that environmental rights grow from a history and a context that shapes how those rights are interpreted).

[59] Stylianos-Ioannis G. Koutnatzis, "Social Rights as a Constitutional Compromise: Lessons from Comparative Experience", 44 *Colum. J. Transnat'l L.* 74 (2005).

[60] Joseph L. Sax, "The Search for Environmental Rights", 6 *J. Land Use & Envtl. L.* 93, (1990): 93-94.

[61] *See e.g.,* Edith Brown Weiss, *In Fairness to Future Generations: International Law, Common Patrimony, and Intergenerational Equity* (1989) (articulating the role of environmental constitutional provisions can play in preserving the environmental rights of future generations)

[62] For an interesting discussion of the myriad roles a constitution can play in society, *see e.g.,* Lawrence Lessig, "What Drives Derivability: Responses to Responding to Imperfection," 74 *Texas L. Rev. 839* (1997).

[63] *See Tahoe-Sierra Preservation Council, Inc. v. Tahoe Regional Planning Agency*, 535 U.S. 302 (2002).

[64] John Rawls, *A Theory of Justice*, (Oxford: Oxford University Press,1971), 126-130 (providing an overview of the circumstances of justice.) The environmental justice movement has produced a voluminous literature. A few articles worth reading include: Regina Austin & Michael Schill, Black, Brown, "Poor & Poisoned: Minority Grassroots Environmentalism and the Quest for Eco-Justice," 1 *Kan. J. L. & Pub. Pol'y* 69, 71 (1991) (discussing why hazardous waste facilities are more likely to wind up in poor communities)

[65] Rebecca Morley, "The Cost of Being Poor: Poverty, Lead Poisoning, and Policy Implementation" 295 *JAMA* (2006), 1711-1712; J. E. Dilworth-Bart and C.F. Moore, "Mercy Mercy Me: Social injustice and the prevention of environmental pollutant exposures among ethnic minority and poor children," 77 *Child Development* 247 (2006); (World Resources Institute, *Environmental change and human health* (1998-99).

[66] Laura Westra and Peter S. Wentz, *Faces of Environmental Racism: Confronting Issues of Global Justice. (*1995); Alan B. Durning, "Apartheid's Environmental Toll," *Worldwatch Paper* 95 (May 1990);. For information about the environmental justice movement in the United States, *see* Robert D. Bullard, *Dumping in Dixie: Race, Class and Environmental Quality* (Westview Press: 2000); Commission for Racial Justice, *Toxic Wastes and Race in the United States* (1987); GAO, *Siting of Hazardous Waste Landfills and Their Correlation with Racial and Economic Status of Surrounding Communities* (1983);

[67] Vicki Been and Francis Gupta, "Coming to the Nuisance or Going to the Barrios? A Longitudinal Analysis of Environmental Justice Claims", 24 *Ecol. L.Q.* 1 (1997).

[68] The phrase environmental justice formally entered the US federal lexicon in 1994 when President Clinton signed Executive Order No. 12,898 addressing "Environmental Justice in Minority and Low-Income Populations." available at 59 Fed. Reg. 7629 (Feb. 11, 1994). The environmental justice movement has taught us much about the unequal distribution of environmental risks. Recent events, as perhaps most graphically illustrated by Hurricane Katrina and its aftermath, underscore this lesson-- environmental burdens are not distributed equally across society. For a discussion of environmental justice, *see generally,* Luke W. Cole and Sheila R. Foster, *From the Ground Up: Environmental Racism and the Rise of the Environmental Justice Movement* (New York, NY: NYU Press, 2001); *see also,* Michele L. Knorr, "Environmental Injustice: Inequities Between Empirical Data and Federal, State Legislative and Judicial Responses", 6 *U. Balt. J. Envtl. L.* 71 (1997).

[69] For example, in a now-infamous 1992 memo, Lawrence Summers, then the World Bank's chief economist posed the question of whether the World Bank should be encouraging more migration of the dirty industries to less developed countries. Summers' rationale for this suggestion was that:

> [t]he measurement of the costs of health-impairing pollution depends on the forgone earnings from increased morbidity and mortality. From this point of view a given amount of health-impairing pollution should be done in the country with the lowest cost, which will be the country with the lowest wages. I think the economic logic of dumping a load of toxic waste in the lowest-wage country is impeccable and we should face up to that.

[70] Basel Convention on the Control of Transboundary Movements of Hazardous Wastes and Their Disposal, 28 I.L.M. 649 (March 22, 1989). In particular, the Basel Ban attempts to remedy this injustice by banning shipment of wastes from OECD countries to non-OECD countries. Basel Ban

Amendment, 34 I.L.M. 850 (Sept. 22, 1995). While the Basel Convention itself entered into force in 1992, the Basel Ban currently has sixty-one ratifications and sixty-two are needed for it to enter into force. *See* Secretariat of the Basel Convention, Status of Ratification, http://www.basel.int/ratif/frsetmain.php. The United States is one of three countries to have signed the convention but not ratified it. Haiti and Afghanistan are the others. *Id.*

[71] Stockholm Convention on Persistent Organic Pollutants (POPS), May 23, 2001, 40 I.L.M. 532 (2001), available at http:// www.pops.int/documents/convtext/convtext_en.pdf.

[72] For a detailed exploration of this topic, *see* Laura Westra, *Ecoviolence and the Law: Supranational Normative Foundations of Ecocrime* (Transnational, 2004).

[73] *See generally,* Penelope Andrews, "Evaluating the Progress of Women's Rights on the Fifth Anniversary of the South African Constitution," 26 *Vt. L. Rev.* 829 (2002): 835 (noting this same phenomenon with regard to other social rights enshrined in the South African Constitution.)

[74] *See supra* note 23.

[75] *Oposa v. Factoran, Jr.* GR No. 101083, 30 July 1993, 224 SCRA 792, 804-805. The court reached this conclusion even though the relevant language was found in the Philippine constitution's Declaration of Principles and State Policies rather than in the Bill of Rights. In reaching this conclusion, the court expressly rejected the contention that the challenge raised political questions best left to the legislature and executive branches of government.For an in-depth discussion of this case and its legacy, *see* Ma. Socorro Z. Manguiat and Vicente Paolo B. Yu III, "Maximizing the Value of Oposa v. Factoran", 15 *Geo. Int'l Envtl. L. Rev.* 487 (2003).

[76] For example, some courts have concluded that environmental provisions are not self-executing and are therefore unenforceable. For a brief introduction to the relevant cases in Hungary, Spain, and Turkey, *see* James R. May, "Constituting Fundamental Environmental Rights Worldwide", 23 *Pace Envtl. L. Rev.* 113 (2005). Korea has reached a similar result. Dae-bup-won [DBW] [Supreme Court] 94 ma 2218 (May 23, 1995) (S. Korea). In the United States, this has been true for many of the environmental provisions in state constitutions. For example, Article XI of the Virginia Constitution provides:

> To the end that the people have clean air, pure water, and the use and enjoyment for recreation of adequate public lands, waters, and other natural resources, it shall be the policy of the Commonwealth to conserve, develop, and utilize its natural resources, its public lands, and its historical sites and buildings. Further, it shall be the Commonwealth's policy to protect its atmosphere, lands, and waters from pollution, impairment, or destruction, for the benefit, enjoyment, and general welfare of the people of the Commonwealth.

This language has been interpreted not to be self-executing and therefore to be a mere indication of public policy principles. *Robb v. Shockoe Slip Fund,* 324 S.E.2d 674, 677 (Va. 1985). Interpreting similar provisions, the Illinois Supreme Court concluded that the constitutional provision created no new cause of action or remedies. *City of Elgin v. County of Cook,* 660 N.E.2d 875, 877 (Ill., 1995). A plurality of the Pennsylvania Supreme court expressed concern about whether such a provision could be considered self-executing. *Commonwealth v. National Gettysburg Battlefield Tower, Inc.,* 311 A.2d 588 (Pa. 1973) (finding that the relevant provision of the Pennsylvania constitution merely stated "the general principle of law that the Commonwealth is trustee of Pennsylvania's public natural resources with power to protect the 'natural, scenic, historic, and esthetic values' of its environment." Id., 594-95. Three years later, however, the same environment provision was held self-executing in the reverse situation -- that is, where it was asserted *against* the state. *Payne v. Kassab,* 361 A.2d 263, 272-273 (Pa., 1976).

For arguments criticizing the interpretation of environmental provisions as not self-executing, *see e.g.,* Richard O. Brooks, "A Constitutional Right to a Healthful Environment", 16 *Vt. L. Rev.* 1063 (1992): 1108; Lynda L. Butler, "State Environmental Programs: A Study in Political Influence and Regulatory Failure", 31 *Wm. & Mary L. Rev.* 823 (1990): 844-60; Lynton K. Caldwell, "The Case for an Amendment to the Constitution of the United States for Protection of the Environment," 1 *Duke Envtl. L. & Pol'y F.* 1 (1991); Robert A. McLaren, "Comment, Environmental Protection Based on State Constitutional Law: A Call for Reinterpretation", 12 *U. Haw. L. Rev.* 123, (1990): 136. For a powerful critique of reliance on judicial decisionmaking to achieve social change, *see* Gerald N. Rosenberg, *The Hollow Hope: Can Courts Bring About Social Change?* (Chicago, IL, Chicago University Press, 1991).

[77] For a powerful critique of the notion that constitutions can secure rights, *see* Hirschl, *Towards Juristocracy*, *supra* note 55.

[78] Costa Rica, for example guarantees that "[e]ach person has the right to a healthy and ecologically balanced environment." COSTA RICA CONSTITUTION, Art. 50. The constitution also guarantees procedural rights to enforce this provision. *See* Robert S. Barker, "Judicial Review in Costa Rica: Evolution and Recent Developments," 7 *Sw. J. L. & Trade Am.* 267, (2000): 279-82.

[79] *See generally* Nicholas A. Robinson, "International Trends in Environmental Impact Assessments", 19 *B.C. Envtl. Aff. L. Rev.* 591 (1992).

[80] Much to the dismay of many environmentalists, in *Robertson v. Methow Valley Citizens Council*, 490 U.S. 332 (1989) the US Supreme Court declared it "well settled that NEPA itself does not mandate particular results, but simply prescribes the necessary process." Thus, as implemented in the United States, NEPA's EIS process imposes only procedural burdens. What I am proposing is a substantive version of this process—one that examines results and not merely processes against an explicit constitutional right to a wholesome environment.

[81] National Environmental Policy Act, 42 U.S.C. §4332(c).

[82] Nicholas A. Robinson, "International Trends in Environmental Impact Assessment", 19 *B.C. Envtl. Aff. L. Rev.* 591 (1992) (describing the global expansion of NEPA)

[83] Principle 17 states: "Environmental impact assessment, as a national instrument, shall be undertaken for proposed activities that are likely to have a significant adverse impact on the environment and are subject to a decision of a competent national authority." Rio Declaration on Environment and Development, U.N. Doc. A/ CONF. 151/26 (vol. 1), *reprinted in* 31 I.L.M. 874 (1992).

[84] In Section 4331(c), NEPA explicitly states that "Congress recognizes that each person should enjoy a healthful environment." Where this NEPA language has been interpreted as wholly procedural and requiring no substantive outcome, a constitutional environmental provision could reshape the EIS process into NEPA with teeth. 42 U.S.C. §4331(c).

[85] *Calvert Cliffs Coordinating Committee v. Atomic Energy Commission*, 449 F.2d 1109, 1114-15 (D.C. Cir 1971) J. Skelly Wright.

[86] This chapter is not the proper place to explore the possibilities of horizontal application of an environmental constitutional right. For the reader interested in the possibilities of horizontal application, the best I can do right now is direct attention to the developing literature on horizontal application of other constitutional rights in Germany and South Africa. *See e.g.*, Christopher J. Roederer, "Post-matrix Legal Reasoning: Horizontality and the Rule of Values in South African Law", 19 *S. African J. H.R.* 57 (2003); Johann van der Walt, "Progressive Indirect Horizontal Application of The Bill Of Rights: Towards a Co-Operative Relation Between Common-Law and Constitutional Jurisprudence", 17 *S. African J. H.R.* (2001); "Federal Constitutional Court Affirms Horizontal Effect of Constitutional Rights in Private Law Relations and Voids a Marital Agreement on Constitutional Grounds", 2 *German L. J.* (2001) *available at* http://www.germanlawjournal.com/past_issues.php?id=61; *see also* Stephen Gardbaum, "The "Horizontal Effect" of Constitutional Rights," 102 *Mich. L. Rev.* 387 (2003).

[87] See, e.g., Thomas T. Ankersen, "Shared Knowledge, Shared Jurisprudence: Learning to Speak Environmental Law Creole (Crillo)", 16 *Tul. Envtl. L.J.* 807 (2003) (describing implementation of constitutional provisions concerning the environment in various Latin American countries.)

[88] Expedeiente 02-002197-0007-CO, Resolución 2002-04397 (Costa Rica). Article 50 had previously been used to stop other environmentally unsound practices. *See, e.g.*, Expediente 98-003684-0007-CO, Resolución 1999-01250 (Costa Rica) (finding that legislation authorizing annual harvest of sea turtles violated article 50); Expediente 01-011865-0007-CO, Resolución 2002- 2486 (Costa Rica) (finding that harvest a species of trees relied upon by the endangered green parrot violated article 50).

CHAPTER 16

READING BETWEEN THE LINES: JUDICIAL PROTECTION FOR SOCIO-ECONOMIC RIGHTS UNDER THE SOUTH AFRICAN AND UNITED STATES CONSTITUTIONS

*Susan N. Herman***

Introduction

Rights discourse can overstate the role of judicially-enforced constitutional rights in effectuating change; critiques of rights discourse can understate the role of the judiciary in implementing constitutional commitments.

The Constitution of the Republic of South Africa contains a number of provisions expressing a commitment to some fundamental principles of socio-economic justice. Sections 26 and 28 create certain rights in connection with the provision of adequate housing,[1] adequate health care, food, water, and social security,[2] and shelter, basic health care services, and social services for children.[3] One major issue that many of the authors of the papers in this book discuss is the extent to which the South African courts can truly be effective in ensuring the fulfillment of those commitments. Is it too much to expect a court to implement a commitment to provision of adequate shelter where there has not been sufficient political will or resources to provide shelter to the people who are resorting to litigation? Will a court's efforts necessarily be futile under such conditions? What is the proper role of the judiciary, as distinct from the political branches, in ensuring that such constitutional promises are kept?

Another issue discussed throughout this symposium is what, if anything, the South African courts can glean from the experiences of other countries in answering these difficult questions of role and responsibility. Some argue that there is nothing relevant in the experience of the United States because the United States Constitution does not guarantee socio-economic rights at all and so American courts have no role to play in promoting socio-economic justice. This is an overly hasty dismissal of a potentially useful comparison. First, even though the eighteenth century United States Constitution did not include any socio-economic rights, there is a strong argument to be made that the post-Civil War amendments reconstructing that Constitution, especially the Equal Protection Clause of the Fourteenth Amendment,[4] provided a basis for federal and hence for federal judicial protection of some socio-economic rights, which has simply been ignored by the United States Supreme Court. Second, the American judicial experience with racial discrimination provides a fruitful basis for evaluating the scope of judicial role in initiating social change in circumstances that are, in some respects, comparable if not truly similar to those in South Africa.

In this essay, I will first describe briefly some of the central questions of role confronting the South African Constitutional Court in interpreting sections 26 and 28. I will then discuss what I think is relevant in choices the American courts have made in battling racial discrimination. The Supreme Court has interpreted even the core of the Equal Protection Clause – protection against racial discrimination – as guaranteeing only a negative right (to be free from government discrimination) as opposed to an affirmative right (to have the government "protect" all persons against racial discrimination). The Warren Court, beginning with Chief Justice Earl Warren's landmark opinion in Brown v. Board of Education,[5] laid the groundwork for a more affirmative vision of what the promise of "protection" entails. But the political and judicial winds shifted radically and the current Court has adopted a blinkered view of the meaning of this guarantee that not only declines to pursue a greater measure of equality than the political branches deem sufficient, but can even prevent Congress from implementing visions of equal "protection" more robust than what the Court has found constitutionally required. In another area where the Court has addressed claims of unequal "protection" on the basis of race — jury selection — on the other hand, the Supreme Court has sought to implement a more affirmative interpretation of the right to be free from racial discrimination. Comparison of the Court's approaches in these two areas provides much grist for discussion about judicial role in implementing constitutional promises of equality, whether the issue is race or socio-economic well-being. I will then discuss my claim that the Equal Protection Clause of the United States Constitution does implicitly offer federal protection of socio-economic rights and explain why the American courts have played no role at all in effectuating that implicit guarantee.

Reflection on both these areas – varying judicial efforts to address racial discrimination and lack of judicial effort to address socio-economic inequality — suggests that, even if the courts cannot by themselves effectuate deep and lasting change, it is both important and worthwhile to include the judiciary, one of three branches of both the United States and South African governments, in national conversations about how to effectuate constitutional commitments. The South African courts can learn from the American judicial experience with combating racial discrimination in different contexts. The United States courts can learn from the South African judicial experience with respect to socio-economic rights, an area where the South African courts are themselves still learning.

The South African Constitution

The Constitution of the Republic of South Africa, written two centuries after the original United States Constitution and one century after the Fourteenth Amendment, was able to build on American as well as other countries' experience in Constitution drafting, both positive and negative. The drafters of the RSA Constitution decided to include explicit provisions not included in the United States Constitution — guaranteeing women's rights,[6] for example, as well as a cluster of socio-economic rights including those described above. Sections 26 and 28 provide good examples of constitutional commitment to providing basic shelter to all, and fuller protection to children. These sections invite people in need of housing to sue the government for not attending to their needs. They also invite interpretation. One well known case, Government of the Republic of South Africa and Others v. Grootboom and others,[7] involved 510 children and 310 adults who waited in a squatter settlement, some for as long as seven years, for the government to provide them with subsidized low-income housing. Despairing of government aid, they decided to occupy a vacant housing project but they were evicted for illegal occupancy and their property was destroyed, leaving them to live under plastic sheeting on a soccer field or in an overcrowded community hall. The Constitutional Court described some of these events as reminiscent of practices under apartheid,[8] the very model of government behavior the RSA Constitution foreswears. Interpreting section 26, the Court found that the State's housing program violated the Constitution with respect to those who are in immediate need, like Irene Grootboom and the other applicants in this case, and issued a declaratory order requiring the State "to act to meet the obligation imposed upon it by section 26(2)." At the same time, the Court declined to interpret section 26 as creating a minimum core entitlement to shelter, ruling instead that what was "reasonable" under the Constitution would have to be decided on a case by case basis.[9] While concluding that the obligation of section 26 had not been met in this case, the Court deferred to the coordinate branches of government to decide which of a range of potential responses to those obligations to adopt.

A landmark opinion like this, of course, attracts criticism from all directions. Some will argue that the Court has not done enough because it has declined to find a minimum core entitlement;[10] others will argue that the Court has done too much because it has not deferred entirely to the decisions of the political branches. And some of those who support government provision of shelter to people like Grootboom herself will argue that having the court force the government to provide housing to these applicants is not an effective long term strategy for generating a societal commitment to providing housing to all in need – a commitment that requires an allocation of resources only the legislature can provide.[11]

This is the same range of praise and critique that met the United States Supreme Court's opinion in its own landmark decision in Brown v. Board of Education.[12] That Court faced many of the same issues in interpreting the United States Constitution's Fourteenth Amendment as the South African Constitutional Court faced in interpreting section 26: 1) to what extent does the Constitution impose affirmative obligations on government, including the courts? and 2) when should a court defer to or include the legislature in effectuating a constitutional guarantee? For that reason, it is worth remembering some relevant United States constitutional history.

The United States Constitution Reconstructed

The eighteenth century framers of the original United States Constitution – James Madison and his founding brothers – had little or nothing to say about embedding aspirations toward a more equal society in a Constitution. The Constitution they created contained no reference to equality or even any provision affording women or those without property any right to vote. Most perniciously, due to a political compromise, the Constitution betrayed the Declaration of Independence's assertion that all men are created equal by countenancing slavery and counting slaves, for political representation purposes, as three-fifths of a person. Not only did enslaved people have no right to vote, they did not enjoy even three-fifths of the rights of other people. It was left to the individual states to decide what protection, if any, to offer them.

That Constitution was reconstructed in the nineteenth century following the American Civil War, an event somewhat comparable to the end of apartheid in the RSA. The Thirteenth Amendment ended slavery;[13] the Fourteenth Amendment superseded the three-fifths clause and included an Equal Protection Clause that introduced a general promise of equality before the law; eventually, the Fifteenth Amendment guaranteed a right to vote regardless of "race, color, or previous condition of servitude."[14] After these amendments, the states were no longer allowed to make their own unconstrained decisions about how equally to treat their residents. The United States Constitution limited their discretion and offered the federal courts as well as the federal Congress the opportunity and obligation to enforce those constitutional limits against recalcitrant states.

Ever since the Reconstruction Era, the question of the extent to which the Fourteenth Amendment limits the states has been one of the central conundrums of American constitutional law jurisprudence. The framers of the Fourteenth Amendment certainly intended the Equal Protection Clause to prevent states from choosing to write or implement their laws on the basis of race. It is also clear that Congress did not intend the federal government to be limited to effecting only formal equality. In the Fourteenth Amendment, more than anywhere else, Congress embedded its understanding of what had been won in the Civil War.[15] The Reconstruction Congress that drafted the Fourteenth Amendment was very much concerned with promoting racial equality beyond the political and legal spheres. That Congress was also concerned with promoting social and economic equality for the freed slaves and sometimes for others, and undertook an affirmative program of federal government provision of basic shelter and sustenance in the form of the Freedmen's Bureau.

However, while the American courts have actively debated the extent to which the Equal Protection Clause should be interpreted as providing an affirmative guarantee of racial equality, in the area of socio-economic justice, a concern implicit in the Fourteenth Amendment, American courts have essentially ignored what was written between the lines.

Affirmative Racial Equality

The American courts' role in the search for racial justice does bear out the argument of many of the authors in this book that Constitutions and the courts enforcing them cannot by themselves effect deep and lasting societal change. The United States Supreme Court decision in Brown v. Board of Education[16] is often given as an example of judicial good intentions failing to achieve results.[17] The Warren Court declared in grand style that racially segregated schools violated the Equal Protection Clause[18] but, fifty years later, racial segregation in American schools is still a pervasive problem.[19] Critics maintain that therefore Brown's promise has not been fulfilled.[20]

The failure to achieve greater success in integrating the schools can be attributed to a lack of political and social will to make racial integration a priority. It can also be attributed to the fact that the Supreme Court itself did not continue to actively pursue that goal. In the decades after Brown, the Court decided to declare victory over inequality as long as racial segregation in public schools is not de jure, even if it remains de facto, defining the constitutional guarantee of equal protection as requiring a formal equality of process, not equality of result.[21] The constitutional injury was redefined as a state action classifying on the basis of race, rather than as a state's failure to "protect" children from the harm of segregated education. The diminishing role of the federal courts in promoting actual integration may be one cause of the lack of progress in racially integrating schools; it is certainly a symptom of the lack of genuine political will to undertake radical change in this area. In such a political climate, the Supreme Court alone could not have achieved deep or lasting results even if it had not retreated.

Brown can also be described as a success story. First, the authority the Court provided to the lower federal courts in jurisdictions which had practiced de jure segregation led to marked changes in the schools in those jurisdictions. The federal courts in those areas did achieve a greater degree of integration than the political process yielded in areas not subject to federal court jurisdiction.[22] One prominent American constitutional law book describes the Court's efforts to administer the implementation of Brown v. Board of Education as "perhaps the most prolonged effort to address how far beyond de jure or purposeful discrimination the Equal Protection Clause should extend."[23] Of course, it remains to be seen to what extent those schools will revert to segregated patterns as the federal courts withdraw. In the long run, what may be the more important success of *Brown* is not any results the courts achieved in desegregating the schools, but the fact that the Court declared racial segregation to be contrary to the Constitution and therefore unequivocally wrong. By this declaration, the Court began a political and social dialogue on behalf of a politically powerless minority.[24] The Supreme Court, realizing that neither the states nor the coordinate branches of the federal government were likely to do so, shouldered responsibility for declaring racial segregation, at least when it was de jure, to be a form of inequality. This declaration began an active national conversation about the evils of segregation. The Court made a moral statement that children are entitled not only to formal equality (separate but equal schools that technically treat white and black children alike), but to "protection" against laws that insult their dignity by declaring that their education and even their worth can depend on their race.[25] We will never know whether, or when, state, local, or federal political actors might have taken up this cause without the Court's leadership, so it is impossible to evaluate how much of a difference the Court's decision actually made. It should not come as any surprise that the Court did not by itself resolve the deeply entrenched American problem of race relations. The Court did serve a critical role in helping to push American society further along the road to racial justice than the country was likely to have gone, at least at that time, without the participation of the judiciary, by acknowledging the problem as a failure of | constitutional commitment.

There is another area in which the United States Supreme Court has taken a more affirmative view of its own responsibility to promote racial equality. In a line of cases concerning racial discrimination in jury selection, the Court has shown a remarkable and consistent commitment to achieving racial integration of juries. The Court's interest in this area began in Strauder v. West Virginia,[26] a case brought shortly after ratification of the Fourteenth Amendment. In that case, the Court invalidated a West Virginia statute prohibiting blacks from serving on juries on the ground that it violated three kinds of equality rights: first, the right of prospective jurors not to be stigmatized on the basis of race, second, the right of black defendants, like white defendants, to be judged by a jury of their peers, and third, the right of defendants to have their life and liberty protected against racial discrimination.[27] This remarkable opinion did not actually lead to racially integrated juries because prosecutors were able to use peremptory challenges to prevent any black person from actually serving on a jury, especially in cases involving black defendants. Even the Warren Court was stymied by the use of peremptory challenges to conceal racial discrimination.[28] But a far more conservative later

Court, in the 1986 case of Batson v. Kentucky,[29] decided to take the next step and enlist trial judges in an active program designed to eliminate racially based peremptory challenges. Throughout changes in its composition, the Court has remained remarkably committed to this judicial affirmative action program for jurors. The Court has applied Batson to anyone, not just prosecutors, who attempts to exclude prospective jurors on the basis of their race.[30] In a 2005 decision, the Court conducted its own extensive analysis of the facts regarding certain peremptory challenges which a state court had found not to be based on race, disagreeing with the state court and the lower federal court's factual conclusions in a habeas corpus case,[31] a remarkable result given the current Court's deeply rooted concerns about federalism and finality.

As in Brown, the Supreme Court did not wait for the political branches to take action to effect more racially integrated juries but made its own declaration of principle. Unlike the recent post-Brown school cases, the jury selection cases show a Court which has not backed down and has continued to insist that the lower courts play an active role in identifying and curing racial discrimination, perhaps because the arena in the Batson cases is not schools, but the courts themselves. Together, these two lines of cases show a Supreme Court willing to take a proactive view of the meaning of racial equality, although not consistently, and willing, at the least, to take the lead in fighting formal inequality. These cases provide a great deal of grist for evaluating whether courts can be successful in implementing affirmative constitutional guarantees and whether, regardless of their ability to achieve deep or lasting success unilaterally, they should try. Declaring a right may not be enough to precipitate immediate and lasting results, but it may be better than not declaring a right at all.

Affirmative Socio-Economic Equality

With some notable exceptions during the Warren Court era, American courts have failed even to confront the parallel and equally difficult issues concerning socio-economic justice that the South African Constitutional Court grappled with in Grootboom. Some of the authors of this book debate to what extent socio-economic rights should be viewed as justiciable, and to what extent courts are competent to make or effectuate ostensibly political judgments involving allocation of resources. American courts have stayed out of the area of socio-economic rights not because of theories about institutional competence, but because of assumptions about lack of authority. The American Constitution, it is said, takes no position on socio-economic rights and therefore affords no role for the courts to play. There are no rights.[32]

Although the Supreme Court has consistently chosen limiting constructions of the Fourteenth Amendment, there has always been sufficient basis for finding the Equal Protection Clause of the Fourteenth Amendment to provide authority for requiring governmental "protection" of the poor. The framers of the Fourteenth Amendment had economic as well as political equality in mind during the drafting process, as shown by the debates surrounding the creation and continuation of the Bureau of Refugees, Freedmen, and Abandoned Lands, commonly known as the Freedmen's Bureau, which supervised much of the transition from slavery to freedom in the South.[33]

The Freedmen's Bureau

W.E.B. Du Bois described the Freedmen's Bureau as "one of the most singular and interesting of the attempts made by a great nation to grapple with vast problems of race and social condition."[34] Congress enacted the Freedmen's Bureau Act[35] on March 3, 1865, during the month before President Lincoln's assassination. Lodged within the War Department, the Bureau's mandate was to manage abandoned lands, to provide freedmen and refugees with shelter and provisions, and to redistribute parcels of abandoned, confiscated, or federally owned lands to loyal refugees and freedmen – the legendary "forty acres."[36] The members of Congress offered a range of justifications for this Act – it was viewed as an attribute of war (because the destitute freed slaves flocked to the Union Army seeking help), as an implementation of the Thirteenth Amendment (then in the process of being ratified),[37] or as simple justice. In addition to providing basic sustenance and a fulcrum for reestablishing the rule of law in the South, the Bureau began redistribution of land under this Act. When General Sherman issued his famous field order providing some freed slaves with forty acres per family of land in the Sea Islands and other portions of South Carolina and later offered the loan of mules, the phrase "forty acres and a mule" flickered throughout the South,[38] embodying the expectation that what DuBois called "poetic justice" would be done: freed slaves would farm the land formerly belonging to their masters.[39]

While the Bureau did accomplish "something,"[40] its mission of land redistribution was doomed to failure by subsequent events.[41] The Bureau was given no budget.[42] The legal status of the abandoned and confiscated lands was unclear. And there was considerable ambivalence, not only among white southerners, about whether it was more important to provide the freedmen with land, or to get Southern agriculture up and running.[43] Perhaps most significantly, President Andrew Johnson, succeeding Lincoln, decided to prioritize pardoning southern landowners, whose lands were then restored to them.[44] This policy resulted in eviction of freedmen who had been settled on those lands[45] and a presidential order to the Freedmen's Bureau to stop distributing land.[46] A restoration model was replacing the ideal of Reconstruction.

The Reconstruction Congress fought back. The Freedmen's Bureau Act was due to expire one year after the end of the war. In December of 1865, a bill was introduced to renew and expand the Act to make the rights it guaranteed more secure. Also in December 1865, Congress began to consider Representative Bingham's proposal to enact a new constitutional amendment to establish a clear and solid basis for federal action on behalf of the emancipated slaves – what ultimately became the Fourteenth Amendment.[47] In February 1866, Congress voted to approve a new expanded version of the Freedmen's Bureau Act, including a right to redistribution of land, establishment of schools, and military assistance to secure the freedmen's rights. The bill was vetoed by President Andrew Johnson and Congress was unable to muster enough votes to override his veto.[48] Congress also passed a Civil Rights Act in April of 1866, creating mechanisms for federal protection for a wide range of civil rights. President Johnson vetoed this bill too, but Congress overrode his veto and then went on to repass the Freedmen's Bureau Act and, this time, to override Johnson's veto.[49]

One of President Johnson's chief complaints in his veto message was that he did not believe that the Constitution, even including the Thirteenth Amendment (which had by then been ratified), conferred sufficient power on Congress to pass these acts.[50] The efforts of the Freedmen's Bureau, some argued, were not appropriate federal action once the war had ended. It was while these debates were taking place that Congress agreed on the text of the proposed Fourteenth Amendment, which was designed to secure a clear basis for their legislative actions beyond that secured by the Thirteenth Amendment and beyond actions dependent on an exercise of federal war powers. While the Civil Rights Act is often the focus of attention when commentators discuss the intent of the Fourteenth Amendment's framers, the provisions of the Freedmen's Act, the first American welfare bill, were also very much on the table and very much on the minds of members of Congress during the discussions of the need for a Fourteenth Amendment.[51]

Throughout congressional discussions of the mandate of the Freedmen's Bureau, the idea that the freedmen deserved "protection" kept recurring.[52] The purpose of the Fourteenth Amendment was to embed in the Constitution itself the understanding that Congress and the Amendment's ratifiers had of the "fruits of the Civil War."[53] Although Congress had initially viewed the Freedmen's Act as temporary,[54] both reenactments of the Act, in 1866 and then in 1868,[55] recognized that even though the war was over, the freedmen were still in need of economic as well as political protection. Congress clearly recognized that Reconstruction was a dynamic process[56] and evidently intended to afford itself sufficient authority, under the enforcement provision of the Fourteenth Amendment,[57] to take whatever measures it believed "appropriate," as time went on, to enable the freedmen to become self-supporting as well as to guarantee them the right to equal treatment under state law.

As northern political will failed and social resistance among white southerners grew, Congress lost the will to exercise that authority. The composition and mood of Congress changed substantially as the former Confederate States were readmitted and their representatives reseated. A later Congress might have been able to resume the Reconstruction project, political climate permitting, if the Supreme Court had not sealed the retrenchment by deciding several cases taking the narrowest possible view of federal and congressional powers under the Fourteenth Amendment. In The Slaughterhouse Cases,[58] the Supreme Court declared the Fourteenth Amendment's Privileges and Immunities Clause to be too hollow to support claims against a state for violations of rights. The "privileges" of United States citizenship, according to the Court, amounted to little more than a right to travel to the seat of the federal government to register a complaint. States were prohibited from erecting a barricade on the road to the nation's capital, but were not prohibited from denying their residents the kinds of rights Congress had almost certainly intended by including this seemingly capacious guarantee in the Fourteenth Amendment.

In The Civil Rights Cases,[59] the Court held that the language of the Equal Protection Clause only prohibited states from taking an active role in racial discrimination and therefore did not protect the broader right of individuals to be free from discrimination. Declining to take an affirmative view of the meaning of providing equal "protection," the Court found that Congress did not have authority under the enforcement section of the Fourteenth Amendment to prohibit denial of access to public accommodations on the basis of race and therefore invalidated the Civil Rights Act of 1875. Discrimination by a non-state actor, the Court ruled, was merely private action, not cognizable under the Equal Protection Clause, and therefore beyond the reach of Congress. States were not required to provide protection against private racial discrimination; Congress was not allowed to provide protection against this form of discrimination either.[60] Like The

Slaughterhouse Cases, The Civil Rights Cases have never been overruled, despite having been subjected to extensive criticism.

The Warren Court and Socio-Economic Inequality

In a celebrated article written in 1969, Professor Frank Michelman argued that the Supreme Court had been wrong in The Civil Rights Cases, and that under the Fourteenth Amendment, the government should have a duty to protect individuals against certain hazards rather than merely having a duty to avoid complicity in unequal treatment.[61] Michelman argued that poverty is a form of inequality and that the courts therefore should be regarded as having authority, based on the Equal Protection Clause, to help "move us towards a condition of economic equality."[62]

Michelman was able to cite a number of cases where the Warren Court had taken the initiative, as it had in Brown, to promote greater equality for the poor. These decisions sought to minimize the extent to which poverty can impede or preclude participation in the political process[63] or fair access to the criminal justice system.[64] He recognized that interpreting the Fourteenth Amendment as providing "minimum protection" would have significant consequences. First, the courts would be involved in correcting some conditions that a more formal articulation of equal protection would tolerate (as in Brown). Second, "[m]inimum protection is likely to demand remedies which cannot be directly embodied in judicial decrees,"[65] either because of justiciability concerns or because legislative action would sometimes be an essential complement to a judicial ruling.

Rather than moving closer to Michelman's view, the Court backed away from the Warren Court's forays into the area of economic equality. When the Warren Court era ended, the mood of the Supreme Court shifted in a manner that has deepened with the continuing changing composition of the Court. Over the past thirty years, although continuing to preserve limiting decisions like The Civil Rights Cases, the Court has, at best, circumscribed even the limited equality rights the Warren Court declared.[66] In a recent series of cases, the Court has even dramatically narrowed the power of Congress by announcing that Congress may generally only use its Fourteenth Amendment enforcement powers to promote equality in situations where the Court would have found a denial of Equal Protection.[67]

As Michelman recognized, and as co-authors of this volume agree, a regime of constitutional rights and judicial review is not a panacea. And a decision to provide the courts with some role does not resolve, as the Grootboom Court understood, questions about the proper scope of the court's role. Important questions about the sweep of justiciability doctrines and about the relative institutional competence of court and legislature remain. But the fundamental premise that the courts do have a role to play in promoting socio-economic as well as racial equality inheres in both Constitutions. The American Supreme Court has abdicated any responsibility to promote socio-economic rights, has sharply limited its own role in promoting racial and other forms of equality, and is actively impeding the ability of Congress to adopt a more robust vision of equality. The South African Constitutional Court has the opportunity the American courts have squandered to play a positive rather than a negative role in the quest for equality. It is easier for that Court to play a role in implementing a vision of a more just society because the socio-economic rights of the South African Constitution are explicit and are explicitly affirmative. It also helps that the South African Constitution is only ten years old, so judges are less likely to be accused of misapprehending the intent of the framers. Indeed, some of those framers went on to serve on the Constitutional Court.

Conclusion

I have argued that under the United States Constitution, like the South African Constitution, there is sufficient authority for courts to raise their voices in the national debate about the rights of the poor. I have not yet offered my own answer to the question of why the courts should seize that opportunity in both countries.

I do believe that substantial and lasting change in the law – whether with respect to race relations, land distribution, or economic entitlements – can only occur if it is accompanied by sufficiently deep changes in society itself. The experiences of the United States after the Civil War and of South Africa after the end of apartheid show that even a profoundly transformative event may not result in a lasting societal commitment to follow through on promised change – like the redistribution of land. In drafting a Constitution, framers may accurately express their constituents' altruistic intentions to help the victims of slavery or of apartheid to build new lives. But when the personal costs of living up to that commitment become apparent, political will can and usually does dissipate. Self-interest, partisan politics, and inertia can all erode the inclination of political actors to live up to earlier promises, no matter how sincere those promises were at the time they were made. It is for that reason that both the United States and South Africa, after transformative and wrenching events, embodied their deeply held beliefs in a Constitution and assigned the responsibility for interpreting that Constitution to politically insulated courts. A Constitution is like a marriage contract, demanding that we follow through on our commitment even at moments when we would prefer not to be reminded of promises that conflict with our very human desires.

Some of my co-authors ask whether judicial involvement in socio-economic matters can be justified. I think that presumption should be reversed. If a Constitution confers socio-economic rights, whether explicitly or implicitly, we should have to provide justification for excluding one branch of our government from the conversation about the meaning of those rights. With three branches of government working on a problem, the odds of someone getting it right may be multiplied.

[1] Constitution of the Republic of South Africa § 26 provides:
"(1) Everyone has the right to have access to adequate housing.
(2) The state must take reasonable legislative and other measures, within its available resources, to achieve the progressive realisation of this right.
(3) No one may be evicted from their home, or have their home demolished, without an order of court made after considering all the relevant circumstances. No legislation may permit arbitrary evictions."
[2] Constitution of the Republic of South Africa § 27.
[3] Constitution of the Republic of South Africa § 28.
[4] "[N]or shall any State . . . deny to any person within its jurisdiction the equal protection of the laws." U.S. CONST., amend. XIV.
[5] 347 U.S. 483 (1954).
[6] Constitution of the Republic of South Africa § 9(3).
[7] 2000 (11) BCLR 1169 (CC), 2000 SACLR LEXIS 126.
[8] Id. at ¶ 32.
[9] Id. at ¶ 43.
[10] See, e.g., David Bilchik, "Giving Socio-Economic Rights Teeth: The Minimum Core and Its Importance," S. African L.J. 119 (2002): 484.
[11] For an interesting description of the government's response to Grootboom, see Theunis Roux, "Legitimizing Transformation: Political Resource Allocation in the South African Constitutional Court" (paper presented at a Workshop in Bergen on "The Accountability Funciton of Courts in New Democracies," November 2002), available at http://www.law.wits.ac.za/cals/lt/pdf/norway_paper.pdf.
[12] 347 U.S. 483 (1954).
[13] "Neither slavery nor involuntary servitude, except as a punishment for crime whereof the party shall have been duly convicted, shall exist within the United States, or any place subject to their jurisdiction." U.S. CONST., amend. XIII, § 1.
[14] U.S. CONST., amend. XV, § 1.
[15] Eric Foner, Reconstruction: America's Unfinished Revolution (New York: Harper/Collins Perennial Classics, 2002), 251.
[16] 347 U.S. 483 (1954).
[17] See, e.g., Gerald Rosenberg, The Hollow Hope: Can Courts Bring about Social Change? (Chicago: University of Chicago Press, 1991).
[18] The Court took a dynamic view of the meaning of the Equal Protection Clause, finding a violation despite the fact that when the Fourteenth Amendment was framed, many states, even northern states, and Congress itself provided segregated or no education for black children. See Richard Kluger, Simple Justice (New York: Vintage Books, 1976), 633-34.
[19] See Gary Orfield and Chungmei Lee, Racial Transformation and the Changing Nature of Segregation (Cambridge, MA: The Civil Rights Project at Harvard University, 2006), 19, available at http://www.civilrightsproject.harvard.edu/research/deseg/deseg06.php.
[20] Rosenberg, The Hollow Hope.
[21] See Keyes v. School District, 413 U.S. 189 (1973). Subsequent cases also narrowed the grounds for federal court intervention. See, e.g., Board of Education of Oklahoma City v. Dowell, 498 U.S. 237 (1991).
[22] Orfield & Lee, "Racial Transformation and the Changing Nature of Segregation."
[23] Kathleen M. Sullivan and Gerald Gunther, Constitutional Law, 15th ed. (New York: Foundation Press, 2004), 697.
[24] A number of scholars have suggested that Brown sparked the civil rights movement, leading to a wide array of federal civil rights legislation. See Michael Klarman, "Civil Rights Law: Who Made It and How Much Did It Matter?" Georgetown Law Journal 83 (1994): 433, 452 n. 91.
[25] For another view of the meaning of Brown and its achievements, see Taunya Lovell Banks, "Brown at 50: Reconstructing Brown's Promise" Washburn Law Journal 44 (2004): 31, 63-64.
[26] 100 U.S. 303 (1880).
[27] Id. at 306-09.
[28] See Swain v. Alabama, 380 U.S. 202 (1965).
[29] 476 U.S. 79 (1986). The procedure the Court established in Batson requires the trial court to determine whether there is a race-neutral explanation for a peremptory challenge if any party can make out a prima facie case that peremptory challenges are being used to exclude members of any cognizable racial group.

[30] See *Edmonson v. Leesville Concrete Co.*, 500 U.S. 614 (1991) (applying *Batson* to civil cases); *Powers v. Ohio*, 499 U.S. 400 (1991) (white defendant can raise claim to vindicate equal protection rights of black prospective jurors); *Georgia v. McCollum*, 505 U.S. 42 (1992) (applying *Batson* to a criminal defendant's peremptory challenges). *See* Susan N. Herman, "Why the Court Loves *Batson*: Representation-Reinforcement, Colorblindness, and the Jury" *Tulane Law Review* 67 (1993): 1807 (explaining *Batson* as the Supreme Court's procedurally based response to perceptions of racism in the criminal justice system that the Court is unwilling to address more directly).

[31] *Miller-El v. Dretke*, 545 U.S. 231 (2005).

[32] The Court has held that the government may not explicitly discriminate against poor people, *Edwards v. California*, 314 U.S. 160 (1941) (invalidating a California law against bringing indigents into the state). Explicit formal discrimination against the poor is not usually the problem.

[33] *See* Horace Edgar Flack, *The Adoption of the Fourteenth Amendment* (Buffalo: William S. Hein & Co., Inc., 2003), 11 (arguing that in order to understand the Fourteenth Amendment, it is "necessary" to begin with an account of the Freedmen's Bureau Act and Civil Rights Act of 1866).

[34] W. E. Burghardt Du Bois, "The Freedmen's Bureau," *Atlantic Monthly* 87 (1901): 354-65, *available at* http://history.eserver.org/freedmens-bureau.txt.

[35] U.S. Statutes at Large, 38th Congress, Session II, ch. 90, pages 507–09.

[36] The commissioner was given discretion to "protect" loyal refugees and freedmen in the "use and enjoyment" of tracts of land not larger than forty acres, for three years at a rent not exceeding six percent of the appraised value. After that time the occupants could purchase the land. Freedmen's Bureau Act of 1865, § 4.

[37] The Thirteenth Amendment's prohibition of slavery, in its first section, was accompanied by a second section providing that "Congress shall have the power to enforce this article by appropriate legislation." U.S. CONST. amend. XIII, § 2.

[38] Foner, *Reconstruction*, 70.

[39] Du Bois, "Freedmen's Bureau." In Du Bois's account, as time went on, poetic justice was translated into prose. *See also* W.E.B. Du Bois, *Black Reconstruction* (New York: Russell & Russell, 1935) 220-27.

[40] John Hope Franklin, *Reconstruction after the Civil War* (Chicago: University of Chicago Press, 1994), 36.

[41] Foner, *Reconstruction*, 143, 158-63.

[42] Id. at 69.

[43] Id. at 153, 156.

[44] Id. at 176-227. Foner describes Johnson as having in effect "abrogated the Confiscation Act and unilaterally amended the law creating the Bureau." Id. at 161.

[45] Id. at 162.

[46] Id. at 159.

[47] Michael Kent Curtis, *No State Shall Abridge* (Durham: Duke University, 1986), 57; Foner, *Reconstruction*, 251-61.

[48] Foner, *Reconstruction*, 245-51.

[49] Id. at 246-51. The House of Representatives also impeached Johnson for refusing to execute the laws as drafted. Franklin, *Reconstruction After the Civil War*, 69-78.

[50] Flack, *Adoption of the Fourteenth Amendment*, 17-18.

[51] Id. at 11-54.

[52] *See, e.g.,* Foner, *Reconstruction*, 148, 159, 169; Du Bois, 'The Freedmen's Bureau.'

[53] Foner, *Reconstruction*, 251. "The aims of the Fourteenth Amendment can only be understood within the political and ideological context of 1866. . . ., the Amendment's central principle remained constant: a national guarantee of equality before the law." Id. at 257.

[54] Id. at 69, 167.

[55] *See* Du Bois, *Black Reconstruction*, 227-30.

[56] Foner, *Reconstruction*, 258.

[57] "The Congress shall have power to enforce, by appropriate legislation, the provisions of this article." U.S. CONST. amend. XIV, § 5.

[58] 83 U.S. 36 (1873).

[59] 109 U.S. 3 (1883).

[60] Decades later, the Court upheld legislation prohibiting racial discrimination in public accommodations based not on Section 5 of the Fourteenth Amendment but on Congress's Commerce Clause power. See *Heart of Atlanta Motel v. United States*, 379 U.S. 241 (1964).

[61] Frank I. Michelman, "Foreword: On Protecting the Poor Through the Fourteenth Amendment," *Harvard Law Review* 83 (1969): 7, 9.

[62] Id. Michelman's view that the Equal Protection Clause authorizes the Court to address the problem of the inequality of the poor would complement the implicit authority given to Congress under Section Five of the Fourteenth Amendment to promote the equal protection of the poor in legislation like the Freedmen's Bureau Acts.

[63] E.g., *Harper v. Virginia State Bd. of Elections*, 383 U.S. 663 (1966) (finding that it is a denial of equal protection to condition the right to vote on payment of a poll tax); *see* Michelman, "On Protecting the Poor," 24-25.

[64] E.g., *Griffin v. Illinois*, 351 U.S. 12 (1956) (requiring state to provide transcripts to those who would be too poor to take an appeal otherwise); *Douglas v. California*, 372 U.S. 353 (1963) (requiring provision of appellate lawyers to the indigent); *see* Michelman, "On Protecting the Poor," 25-33.

[65] Michelman, "On Protecting the Poor," 39.

[66] For example, the Warren Court found that indigent criminal defendants have the right to appointment of counsel in felony cases, in the landmark case of *Gideon v. Wainwright*, 372 U.S. 335 (1963). The Court extended that holding to defendants charged with misdemeanors. *Argersinger v. Hamlin*, 407 U.S. 25 (1972). As the composition of the Court changed, the Court put an end to the right to counsel, ruling that indigent defendants have no right to counsel unless they are actually sentenced to incarceration; *Scott v. Illinois*, 440 U.S. 367 (1979); and no right to counsel in post-conviction challenges; *Ross v. Moffitt*, 417 U.S. 600 (1974).

[67] The Court held, for example, in *Kimel v. Florida Board of Regents*, 528 U.S. 62 (2000), that Congress had exceeded its constitutional authority in allowing state employees to seek damages for the state's violation of their rights under the federal Age Discrimination in Employment Act. See also *Board of Trustees of the University of Alabama v. Garrett*, 531 U.S. 356 (2001) (invalidating Congress's attempt to provide a damages action for state employees denied rights provided in another federal civil rights statute, the Americans with Disabilities Act).

** Thanks to Penelope Andrews and Susan Bazilli for organizing the extraordinary conference that generated this book, to Tim Stapleton for his research assistance, to Ursula Bentele and Paul Gangsei for their contributions to this paper, and to Brooklyn Law School for its generous research stipend program.

CHAPTER 17

IMPLEMENTING THE SOCIAL AND ECONOMIC PROMISE OF THE CONSTITUTION: THE ROLE OF SOUTH AFRICAN LEGAL EDUCATION

Peggy Maisel and Susan R. Jones

Introduction

Currently, progress towards social and economic justice is South Africa's greatest challenge. This is complicated by an AIDS pandemic, a catastrophe that perpetuates the pain of poverty and economic inequality. The South African Constitution recognizes socio-economic rights as a necessary foundation for the enjoyment of civil and political rights. The challenge is translating these rights into opportunities for social and economic advancement by the vast majority of South Africans living in poverty.

The South African Constitution, one of the most progressive in the world, contains many important protections such as the rights to equality, housing and education.[1] The Broad-Based Black Economic Empowerment Law (BEE), discussed later in this chapter, was designed to address the economic inequities of apartheid.[2] South Africa's commitment to economic justice is also evidenced by the fact that it is a signatory to the International Covenant on Economic, Social and Cultural Rights (ICESCR) which recognizes the "right of everyone to an adequate standard of living for himself, and his family, including adequate food, clothing and housing, and to the continuous improvement of living conditions."[3]

Lawyers are among the most highly educated professionals in every society and are needed to support and lead the transformation away from poverty and inequality by helping to actualize these constitutional provisions and international covenants.[4] For this to occur, however, law students must learn about how law can be used as a tool to promote, rather than inhibit, social and economic development, and they must gain the skills, values, and knowledge to assist.[5] Under apartheid, law schools educated lawyers to maintain a system of subordination, but even with governmental change, the economic system remains virtually the same.[6]

This chapter first identifies ways in which legal education must continue to change in order to educate lawyers who are able to assist with South Africa's development. Second, it analyzes the contributions of clinical legal education since apartheid and some of the obstacles to its growth. Third, the chapter discusses community economic development (CED) law school clinics in the United States and the ways they may provide new ideas for South African legal education. Finally, the chapter discusses specific CED opportunities that exist in South Africa. The article argues that legal education in contemporary Africa must relate to the development needs of the country. In fact, the South African clinical movement is advancing this perspective.

Changes in Legal Education Post-Apartheid

A 1993 article suggests three needed substantive and procedural changes in legal education to support the new South African political democracy.[7] The first change is for the black majority to be demographically represented in law schools, and therefore eventually in the legal profession. The second need is for a radical change in pedagogy away from large lecture classes.[8] The third change is curriculum reform to teach law students to engage with constitutional rights and to know how to enforce them. The article agrees that law students must learn about human rights, particularly the rights of women, the disabled, homosexuals, children, the aged and the environment. These concepts as legal rights were new to most South Africans in 1993 and had not been taught in most law schools. In the past thirteen years, however, it has become clear that law students must also learn about the socio-economic rights and laws designed to promote economic justice if they are to contribute to the development of South African communities.

A 2002 critique of legal education in Africa further recognizes the problems created by a system of curriculum design, including pedagogy, that mirrors the British common law or European civil law educational systems developed in an entirely different socioeconomic cultural context.[9] In South Africa the received legal system is a combination of English and Roman-Dutch law. The law courses under apartheid did not reflect the development needs of the society, and the training of lawyers was based on teaching geared to an "adversary setting catering to litigation for the fortunate few at the cost of social injustice to the deprived many."[10]

There has been progress in changing legal education over the past ten years of constitutional rule but there is still a long way to go. Clinical legal education has been at the forefront of curriculum and pedagogical change. Law school clinics have also contributed to providing more opportunities for black students to obtain articles and thus be better represented in the profession.[11]

In its broadest definition, clinical legal education implies pedagogy which requires law students to think and act like lawyers.[12] It usually has a social justice focus, and includes in-house live client clinics, externships, community education projects, simulation courses, and other skills courses. All of these curriculum reforms exist to some degree at South African law schools. This chapter focuses on the opportunities provided by the university based law clinics, where final year law students work with clients, while enrolled in a course for credit. However, the other types of courses mentioned above are also important to preparing law students to contribute to socio-economic change.

For example, Street Law courses exist at many South African law schools, where law students teach about human rights, including socio-economic rights, at secondary schools, prisons and juvenile detention centers.[13] The Street Law students not only learn about these rights in their law school classrooms, but spread this knowledge through their teaching in the community.

The teaching of legal skills, such as legal analysis, problem solving, legal research and writing, is also critical in the first three years of law school.[14] This preparation is necessary before law students enroll in law clinics during their final year, otherwise clinical faculty are forced to teach these skills for the first time in the context of working on client cases.

An example of a strong skills curriculum is one developed by the University of Kwa-Zulu Natal (UKZN) law faculty in 2000 as part of its LLB degree.[15] The students take at least one skills course each semester. In the first year there are two courses taught in small groups called Introduction to Law and Foundations of South African Law.[16] The latter course also introduces all first year students to critical constitutional issues with sections on the right to equality, access to justice, and HIV/AIDS. In the second year, the curriculum covers computer skills, legal research, numeracy and legal drafting.[17] Third year students learn interviewing, counseling, negotiation and transactional skills.[18] In the fourth year, the students choose between the Legal Clinic, Street Law, or a course called Teaching Legal Skills. In the latter course the final year students learn how to tutor the first year students in small groups on the legal skills taught in the Introduction and Foundation courses.[19]

One of the reasons given for the difficulty in changing pedagogy from the large classroom lecture method to smaller interactive classes is the shortage of law faculty.[20] The Teaching Legal Skills course and a companion legal education course for LLM students help to increase faculty resources for legal skills teaching.[21]

The Expansion of Law School Clinics

The expansion of South African law school clinical programs has been an important step in educating law students about social justice issues and providing legal services to poor communities. The first law school clinic started at the University of Cape Town in 1971.[22] Under apartheid this clinic was a voluntary effort on the part of law students and lawyers to provide free legal services to the poor and not a part of the curriculum. Since the end of apartheid, law school clinics have been established at every law school with students participating for credit as part of final year coursework.[23]

The educational goals of clinics are, first, to add balance to the law school curriculum with the introduction of poverty and development law issues into a curriculum that has historically ignored these subjects in favor of commercial and middle class interests. Second, to improve legal education by taking students out of a passive classroom learning environment to instead actively engage with clients, learning the skills of lawyering such as interviewing, negotiating and performing legal analysis, while confronting the ethical issues that are raised in legal practice. Further, in legal clinics students receive individual and small group supervision that provides one to one learning. Finally, law school clinics expand the resources available to poor people and communities.

Because of the lack of Legal Aid Board (LAB), resources the South African law school clinics have primarily focused on civil cases where clients would otherwise be unrepresented.[24] These are issues vital to people's survival, and include public benefits, such as shelter, family matters and civil rights. As this chapter suggests, an important expansion to this work would be to introduce more clinics with a specific focus on community economic development.

Challenges to Implementing Curriculum Reform and Clinical Education

There are still substantial barriers to the development of law school clinics and curriculum reform, in spite of a supportive government and the commitment of some within the university. The biggest problem is that legal clinics are more expensive than classroom courses and clinics receive limited, if any, financial support from their universities.[25] Related is a lack of some faculties' understanding of clinical legal education as a vital component of a law school curriculum and what is required for its success. In addition, there is the need to build capacity within all law schools, but particularly those previously disadvantaged schools, so that clinical programs can provide high quality legal education and legal services. Finally, there is the pressing need for free legal services in South Africa, which makes it more difficult to control caseloads and achieve both the educational and service missions of the law school clinics.

When the Constitution was adopted, legal clinics existed at all twenty-one law schools. There was a great disparity in resources, however, between clinics at historically black universities (HBU's) and those at historically white universities privileged under apartheid.[26] Some clinics functioned with few resources, inexperienced directors, and limited support. In the past ten years, clinical law faculty and their supporters have successfully implemented several strategies to overcome these obstacles.

The most important strategy has been the formation and effective work of the Association of University Legal Aid Institutions (AULAI), whose members include all of the law school clinics.[27] AULAI was formed in the late 1980s, but became active in the mid 1990s when it ran a national conference on clinical education. Since then the organization has successfully raised funds, lobbied law schools and the government on legal aid policies and curriculum development, and provided program support and training at workshops twice a year. In 1998, AULAI established a separate Trust to help fund and support the development of clinical education throughout South Africa.[28] The Trust raises funds from donors to distribute among the twenty-one university based law clinics, on a basis determined by the Trust Board, that is composed of directors committed to clinical education, from academia, non-governmental organizations, the private sector and government. This Trust is a model that does not exist in any other country and has helped sustain and build the law clinics, by increasing their staff. Special attention has been paid by the Trust to the needs of clinics at the HBUs. Unfortunately, the Trust endowment has been almost completely spent and the problem remains how to sustain both the Trust itself and the clinics it supports. The stability and continued growth of law clinics is central to achieving the educational goals of preparing law students to promote constitutional rights and economic justice.

New Opportunities for Law School Clinics

Law school clinical faculty have also worked to maximize the impact of the legal work of the clinics, and in the process teach students how to find solutions for some of South Africa's pressing social and economic justice issues. One effective strategy has been for law clinics to specialize in their legal work. For example, in 1996 the legal clinic at the University of Natal in Durban was a general practice clinic with a high caseload of divorces.[29] The new Director of the clinic led a strategic planning process in 1997, resulting in establishing three units focused on priority work: The Gender and Children's Rights Unit focused on domestic violence cases; the

Administrative Justice Unit focused on HIV/AIDS cases and police abuse; and the Development Law Unit on development issues.

The Development Law Unit has represented land claimants since 1997, enforcing rights under statutes passed pursuant to the new Constitution.[30] It has also engaged in assisting micro-businesses. One of the clinic's first cases was to represent 2,500 applicants who had been removed during apartheid from an area of prime real estate called Cato Manor.[31] This case is an example of how law students can learn about economic justice by engaging in development work. The Director of the Clinic described some of the case lessons learned, including the importance of interdisciplinary collaboration; a lesson which is usually missing from law courses.

> We started by embarking on what was at first a desperate search for a historian who would paint a clearer picture for us and an urban planner who would understand the planning implications of the application.......We realized that we as lawyers were not going to be able to do this on our own. A technical legal approach would not work. It was clear that a holistic approach that included social processes, participation of clients and members of other disciplines was needed.[32]

A second effective strategy for increasing the impact of legal work has been for the law clinics to enter into cooperative agreements with the National Community Based Paralegal Association and with the Legal Aid Board. During apartheid, paralegals from rural communities and townships were the only source of legal assistance for many black South Africans.[33] In 1996 many of the 750 paralegals working in 250 advice offices formed the National Community Based Paralegal Association.[34] Law school clinics, which are geographically spread out across the country, have more recently entered into partnerships to provide back-up legal services to the advice offices. This is a wonderful opportunity for law students to assist with the development problems of poor rural and urban communities.

Another type of partnership educating law students has been cooperative agreements between law school clinics and the Legal Aid Board. The LAB, which is funded by the South African government to provide legal services to indigent people in both criminal and civil cases, has struggled to fulfill this mandate.[35] The constitutional imperatives and demands of the new democracy have created an increasing need for legal representation, but the LAB has prioritized representation in criminal over civil cases.[36] In recent years the LAB has opened a network of Justice Centres located throughout the country as a means of making legal services more available. The LAB has formed partnerships with law school clinics to do outreach, and provide legal services on civil matters in communities located in rural areas and townships that are not accessible to these Centres.[37] This provides more opportunities for students to engage in development work.

Development law clinics provide an opportunity for students to learn the tools and practice required to assist the economic growth and development needed in African countries. Professor Grady Jessup, while working in Ghana, suggested the implementation of a Development Law Clinic, but he cautioned that customary law and indigenous norms must be taught to insure a vital link to communities. He argued for a problem driven methodology where work could include legislative reform, infrastructure project development, law reform or demographic studies.[38]

Three South African law school clinics have specifically specialized in development work employing all of these strategies. As previously discussed, the University of Kwa-Zulu Natal clinic represented land claimants and has provided legal assistance to some micro-enterprises. The law clinic at Rhodes University has provided legal assistance to the micro-lending industry and the University of Pretoria has a debt relief clinic.[39] These clinics are teaching law students about the new laws passed to encourage economic growth and redistribute land. They have pioneered in South Africa the type of community economic development work described in the next section.

Community Economic Development Clinics in the United States

The U.S. experience with CED clinics may be helpful to South African law schools as this type of work grows and develops.[40] It is important to note that while South African clinical programs have been influenced by the American model of clinical legal education, the social and economic issues confronting South Africa are more complex and different from those in the U.S. At the same time, historically underserved minority communities in the U.S. have much in common with South Africa.[41]

In her book, *New News Out of Africa: Uncovering Africa's Renaissance*, journalist Charlayne Hunter-Gault compares South Africa's emerging democracy to the American civil rights movement.

> A little over a decade into its new democracy, South Africa is in some ways where America was in 1968, when the country's inner cities erupted in flames sparked by rage. Back then, President Johnson's Kerner Commission reached a conclusion that took most Americans by surprise: America was in fact two societies, one white and prospering, one black and in decline. While there are no signs yet of such an explosion in South Africa, there are worries about poverty, still holding at some 45 percent, and unemployment, which was over 26 percent in 2005.[42]

Given the realities of the global economy,[43] the contemporary American civil rights movement must emphasize economic justice within the context of global human rights. Accordingly, within the legal profession, legal activists and public interest and human rights lawyers are examining ways to advance social and economic justice. The creation of CED and small business clinical programs is contributing to this effort.

Influenced by the international microfinance[44] and microcredit[45] movement, a social (and economic justice) perspective has been embraced in the U.S. clinical legal education movement. There are now at least 50 community economic development and/or small business clinical programs at American law schools.[46] While small business clinics were once considered an oxymoron, they are now representative of the "new public interest law".[47] CED and small business clinics are engaged in transactions rather than litigation. Second and third-year law students, enrolled in a law school course for academic credit, represent a myriad of clients. These students are engaged in improving the quality of life for low-income people in underserved communities.

Community Economic Development is a term of art that involves many kinds of strategies for revitalizing poor communities.[48] Historically, quite a few laws in the U.S. have supported community economic development. Examples include The Low Income Housing Tax Credit Program and most recently the New Market Tax Credit Program.[49]

CED facilitates the economic growth of communities through "business development jobs, affordable housing and affordable healthcare, childcare, environmental justice", and "other necessities in a manner that enables community residents to improve the quality of their lives and exercise greater determination over the affairs that shape their daily existence."[50] CED strategies include supporting economic independence through entrepreneurship, encouraging joint ventures between the private sector, government and local institutions, encouraging greater citizen participation in political, civil and social rights movements and translating, applying and challenging the various laws that impact CED.[51] CED lawyers typically represent nonprofit organizations such as nonprofit housing developers, health care and day care centers, business cooperatives and microbusinesses—very small businesses comprised of 1-5 people with less than $35,000 in start up capital.[52]

In the late 1960s during the U.S. Civil Rights movement and the national "War on Poverty", U.S. Legal Services attorneys recognized that the problems of the individual poor people they represented had to be seen from a broader perspective. They began to look for strategies to alleviate poverty. Clinical programs in domestic violence, HIV/AIDS, intellectual property, small business and community economic development emerged, in part, by responding to these social needs and funding opportunities. For example, small business clinics emerged in the late 1970s because of funding from the U.S. Small Business Administration to provide legal assistance to small business owners.[53]

One continuing strategy is to work with nonprofit community development corporations (CDCs) and other community-based organizations (CBOs) also known as Neighborhood-Based Organizations (NBOs). These are Non-Governmental Organizations (NGOs) or Private Voluntary Organizations (PVOs) in the South African and international context. In the U.S. local and national bar associations are recognizing the need to assist low income communities as part of a commitment to pro bono service.

Pro bono business law is gaining momentum through the American Bar Association pro bono challenge and internal law firm pro bono requirements.[54] Indeed, a number of pro bono legal assistance programs have devoted attention to providing legal assistance to CBOs, and CDCs working to address affordable housing, small business development, health care, child care, environmental issues, juvenile delinquency, public safety and crime prevention.[55]

Opportunities For CED Clinics

Civil society has been critical to the goal of realizing social and economic opportunities in the US and South Africa. Indeed, in the South African context, Chapter 2, Section 18 of the South African Constitution guarantees everyone the right to freedom of association.[56] Civil society groups have been instrumental in organizing the mass movements to advocate for socio-economic rights. Despite formal legal rights to equality in both South Africa and the United States, serious poverty and racism persist. The U.S. poverty rate is 12.7%.[57] The South African poverty rate is reported as high as 57%.[58] Even though there are vast differences socially, politically and economically between the two countries, there are also some interesting parallels when in comes to examining opportunities for advancing social and economic opportunities.

For example, microenterprise development as a scheme for alleviating poverty is being vigorously pursued in both countries and other parts of the world. A pressing problem for South Africa is how to employ unemployed and unemployable citizens in the formal business sector.[59] Terreblanche reports in his book, *A History of Inequality in South Africa*, that

> about 50% of African entrants to the job market could not find jobs in the formal sector. This lack of employment is a major reason for the poverty of 60% of the black population. This situation of structural unemployment and poverty has a compulsory character because it is beyond the control of the unemployed.[60]

Advances in technology and globalization have changed the nature of work creating more skilled and fewer unskilled jobs.

Globally, small businesses create most new jobs[61], and China, for example, which is moving toward privatization and closing state owed enterprises, is looking to small and medium sized enterprises (SMEs) to employ former state-owned workers.[62] This means that SME development and the creation of opportunities for self-employment will be an important part of global economic development strategies. In his book, *Ending Global Poverty: A Guide to What Works*, economist Stephen Smith identifies the importance of assets, credit and market development as keys to ending global poverty. He points out that microfinance works, but poor families need assets and better market access as well.

While small businesses are creating most new jobs in America today, the nonprofit sector is also formidable.[63] South Africa, too, has a large and vibrant nonprofit sector.[64] Studies have found that "civil society is a significant economic sector…and that its civil society is as large in proportional terms and as vibrant as in all but a handful of advanced industrialized countries."[65] South African NGOs are concerned about the withdrawal of international aid to these groups and assert that aid is now being given to government.[66]

Another area for legal analysis is cooperation and coordination amongst government, the nonprofit and business sectors. The proliferation of legal clinics in small business and community development is introducing students to the idea that business law can help transform communities.[67] Concepts of social venture philanthropy, a model of charitable giving influenced by venture capital, social entrepreneurship, a blend of social, philanthropic and business values and social purpose business must be a core part of CED or development work. Neighborhood entrepreneurs often employ local residents and demonstrate to the community that starting a small business is indeed possible. By working to create community-based jobs and self-employment, the CED movements help to address the growing problem that "workers are far from potential jobs, a phenomenon researchers call "spatial mismatch".[68]

Given issues of economic, racial and gender disparity in the U.S. and South Africa, economic justice ought to be taught as part of the core law school curriculum.[69] Just as legislation in the U.S. has encouraged CED, The Broad Based Black Economic Empowerment Act of 2003 was enacted to address economic disparity in South Africa.[70] The purpose of the Act is to "establish a legislative framework for the promotion of black economic empowerment, to empower the

Minister to issue codes of good practice and to publish transformation charters, to establish the Black Economic Empowerment Advisory Council, and to provide for matters connected therewith."[71] The Preamble to the Act acknowledges that during apartheid "race was used to control access to South Africa's productive resources and access to skills"; that the "economy still excludes the vast majority of its people from ownership of productive assets and the possession of advanced skills," and that "that the economy performs below its potential because of the low level of income earned and generated by the majority of its people."[72] The Preamble recognizes that

> unless further steps are taken to increase the effective participation of black people in the economy, the stability and prosperity of the economy in the future may be undermined to the detriment of all South Africans, irrespective of race.[73]

The BEE creates a score card to facilitate broad based economic development.[74] This score card increases capital to black owned businesses, and is intended to boost skills particularly among the black unemployed to levels that will enhance economic growth. Companies have to achieve BEE status which qualifies them for lucrative business opportunities. One way that corporations can achieve BEE status is through corporate social investment initiatives. The Black Economic Empowerment Commission created in 1998:

> [e]xtends the definition of empowerment beyond transferal of ownership of companies, describing it as 'an integrated and coherent socio-economic process... which aims to redress past imbalances by transferring and conferring ownership, management, and control of South Africa's financial and economic resources to the majority of its citizens and ensure broader participation of black people in the economy in order to achieve sustainable development and prosperity.[75]

The commission also reports that "continuing racism across all sectors of society acts as a social impediment," distorting the functioning of markets and reinforcing the marginalization of black South Africans.[76] There are also a number of other laws that work in tandem with the BEE.[77]

The BEE has been controversial and the subject of much debate. The need to build a broad-based middle class must be balanced against social values of "Ubuntu", an African humanist philosophy which says that people are people because of people. South African clinicians should consider engaging in a careful analysis and critique of the BEE to determine where there might be creative uses of NPO law. Legal research might be conducted to assess, for example, the use of BEE in the creation of worker owned cooperatives and other corporate legal entities for businesses that create work for unemployed persons.

Conclusion

Changes in universities since the end of apartheid have resulted in law students now more closely representing the demographics of South Africa. The new law school curriculum and pedagogy recognize the importance of teaching students about the Constitution and legal skills needed for problem solving. The expansion of clinical legal education has been central to many of these law school reforms. However, more radical innovation in legal education is needed if South African lawyers are to be adequately prepared to solve the pressing socio-economic problems in the country.

Development law clinics can help law students learn the tools necessary to promote economic justice and achieve the promise of the Constitution and related laws. This chapter considered the development of the South African clinical law movement and the importance of community economic development opportunities. It also surveyed the growth of community economic development clinics in the United States that may provide some new ideas and guidance if adapted to the South African context. Legal education that provides students with the skills to help implement the social and economic promise of the Constitution is the challenge for its second decade.

[1] See Chapter 2 of the Constitution of the Republic of South Africa, Act 108 of 1996.
[2] See Broad-Based Black Economic Empowerment Act 53 of 2003 (S. Afr.) pmbl., available at http://www.info.gov.za/gazette/acts/2003/a53-03.pdf (last visited July 18 2006).
[3] International Covenant of Economic, Social and Cultural Rights art. 11, para. 1, Dec. 16, 1966. S. Treach Doc No 95-19 U.N.T.S. 4. South Africa became a signatory to the Covenant on Oct. 3, 1994 and has yet to ratify it.
[4] Historically black lawyers have led the struggle for equality in South Africa. See KENNETH S. BROUN, BLACK LAWYERS, WHITE COURTS: THE SOUL OF SOUTH AFRICAN LAW 235-43 (Ohio University Press 2000).
[5] Motivation to become a public interest lawyer either full-time or in pro bono work is also required. In the United States articles discuss how law students may lose their justice orientation during law school and graduate with a large debt that causes them to pursue legal careers with no public interest work. See Lawrence S. Krieger , The Inseparability of Professionalism and Personal Satisfaction: Perspectives on Values, Integrity and Happiness, 11 Clinical. L. Rev. 425 (2005).These economic pressures also exist for African law students, particularly black law students who may be the first in their families to be able to attend university and have extended families to support.
[6] Blacks still control only 3% of the market value of companies listed on the Johannesburg stock market. Whites, who constitute 10% of the population, still hold 85% of all senior management posts. See Sharon LaFraniere, South Africa's Shift Gradually Accelerates, N.Y. Times, June 8, 2004.
[7] See Joanne Fedler, Legal Education in South Africa, 72 Oregon. L. Rev. 999 (1993).
[8] Previously, large lectures, extensive reading, and exams, particularly oral ones, created a huge burden for black students, whose first language was usually not English. Id. at 1002.
[9] Grady Jessup, Symbiotic Relations: Clinical Methodology—Fostering New Paradigms In African Legal Education, 8 Clinical L. Rev. 377, 387 (2002).
[10] Id.
[11] The Attorney's Act 53 of 1979 (1979) was amended by Act 115 of 1993 (1993) to allow candidate attorneys to perform their articles at legal aid organizations such as law school clinics. Historically, many black lawyers were excluded from the profession by their difficulty in obtaining articles. See Lisa R. Pruitt, No Black Names on the Letterhead? Efficient Discrimination and the South African Legal Profession, 23 MICH. J. INT'L L. 545, 573 (2002).
[12] See Adam Babich, The Apolitical Law School Clinic, 11 Clinical L. Rev. 447, 452 (2005); Michael Jordan, Law Teachers and the Educational Continuum, 5 S. Cal. Interdisc. L.J. 41, 46 (1996).
[13] See Tony Axam Jr., A Model for Learning and Teaching – Rights and Responsibilities in the New Legal Order, 17 S. Afr. J. on Hum. Rights 3 (2001).
[14] Previously, five years were required for an LLB degree. This was changed in 1997 so that black students, who could not afford five years of university education, could compete with white students who had previously graduated with LLB degrees. See Thuli Mhlungu, Educating and Licensing Attorneys in South Africa, 20 Ga. St. U. L. Rev. 1005, 1005-22 (2004).
[15] In adopting the four year LLB degree, the law school Deans agreed that skills courses should be introduced into the curriculum. The law faculty at UKZN decided to create new courses for the first three years of the curriculum and add Teaching Legal Skills as a final year elective.
[16] See PEGGY MAISEL AND LESLEY GREENBAUM, INTRODUCTION TO LAW AND LEGAL SKILLS, (Butterworths 2001) (and accompanying Teacher's Manual); and PEGGY MAISEL AND LESLEY GREENBAUM, FOUNDATIONS OF SOUTH AFRICAN LAW, CRITICAL ISSUES FOR LAW STUDENTS, (Butterworths 2002). These are the textbooks for the first year courses.
[17] See ROBIN W. PALMER, A. CROCKER & M. KIDD, BECOMING A LAWYER; FUNDAMENTAL SKILLS FOR LAW STUDENTS (LexisNexis Butterworths 2003)
[18] This course has been taught to all third year law students by faculty from the law clinic. They use simulations and the course helps to prepare the students to practice in the law clinic during the following year.
[19] See Lesley A. Greenbaum, Teaching Legal Writing At South African Law Faculties: A Review Of The Current Position and Suggestions For The Incorporation Of A Model Based On New Theoretical Perspectives, 15 Stellenbosch L. Rev. 1, 18 (2004).
[20] See Fedler, supra note 7, at 1003.
[21] In the LLM course, graduate students lecture small sections of first year students while learning an approach to teaching legal skills.
[22] See DAVID J. McQUOID-MASON, AN OUTLINE OF LEGAL AID IN SOUTH AFRICA 27 (Butterworth & Co. (SA) 1982).

23 *See* BODENSTEIN, BONIFACE, DE KLERK, HAUPT, KOK, MAHOMED, STEENHUISEN, STILWELL, WIMPEY, CLINICAL LAW IN SOUTH AFRICA 2 (LexisNexis Butterworths 2004).

24 *See* David J. McQuoid-Mason, *The Delivery of Civil Legal Aid Services in South Africa,* 24 FORDHAM INT'L L.J. S120 (2000). See also *infra* note 35 and accompanying text.

25 In 2000, one of the authors of this chapter conducted a survey of the twenty-one university based law clinics in South Africa to obtain information about the then current state of the law clinics. *See* Peggy Maisel, The Position of Clinicians in South African Law Schools, (July 2000) (unpublished paper on file with the author).

26 *See* M. Shanara Gilbert, Report on the Status of University Law Clinics in South Africa 1-2 (Nov. 15, 1993) (prepared for the South Africa-Nambia office, The Ford Foundation) (on file with author).

27 Schalk Meyer, President of AULAI, at the First All African Clinical Legal Education Colloquium, Durban South Africa: Legal Service Delivery through University Law Clinics at South African Universities (2003) (on file with author).

28 *Id.*

29 In 2005, the University of Natal merged with the University of Durban – Westville, a university designated under apartheid for students of Indian origin. The university is now called the University of Kwa-Zulu Natal. The merger was mandated by the national government to rationalize spending and as one of the methods of overcoming the educational legacies of apartheid.

30 *See* The Restitution of Land Rights Act 22 of 1994, The Land Reform (Labour Tenants) Act 3 of 1996, and the Extension of Security of Tenure Act 62 of 1997.

31 *See* Asha Ramgobin, *Reflections on the Challenges Facing Public Interest Lawyers in Post-Apartheid South Africa,* 7 Wash. U. J.L. & Pol'y 77, 82 (2001).

32 *Id.* At 88. She also noted that "The law students involved in the project still talk about how meaningful the experience was for them because for once they were doing something that actually had a direct impact on both the life of the claimants and on the political and historical development of land reform in the country." *Id.* at 87.

33 McQuoid-Mason, *supra* note 24, at S125.

34 *See* Asha Ramgobin, Justice For All? Law Clinics in South Africa. And in Sweden? 39. (2004). (Unpublished Thesis for LLM degree from Lund University). (On file with author).

35 Legal Aid Act 22 of 1969 (1969) (S. Afr.), as amended by Legal Aid Amendment Act 20 of 1996 (1996) (S. Afr.). See Peggy Maisel, An Alternative Model to United States Bar Examinations: The South African Community Service Experience in Licensing Attorneys, 20 Ga. St. U. L. Rev. 977, 986 (2004).

36 *Id,* Maisel at 986, 987.

37 *Supra,* Note 35 at 55.

38 *See* Jessup *supra* note 9, at 401.

39 Information from presentation by Thuli Mhlungu, "Advancing Social and Economic Opportunity: Perspectives from Law and Society" at the Comparative Constitutionalism and Rights: Global Perspectives Conference, University of KwaZulu Natal, Durban South Africa, December 10-13, 2005.

40 The U.S. clinics also have much to learn from the South African experience of working more closely with groups and social movements, such as land claimants. See *supra* note 31.

41 Some of the common issues include violence, unemployment, community safety, drug and alcohol abuse, and teen pregnancy. For example, statistics show that in New York City 50% of black men are unemployed, and one national study found that "[b]y 2002, one of every four black men in the U.S. was idle all year long." Susan R. Jones, *Dr. Martin Luther King, Jr.'s Legacy: An Economic Justice Imperative,* 19 WASH. U. J.L. & POL'Y, 39, 44 (2005) [hereinafter *King's Legacy*] (citing Janny Scott, *Nearly Half of Black Men Found Jobless,* N.Y. TIMES, Feb 28, 2004, at B1, Bob Herbert, *An Emerging Catastrophe,* N.Y. TIMES, July 19, 2004, at A17 (noting a study by Andrew Sum, Director of the Center for Labor Market Studies at Northeastern University in Boston); see U.S. Dep't of Labor, Bureau of Labor Statistics, Labor Force Statistics from the Current Population Survey, *available at* http://www.bls.gov/cps/home.htm *(last visited July 25, 2006)).*

42 CHARLAYNE HUNTER-GAULT, NEW NEWS OUT OF AFRICA: UNCOVERING AFRICA'S RENAISSANCE 57-58 (Oxford University Press 2006) (quoting South African Labour and Development Research Unit, University of Cape Town, October Household Survey (OHS) and Labour Force Survey (LFS), data from Statistical Releases of Statistics South Africa, *available at* http://www.saldru.uct.ac.za (last visited July 18, 2006).

[43] For more information on the global economy see, WAYNE ELLWOOD AND JOHN MCMURTY, NO NONSENSE GUIDE TO GLOBALIZATION, (Verso 2001), THOMAS FRIEDMAN, THE WORLD IS FLAT: A BRIEF HISTORY OF THE TWENTY-FIRST CENTURY (Farrar, Straus and Giroux 2005).

[44] Microfinance, Microcredit and Microlending are used interchangeably. Microfinance, generally, "refers to a broader array of financial services used by microenterprise programs, including assistance with credit repair, microloans, asset development activities ... or access to credit through credit unions or other community development financial institutions . . ." SUSAN R. JONES, LEGAL GUIDE TO MICROENTERPRISE DEVELOPMENT, (American Bar Association 2004) at 6 [hereinafter *Microenterprise Development*].

[45] "Microcredit is often uses by international practitioners and is preferred by some over microfinance." *Id.*

[46] *See* Lawbus Listserv Directory maintained by Prof. Thomas Morsch, Northwestern University School of Law, lawbus@listserv.it.northwestern.edu,[on file with the author]. For a comprehensive discussion of small business and community economic development clinics, *see* Susan R. Jones, *Small Business and Community Economic_Development: Transactional Lawyering for Social Change and Economic Justice*, 4 CLINICAL L.REV. 195 (1997) [hereinafter *Small Business*]. It is important to note that not all of these programs have an explicit social and economic justice mission.

[47] *Id.* at 204.

[48] There is no established legal definition for CDCs. The National Congress for Community Economic Development, the service organization for an estimated 3,600 CDCs across America, described them as having community-based leadership and working primarily on job creation and housing production. These organizations are formed by local stakeholders – community residents, faith-based congregations, and small business owners. They often provide social services and help to create jobs through commercial development projects and small and micro business loans. Funded from public and private sources, CDCs are notorious for producing private sector jobs (774,000 in 2005) and substantial units (1,252,000 in 2005) of affordable housing. *See* National Congress for Community Economic Development's 5th National Community Development Census – *Reaching New Heights: Trends and Achievements of Community-Based Development Organizations* (2005) (unpublished report, *available at* http://www.ncced.org/documents/NCCEDCensus2005FINALReport.pdf, last visited July 25, 2006).

[49] *See* Scott L. Cummings & Benjamin S. Beach, *The Federal Role in Community Economic Development*, CLEARINGHOUSE REV. J.L. & POL'Y., May-June 2006, 89; Peter Edelman, *The War on Poverty and Subsequent Federal Programs: What Worked, What Didn't Work and Why? Lessons for Future Programs*, CLEARINGHOUSE REV. J.L. & POL'Y., May-June 2006, 7; James D. Weill, *The Federal Government – the Indispensible Player in Redressing Poverty*, CLEARINGHOUSE REV. J.L. & POL'Y., May-June 2006, 19.

[50] Jones, *Small Business, supra* note 46, at 199 (citing National Economic Development and Law Center, A Lawyers Manual on Community-Based Economic Development, I-3 (revised 1994).

[51] *Id. See also* Brian Glick & Matthew Rossman, *Neighborhood Legal Services as House Counsel to Community-Based Efforts to Achieve Economic Justice: The East Brooklyn Experience*, 23 N.Y.U. REV. L. & SOC. CHANGE 105, 107-08 (1997).

[52] *See* JONES, *Microenterprise Development, supra* note 44. *See also* Susan R. Jones, *Promoting Social and Economic Justice Through Interdisciplinary Work in Transactional Law*, 14 WASH. U. J.L. & POL'Y., 249 (2004).

[53] Jones, *Small Business, supra* note 46 at 206..

[54] James L. Baillie, *Fulfilling the promise of Business Law Pro Bono*, 28 WM. MITCHELL L. REV. 1548.

[55] It is noteworthy that both the U.S. and South Africa have legal regimes that enable the nonprofit sector. Section 21 of the Nonprofit Organizations Act of 1997 provides for the registration of NPOs including companies, trusts, religious institutions, trade unions, or co-operatives. Nonprofit Organizations Act 71 of 1997 (S. Afr) § 21. The Minister of Welfare can also prescribe benefits or allowances for registered NPOs. *Id.* § 11. In the U.S., nonprofit corporations are generally established under state corporate charters, apply for federal and state tax exemption and comply with regulatory charitable solicitation laws.

[56] S. AFR. CONST, § 18 *supra* note 1.

[57] *See* Carmen DeNavas-Walt, Bernadette D. Proctor, & Cheryl Hill Lee, U.S. Census Bureau, *Current Population Survey, P60-229, Income, Poverty and Health Insurance Coverage in the United States: 2004* (2005), *available at* http://www.census.gov/prod/2005pubs/p60-229.pdf (last visited July 18, 2006).

[58] *See Human Sciences Research Council Fact Sheet: Poverty in South Africa: 2004, available at* http://www.sarpn.org.za/documents/d0000990/P1096-Fact_Sheet_No_1_Poverty.pdf (last visited July 18, 2006).

[59] FLICK ASVAT, LET US DO THIS THING: WHERE BUSINESS, GOVERNMENT AND SOCIAL TRANSFORMATION MEET, 19 (Colette Braudo ed., Altered Attitudes 2004).

[60] HUNTER-GAULT, *supra* note 4, at 57 (quoting SAMPIE TERREBLANCHE, A HISTORY OF INEQUALITY IN SOUTH AFRICA 13-14 (Pietermaritzburg: University of Natal Press 2002)).

[61] *See* STEPHEN C. SMITH, ENDING GLOBAL POVERTY: A GUIDE TO WHAT WORKS (Palgrave Macmillan 2005).

[62] Professor Jones served as a foreign expert to GTZ, a German based NGO, on China's SME law. *See* Susan R. Jones, *Comments on Chapter II, Articles 7-11, 19, Direct Public Subsidies – Annotations from the American Perspective, in* THE LAW OF THE PEOPLE'S REPUBLIC OF CHINA ON THE PROMOTION OF SMALL AND MEDIUM-SIZED ENTERPRISES, PART ONE: MATERIALS ON THE DRAFTING PROCESS 715 (Immanuel Gebhardt & Zhu Shaoping eds., Citic 2004), *Id. Articles 12-18, Facilitating Loans – Annotations from the American Perspective* at 723, *Id. Chapter III, Technology Innovation – Annotations from the American Perspective* at 734, Id. *Chapter IV, Market Development – Annotations from the American Perspective* at 743. *See also* Susan R. Jones, *The Second Draft – Annotations on Chapter IV from the American Perspective, in id.* PART TWO at 391, *id. Chapter V* at 392, *id. Chapter VI* at 412.

[63] In the U.S. it is reported that there are more than 1.8 million tax exempt organizations, although the actual number is much higher. These organizations generate in excess of 1.2 trillion dollars annually and their assets have a total value of at least 3.7 trillion. Tax exempt organizations account for 12% of the U.S. gross domestic product. Charitable giving totaled $241 billion in 2003. Bruce R. Hopkins, Professional Education Systems Institute, LLC, Seventh Annual, The Law of Tax Exempt Organizations Conference materials page 2 [on file with the Prof. Susan Jones].

[64] There are 98,920 nonprofit organizations in South Africa. Fifty-three percent (53%) of these are less formalized and do not receive large amounts of aid. *See* ASVAT, *supra* note 59, at 39-40.

[65] A.E. Rippon, A Strategic Approach for Not-For-Profit Organisations 21(Oct. 2002) (unpublished report, on file with the author).

[66] HUNTER-GAULT, *Supra,* Note 42 at 30.

[67] "[T]there are examples of fresh new economic justice initiatives in the progressive corporate world. Greyston Bakery is a social experiment started more than twenty years ago by Bernie Glassman. Greyston Bakery was established with the goal of employing the chronically unemployed. Profits from the bakery, a $5 million a year business that sells to businesses such as Ben and Jerry's Ice Cream, are used to fund day care centers, health clinics and counseling services. Greyston makes cakes in order to hire people, and currently employs some sixty-five workers, including former drug dealers and homeless people. These examples show us that the opportunities for creating good jobs as part of a larger mission to end homelessness and poverty are truly possible, and lawyers play a critical role in the process of nonprofit and for-profit business development." Jones, *King's Legacy, supra* note 6, at 63. Greyston Bakery, *The Greyston Bakery Story, available at* http://www.greystonbakery.com (last visited July 18, 2006).

[68] Susan R. Jones, *Self-Employment: Possibilities and Problems, in* HARD LABOR: WOMEN AND WORK IN THE POST-WELFARE ERA 76, 82 (Joel F. Handler & Lucie White eds., M.E. Sharpe 1999).

[69] See for example, EMMA C. JORDAN & ANGELA P. HARRIS, ECONOMIC JUSTICE: RACE, GENDER, IDENTITY AND ECONOMICS (Foundation Press 2005). Courses on community economic development, race and the law, poverty law, and international human rights courses and clinics also provide opportunities to teach about economic justice.

[70] Broad-Based Black Economic Empowerment Act, *supra* note 2.

[71] *Id.*

[72] *Id.*

[73] *Id.*

[74] Broad-based includes women, workers, youth, people with disabilities and people living in rural areas.

[75] DUMA GQUBULE & ANDREA BROWN, BLACK ECONOMIC EMPOWERMENT COMMISSION REPORT (Skotaville Press 2001), *available at* http://www.capegateway.gov.za/text/2004/5/beecomreport.pdf (last visited July 20, 2006).

[76] *Id.*

[77] They include the Qualifications Authority Act 58 of 1995; the National Small Business Act 1901 of 1996; and the Employment Equity Act 55 of 1998. The Skills Development Act 97 of 1998, and the

Skills Development and Employment Equity Acts of 1998 are designed to address disparities in the workplace and train the country's workforce. The Skills Development Levies Act of 1998 provides for funds for companies to develop human capital to achieve employment equity and creates the basis for a National Skills Development Strategy. A skills levy has been instituted on corporate South Africa and 24 Education and Training Authorities (SEATS) were created by the Skills Development Act.

CHAPTER 18

INTERNATIONAL LAW AND THE SHRINKING SPACE FOR POLITICS IN DEVELOPING COUNTRIES

J. Patrick Kelly

There is an emerging worldwide debate between democratic constitutionalists and populist or majoritarian constitutionalists about the appropriate institution or institutions of government to engage in constitutional interpretation. Democratic constitutionalists view a constitution as foundational law, approved by the people as an act of democratic self-government, superior to and constraining of later majoritarian law expressed through legislative or executive decisions.[1] In the United States, South Africa and other democracies with a written constitution that must be interpreted, courts have assumed the role of final constitutional authority under the doctrine of judicial supremacy to overturn unconstitutional actions of the other branches.[2] Populist constitutionalists such as Mark Tushnet[3] and Ran Hirschl[4] argue that the elected branches of government, more reflective of popular will, should dominate constitutional interpretation. Their concern is that the constitutionalization of rights has expanded the role of the judiciary transferring issues of right articulation and distributive justice from democratic processes to the courts.[5]

In this debate between adherents of constitutional democracy (constitutional rights as judicial trumps) and populist constitutionalism (legislature as guardian of constitutional interpretation) there is an often overlooked dynamic affecting the articulation of rights and the allocation of resources—the place of international law in domestic constitutionalism. The question may be posed: to what extent and by what processes should international legal norms be incorporated into domestic constitutions. The reception of international norms into constitutions may provide courts with increased authority to overturn legislative decisions and thereby insulate important policy issues from democratic processes

This article raises several concerns about the democratic legitimacy of many international legal norms and therefore about the wisdom of the ready importation of international legal norms into domestic law. International norms may be imported by listing such norms in long, encyclopedic constitutions attempting to solve social problems. More frequently, international norms are infused into constitutions through interpretation by judges with defined policy perspectives or the perception that international legal norms are, in some sense, superior to domestic democratic decisions.

The internationalization of constitutional interpretation rests on several problematic assumptions. First, proponents of internationalization of constitutional interpretation assume that several international norms, originally only human rights but now increasingly environmental norms, are universal and should be incorporated without specific democratic approval. Second, other international norms, delineated as customary international norms, are perceived to be formed by the consent of the world community of nations and are therefore obligatory.

The importation of international norms by developing countries is especially problematic because they have so little input into international norms and institutions. Developing countries are receivers of international law, not makers of international law. Such norms are therefore of questionable legitimacy in these societies, and may be inappropriate policy choices in countries at a different stage of economic development than more developed western countries.

International law as a source of legitimate norms suffers from an existential problem. How do we know that it exists? There is no international legislature with the authority to make law; no authoritative court with mandatory jurisdiction to find and interpret law; no executive with delegated authority to make law or execute legal norms; and no international police force to enforce it. Rather under conventional theory, substantive international law is by and large consensual. International law is said to be formed by express consent in the case of treaty law and implied consent in the case of customary international law (CIL).

My concern is that with globalization and the increased dominance of the United States there has been a turn away from consent as the basis of international law making and towards "Naturalism"[6] This paper will analyze several techniques of naturalism including the misuse of CIL, the adoption of a universal ideology of human rights beyond state consent, and expansive interpretations at treaty regimes that inhibit consensual norm development. This rise of naturalism is not accidental. It reflects an underlying value struggle within the domestic polities of a few wealthy developed countries without the input or an appreciation of the different values and perspectives of most nations of the world. The premature touting of the values of the wealthy western nations as international legal obligations rather than as part of a moral or policy discourse forces unattainable and, at times, inappropriate norms on developing countries. In some cases, these norms are contrary to their interests. Premature international legalism[7] may take normative development and sensible trade-offs out of the realm of both international and domestic politics without the necessary political deliberation. Environmental and even human rights have costs both in financial resources and political resources that should be assessed along with competing claims.

These concerns about the legitimacy and undemocratic nature of many international legal norms do not necessarily constitute an argument for the elimination of judicial review under populist or majoritarian constitutionalism.[8] Rather, these concerns serve both as a democratic caution to the importation of international norms into domestic societies through judicial interpretation, and as a justification for allocating some types of policy decisions, such as many environmental and other social policy decisions, to majoritarian processes where the virtues and disadvantages of alternative courses of action can be debated and formulated in a wider context.

The undemocratic nature of international law

With increased globalization there is a need for legal norms to regularize and regulate human interactions. A fundamental question that international society must confront is: by what processes should international law be made. Much of international law touted as consensual is, in fact, propounded by judges, academics, NGOs, and a few powerful nations with little input from developing countries. In this section the article demonstrates that much of international law is undemocratic and formed outside of domestic political processes.

Turning first to customary international law (CIL), it has historically been the most important source of international norms. Custom's primacy is reflected in the understanding that treaties are considered binding because there is a prior customary norm, *pacta sunt servanda*, obligating nations to observe treaties. CIL is said to be consensual based on state practice generally accepted as law.[9] States impliedly consent to norms by their participation in state practice and their demonstrated attitude of acceptance of the norms imbedded in practice. It consists of two elements: (1) the practice of states is the material element that provides evidence of customary norms and (2) the general acceptance of a norm as a legal obligation by the world community is the attitudinal requirement.[10] Yet much of international law is announced in books and articles with little input from nations. If one reads the international law literature, there is a rising tide of customary human right norms, environmental norms, and jurisdictional limitations without nations either accepting these norms as legal obligations or participating in relevant state practice. Much of CIL is a fiction.

Customary law, properly so called, is empirical law. Customary norms are binding because they are, in fact, accepted by all normal members of a society.[11] Empirical acceptance is the touchstone. Empirical acceptance, which has a certain popular democracy component, gives customary law its legitimacy. But CIL has taken a different path—it is the law of scholars, NGOs, and at times international tribunals not of nations or people.

The modern paradigm of CIL can be simply stated as follows. CIL is formed by the general and consistent practices of states accepted by them as law. CIL binds all states. New members of the international community of states are bound by existing customary law. However, an existing state is not bound by emerging customary law if it persistently objects.[12]

All aspects of this paradigm are subject to debate.[13] There is no common understanding of how to determine CIL beyond the ritualistic words of "general state practice accepted as law." There are several significant problems of applying this conception of law to international society.

First, international society is composed of states with widely different values, perspectives, and interests spread throughout the globe. Few states participate in or contribute to state practice. Thus state practice may not reflect a generalized acceptance of norms imbedded in practice.

Second, there is no agreement on what constitutes state practice. Do only physical actions such as repelling a ship from territorial waters count as state practice[14] or do formal protests count to help prevent the formation of CIL?[15]

Third, how does one know if a norm has been generally accepted? Does assent to a non-binding Declaration at an international conference or at the United Nations General Assembly indicate general acceptance of the norm as law or does it suggest only a concern about a vague goal? Are votes in favor of resolutions such as the Stockholm or Rio Declarations state practice, acceptance or both?

Fourth, are new nations including those that emerged from the colonial era bound by prior customary norms? The reigning paradigm appears to so require because custom once it is accepted by common consent binds all universally. Is this the case when the majority of nations did not participate and would not consent to several such norms? This example exposes a hidden conundrum in customary theory: is CIL based on common consensus or specific implied consent. While custom has historically been considered universal, the paradigm, as recently described in the western literature, permits a nation that persistently objects during the process of formation to opt out of norms, suggesting a consent theory.[16] This persistent objector principle emerged after new nations became a majority at the United Nations and the west began to lose control over the development of customary legal regimes particularly the protection of foreign investment.[17] The effect of this incoherence is to make custom consensual for older nations and universally binding on new nations.

Accordingly, customary international legal theory is incoherent and undefined. There are no defined criteria for determining customary norms. The methodology of customary international law is so malleable that both the left and right in wealthy developed countries manipulate it to advance their own normative agenda, without the participation or consent of most of the nations and peoples of the world. Progressive internationalists, including judges of the International Court of Justice, the World Trade Organization, and the European Court of Human Rights utilize general resolutions and treaties to make environmental and human rights norms universally binding. On the right scholars and unilateralists, operating under a theory that only physical acts count as state practice, use custom theory to protect foreign investment and to promote a right of unilateral humanitarian intervention that is said to justify US interventions in Grenada and Panama, and Viet Nam's takeover of Cambodia contrary to the norm against the use of force in the UN Charter.[18] Despite near unanimous condemnation by States, the putative norm of international humanitarian intervention has considerable resonance within the academy.

Progressives use the Declarative Model of CIL to construct norms without their acceptance as legal norms by States. The repetitive iteration (declarations) of norms such as the transboundary harm norm or the norm of sustainable development in resolutions at international fora is said to indicate general acceptance of the norm. It is axiomatic in international environmental circles that the transboundary harm norm originally articulated in the Trial Smelters Arbitration[19] and repeated in a different form in the Stockholm Declaration[20] as well as other international instruments is customary international law. This conclusion is reinforced in the Restatement of Foreign Relations Law of the United States.[21] The idea is that state acceptance of the norm in this and other declarations reinforce the arbitrator's conclusion in the judgment which is a kind of state practice. Yet the arbitrator in Trial Smelters found no evidence of international state practice. Instead he chose to assume that international law was the same as US law and then applied US law. The Stockholm Declaration and the subsequent Rio Declaration[22] containing this norm are non-binding. They are further qualified by contradictory language declaring that States have the sovereign right to exploit their resource according to their own environmental and now development policies. Indeed there is little empirical evidence that states accept it as norm. The Trail Smelter in Canada, itself, continues to pour sulfur dioxide into the atmosphere. The US produces acid rain that drifts into Canada. Yet by what authority does the repetition of non-binding norms, such as sustainable development, the precautionary principle, or the transboundary harm norm in declarations become binding when they are ignored in practice and nations are unwilling to accept them in binding treaties? These are paper norm in books and articles written by the converted.

Similarly, the universalizing of limited incidents of state practice by scholars on the right and the current Bush administration reifies power at the expense of democracy. This methodology redefines customary law in a manner that minimizes the essential legitimizing element of custom, the general acceptance of the community. It encourages violence rather than legal processes to solve disputes making international law an undemocratic exercise with little persuasive authority.

All these approaches are tenable because there is no agreement on how to construct CIL norms. The concept of CIL as empirical law has disappeared. CIL is now a metaphor for a "Naturalist" methodology of lawmaking not empirical law. If we take the general acceptance requirement seriously, it may be nearly impossible to form legitimate substantive customary norms in an expanded world of many different cultures, values, and perspectives. Moreover, in my view, CIL is not necessary in an era of rapid transportation and communications. If there is, in fact, the political will to accept international legal norms, then a binding treaty is possible. CIL is the preferred technique for normative scholars and judges precisely because there is a lack of political will to create binding obligations.

This discourse on custom theory serves as a caution to a democratic constitutionalism that imports international norms through judicial interpretation. Many CIL norms lack legitimacy as law because nations have not, in fact, accepted them as law and would not. The West, by and large, controls the literature; and the discourse reflects the political debate in Western societies without consideration or understanding of the impact on developing countries. The current free-form approach to CIL by judges, as if it were common law, therefore contains a kind of "double democratic deficit". Few nations actually participate in the incidents of state practice that form law, and then these norms are incorporated into domestic constitutional law by unelected judges.

Few substantive CIL norms have a legitimate pedigree as law. Environmental principles, such as sustainable development or the precautionary principle, articulated as law in much of the literature may be wise policy guides, but they are inappropriate as legal norms. Sustainable development is a useful concept for organizing one's thinking about how to allocate resources to minimize harm and maximize the availability of resources for the future. Its delineation does, however, inherently impose costs and require tradeoffs with other worthy goals that should be the providence of the legislature rather than the judiciary.

The universal nature of human rights

The Second "Naturalist" approach is the imbedded notion in recent international legal theory that international norms are an expression of universal rights that apply regardless of national boundaries or political choice by domestic majorities.[23] These norms are said to be binding without state consent or domestic democratic processes. Jed Rubenfeld terms this conception "international constitutionalism" because these rights are determined by international judges or experts irrespective of democratic politics.[24] This underlying normative structure is then expressed by the use of traditional sources that reveal these fundamental norms. Sometimes this argument is made as a form of CIL, as discussed above, such as the claim by scholars that many of the norms in the nonbinding Universal Declaration of Human Rights are now generally accepted as CIL because of their repetition in declarative documents and by judicial tribunals.[25]

Universal norms are also revealed through interpretation of consensual treaties in a manner that expands the norms beyond any intended bargain. Article 7 of the International Covenant on Civil and Political Rights (ICCPR), for example, that prohibits "cruel, inhuman or degrading treatment or punishment" has been declared to prohibit the death penalty, caning, and other forms of physical punishment even though these punishments are widely permitted within domestic legal systems and many, if not a majority of nations in the case of the death penalty, would not accept such limits on their prerogatives. What a given society considers as "cruel or inhuman" may be a question of perception affected by culture and religious beliefs. Agreement on the interpretation of a general standard of human rights like "cruel or inhuman" is unlikely without an extended dialogue among cultures.[26]

Similarly, article 1 of The Convention on the Elimination of all Forms of Discrimination Against Women (CEDAW) prohibits discrimination that has the effect or purpose of "impairing or nullifying the recognition, enjoyment or exercise by women, irrespective of their marital status, on the basest of equality of men and women, of human rights and fundamental freedoms...."[27] The Committee on CEDAW, the treaty body established to review national reports and make recommendations, declared that female circumcision was a gender-based form of violence and that states may be responsible even for private acts if they fail to act with due diligence.[28] Even though female genital mutilation or female circumcision may be abhorrent and injurious to health, it is not clear that it is a form of discrimination that violates the Convention when the participants (women and young girls) believe that this traditional practice is a constituent part of their culture.[29] Nor is it necessarily either a treaty or customary norm when 53 nations that did sign entered reservations for religious or cultural reasons.[30]

A further example is the universalizing of human rights beyond state consent by the Human Rights Committee of the United Nations. One may deplore the hypocrisy of the U.S. government in using the ICCPR as a sword against other countries while submitting reservations, declarations, and understandings to its ratification that effectively preclude undertaking any significant international legal obligation.[31] Nevertheless, the Human Rights Committee in rejecting the U.S. reservations as unacceptable revealed that it regarded human rights as universal obligations beyond the normal exchange of obligations through consensual treaty law.[32]

These techniques of universalizing rights beyond politics are, of course, not just the province of progressives. The Restatement of Foreign Relations Law, for example, proclaims the standard of full compensation for expropriation of foreign investment as not subject to change by a majority of nations.[33] The Bush administration propounds a right to democracy as justification for selective military intervention to vindicate this right. Both the pedigree and content of such a right are open to question.[34]

The point is not to approve or disapprove of the death penalty, female genital mutilation, a right to democracy or any specific norm, but to raise the issue of which system of law, international or domestic, should make these determinations and by what processes. The universal theory of human rights applied by many judges and practitioners is, in many circumstances, inconsistent with the consent theory of international law and democratic governance within domestic societies. One of its manifestations is found in the rise of transnational litigation of human rights in domestic courts under the notions of universal jurisdiction or transitory torts.[35] Judges should be careful in importing norms without prior approval through domestic democratic processes. Expanding human rights in a manner contrary to traditional and non-western cultural values raises issues both of the legitimacy of the project and its practical utility when it engenders widespread opposition rather than compliance. Differences in values, in many circumstances, might better be characterized as moral dialogue rather than as legal imperatives. Any expansion beyond a small core of negative freedoms (freedom from government interference with personal autonomy and the electoral process)[36] has and may continue to degenerate into cultural imperialism.

Judicial activism at international forums

There is a third form of "Naturalist" in international law formation that is inhibiting domestic political debate and policy-making: norm expansion through judicial activism within treaty regimes. The formation of the World Trade Organization (WTO) in 1995 inaugurated a new era of compulsory judicial-like settlement of trade disputes.[37] A new Appellate Body (AB) is empowered to review decisions of expert panels for fidelity to WTO law. The Dispute Settlement Understanding (DSU), the agreement regulating the authority and process of dispute settlement, severely curtails the discretion of the AB in lawmaking.[38] The debate at the WTO, however, has been between those who view the regime as essentially contractual (with a measure of democratic legitimacy) and those who would incorporate other norms including a wider body of CIL norms in a manner to trump previously negotiated treaty norms.[39] Environmentalists and progressives would expand the range of social policies that might justify limits on the treaty right to market access.[40] This debate may be seen as a struggle between different interest groups in the west: environmental and labor activists, on the one hand, and multilateral corporations on the other. This debate, however, again ignores the views and interests of developing countries.

The battlefront of this debate has been a series of environmental conservation cases beginning with the Tuna/Dolphin[41] litigation under the more voluntary General Agreement on Tariffs and Trade dispute settlement system and culminating with the Shrimp/Sea Turtle[42] litigation under the mandatory WTO dispute system. In the Tuna/Dolphin cases GATT panels had found that U.S. regulations that prohibited the importation of tuna captured beyond the territorial waters of the U.S. in a manner that killed more dolphin than permitted violated Article XI as a non-tariff barrier to imports. In doing so they held that the general exceptions in Articles XX(b) and (g) for measures necessary for human or animal life or health and for the conservation of natural resources did not apply.[43] The measure was not necessary because there were other methods more consistent with GATT obligations such as multilateral negotiations and labeling that could be used to resolve the problem. The GATT panel also found that the measures could not be applied extraterritorially. A nation may regulate the products that enter its jurisdiction but not how they are caught or produced abroad—the so-called process/production distinction. The cases engendered much critical comment from environmentalists and lead to massive demonstrations and riots at WTO ministerial meetings.

In the Shrimp/Sea Turtle case the new Appellate Body (AB) of the WTO reexamined these issues and used an "evolutionary methodology" to expand the conservation exception to GATT obligations in article XX(g).[44] The AB said that article XX(g) must be interpreted in light of the contemporary concerns of the international community.[45] It upheld a unilateral US ban on imported shrimp caught in foreign waters in a manner contrary to US law, but found that the measure was applied in a discriminatory manner.[46] It is important to understand that the US was banning a product not because of defects in the product itself which would be permissible, but because it objected to how the shrimp were caught within the territorial waters of Thailand. That is the US was using the lever of market access to prescribe environmental policy within Thailand. It was not a health or safety issue for consumers in the US.

The decision appears to be quite broad permitting unilateral bans of products produced in a manner contrary to one nation's environmental policy. In many ways the AB should be applauded for their candor in expanding the agreements exceptions. It openly used an "evolutionary" method of interpretation that ignored the original intent of the parties, past GATT decisions, and the declared positions of the vast majority of nations rather than hide their decision, as is often done, behind textualism.[47]

My technical objections to this decision are discussed in depth elsewhere.[48] The core concerns are: first, the "evolutionary methodology" the AB utilized is inconsistent with the structure of governance in the WTO agreements and the interpretive methodology of the VCT required by the DSU.[49] The WTO is essentially a contractual regime where nations negotiate rather specific norms and standards. As a state-centered contractual treaty regime, lawmaking authority properly resides in the Ministerial Council, not the AB.[50] Second, the proper interpretation of the Article XX(g) exception does not include living creatures as "exhaustible natural resources" rather regulation of human, animals and plants properly fall under the XX(b) exception. Article XX(b) wisely contains a "necessary" requirement as a filter for protectionist uses of this exception. Third, neither the Article XX(b) or (g) exceptions, properly interpreted, apply to the unilateral regulation of production methods abroad.

More importantly for the purposes of this article, even if we assume, contrary to the DSU, that the AB does have the authority to engage in this type of broad "evolutionary" interpretation, it is apparent that this methodology was being used as a form of the Naturalist approach to lawmaking. The AB did not engage in an empirical or even systematic investigation to determine the contemporary community's concerns about this issue.

In determining the contemporary concerns of the international community about the conservation of endangered species, the AB did not even look to the most relevant treaty, The Convention on the International Trade in Endangered Species (CITES) for guidance. CITES does not permit the regulation of how a nation treats its endangered species within its own territory leaving such regulation to the sovereign prerogative of each nation. Rather the AB placed great reliance on the preamble of the 1994 WTO Agreement, explicitly acknowledging the broad, undefined norm of sustainable development as one of the many objectives of the WTO regime. The preamble of the WTO Agreement, for example, does not raise environmental concerns above others. The Preamble actually includes primarily economic objectives such as raising living standards in developing countries and growth in income, production and employment. The one-hundred word, internally inconsistent preamble gives no guidance on how these general and conflicting mass of goals and concerns are to be reconciled.

The AB's selective use of a small portion of the preamble provides it with the unfettered discretion to choose the policy concern in the preamble that supported its policy choice. It could just as well have referred to language in the preamble to justify the opposite conclusion because the measure would close members' borders to developing countries' products, shrink employment and economic growth in the

Thai shrimp industry, and interfere with rather than preserve the objectives of the trading system.

The AB's misuse of the "evolutionary" interpretation methodology illustrates the dangers of the Naturalist approach. The "evolutionary interpretation" methodology provides the means for judges to expand exceptions and other norms when there is a no community agreement or consensus. The AB's interpretive methodology raises fundamental issues of global governance. Implicit is the premise that major substantive policy issues not negotiated by Member states in treaty regimes may, nevertheless, be decided by judicial panels beyond state consent.

The AB's judicial activism not only disenfranchises developing countries from important international policymaking, it also, as a practical matter, diminishes the ability of LDCs to determine their own environmental policies within their territory. It is important to understand that this is a game only for the wealthiest of nations with large markets. Now wealthy developed countries may unilaterally deny access to their markets increasing production costs of competitor nations unless other countries adopt their preferred environmental policies.

The decision and the use of the evolutionary methodology removes environmental and potentially other social policy from both international and domestic politics where costs and benefits could be debated. Instead in a world of many different interests and levels of economic development, important policy decisions on the appropriate balance of environmental protection and economic development are left to the vagaries of the domestic political arena of a few powerful nations.

Conclusion: internationalism in democratic constitutionalism

The discussion above demonstrates that the link between state consent and international norm development is increasingly attenuated. As international institutions proliferate and judicial bodies expand their province, international obligations are being created and authoritative decisions being made beyond domestic democratic processes. All forms of "Naturalism" discussed above (the misuse of malleable CIL, the adoption of a universal ideology of rights by domestic and international tribunals, and "evolutionary" or expansive interpretation of treaty regimes) diminish democratic decision-making. This lack of democratic legitimacy is particularly true with regard to LDCs who may have little input into norm development and lack the power or influence to significantly affect the outcome.

This suggests two broad areas of concern: the democratization of the structure of international law making and the reception of international legal norms into domestic legal systems.

Democratic values will be enhanced by decreasing reliance on CIL as a legitimate source of legal norms. The legitimacy of international law would be improved by greater use of consensual treaties and treaty regimes. Treaties and treaty regimes permit greater participation by developing countries with the greater likelihood that their voices and interests will be heard affecting the outcome. LDCs will increase their power and influence in treaty regimes by creating a unified block of nations around issues of common concern. Greater resources need to be allocated to improve the quality of LDC participation within treaty regimes particularly the WTO.

The decreased role of state consent in international law formation suggests that nations should exercise great care in incorporating such norms into their constitutions either directly in drafting or indirectly through judicial interpretation without prior democratic processes. The proliferation of naturalist forms of lawmaking in international law threatens the democratic claims of democratic constitutionalists when norms that trump legislation were themselves not previously approved by the people or their representatives.

Even if it were true that CIL norms represented a consensus of the world community, the proper interpretation of a nation's own constitution should reflect its fundamental commitments. The question should be: is this right or norm adequately grounded in a domestic consensus appropriate for the judiciary to interpret or is its application best determined by a legislature that can make the appropriate tradeoffs. International legalism may take normative development and sensible trade-offs out of the realm of domestic politics without the necessary political deliberation. Environmental and even human rights have costs both in financial resources and political resources. These costs should, in most cases, be balanced with other pressing goals such as economic development and health demands. Norms, particularly environmental norms, must be balanced with costs and alternative uses of resources, and then subjected to domestic political processes if they are not to be seen as cultural imperialism.

Expanded human rights such as Europe's opposition to the death penalty or a prohibition on corporal punishment should be seen as a form of moral rather than legal discourse subject to local political decisionmaking. The claims of universal legal rights are even less persuasive when the US, for example, does not accept these same norms as domestically enforceable obligations or limitations on their sovereignty.

All nations, particularly developing countries, should be cautious about importing the putative international norms of NGOs, scholars, and international conference declarations. International environmental principles, such as sustainable development and the precautionary principle[51], may be wise policy guides, but tell us little about how to reconcile competing interests when resources are scarce.

Declarations of broad environmental rights or a requirement of sustainable development placed in constitutions may be unwise. The legitimacy of these as legal norms is questionable and their content uncertain. The Shrimp/Sea Turtle case, for example, illustrates how broad, undefined norms such as sustainable development could be used by the judiciary to trump democratic compromises between environmental concerns and economic development. Important resource questions such as environmental policy should not be allocated to the judiciary, the branch least qualified to appreciate the potential costs and weigh them against competing needs such as poverty elimination, and life saving strategies against widespread diseases such as HIV and malaria. While I agree with the goals of expanding human rights and sustainable development, it is unwise to adopt methodologies that bypass inconvenient democratic processes. Resource and goal balancing are the proper domain of the legislature and, when delegated, of the executive. All too often western NGOs and academics, including myself, have no understanding of the experiences and perspectives of the majority of people of the world who live at a different stage of economic development.

Despite these serious concerns about the democratic legitimacy of international legal norms and institutions, each may play a valuable role in helping democratizing domestic societies. The United Nations Security Council, itself an undemocratic institution, has and will play an important role in stopping massive human suffering, oppression and genocide as well as separating warring parties to encourage the peaceful resolution of disputes. Democratic legitimacy is not the only value. There are other values such as the elimination of poverty, security, and freedom from oppression that must share the value stage.

While suggesting that international norms not be directly imported into domestic constitutions without democratic deliberation, this is not an argument for a populist or majoritarian constitutionalism that eliminates judicial review. Judicial review that holds executive and legislative decisions within the bounds of the constitution is essential to securing not only minority rights but the rights of all citizens. Democracy can be illiberal and violent as Fareed Zakaria reminds us.[52] Slobodan Milosevic was elected in a landslide and remains popular today among Serbs despite his incitement of ethnic cleansing. International norms, moral outrage, and constitutional restraints may limit oppression and encourage nations to act.

Nations that hold elections may not be democracies at all or may possess only a limited form of democracy. The electoral process can be manipulated, fixed, or ignored. Democracy may be seen as only as a set of procedures including elections or it may be seen as having substantive content that includes, at a minimum, a core of political rights that ensure effective participation.[53] A government may be a kleptocracy, a form of organized crime utilizing elections as a fig leaf of authority.

The judiciary within a country may play a useful role in limiting the excessive use of executive power or at least delegitimizing its excesses. Constitutional reforms in a number of African countries, for example, have increased the role of the judiciary in interpreting and enforcing the constitution against executive attempts to undermine democracy and constitutional commitments.[54] The authority to review and declare oppressive acts of the executive or legislature as incompatible with the constitution gives both legal and moral legitimacy to claims of overreaching and may affect future elections.

There is value in a democratic constitutionalism that restricts the oppressive use of power. Countermajoritarian decisions of judges upholding constitutional rights may, in some circumstances, be seen as a form of democracy and protective of the institutions of democracy. At a minimum, the judiciary must preserve the process of democracy from manipulation and fraud. The constitution with individual rights and restraints on governmental action was itself enacted by democratic processes and is subject to later amendment. Democracy is not just the present will of the people, but includes the development and fidelity to long-term political and legal commitments.[55] One democratic majority, generally a supermajority, by creating a constitution, is making a commitment to democracy over time that is not subject to political whim. This gift from one generation to another promotes a deeper form of democracy.

[1] Bruce Ackerman, *We the People: Foundations* (Cambridge: Harvard University Press, 1991), 1-16. Ackerman terms democratic constitutionalists 'dualists' because they allow two sources of democratic authority: the people in enacting a constitution and the people's representatives in enacting laws. He further distinguishes 'rights foundationalists', who accept the primacy of fundamental rights even contrary to democratic processes, from dualists. Foundationalists share a common perspective with advocates of universal human rights that transcend state sovereignty.

[2] Chief Justice Marshall expounded the doctrine of judicial supremacy in Marbury v. Madison, 5 U.S. (1 Cranch) 137 (1803). For a modern defense, *see* Larry Alexander and Frederick Schaur, "On Extrajudicial Constitutional Interpretation", *Harv. L. Rev.* 110 (1997): 1359.

[3] Mark Tushnet, *Taking the Constitution Away From Courts* (Princeton: Princeton University Press, 1999). Tushnet calls for the abolition of judicial review at 154-76.

[4] Ran Hirschl, *Toward Juristocracy: The Origins and Consequences of the New Constitutionalism* (Cambridge: Harvard University Press, 2004). Using four case studies the author demonstrates that judicial empowerment through constitutionalism has insulated important policy issues from democratic politics and served to preserve the status quo.

[5] Tushnet, *supra* note 3, 177-94; Hirschl, *supra* note 4, 219-223.

[6] By 'naturalism' I mean the application of legal rules or principles extrinsic to positive enactment by the relevant political community. The forms of naturalism include the application of natural law, fundamental rights, constructivist norms, or, as discussed below, customary international law in a manner to find one's own values.

[7] *See e.g.*, Lawrence R. Helfer, "Overlegalizing Human Rights: International Relations Theory and the Commonwealth Caribbean Backlash Against Human Rights Regimes", *Colum. L. Rev.* 102 (2002): 1832.

[8] For the position that judicial review should be eliminated, *see* Tushnet, *supra* note 3. For an interesting modification of judicial review that would authorize the Congress by a majority vote to overrule a Supreme Court decision as unconstitutional after a subsequent election in which to debate the issue, *see* Robert Justin Lipkin, "The New Majoritarianism", U. Cinn. L. Rev. 69 (2000): 154.

[9] Ian Brownlie, *Principles of Public International law*, 6th ed. (Oxford: Oxford University Press, 2003), 39.

[10] Anthony D'Amato, *The Concept of Custom in International Law* (Ithaca: Cornell University Press, 1971), 47-72.

[11] Customary law is a social fact subject to observation that the relevant community invests with binding authority. *See* Ian Hamnett, "Introduction" in *Social Anthropology and Law*, ed. Ian Hamnett (New York: Academic Press, 1977), 7-11.

[12] The major treatises agree on the formal elements of this paradigm as well as the U.S. Restatement. *See* for example, Ian Brownlie, *supra* note 9, 6-11 and *Oppenhiem's International Law*, 9th ed., ed. Robert Jennings & Arthur Watts (London: Longman, 1997), 35-41.

[13] For a fuller discussion of the problems with the CIL paradigm, *see* J. Patrick Kelly, "The Twilight of Customary International Law", *Va. J. Int'l L.* 40 (2000): 449.

[14] Anthony D'Amato, *The Concept of Custom in International Law* (Ithaca: Cornell University Press, 1971), 87-91.

[15] Michael Akehurst, "Custom as a Source of International Law", *Brit. Y.B. Int'l L.* 47 (1977): 40.

[16] *Oppenheim's 9th*, *supra* note 12, 29.

[17] *See* Kelly, *supra* note 13, 508-19. The author describes the history of the struggle between the consent and universal paradigms and the recent rise of the persistent objector principle.

[18] The Yale policy-oriented school of jurisprudence associates authority with effective power and has had significant influence at the U.S. Department of State. *See* W. Michael Reisman & Andrew Williard eds., *International Incidents: The Law That Counts in World Politics* (New Haven: Yale University Press, 1988).

[19] Trial Smelter (U.S. v. Canada) 3 U.N. Rep. Int. Arb. Awards 1905 (1941).

[20] Stockholm Declaration of the United Nations Conference on the Human Environment, U.N. Doc A/Conf.48/14 (1972).

[21] Restatement (Third) of the Foreign Relations Law of the United States, § 601.

[22] Rio Declaration on Environment and Development, U.N. Doc. A/Conf.151/26 (1992). Principle 2 of the Rio Declaration restates and weakens Principle 21 of the Stockholm Declaration by clarifying that the sovereign right to exploit resources is pursuant to both developmental and environmental policies.

[23] For a discussion of this approach, *see* Louis Henkin, "Human Rights: Ideology and Aspiration, Reality and Prospect", *in* Samantha Power and Graham T. Allison, eds., *Realizing Human Rights: Moving From Inspiration to Impact* (New York: St. Martin's Press, 2000).

[24] Jed Rubenfeld, "Unilateralism and Constitutionalism", *N.Y.U. L. Rev.* 79 (2004): 1991-99.

[25] See e.g., Hurst Hannam, "The Status of the Universal Declaration of Human Rights in National and International Law", *Ga. J. Int'l & Comp. L.* 25 (1995-96): 289.

[26] Abdullahi Ahmed An-Na'im, "Toward a Cross-Cultural Approach to Defining International Standards of Human Rights" in *Human Rights in Cross-Cultural Perspective*, ed. An-Na'im (Philadelphia: University of Pennsylvania Press, 1992), 37-39.

[27] 1249 U.N.T.S. 13 (1981).

[28] CEDAW Committee, General Recommendation No. 19, U.N. Doc. A/37/38 (1992).

[29] For a survey of the diversity of views on this controversial subject, *see* Hope Lewis, "Between Irua and 'Female Genital Mutilation: Feminist Human Rights Discourse", *Harv. H. R. J.* 8 (1995): 1.

[30] The CEDAW Committee in analyzing the many reservations indicated that traditional or religious beliefs do not justify violations and offered its view that such reservations were incompatible with the Convention and should be withdrawn. "Contribution to the Commemoration of the Fiftieth Anniversary of the Universal Declaration of Human Rights", in *Status of the Convention on the Elimination of All Forms of Discrimination Against Woman,* Report of the Secretary-General, Annex X, 29, UN Doc. A/53/318 (1998).

[31] Louis Henkin, " United States Ratification of Human Rights Conventions: The Ghost of Senator Bricker", *Am J. Int'l L.* 89 (1995): 341.

[32] Human Rights Committee, Comment 24, UN. Doc. A/50/40, Vol. 1 (1995), §§ 17 & 18, 119.

[33] American Law Institute, *Restatement (Third) of the Foreign Relations Law of the United States*, §§ 711-13 (1987).

[34] For a summary of the arguments for and against a right to democracy, *see* Gregory H. Fox and Brad R. Roth, "Introduction: The Spread of Liberal Democracy and its Implications for International Law" in *Democratic Governance and International Law,* ed. Fox and Brad R. Roth (Cambridge: Cambridge University Press, 2000), 1-22. Even in his classic argument for a right to a democratic form of government, Thomas Franck warns that such a democratic entitlement should be delinked from the unilateral use of military force to compel compliance. Thomas M. Franck, "The Emerging Right to Democratic Governance," *Am. J. Int'l L.* 86 (1992): 84.

[35] *See* William J. Aceves, "Liberalism and International Legal Scholarship: The Pinochet Case and the Move Toward a Universal System of Transnational Law Litigation", *Harv. Int'l L. J.* 41 (2000): 129.

[36] For an extended argument for this position, *see* Michael Ignatieff, *Human Rights as Politics and Idolatry* (Princeton: Princeton University Press, 2001).

[37] The World Trade Agreement: Final Act Embodying the Results of the Uruguay Round of Trade Negotiations, Apr. 15, 1994, *Legal Instruments-Results of the Uruguay Round.*

[38] Ibid., Understanding on Rules and Procedures Governing the Settlement of Disputes (DSU), Apr. 15, 1994, WTO Agreement, Annex 2. The DSU cautions the AB in Art. 3.2 that the purpose of the dispute settlement system is "to preserve the rights and obligations of members under the covered agreements" and that rulings "cannot add to or diminish the rights and obligations under the covered agreements." (emphasis added).

[39] David Palmeter & Petros Mavroidis, "The WTO Legal System: Sources of Law", *Am. J. Int'l L.* 92 (1998): 398.

[40] *See e.g.*, Steve Charnovitz, "The Moral Exception in Trade Policy", *Va. J. Int'l L.* 38 (1998): 689.

[41] GATT Panel Report, *United States-Restrictions on Imports of Tuna*, DS21/R-39S/155 (Sept. 3, 1991) (not adopted) and GATT Panel Report, *United States- Restrictions on Imports of Tuna*, DS29/R (June 16, 1994) (not adopted).

[42] WTO Appellate Body Report, *United States- Import Prohibition of Certain Shrimp and Shrimp Products,* WT/DS58/AB/R (Oct. 12, 1998).

[43] GATT Panel Report, *United States-Restrictions on Imports of Tuna*, Sept. 3, 1991, *supra* note 41, ¶ 7.1 (a). The Article XX (b) exception from Member obligations provides: (measures) "necessary to protect human, animal, or plant life or health...." The article XX (g) exception includes measures "relating to the conservation of exhaustible natural resources..."

[44] WTO Appellate Body Report, *United States- Import Prohibition of Certain Shrimp and Shrimp Products,* Oct. 12, 1998, supra note 42, ¶¶ 129-30.

[45] Ibid., ¶129.

[46] Ibid. at ¶¶ 161-87.. The United States subsequently modified its procedure to eliminate the discriminatory treatment, and the AB upheld the measure and its application as consistent with the agreements. WTO Appellate Body Report, *United States- Import Prohibition of Certain Shrimp and Shrimp Products, Recourse to Article 21.5 of the DSU by Malaysia,* WT/DS58/AB/RW (Oct. 22, 2001).

[47] For the AB's discussion of its evolutionary methodology, *see Shrimp/Sea Turtle I, supra* note 42, ¶¶ 129-30.

[48] J. Patrick Kelly, "The Seduction of the Appellate Body: Shrimp Sea Turtle I and II and the Proper Role of States in WTO Governance", *Cornell J. Int'l L.* 38 (2005): 459. Recognizing that the AB is unlikely to fully reverse its position, the author proposes that article XX (g) be limited to an emergency exception for endangered species.

[49] The DSU, establishing the terms of WTO mandatory dispute settlement, further cautions the AB in Art. 3.5, "All solutions to matters formally raised under the… dispute settlement provisions of the covered agreements… shall be consistent with those agreements and shall not nullify or impair benefits accruing to any Member under those agreements…." DSU, *supra* note 38, art. 3.5.

[50] *See* WTO Agreement, *supra* note 37, arts. IX and X.

[51] The precautionary principle, for example, has many incompatible definitions. *See* Cass R. Sunstein, "Irreversible and Catastrophic", *Cornell L. Rev.* 91 (2006): 848-50.

[52] Fareed Zakaria, *The Future of Freedom: Illiberal Democracy at Home and Abroad* (New York: W.W. Norton & Company, 2004).

[53] For a discussion of procedural and substantive democracy, *see* Gregory H. Fox and Georg Nolte, "Intolerant Democracies" in *Democratic Governance and International Law,* ed. Gregory H. Fox and Brad R. Roth (Cambridge: Cambridge University Press, 2000), 389.

[54] H. Kwasi Prempeh, "Marbury in Africa: Judicial Review and the Challenge of Constitutionalism in Africa", *Tulane L. Rev.* 80 (2006): 1239-47.

[55] Jed Rubenfeld, *Freedom and Time: A Theory of Constitutional Self-Government* (New Haven: Yale University Press, 2000).

CHAPTER 19

WAR POWERS UNDER THE SOUTH AFRICAN CONSTITUTION

Stephen Ellmann[*]

It may seem strange to inquire into the nature of war powers under South Africa's Constitution – for surely South Africa is not a nation that considers itself embarked on a policy of war. But I believe the topic is important nonetheless.

As a matter of principle, there are few greater destroyers of rights, or creators of utter and arbitrary inequality, than war, which orders soldiers to kill, sacrifices others, and potentially rips apart the fabric of civil society. The power to make war is the power to protect and to destroy perhaps the most fundamental right of all, the right to live in an ordered society. A state which leaves this power loosely governed is a state where rights are not entirely secure, no matter how extensively that state protects rights in situations short of war.

Nor are these abstract considerations for South Africa. South Africa is not a warlike state, but it is, compared to other nations in Africa, a well-armed state.[1] Its spending to maintain that military strength is at the heart of a bribery scandal that as of 2008 still threatens to bring down Jacob Zuma, now President of the African National Congress, and may taint others as well.[2] Its troops are already serving, or have served, in peacekeeping or election-support missions in several other African states, including Burundi, the Democratic Republic of the Congo (DRC), and Darfur in the Sudan, as well as the Comoros, Côte d'Ivoire, Eritrea, Ethiopia, Lesotho, Liberia, Mozambique, and Uganda – and also in Nepal.[3] Some, fortunately a small number, have died in combat outside its borders, in an intervention in Lesotho in 1998 and more recently in the DRC.[4] War is not entirely absent from South Africa's politics, even today – and there is of course no telling what the future may hold. South Africa's peacekeeping efforts in fact have stretched the nation's current military resources,[5] and the goal of establishing an African Union peacekeeping force will certainly call on South African resources as well.[6]

The South African Constitution addresses the possibility of war, and the deployment of troops, but not at great length. The brevity of these provisions is entirely understandable. No doubt the reason for it was, at least in good part, that South Africa's constitution writers – like their counterparts in every nation – wrote a constitution not for abstract review but for the governance of their nation with its particular and painful history. The legacy of human rights abuses, especially in states of emergency, was fresh in the drafters' minds, and they addressed these dangers in detail in the new Constitution, but they did not envision their renewed country as a war-making state. Perhaps they also did not expect that the new South

[*] Associate Dean for Faculty Development and Professor of Law, New York Law School. I presented earlier drafts of this paper at the University of KwaZulu-Natal conference from which this book has come, and at the conference on 'Law, Politics, Culture, and Society in South Africa: The Politics of Inequality Then and Now,' sponsored by the University of Florida, in March 2006. I thank the conference organizers for those opportunities and the participants, as well as other readers, for their helpful comments. I also thank Sarah Valentine (now at CUNY School of Law) and Michael McCarthy of NYLS' Mendik Law Library for their timely help with research.

Africa would play as active a role as it does in deploying military force on behalf of peace – a constructive and admirable role, but one not without risks.

Meanwhile, we in the United States have re-encountered the issues of war powers, as we have faced an unconventional enemy and our government has pressed the boundaries of many uncertain constitutional powers while it fashions its response to this enemy and others. In the grim light of 9/11 and its aftermath, issues of war power that might at one time have seemed obscure or implausible have turned out to be present and pointed. War is hell, and havoc, and it is also extremely hard to govern constitutionally; the pressures of military necessity drive the meaning of constitutional language in ways that only experience may fully reveal. South Africa so far has, happily, had little occasion to encounter these questions in its own governance. But war is a great danger, even in a country that takes pride in its commitments to peace. While I will offer few prescriptions in this paper, I hope that it will be useful to South Africans as they develop the constitutional understandings that may someday guide the interpretation of their nation's powers of war.

Let me add one more word of explanation of the inquiry I make in this paper. It should surprise no one that South Africa's constitutional provisions dealing with war and fighting have some ambiguities – all texts have some ambiguities. I do not mean to score debater's points by highlighting linguistic possibilities that may be grammatically coherent but are inconsistent with the fundamental themes of the South African Constitution. On the contrary, where ambiguity in specific clauses can be interpreted by reference to general principles of South African constitutional law I will hope to do just that.

Three such general principles are particularly important. First, and most fundamental, all acts of the South African government are subject to the Constitution[7] – so the notion of war powers that are wholly beyond the reach of judicial review is implausible.[8] Moreover, the protection of human rights is an absolutely integral part of the South African constitutional order.[9] Second, the Constitution contains a specific commitment to subject military power to law. The Constitution declares that the security services (including military, police and intelligence services) 'must act ... in accordance with the Constitution and the law'.[10] This is not just an abstract sentiment; for the ANC the issue of the armed forces' loyalty during the constitutional transition was a critical and delicate one.[11] Third, the Constitution rejects the idea that war is the province of the executive alone. Section 198(d) lays out, as one of the 'governing principles' for the security services, that '[n]ational security is subject to the authority of Parliament and the national executive'.[12]

As important as these general principles are, however, they do not remove the need to look carefully at the specific provisions of the South African Constitution that deal with war. We will first look at the provisions governing the declaration of a state of national defence – the clearest route provided by the Constitution for South Africa to enter war. As we will find, the procedural requirements for such declarations are distinctly less demanding than those governing the declaration of a state of emergency. At the same time, the substantive powers conferred on the President by such a declaration – though not beyond Parliament's authority to regulate – are potentially far-reaching, both in military terms and in terms of their impact on at least some human rights. Next, we will ask whether South Africa can become involved in military action without a declaration of a state of national defence. The answer appears to be 'yes', and moreover it appears that the President has authority to initiate a range of potentially risky military involvements without any direct approval by Parliament – although, again, Parliament may approve, or disapprove, if it so chooses. Finally, in light of the extent of military and Presidential authority that this analysis has identified, we will consider the role of Parliament's power over the budget as a check, albeit not a perfect one, on executive military decisions.

(1) The procedural requirements for a state of national defence

The Constitution gives no explicit power to anyone to declare 'war'. Perhaps such an authority is still implicit in the general powers of the President and Parliament, but probably not. Instead, it appears that the drafters of the Constitution carefully avoided giving the nation a power to declare war, and instead gave it a power to declare a 'state of national defence'.[13] Does this mean that South Africa cannot fight a war, or engage its troops in combat 'hostilities'?[14] Surely not. There is no sign that South Africa chose to abandon its military when it abolished apartheid, and a country with a military is a country prepared, at least in some circumstances, to fight. If the country were to be attacked, the declaration of a state of national defence must have been meant as a way of declaring that the nation was going to fight to defend itself.[15] It may well be that South Africa has no constitutional power to fight a war of aggression,[16] but, as we will see, that constraint still leaves room for many potential military engagements.

What are the procedural requirements for the declaration of a state of national defence? The first part of the answer to this question is explicit, or almost explicit. Section 203(1) says that '[t]he President as head of the national executive may declare a state of national defence'. Although this language doesn't in so many words prohibit Parliament from also issuing such a declaration on its own, the overall content of § 203 (with its focus on the President's reporting to Parliament, and Parliament's approving the declaration after it has been made) makes clear that only the President has this authority.

More precisely, only the President, or whoever may be serving as Acting President, can exercise this authority. Because the authority is transferable, it is quite possible that a declaration of a state of national defence could be made by someone chosen by the President to serve as Acting President rather than by anyone elected by Parliament to play this role.[17] In actual fact, South Africa's intervention into Lesotho in 1998, though apparently not based on a declaration of national defence but simply on a decision to send troops on the mission, was ordered by Mangosothu Buthelezi in his capacity as Acting President while President Nelson Mandela was out of the country[18]; Mandela's choice of Buthelezi surely was related to the ANC's efforts to improve relations with this long-time opponent.[19]

It is striking that this power is given to the President. Clearly, explicitly, he or she can declare the nation's involvement in war without any prior approval from Parliament. (It may be that the President must obtain the approval not only of the relevant Cabinet minister but also, for a decision of this magnitude, of the Cabinet as a whole.[20]) Presumably the war can then be fought as well. But the declaration 'lapses unless it is approved by Parliament within seven days of the declaration'.[21] This requirement of affirmative approval by Parliament means that in South Africa, as has also been the practice in the United States,[22] a formal declaration of the nation's martial intent (a declaration of war in the US, a declaration of a state of national defence in South Africa) rests on the approval of both of the political branches of government. But it must be said that within a week a lot can happen, politically and militarily. If the President begins the war on Monday, and South African troops have fallen by Saturday, will Parliament be prepared to withhold its approval? It has often been suggested that the Presidential power to involve the United States in fighting presents our Congress with something approaching a *fait accompli*.[23] In any event, the more firmly the executive maintains political control of Parliament – and that control in general seems considerably firmer under South Africa's system of government than it would be in the United States – the less likely that Parliament will withhold its approval.

Though Parliamentary approval is required for a declaration of a state of national defence, it is clear that overall the Constitution imposes much clearer and more stringent requirements for a declaration of a state of emergency than it does in connection with the declaration of a state of national defence. Specifically:

First, § 37(1) specifies the grounds on which a state of emergency can be declared (a threat to 'the life of the nation'), whereas no specific grounds are spelled out for declaring a state of national defence. A state of emergency can only be declared in terms of an Act of Parliament,[24] but no statute is required as a basis for declaring a state of national defence. In fact, the Defence Act does set out grounds for declaring a state of national defence,[25] but these are not mandated by the constitutional text.

Second, while a state of emergency can last for 21 days without legislative endorsement – compared to 7 days for a state of national defence – once initial approval has been given by Parliament for a state of emergency, this approval must be renewed at least every three months.[26] A state of national defence, by contrast, appears to extend indefinitely.

Third, § 37(2) spells out which chamber of Parliament has the power to give or withhold approval of a state of emergency – the National Assembly – whereas the allocation of this authority for states of national defence is not made explicit. What § 203(3) says is that 'Parliament' must approve the declaration, and § 42(1) declares that Parliament consists of the National Assembly and the National Council of Provinces (NCOP).[27] It is not easy to see why the National Assembly should be relied upon to approve or disapprove states of emergency, while the National Council of Provinces as well as the National Assembly are needed for approval or disapproval of states of national defence, but on its face this is what the text dictates.[28] Conceivably, however, the NCOP is not meant to play a part in approving a declaration of a state of national defence. It might be argued that the NCOP's powers are limited to 'legislative power', and that approval or disapproval of a declaration of a state of national defence is not actually legislation. Rather, this function might be seen as a form of oversight over executive power, a responsibility apparently reserved to the National Assembly.[29]

If, on the other hand, the NCOP does have a role to play in the approval of a declaration of a state of national defence, then how great is that role? If this decision is viewed as a form of legislation, presumably it is legislation of national rather than distinctively provincial concern.[30] If so, then even if the NCOP withholds approval of the declaration after the National Assembly has given its endorsement, the National Assembly can give *Parliament's* approval by re-enacting it.[31] But if this approval did count as legislation triggering the special NCOP powers applicable to bills 'affecting provinces', then very different dispute resolution provisions would apply.[32] Finally, it could be maintained that the approval of a declaration of a state of national defence is not governed by either of the two sets of procedures for normal legislation, and that some further process, such as an absolute requirement of approval by each House of Parliament, must be inferred for this very special function. The failure to fully clarify this complex of issues is a significant omission, and a potential source of great difficulty should a state of national defence ever be declared.

Fourth, § 37(2) also forbids the National Assembly from approving or extending a state of national emergency without a public legislative debate. No such rule is imposed for approval of a state of national defence, though other sections require that Parliament's rules in general must have 'due regard' for 'transparency and public involvement'.[33] It is hard to accept the idea of a state of national defence being approved without a public debate – but perhaps the sheer unlikelihood of such a step makes the absence of this textual requirement less important.

Fifth, the required majorities for approval differ. The National Assembly can only approve a state of emergency by 'a supporting vote of a majority of the members of the Assembly', and can only extend it by 'a supporting vote of at least 60 per cent of the members of the Assembly'.[34] The Constitution imposes no supermajority voting requirement for Parliament's approval of a state of national defence. Presumably, therefore, Parliament is to treat this declaration according to one or the other of the two standard models the Constitution provides. If the declaration is treated as equivalent to a 'Bill', then the required quorum in the National Assembly is one-half of the members, and the required vote appears to be simply a majority of those voting.[35] If, on the other hand, the declaration is not treated as a bill, then the required quorum in the National Assembly is only one-third of the members; again, approval or disapproval would require simply a majority of the votes cast.[36]

Sixth, the Constitution explicitly provides for judicial review of the validity of states of emergency – their declaration, the approval and extension of their declaration, and any legislation or action taken in consequence of their declaration.[37] It is likely that some form of judicial review of a state of national defence is also available, because of the fundamental principle that all government action is subject to the Constitution.[38] But the Constitution contains no explicit, specific provision for such review, and that silence might well support arguments that the available judicial review must be particularly deferential.

(2) The powers granted by the declaration of a state of national defence

To address this matter, we must consider three issues: (a) If Parliament approves a declaration, without more, what powers does the declaration confer on the President to wage war?; (b) To what extent can Parliament limit the authority that the declaration confers by adding restrictions to it?; and (c) To what extent can the President and Parliament together limit otherwise-applicable constitutional rights based on a declaration of a state of national defence? Let us take up these three questions in order.

What powers is the President authorized to employ, if the President declares and Parliament authorizes a state of national defence? The text does not explicitly answer this question. The most straightforward inference from the text, however, is that when a state of national defence has been declared and authorized, the President has full authority (acting with the responsible cabinet minister and the cabinet as a whole) to deploy and direct the troops, as their Commander-in-Chief, at least until Parliament in some way restricts that authority.

The President is always the Commander-in-Chief, of course.[39] But what are the powers of a Commander-in-Chief? The text does not specify these authorities, but, again, the most plausible answer is that as Commander-in-Chief, the President has the authority to order any lawful military action,[40] from preparation for war to actual fighting. Suppose, for instance, that troops from one of South Africa's neighbors massed on the border. One might imagine that South Africa would move its troops to the border in response, and this positioning of forces would be an appropriate exercise of Commander-in-Chief powers under a 'state of national defence'. By the same logic, Parliament's approval of the state of national defence would also authorize the President to launch a preemptive attack on the threatening troops (assuming that such an attack could be justified under international law as self-defence against an imminent invasion). Similarly, it would allow the President to repel an attack and pursue the attackers deep into the attacking country's territory, assuming that such a response fell within legitimate self-defence under the UN Charter and other binding international law. On the same basis, Parliament's approval of the declaration of a state of national defence could authorize, without further legislative action, the President's taking the attacking country's capital by force and overthrowing the aggressor government.

It might be argued, however, that Parliament's approval is narrower than this. Section 203(1), which empowers the President to declare a state of national defence, also requires the President to report to Parliament:

      (a) the reasons for the declaration;

      (b) any place where the defence force is being employed; and

      (c) the number of people involved.

Parliament's approval of the declaration might be thought to be limited to approving the particular rationale and the particular level of troop engagement that the President has reported to it. This is a possible reading but not, I think, the most plausible one. Section 203 does not say that the President's use of troops lapses if it is not approved within seven days; rather, it says that the *declaration* lapses if not approved within that period. It seems inevitable that in a war, whatever uses are being made of troops in the first seven days will change over the next seven, or seven hundred, and there is no sign in the text that each such change requires a fresh declaration and a fresh Parliamentary approval.

It is important to add that the question of Presidential power is not only a question of 'what powers' but of 'against whom'. Who can be the target of a declaration of a state of national defence? The broader the range of potential targets, the wider the potential occasions when the war powers of the nation can be brought into play under this mantle. The text does not say who the targets of such declarations can be. It seems reasonable to infer, however, that in rejecting the rubric of 'declarations of *war*' the Constitution also puts to one side any possible argument that a declaration can only be directed against another nation-state, as might have been the case with a declaration of war. Assuming that the declaration must be against *someone* (rather than being, simply, a declaration that the nation is in peril, with no specification of the source of the danger), how well must that someone be specified? Would it be constitutional for the President to declare a state of national defence against, say, all those who participated in an act of terrorism against South Africa, or who aided or harbored those who did? Or all those whom the President *concludes* or *finds* participated in the act of terrorism, or aided or harbored those who did?[41] Or who commit acts of terrorism in the future?[42] The answers to these questions will help measure the breadth of the President's, and Parliament's, authority under a state of national defence.

Can Parliament limit the authority conferred on the President by its approval of a state of national defence? If Parliament's approval of the declaration of a state of national defence ordinarily operates to authorize all lawful military action that the President may order, still it might be that Parliament can, if it chooses, impose limitations on this authorization. The text does not make clear whether Parliament has this power, and this is an important and potentially troublesome ambiguity. Given that only the President can issue a declaration of a state of national defence, it is possible (as a reader suggested) that Parliament's only power as to declarations is to approve them or disapprove them, since any Parliamentary modification of the declaration might begin to constitute a new declaration, issued by Parliament. The basic principle that national security is subject to both Parliamentary and Presidential authority, on the other hand, argues in favor of finding that Parliament *can* amend a declaration before approving it. Even if the division of powers with regard to declarations impliedly limits Parliament's authority in this respect, moreover, a sufficiently independent Parliament might be able to compel a President to modify and re-issue a declaration, in order to win Parliamentary approval for it.

In addition, Parliament might well retain authority to approve or disapprove the broad policies that the President undertakes by virtue of the declaration. So, for example, I would argue that Parliament could choose to forbid the President to invade the aggressor nation I imagined earlier, even if the President believed that invasion was necessary to erase the peril that nation posed to South Africa and even though Parliament had approved the declaration of a state of national defence in response to that peril.[43] The constitutional text does not spell out such a power to approve or disapprove military policies, but it is not precluded by the text, and the principle of joint Parliamentary-Presidential responsibility counsels in favor of it. Indeed, precisely because a declaration of a state of national defence can last for an unlimited time, principles of accountability strongly argue in favor of finding Parliamentary power to regulate what is done during the potentially extended duration of hostilities.

In this regard, it is noteworthy that the Constitution, in addition to requiring the President to provide Parliament with certain information in connection with a declaration of a state of national defence, also imposes in § 201(3) a requirement that the President provide information to Parliament concerning a range of 'employment[s] of the defence force', notably including employment 'in defence of the Republic'.[44] If this section is understood to create an ongoing duty of reporting, even during an already-approved state of national defence, and if the function of this reporting is inferred to be not simply to inform Parliament but to empower it to act, then we have reason to find a continuing Parliamentary authority to regulate the military course of a state of national defence.[45] (Parliament's funding power is a further check, as we will see.)[46] It is important to recognize, however, that this reading affirms Parliamentary review power but does not establish any requirement of Parliamentary approval as a predicate for Presidential action. As long as Parliament does not order otherwise, it seems quite likely that the declaration of a state of national defence confers, or accepts, unlimited Commander-in-Chief authority bound only by general South African or international law.

Moreover, assuming that Parliament does have this implied authority to limit the President's freedom of action in a state of national defence, it would appear to be subject to a possibly significant limit: Parliament presumably cannot impose modifications that in effect prevent the President from performing the role of Commander-in-Chief. What this limit would entail is by no means certain, and I do not mean to suggest that aggressively expansive notions of executive war-making power would be compatible with South Africa's constitutional order. But still this limit does seem to have at least some content. Parliament probably could not, for example, require that Presidential military orders be co-signed by the Speaker of the National Assembly; the President, not the Speaker, is the Commander-in-Chief.[47] Parliament also cannot order the 'employment' of troops in defence of the nation; '[o]nly the President, as head of the national executive', has that authority, under § 201(2) of the Constitution.[48] If Parliament cannot order the 'employment' of troops, its power to order, or to compel the President to order, their 'deployment' during a state of national defence may also be limited. Thus, although I have already urged that Parliament would have the power to regulate the broad outlines of war (for example, to forbid an invasion as a form of self-defence), it is open to question whether Parliament could direct the President in a state of national defence to attack one base rather than another, to defend one town but not a second, or to use armored personnel carriers but not tanks.[49] Once a state of national defence has been declared and approved, some considerable authority may pass to the President in a way that Parliament cannot restrict.

To what extent does the declaration of a state of national defence authorize limitations on otherwise protected human rights? We can begin to answer this question by asking another: Does the declaration of a state of national defence also declare a state of national emergency? The answer to this question is clearly 'no'. A state of national defence is not a state of emergency, and a state of emergency is not a state of national defence. The brief constitutional text bearing on states of national defence does not suggest a recognition that constitutional rights would be subject to extensive abridgment, whereas the text addressing states of emergency focuses elaborately on exactly this prospect. It seems reasonable to say that in South Africa the only time that constitutional rights can be 'derogated' from is in a state of emergency, although the text of § 37 (on states of emergency) does not actually say this in so many words.

As we have seen, the constitutional provisions governing the declaration and continuation of states of emergency are in general more demanding than those governing states of national defence. It appears to follow, therefore, that in South Africa the government is considerably freer to engage troops in battle than it is to deprive people of constitutional rights. This statement is somewhat startling, but not necessarily cause for concern. It may be that states of national defence are so much less tempting as instruments of potential authoritarian oppression than states of emergency are that fewer constitutional limits need to be imposed on their use; *realpolitik* itself will protect the nation.

While this may be so, it is important to recognize that the powers employed in a state of national defence do have important human rights implications. Sending troops into battle risks depriving them of their lives. Section 11 of the Constitution protects the right to life, which cannot be derogated from even in a state of emergency, under § 37(5)(c). It must follow that orders sending troops into battle in a lawfully-undertaken war are *justified* under § 36 as a limitation on the soldiers' right to life, and so can be issued without effecting a derogation from that right.[50]

There are other ways in which the violent clashes that a state of national defence would authorize would inevitably impair otherwise fully-protected constitutional rights, even if a state of national defence is not meant to authorize limitations of the sort contemplated in states of emergency. I will put aside here the possibility of military conflict so grave that the civil courts cannot stay open; there lies the ultimate recourse of martial law, unmentioned in the South African Constitution (as it is unmentioned in the United States Constitution) yet still present somewhere in the wings.[51]

Far from the realm of martial law, the existence of a state of national defence would raise other issues of limitation of constitutional rights. Suppose, for example, that South Africa faced the likelihood of imminent terrorist attack by a foreign terrorist group, and had declared a state of national defence as a result. Unless Parliament enacted limitations, presumably the President would be entitled to use all normally lawful military steps to ward off the attack. In an actual war, the armies of one side monitor the communications of the other, and they do not usually stop to obtain court authorization first. It would seem that the President, as commander-in-chief of the South African National Defense Force, would have the authority to order electronic surveillance of communications among members of this foreign terrorist group abroad, without case-by-case judicial review, though doing so would certainly impair their privacy of communications under § 14(d).[52] Would the President have the same authority as to communications by members of the group abroad to their (known? suspected?) confederates within South Africa, assuming those confederates are also not South African citizens? What about communications from outside South Africa into the country, when either the sender or recipient *is* a South African citizen? And what about communications going the other way?[53] And, finally, what if the group against which the state of national defence has been declared is a domestic, South African terrorist group?[54]

I don't mean that these questions are unanswerable, or that the exercise of such wartime authority would be beyond review by the courts or regulation by Parliament. But it is hard to believe that the rules governing surveillance in a state of national defence would be the same as those applying in ordinary circumstances; *some* limitations on normally available rights would likely be justified by the needs of the state of national defence. The power to declare a state of national defence means that military need and domestic constitutional liberty may overlap and conflict, and the exact contours of the boundary between them have not yet been worked out.

These inferences may seem feverish. In fact, however, the Defence Act appears to go considerably further. Section 91(1) gives the President broad authority to make regulations to deal with the tasks of a state of national defence, and § 91(2) makes clear that such regulations can have a very substantial effect on constitutional rights. It remains to be seen, of course, whether the powers conferred in these sections are constitutional, but the existence of the statute presumably reflects at least the view of Parliament and the President that the Constitution does permit these provisions.

The subsections of § 91 cover a considerable range of issues affecting human rights. To begin with, §§ 91(2)(a) – (f) appear to authorize the President to impose a draft (referred to as a 'mobilization'). Section 91(2)(g) authorizes regulations dealing with 'the security of national key points and other places that may be designated', but does not specify what steps such regulations might require. Section 91(2)(h) provides for 'censorship of information', clearly a limitation on free speech. Section 91(2)(i) empowers the President to make regulations dealing with 'the evacuation or concentration of persons, including curfew laws'. All such laws impinge on freedom of movement and association, and an American reader cannot help but think of the worst instance of the use of such power in our history, the exclusion of Japanese-Americans from the West Coast early in World War II, and their confinement in camps for years thereafter. A South African reader may think just as quickly of the disease-ridden concentration camps created by the British during the Boer War.

Finally, § 91(2)(l) addresses regulations of 'places of custody or detention'. On this score, it is worth noting that § 37(8) of the Constitution makes clear that the many provisions of § 37 which protect detainees during states of emergency

> do not apply to persons who are not South African citizens and who are detained in consequence of an international armed conflict. Instead, the state must comply with the standards binding on the Republic under international humanitarian law in respect to the detention of such persons.

Section 37(8) appears to apply whether or not a state of emergency is in place, and seems to say that the rules of detention applicable to foreigners detained in consequence of an international armed conflict are simply those required by international humanitarian law, not those that might otherwise be inferred from other provisions of the Constitution. Thus a non-South African detained in these circumstances would have neither the rights of a normal detainee under § 35 of the Constitution, nor the rights of an emergency detainee under § 37 (unless international humanitarian law binding on South Africa provided otherwise, either by directly mandating such protections or by requiring that non-South Africans receive the same protections as South Africans enjoy). And this would be true even if the non-South African was detained or (to use a more military term) taken prisoner on South African soil and thereafter detained inside South Africa as well.

To all of this, it is important to add that the list of topics in § 91(2) may not be exclusive. Indeed, the breadth of § 91(1)'s general authorization suggests that the specific powers given in § 91(2) might be viewed as exemplifying a range of other authorities to impinge, where necessary, on constitutional liberties. Whether § 91(2)'s provisions, or broader implications from them, are constitutional remains to be litigated, and of course the constitutionality of any particular exercises of the Defence Act powers will also be subject to constitutional review. But the statute does at least confirm the possibility that states of national defence will involve significant limitations on otherwise protected rights, limitations with some resemblance to the 'derogations' that are authorized, but much more carefully addressed, in the state of emergency provisions of the Constitution. It might be argued that the differences do not matter, since South Africa can always declare and approve declarations of a state of national defence and of a state of emergency simultaneously. A state of emergency is harder to start and harder to maintain, however, and so the existence of this partially overlapping, less regulated authority is troubling.

(3) Hostilities *without* a declaration of a state of national defence

Although the declaration of a state of national defence under § 203 of the Constitution appears to be the way that South Africa can declare its fullest engagement in the use of military force, it is clearly not the only path by which the country can employ its armed forces. Instead, § 201(2) creates another route, and one which the President may take the nation along without affirmative Parliamentary ratification. This section declares that:

Only the President, as head of the national executive, may authorize the employment of the defence force –

    (a) in cooperation with the police service;

    (b) in defence of the Republic; or

    (c) in fulfillment of an international obligation.

Action in defence of the Republic under § 201(2)(b) presumably is, or at least may be, taken pursuant to a declaration of a state of national defence. The distinction drawn in § 201(2) between such defence and the use of force 'in fulfillment of an international obligation', however, suggests that the latter is not encompassed in a 'state of national defence'.[55] Moreover, this reading of §§ 201(2) and 203 accords both with the natural sense of the words 'national defence' – for surely national defence is not directly implicated by peacekeeping missions far from South Africa's borders – and with South African practice, under which troops have been sent to a number of countries for peacekeeping purposes without, as far as I am aware, any declarations of a state of national defence.[56]

Peacekeeping missions do not seek combat, but combat can certainly arise in them. In point of fact, as we have seen, South Africans engaged in interventions of this sort have taken casualties in both Lesotho and the DRC. Once troops are deployed in a situation of potential strife, active fighting and war are always possibilities; indeed, even deployments under conditions of peace (say, a deployment of troops to Namibia as a check on any potential rise of territorial ambitions against Namibia in other nations) ultimately pose this risk.

Given that peacekeeping missions carry with them some risk of involvement in actual fighting, as might other military deployments ordered by the President[57], is affirmative Parliamentary approval required for these steps? The answer seems clearly to be 'no'; as long as Parliament does not affirmatively *disapprove* (and as long as funds are available), the military action can continue. This is apparent from section 201(3), which requires the President to 'inform Parliament, promptly and in appropriate detail', of a range of information about any employment of the defence force which he or she has ordered under 201(2). This reporting requirement is a wise one, but what the section requires is only reporting; it does not require any vote by Parliament on the matter. In fact, the text does not even explicitly authorize Parliament to vote on the matter, though I believe, as I have already argued in connection with declarations of a state of national defence[58], that the principle of joint Parliamentary-Presidential control over the military does mean that Parliament *can* vote if it so chooses.[59]

It is important that Parliament have this authority. But it is also important to recognize that if Parliament has this authority, and chooses to take no action whatsoever, the President's decision stands. Only an affirmative decision by Parliament to modify or reject the President's choice constrains his power; inaction constitutes acceptance (at least as long as funds are available). As I have already suggested, it is also important to recognize that if the President makes decisions that embroil the nation in fighting, Parliament may find it very hard to respond then by demanding a reversal of the President's judgments. The President has the authority, as long as Parliament does not affirmatively object, to take the nation a substantial distance, perhaps politically an irreversible distance, along the road towards war.

Suppose now that in the course of a deployment of troops ordered by the President, and not objected to by Parliament, fighting does break out. Must a state of national defence now be declared, and Parliamentary approval obtained? Parliament might find it hard to withhold its approval, as I've just noted, but still it would have a chance, and indeed an obligation, to endorse or not endorse such a declaration if it was issued – and unless it gave its approval, the declaration would lapse.

But the constitutional text does not say that a state of national defence must be declared whenever actual fighting breaks out. The fact is that the text does not say that a declaration of a state of national defence is required as a prerequisite, or an accompaniment, even to a full-scale war. Nor is it clear that such a declaration plays any international law role (as a declaration of war might have, especially in earlier times), and so it may be that no implied requirement of such declarations can be inferred in the text based on international law. It would have been possible for the Constitution to have explicitly forbidden war or fighting in the absence of a declaration, but no such prohibition has been spelled out.[60] I would infer nevertheless that a full-scale war (unlike the sorts of smaller-scale hostilities discussed above) does need to rest on such a declaration, since the declaration process seems designed to provide notice to the nation and to insure that Parliament's assent is obtained as part of the country's going to war – but the point remains debatable because the text is not explicit.

As to lesser military engagements, moreover, I do not think the same inference follows. The Constitution empowers the President to send troops abroad for peacekeeping, as long as Parliament does not object. Peacekeeping can be violent. To authorize a peacekeeping mission, it seems to me, is to authorize some limited amount of actual fighting in the course of that mission – and the Constitution authorizes the President to undertake such missions so long as Parliament does not affirmatively object. There may, in addition, be legitimate reasons for a President's *not* wanting to declare a state of national defence. Such a declaration might trigger domestic powers that the President fears would burden, or upset, the country. It might also carry foreign policy connotations that would fuel a crisis atmosphere internationally that the President would like to dissipate, precisely in order to accomplish the peacekeeping objectives for which the troops have been deployed.[61] Finally, even after South African troops have been shot at, it may not really be the case that 'national defence' is at stake, and so the provision for a declaration of a state of national defence may not truly be applicable in these circumstances. For all of these reasons, it seems to me that some level of combat is possible in the course of an authorized employment of South African troops without the need for a declaration of a state of national defence and therefore, once again, without any need for Parliament to give or withhold its approval for the enterprise. Exactly what level of combat triggers the need for a declaration remains, inescapably, unclear in the text.

Suppose, finally, that the President does declare a state of national defence, but Parliament refuses to approve it. Then must the fighting stop? Again, the text does not say this, but surely it must be the case that where a declaration is constitutionally required, its absence means the fighting must come to a halt. As we have just seen, however, it is not by any means certain just when a declaration is constitutionally required. Perhaps the President would argue that the fighting in question didn't actually rise to the level (whatever it might be) for which a declaration of national defence was required, and therefore that although he or she had issued the declaration and sought Parliament's approval as a matter of prudence, Parliament's failure to approve did not remove the President's prerogative to continue the fighting. That position would be especially forceful if Parliament did not actually disapprove the declaration, but simply never brought it to a vote and so failed to approve it. So, too, the President's position would have force if Parliament disapproved the declaration, but at the same time rejected a proposal to de-fund the fighting.[62] Or perhaps the President would argue that although Parliament's failure to approve the declaration meant that the fighting had to be brought to an end, Parliament couldn't possibly have meant that South African troops should be placed in jeopardy as the process of disengaging from the enemy took place, and therefore that the fighting would have to continue for a considerable period in order to insure the safe extrication of South African troops.[63] Whatever the correct view of this matter, it is quite clear that the text leaves it ambiguous, and that makes it equally clear that in a situation where this point became important, the President could claim various forms of authority to continue. Though a South African court might well be readier to review such claims of authority than an American judge today, still it would not be easy for a court to reject a President's claim of authority while battle actually raged.

(4) The power of the purse?

Let us begin our examination of Parliament's power to limit war by restricting spending somewhat indirectly, by considering the problem of how, once the President has declared a state of national defence, and Parliament has approved it, it comes to an end. No doubt, if the President wages war and achieves victory, both branches of government will be happy to recognize the end of the state of national defence. But can the President un-declare a state of national defence without Parliament's approval? If an Acting President declares it, can the President, on returning to his or her duties, revoke it? If the President has some revocation power, does it last only until Parliament has actually approved the state of national defence, or go on indefinitely? Perhaps more importantly, can Parliament withdraw its approval once it has given it? Can a single chamber of Parliament withdraw its approval, or must both chambers concur?

All of these points are left unspecified by the text. It is plausible to infer that since a state of national defence must rest on the assent of both political branches of South Africa's government, each branch can also revoke its consent. But as a practical matter, it may be very hard for either branch to overturn a state of national defence to which the other is committed, and, continuing as a practical matter, it may be very hard in particular for Parliament to abrogate a state of national defence to which the President remains committed. Moreover, the logic of the basic inference of a power for a single branch of government to revoke the declaration is uncertain: once both branches have assented to the declaration of a state of national defence, it might be argued that only a decision by both branches can revoke it. Or (as a reader has suggested) perhaps the declaration of a state of national defence, once approved by Parliament, is so profound a vesting of authority in the President that only the President can end it.

The most important powers Parliament may have to control executive uses of military force may lie elsewhere. I have already argued that Parliament can disapprove the President's uses of force even after approving a declaration of a state of national defence under section 203 of the Constitution (as long as it does not interfere with the President's commander-in-chief authority). So, too, I've argued that Parliament can disapprove any Presidential employment of troops under section 201 of the Constitution. But Parliament does not have to exercise these powers. In contrast, Parliament also has authority to give or withhold funding for the nation's military engagements, and this power Parliament at least to some extent cannot escape exercising.

As a general proposition, the President cannot spend money without Parliament's having authorized it. The Constitution establishes this rule by requiring that all revenues received by South Africa must be paid into the 'National Revenue Fund', unless Parliament legislates to the contrary.[64] Once revenue has been deposited in this Fund, the Constitution specifies that it normally can only be withdrawn if Parliament appropriates or authorizes the withdrawal.[65] Hence even if the President engages in peacekeeping missions for which, say, the United Nations provides reimbursement, those UN funds apparently will go into the National Revenue Fund and become subject to Parliamentary control rather than unilateral Presidential disposition. Whether the revenues to be spent come from the United Nations or domestic taxes, unless Parliament has provided the President with spending authority, the President cannot carry on.[66]

In principle, this funding authority appears to be the strongest check on Presidential power in the field of war. I would assume – as elsewhere, in part on the basis of the fundamental principle of shared Parliamentary and Presidential authority – that this power applies whether or not the President has obtained approval of a declaration of a state of national defence, and even if the President is in the midst of exercising his or her commander-in-chief and foreign affairs authority in the prosecution of some military objective. The President is commander-in-chief only of those forces Parliament provides, as Justice Robert Jackson pointed out in an important war powers case in the United States.[67] In the United States, this power has on occasion been used with some effect, notably in bringing an end to the late Vietnam War bombing of Cambodia.[68] It has also been notoriously circumvented, in the Iran-Contra affair.[69]

Though it is possible to argue for an implied Presidential authority to take otherwise unauthorized action, including spending money, in a dire emergency,[70] I believe that a general argument for an implied Presidential power to fund wars without Parliamentary approval would be alien to South African constitutionalism, and therefore that Parliament can end a war by de-funding it. A more difficult issue is whether Parliament can use its funding power to constrict the President's commander-in-chief authority in a war that Parliament has not chosen to end. If there are limits on Parliament's power to directly control the tactical choices the President may make in an ongoing, duly authorized war,[71] then Parliament might well also be barred from using its funding power to impose restrictions on the conduct of the war that it could not directly require. Exactly where the line is between Parliament's authority to decide what wars South Africa's money is to be spent on, and the President's authority to decide how to spend the money Parliament has appropriated for war, is no easy question. Despite this ambiguity, the power to end a war by ending its financing is a profound one.

Yet it will undoubtedly be difficult for Parliament to wield this authority, and probably more difficult, politically, than in the United States (given the greater overlap of the executive and legislature in South Africa than in the US). Moreover, there are two other reasons for some hesitation about the efficacy of this power in South Africa. The first is the special legislative authority that the executive holds in the area of budgeting, under the Constitution. Under § 73(2) 'only the Cabinet member responsible for national financial matters may introduce [a money Bill] in the Assembly'.[72] The United States Constitution, by contrast, provides that 'All Bills for raising Revenue shall originate in the House of Representatives'.[73] No member of Parliament seeking to end a war to which the President and the Cabinet are committed, therefore, can introduce a bill proposing to cut off the war's funds.

This limitation should not mean that Parliament is without power to make spending decisions.[74] Most clearly, Parliament can reject the Executive's war when the Executive proposes legislation to fund it. But this power is less salient than it would be in the United States, because the President may not need to apply to Parliament for more money for a considerable time. There does not appear to be a constitutional limit on the period of time for which Parliament can appropriate military spending funds (in contrast to the US Constitution's two-year limit),[75] and so, at least in theory, an extended appropriation at one point could fund a considerable length of military activity without further specific approval.[76]

In addition, Parliament should be able to amend a money bill already introduced, so as to include a provision barring any further spending for the military operation in question, and to revoke, if need be, any previously-granted appropriation. Section 77(3) of the Constitution seems meant to insure Parliament's authority to amend money bills, since it declares that '[a]n Act of Parliament must provide for a procedure to amend money Bills before Parliament'.[77] It is somewhat disquieting that this legislation has not yet been enacted, as of May 2008.[78] In practice, the result apparently is that money bills normally cannot be amended in the National Assembly.[79] While the National Assembly arguably might exercise the power to amend even in the absence of implementing legislation, it would seem that the practical value of amending appropriations bills as a tool for controlling executive war will be determined by the shape of that legislation, if and when it is enacted.

The second reason for hesitation about the efficacy of the funding power is, perhaps, simply an illustration of the political difficulties of wielding this authority: in practice, so far, it appears that the executive has at least on occasion been able to undertake military missions without seeking specific funding approval in advance. At a 2003 parliamentary committee discussion of the White Paper on Peace Missions, General Rautie Rautenbach, Budget Director for the Department of Defence, reportedly 'noted that for the most part peace missions were an unforeseen occurrence and that by that very nature there was normally no budgetary provision for this development. He informed the Committee that the DOD had a deficit of

R200 million that had been occasioned by peace-keeping expeditions noting that the current budget did not provide for this kind of money'.[80] That deficit may have been unusual, but budget adjustments to cover unanticipated spending are quite permissible under South African law.[81]

The National Assembly does, finally, have one further recourse: it can eject the President from office, by either of two possible routes. First, it can 'remove the President from office' under § 89. That step, however, requires a vote of two-thirds of the members of the Assembly. Moreover, it is not entirely self-evident that the President's determination to continue fighting an unpopular war would constitute one of the specified grounds on which a vote of no confidence can be based: serious illegal conduct, serious misconduct or inability to perform the functions of the office.[82]

Second, and more easily, the National Assembly can require the President (and the entire Cabinet at the same time) to resign, by approving a 'motion of no confidence'. But even this step is not altogether simple – even assuming Parliament is prepared to bring down the entire existing executive – because it requires 'a vote supported by a majority of [the National Assembly's] members'.[83] National Assembly members determined to end a war might find it easier to do so by exercising Parliament's appropriations power. To pass a bill cutting off funding for a war, as few as one-fourth-plus-one of the members of the Assembly would be sufficient,[84] even though they would also have to vote to override the National Council of Provinces, if that body opposed the legislation.[85]

Conclusion

The text of the South African Constitution, in short, imposes only partial limits on the power of South Africa's President to involve the nation in fighting or war (within the limits of international law), and on the simultaneous potential for limitation of constitutional rights South Africa otherwise holds dear. Perhaps South Africa will not actually face the agonizing possibilities of war with any frequency. But it is difficult to be confident of such predictions. Moreover, it is hard to be confident that military power, if it exists and is used, will not be subject to misuse as well. In other areas of human rights protection, South Africa's constitutional drafters chose to take few chances; they defined a wide range of rights, mandated governmental protection and respect for them, and created a powerful Constitutional Court, among other institutions, to make those commitments enforceable. In these areas, South Africans developed an apparatus of constitutional protection that is profoundly impressive. In the field of war, however, the Constitution took fewer precautions.

South Africans themselves will be better suited than I to decide whether to seek changes in the constitutional text or instead to rely on the growing strength of South Africa's constitutional traditions to guide interpretation of the current text if and when these issues must be addressed. This paper has sought both to outline a rights-protective interpretation of the present text and to point to aspects of the text – the procedures for Parliamentary approval of a declaration of a state of national defence, and the absence of a requirement of affirmative Parliamentary approval for Presidential decisions to employ troops, particularly in peacekeeping abroad – where stronger provisions would be desirable. I hope this paper will suggest other areas as well that may deserve attention, but I take very seriously a reader's caution that interpretation might be preferable to amendment, because efforts to amend the constitutional text today might increase rather than limit executive prerogative. Finally, I must close by saying that experience in the United States, hard experience, shows that to regulate killing and chaos – war – by law is always, to some extent, impossible.

---

[1] Even while recognizing that South Africa is a peaceful state, we should not overlook the considerable military force it is accumulating. *See, e.g.,* Shaun Benton, 'First of SA's Three New Submarines Cruises into Simonstown After 49-Day Voyage', AllAfrica.com, Apr. 7, 2006 (available on Westlaw – WIRES database).

[2] *See, e.g.,* Mandy Rossouw, Matuma Letsoalo & Rapule Tabane, 'Mbeki Faces Amnesty Pressure', *Mail & Guardian Online,* Mar. 20, 2008, *available at* http://www.mg.co.za/articlePage.aspx?articleid=335115&area=/insight/insight_national/ ; 'Cabinet Dismisses Arms-Deal Allegations Against Mbeki', *Mail & Guardian Online,* Mar. 20, 2008, *available at* http://www.mg.co.za/articlePage.aspx?articleid=335107&area=/breaking_news/breaking_news_natio nal/; Sam Sole & Stefaans Brümmer, 'Arms Broker *Did* Give Cash to the ANC', *Mail & Guardian Online,* Mar. 14, 2008, *available at* http://www.mg.co.za/articlePage.aspx?articleid=334629&area=/insight/insight_national/ (all last visited Apr. 20, 2008).

[3] 'Foreword by the Honourable M.G.P. Lekota, Minister of Defence', in Department of Defence, Annual Report FY 2006 – 2007, pp. xiii, xiv, *available at* http://www.info.gov.za/annualreport/2006/defence_annual_rpt07.pdf (last visited Apr. 20, 2008); Parliamentary Monitoring Group, 'Transformation Management Developments; SANDF Deployment to West Indies, Nepal, Mozambique', *available at* http://www.pmg.org.za/node/9056 (last visited Apr. 20, 2008); Mosiuoa Lekota, 'Address by the Minister of Defence, the Honourable Mosiuoa Lekota, at media breakfast at the Defence Headquarters, Pretoria', Sept. 5, 2005, *available at* http://www.info.gov.za/speeches/2005/05090712451003.htm (last visited Mar. 3, 2007); Clive Ndou, 'South Africa Beefs Up Peace Missions in Africa', AllAfrica.com, Mar. 23, 2006 (available on Westlaw – WIRES database). SANDF troops have also been employed in the Central African Republic. Shaun Benton, 'Cabinet Approves SANDF Deployment in Uganda', *BuaNews* (Tshwane), Mar. 20, 2008), *available at* http://allafrica.com/stories/printable/200803200328.html.

[4] At least nine South African soldiers died in the intervention in Lesotho in 1998. Suzanne Daley, 'How Did Pretoria Err? Lesotho Counts the Ways', *New York Times,* Sept. 27, 1998, 16. Ten have died in the Democratic Republic of the Congo more recently, mostly not in combat. *See* Boyd Webb, 'Defence Chief Visits Injured Soldiers', June 10, 2004 (SAPA); 'Five of Six Soldiers Drowned in DRCongo to Be Buried Saturday', Apr. 16, 2004 (SAPA); 'Full Military Honours for SANDF Soldier Killed in DRC', Apr. 6, 2004 (SAPA); 'South Africa: Army to Investigate Officer's Death', Mar. 31, 2004 (UN Integrated Regional Information Networks) (all available on Westlaw – ALLNEWS database).

[5] These resources have also been affected by AIDS, with an estimated 23 % of SANDF troops – and perhaps more – HIV-positive. Xan Rice, 'South African Army Facing HIV Crisis', *The Times* (UK), Aug. 19, 2004 (available on Westlaw – ALLNEWS database).

[6] *See* Peter Honey, 'Defence. Battle for Force Readiness', *Financial Mail,* Sept. 16, 2005, 46 (available on Westlaw – ALLNEWS database); Shaun Benton, 'Darfur Peace Mission Is Hurting AU, SA, Financially', allAfrica.com, March 16, 2006 (available on Westlaw –WIRES database). In 1999 South Africa anticipated employing one battalion (approximately 1000 soldiers) in peacekeeping operations outside its borders at any one time, *see* Department of Foreign Affairs, *White Paper on South African Participation in International Peace Missions,* 25 (approved by Cabinet, Oct. 21, 1998; tabled in Parliament, Feb. 24, 1999). In 2004-05, it had three times that number of soldiers stationed in other nations on such missions. Prakash Naidoo, 'African Peacekeeping Force. SA Stretched to Its Limits', *Financial Mail,* June 18, 2004, 24 (available on Westlaw – ALLNEWS database). South African troops are also part of the Southern African Development Community 'stand-by brigade', officially launched in 2007 and part of the larger African Union stand-by force. David Masango, 'Southern Africa: Stand-By Brigade to Maintain Peace in SADC', *BuaNews* (Tshwane), Aug. 17, 2007, *available at* http://allafrica.com/stories/20070817075.html.

[7] Sections of the South African Constitution, Constitution of the Republic of South Africa, 1996 (Act 108 of 1996), are cited hereafter simply by section number; all other sources are fully identified. South African constitutional and statutory citations in this chapter are current as of the March 2008 update of Butterworths Statutes of South Africa, available on LEXIS.

[8] *See, e.g.,* Kaunda and Others v. President of the Republic of South Africa and Others, 2005 (4) SA 235 (CC), 2004 (10) BCLR 1009 (CC), para 78 (judgment of Chaskalson CJ). However, where issues primarily for other branches are involved – as is surely the case with foreign affairs and war -- courts'

review will be relatively more deferential. *See id.*, para 244 (judgment of O'Regan J). I am grateful to a reader for calling this decision to my attention.

[9] *Id.* para 66 (judgment of Chaskalson CJ); para 159 (judgment of Ngcobo J); para 221 (judgment of O'Regan J). *See* § 7(2) of the Constitution, declaring that "[t]he state must respect, protect, promote, and fulfill the rights in the Bill of Rights."

[10] § 199(5). *See generally* South African National Defence Union v. Minister of Defence and Another, 1999 (4) SA 469 (CC), 1999 (6) BCLR 615 (CC); South African National Defence Union v. Minister of Defence and Others, 2007 (8) BCLR 863 (CC) (both examining the constitutional rights of members of the South African National Defence Force).

[11] *See* Nico Steytler & Johann Mettler, 'Federal Arrangements as a Peacemaking Device During South Africa's Transition to Democracy', *Publius*, Oct. 1, 2001, 93, 95-96. Assuring the military's loyalty to civilian rule is essential in any democracy, and may still require attention in South Africa. *See* Max du Preez, 'SANDF Is a Crumbling Excuse for an Army: Strong Leadership and Discipline Are Needed to Validate This Force and Massive Expenditure', *Daily News*, Feb. 14, 2008, available at http://www.dailynews.co.za/index.php?fArticleId=4253049.

[12] Moreover, the Constitution provides that '[t]o give effect to the principles of transparency and accountability, multi-party parliamentary committees must have oversight of all security services'. (§ 199(8)).

[13] § 203. This language may owe something to the German Constitution's provision for declaration of a 'state of defence', though the relevant South African and German sections differ in many ways. *See generally* Grundgesetz, arts. 115a – 115l (available in English translation at http://www.psr.keele.ac.uk/docs/german.htm) (last visited Sept. 15, 2006). The same may be said of the Namibian Constitution, *see* Constitution of the Republic of Namibia 1990, art. 24, in Gisbert H. Flanz, ed., *Constitutions of the Countries of the World* (Dobbs Ferry: Ocean Publications, 2003), pp. 19-20. In any event, as a reader pointed out to me, South Africa's final Constitution here elaborates on an idea that appeared in the Interim Constitution as well, *see* Constitution of the Republic of South Africa, Act 200 of 1993, § 82(4)(b)(i) (empowering the President 'with the approval of Parliament, [to] declare a state of national defence'). (This Interim Constitution provision retained a tenuous legal existence under Schedule 6, Item 24(1) of the 1996 Constitution, *see* Iain Currie & Johan de Waal, with Pierre de Vos, Karthy Govender & Heinz Klug, *The New Constitutional & Administrative Law*, 2 vols. (Cape Town: Juta & Co., rev. ed. 2002), vol. I, p. 252 n.163.) The last Constitution of apartheid South Africa, by contrast, had authorized the 'State President' to 'declare war and make peace'. Republic of South Africa Constitution Act, No. 110 of 1983, § 6(3)(g).

[14] I do not seek here to precisely define the term 'war'. My focus is on the Constitution's provisions for the engagement of South African troops in combat, short or prolonged; exactly when the term 'war' becomes applicable to these engagements is not the central issue, for the Constitution itself does not make it so.

[15] Again, whether South Africa can also fight *without* a declaration of a state of national defence is a separate question, to which we will return. *See* text at notes 55-63 below.

[16] Currie and de Waal point out that wars of aggression are now violations of international law as well. Currie & de Waal, *The New Constitutional Law*, vol. I, p. 252.

[17] *See* § 90(2). The Acting President could even be a Minister chosen from outside Parliament, and thus entirely unelected. §§ 90(1) & 91(2)-(3).

[18] Buthelezi reportedly did, however, consult with both President Mandela and Deputy President Mbeki (who also was out of the country at the time), before ordering the military entry into Lesotho. Both 'approved the operation'. Gilbert A. Lewthwaite, 'South Africa Weighs Withdrawal from Messy Lesotho Intervention [–] Resistance Was Fiercer, and Intelligence Less Reliable Than Expected', *Baltimore Sun*, Sept. 26, 1998 (available on Westlaw – ALLNEWS database). South Africa apparently expected its entry to be quite uneventful, and initially its troops were supplied only with blank ammunition. *Id.*

[19] *See* Steytler & Mettler, 'Federal Arrangements', 102; Richard Ellis, 'Zulu Chief Keeps Low Profile on the Campaign Trail', *Scotsman*, June 2, 1999 (available on Westlaw – ALLNEWS database).

[20] Currie & de Waal maintain that the President must obtain the countersignature of the relevant Cabinet minister for any action within the sphere of that Minister's authority, *see* § 101(2), but also that '[i]f the issue has implications for government as a whole or concerns matters of real political importance, the President cannot act with the concurrence of a Minister, but the approval of Cabinet must be obtained', *see* § 85(2). Currie & de Waal, *New Constitutional Law*, vol. I, p. 246. Thus the President would need the signature of the Minister of Defence for orders to the troops, *see* §§ 201(1),

202(2), and perhaps the approval of the Cabinet as a whole for a declaration of a state of national defence or other commitments of troops to potential combat. It seems unlikely that these requirements would ordinarily prevent a President convinced of the need for warlike action from proceeding.

[21] § 203(3).

[22] *See* J. Gregory Sidak, 'To Declare War', (1991) 41 Duke L.J. 27, 81-85.

[23] In the United States, if the President undertakes military action without a declaration of war, the War Powers Resolution (a statute) normally requires an end to the operation if it does not receive Congressional approval – but 60 days can elapse before that approval is obtained. War Powers Resolution, § 5(b), 50 USC § 1544(b) (2000).

[24] § 37(1).

[25] Defence Act, Act No. 42 of 2002 (cited hereafter as "Defence Act"), § 89, says that the President may declare a state of national defence 'if, among other things, the sovereignty or territory of the Republic –

   (a)   is threatened by war, including biological or chemical warfare, or invasion, armed attack or armed conflict; or

   (b)   is being or has been invaded or is under armed or cyber attack or subject to a state of armed conflict'.

[26] § 37(2)(b).

[27] I am grateful to a reader for pointing this out to me.

[28] Abstractly, it might seem harder for the executive to obtain the approval of two houses of Parliament than of just one, and so a requirement of bicameral approval might be seen as a way of slowing the march towards war – though it would remain unclear why a similar check on the move to a state of emergency was unnecessary. As a practical matter, however, at least in today's South Africa, the chance of such disagreement between the two houses of Parliament seems small.

[29] *See* Steven Budlender, 'National Legislative Authority', in S. Woolman et al. (eds.), *Constitutional Law of South Africa*, 2 vols., 2d ed. (Lansdowne: Juta and Co., 2004), vol. I, pp. 17-1, 17-3 ('The national executive is accountable to the National Assembly and not to the NCOP.'); *compare* § 68 (section on 'Powers of National Council' detailing only "legislative power") *with* § 55 (section on 'Powers of National Assembly' separately describing the Assembly's legislative power and its accountability/oversight power). Even if the NCOP does perform oversight functions in practice, perhaps its oversight role is not sufficiently secured by the Constitution to extend to 'oversight' of the declaration of a state of national defence.

[30] *See* §§ 75-76.

[31] § 75(1); Budlender, 'National Legislative Authority', p. 17-15.

[32] § 76. The NCOP also follows substantially different voting procedures ('one legislator, one vote' or 'one provincial delegation, one vote'), depending on which category of legislation it is considering. *See* §§ 65, 75(2); Budlender, 'National Legislative Authority', pp. 17-4 to 17-6.

[33] *See id.*, p. 17-37, citing §§ 57(1)(b), 70(1)(b).

[34] § 37(2). Bruce Ackerman characterizes the 60-percent majority requirement for extending a state of emergency as 'the first supermajoritarian escalator in the constitutional world', and sees in it a confirmation of the value of similar structures for the United States. Bruce Ackerman, 'The Emergency Constitution', (2004) 113 Yale L.J. 1029, 1055.

[35] § 53(1).

[36] *See* § 53(1). For the decision rules potentially applicable in the NCOP, see §§ 65(1), 75(2).

[37] § 37(3).

[38] *But see* Ziyad Motala & Cyril Ramaphosa, *Constitutional Law: Analysis and Cases* (Cape Town: Oxford University Press, 2002), pp. 218-20 (suggesting that the President's use of defence powers would be largely or entirely non-justiciable).

[39] § 202(1).

[40] Lawful, that is, under South African law and also lawful under the international law of war to the extent South Africa is bound by it. §§ 231-32. So, for example, South African legislation or the Geneva Conventions would constrain the President's authority to direct the treatment of prisoners of war who were taken during the fighting that the declaration of a state of national defence authorized.

[41] *Cf.* Authorization for Use of Military Force (AUMF), Pub. L. 107-40, 115 Stat. 224, § 2(a) (Sept. 18, 2001) (authorizing the use of force against those the President 'determines' were connected to the September 11 attacks or to the attackers).

[42] Proposed language for the AUMF would have authorized the use of force not only against those connected to the September 11 attacks, but also to 'deter and pre-empt any future acts of terrorism or aggression against the United States'. Tom Daschle, 'Power We Didn't Grant', *Washington Post*, Dec. 23, 2005 (available on Westlaw – ALLNEWS database).

[43] Though US law on this question is decidedly ambiguous, there are early Supreme Court cases supporting the conclusion that Congress retained a power to limit Presidential warmaking discretion, in

undeclared wars and even in declared ones. *See* Little v. Barreme, 6 US (2 Cranch) 170 (1804); Brown v. US, 12 US (8 Cranch) 110 (1814). Language in an important Civil War decision, however, suggests a broader scope for Presidential discretion. *See* The Prize Cases, 67 US (2 Black) 635 (1863).

[44] These instances of employment of the defence forces are specified in § 201(2), and discussed further in the text at notes 55-63 below. For uses of the military covered by § 201(2), § 201(3) requires the President 'to inform Parliament, promptly and in appropriate detail, of –

    (a) the reasons for the employment of the defence force;
    (b) any place where the force is being employed;
    (c) the number of people involved; and
    (d) the period for which the force is expected to be employed'.

The Defence Act, §§ 18(2)(e) & (4), adds the requirement of a report on 'expenditure incurred or expected to be incurred'. This information is somewhat more extensive than what the President must report in connection with a declaration of a state of national defence; in that context, § 203(1)'s reporting requirements do not include discussion of the period for which the declaration is expected to last or of costs. I would view the several requirements as complementary rather than conflicting.

[45] § 18(5) of the Defence Act explicitly establishes Parliamentary review power over the President's uses of troops for a variety of purposes. It applies under circumstances specified in § 18(1), which provides:

    In addition to the employment of the Defence Force by the President as contemplated in section 201(2) of the Constitution, the President or the Minister may authorize the employment of the Defence Force for service inside the Republic or in international waters, in order to –

        (a) preserve life, health or property in emergency or humanitarian relief operations;
        (b) ensure the provision of essential services;
        (c) support any department of state, including support for purposes of socio-economic upliftment;
        (d) effect national border control.

In these circumstances, under § 18(5), Parliament

    may by resolution within seven days after receiving information [about the employment of troops in question] from the President or the Minister –

        (a) confirm any such authorization of employment;
        (b) order the amendment of such authorization;
        (c) order the substitution for such authorization of any other appropriate authorization; or
        (d) order the termination of the employment of the Defence Force.

As a reader has pointed out to me, however, this provision appears to cover only the employment of troops in South Africa or in international waters, and only for purposes in addition to those functions, notably including national defence and fulfillment of international obligations, for which § 201(2) of the Constitution authorizes the President to employ troops. It appears, therefore, that Parliament has not yet asserted the broader review power which I argue it possesses under the Constitution.

[46] *See* text at notes 64-81 below.

[47] *Cf.* Michael D. Ramsey, 'Torturing Executive Power', (2005) 93 Geo. L.J. 1213, 1241 (US 'Congress cannot appoint a commander who does not answer to the President').

[48] I discuss this provision in much more detail below. *See* text at notes 55-63 below.

[49] In the United States, '[t]here is ample evidence that the legislature was not meant to make tactical military decisions once war was initiated', according to Stephen Dycus et al., *National Security Law*, 4th ed. (New York: Aspen Publishers, 2007), p. 26. But a number of scholars have recently argued that although Congress wisely does not intervene in such decisions, constitutionally it could. *See* David J. Barron & Martin S. Lederman, 'The Commander in Chief at the Lowest Ebb – Framing the Problem, Doctrine, and Original Understanding', (2008) 121 Harv. L. Rev. 692; Jules Lobel, 'Conflicts Between the Commander in Chief and Congress: Concurrent Power Over the Conduct of War', Ohio St. L.J. (forthcoming), *available at* http://ssrn.com/abstract=1028526; David Luban, 'On the Commander-in-Chief Power', available at http://ssrn.com/AbstractID=1026302.

[50] Section 36, to be sure, requires not just a weighing of national need and democratic reasonableness, but also the presence of 'law of general application' or authority elsewhere in the constitution to sustain a limitation on rights. If a statute such as the Defence Act did not provide the necessary legal basis, Parliamentary approval of the declaration of a state of national defence might, or the Constitution itself might indeed be seen as the foundation for orders to fight under such a declaration.

[51] *Cf.* Ex parte Milligan, 71 U.S. 2, 78-82 (1866) (on the circumstances in which martial law may and may not be declared).

[52] No constitutional question would arise, of course, if the Constitution does not apply to actions taken by the South African government outside its own borders and directed at noncitizens whose only

connection with South Africa is their intent to attack it. *See generally Kaunda*, paras 41-44 (judgment of Chaskalson CJ); *id.* para 228 (judgment of O'Regan J).

[53] These questions of course recapitulate the argument in the United States over whether our President has authority, under the post-9/11 Authorization for Use of Military Force, Pub. L. 107-40, 115 Stat. 224 (Sept. 18, 2001), to order warrantless electronic surveillance of people suspected of links with Al Qaeda. South Africa has prohibited surveillance inside the country even in national security matters absent a judicial order, *see* Regulation of Interception of Communications and Provision of Communication-Related Information Act, Act No. 70 of 2002, §§ 2 -3. This statute does, however, permit emergency 'interception' of communications without such an order, in order to locate their sender, when a law enforcement officer, including a member of the Defence Force, 'has reasonable grounds to believe that an emergency exists' because another person is in danger of dying or being seriously injured. *Id.*, §§ 1, 8(1)(b); *see also id.* § 7 ("[i]nterception of communication to prevent serious bodily harm"). Moreover, it seems arguable that Parliament did not craft this Act's limits with the needs of a state of national defence in mind, and that the President might exercise the authority granted in the Defence Act (discussed *infra* in the text) to establish different rules to govern surveillance in that context.

[54] As noted earlier, *see* text at notes 41-42 above, the constitutional text does not make clear who a declaration of a state of national defence can be made against. But it is certainly possible to imagine domestic threats that are as grave as foreign ones, and so it is quite possible that a declaration could target a domestic group.

[55] But are there actually any interventions that are mandated by 'international obligation'? It may be that no international agreements to which South Africa is a party actually *demand* the commitment of South African troops, but it is also true that South Africa, as a member of the United Nations, the African Union, and the Southern African Development Community, has obligations to preserve human rights in other parts of the world. Section 201(2) can easily be read to refer to this broader, less insistent form of 'obligation', and to authorize the deployment of troops in its service. The White Paper on South African Participation in International Peace Missions also can be read to reflect such a view, *see* 'White Paper on Peace Missions', 34. In any event, it would seem from § 201(2)(c) itself that South Africa must have the power to enter into international obligations whose fulfillment will entail the employment of troops.

[56] So, too, it appears that 'employment of the defence force … in cooperation with the police service' does not require any declaration. (It is also noteworthy that the list in § 201(2) is not explicitly exclusive, Motala & Ramaphosa, *Constitutional Law*, p. 218, and in fact the Defence Act, § 18(1), provides for *other* uses of the defence forces as well, *see* note 45 above.) The question of how deeply the South African military is, or should be, involved in domestic law enforcement has important potential implications for the long-run strength of civilian democracy. The Defence Act as it now stands appears to empower the defence forces to exercise a considerable range of domestic law enforcement authorities, *see* Defence Act, §§ 20(1) & 22. For an American response to this problem, see the longstanding, though ambiguous, Posse Comitatus Act, 18 USC § 1385 (2000). But these issues are beyond the scope of the present paper.

[57] There would be risks entailed in a variety of actions the President might take as part of routine military protection of the nation, especially if South Africa were actually to face any external threats. Today, fortunately, South Africa 'faces no known immediate threat', according to Major-General Roy Andersen, head of the SANDF Reserve Force. Jonathan Katzenellenbogen, 'Overlooked Reservists Bolster Ranks of Cash-Strapped SANDF', *Business Day*, Oct. 13, 2004 (available on Westlaw – ALLNEWS database).

[58] *See* text at notes 43-49 above.

[59] Parliament, however, has not asserted this power in the Defence Act. *See* note 45 above. Vanessa Kent and Mark Malan have pointed out that the 'White Paper on Peace Missions' (which they report was adopted by Parliament in October 1999) envisioned greater responsibility for Parliament than the Defence Act Mandates. The White Paper appeared to see Parliamentary approval as a prerequisite to the President's authorizing the deployment of troops where 'military enforcement measures' might be required, and seemed to contemplate, as a standard procedure, the President's 'tabling a proposal for ratifying the participation of a South African military contingent in a particular peace support operation'. 'White Paper on Peace Missions', 32; *see* Vanessa Kent & Mark Malan, 'Decisions, Decisions – South Africa's foray into regional peace operations' (Pretoria: Institute for Security Studies, Occasional Paper 72, April 2003), *available at* http://www.iss.co.za/index.php?link_id=14&slink_id=576&link_type=12&slink_type=12&tmpl_id=3. I have found no instance of such a proposal being presented to Parliament or voted on by it, and Kent and Malan in 2003 argued that troop deployment decisions were being taken 'at the level of the Presidency' with little input from Parliament (or other actors). In one instance, however, Parliamentary

committees decided to draft and support a resolution approving the already-underway employment of South African troops in Burundi. Parliamentary Monitoring Group, 'Joint Standing Committee on Defence; Select Committee on Security and Constitutional Affairs: Joint Meeting, 14 November 2001, Deployment of the SANDF in Burundi', *available at* http://www.pmg.org.za/viewminute.php?id=1240. It is conceivable that this resolution was voted on by Parliament, but perhaps more likely that the committee itself voted on the resolution and reported its vote to Parliament, which then took no further action. For examples of the Joint Committee on Defense apparently proceeding in this way -- reviewing troop deployments and then reporting the conclusion of its deliberations to Parliament (and on one occasion raising some concerns in the course of its deliberations) -- see Parliamentary Monitoring Group, 'SANDF Deployment to DARFUR, Sudan & within South Africa, Committee Annual Report', Feb. 21, 2008, *available at* http://www.pmg.org.za/node/10543 (last visited Apr. 20, 2008); Joint Standing Committee on Defence, 'Annual Report: January – November 2007', *available at* http://www.pmg.org.za/docs/2008/comreports/080304jcdefencereport.htm (last visited Apr. 20, 2008).
[60] A similar argument has been made by John Yoo to support the inference that the President does not need a declaration of war by Congress. Yoo notes that the United States constitutional text *does* explicitly prohibit the states from making war without Congress' consent, and contrasts that to the absence of any explicit textual requirement that the President obtain consent. John C. Yoo, 'Exchange: War Powers – War and the Constitutional Text', (2002) 69 U. Chi. L. Rev. 1639, 1666-67, *citing* U.S. Const., art. I, § 10. I would not take this argument so far, either for South Africa or for the United States, but the absence in the South African Constitution of any textual requirement of Parliamentary assent to fighting does have to be reckoned with.
[61] Cf. Orlando v. Laird, 443 F.2d 1039, 1043 (2d Cir.), *cert. denied*, 404 US 869 (1971) (noting that a declaration of war might be seen by Congress and the President as 'plac[ing] the nation in a posture in its international relations which would be against its best interests'). The Constitutional Court has recognized 'the government's special responsibility for and particular expertise in foreign affairs'. *Kaunda*, para 144, subsection 6 (judgment of Chaskalson CJ). *See also id.*, para 172 (judgment of Ngcobo J); *accord, id.*, para 243 (judgment of O'Regan J).
[62] Such paradoxical votes are possible, and in fact were cast by the members of the US House of Representatives on Operation Allied Force, the NATO bombing campaign against the Federal Republic of Yugoslavia in 1999. *See* Stephen Dycus et al., *National Security Law*, 3d ed. (New York: Aspen Law & Business, 2002), p. 412.
[63] For an account of the US courts' unwillingness to second-guess the President's efforts to withdraw from Vietnam, despite the intense fighting that took place over several years in the process, see Dycus et al., *National Security Law*, 4th ed., pp. 230-39.
[64] § 213(1) (limiting exceptions to those 'reasonably' made by Parliament).
[65] Parliamentary may either enact appropriations, § 213(2)(a), or by statute authorize 'direct charge[s]' against the National Revenue Fund. § 213(2)(b). Parliamentary action is not required when a direct charge 'is provided for in the Constitution'. *Id.*
[66] The President cannot carry on, that is, unless the spending is a direct charge 'provided for in the Constitution'. *Id.* But § 213 itself identifies only one such direct charge, and that one –for revenue sharing with the provinces, § 213(3) – is far from the field of defence.
[67] Youngstown Sheet & Tube Co. v. Sawyer, 343 US 579, 643-44 (1952) (Jackson, J., concurring).
[68] *See generally* Holtzman v. Schlesinger, 484 F.2d 1307 (2d Cir. 1973); Dycus et al., National Security Law, pp. 285-91.
[69] For an extensive account of Congress' efforts to cut off funding to the Nicaraguan Contras, and the Reagan administration's efforts to circumvent this cut-off with funds received from covert sales of arms to Iran, see *id.* pp. 473-522.
[70] *See* Motala & Ramaphosa, *Constitutional Law*, pp. 216-17, *discussing* Executive Council, Western Cape Legislature, and Others v. President of the Republic of South Africa and Others, 1995 (4) SA 867 (CC), 1995 (10) BCLR 1289 (CC), paras 62 (judgment of Chaskalson P) & 149-50 (judgment of Ackermann & O'Regan JJ).
[71] *See supra* note 49 and accompanying text.
[72] *See also* § 55(1)(b), giving the National Assembly power to 'initiate or prepare legislation, *except money Bills*' (emphasis added).
[73] US Const., art. I, § 7.
[74] Moreover, if Parliament is really determined to block some exercise of executive war powers, it probably can do so directly, as already noted.
[75] US Const., art. I, § 8, cl. 12.

[76] The procedures specified for the National Assembly's consideration of appropriation bills also seem more likely to curtail Parliamentary resistance than to facilitate it. In the Rules of the National Assembly as of June 1999, *available at* http://www.pmg.org.za/parlinfo/narules (last visited May 12, 2008), a section on 'Specific Rules applicable to money bills' lays out a 'special procedure' which must be used for 'a bill appropriating money for the ordinary annual services of the government or imposing taxes, levies or duties for this purpose'. Rule 286(2). Under this procedure, it appears that committee consideration of a 'main appropriation bill' must be completed within 'a maximum of ... seven consecutive Assembly working days'. Rule 290(3). Moreover, if a money bill is subsequently amended by the National Council of Provinces, and is returned to the National Assembly for reconsideration, '[t]he debate on the reconsideration of the bill, including the consideration of any amendment, may not continue for more than one hour'. Rule 295(3).

[77] As the Congress of South African Trade Unions (COSATU) has pointed out, it is also noteworthy that ss 55(1)(a) and 68(a) of the Constitution, which describe the legislative powers of the National Assembly and the National Council of Provinces, respectively, both refer to these Houses' authority to amend, or in the National Council of Provinces' case to amend or propose amendments to, '*any* legislation' (emphasis added). *See* Congress of South African Trade Unions (COSATU), 'COSATU Submission on the Republic of South Africa Second Amendment Bill, Submitted to the Portfolio Committee on Justice and Constitutional Development, 21 September 2001', s 4.2, *available at* http://www.cosatu.org.za/docs/2001/const.htm (last visited May 12, 2008).

[78] A National Council of Provinces webpage, http://www.parliament.gov.za/live/content.php?Item_ID=34&Revision=en/13&SearchStart=0 (last visited May 11, 2008), indicates that this legislation has yet to be enacted. In early May 2008, a 'tripartite alliance summit' of the African National Congress, the South African Communist Party, and the Congress of South African Trade Unions reportedly decided 'to allow Parliament to amend money bills' – one of several decisions seen as 'suggest[ing] much greater influence of the ANC's leftist allies on economic policy ...' Karima Brown & Amy Musgrave, 'South Africa: Leftward Leap If ANC Allies Get Their Way', *Business Day* (Johannesburg), May 12, 2008, *available at* http://allafrica.com/stories/200805120351.html. COSATU has in the past called for 'the tabling of an adequate money bills amendment procedure bill as a matter of urgency'. 'COSATU Submission', s. 4.2. As COSATU noted in that submission, *id.*, Article 21(1) of Schedule 6 of the Constitution provides that '[w]here the new Constitution requires the enactment of national or provincial legislation, that legislation must be enacted by the relevant authority within a reasonable period of the date the new Constitution takes effect'.

[79] The Parliamentary Monitoring Group's description of 'The Legislative Process', http://www.pmg.org.za/parlinfo/sectionb3 (last visited May 12, 2008), observes that '[a]t present Money Bills may only be debated and not amended as, according to the Constitution, Parliament must still devise legislation for a procedure to amend Money Bills'. COSATU cites an example of a bill that could not be amended because of its status as a money bill in 'COSATU Submission', s 4.2.

Parliamentary rules appear to produce a particularly odd result – that the National Assembly cannot amend money bills, but the National Council of Provinces (in general the less powerful house with respect to matters of national rather than provincial concern) can. Under the National Assembly's 'special procedure' for money bills, *see* note 76 *supra*, there is simply no provision for amendments – either by committees or by individual members of Parliament – in the Assembly's initial decision on such a bill. Oddly enough, there is also no explicit prohibition of amendments in these provisions; they simply are not mentioned.

Under ss 75 & 77(3) of the Constitution, the bill then goes to the National Council of Provinces. Draft National Council of Provinces rules adopted by its Rules Committee in 1999 do authorize amendments of 'Ordinary Bills not affecting provinces' – for which s 75 of the Constitution specifies the appropriate Parliamentary processes -- while noting that '[i]t is unclear whether money Bills should have a procedure separate from the standard procedure for section 75 Bills'. Note to 'Part 4: Section 75 Bills', Draft Rules of the National Council of Provinces, *available at* http://www.pmg.org.za/parlinfo/ncoprules (last visited May 12, 2008); for the rules applicable to amending section 75 bills, *see* Rules 203(i) & 205(1)(a), *id.*

If the National Council of Provinces does follow the rules for section 75 bills and amends a money bill, then the bill, as amended, returns to the National Assembly. At that point, according to National Assembly Rule 295(1), further amendments are possible, but only certain amendments: 'The Assembly must consider any amendments proposed by the Council. No further amendments may be considered unless moved by the Minister in charge of the bill, who may do so without prior notice'. As mentioned in note 76 *supra*, the debate over the amended bill, and over any amendments moved by the Minister, must be completed within an hour.

[80] Parliamentary Monitoring Group, 'Minutes for Defence Joint Committee, 26 March 2003, White Paper on Peacekeeping: Discussion' (*available at* http://www.pmg.org.za/viewminute.php?id=2596)

(last visited Jan. 26, 2007). For another suggestion of the degree of operational flexibility that current defence budgeting gives the Executive, *see* Wyndham Hartley, 'African Peace Burden Cannot Be SA's Alone, Warns Lekota', *Business Day*, Feb. 16, 2005 (available on Westlaw, ALLNEWS database).
[81] The statutory basis for such adjustments ultimately lies in the Public Finance Management Act, Act No. 1 of 1999, as amended, under which a government department has a number of statutory routes by which it can increase its spending on a particular function, such as peacekeeping, without prior specific Parliamentary authorization. *See id.* §§ 16, 30, 34, 43, & 92; *see* Kent & Malan, *Decisions, Decisions* (discussing §§ 16 & 30). For an illustrative recent funding bill, see 2006/07 Appropriation Bill, as introduced, Schedule, Vote 21 (Defence), *available at* http://www.info.gov.za/gazette/bills/2006/b2-06.pdf (last visited Mar. 5, 2007) (allocating R820 million specifically and exclusively to 'peace support operations' within a 'force employment' budget of R1.41 billion). For an example of a peacekeeping mission whose costs were expected to be covered without the need for new legislation, see Letter from President T.M. Mbeki to Speaker of the National Assembly, 'Employment of the South African National Defence Force in Sudan in Fulfilment of the International Obligations of South Africa Towards the African Union', July 2, 2004, *available at* http://www.pmg.org.za/docs/2003/comreports/040729presletters.htm (last visited Mar. 5, 2007) (noting that costs would be accommodated within the Department of Defence's 'current allocation for Peace Support Operations').
[82] § 89(1).
[83] § 102(2). I am grateful to Christina Murray for calling this section to my attention.
[84] § 53(1).
[85] §§ 77, 75.

CHAPTER 20

THE UK RESPONSE TO TERRORISM: HUMAN RIGHTS AND A WIDER PERSPECTIVE

Christopher JS Gale

Introduction

Governments around the world have used the terrorist attacks on the United States of 11 September 2001 (9/11) as an opportunity to review anti-terrorism laws and security procedures. As a part of its own immediate response the United States rushed the Patriot Act 2001 through Congress. The United Kingdom followed suit with the Anti-terrorism, Crime and Security Act 2001 (ATCSA), the Prevention of Terrorism Act 2005 (PTA) and now another Terrorism Bill (TB) is presently being debated in Parliament. All have contributed (or will contribute) to a number of far-reaching infringements of civil liberties, possibly of global significance, in ultimately reinforcing the messages of international terrorism.

The United Kingdom is, and remains in, a state of emergency that appears unlikely to end in the near future. In enacting ATCSA the UK has derogated from Article 5 of the European Convention on Human Rights (ECHR). The Act introduced indefinite detention for non-UK nationals suspected of being concerned in terrorism.[1] Following a series of legal challenges this has now been modified to a form of "house arrest" contained in PTA. The right of access to evidence and reasons for detention granted to detainees remains restricted.

Until the decision of the US Supreme Court in *Rasul et al v George W Bush et al*,[2] detainees at the Guantanamo Bay Naval Base were denied the right of habeas corpus. Similarly, a US citizen captured in Afghanistan and detained in the US was denied his due process guarantees to challenge the legality of his detention until the decision of the Supreme Court in *Hamdi v Donald Rumsfeld*,[3] In *Hamdi* Justice Scalia, who dissented in *Rasul*, echoed the words of Lord Atkin[4] in *Liversedge v Anderson*[5] and seemed timely:

> Many think it is not only inevitable but entirely proper that liberty give way to security in times of national crisis—that, at the extremes of military exigency "inter arma silent leges". Whatever the general merits of the view that war silences law or modulates its voice, that view has no place in the interpretation and application of a constitution designed precisely to confront war, and, in a manner that accords with democratic principles, to accommodate it....[6]

Probably the real issues are these: does the UK (or indeed any government if the argument is globalised) have a rational policy for dealing with terrorism and, whether it does or not, do the measures enacted affect human rights adversely and if they or some of them do, is that result intended or accidental?

Overview of anti-terrorism legislation in the UK

The experience of the UK in dealing with political violence in Northern Ireland has played an important part in forging the current approach to combating terrorism.

The focus for the UK has now shifted to the global war against terror, not only as a consequence of the attacks of 9/11, but also of those in Bali, Madrid and London itself, amongst others. The strategies that have emerged in UK law to combat terrorism have been determined by international alliances and obligations.[7]

The UK has a raft of existing criminal legislation under which terrorists could, arguably, be charged without the need for creating specific anti-terrorism measures. For instance, it is often possible to prosecute under the Explosives Substances Act 1883.[8] Where a terrorist attack results in loss of life, individuals can be charged with murder and/or a conspiracy to commit explosions, depending on the nature of the attack. The perceived need for specific legislation may arguably be nothing more than a knee-jerk reaction to public panic in a manner echoing the introduction of Official Secrets Act 1911[9] and the Public Order Act 1936.[10] One of the major problems with such legislation is that it often continues beyond its original intended shelf-life. The Criminal Law and Procedure (Ireland) Act 1887, originally introduced to curtail the activities of the Land League in Ireland,[11] prohibited "unlawful associations."[12] This continued as "proscribed organisations" under the Prevention of Terrorism Act (Temporary Provisions) 1974 and in current anti-terrorism legislation.

Modern anti-terrorist legislation probably originates in the Civil Authorities (Special Powers) Act (Northern Ireland) 1922 (SPA) and Regulations. SPA was re-enacted and made permanent in 1933, providing a number of powers. These included stop and search, arrest and detention, unlawful associations and assemblies and promotion of their aims. Most notably, detention without trial was introduced.[13]

Internment has been used regularly since the introduction of SPA, but it was not until 1971 that it provided a catalyst for conflict. Internment received widespread criticism, as those interned often had no connection with any proscribed organisation.[14] Consequently, Westminster was forced to introduce limited procedural safeguards "which provided a measure of judicial oversight."[15] This was completed by the introduction of the Detention of Terrorist (Northern Ireland) Order 1972 enabling the Secretary of State for Northern Ireland to order the detention, without trial, for 28 days of "a person suspected of having been concerned in the commission or attempted commission of any act of terrorism, or in the direction, organisation or training of persons for the purpose of terrorism."[16]

In December 1995, Lord Lloyd of Berwick carried out an inquiry

> to consider the future need for specific counter-terrorism legislation in the United Kingdom if the cessation of terrorism connected with the affairs of Northern Ireland leads to a lasting peace, taking into account the continuing threat from other kinds of terrorism and the United Kingdoms obligations under international law; and to make recommendations.[17]

It was predicted that the threat to mainland UK would recede following the initiation of the peace process in Northern Ireland but, with ominous prescience, that the threat from global terrorism would increase and demanded a response.

Terrorism and terrorists

An exploration of the definition of terrorism is useful in understanding the purpose of such attacks. Terrorism is a type of violence that is equally available to governments[18] and subversive groups. For many terrorist groups it is a form of communication. The contemporary non-legal definition conveys the deliberate or reckless killing of civilians, the causing of extensive damage to property, thus communicating a political message of some sort to a third party[19]. The definition of what constitutes a "terrorist" is difficult to determine without reference to moral and ethical opinion.

It is important to assert that terrorism refers to a type of violence rather than to a type of person.[20] It is a technique that is capable of being used by any individual, and describes their actions. The use of terror is a tactic, and terrorism a description of that tactic. Walter Laqueur states "political terrorism is the weapon of the weak."[21] It has, nonetheless, been a dominant form of terrorism for many years. Such terror has not been limited to dictatorships. The carpet bombing of Dresden and the two atomic bombs dropped on Hiroshima and Nagasaki in 1945 were, arguably, acts of political terror. Acts of terror committed by Governments are often more effective than subversive terror because there is generally a better means of achieving the terror goals.[22]

Exponents of subversive terror (still referred to for ease as "terrorists" despite the above) are no longer viewed as "ambitious revolutionaries" thriving to make a change, or challenging the power of the ruling elite.[23] Rather, the attacks of and subsequent to 9/11 suggest that they are groups who, in their determination to induce a reaction in the civilian population, and hence, the target Government(s), care little for loss of life, even amongst their own members.

The purpose of counter-terrorism is to defeat terrorism, regardless of the means used. Ironically, the acts of war between sovereign nations (the counter-terrorists), and those who seek change for whatever reason (the terrorists) provides an explanation of how government has managed to secure power.[24] It is government that bears responsibility for the categorisation of individuals. Those that wear the legitimate uniform of the state are "counter-terrorists". Alternatively, those who have no army, no uniform[25] and no government allegiance, will be identified as indiscriminate murderers for political ends and classified as terrorists.

Human rights and terrorism

The Terrorism Act 2000 (TA) was passed, obviously before 9/11, as a "clean up" operation to re-enact the law on terrorism in the light of the reduced Irish threat and along the lines of the thinking of Lord Lloyd's report[26] has almost inevitably given rise to breaches of Articles of the ECHR. This does not arise out of a general incompatibility of the Act with Convention Articles, but because the facts of individual cases may produce specific violations. The powers granted by the TA may contravene a number of rights. The powers include:

- exercise of stop and detain and arrest powers[27]
- a burden of proof on the defendant in a criminal case[28]

- questioning and search powers[29]
- disclosure of information[30]
- proscription[31]

One of the problems is that the law in this area is not precise. This lack of precision militates against due process of law. The cases of *Steel and others v United Kingdom*[32] and *Hashman and Harrup v United Kingdom*[33] have confirmed that domestic law should be precise and foreseeable. Whilst this is undoubtedly a desirable feature of law generally, it can be argued that because of the nature and characteristics of terrorism, anti-terrorism legislation should be regarded in a special way. Thus, the interference with a right or freedom may be more willingly justified in the case of terrorism.

This issue was considered in the case of *R v DPP, ex parte Kebilene,*[34] where the House of Lords considered the provisions of the Prevention of Terrorism (Temporary Provisions) Act 1989, which created the offence of possession of articles for the purposes of terrorism.[35]

The defendants claimed that the reversal of the burden of proof was a breach of Article 6 ECHR. Lord Cooke suggested that one might "read down"[36] s16(a) by reference to the words "according to law" in Article 6, and that one might treat terrorism as a special subject, suggesting that it might not be disproportionate to place the burden of proof on the defendant in cases of terrorism.

In *McVeigh and others v United Kingdom,*[37] the applicants claimed that there had been violations of Articles 5 and 8 ECHR. The Commission held that the applicants had been detained "in order to secure the fulfilment of an obligation" within the meaning of the word, "obligation", in Article 5(1)(b).[38]

In instances involving a potential breach of Convention rights it will be important for the Court to consider whether the power exercised has been lawful and proportionate. The test is whether the interference is necessary in a democratic society and whether it is "proportionate to the legitimate aim pursued."[39] As Wadham and Mountfield confirm, the fact that a violation of a Convention right occurs as the result of the pursuit of a legitimate aim of social policy, such as the prevention of terrorism, will not in itself provide justification if the means used are regarded as excessive.[40]

Human rights have been under State attack as a result of 9/11. This is more apparent in the United States where debates have concerned the appropriate use of torture issued by judicial warrant.[41] However, in the UK, despite approval (for the period August 2004 to December 2005) of the use in proceedings of evidence obtained abroad by torture in *A and others v Secretary of State for the Home Department ,*[42] there has been no general attempt to derogate from Article 3 of the Convention, which is, of course, an absolute right. Consequently, as a means of controlling those facing allegations of involvement in terrorist activity the UK has resorted to indefinite detention without trial.[43] Although this action is not as physically brutal as torture, it must be highlighted that with regard to individuals detained under ATCSA and, presumably also PTA, the authorities did or do not have sufficient evidence to bring criminal charges against them.

Section 1 Terrorism Act 2000

The difficulty in defining or accurately describing "terrorists" or "terrorism" in lay language translates to statute. Whilst most people would recognise acts they consider to be "terrorism", a true definition remains elusive. The US State Department defines terrorism as:

> premeditated, politically motivated violence perpetrated against non-combatant targets by sub national groups or clandestine agents.

The FBI divides terrorist-related activity into three categories:

1. A terrorist incident is a violent act or an act dangerous to human life, in violation of the criminal laws of the United States or of any state, to intimidate or coerce a government, the civilian population, or any segment thereof, in furtherance of political or social objectives.
2. A suspected terrorist incident is a potential act of terrorism in which responsibility for the act cannot be attributed at the time to a known or suspected terrorist group or individual.
3. Terrorism prevention is a documented instance in which a violent act by a known or suspected terrorist group or individual with the means and a proven propensity for violence is successfully interdicted through investigative activity.[44]

Thus the term "terrorist" becomes difficult to define without reference to moral and ethical criteria. The UK Parliament has given a very broad definition of "terrorism" and one that is not subject to territorial restrictions. Consequently, groups supporting struggles against repressive regimes, protestors and even unions on strike may fall within the category.

Whilst the Act does not create a specific offence of terrorism, the wide definition contained within s1 applies to terrorism of any kind, whether national or international, and applies wherever the term is used in the Act in relation to the prevention, detection, and investigation of terrorism, and the interception of terrorist funds and property.[45]

Therefore, in order to establish a case, proof is required of three elements:

1. Any action falling within s1(2).
2. An intention to influence government or intimidate, and a political, religious, or ideological cause.
3. By virtue of section 1(4) of the Act, any activity may amount to terrorism if committed outside the United Kingdom or may be referable to persons and events outside the United Kingdom.

It is therefore possible that activity otherwise considered lawful may fall within the ambit of the definition:

> It is important that the definitions in the Bill should not catch actions in connection with industrial disputes, large demonstrations or even politically motivated mass boycotts of major oil companies.... to suggest, for instance, that the nurses' dispute could be a terrorist act is wrong. It would not cause a serious risk, nor would it be driven by a political, religious or ideological cause. It would be a trade dispute, which is not a political, religious or ideological cause.[46]

Clause 33 TB proposes alterations to the definition of terrorism, underlining the theory that whatever it may be is a movable feast depending on current Governmental feeling.

Police powers

The Terrorism Act 2000 has effectively increased police powers in relation to stop and search. Section 44 permits senior police officers to authorise extended stop and search powers within specified areas. The authorisation is only to be granted where the Senior Officer considers it "expedient" for preventing acts of terrorism.[47] This extended power entitles police officers in uniform to stop and search persons and vehicles[48] and remove items that they reasonably suspect may be used for terrorism.[49] Failure to stop when requested to do so may be punishable under s47 as a criminal offence. There are limits to the use of such powers, and authorisation can only be given for a period of 28 days and is subject to confirmation by the Home Secretary within 48 hours of being made.[50] There are clearly arguments here relating to the infringement of individual liberty, as demonstrated in *R (on the application of Gillan & Another) v Commissioner of Police for the Metropolis & Another.*[51]

The case[52] raised cause for concern because of the wide coercive powers of stop and search. The Court of Appeal stated that the power was "not to be used arbitrarily or capriciously", and that the police were obliged to take extra care not to infringe the rights of the individual.

The authorisations and confirmations are subject to judicial review. However, the Court is limited to considering the proportionality issue. Lord Woolf stated that:

> The disadvantage of the intrusion and restraint imposed on even a large number of individuals by being stopped and searched cannot possibly match the advantage that accrues from the possibility of a terrorist attack being foiled or deterred by the use of the power.

However, the existence of safeguards within the legislation does not provide failsafe protection of individual freedoms. The authorisations and confirmations can be renewed ad infinitum effectively undermining their efficacy. It is also arguable that the potential interpretation of "articles of a kind which could be used in connection with terrorism" is wide and of limited effect as a safeguard. However, even though the Court of Appeal criticised the use of these powers in respect of the first applicant who had no such articles in his possession it was nonetheless satisfied that the powers were compatible with the European Convention on Human Rights, and that Article 5 had not been breached.

The case illustrates the difficulty the courts face. There is clearly a need for some discretionary power when dealing with suspected terrorists. The problem lies in their extent and controls over their use. The courts have a constitutional role as a check on the Executive but the area of national security has been one in which they have traditionally been fearful of treading.

The use of the stop and search powers may be necessary, but there may be a danger of a "rolling programme", in the sense that such "special" powers may become the norm.[53] This may eventually extend to other areas of the criminal justice system and lead to authoritarian policing subject to fewer challenges.

The ability to undertake action designed to influence government is the guarantee of a democratic society. However, it appears that any action that seeks to influence government, but involves no threat, violence or intimidation against the public has the potential to fall within the definition of terrorism.[54]

Direct response to 9/11 in the UK

The UK government responded to the terrorist attacks of 9/11 by declaring a state of emergency and, by 14 December 2001, enacting the Anti-Terrorism, Crime and Security Act 2001 (ATCSA). The provisions of Part IV of the Act, which permitted unlimited detention of non-nationals suspected of terrorism, without charge, where it is not possible to deport them[55] forced a derogation from Convention rights less than two years after they had been given direct applicability in UK law by the Human Rights Act 1998.[56]

As Fenwick confirms[57] the Government was only able to declare the Act compatible with Convention rights under s19 HRA[58] by entering a derogation to Article 5(1) as provided for under s14(1) of the HRA. The result even at that stage was arguably the most draconian anti-terrorist legislation of any advanced nation. The legislation was introduced hurriedly as a knee-jerk response to outraged public opinion. As a result, the Bill largely by-passed usually stringent Parliamentary scrutiny procedures. This is by no means a new phenomenon. The Official Secrets Act 1911 was forced through Parliament in a single day in response to a spy scare. The wide-ranging s2[59] prohibited disclosure of any official information, however trivial, and remained in force for 78 years. The Public Order Act 1936, aimed at controlling the activities of the Fascist movement in the UK, gave the Home secretary the power to ban marches in the London area and to give authority to Chief Constables to do so elsewhere and was used in a way that far exceeded its original purpose. The Prevention of Terrorism Bill was enacted in only four days as a direct response to the Birmingham pub bombings of 1974. The problem with legislation introduced in this way is that it often, as detailed above, remains in force long beyond the existence of the "emergency" it was enacted to deal with and often has implications that are far more wide ranging than the original intention.

The Anti-Terrorism Crime and Security Act 2001

The object of ATCSA was to ensure the Government had adequate powers to counter the perceived increased threat of terrorism. Given the extent of existing criminal law, including the Terrorism Act 2000 enacted only a little over a year earlier, it is more than possible that the Government was simply pandering to popular opinion and needed to be seen to respond. In doing so, it may have been tempted to ask Parliament (and receive!) powers it would never have dared to do in a more ordered Act passed at a more reflective speed.

ATCSA contained a number of wide ranging provisions including

- measures against terrorist funds[60]
- provisions for the disclosure of information by public authorities for the purpose of facilitating the work of the intelligence services[61]

- power for the Home Secretary to certify a non-UK national as a "suspected international terrorist" and to order his removal from the UK, or if this is prevented, his detention indefinitely without charge if the Home Secretary reasonably believes his presence is a threat to national security[62]
- provisions extending police powers, including the taking and indefinite retention of fingerprint records for the purposes of terrorist investigation and the removal of items believed to be worn for concealing identity[63]
- re-introduction of the offence of general failure to disclose information about terrorism[64]
- measures for the implementation of the third pillar of the European Union so that the EU wide anti-terrorist measures on policing, extradition and sentencing can be given effect if necessary.[65]

The effect of this last measure is being strengthened by the new criminal co-operation agreements between the EU and the US. Since 9/11, the Europol-US negotiations on mutual legal assistance and extradition conventions have progressed and closer co-operation between Eurojust, a co-ordination body composed of magistrates, prosecutors and police authorities and relevant US authorities is being progressed. Extensive EU co-operation is based on the principle of mutual recognition, which in turn rests on the presumption of equivalent systems of criminal justice by virtue of the fact that all EU member states have ratified the ECHR. The USA however does not seem to have comparable protection and has not ratified the equivalent Inter-American Convention on Human Rights.

By the time the Bill was enacted on 14 December 2001,despite it being just one month after its publication, it had suffered a total of 12 report stage defeats some of its most was commented in *The Independent* commented that it

> was improved by the compromises agreed at the last minute, but it remains a deeply offensive, illiberal and unnecessary set of measures.[66]

Compromises (not withdrawals) introduced included a right of appeal to the Special Immigration Appeals Commission (SIAC)[67] and an amendment to s1 of the Special Immigration Appeals Commission Act 1997 to enable challenges to orders of the Home Secretary against non UK nationals suspected of being "international terrorists", with a right of appeal to the Court of Appeal on a point of law.

Although supportive of some measures including those relating to terrorist funds, human rights bodies were vociferous in condemning controversial issues on the grounds that many of the measures in the Act were not "necessary", were unlikely to avert or deter terrorists and were liable to be counter-productive. It has to be asked why the UK, alone amongst signatories to the ECHR and soon after the passing of the Human Rights Act, felt it necessary to derogate one of the basic provisions of the ECHR in order to fight terrorism. The issue seems to be that there was no way of testing whether the actions of the relevant authorities were proportionate having regard to the secrecy surrounding them. Gareth Pierce, a prominent human rights lawyer, commented on the inability of the police and intelligence services to understand the distinction between resistance to oppression and support for terrorism, which recalls a similar comment on the debates in the House of Lords on the attitude which would have been adopted towards those who fought against apartheid, the so-called *Nelson Mandela Point.*

In support of the legislation, the UK government cited the recognised threat to international peace and security proclaimed in *UN Resolutions 1368 and 1373* and the requirement in *Resolution 1373* that all States "take action", including denying refuge to those who finance, plan, support or commit terrorist acts. They said there existed a state of emergency threatening the nation by virtue of

> foreign nationals present in the UK who are suspected of being concerned in the commission, preparation or instigation of acts of international terrorism…and who are a threat to its national security.

The ECHR has allowed a wide margin of appreciation on this issue:

> [It] will give appropriate weight to such relevant factors as the nature of the rights affected by the derogation, the circumstances leading to, and the duration of the emergency situation.[68]

The 2004 position

Following the introduction of ATCSA, 14 foreign nationals were arrested. Two chose to leave the UK and the remaining 12 were detained at Belmarsh and Woodhill high security prisons and one at Broadmoor Hospital under the provisions of the Act. They immediately began an appeals process before SIAC.

It is important, at this stage, to understand the criteria under which SIAC was initially established and under which it continues to function. SIAC was established as the UK's response to the adverse ruling of the European Court of Human Rights (EctHR) in *Chahal v United Kingdom.*[69] The case related to C, an Indian national who had been granted indefinite leave to remain in the UK, having entered illegally in 1974. He returned on a visit to the Punjab in 1984, where, following his involvement in the organisation of passive resistance in support of a Sikh homeland, he was detained and tortured by the authorities. In 1990 he was ordered to be deported from the UK in the interests of national security and the prevention of terrorism. He was held in custody from where he applied for political asylum. This was refused and due to the involvement of issues of national security he was denied a right of appeal. However, in 1991, an advisory panel was appointed to examine the case, though C was allowed no access to representation, or to any of the evidence against him. His application for judicial review was refused as in the absence of any evidence of the risk posed to national security the court would be unable to assess whether the Secretary of State's decision was irrational or not. An application was made to the ECtHR who decided, in line with the previous decision in *Soering v UK*[70] that:

1. Any attempt to deport C would amount to a breach of Article 3.
2. The refusal to allow C access to domestic appeals procedures amounted to a breach of Article 5(4) on the basis that it must be possible to find a

way of allowing access to the court system without compromising national security.

3. That C's rights under Article 13 had also been breached.

The response of the UK in respect of the breach of Article 5 rights was to enact the Special Immigration Appeals Commission Act 1997 to provide appellants in similar circumstances with access to security-vetted lawyers, known as "Special Advocates" operating outside of their own legal team[71]. The Special Advocates have access to secure information and in this way are supposedly able to test the evidence on behalf of the appellant. However, even though they are acting to safeguard the appellant's interests and ensure that Article 5 rights are not breached they are unable to discuss the evidence with the appellant or his defence team. Indeed, once they have seen the evidence they are allowed no further direct contact with the appellant or his lawyers. It is questionable as to whether this meets the obligations imposed under Article 5(4) ECHR.

The 12 Belmarsh detainees held under the provisions ATCSA appealed to SIAC in accordance with s2 of the Act.[72] However their appeals against their certification by the Secretary of State for the Home Department as "suspected international terrorists and security risks" were rejected. The appeals took place in both open and closed session and, according to Amnesty,[73] fell far short of international fair trial standards on a number of counts, not least on the reliance on secret evidence alleged to have been adduced by torture. As one detainee commented:

This sort of court reminds me exactly what my country did with the detainees in Libya—exactly the same—I believe I'm an innocent man and I did nothing against this country. (Released suspect "M") [74]

The detainees appealed to the Court of Appeal[75] on four grounds[76]. The appeal was rejected in respect of the first two, but it was determined that the Commission should have accepted jurisdiction in respect of the deported appellants and that no fair trial could result where evidence had been obtained against the party bringing the appeal by means of torture.

The appellants were given leave to appeal to the House of Lords on three grounds.[77]

It was held that the Government was entitled to conclude that a state of emergency existed (Lord Hoffman dissented on this point). It was further held that the detentions were disproportionate as they failed to address rationally the threat to security posed by foreign nationals because they did not address the threat posed by UK nationals and that they permitted foreign nationals to continue their activities abroad. In addition it was held that if the threat to UK national security posed by UK nationals could be addressed without infringements to personal liberty then it should be possible to do so with regard to the threat posed by foreign nationals. Therefore the measures were not "strictly required" by the exigencies of the situation within Article 15. Article 14 was also breached. Any decision to retain one group of individuals based on nationality or immigration alone is clearly discriminatory. The House firmly declared under s4 of the HRA that s23 of ATCSA was incompatible with Articles 5 and 14 of Sch.1 Part 1 of that Act.

The impact of the House of Lords' decision

Whilst, prima facie, the decision of the Lords' in *A v SoS for the Home Department* is a clear demonstration of the willingness of the judiciary to exercise the powers allocated to them under the HRA and to make declarations of incompatibility[78] where justice demands that they do so, the response of the UK government has been disappointing. The Home Secretary, Charles Clarke, issued a response to the ruling on the 26th January 2005. Whilst the statement accepted declaration of incompatibility and also that any new legislative measures must apply equally to nationals as well as non-nationals, the steps taken to rectify the situation are the minimum necessary to ensure equality and to avoid the need for high-security detention in such circumstances.

Control orders (see below) replaced Part IV orders allowing the indefinite detention of foreign nationals certified as terrorism suspects on 13 March 2005. Parliament passed the legislation after a marathon day-and-night sitting, during which the House of Lords sent the bill back to the House of Commons four times. The new controls orders, now enacted as the Prevention of Terrorism Act 2005, apply equally to nationals and non-nationals and to all forms of terrorism, both national and international. The control orders enable the authorities to impose conditions ranging from prohibitions on access to specific items or services, and restrictions on association with named individuals, to the imposition of restrictions on movement or curfews. Control orders are made for a period of 12 months and appear to be infinitely renewable[79]. Any breach of a control order will be subject to punishment by the criminal law.

The 2005 legislation

Whereas the ATCSA had allowed the indefinite imprisonment of foreign terror suspects without trial, the PTA introduced as mentioned above, "control orders". Any change that followed such a ruling from the Law Lords as that in *A v SoS for the Home Department* surely should have represented a renewed government commitment to human rights from the very administration responsible for the enactment of the Human Rights Act less than seven years earlier.

Unfortunately, that seemed to be far from the case. In June 2005, both the Council of Europe's Committee for the Prevention of Torture and the Commissioner for Human Rights, Alvaro Gil-Robles, criticised the UK's treatment of terrorist suspects as violating basic rights. Those reports joined sustained criticism mounted by organisations including Amnesty International and Liberty, and disquiet amongst peers and MPs, Conservatives, Liberal Democrats and Labour backbenchers alike.

Under a control order, suspects can have indefinite restrictions placed upon their movements, from tagging to effective house arrest, as well as upon their associations and work. They can be prohibited from using communications services, or be forced to surrender their passports[80]. Failure to adhere to such restrictions can result in a fine or imprisonment. The possible implications are wide-ranging, with many clearly violating domestic and international human rights legislation. Indeed, such orders are acknowledged to breach Article 5 of the European Convention for the Protection of Human Rights and Fundamental Freedoms, being specifically denoted as "derogating control orders".

The initial PTB raised serious concerns, as it gave the executive what many considered unprecedented and improper power and restricted the right to be brought before a judge or other officer authorised by law to exercise judicial power. It was proposed that politicians, rather than judges, would impose control orders. This was condemned by some as the greatest threat mounted against civil freedoms in the UK in over 300 years and a death knell to the principle of the separation of powers. The government eventually capitulated over this matter, and the PTA states that judges should have the last word on the imposition of control orders[81]. Despite this concession, however, it can be maintained that the real travesty of justice remains. The reality for a suspect who suffers violations of his or her basic rights is unchanged.

Furthermore, even the principle of upholding proper judicial authority remains ill-served. Mr Gil-Robles asserts that in practice, the issuing of control orders involves only weak judicial involvement, not comparable to that exercised in criminal proceedings. Since a suspect's response is not considered in a judge's assessment of the veracity or relevance of evidence, for Mr Gil-Robles the review procedure is "inherently one-sided".

This one-sidedness arises from the fact that suspects are deprived of the right to be given prompt and detailed information regarding accusations, and consequently the right to mount a defence and seek self-chosen legal assistance, if desired. Three main reasons are offered for withholding evidence from public scrutiny, consequently delaying charge and trial of the suspect. Firstly, certain methods of procurement, such as bugging, currently render evidence inadmissible in court. Secondly, the revelation of some intelligence may compromise national security. Lastly, evidence is often of an insufficient quality to uphold criminal conviction. Furthermore, UK authorities are not obliged to disclose to judges evidence which may exculpate the suspect, nor whether evidence has been obtained under torture or similarly unlawful circumstances, if no UK agent is directly implicated.

On top of this bias against suspects, such practices not being sanctioned in criminal trial proceedings, a judge need only have "reasonable suspicion"[82] that someone is involved in terrorism for a control order to be imposed. As such, not only is the integrity of judges' decisions being undermined, but suspects lose the right, otherwise accorded by the criminal justice system, to be presumed innocent until guilt is proven "beyond reasonable doubt". As far as the right to have criminal charges brought by an independent and impartial tribunal is upheld, Mr Gil-Robles concludes that "the review proceedings described can only be considered fair, independent and impartial with some difficulty".

These legal arguments may appear abstract but are fundamentally important. What must not be obscured is what human rights legislation essentially seeks to protect: the well-being of individuals. In January 2005, the Royal College of Psychiatrists stated that "indeterminate detention, lack of normal due legal process and the resultant sense of powerlessness, are likely to cause significant deterioration in detainees' mental health". These claims are substantiated by a visit to Belmarsh prison by the Council of Europe's Committee for the Prevention of Torture that found prisoners held under the ATCSA to be in a physical and mental state so poor as to reflect "inhuman and degrading treatment". Simply deinstitutionalising this detention, by moving detainees from prisons to their homes, will do little to alleviate any psychological strain.

Ultimately, this all amounts to the inescapable fact that under the PTA, individuals can be stripped of many rights concerning their liberty, the receipt of a fair trial and equality before the law, and in the damning words of Mr Gil-Robles, "control orders are intended to substitute the ordinary criminal justice system with a parallel system run by the executive".

The UK authorities point to the continued existence of a "public emergency threatening the life of the nation" making such measures necessary. However, great the threat of terrorism may be, it remains and cannot simply be legislated away. Ostensibly an attempt to do so, the PTA is described by Professor Paul Wilkinson, chairman of the Centre for the Study of Terrorism and Political Violence at St Andrew's University, as "dangerously counter-productive ... draconian ... a recruiting sergeant for terrorist organisations".[83]

There is hope yet that the trend for hurried anti-terrorist legislation will eventually be reversed. Indeed, Mark Oaten, Liberal Democrats home affairs spokesman, believes that Mr Gil-Robles' report signalled "the beginning of the end" for control orders. The new TB has been brought forward in response to the London bombings on 7th July and attempted bombings a fortnight after, but more controversial aspects, including control orders, were to be left until January 2006 for further consideration[84]. Although, with Mr Blair suggesting that human rights legislation may be amended in order to facilitate his fight against terrorism in the UK, is there more cause for fear that, in the wake of the atrocities in New York on 11th September 2001, human rights are increasingly becoming a mere, easily breached inconvenience for politicians?

Cl 23 of TB contains the recently debated provisions about extending the period of detention for terrorist suspects, without need for charge or trial, to three months. This resulted in a Government defeat in the House of Commons but it still seems keen to try to force the measure through, citing "police requirements" as the main requirement for this draconian provision. The original detention period in s 41 TA was seven days and was increased to fourteen days by s 306 (4) Criminal Justice Act 2003. The TB's Parts and Schedules are as follows:

Part 1 (Offences) provides for new offences, amendments to existing offences, and makes incidental provisions about terrorism offences. Part 1 creates offences relating to the encouragement of acts of terrorism, and to the dissemination of terrorist publications. Part 1 makes specific provision about how these two new offences are to apply to those providing and using the internet and other electronic services. It also creates offences relating to the preparation of terrorist acts and terrorist training; the making, possession or use of radioactive devices and materials; the making of terrorist threats relating to radioactive devices, materials, or nuclear facilities; and trespass on nuclear sites. The Bill increases penalties for possession for terrorist purposes; offences relating to nuclear material; and offences relating to the contravention of a notice relating to encrypted information. Part 1 also sets out new procedures to be followed in the preparation of terrorist cases for trial. Schedule 1 sets out a list of "Convention offences" that are referred to in Part 1. These represent the parallel offences in UK law to those offences mentioned in the Council of Europe Convention on the Prevention of Terrorism.

Part 2 (Miscellaneous provisions) includes an amendment to the grounds on which the Secretary of State is empowered to proscribe organisations, a process through which a proscribed organisation may be identified by another name, and amendments to police and investigatory powers. [85]

Schedule 2 sets out the method by which forfeiture proceedings should be carried out, following a seizure of terrorist publications.

Part 3 (Supplemental provisions) provides for the oversight of the operation of Part 1 of the Bill and the TACT through an independent annual review to Parliament. It also contains a specific provision which provides that clause 23 (extension of period of detention of terrorist suspects) will expire one year after its commencement unless continued in force by an order made by the Secretary of State. Finally, it includes a number of consequential amendments and repeals.

2006

The Terrorism Act 2006 was introduced to tighten the law yet again following the attacks on the London underground and buses in July 2005. It extends the definition of terrorism to include actions or threats or using noxious substances or things to influence or intimidate a government. [86]

Section 1 creates the offence of encouragement of terrorism, and applies to a statement "that is likely to be understood by some or all of the members of the public to whom it is published as a direct or indirect encouragement or other inducement to them to the commission, preparation or instigation of acts of terrorism or Convention offences". It is an offence to publish such a statement, or to cause another to publish such a statement with the intention that members of the public be "directly or indirectly encouraged to commit, prepare or instigate acts of terrorism or Convention offences." [87] It is also an offence to be "reckless as to whether members of the public will be directly or indirectly encouraged….etc". An indirect encouragement is defined as being a statement "describing terrorism in such a way that the listener would infer that he should emulate it."

Section 2 creates the offence of disseminating a terrorism publication with the intention, or being reckless, of directly or indirectly encouraging or inducing the commission, preparation or instigation of acts of terrorism. The criminal offences under Section 1 and Section 2 extend to internet activity.

The Act extends the law to cover *any* conduct undertaken in preparation for committing, or assisting another to commit, acts of terrorism. Conviction carries a maximum sentence of life imprisonment. Providing or receiving instruction for or training in skills relating to terrorism is criminalized. The making and possession of radioactive material or devices, or the misuse of devices or material, or demands or threats relating to such items are offences punishable with a maximum of life imprisonment. [88] Conduct outside the UK is a criminal offence inside the UK if it would amount to an offence listed in section 17 (2).

The period in which a terrorist suspect may be held without charge is extended to 28 days, and this came into force in July 2006 (the rest of the Act having come into force in April 2006), just in time to be taken advantage of in the investigations of the alleged plot in August 2006 to blow up transatlantic flights. Some 11 suspects out of the 25 originally arrested were held under this provision beyond the 14 days previously permissible. The Blair Government had wanted a 90 day detention period but eventually agreed on 28 after opposition in Parliament during the passage of the Bill. In the days following the alleged plot in August 2006, Government ministers were speaking of looking to Parliament to extend the limits again. The Terrorism Act 2006 extends the grounds on which detention may be authorized as set out in Schedule 8 to the Terrorism Act 2000 by including continued detention pending the result of an examination or analysis of relevant evidence, to obtain relevant evidence whether by questioning or otherwise and to preserve relevant evidence.[89] Detention beyond 14 days must be authorized by a High Court judge, whereas up to that point a District Judge's order will suffice.

Conclusion

It seems that, again and again, legislation is enacted hastily in response to a new and urgent situation. Whilst in many circumstances this would be laudable there seems to have been little questioning of the principles underpinning this issue; Why for instance has the fundamental matter of charging terrorists with specific offences not been addressed? Clearly there is an issue that, because of their secretive and covert nature, allegations of involvement in terrorism are difficult to investigate, but to subject individuals to such indeterminate restraints of liberty, albeit the least worst option, seems to fly in the face of due process and continue to militate against those basic rights set out in a multitude of International Charters on Human Rights. There is always a balancing act to be performed, the rights of citizens to live in peace and security set against the rights of individuals who may seek to threaten this. However, our criminal justice systems are founded on a presumption of innocence and we should be exploring ways in which that presumption can be preserved, investigations expedited and individuals charged or released.

History shows that legislation passed in haste, however laudable the motive, be it Official Secrets Act 1911, Public Order Act 1936 or Prevention of Terrorism (Temporary Provisions) Act 1974, far outlives the perceived crisis for which it is apparently designed and is used by future Governments in ways never envisaged at r birth such as the use of The Official Secrets Act 1911 against "whistleblowers" in the 1980s following the Falklands conflict and the use of Public Order Act 1936 against anti-nuclear protestors is the 1950s, 1960s and 1980s and its use against mine workers in their national strike in the 1980s. It seems that the population as a whole is keen for new powers to be taken to deal with an apparent crisis and the Government of the day, mindful both of public opinion and the usefulness of draconian powers never likely to be given to them in more tranquil times, is keen to oblige. Seldom would the ordinary pre-existing criminal law have been inadequate—and with powers of arrest for breach of the peace and with conspiracy and incitement being offences in the UK in certain circumstances it is hardly surprising that a virtually all encompassing set of powers already exists. The "additional powers" usually offend, or risk offending, what we now call the "human rights" of those arrested under them. If they are not necessary, this is an indictment of a so called "liberal democracy". They become more and more ridiculed and less and less workable while extreme if unconvincing political effort is made to shore them up. If they truly are needed, then the dam in a civilised human rights respecting State can surely be held by pre-existing powers until well reasoned and discussed law can be agreed through Parliament after full debate. Anything less results in accusations that the State is as morally corrupt as those who would attack it are hard to refute.

---

[1] S23 ACTSA

[2] Case Nos 03-334 and 03-343, 542 US (2004)

[3] Case No 03-6696. 542 US (2004)

[4] 'In this country, amid the clash of arms, the laws are not silent. They may be changed, but they speak the same language in war as in peace.'

[5] [1942] AC 206 at page 244

[6] dissenting opinion of Justice Scalia, p 21

[7] Terrorism, Human Rights and the Rule of Law: 120 Years of the UK's Legal Response to Terrorism, Brandon.

[8] The Act was a result of Fenian and anarchist bombing in London in the 1870s.

[9] An Act passed to deal with a supposed influx of German spies in the years before World War 1. Any British subject behaving in a way liable to prosecution under the Act could probably have been prosecuted for treason, and any alien could have been prosecuted for a number of pre-existing offences under the ordinary criminal law. Once the 'German threat' had passed, the Act remained substantially in force until 1989.

[10] An Act passed in response to activities of Oswald Moseley and his supporters in the British Union of Fascists. Again, they could have been prosecuted under statutes forbidding criminal damage, violence against the person, or common law offences such as conspiracy as well as the catch all 'breach of the peace'. The statute remained until 1986 when the situation was made even more restrictive by Public Order Act 1986.

[11] Established in 1879 to improve the rights of tenant farmers in Ireland

[12] See s7:
"... the Lord Lieutenant in Council, may from time to time, by order to be published in the prescribed manner, prohibit or suppress in any district specified in the order any association named or described in such special proclamation, or any association which appears to the Lord Lieutenant to be a dangerous association...From and after the date of such an order, and ensuring the continuance thereof, every assembly or meeting of such association, or of the members of it as such members in the specified district shall be an unlawful assembly, and the association itself shall be an unlawful association..."

[13] "The civil authority may by order require every person within any area specified in the order to remain within doors between such hours as may be specified in the order, and in such case, if any person within that area is or remains out between such hours without a permit in writing from the civil authority or some person duly authorised by him, he shall be guilty of an offence against these regulations"

[14] Report of the Commission to Consider Legal Procedures to Deal with Terrorist Activities in Northern Ireland, Cmnd.518 (1972). Chairman: Lord Diplock. See p. 15: "it is now recognised by those responsible for collecting and collating this kind of information that when internment was re-introduced in August 1971, the scale of the operation led to the arrest and detention of a number of persons against whom suspicion was founded on inadequate and inaccurate information."

[15] Terrorism, Human Rights and the Rule of Law: 120 Years of the UK's Legal Response to Terrorism, Brandon, Crim LR 2004

[16] Detention of Terrorists (Northern Ireland) Order 1972, s.4 (SI 1972/1632) (N.I.15)

[17] Inquiry into Legislation against Terrorism by the Rt Honourable Lord Lloyd of Berwick, Cm.3420 (1996), p.v.

[18] Robert Mugabe's ZANU-PF has been in power since 1980 and has often used terror to achieve his political ambitions, for example, seizing white-owned farmland in Zimbabwe. For further information see: http://en.wikipedia.org/wiki/Robert_Mugabe

[19] This does not necessarily have to be the Government. Although the message is not political, many individuals would class domestic violence and child abuse as terrorism. See Terrorism and Morality by Conor Gearty. European Human Rights Law Review.

[20] The idea of the "terrorist" as a type of person rather than a technique of violence grew out of the concept of the "urban guerrilla" which in turn was a kind of revolutionary—mainly based in South America—who sought in the 1960s to bring Castro's and Che Guevara's insights about rural guerrilla subversion to the cities. See

[21] W. Laqueur (1987). The Age of Terrorism. Boston: Little, Brown and Company.

[22] Such as intelligent weapons and money.

[23] Fighters engaged in a restrained military campaign against an undemocratic, racist or those active in genocide type of Government, are still "terrorists", with the Government forces that oppose them being the "counter-terrorists". Mugabe See Note and literature.

[24] Oliver Cromwell.

[25] Note: Terrorist groups such as the IRA, will often declare themselves to be an 'army' and choose to wear a 'uniform'

[26] Supra—footnote 22

[27] ss42-47 potential for breach of Article 5 rights

[28] Article 6

[29] ss40-43 potential for breach of Article 8 rights

[30] s20 potential for breach of Article 10 rights

[31] s3 potential for breach of Article 10 and 11 rights

[32] (1999) 28 E.H.R.R. 603. At para. 54; "The Court recalls that the expressions "lawful" and "in accordance with a procedure prescribed by law" in Article 5(1) stipulate not only full compliance with the procedural and substantive rules of national law, but also that any deprivation of liberty be consistent with the purpose of Article 5 and not arbitrary. In addition, given the importance of personal liberty, it is essential that the applicable national law meets the standard of "lawfulness" set by the Convention, which requires that all law, whether written or unwritten, be sufficiently precise to allow the citizen—if need be, with appropriate advice—to foresee, to a degree that is reasonable in the circumstances, the consequences which a given action may entail."

[33] (2000) 30 E.H.R.R. 241. At para. 31; "The Court recalls that one of the requirements flowing from the expression "prescribed by law" is foreseeability. A norm cannot be regarded as a "law" unless it is formulated with sufficient precision to enable the citizen to regulate his conduct. At the same time, while certainty in the law is highly desirable, it may bring in its train excessive rigidity and the law must be able to keep pace with changing circumstances. The level of precision required of domestic legislation—which cannot in any case provide for every eventuality—depends to a considerable degree on the content of the instrument in question, the field it is designed to cover and the number and status of those to whom it is addressed."

[34] [1999] 3 W.L.R. 972.

[35] Section 16a of the Prevention of Terrorism (Temporary Provisions) Act 1989. "A person is guilty of an offence if he has any article in his possession in circumstances giving rise to a reasonable suspicion that the article is in his possession for a purpose connected with the commission, preparation or instigation of acts of terrorism to which this section applies".

[36] [1999] 3 W.L.R. 972.

[36] Section 16a of the Prevention of Terrorism (Temporary Provisions) Act 1989. "A person is guilty of an offence if he has any article in his possession in circumstances giving rise to a reasonable suspicion that the article is in his possession for a purpose [36] Reading down in this instance means either reading the section in the Act according to a quality of law which does not put a high burden on the defendant, so that there is no violation of the presumption of innocence; or alternatively reading it according to a proportionate law, which must take account of present terrorism and the danger to the state, so the section is not disproportionate in the circumstances, and so not in violation of Article 6.

[37] (1981) 5 E.H.R.R. 71. The applicants were arrested by police in 1977 when they arrived at Liverpool from Ireland. They were detained for 45 hours for "examination" under the PTA, searched, questioned, photographed, and fingerprinted; but no charges were preferred.

[38] "Everyone has the right to liberty and security of person. No one shall be deprived of his liberty save in the following cases and in accordance with a procedure prescribed by law...(b) the lawful arrest or detention of a person for non-compliance with the lawful order of a court or in order to secure the fulfilment of any obligation prescribed by law."

[39] *Handyside v UK (1976) 1 EHRR 737*

[40] J. Wadham & H. Mountfield. (1999). *Blackstone's Guide to the Human Rights Act 1998.* London. Blackstone Press Ltd. p14

[41] Alan Dershowitz, Professor of Law at Harvard University, has controversially proposed calls for the use of judicially sanctioned torture to force a terrorist suspect to reveal information that would prevent an imminent terrorist attack. For further information see Dershowitz, A. (2002) *Why Terrorism Works*, New Haven and London, Yale University Press.

[42] [2004] EWCA CIV 1123, [2004] All ER (D) 62 (Aug), (Approved judgment) saw this decision made by the Court of Appeal. It was overturned by the House of Lords on 8 December 2005. [2005] UKHL 71

[43] See later discussion on ATCSA and PTA .

[44] US Counter-Terrorism Threat and Warning Unit. Counter-Terrorism Division. *Thirty Years of Terrorism: Terrorism in the United States 1999* http://www.fbi.gov/publications/terror/terror99.pdf Accessed 16.05.05

[45] . S1 of the Act provides:

(2) Action falls within this subsection if it—

      (a) involves serious violence against a person,

      (b) involves serious damage to property,

(c) endangers a person's life, other than that of the person committing the action,

(d) creates a serious risk to the health or safety of the public or a section of the public, or

(e) is designed seriously to interfere with or seriously to disrupt an electronic system.

(3) The use or threat of action falling within subsection (2) which involves the use of firearms or explosives is terrorism whether or not subsection (1)(b) is satisfied.

(4) In this section-

    (a) "action" includes action outside the United Kingdom,

    (b) a reference to any person or to property is a reference to any person, or to property, wherever situated,

    (c) a reference to the public includes a reference to the public of a country other than the United Kingdom, and

    (d) "the government" means the government of the United Kingdom, of a Part of the United Kingdom or of a country other than the United Kingdom.

[46] H.C. Deb. S.C.D., col. 31. Mr Charles Clarke M.P

[47] Section 44(3) TA 2000

[48] Section 45(1)(a)

[49] Section 45(3)

[50] Section 46(4)

[51] [2004] EWCA Civ 1067

[52] The case challenged the lawfulness of two stop and searches that were carried out

The facts of the case are as follows: On the 13th August 2003 a section 44 authorisation was made and confirmed by the Home Secretary on the 11th September 2003. On the 9th September 2003, one of the applicants was stopped and searched on his way to an arms fair. The search lasted 20 minutes. The items seized were nothing to with terrorism. The other applicant, a photographer was also stopped and searched. The applicants sought a judicial review of the lawfulness of the police action. The Administrative Court dismissed the applications, but granted permission to appeal on the basis that the case raised important issues in relation to national security and the liberty of individuals.[52]

The Court of Appeal considered the issues upon which the grounds were based. These included the interpretation of the Terrorism Act 2000, the decision by the Assistant Commissioner to grant a section 44 authorisation, the Home Secretary's decision to confirm the authorisation, the actions of the Commander on the day, and the actions of officers exercising the powers.

The Court of Appeal adopted a literal approach to interpretation, giving the wording of the Act its ordinary meaning. The Court noted that the power was wide but subject to a number of safeguards, including the need to obtain authorisation that, in turn, also needed to be confirmed by the Home Secretary. In addition limits to the authorisation exist. Due to the scale of the threat of terrorist activity at the time the Court determined the decisions to grant and confirm the authorisation were lawful. The Commander needed to ensure that officers were given proper instruction on the use and exercise of the powers, and the Court advised the police to 'review very carefully' the exercise of the powers.

[53] see I. Sim and P.A. Thomas, The Prevention of Terrorism Act: Normalising the Politics of Repression' (1983) 10 Journal of Law and Society 71).

[54] Such would be the case with fox-hunting. For further information, refer to section 1 of the Terrorism Act 2000.

[55] S22(1)

[56] Which came into force on 2 October 2000

[57] H Fenwick. The Anti Terrorism, Crime and Security Act 2001: A proportionate response to 11 September? MLR September 2002. Vol 65 (5) p724 at 727

[58] s19(1) provides that a minister of the Crown (in either House)must, prior to the second reading of the Bill, make a statement either (a)to the effect that the provisions of the Bill are compatible with Convention rights or (b) make a statement to the effect that he unable to make a statement of compatibility but that the government nonetheless wishes to continue with the Bill

[59] s2 received no Parliamentary consideration whatsoever

[60] Part 1 s1-3 and Part 2 s4-8

[61] Part 3 s17-20

[62] Part 4 s21-32

[63] Part 10 s89-95

[64] Part 13 s117

[65] Part 13 s111 & 112

[66] *The Independent*, 15 December 2001

[67] under s30(2) of the Act

[68] *Brannigan and McBride v UK* (1994) 17 EHRR 539 at para 43
[69] (1997) 23 E.H.R.R. 413
[70] [1989] 11 E.H.R.R. 439
[71] s6
[72] A v Secretary of State for the Home Department, [2002] H.R.L.R. 45; [2002] A.C.D. 98 (Sp Imm App. Comm)
[73] http://web.amnesty.org/library/index/ENGEUR450292003 Accessed 23.05.05
[74] http://news.bbc.co.uk/1/hi/uk/3652141.stm Accessed 23.05.00
[75] A (and others) v Secretary of State for the Home Department [2004] EWCA Civ 1123
   1.   [76] SIAC had not sufficiently scrutinised the Secretary of State's case
   2.   that there had been too wide an interpretation of the scope of the derogation from Article 5
   3.   that evidence obtained from a third party in breach of Article 3 should have been regarded as inadmissible
   4.   that jurisdiction in respect of deported applicants should not have been declined

   1.   [77] that no 'public emergency threatening the life of the nation' within the meaning of Article 15 existed and that as such the test for reliance had not been satisfied
   2.   that the detentions were disproportionate to the objective which could be achieved by less draconian measures
   3.   that s23 was discriminatory in allowing for the detention of foreign nationals suspected of terrorism but not allowing for the detention UK nationals similarly suspected.
[78] s4
[79] Prevention of Terrorism Act 2005 s2(4)(a) & (b)
[80] S1 PTA
[81] Ss 3 and 4 PTA
[82] S4 PTA
[83] Dick Oosting of Amnesty International maintains: 'Respect for human rights is often portrayed as hampering efforts to defeat terrorism but ... genuine security is undermined if basic human rights and the rule of law are not respected'. Such an apparently scant regard for human rights as demonstrated by this government cannot be tolerated.
[84] Their continuation for another year was approved by Parliament in February 2006
[85] These changes affect:
   - Powers to detain terrorist suspects under the TA, and the grounds on which such detention may be authorised
   - Powers to search premises, and seize material under Schedule 5 to the TA
   - Powers to seize, and seek forfeiture of, terrorist publications
   - Powers to search at ports under Schedule 7 TA, and to issue authorisations to stop and search under Section 44 TA
   - Powers to issue authorisations or warrants to carry out acts under the Intelligence Services Act 1994
   - Powers to issue, and amend the schedules of intercept warrants
   - Powers to seek disclosure notices under the Serious Organised Crime and Police Act 2005
   - The definition of terrorism, as set out in the TA
   - The process under which terrorist cash-seizure hearings are heard under the TA
[86] Amending s 1(1)(b) of Terrorism Act 2000 and s 113 (1)(c) Antiterrorism Crime and Security Act 2001
[87] Convention offences are those listed in Schedule 1 to the Act.
[88] Ss 9-11 Terrorism Act 2006
[89] Ss 23-25 Terrorism Act 2006

CHAPTER 21

AMERICAN TORTURERS AND THEIR KNOWN VICIOUS PROPENSITIES[1]

Paul H. Brietzke[**]

An old saw of the Anglo-American common law of tort is that "every dog gets its first bite," since dogs are not deemed inherently vicious. But once that dog has bitten, its owner becomes strictly liable to prevent future bites; the dog is then said to have a known vicious propensity.[2] Even giving the U.S. military/intelligence/ private contractor/civilian hierarchy the benefit of the doubt, by treating it as not inherently vicious, this hierarchy has now bitten so hard, so often, and in so many contexts since September 11, 2001 that the owner is clearly obliged to take the strictest of precautions. In a democracy, the ultimate owner of this beast is the people of the U.S., but they can only exert control through the president, his bureaucratic hierarchy, Congress, the courts, the ballot box, and/or activist media and nongovernmental organization (NGO) networks.[3] Continued savagery under the rubric of torture shows the failure of such accountability devices that otherwise guarantee civilized behavior in mature democracies. Alternatives must therefore be pursued, to call these known vicious propensities to account.

The dog metaphor is appropriate because dogs are "unclean" animals among Muslims, objects for disdain and avoidance. Many others misbehave of course, in the Muslim world and elsewhere. If it did not conflict with other perceived U.S. interests—as it does in Pakistan or Saudi Arabia for example, the U.S. calls miscreants to account for, e.g., sanctioning torture on grounds of national security—in Algeria and Uzbekistan for example. (Regrettably, such criticisms by the U. S. were too little and too late concerning former juntas in Chile and Argentina.) Such criticisms issue from a moralistic "us versus them" high ground: *our* sincere (but selective) dedication to the Rule of Law, versus *their* systematic violations of human rights. But this vision is now unhinged and U.S. torturers' hands are unclean, in ways the world has not seen since the 1968 My Lai massacre during the Vietnam War. Haditha (but apparently not Ishaqi) in Iraq is a May 2006 re-enactment of My Lai. Ostensible enemies of the U.S. were handed a propaganda coup that trumps their own best efforts, and some would draw parallels between torture and abuses of "ordinary" Americans in prisons, mental hospitals, old-age homes, etc.[4]

An arrogant and insensitive Bush Administration showed a contempt for significant international laws by rejecting the International Criminal Court, the Anti-Ballistic Missile Treaty, and the Kyoto Protocol, and then rejecting a multilateral diplomacy, the Geneva Conventions—at least as they apply to "enemy combatants" (*infra*), and the Torture Convention and domestic laws that, Bush and his neo-conservatives allege, impermissibly infringe a breathtakingly-broad definition of the President's "Commander—in—Chief" powers under the Constitution.

Even Shiites and Sunnis found they could often unite in opposition to a not—so—benevolent U.S. imperialism in Iraq: events lent credence to arguments that the U.S. is in the Middle East and West Asia, not to promote democracy and freedom, but for oil, protecting Israeli interests, a vindictiveness harkening back to the Crusades, and spreading a secular depravity. Even U.S. Defense Secretary Donald Rumsfeld knows that new terrorists are being created faster than the older ones are being captured or killed.[5] The U.S. is losing a struggle for the hearts and minds of those who are not yet its enemies, regardless of how the Administration responds to its torturers, as well as winning battles but losing the Wars that, you will recall, were started to capture Osama bin Laden and Saddam's weapons of mass destruction (that were re-named weapons of mass deception by American wags).

A Vicious Cycle

The behavior of U.S. jailers in Iraq's Abu Ghraib prison was shown in widely-available digital photographs and a movie. Conceptually, Abu Ghraib represents the transplantation of inattention to law, and thus an adoption of torture techniques which the U.S. military, CIA, and private contractors used, first in prisons in Afghanistan and then as transplanted along with Afghan prisoners to Guantanamo. This cycle was then completed when 'improved' Guantanamo techniques were transplanted to Iraq and, as 'refined' further, back to Afghanistan.

In Afghanistan, Pulitzer Prize-winning WASHINGTON POST reporters demonstrated that senior military officers stonewalled about torture, bombing "mistakes", etc. and that they and their juniors got away with such behavior. As in other U.S. detention facilities set up later, error was not admitted nor responsibility assigned. A former intelligence officer gave as the "operating principle" for Afghanistan: "Grab whom [sic.] you must. Do what you want."[6] Only a few of the deaths in the prison at Bagram air base were investigated, and only one "conviction" has been reported. As was his wont until the Abu Ghraib prison photos first appeared, President Bush dismissed or denied media and NGO reports of torture. But he did term prisoners in Afghanistan (and later in Guantanamo, but not in Iraq) "enemy combatants," who are *thus* not entitled to protections under the Geneva Conventions because they are not "prisoners of war."[7] (Bush conveniently ignored the common Art. 3 of the Conventions, and Convention No. 4 which protects "civilians" and others who are not "prisoners of war", in ways broad enough to encompass Bush's prisoners.) "Enemy combatant" is a category known only from that blot on American jurisprudence, *Ex Parte Quirin*,[8] where both the facts and the law were manipulated by Justice Department prosecutors to save then-F.B.I. Director J. Edgar Hoover from embarrassment, and to execute the defendants *before* the Supreme Court's opinions were written—because President Roosevelt wanted it that way. Regrettably, the Supreme Court gave limited credence to *Quirin* and its "enemy combatant" characterization in *Hamdi* (2004).[9]

An unknown number of prisoners from the Afghan War (and, later, Iraqi War II) were "rendered" by the U.S.: transferred to authorities in Uzbekistan, Pakistan, Egypt, Jordan, Saudi Arabia, Morocco. It became clear in March 2006 that some of these and other prisoners were also transferred to places unknown, after transit through major European cities. In all of these countries, the CIA knew that prisoners could be tortured even more thoroughly and with less compunction than they could be while in U.S. custody. In April 2006, Amnesty International discomfited Secretary of State Rice, with a Report detailing the CIA's covert rendition airplane fleet. "Rendition" is prohibited without exception by international law, under its correct name of refoulement.[10] Some 700 Afghan War prisoners were initially rendered to Guantanamo, a U.S. military base on perpetual lease from Cuba and thus (mistakenly, it turned out) thought by the Bush Administration to be beyond the jurisdiction of the U.S. courts.

The Red Cross made a rare public complaint about abuses and the "worrying deterioration" of detainees' mental health at Guantanamo. It was later disclosed that interrogators have access to detainees' health records, to better probe for weaknesses. Protests from military lawyers caused Secretary of Defense Rumsfeld to order a review of Guantanamo interrogation techniques (*infra*). In June 2004, the Pentagon released hundreds of documents about these interrogations, and stated that "extreme measures" now require Rumsfeld's approval. Military defense lawyers believe that potential witnesses against their clients have been coerced or manipulated at Guantanamo. Then-Deputy Defense Secretary (and leading neo-conservative; now head of the World Bank) Paul Wolfowitz admitted that the Bush Administration "paid a heavy price" for denying Geneva Convention protections to Guantanamo's "enemy combatants"—while ignoring the heavy price that the detainees themselves paid. Tribunals for the detainees which comply with U.S. treaty obligations under the Political and Torture Conventions would have offered a measure of oversight without interfering with Guantanamo's legitimate functioning—as the Supreme Court eventually held.[11]

Major General Miller, who commanded Guantanamo with no training in prisons or intelligence, was transferred to Iraq to (in Miller's words) "Gitmo-ize" (Guantanamo-ize) the "successful interrogation and exploitation" of detainees at Abu Ghraib prison. Guantanamo techniques approved by Defense Secretary Rumsfeld were to be applied, free (it was thought) of prying eyes and both civilian and military law. Lieutenant General Sanchez, commander of the U.S. forces in Iraq, signed off on the process, as did Rumsfeld—according to Brigadier General Janis Karpinski. This carried responsibility for torture to the very highest levels, although Karpinski, the first woman commander in combat—who ran the prisons in Iraq, was framed to be the "fall guy" when evidence of bestiality at Abu Ghraib first leaked out. In any event, there was a total lack of supervision and monitoring of the military and CIA in Abu Ghraib.[12]

The photos and movie from Abu Ghraib provoked the revulsion in the U.S. and around the world that similar verbal accounts about Afghanistan and Guantanamo did not. The photos show the guards, from a military police reserve unit, absolutely certain of their legal and moral right gleefully to torture, when they had a clear choice to do otherwise. Iraqis thus had their suspicions confirmed, that the U.S. occupation is bent on their humiliation. Lieutenant General Sanchez recommended "the highest form of administrative rebuke" against six of the guards: an exceedingly mild punishment. One guard, Charles Graner, is a serial wife beater who was guilty of abuses as a jailer in a Pennsylvania county prison, and who impregnated a hapless woman soldier who also appears in the Abu Ghraib photos— Lynndie England. In addition to Sanchez and Miller, Assistant Secretary of Defense Stephen Cambone played a pivotal role in the tortures, and he then lied to Congress about the whole affair. Sanchez violated Army doctrine by subordinating his military guards to interrogators from the CIA *and* from private contractors. The Red Cross found that up to 90% of those detained in Iraq had been arrested by mistake, and that "excessive and disproportionate force" was "standard operating procedure" by the U.S.—a "war crime" under the Geneva Conventions that the Red Cross administers.[13]

The interrogation tactics used by the U.S. are described in a footnote,[14] to spare readers disgusting details that play no significant role in subsequent analyses. If civilian trials are held, evidence from detainees who were tortured would be inadmissible, as coerced and thus unreliable, in decisions designed to deter torture in the future. As Tom Malinowski of Human Rights Watch puts it, such "[s]tress and duress interrogation techniques were invented in the dungeons of the world's most brutal regimes for only one purpose—to cause pain, distress, and humiliation, without physical scars."[15] William Burke adds: "If torture was effective, the French would still control Algeria and a land of milk and honey would surround Israeli military prisons."[16]

Under torture, a detainee will tell interrogators what he thinks they already know or offer false leads, or say anything which may make the pain stop. Yet torture persists *because the torturer needs it*. Leaders, frustrated by an absence of weapons of mass destruction in Iraq for example, who know not what to do—Secretary of Defense Rumsfeld for example, will sponsor a hyper-aggressiveness because they fear being seen as shiftless appeasers. This is especially so if, like Bush, Rumsfeld, (Attorney) General Ashcroft/Gonzales, and many of their underlings, they develop a (neo-conservative) ideological rigidity because they are unwilling to get into the details and divergent views, to admit mistakes, and to change direction. The political commodity of fear among soldiers and detainees (and citizens) has no limits, since government can always manufacture more of it.[17]

No one's behavior in extreme circumstances is predictable. The risk of torture is thus huge when military personnel, whose pre-service and in-service records show a pattern of brutal or otherwise-substandard behavior, are encouraged to misbehave by defective descriptions of their warrior ethos (or whatever), and are given what Stanford psychologist Phillip Zimbardo calls "the power of the situation," and are then left unsupervised.[18] Somewhat like Nazi and Soviet camp guards, those from the U.S. are capable of treating detainees from a different culture as subhuman, especially if they are told that "this is how military intelligence wants it done."[19]

If they survive, many tortured detainees (those from East Germany have been studied extensively) suffer from what psychologists call Post-traumatic Stress Disorder. They feel defeated (having lost their perceived integrity and autonomy), alienated, and unable to influence their environment. Detainees may thus go on hunger strikes or attempt suicide, as documented at Guantanamo, in an attempt to assert control by being stricter on themselves than are their captors, or they may disassociate and perhaps live in a fantasy world. U.S. policy is thus creating many cripples, with very little or no useful intelligence to show from it.[20]

Y

Who Knew What?

The U.S. military/intelligence/private contractor/civilian hierarchy responded to rumors, reports, photos, and a movie of the vicious cycle just discussed with a cynical, shameful, and ultimately futile attempt to deflect responsibility onto "a few rotten apples:" untrained members of the army reserves at the bottom of the chain of command. (Many of those are receiving paltry punishments.) The Pentagon then boasted of the multiple investigations (37 according to one report) and the Office of Detainee Affairs it has launched, calling these proof of an ability to self-police— even though those responsible at the top remain in control of the investigations. Defense Secretary Rumsfeld and General Keith Alexander ducked Senate Armed

Services Committee questions by pleading the need to protect the rights and privacy of their juniors being court-martialed. Regardless, established facts show that commanding officers and Rumsfeld authorized the relevant interrogation programs, and "informed" President Bush about them. A Colonel reported to General Antonio Taguba (whose 6,000 page investigative report for the Defense Department was made public) that "White House Staff" requested certain information about Abu Ghraib, and that Bush's top counterterrorism advisor put pressure for results on interrogators while touring Abu Ghraib in November 2003.[21] When asked by a Senate Committee why everyone fumbles the question of who was in charge, Rumsfeld replied: "Responsibility shifted over time."[22] Indeed, the record shows a fitful and contradictory policymaking, often on an ad hoc, case—by—case basis that fosters abuses, although some detainees were nonetheless hidden from the Red Cross and the details of detainees' deaths were concealed.[23]

A February 2002 directive from President Bush, concerning the treatment of prisoners in Afghanistan and Guantanamo, required that the Geneva Conventions be respected "to the extent appropriate and consistent with military necessity"—despite the fact that U.S. military judges almost always reject "military necessity" as a defense to liability for, e.g., torture.[24] Allies, human rights NGOs like Amnesty International, and the Red Cross began to complain of torture in Iraq as early as May 2003, a month after Iraqi War II began. They were soon joined by then—Secretary of State Colin Powell and the then—U.S. civilian governor of Iraq, L. Paul Bremer. The Red Cross sent a fuller report in February 2004, but some senior Pentagon officials deny receiving it. General Taguba's report confirmed Red Cross concerns in May 2004, attributing the tortures to failures of leadership, training, communication, and supervision, under conditions of constantly shifting responsibilities. No one in the Pentagon thought that any of this deserved more than a routine examination, at least until the Abu Ghraib photos appeared. Under sharp questioning by the Senate Armed Services Committee, then—Assistant Defense Secretary Wolfowitz admitted that the Geneva Conventions had been violated. But his boss, Rumsfeld, equivocated: "Geneva doesn't say what you do when you get up in the morning."[25]

About the only changes resulting from five years of the Bush Administration's "military transformation" concern a few modifications in the way the military is organized and thinks about itself—although the power of the military within the U.S. Government grew markedly, beginning in 2005. The tortures, and especially the responses to them, clearly show a heavily bureaucratic "business as usual." Secretary of Defense Rumsfeld doubted whether "we [are] organized to handle this kind of problem," while one commentator saw the various bureaucracies that are involved "tip into death spirals ...."[26] Steven Pearlstein stresses that a failed "management model" is in operation:

An over-emphasis on hierarchy and orderliness; a penchant for secrecy and keeping decisions closely held; an instinct to discount information or dismiss views that don't comport with the company line; a habit of pronouncing rather than engaging intellectually with those outside the inner circle; an unhealthy arrogance and sense of entitlement.[27]

In no small measure, confusion and violent miscalculations occur because the defective metaphor of a 'War' on Terror is so widely accepted—for what should be seen as an exercise in criminal enforcement. (Osama bin Laden then becomes a Timothy McVeigh—in—robes, rather than a Saladin.)[28]

The military, the CIA, and private contractors formed separate hierarchies, giving their underlings conflicting instructions. Disaffected people within these hierarchies complained to human rights NGOs and leaked classified documents to the media. In the absence of political support, the military apparently cannot determine who gave which orders, and which political decisions made torture possible. In July 2004, the Justice Department pressed the CIA publicly to reveal interrogation techniques authorized by the Bush Administration, just as the CIA earlier asked the Department to approve specific techniques (or not). Bureaucracies ostensibly on the same side are thus unable to communicate with each other. The CIA (ostensibly) halted "extraordinary" interrogation tactics in June 2004, claiming that confusion over the legal limits on interrogation, and whether these give rise to administrative or criminal sanctions, has slowed efforts to obtain information. The CIA resents the rival Pentagon intelligence operations that are slowly engulfing it, while others refer to the CIA's detainees as "ghosts" or "the disappeared" —names given the victims of The Terror under juntas in Chile and Argentina. The CIA took the lead in employing private contractors as interrogators and interpreters, and it operates where U.S. troops are ostensibly forbidden: e.g., Pakistan.[29]

Much detainee interrogation and translation in Iraq was carried out by U.S. corporations as private contractors: CACI International and Titan in particular. (CACI was subsequently cleared of unethical behavior and violating federal contracting rules by a government agency.) Many of the contractors' employees are ex-military or ex-CIA, and they are ostensibly supervised by the CIA. They are apparently used to save money—although many doubt that savings occur in fact, but they also help to shield government activities from the public eye. Private contractors are independent of and have power over military units, and are widely believed to be beyond military law and the jurisdiction of the moribund local courts. They might be liable under the U.S. War Crimes Act of 1996, the Geneva Conventions or the U.S. Alien Tort Claims Act (infra), however. In his Report, General Taguba blamed private contractors for some of the Abu Ghraib abuses, and identified two individuals for "reprimand." The longstanding policy of banning private contractors from military intelligence work was enforced beginning only in June 2004.[30]

Defective advice from politicized government lawyers played a major role in the tolerance for torture displayed by the upper levels of the bureaucratic hierarchies being surveyed. President Bush allegedly said that "new thinking in the law of war" is required, but "[m]ake sure it is lawful," and the drafters of the August 2002 Justice Department memo (who are now a federal court of appeals judge and a Berkeley law professor, and were then voicing the "conscience" of the executive branch) and of the April 2003 Defense Department memo cheerfully obliged.[31] They posed arguments which are simply not credible, since they counsel criminal acts on the basis that the President's "Commander—in—Chief" power under the Constitution trumps the rest of the Constitution and other U.S. and international laws—the latter's prohibitions being deemed "situational" rather than absolute.[31] Under this Justice Department memo, torture is:

Equivalent in intensity to the pain accompanying serious physical injury, such as organ failure, impairment of bodily function or even death.[32] [I]f the interrogator knows that his actions will inflict severe harm, but he does not "specifically intend" them to do so, he is off the hook. Threats of death are permissible, so long as they are not threats of "imminent death." Drugs designed to disrupt a suspect's personality may be administered if they do not "penetrate to the core of an individual's ability to perceive the world around him." Mental harm is fine if it is not "prolonged." ... The interrogator can claim torture was a "necessity", that he was torturing "in self-defense" or that he was following "superior orders.[33]

The Nation found all of this "periously close to totalitarianism."[34] A politically-moderate legal academic, Cass Sunstein, called it "egregiously bad, very low level ... embarrassingly weak, just short of reckless."[35] The former head of the New York Bar's international human rights committee said the memo's lawyer/authors "could and should face professional sanctions."[36] Human Rights Watch's Tom Malinowski called it "embarrassingly, bizarrely bad logic" in aid of avoiding a legal accountability and overthrowing years of military doctrine.[37]

When these secret memos were leaked to the media in June 2004, congressional and international outrage led President Bush to disown them: "I will never order torture. The values of our country are such that torture is not a part of our soul and our being."[38] But at the end of the day, Bush, Rumsfeld, and Ashcroft seemed to dodge the bullet: impeachment is too blunt an instrument—although it was tried (and failed) for the less serious crimes and misdemeanors allegedly committed by Bill Clinton—and the Administration's behavior over torture did not figure prominently in the November 2004 (presidential) elections. The evidence is certainly sufficient to justify appointing a special prosecutor—Ken Starr went after Clinton with much less—but Defense Secretary Rumsfeld or a Republican-led Congress will not initiate this process. The Administration is understandably worried that the Democrats will gain control of Congress in the November 2006 elections and force further investigations, however.

In May 2004, Rumsfeld (or "Rumstud," as Bush calls him) refused suggestions that he resign, apologized, offered "appropriate compensation" for the Abu Ghraib tortures, and apologized for failing to advise Congress. But he did not commit himself to correct the situation, complaining (like Bush) of "peacetime {N.B.} constraints" on dealing with the "isolated acts of individuals." Most Americans then wanted him to remain in office. He complains of the lack of a "coherent approach" to the "War" on Terror, despite his being ideally positioned to come up with such an approach, by himself or along with other officials.[39]

In a June 2003 statement, Bush promised to "prevent other cruel and unusual punishment," but never moved to implement this statement and was subsequently "informed" of practices and rules that directly contradicted it. In May 2004, he mentioned an apology made privately to King Abdullah of Jordan—rather than apologizing while he was interviewed by two Arab television stations, days earlier. But like Rumsfeld's, this apology distances the speaker from any connection to the events, relieving the speaker of the need to admit mistakes or even to engage in self-examination.[40]

Lawyers re-write, CIA interrogators ostensibly change techniques—from which private contractors supposedly abstain. In Iraq, untold billions of dollars have been 'invested' to produce ridiculously overpriced ("pork barrel") contracts, chaos, pain, death, and mistrust at home and abroad. Three times, Rumsfeld maintained that "the system works."[41] He can only mean that routine and inertia prevail: like dead fish, the relevant bureaucracies are rotting from the head down, separately and especially together.

Alternatives

A WASHINGTON POST Editorial would apply a biblical Golden Rule or a Kantian categorical imperative: "No [torture] technique should be used that, if used by an enemy on an American, would be regarded as a violation of U.S. or international law"—even if a foreign leader thinks that such a step is justified as protecting his/her country's security.[42] The bureaucratic pathologies documented in the last Section, the ideological orientations of the Bush Administration's neo-conservatives, and their antipathy toward legal traditions in the U.S. and internationally, mean that nothing like this Golden Rule will be implemented by an executive branch much given to slipshod behavior. The Administration has shattered notions of a separation of powers in the US, in pursuit of a strong national security State for purposes of War (and 'War' on Terror) mobilizations—and concerns over torture only detract from this goal. As Dana Milbank puts it, "Bush aides are as loyal as Vatican cardinals in defense of an informal Doctrine of Presidential Infallibility."[43]

Congress issued two blank checks to cover executive branch power, soon after 9/11. Some congresspeople now complain of a lack of information from a hyper-partisan Administration obsessed with secrecy but, earlier, conservative Republicans waved the "bloody shirt" of September 11 and Democrats quickly fell into line. A (fluctuating) congressional interest in torture-related topics *may* change this somewhat. Oversight and creating the missing domestic legal framework for handling foreign detainees does not seem to be forthcoming, however. Congress has no reelection or campaign-funding motives to get to the bottom of this morass or to devise meaningful solutions. A Republican-controlled Senate refused the Democrats' demand for the release of more torture-related documents. The Republican Chair of the Senate Armed Services Committee, John Warner, vowed to hold more meetings concerning torture, but has so far failed to do so.[44]

In other words, politics as usual. In the U.S. today, most people expect their courts to be similarly political beasts—rather than neutral appliers of "the law." The Supreme Court decided three cases concerning terrorism in June 2004;[45] one is generally relevant to our topic, *Hamdi*, while *Rasul* is of specific relevance. Given the Court's increasingly loose application of *stare decisis* (the common law idea that past court decisions determine current outcomes), and the Justices' penchant for balancing everything, here of fundamental constitutional rights against national security concerns, the outcomes did not please either side much or have an inherent advantage over a congressional balancing—especially as the reader senses that some of the Justices, like some congresspeople, panicked over terrorism. By a 6-3 vote among the Justices, *Rasul* allows Guantanamo detainees to apply for habeas corpus (a writ under which a court can order the prisoner's release), since Guantanamo (in Cuba) falls within the court's jurisdiction—as prisons in Afghanistan and Iraq manifestly do not. But the detainee is to receive a "hearing" at Guantanamo first, and courts considering subsequent habeas applications will defer to the decision from this hearing to an uncertain extent. The structure of the Guantanamo "hearing", created by the Bush Administration after *Rasul*, gives cause for concern: the detainee is not entitled to a lawyer who is not approved by the military (to, e.g., advise about the details of habeas corpus rights), and the military "judges" are far from independent of their commanding officers. This case paved the way for undercutting the Bush Administration's legal strategy in other ways, culminating (so far) in Boumediene in June 2008—vaguely stating Guantanamo prisoner's entitlement to habeas corpus.[46]

Hamdi held that a *U.S. citizen* has a "due process" right to contest the factual basis for detention as an "enemy combatant" (the nature of which is to be developed by the lower courts, rather than by the executive branch—based on its understanding of *Quirin*) before a "neutral decision maker:" not necessarily a court. (The Supreme Court ignores the fact that, under the Fifth Amendment to the Constitution, due process is the right of "persons", including corporations, rather than of "citizens" alone.) Since *Rasul* is applicable only to non-citizens, they may have greater access to a court through habeas corpus than citizens will. But Justice O'Connor bluntly wrote in *Hamdi*: "[A] state of war is not a blank check for the President when it comes to the rights of the Nation's citizens."[47] Despite her buying into the defective 'War' on Terror metaphor, this should be (but apparently isn't) the definitive nail in the coffin of the breathtakingly-broad "Commander—in—Chief" constitutional powers asserted by the Bush Administration since 2001, an assertion evident in his Justice and Defense Departments' memos (*supra*). So, the Court's terrorism cases were not a whitewash or a vulgar, politicized pastiche like *Quirin*, but they protect only some rights not directly related to torture and in a limited fashion.[48]

In sum, Guantanamo detainees are now less likely to be tortured, if this can later be disclosed in, and punished by, U.S. courts. But this is of no help to detainees tortured in Afghanistan, Iraq or "third countries" —as a result of "renditions." Attorney General John Ashcroft mentioned the possibility of criminally prosecuting civilian contractors, but his successor General, Gonzales, is unlikely to exercise his abundant discretion to prosecute in politically-sensitive areas.

It was the good fortune of detainees and the American public that dissidents from Administration policies leaked photos and documents to the media. These leaks forced the mainstream media to abandon, temporarily at least, its conservative, cautious predispositions. NGOs like Human Rights Watch and Amnesty International served detainees and public opinion in the U.S. much better than did the media but, at least until the Abu Ghraib tortures became public, NGO analyses seldom gained conspicuous media coverage or attention in a somnolent Congress.[49]

People in the U.S. may be naïve, but few are stupid brutes. The tortures shook the self-image of many, accustomed as they are to a government which mirrors their values. Critics reminded them that much in the Bush Administration agenda has never been openly presented to the public.[50] There is strong public support for ending torture, and Human Rights First has a useful "10-Point Strategy" for doing this, a strategy which calls on both international and domestic laws.

1. Commit to upholding the law on interrogation and detention.
2. Report, investigate, and prosecute all acts of torture and abuse.
3. Ban torture to the extent that it is not already prohibited, under the rubric of "cruel, inhuman or degrading treatment" (*infra*), including banning those interrogation tactics mentioned in note 13, plus shaking and prolonged incommunicado detention—without access by family, consular officials, and/or lawyers.

4. Rescind all orders or regulations permitting torture or abuse.

5. Compensate and rehabilitate victims, and notify their families.

6. Mandate rigorous training for interrogators and ban interrogation by civilian contractors.

7. Disclose the location of all detention facilities and account for all detainees.

8. Inspect all facilities, with regular inspectors' reports to Congress.

9. Provide for regular Red Cross visits and a due process for all detainees, wherever located.

10. Ban the transfer of prisoners to countries that use torture.[51]

We have seen that the Bush Administration is ideologically unwilling and, given the many bureaucratic pathologies discussed earlier, probably unable to implement something like this "Strategy." Similarly, Congress is unwilling (unless the Democrats gain control in the 2006 election, perhaps) and, given the huge number of vested interests involved, probably unable to implement it. The Supreme Court depends on the right kinds of cases coming to it, and the terrorism cases just discussed indicate that a moderately conservative Court with little fondness for international law would be similarly unwilling and unable.

All of this has the effect of putting more pressure on international and foreign laws and venues. As Anne-Marie Slaughter ably puts it: "In international law, the standard is not only whether you knew, but whether you had reason to know. The question is: How far up the chain of command should people have been vigilant about the practices going on?"[52] No military officer has been convicted under a US military law imposition of liability, where an officer "knew or should have known" of his subordinates' abusive behavior.   By such standards, Defense Secretary Rumsfeld is guilty—he helped create the rules and the atmosphere that made torture possible—even though he says: "The set of facts that exist today with the al Qaeda and the Taliban were not necessarily the set of facts that were considered when the Geneva Convention [*sic*] was fashioned."[53] Reputable academics can even get a lengthy article out of: *Is the President Bound By the Geneva Conventions?*[54]

The U.S. has ratified both the Civil and Political Covenant and the Torture Convention, as well the Geneva Conventions[55], but a problem arises: a U.S. reservation to the treaties defines torture in a manner consistent with the Eighth Amendment to the U.S. Constitution—"cruel and unusual punishment." Especially as the Supreme Court defined this language over the past twenty years, it has a much narrower meaning than does the "cruel, inhuman, and degrading" standard known under international human rights law (*and* under the longstanding regulations of the U.S. military). During his Senate Armed Services Committee testimony, Defense Secretary Rumsfeld admitted that the U.S. violated the Torture Convention. However, in response to requests from human rights NGOs, Bush declared that the Torture Convention will never be violated—even with regard to "enemy combatants."[56] But does he mean "torture" as the 2002 Justice Department memo defines it, or as the rest of the world understands it?

Regardless, much of the abusive conduct discussed here[57] is so egregious that it violates both the Eighth Amendment and international standards. The problem then becomes the "globalization" of torture, its extraterritorial nature—with little or no formal participation by the government of the country where the detention occurs.

The Red Cross, and the successor to the U.N. Human Rights Commission will arguably not be deterred by this extraterritoriality from criticizing the U.S.

The Committee Against Torture, an expert U.N. body administering the Torture Convention, determined that Israeli techniques similar to those used by the U.S. amount to torture. (The European Court of Human Rights found that similar techniques used by Britain in Northern Ireland are torture.) In May 2006, this Committee Against Torture considered the regular Report from the US that was filed six years late—as is common—with NGO recommendations considered by the Committee as well. The US took the process seriously, appearing by large numbers of senior officials, and preparing a 184-page report. In its own 15 page report, the Committee demanded that the US close Guantanamo, that interrogation techniques which constitute torture, sexual violence, or cruel, inhuman or degrading treatment be banned in all places under US control; that perpetrators of torture be investigated and prosecuted, including those whose responsibility stems from occupying senior positions in the chain of command; and that renditions to countries where torture was likely are to be prohibited. The US reaction is that detainee abuse was a thing of the past, that the Committee did not give the US a fair hearing, the Committee overreached its authority, and it issued a report riddled with errors.[58]

International organizations like this Committee have no formal means of enforcing their decisions. Hostile toward international law and a multilateralism generally, the Bush Administration would likely try to ignore such decisions. Still unwilling to tie the CIA's hands, and refusing to see compliance with such decisions as part of a commitment to the Rule of Law, the Administration's neo-conservatives might not even grasp the hortatory, moral persuasion of such decisions. Fortunately, a president who is an international law renegade can only serve eight years: Reagan noisily marched out of the World Court and UNICEF, while Clinton quietly marched back in. The UN General Assembly might be convinced to take action—to improve the monitoring of detainee torture, as NGOs advocate, for example; the U.S. never had many scruples about wielding the veto it has in the Security Council, thereby rendering the Council ineffective.

If he can see that his nationalist ideology has failed, Bush might find the UN useful, applying its criminal, financial, and administrative remedies to terrorism, and using the UN's symbolic role as the guarantor of independence and security in Iraq, Afghanistan, and even Palestine. A carefully managed, multilateral diplomacy works well alongside the reality of the unipolar power of the U.S.—if only neo-conservatives recognize this. Using such diplomacy might help counter the unsavory image of the U.S. as occupier, torturer, and even state terrorist.

Civil suits under the (U.S.) Alien Tort Claims Act (ATCA) are too complex to be more than outlined here. The ATCA dates back to 1789 and was seldom used until Filartiga[59] allowed a Guatemalan to recover against a Guatemalan torturer in a U.S. court. Even though the tort did not occur in a U.S. jurisdiction, the court asserted a universal jurisdiction against a torturer deemed the enemy of all mankind. (Personal jurisdiction was conferred while the torturer was holidaying in New York City.) Holocaust survivors often succeed under the ATCA. A suit is proceeding against 205 Saudis for the September 11 terrorist attacks, despite (so far) the argument that plaintiffs' lawyer, who has spent $12 million investigating his case, is meddling in U.S. foreign policy. The Center for Constitutional Rights has filed against CACI International and Titan, their subsidiaries, and individual defendants under the ATCA, *and* under the Racketeer Influenced and Corrupt Organizations Act (RICO)—for conspiring to torture so as to make more money; RICO permits plaintiffs to multiply their actual damages by three. One stumbling block is that the

Supreme Court, at the same time as it was deciding the terrorism cases[60] gave a rather narrow interpretation of plaintiffs' entitlements under the ATCA in Alvarez-Machain.[61] Another stumbling block is that people employed by the U.S. government will claim a "sovereign immunity," although a growing consensus in international law is that persons who violate "preemptory" norms of international law (such as the prohibition on torture) are not entitled to claim a sovereign immunity. In both civil and criminal cases, the Bush Administration tries to invoke the "state secrets" privilege, to avoid disclosing possibly secret but always damaging information. Courts almost always defer to this assertion rather than, e.g., appoint a master with the appropriate security clearance to hear the information and then advise the judge about disclosure.

Saving the most intriguing possibility for last, a "progressive" country might indict Rumsfeld, General Miller and/or General Sanchez, and even Bush himself, under the universal jurisdiction conferred (as in *Filartiga*) by the violation of a preemptory norm of international law. Belgium is most interesting in this regard, having indicted then—Israeli Prime Minister Sharon (for war crimes committed some time ago, at refugee camps in Lebanon) and a Congolese minister. The latter indictment was struck down by the International Court of Justice, and Belgium reportedly repealed the statute under which such indictments were brought. But universal jurisdiction presumably requires no domestic statute to give it effect. It would be a brave Rumsfeld/Rumstud, Miller or Sanchez who would travel to Belgium on, e.g., NATO business, and thus confer personal jurisdiction on the Belgians—as Sharon never did. At the least, the media is likely to report Belgian demonstrations in favor of indictment. A less likely country may spring universal jurisdiction on an unsuspecting traveler, as when Philippines President Marcos "retired" to Hawaii—only to face a blizzard of ATCA suits.

CONCLUSION

There are thus a variety of domestic and international alternatives, imperfect in varying degrees but imperfect nonetheless, to remedy serious U.S. abuses of human rights revolving around torture. But we also want to know *why* the abuses occurred in the first place. For this we consult the distinction that the eighteenth-century German philosopher Immanuel Kant drew in PERPETUAL PEACE, *between political moralists and moral politicians.* For Kant, peace requires that both republican countries and their international federation be governed by moral politicians.[62] Kofi Annan fits this description nicely, while the warlike Bush (and Blair and Chirac to a lesser extent, and others like Zimbabwe's Mugabe to a greater extent) is the quintessential political moralizer. Bush detracts from everyone's (Kantian) freedom by constantly using his considerable power in efforts to force people to do what he wants them to do.[63]

In foreign affairs, a *pax Americana* is peace in Bush's mind (if we can dignify it with that term), no matter how immoral or irrational the means to that end. Expediency consistently trumps moral principle based on, e.g., the international humanitarian and human rights law to which Bush only gives lip service. For Blair as well as Bush, Iraqi War II is a passionately-held belief, desperately in search of a saleable moral justification. This is the logic of a criminal regime, of a dictatorship (the parliamentary kind, in Blair's case).

Seen in context, Bush's concentration camps (for that is what they are, inhabited mostly by Semites—Arabs) lay a strong foundation for fascism, along with: a growing corporatism in U.S. politics as well as the economy; trying to create a "living room" (*Lebensraum* or Mussolini's *Mare nostrum*) through a Romantic adventurism concerning Mideast democracy—as Bush understands this, with governments too weak to threaten U.S. oil and other interests; trashing American civil liberties under the Orwellian-sounding USA PATRIOT Act; and a martial spirit inculcated by Bush for Wars (and the 'War' on Terror) without end. Edmund Burke put it more succinctly than Kant: "All that is necessary for the triumph of evil [which Bush claims to be battling] is that good men [and women and institutions] do nothing."[64] To keep their Republic, people in the U.S. must be willing to fight tenaciously and courageously.[65] All of this may simply end with the inauguration of Bush's successor. But the anti-democratic foundations of a strong and military state will continue to threaten Americans and the world, especially if enough Americans continue to take neo-conservatives and/or their perpetual 'War' on Terror seriously.

[1] Presented to the Durban Conference, in December 2005.

[2] *See* W. Page Keeton et al., *Prosser & Keeton On Torts*, 5th ed. (St. Paul: West Publishing Co., 1984, with 1988 pocket part), 197-98, 542-43.

[3] Poll: Two-Thirds of Americans Against U.S. Physical Torture," *USA Today*, July 23, 2004 (*available at* http://www.usatoday.com) (also, 55% thought mental torture should never be used, 4 of 5 supported the right of a detainee to have a hearing, and 3 of 4 saw the U.S. as "a moral leader in the world" which thus should not torture or degrade detainees).

[4] Gordon Morse, "Health Care in Need of Life Support," *Washington Post*, June 6, 2004, Section B8 ("Abu Ghraib? In Virginia, We Call it Assisted Living") id. ("Hand-wringing follows, along with official finger-pointing" but nothing happens) parentheticals are quotes from Morse article; Megan Stack and Raheem Salman, "A Town Awoke to Slaughter," *L.A. Times*, June 1, 2006 (*available at* http://www.latimes.com); (no author listed) "Probe Clears US Troops of Misconduct at Ishaki," *Jordan Times*, June 4, 2006, 1 &5. See Mark Bowden, "The Lessons of Abu Ghraib," *The Atlantic Monthly* (July/Aug. 2004): 37; Fred Hiatt, "Shadow on the U.S. Beacon," *Washington Post*, May 16, 2004, B7 (listing among "the victims of ... Abu Ghraib ... those who ... live in Libya and Hong Kong, Venezuela and Burma, and anywhere human rights are in jeopardy.").

[5] Robert Burns, "Rumsfeld Fears Losing War on Extremism," *Washington Post*, June 5, 2004, AP dispatch, 9:47 p.m. (*available at* http://www.washingtonpost.com).

[6] James Harding, "Abu Ghraib Leaks Expost CIA-Pentagon Schism," *Financial Times*, May 17, 2004, 2.

[7] Don Eggan & Diana Linzer, "9/11 Commission Offer Critiques on Many Fronts," *Washington Post*, July 22, 2004, Section A1 (the Commission, criticizing Bush's "controversial enemy combatant characterization" and citing the common Art. 3 of the Geneva Conventions, as offering protections in "cases in which the usual laws of war do not apply."); Seymour Hersh, "Torture at Abu Ghraib," *The New Yorker*, May 10, 2004, 42, 45 (in Afghanistan, "the Ryder report said that MPs had worked with intelligence operatives to set favorable conditions for subsequent interviews'—a euphemism for breaking the will of prisoners"); Amir Shah, "Afghans Allege Three Americans Ran Jail on Kabul," *Washington Post*, July 9, 2004, Section A15 (posing as military, three men ran an "illegal" jail where prisoners were beaten and hung upside down).

[8] 317 U.S. 1 (1942), (discussed in Paul Brietzke, "September 11 and American Law," (2007) (available at http://ssrn.com/abstract=453522).

[9] *See* text accompanying notes 46-47, *infra.*

[10] Lubna Freih, "Human Rights and Terrorism" (comments by Geneva Dir., Human Rights Watch at World Forum on Human Rights, Nantes, France, May, 17, 2004) (on file with author) (citing refoulement prohibitions in Civil and Political Covenant, Art. 7 and the Convention Against Torture, Art. 3, both of which the U.S. has ratified, as well as the Convention Relating to the Statutes of Refugees, and several regional treaties). *See* William Fisher, "Report Details CIA's Covert Rendition Fleet," *Inter Press News Agency (IPS)*, April 6, 2006 (*available at* http://www.ipsnews.net); Craig Whitlock, "A Secret Deportation of Terror Suspects," *Washington Post*, July 25, 2004, Section A1 (at U.S. insistence, Swedish security police deported two men to Egypt aboard a U.S.-registered plane. The Swedes received Egyptian reassurances that the men would not be subjected to "inhuman treatment," but they were tortured as soon as they landed in Cairo).

[11] *See* text accompanying note 45, *infra.*

[12] Julian Coman, "Rumsfeld Gave Go-Ahead for Abu Ghraib Tactics, Says General in Charge," *Daily Telegraph*, July 4, 2004 (*available at* http://www.portal.telegraph.co.uk); Hersh, "Torture at Abu Ghraib," 47 ("Abu Ghraib had become, in effect, another Guantanamo.").

[13] Anne Applebaum, "So Torture is Legal," *Washington Post*, June 16, 2004, Section A27; Applebaum, "What Would You Do?," *Washington Post*, May 12, 2004, Section A23; Sewell Chan & Fred Barbash, "Six Prison Supervisors Will Receive Highest Rebuke," *Washington Post*, May 3, 2004, 12:51 p.m.; David Finkel & Christian Davenport, "Records Print Dark Portrait of Guard," *Washington Post*, June 5, 2004, Section A1.

[14] As recorded in a classified document, 24 of 35 "techniques" to "break down prisoners for interrogation" survived the review of Secretary of Defense Rumsfeld called for in April 2003. Regardless of how widely-publicized these restrictions are, the following techniques were credibly reported. Food is denied to the detainee or made unpalatable. The detainees' environment was manipulated: made too hot, cold, light, dark, wet, and/or full of loud music and strobe lights. Detainees were hooded and/or placed in solitary confinement, beaten, denied pain medication, covered with wet towels or strapped to a "waterboard"—to simulate drowning, threatened with and frequently bitten by

dogs, chained to the floor in a painful position, forced to stand or assume painful positions or repetitive motions for long periods, deprived of sleep, and subjected to mock electrocution, rape, sexual harassment, and humiliation—e.g., forcing Muslim men to remain nude, wear women's underwear and/or masturbate. Bradley Graham & Thomas Ricks, "Leadership Failure is Blamed in Abuse," *Washington Post,* May 12, 2004, Section A1; John Mintz, "Britons Allege Guantanamo Abuse in Letter to Bush," *Washington Post*, May 14, 2004, Section A16; Dana Priest & Bradley Graham, "Guantanamo Lists Approved Interrogation Methods," *Washington Post*, June 10, 2004, Section A13; Dana Priest & R. Jeffrey Smith, "Memo Offered Justification for Use of Torture," *Washington Post,* June 8, 2004, Section A1. Jackie Spinner, "Soldier: Unit's Rule Was to Break Down Prisoners," *Washington Post,* May 8, 2004, Section A1; "Report: CIA Halts Interrogation Tactics," *USA Today,* June 27, 2004 (*available at* http://www.usatoday.com).

[15] Tom Malinowski, "The Logic of Torture," *Washington Post*, June 27, 2004, Section B7.

[16] William Burke, "Letter to the Editor," *The Economist*, May 15, 2004, 14. *See* Hersh, "Torture at Abu Ghraib," 47 (citing Willie Rowell, who has 36 years experience as a CIA agent--"the use of force or humiliation with prisoners is invariably counterproductive").

[17] Steven Pearlstein, "War Management Follows the Wrong Corporate Model," *Washington Post*, May 12, 2004, Section E1 (citing Michael Maccahy, psychoanalyst and management consultant). *See* Burns, "Rumsfeld Fears Losing War on Extremism" (quoting and citing Rumsfeld--"we do not have a coherent approach" to a "troubling unknown," so we must take the offensive lest we make the mistake of Hitler's appeasers); Richard Cohen, "The Accountability Pact," *Washington Post*, May 11, 2004, Section A19 (the Bushies (members of the Administration) will not take responsibility, because they exist in "a corporate suite of yes men" who see the war as "a Baghdad version of Pasadena, Tournament of Roses").

[18] M.S. Embser Herbert, "When Women Abuse Power, Too," *Washington Post*, May 16, 2004, Section B1. *See* Mark Bowden, "The Lessons of Abu Ghraib," *The Atlantic Monthly* (July/Aug. 2004): 37, 40 (in an infamous 1971 Stanford experiment, students were randomly assigned to play "guards" and "inmates," and abuses began immediately—including sexually humiliating role-playing); Coman, "Rumsfeld Gave Go-Ahead for Abu Ghraib Tactics, Says General in Charge," (six recent studies leaked to the media criticize the military for failing to screen recruits for violent and criminal backgrounds); Finkel & Davenport, "Records Print Dark Portrait of Guard" (discussing Graner, one of the Abu Ghraib guards). But, *see also* Shankar Vedantam, "The Psychology of Torture," *Washington Post,* May 11, 2004, Section A14. Troops who abused Iraqis were not sadists but ordinary people who thought they were doing dirty work in a new kind of battle, from a high moral ground. *Id.* (quoting Zimbardo: "In my study, we put good people into a bad barrel, then they come out rotten apples.").

[19] Anne Applebaum, "Willing Torturers," *Washington Post,* May 5, 2004, Section A29.

[20] Colin Brietzke, "Article Critique," April 20, 2004 (MS on file with the author).

[21] Jackson Diehl, "Officers' Unheroic Example," *Washington Post,* July 19, 2004, Section A17; National Public Radio (NPR) Testimony before the Senate Armed Forces Committee, May 6, 2004, 10:30 CDT (Lt. Gen. Lance Smith); R. Jeffrey Smith, "Bush Advisor Toured Abu Ghraib," *Washington Post*, June 18, 2004, Section A11; "Soldier Described White House Interest," *Washington Post*, June 9, 2004, Section A3 (Lt. Col. Steven Jordan, to Gen. Taguba); "What Did He Know," *The Economist*, May 22, 2004, 48; "Editorial: Unanswered Questions," *Washington Post*, July 11, 2004, Section B6. *See* Human Rights Watch (HRW), *Bush Policies Led to Abuse in Iraq,* 6/9/04 (*available at* http://www.hrw.org) (the HRW report, *The Road to Abu Ghraib* "examines how the Bush Administration adopted a deliberate policy of permitting illegal interrogation techniques—and then spent two years covering up or ignoring reports of torture").

[22] NPR, *supra* note 20 (Rumsfeld testifying).

[23] **Smith & White. See id. (General Taguba found that the Iraq command "changed their rules of engagement ... four times"). I regret having loss the source of this quote.**

[24] Dana Priest & Bradley Graham, "U.S. Struggled Over How Far to Push Tactics," Washington Post, June 25, 2004, Section A1 (quoting Bush's directive).

[25] Editorial: "Double Standards," *Washington Post*, May 14, 2004, Section A24 (quoting Rumsfeld). *See* Julian Boyer, "Jailed Iraqis Hidden From Red Cross," *Guardian*, MAY 5, 2004 (*available at* http://www.guardian.com.uk); David Cloud, "Red Cross Cited Detainee Abuse Over a Year Ago," *Wall Street Journal*, May 10, 2004, 1 (the Red Cross Final Report was leaked to the Wall Street Journal); Alexander Higgins, "Red Cross: Iraq Abuse Widespread, Routine," Washington Post, May 11, 2004, 1:11 A.M. (AP dispatch, *available at* http://www.washingtonpost.com); Matt Kelley, "Army Reports New Allegations of Abuse," July 23, 2004, 9:03 a.m. (AP dispatch, *available at* http://www.washingtonpost.com) (Lt. Gen. Mikolasheck, the Army Inspector General, reported 94

cases of abuse and 39 deaths, 20% of which were ruled homicides or are under investigation); Neal Lewis & Eric Lichtblau, "Red Cross Says That for Months it Complained of Iraq Prison Abuses to the U.S.," *New York Times*, May 7, 2004 (available at http://www.nytimes.com); Josh White & Scott Higham, "Army Calls Abuses 'Aberrations'," *Washington Post*, July 23, 2004, Section A1 (Lt. Gen. Mikolashek, the Inspector Gen. found that Abu Ghraib reflects "aberrations", rather than the need to alter Army doctrine); Editorial: "An Inadequate Reponse," *Washington Post* (Rumsfeld claimed Abu Ghraib guards had been instructed to follow the Geneva Conventions, but General Taguba discovered no such instruction while preparing his report).

26 Jim Hoagland, "End of Empire," *Washington Post*, May 9, 2004, Section B7 (quoting Rumsfeld). *See* R. Jeffrey Smith, "Knowledge of Abusive Tactics May Go Higher," *Washington Post*, May 16, 2004, Section A2 (testifying before a Senate Committee, Gen. Alexander said—"Well ma'am, … I think that the difficult part is to find out who told whom what to do.").

27 Pearlstein, "War Management Follows the Wrong Corporate Model." *See* Lt. Col. Karen Kwiatkowski, "The New Pentagon Papers," March 10, 2004, *available at* http://www.salon.com.

28 *See* Brietzke, "September 11 and American Law;" Glenn Kessler, "War on Terror Criticized for Lack of Focus," *Washington Post* (the September 11 Commission's "broad critique" of Bush's "war on terrorism" as too vague, too diffuse, and tending to the neglect of "law enforcement, economic policy, foreign aid, public diplomacy, and homeland defense."). McVeigh was the right-wing American who bombed the Oklahoma City Federal Building; Saladin was the adroit Muslim commander who defeated European troops on several occasions during the Crusades.

29 Joshua Chaffin, "US Turns to Private Sector for Spies," *Financial Times*, May 17, 2004, 3; David Johnson, "Uncertainty About Interrogation Rules Seen as Slowing the Hunt for Information on Terrorists," *New York Times*, June 28, 2004 (*available at* http://www.nytimes.com); Dana Priest, "CIA Puts Harsh Tactics on Hold," *Washington Post*, June 27, 2004, Section A1. *See* Diehl, "Officers' Unheroic Example" (among senior commanders, "the standard procedure of evasion and denial still seems to be in effect"--e.g., Gen. Miller testified that the "interrogation rules of engagement" for Abu Ghraib "were not briefed to me"—when they were drawn up on his own recommendation, as based on those he used in Guantanamo); Dana Priest & Joe Stephens, "Secret World of U.S. Interrogation," *Washington Post*, May 11, 2004, Section A1. In Afghanistan, the CIA's prison is called "The Pit," for its despairing conditions--some CIA prisons are as small as shipping containers. *Id.* Such facilities overlap with those of foreign intelligence services, to which mid- or low-level suspects are "rendered." "Ghost detainees" are moved around by the CIA, to hide them from the Red Cross and in violation of international law prohibitions on refoulement. *Id.*

30 Deborah Avant, "What Are Those Contractors Doing in Iraq?," *Washington Post*, May 9, 2004, Section B1; Center for Constitutional Rights, CCR Files Lawsuit Against Private Contractors for Torture Conspiracy, June 21, 2004, http://www.ccr-ny.org (suit under Alien Tort Claims Act); Ariana Cha & Ellen McCarthy, "Prison Scandal Indicates Gap in U.S. Chain of Command," *Washington Post*, May 5, 2004, Section A20; Chaffin, "US Turns to Private Sector for Spies;" Ellen McCarthy, "Government Clears CACI for Contracts," *Washington Post*, July 8, 2004, Section E1; NPR, *supra* note 20 (Rumsfeld, testifying about private contractors); "Army Policy Bans Contractors from Interrogations," *Houston Chronicle*, June 12, 2004, AP Dispatch, 9:45 a.m. (*available at* http://www.chron.com); Editorial: "Outside Contractors Outside Military Law," *Washington Post*, May 9, 2004, Section B5. *See* Comment: "Outsourcing is Hell," *The Nation*, June 7, 2004, 5, 6 (private companies make accountability over the use of force difficult and, e.g., their use jeopardized delivery of food and water to U.S. troops); "The View from Within," *The Economist*, May 15, 2004, 38 (Titan claimed commercial confidentiality when human rights groups asked about safeguards).

31 Mike Allen & Susan Schmidt, "Memo on Interrogation Tactics is Disavowed," *Washington Post*, June 23, 2004, Section A1; "Justice Department Memo to the White House Counsel," August 1, 2002 (*available at* http://www.Findlaw.com); "Report of the Pentagon Working Group," *Washington Post*, April 16, 2003 (*available at* http://www.washingtonpost.com). *See* Priest & Smith, "Memo Offered Justification for Use of Torture," (the Pentagon memo uses language very similar to the Justice Department's); "Letter to President Bush from the Attorney General," February 1, 2002 (available at http://www.Findlaw.com) (Ashcroft stating why the Geneva Conventions did not apply to al Qaeda and Taliban detainees).

32 "What on Earth Were They Thinking?," *The Economist*, June 19, 2004, 31 (*quoting* the Justice Department memo). *See* R. Jeffrey Smith, "Slim Legal Grounds for Torture Memos," *Washington Post*, July 4, 2004, Section A12. Disagreeing with the Justice Department, the State Department was strongly and consistently of the view that the Geneva Conventions apply to all U.S. detainees. R. Jeffrey Smith, "U.S. Liability Key Concerns in '02 Debate on Detainees," *Washington Post*, June 23,

2004, Section A13. This led William Howard Taft IV, legal advisor to the State Department, to call the Justice Department memo "seriously flawed, ... incorrect as well as incomplete," and "contrary to the official position of the United States, the United Nations and all other states that have considered the issue." This letter was omitted from the documents the White House disclosed on the subject. R. Jeffrey Smith, "Lawyer for State Department Disputed Detainee Memo," *Washington Post*, June 24, 2004, Section A7.

[33] Comment: "Torture and Democracy," *The Nation*, July 5, 2004, 3 (quoting and interpolating the Justice Department memo). *See* Priest & Smith, "Memo Offered Justification for Use of Torture," *Washington Post*, June 8, 2004, Section A1. The Justice's memo states "it is difficult to take a specific act out of context and call it torture." *Id.* Mental pain must last for months to amount to torture . . . even then, there is a "good faith" defense—that most would see as dubious. *Id.*

[34] Comment: "Torture and Democracy," 4.

[35] Adam Liptak, "Legal Scholars Criticize Memos on Torture," *New York Times*, June 25, 2004 (*available at* http://www.nytimes.com) (*quoting* Sunstein).

[36] Nat Hentoff, "What Did Bush Know?," *Village Voice*, June 28, 2004 (available at http://www.villagevoice.com) (*quoting* Scott Horton). *See* Kathleen Clark & Julie Mertus, "Torturing the Law," *Washington Post*, June 20, 2004, Section B3 (a lawyer arguing to a court can be disingenuous, but a lawyer "writing an opinion letter is ethically bound to be frank" —rather than writing "such a scandalous opinion").

[37] Tom Malinowski, "Transcript: Torture Guidelines," June 14, 2004, 1 p.m. (available at http://www.washingtonpost.com); *See id.* (by the criteria in the memos, the Abu Ghraib photos do not disclose torture); Priest & Smith, "Memo," (Army Field Manual 34-52 prohibits pain or psychosis induced by chemicals or bondage, forcing a person to assume abnormal positions for prolonged periods, food or sleep deprivation, and mock executions).

[38] Allen & Schmidt, "Memo on Interrogation Tactics is Disavowed" (quoting Bush). *See* Richard Cohen, "A Plunge From the Moral Heights," *Washington Post*, June 10, 2004, Section A19 (testifying before a Senate committee, Attorney General Ashcroft stated that the memos were of no consequence, "internal" stuff, "the scribblings of lawyers"). Cohen argues a 50-page memo is not an hour's work; "someone had torture in mind," and a little bit of torture is like being a little bit pregnant.

[39] Burns, "Rumsfeld Fears Losing War on Extremism;" Bradley Graham, "Rumsfeld Takes Responsibility for Abuse," *Washington Post*, May 8, 2004, Section A1; Graham & David Van Dreble, "Bush Apologizes for Abuse of Prisoners," *Washington Post*, May 7, 2004, Section A1; Richard Marin & Claudia Deane, "Most Want Rumsfeld to Stay, Poll Says," *Washington Post*, May 8, 2004, Section A12. *See* Bruce Hoffman, "Plan of Attack," *The Atlantic Monthly* (July/Aug. 2004): 42. "We know we're killing a lot, capturing a lot, collecting arms. We just don't know whether that's the same as winning." (Quoting Rumsfeld). *Id.* As in Iraq, in counterterrorist campaigns involving Malaysia, Kenya, Cyprus, Northern Ireland, Germany, Italy, and Rhodesia, government was not sufficiently integrated with the military to mount a decisive initial response to counterinsurgency, so that rebels had time to entrench themselves in the civilian population. *Id.*

[40] Mike Allen, "Bush Apologizes, Calls Abuse 'Stain' on Nation," *Washington Post*, May 7, 2004, Section A1; Graham & Van Dreble, "Bush Apologizes;" Robin Wright & Glenn Kessler, "Rejection of Prison Abuse Was Sought," *Washington Post*, May 16, 2004, Section A28.

[41] David Broder, "McNamara Moment," *Washington Post*, May 9, 2004, Section B7 (quoting Rumsfeld). *See* Robert Byrd, "Follow the Exit Signs," *Washington Post*, April 9, 2004, Section A19; Sewell Chan, "Rage is on Display During Prison Tour," *Washington Post*, May 6, 2004, Section A19 (quoting General Miller) (the tortures have "brought a cloud over the enormous efforts of hundreds of thousands of our soldiers", but we'll work hard to re-establish Iraqi and American trust); Tom Lantos, "Investigate, Don't Incapacitate," *Washington Post*, May 18, 2004, Section A19.

[42] *See* Kwiatkowski, "The New Pentagon Papers." Many of us in the Pentagon, conservatives and liberals alike, felt that this agenda, whatever its flaws or merits, has never been openly presented to the American people. Instead, the public storyline was a fear peddling and confusing set of messages, designed to take Congress and the country into "a war based on false pretenses." *Id.*

[43] Dana Milbank, "A Doctrine of Presidential Infallibility," *Washington Post*, January 8, 2002, Section A15. *See* Brietzke, "September 11 and American Law."

[44] Applebaum, "So Torture;" Brietzke, "September 11 and American Law;" Helen Dewar & Don Morgan, "Senate Rejects Request for Abuse Documents," *Washington Post*, June 24, 2004, Section A7. *But see* Charles Babington, "Senator Critical of Focus on Prisoner Abuse," *Washington Post*, May 12, 2004, Section A18 (Sen. Inhofe, R-Okla., is "outraged that we have so many humanitarian do-

gooders right now crawling all over those prisons looking for human rights violations while our troops are fighting and dying," and by the "press ... and the political agendas that are being served by this."). The "blank checks" referred to in the text are the Congressional Joint Resolution For Use of Military Force that delegated so much power to Bush, and the USA PATRIOT Act, that truncated civil rights and liberties—ostensibly to fight terrorism. Brietzke, "Unanswered Questions."
[45] *Hamdi v. Rumsfeld*, 542 U.S. 507 (2004); *Rasul v. Bush*, 542 U.S. 466 (2004); *Rumsfeld v. Padilla*, 542 U.S. 426 (2004). In *Padilla*, the Court held 5-4 that the detainee filed for habeas corpus in the wrong jurisdiction, New York, since he was being held in a military prison in South Carolina. *See* Hoagland, "Normality" (the Court hints that the danger of "terrorism ... looks different today than it did in the autumn of 2001").
[46] *Boumediene, et al. v. Bush* (Nos. 06-1195 and -1196), reversing and remanding 476 F. 3d 981 (D.C. Cir. 2007). The 5-Justice majority in *Rasul* chose a procedure which cut the guts out of the case that was *Rasul's* biggest stumbling-block, in *stare decisis* terms. *Johnson v. Eisentrager*, 339 U.S. 763 (1950). The concurring Justice (creating the 6-3 vote) distinguished *Johnson* (decided it did not apply to these facts), as did the Boumediene Court—by a 5-4 vote.
[47] David Ignatius, "The Balance of Justice Amid a War," *Washington Post*, July 2, 2004, Section A15 (singling the O'Connor quote out to typify "America's commitment to the 'rule of law' "). *Id.* "It is during our most challenging and uncertain moments that our Nation's commitment to due process is most severely tested; ... we must preserve our commitment at home to the principles for which we fight abroad." *Id.* (quoting O'Connor); Robin Wright, "U.S. Immunity in Iraq Will Go Beyond June 20," *Washington Post*, June 24, 2004, Section A1 (U.S. Governor of Iraq hopes that his Order 17 has permanent force in granting criminal, civil, and administrative immunity to all foreign personnel).
[48] *See* Brietzke, "September 11 and American Law;" Smith, "Slim" (quoting David Cole); David Von Dreble, "Executive Branched Reined In," *Washington Post* ("a nearly unanimous," except for Justice Thomas, "repudiation of the Bush administration's sweeping claims to power over those captives"); Editorial: "A Supreme Rebuke," *Washington Post*, June 29, 2004, Section A29 (the terrorism cases show "that the judiciary will not sit still for assertions of unbridled executive power," "oversight and transparency" will be required). *But see* **Quirin**, *supra* **note 48** (which was given a limited credence by the Court).
[49] *See* Brietzke, "September 11 and American Law;" William Greider, "Under the Banner of the War on Terror," The Nation, June 21, 2004, 11, 13 ("Major media played an important role in the political passivity, as they whipped up the fear factor and fell in line behind Bush's 'war.' "); **Id,** (Bush Administration tactics so disturbed legal professionals in the military that they took their concerns to the Red Cross and watchdog NGOs).
[50] **Hoaglund,** *supra* **note 26** ; Kwiatkowski, "The New Pentagon Papers." *See* Poll: "Two-Thirds."
[51] Human Rights First, 10-Point Strategy, June 9, 2004 (*available at* http://www.humanrightsfirst.org).
[52] "U.S. Sent Specialists to Train Prison Units," *Washington Post*, June 3, 2004, Section A 31 (*quoting* Slaughter).
[53] Applebaum, "Willing" (*quoting* Rumsfeld). *See* Jim Lobe, "Impunity Endures Two Years After Abu Ghraib," *Inter Press Service News Agency (IPS)*, April 26, 2006 (available at http://www.ipsnews.net).
[54] Derek Jinks & David Sloss, "Is the President Bound by the Geneva Conventions?," Chicago Public Law and Legal Theory Working Paper No. 61 (2004) (*available as* SSRN Paper No. 517683).
[55] *See* Eggan & Linzer, "9/11 Commission" (the 9/11 Commission Report States that the Common Art. 3 of the Geneva Conventions amount to a "customary international law ...designed for those cases in which the usual laws of war did not apply."); Editorial: "Protecting the System," *Washington Post*, May 12, 2004, Section A22 (under the Third Convention, prisoners of war and captured insurgents "may not be threatened, insulted, or exposed to any unpleasant or disadvantageous treatment of any kind"). The Fourth Convention, covering people under foreign occupation, says "no physical or moral coercion shall be exercised," especially "to obtain information from them or from third parties." *Id.* Interestingly, the use of dogs (with known vicious propensities) is not explicitly dealt with.
[56] NPR, *supra* note 20 (quoting Rumsfeld).
[57] *See* **notes 31-37, supra** .
[58] Eitan Felver, "The Painful Lesson Israel Learned About Torture," *International Herald Tribunal*, June 11, 2004, 7; Frieh, *supra* note 10; Colum Lynch, "Military Prison's Closure is Urged," *Washington Post*, May 20, 2006, Section A1; "U.N. Report to Urge End to Torture by U.S.," *International Herald Tribunal*, May 19, 2006; "Global Rights Applauds Recommendations from the UN's Committee Against Torture," May 19, 2006, http://www.globalrights.org.
[59] *Filartiga v. Pena-Iralia*, 630 F. 2d 875 (2d Cir. 1980).
[60] See notes 45-48 and accompanying text, supra.[lxi] See notes 45-48 and accompanying text, supra.

[61] U.S. v. Alvarez-Machain, 542 U.S. 692 (2004).

[62] Paul Guyer, *Kant on Freedom, Law, and Happiness* (Cambridge: Cambridge University Press, 2000), 418, 430 (Kant being more read about than read). Kant's republican commitments include an equality for all and the impetuous to promote the justice that manifestly do not exist in the U.S. *See id.* at 419-20. Leaders can make war impersonally, if their children and fortunes are not at stake. *Id.* at 420. Poll: "Two-Thirds" ("Three-fourths agreed with the statement that the United States is a moral leader in the world and should not set a bad example by torturing or degrading people in detention.").

[63] *See* Tony Judt, "A Sorry State," *Washington Post*, May 9, 2004, Section B1 (Blair is the most "American" of British prime ministers, "in his well-advertised religiosity and his propensity to wax moralistic"); Colin McGinn, "Review," *Washington Post*, March, 14, 2004, Section BW 6 (reviewing Peter Singer, *The President of Good and Evil: The Ethics of George W. Bush* (New York: Dutton, 2004) ("the book is a litany of moral inconsistencies ... of persistent hypocrisy and doublethink" whereby political expediency triumphs over declarations of principle.")). "States' rights are to be respected, except when gay marriage is at issue." *Id.* "Lying about your sex life is excoriated, but systematic dishonesty about the reasons for going to war is ... morally above board." *Id.* "Bush is a man of sporadically good moral instincts, ... but he sways inconsistently and opportunistically in the political breeze, and has no idea how to make his beliefs fit coherently together." *Id.*

[64] Applebaum, "So Torture" (*quoting* Burke). *See* Brietzke, "September 11 and American Law;" Frieh, *supra* note 10 (violating international human rights and humanitarian law "in the name of counterterrorism enters into the same logic as terrorism: that the end justifies the means.").

[65] Kwiatkowski, "The New Pentagon Papers" ("we may have already failed" to keep Franklin's Republic) (paraphrasing Ben Franklin).

LIST OF CONTRIBUTORS

Penelope E. Andrews (B.A. LL.B (Natal), LL.M. (Columbia), is a Visiting Professor at the Valparaiso University School of Law (on leave from The City University of New York School of Law.) She was the Chamberlain Fellow in Legislation at Columbia Law School, and has worked at the Legal Resources Center in Johannesburg, and the NAACP Legal Defense Fund in New York. She was on the faculty of the Department of Law and Legal Studies at La Trobe University in Melbourne, Australia and has taught in the USA, South Africa and Europe. She has written extensively on constitutional and human rights issues and is the contributing co-editor of THE POST-APARTHEID CONSTITUTIONS: REFLECTIONS ON SOUTH AFRICA'S BASIC LAW. She has held several distinguished visiting positions, including the Stoneman Professor of Law and Democracy at Albany Law School, the Parsons Visitor at the University of Sydney, Australia, and the Ariel F. Sallows Professor of Human Rights Law at the University of Saskatchewan in Canada. During 2004 she was a scholar in residence at the Rockefeller Study Center in Bellagio, Italy. She is a Board member of the East Africa Journal of Peace and Human Rights, the Journal of Law and Policy, and Human Rights and the Global Economy, an SSRN journal.

Taunya Lovell Banks, the Jacob A. France Professor of Equality Jurisprudence and the Francis & Harriet Iglehart Research Professor of Law at the University of Maryland School of Law, teaches constitutional law, torts, and seminars on law in popular culture, citizenship and critical race theory. Her recent publications explore racial reconciliation and reparations, racial formation and new legal theories of racial equality. She is a contributing co-editor of SCREENING JUSTICE- THE CINEMA OF LAW: FILMS OF LAW, ORDER, AND SOCIAL JUSTICE (2006). Professor Banks, a former member of the Association of American Law Schools' Executive Committee, and Trustee of the Law School Admissions Council, served on the Editorial Board of the JOURNAL OF LEGAL EDUCATION and the advisory committee of the LAW & SOCIETY REVIEW.

Susan Bazilli (B.A. Hons. Queens, LL.B. (Osgoode Hall, York University), is the Director of The International Women's Rights Project (IWRP) based at the Centre for Global Studies, University of Victoria, Canada, and in Johannebsurg, South Africa. Her career has encompassed professional and technical experience in over thirty countries as a lawyer, independent consultant, author, executive director, social entrepreneur, trainer, researcher, and advocate on issues of violence against women and girls, women's human rights, civil society, democracy, governance, and international development. Bazilli was the coordinator of the conferences, *Putting Women on the Agenda 1 and 2* (held in 1991 and 2006 respectively) in South Africa. She edited the influential text, PUTTING WOMEN ON THE AGENDA (1992), and the follow-on text PUTTING FEMINISM ON THE AGENDA (2008). She was a Planning Committee member with the Department of Justice South Africa for the launch of the South African Women Lawyer's Association; Gender Issues Expert for the American Bar Association CEELI program in Russia; and the Legal Specialist for the Women's Legal Rights Initiative program in Southern Africa .

Rebecca Bratspies is an Associate Professor of Law at the CUNY School of Law where she teaches property, environmental law, and administrative law. Her scholarly research focuses on environmental regulatory regimes, and she is particularly interested in the international dimensions of environmental regulation. Professor Bratspies has published widely on the topics of environmental liability, international fisheries, and genetically modified food crops. She is the co-organizer of the annual University of Idaho College of Law Symposium on International Law and co-editor of TRANSBOUNDARY HARM IN INTERNATIONAL LAW: LESSONS FROM THE TRAIL SMELTER ARBITRATION (Cambridge 2006) and PROGRESS IN INTERNATIONAL ORGANIZATION (forthcoming Martinus Nijhoff 2007). Professor Bratspies holds B.A. in Biology from Wesleyan University and a J.D. cum laude from the University of Pennsylvania Law School.

Paul H. Brietzke has a BA in Economics from Lake Forest, a JD from the University of Wisconsin, and a Ph. D. from the University of London. He has taught in Malawi, Ethiopia, Malaysia, Vietnam, and England (Brunel University), and is currently Professor at Valparaiso University--just outside Chicago. Brietzke has consulted on economic law and human rights reforms in Hungary, the Czech Republic, Mocambique, Kenya, Eritrea, China, Indonesia, and Mongolia. He is perhaps best known for a 'progressive' economics approach to law, although his most recent articles concern the mostly non-legal topics of global warming and bird flu. A keen photographer, he is overweight because he loves to cook as well as eat.

Janet Calvo is a Professor of Law at the City University School of Law in New York City. The courses she teaches include those that focus immigration and citizenship law. She has also integrated citizenship and immigration issues into a number of courses with a broader legal focus such as Procedure and Health Law. Her scholarship has particularly addressed issues that affect women in the immigration and citizenship context and limitations on access based in citizenship status. In conjunction with the CUNY Law School's clinical programs, she has also assisted law students in the counseling and representation of persons with citizenship and immigration issues.

Martin Chanock is a Professor and Deputy-Dean of the Faculty of Law, La Trobe University, Australia. After completing his doctorate at Cambridge, Chanock taught in Universities in East and West Africa, England (the University of Sussex) and the USA (the University of Texas at Austin). He has held visiting appointments at Harvard, Wellesley, North Carolina; London, and Cape Town and was Smuts Fellow in Commonwealth Studies at Cambridge in 2004/5. His fields of research have been legal colonization, customary law and globalization; constitutionalism and constitutional law; comparative law; African and South African law; anthropology and law; and law and cultural heritage. He is currently working on the constitutional aspects of democratization in developing countries.

Chanock is an editor of CAMBRIDGE STUDIES IN LAW AND SOCIETY. His sample publications include, THE ROLE OF CUSTOMARY LAW IN SUSTAINABLE DEVELOPMENT Cambridge 2005 (with P Orebach et al), THE MAKING OF SOUTH AFRICAN LEGAL CULTURE Cambridge 2001, LAW, CUSTOM AND SOCIAL ORDER Cambridge 1985 (republished 1998).

Stephen J. Ellmann is a Professor and Associate Dean for Faculty Development at New York Law School. An award-winning author on legal ethics and an expert in clinical legal education, constitutional law, and South African law, he co-chairs with Penelope Andrews the Law School's South Africa Reading Group, an interdisciplinary group of scholars who focus on South Africa from a variety of perspectives. Ellmann earned the Sanford D. Levy Memorial Award from the New York State Bar Committee on Professional Ethics for an article "Lawyering for Justice in a Flawed Democracy," 90 *Columbia Law Review* (1990). He has also authored a variety of works concerning human rights in South Africa, as well as America, including "The Rule of Law and the Achievement of Unanimity in Brown," 49 *New York Law School Law Review* (2004–2005). Ellmann holds both a B.A. and J.D. *magna cum laude* from Harvard and served as Law Clerk to Hon. Elbert Tuttle, U.S. Court of Appeals, Fifth (now Eleventh) Circuit. As a staff attorney at the Southern Poverty Law Center in Montgomery, Alabama, his practice included institutional reform litigation for mentally disabled people and prison inmates, voting rights cases, anti-Ku Klux Klan suits, and defense work in capital murder trials.

Brian Flanagan is a Foley-Bčjar Scholar at Balliol College, Oxford. His research interests for his DPhil are focused on human rights legislation and comparative law.

Christopher Gale (LL.B. Wales, LL.M. Leicester), is a Professor of Law and Director of Legal Studies at Bradford University. Gale graduated from University College Cardiff in 1977 and qualified as a solicitor in 1980. He moved to academia in 1990 with an appointment at the Polytechnic of North London and joined Leeds Metropolitan University (Leeds Law School) in 1994, becoming head of undergraduate studies. He joined Bradford University Law School as the inaugural Director of Legal Studies in July 2005. His research interests include human rights, public law and sports and the law. Amongst other projects, Gale is currently examining whether the public has confidence in the executive, particularly the court system, the police and other enforcement agencies.

Susan N. Herman, Centennial Professor of Law at Brooklyn Law School, teaching courses in Criminal Procedure and Constitutional Law. Her recent publications include a book on the Sixth Amendment right to speedy and public trial, and articles in the Harvard Civil Rights-Civil Liberties and other law reviews.
Professor Herman received a B.A. from Barnard College and a J.D. from New York University School of Law. She has worked as Pro Se Law Clerk for the United States Court of Appeals for the Second Circuit, and as Associate Director of Prisoners' Legal Services of New York. She also serves as a member of the National Board of Directors and Executive Committee, and as General Counsel of the American Civil Liberties Union.

Susan R. Jones, is a Professor of Clinical Law at the George Washington University Law School and the 2006 Chair of the Association of American Law Schools (AALS) Section on Clinical Legal Education. She is also an Executive Committee member of the AALS Section on Africa and she is on the Governing Committee of the American Bar Association Forum on Affordable Housing and Community Development Law.

J. Patrick Kelly is Professor of Law at Widener University School of Law in Wilmington, Delaware and Founder and Director of the Nairobi International Law Institute, Nairobi, Kenya. He served as a Fulbright Professor of Law at Makerere University in Kampala, Uganda from 1980-82. He is the author of numerous articles on international law and trade including recent publications in the international law journals of Cornell University, Northwestern University and the University of Virginia.

Craig Lind holds law degrees from the University of the Witwatersrand and the London School of Economics. He has taught at the University of the Witwatersrand, the University of Wales in Aberystwyth and is now a Senior Lecturer in Law at the University of Sussex in Brighton where he teaches (amongst other things) Family Law, Constitutional Law, and Law and Politics in Britain and the U.S.A. He also teaches Masters courses in Family and Child Law on a Masters program aimed at exploring the legal regulation of family responsibility. His major research interests lie in the areas of Family Law and Sexuality and has a strong cultural focus.

Margaret (Peggy) Maisel is Associate Professor and the founding Director of Clinical Programs at Florida International University College of Law where she teaches a Community Development Clinic. In 1996 she went on a Fulbright to the University of Natal in Durban, South Africa and joined the faculty there as an Associate Professor from 1997-2001.

Kirsty Mclean, BMus, LLB (University of the Witwatersrand). Kirsty McLean is currently reading for a DPhil in law at Magdalen College, Oxford. Her thesis is entitled "The Judicial Interpretation and Enforcement of Socio-Economic Rights in South Africa" and deals with the way in which courts define their role in socio-economic rights' adjudication, providing both a theoretical and normative analysis of adjudication of these rights in South Africa. Prior to undertaking her doctorate, Kirsty clerked for Justice Kate O'Regan of the South African Constitutional Court and has lectured in law, part-time at the University of the Witwatersrand. Kirsty also works as a legal consultant for Ashira Consulting, a public-sector legal consultancy, providing advice mainly to clients within government.

Denise Meyerson is currently a Professor in the Division of Law at Macquarie University and an Honorary Professor in the Law Faculty at the University of Cape Town. Previously she held the W P Schreiner Chair in the Law Faculty at the University of Cape Town. She was appointed a Visiting Fellow at All Souls College, Oxford in 1996. She holds the degrees of BA from the University of the Witwatersrand, LLB from the University of Cape Town, and B Phil and D Phil (in philosophy) from the University of Oxford. Her research interests are principally in the areas of jurisprudence, the theoretical foundations of public law, comparative constitutionalism and human rights law. She has written four books as well as numerous articles and book chapters on these topics.

Qudsia Mirza is Senior Lecturer in Law at the University of East London, UK and works in the areas of Islamic Law, Discrimination Law, Critical Race Theory and Ethnic Minorities and the Law. Her primary area of research focusses on feminist perspectives of Islamic law, as well as legal pluralism in the operation of state and Islamic laws in the British and wider European context. She has published extensively in both these areas and is editor of ISLAMIC FEMINISM AND THE LAW (London: Glasshouse Press, 2007). Before becoming an academic, she qualified as a solicitor and is a member of the Centre on Human Rights in Conflict, University of East London, and an Executive Committee member of the Joint Council for the Welfare of Immigrants.

Dwight Newman is an Assistant Professor and Associate Dean at the University of Saskatchewan College of Law, where he teaches in the constitutional and international law areas. After his law degree at the University of Saskatchewan, he clerked for Chief Justice Lamer and Justice LeBel at the Supreme Court of Canada. He worked for the Canadian government and for human rights organizations in China and South Africa and completed graduate work at Oxford University, where he studied as a Rhodes Scholar and a Social Sciences and Humanities Research Council of Canada Doctoral Fellow. In his D.Phil. thesis, completed in 2005, he sought to develop a theoretical account of collective rights. His current research focuses on theoretical dimensions of indigenous rights and theoretical dimensions of international criminal law.

Wendy Pettifer has worked to use social welfare law as a tool to redress the imbalance of justice since working in Manchester Law Centre in the 1970s. She qualified as a solicitor in 1991 and ran two Legal Aid Housing Departments in North London focusing on issues affecting asylum seekers. She had conduct of the successful case of Harrow v Fahia (1998 – 30 HLR 1124) in the House of Lords. She trained interns at AMERA in Cairo in 2002 to support asylum seekers' appeals against negative refugee determinations by UNHCR Egypt as part of her Masters in Refugee Studies. Since 2004 she has developed the Trainee Litigation Scheme at the College of Law where corporate trainees represent clients pro bono in the areas of housing, asylum support and bail for immigration detainees.

Michael Plaxton (BA (Hons) (Western Ontario), LLB, LLM (Alberta), SJD (Toronto))is a Lecturer at the University of Aberdeen, School of Law. He teaches jurisprudence, criminology and various other related subjects. While in Canada, he lectured in evidence, professional responsibility, and jurisprudence. Dr. Plaxton also worked as a factum specialist and appellate consultant, assisting with written submissions that have appeared before several provincial appellate courts, as well as the Federal Court of Appeal and the Supreme Court of Canada. His scholarship addresses a range of issues in criminal law and procedure, the law of evidence, constitutional law and theory, and professional conduct. His publications include,Review of Victor Tadros 'Criminal Responsibility' (Oxford, 2005), CRIMINAL LAW AND PHILOSOPHY, 1(2) 2007, Irruptions of Motive in the War on Terror, CANADIAN CRIMINAL LAW REVIEW, 11 (2007), Torture warrants, hypocrisy and supererogation: justifying bright-line rules as if consequences mattered, THE WARRIOR'S DISHONOUR: BARBARITY, MORALITY AND TORTURE IN MODERN WARFARE, Ashgate, (2006. G Kassimeris, ed.)

Ruthann Robson is Professor of Law at the City University of New York where she teaches in the areas of Law and Sexuality, Constitutional Law, and Family Law. She is the author of SAPPHO GOES TO LAW SCHOOL, LESBIAN (OUT)LAW, and numerous articles developing a lesbian legal theory, as well as works of fiction, creative nonfiction, and poetry. During 2006-2007, she has a fellowship leave from

CUNY and will spend her time as a resident at the Djerassi Residents Artists Program in California, a fellow at the University of Sydney, in the Collaborative Research Program, and a visiting professor for the Bram Fischer Visiting Program at the University of Witwatersrand, Johannesburg.

Valorie Vojdik B.A. (Brown) JD (NYU), is an Associate Professor at the Virginia University College of Law. She is the deputy director of WVU's law clinic and also teaches Constitutional Litigation and Legal Ethics. She also has taught courses in Gender and the Law, International Women's Rights, Employment Discrimination, and Business Organizations. She received an A.B. from Brown University in Development Studies and a J.D. from New York University School of Law. She worked as an associate at Shearman & Sterling in New York City before joining the faculty at New York University School of Law, where she taught in its Lawyering Program. She was a visiting research scholar at the University of Cape Town Law School, where she researched comparative gender jurisprudence and the impact of HIV on women in Africa.

Gregoire Webber B.C.L., LL.B. (McGill) D.Phil. (Law) (University of Oxford), is currently a Scholar at the Trudeau Foundation. He is the co-author with Graham Gee of *A Confused Court: Equivocations on Recognizing Same-Sex Relationships*, in the South Africa Modern Law Review.

LaVergne, TN USA
14 December 2009
166927LV00001B/1/P